ISBN 978-0-428-94546-6
PIBN 10015485

BOHN'S STANDARD LIBRARY.

Post 8vo., Elegantly Printed, and bound in Cloth, at 3s. 6d. per Vol.

2 b

BOHN'S STANDARD LIBRARY.

3 b

BOHN'S STANDARD LIBRARY.

92. DANUBIAN PROVINCES.—RANKE's History of Servia. The Servian Revolution, The Insurrection in Bosnia, and The Slave Provinces of Turkey. Translated by MRS. KERR.

93. GOETHE'S ELECTIVE AFFINITIES, SORROWS OF WERTHER. GERMAN EMIGRANTS, GOOD WOMEN; and A NOUVELETTE.

94. THE CARAFAS OF MADDALONI: Naples under Spanish Dominion. Translated from the German of ALFRED DE ROUMONT. *Portrait of Masaniello.*

97 & 109. CONDÉ'S HISTORY OF THE ARABS IN SPAIN. Translated from the Spanish by MRS. FOSTER. In 3 vols. Vols. I. and II. *Frontispiece.*

98 & 104. LOCKE'S PHILOSOPHICAL WORKS, containing the Essay on the Human Understanding, the Conduct of the Understanding, &c., with Notes by J. A. ST. JOHN, Esq. General Index and a Portrait. In 2 vols.

100. HUNGARY: ITS HISTORY AND REVOLUTIONS. With a copious Memoir of KOSSUTH, from new and authentic sources. *Portrait of Kossuth.*

101. HISTORY OF RUSSIA to the present time, compiled from KARAMSIN, TOOKE, and SEGUR, by W. K. KELLY. In 2 vols. Vol. I., *Portrait of Catherine the Second.*

107 & 108. JAMES'S (G. P. R.), LIFE OF RICHARD CŒUR DE LION, King of England. New Edition, with portraits of Richard, and Philip Augustus. Complete in 2 vols.

BOHN'S EXTRA VOLUMES.

Uniform with the STANDARD LIBRARY, *price 3s. 6d.*

1. GRAMMONT'S MEMOIRS OF THE COURT OF CHARLES II. *Portrait.*
2 & 3. RABELAIS' WORKS. Complete in 2 Vols. *Portrait.*
4. COUNT HAMILTON'S FAIRY TALES. *Portrait.*
5. BOCCACCIO'S DECAMERON, a complete translation, by W. K. KELLY, Esq. *Portrait.*

UNIFORM WITH THE STANDARD LIBRARY,

BARBAULD'S (MRS.) SELECTIONS FROM THE SPECTATOR, TATLER, GUARDIAN, AND FREEHOLDER. In 2 Vols. *3s. 6d.* per Volume.

BRITISH POETS, from MILTON to KIRKE WHITE. Cabinet Edition, comprising, in a very small but remarkably clear type, as much matter as the sixty volumes of Johnson's Poets. Complete in 4 Vols. *Frontispieces.* 14s.

CARY'S TRANSLATION OF DANTE. Extra cloth. *7s. 6d.*

CATTERMOLE'S EVENINGS AT HADDON HALL. 24 exquisite Engravings on Steel, from Designs by himself; the Letter-Press by the BARONESS DE CALABRELLA. Post 8vo. *7s 6d.*

CHILLINGWORTH'S RELIGION OF PROTESTANTS. *2s. 6d.*

CLASSIC TALES; comprising The Vicar of Wakefield, Elizabeth. Paul and Virginia, Gulliver's Travels, Sterne's Sentimental Journey, Sorrows of Werter, Theodosius and Constantia, Castle of Otranto, and Rasselas. 12mo. 7 *Portraits. 3s. 6d.*

DEMOSTHENES. Translated by LELAND. *Portrait.* 3s.

DICKSON AND MOWBRAY ON POULTRY, Edited by MRS. LOUDON, Illustrations by HARVEY (including the Cochin-China Fowl). *5s.*

HORACE'S ODES AND EPODES, translated literally and rhythmically, by the REV. W. SEWELL. *3s. 6d.*

IRVING'S (WASHINGTON) WORKS. Complete in 10 Vols., £1 15s., or 3s. 6d. per Vol.

JOYCE'S SCIENTIFIC DIALOGUES. Greatly Improved Edition, with Questions, &c., by PINNOCK. (Upwards of 600 pages). *Woodcuts. 5s.*

JOYCE'S INTRODUCTION TO THE ARTS AND SCIENCES. 5s.

LAMARTINE'S HISTORY OF THE RESTORATION. 4 vols., post 8vo., new Edition, with a General Index, and 5 additional *Portraits, viz.,* Lamartine, Talleyrand, Lafayette, Ney, and Louis XVII. Cloth.

LAMARTINE'S THREE MONTHS IN POWER. Sewed, 2s.

LAMARTINE'S POETICAL MEDITATIONS AND RELIGIOUS HARMONIES, with Biographical Sketch. *Portrait.* Cloth, 3s. 6d.

LAWRENCE'S LECTURES ON COMPARATIVE ANATOMY, PHYSIOLOGY, ZOOLOGY, AND THE NATURAL HISTORY OF MAN. *Frontispiece and Plates.* 5s.

LILLY'S INTRODUCTION TO ASTROLOGY. A New and Improved Edition, by ZADKIEL, with his Grammar of Astrology, and Tables of Nativities. *5s.*

LOUDON'S (MRS.) ENTERTAINING NATURALIST, a Description of more than Five Hundred Animals, with Indexes of Scientific and Popular Names. *With upwards of* 500 *Woodcuts, by* BEWICK, HARVEY, &c. Revised and enlarged. *7s. 6d.*

LOWTH'S LECTURES ON THE SACRED POETRY OF THE HEBREWS. *3s. 6d.*

MICHELET'S HISTORY OF THE FRENCH REVOLUTION. 4s.

MILLER'S PHILOSOPHY OF HISTORY. Third Revised and Improved Edition, 4 Volumes, at 3s. 6d. per Volume.

MITFORD'S (MISS) OUR VILLAGE. 2 Vols., New Edition, *with Woodcuts and beautiful Frontispieces on Steel,* gilt cloth. Each Vol. 5s.

NORWAY. A Road Book for Tourists in Norway, with Hints to English Sportsmen and Anglers, by THOMAS FORESTER, Esq. Limp cloth. 2s.

PARKES' ELEMENTARY CHEMISTRY. New Edition, revised, 5s.

5 b

UNIFORM WITH THE STANDARD LIBRARY.

SHAKSPEARE'S PLAYS AND POEMS, with Life, by CHALMERS. I1 1 Vol. 3s. 6d.

———————— the same, Embellished with 40 pleasing *Steel Engravings,* elegantly bound i1 red Turkey cloth, gilt edges. 5s.

STANDARD LIBRARY CYCLOPÆDIA OF POLITICAL, CONSTITUTIONAL, STATISTICAL, AND FORENSIC KNOWLEDGE. 4 Vols. 3s. 6d each.

This work contains as much as eight ordinary octavos. It was first published in another shape by Mr. Charles Knight, under the title of Political Dictionary, at £1 16s. The Compiler, MR. GEORGE LONG, is one of the most competent Scholars of the day.

STURM'S MORNING COMMUNINGS WITH GOD. New Edition. 5s.

UNCLE TOM'S CABIN, with Introductory Remarks by the REV. J. SHERMAN (printed i1 a large clear type, with head-li1es of Co1te1ts). 2s. 6d.

———————— The same, o1 fine paper, with 8 *new Illustrations by* LEBCH *and* GILBERT, *and a beautiful Frontispiece by* HINCHLIFF. 3s. 6d.

THE WIDE, WIDE WORLD, by ELIZABETH WETHERELL. Complete i1 1 Vol, *with Frontispiece,* gilt edges. 3s. 6d.

———————— The same, *Illustrated with 9 highly finished Engravings on Steel,* richly bou1d in cloth, gilt edges. 5s.

BOHN'S SCIENTIFIC LIBRARY.

U1iform with the STANDARD LIBRARY, *price 5s., (excepting "Cosmos," Kidd, and Whewell, which are 3s. 6d., and Mantell's "Petrifactions," which is 6s.)*

1. **STAUNTON'S CHESS PLAYER'S HAND-BOOK,** *with Diagrams.*

2. **LECTURES ON PAINTING,** by THE ROYAL ACADEMICIANS.

3, 4, 8, & 15. **HUMBOLDT'S COSMOS;** or, Sketch of a Physical Description of the Universe. Translated, with Notes, by E. C. OTTE. In 4 Vols., *with fine Portrait.* This Translation (though published at so low a price) is more complete than a1y other. The Notes are placed beneath the text. Humboldt's analytica summaries, and the passages hitherto suppressed, are included; and comprehensive Indices subjoined. 3s 6d. per Volume.

5. **STAUNTON'S CHESS PLAYER'S COMPANION,** comprising a New Treatise on Odds, a Collectio1 of Match Games, Original Problems, &c.

6. **HAND-BOOK OF GAMES,** by VARIOUS AMATEURS and PROFESSORS.

7. **HUMBOLDT'S VIEWS OF NATURE,** *with coloured view of Chimborazo, &c.*

9. **RICHARDSON'S GEOLOGY, AND PALÆONTOLOGY,** Revised by Dr. WRIGHT, *with upwards of 400 Illustrations on Wood.*

10. **STOCKHARDT'S PRINCIPLES OF CHEMISTRY,** Exemplified i1 Simple Experiments, *with upwards of 270 Illustrations.*

11. **DR. G. A. MANTELL'S PETRIFACTIONS AND THEIR TEACHINGS; A** Hand-Book to the Fossils i1 t1e British Museum. *Beautiful Wood Engravings.* 6s.

C b

AGASSIZ AND GOULD'S COMPARATIVE PHYSIOLOGY. New and Enlarged Edition, *with nearly 400 Illustrations.*

3, 19, & 28. HUMBOLDT'S PERSONAL NARRATIVE OF HIS TRAVELS IN AMERICA. With General Index.

PYE SMITH'S GEOLOGY AND SCRIPTURE. Fifth Edition, with Memoir.

OERSTED'S SOUL IN NATURE, &c. *Portrait.*

7. STAUNTON'S CHESS TOURNAMENT, *with Diagrams.*

3 & 20. BRIDGEWATER TREATISES. KIRBY on the History, Habits, and Instincts of Animals; Edited by T. RYMER JONES. In 2 Vols. *Many Illustrations.*

1. BRIDGEWATER TREATISES. KIDD On the Adaptation of External Nature to the Physical Condition of Man. *3s. 6d.*

2. BRIDGEWATER TREATISES. WHEWELL'S Astronomy and General Physics, considered with reference to Natural Theology. *Portrait of the Earl of Bridgewater. 3s. 6d.*

3. SCHOUW'S EARTH, PLANTS, AND MAN, and KOBELL'S SKETCHES FROM THE MINERAL KINGDOM, Translated by A. HENFREY, F.R.S., &c., *with Coloured Map of the Geography of Plants.*

4. BRIDGEWATER TREATISES. CHALMERS on the Adaptation of External Nature to the Moral and Intellectual Constitution of Man, with the Author's last Corrections, and Biographical Sketch by the REV. DR. CUMMING.

5. BACON'S NOVUM ORGANUM AND ADVANCEMENT OF LEARNING. Complete, with Notes, by J. DEVEY, M.A.

6 & 27. HUMPHREY'S COIN COLLECTOR'S MANUAL: a popular introduction to the Study of Coins, ancient and modern; with elaborate Indexes, *and numerous highly-finished Engravings on Wood and Steel*, 2 Vols.

9. COMTE'S PHILOSOPHY OF THE SCIENCES, Edited from the 'Cours de Philosophie Positive,' by G. H. LEWES, Esq.

0. MANTELL'S (DR.) GEOLOGICAL EXCURSIONS, including THE ISLE OF WIGHT. New Edition, with Prefatory Note by T. RUPERT JONES, Esq., *numerous beautiful Woodcuts, and a Geological Map.*

1. HUNT'S POETRY OF SCIENCE; or, Studies of the Physical Phenomena of Nature. 3rd Edition, revised and enlarged.

2 & 33. ENNEMOSER'S HISTORY OF MAGIC. Translated from the German by WILLIAM HOWITT. With an Appendix of the most remarkable and best authenticated Stories of Apparitions, Dreams, Second Sight, Predictions, Divinations, Vampires, Fairies, Table Turning, and Spirit Rapping, &c., by MARY HOWITT. In 2 Vols.

4. HUNT'S ELEMENTARY PHYSICS; an Introduction to the Study of Natural Philosophy. New Edition, revised. *Numerous Woodcuts and Coloured Frontispiece.*

BOHN'S ILLUSTRATED LIBRARY.

Uniform with the STANDARD LIBRARY, *at 5s. per volume,*

1 to 8. LODGE'S PORTRAITS OF ILLUSTRIOUS PERSONAGES OF GREAT BRITAIN. 8 Vols post 8vo. 240 *Portraits.*

9. CRUIKSHANK'S THREE COURSES AND DESSERT, *with 50 Illustrations.*

0. PICKERING'S RACES OF MAN, *with numerous Portraits (or Coloured 7s. 6d.)*

1. KITTO'S SCRIPTURE LANDS, AND BIBLICAL ATLAS, *with 24 Maps, (or Coloured, 7s. 6d.)*

7 b

GENERAL HISTORY

OF THE

CHRISTIAN RELIGION AND CHURCH:

TRANSLATED FROM THE GERMAN OF

DR. AUGUSTUS NEANDER,

BY

JOSEPH TORREY,

PROFESSOR OF MORAL PHILOSOPHY IN THE UNIVERSITY OF VERMONT.

NEW EDITION, CAREFULLY REVISED.

"Let both grow together until the harvest."—*Words of our Lord.*
"Les uns Christianisant le civil et le politique, les autres civilisant la
Christianisme, il se forma de ce melange un monstre."—*St. Martin.*

VOLUME THIRD.

LONDON: PRINTED BY W. CLOWES AND SONS, STAMFORD STREET.

CONTENTS OF VOL. III.

SECOND PERIOD OF THE HISTORY OF THE CHRISTIAN CHURCH.
FROM THE END OF THE DIOCLESIAN PERSECUTION TO THE
TIME OF GREGORY THE GREAT, BISHOP OF ROME; OR FROM
THE YEAR 312 TO THE YEAR 590.

SECTION FIRST.

RELATION OF THE CHRISTIAN CHURCH TO THE WORLD. ITS EXTENSION
AND LIMITS, p. 1—183.

Within the Roman Empire, 1—146.

A. *Relation of the Roman Emperors to the Christian Church,* 1—120.

SECTION SECOND.

History of Church Discipline, 253—257.

Persons convicted of gross offences, excluded from the fellowship of the church. (In case of sincere repentance, none
refused the communion in the hour of death.) Different
classes of penitents. Conditions of re-admission. Difficulties attending the application of the principles of
church penance—partly in the case of schisms, partly in

SECTION THIRD.

Lights and Shades of Monachism.

Different Spiritual Tendencies in Religion, in their Relation to Monachism and Asceticism, 375.

Christian Worship, 393—487.

SECTION FOURTH.

HISTORY OF CHRISTIANITY APPREHENDED AND DEVELOPED AS A SYSTEM OF DOCTRINES, p. 488.

General Introductory Remarks, 488.

CHURCH HISTORY.

SECOND PERIOD OF THE HISTORY OF THE CHRISTIAN
CHURCH. FROM THE END OF THE DIOCLESIAN PER-
SECUTION TO THE TIME OF GREGORY THE GREAT,
BISHOP OF ROME, OR FROM THE YEAR 312 TO THE
YEAR 590.

SECTION FIRST.

RELATION OF THE CHRISTIAN CHURCH TO THE WORLD. ITS EXTENSION AND LIMITATION.

I. WITHIN THE ROMAN EMPIRE.

A. *Relation of the Roman Emperors to the Christian Church.*

THE Christian Church had come forth victorious out of its
last bloody conflict in the Dioclesian persecution. The very
author of the persecution, the Emperor Galerius himself, had
been forced to acknowledge that the power of conviction
was not to be overcome by fire and sword. But in truth no
experience can subdue the obstinacy of fanaticism and of despotism ; and had not everything assumed another shape, under
the influence of a great political change in the Roman empire,
deeply affecting the history of the world, the attempt would,
perhaps, even after that last edict of toleration, have been renewed in many districts to suppress Christianity by force ; as
indeed it had often been the case before that the persecution,
after a momentary pause, broke forth again with increased
violence.

One of the regents of that period was Caius Galerius Valerius Maximinus, who ruled at first over Egypt and Syria ; then,
after the death of his uncle Galerius in the year 311, made

himself master of all the Asiatic provinces;—the bitterest
enemy of Christianity and of the Christians. Sprung from
the lowest condition,—having been originally a shepherd,—
he was blindly devoted to all the popular superstitions of
paganism, inclined by his own disposition to serve as a tool to
the priests, and possessed withal of a rough, violent, despotic
temper. He had no wish now, it is true, to be the only one
among the regents of the Roman empire to oppose the edict
which had been issued by the oldest Augustus ; but still he
could not be satisfied to publish it in the same open manner in
which it had been published in the other parts of the empire.
He had only directed, under the hand of his first officer of
state, Sabinus, the prætorian prefect, that it should be announced to all the provincial magistrates, as the emperor's will,
that the Christians should no longer be molested. The prefect issued a mandate, which agreed in substance with the edict
of Valerius, "That it had long been with the emperors an
object of their most anxious desire to bring back the souls of
all men to the right ways of a pious life ; so that those who
followed any usage foreign from that of the Romans might be
induced to pay to the immortal gods the homage which is due
to them ; but such had been the obstinacy of many people, that
they would neither be drawn away from their purpose by a
reasonable obedience to the imperial command, nor awed by
the punishments with which they were threatened. Inasmuch,
then, as their imperial majesties* had graciously considered
that it would be contrary to their mild intentions to involve
so many in danger, they had resolved that, for the future, no
Christian should be punished or disturbed on account of his
religion ; since it had been made evident by the experience of
so long a period that they could in no way be persuaded to
desist from their own wilful determination."†

The more violent the persecution had been, especially in the
countries subject to the government of Maximinus, the greater
was the joy of the Christians in those countries when this
command of the emperor was everywhere put in execution.
From their different places of exile, from the prisons, from

* The Numen dominorum nostrorum, ἡ θειότης τῶν δεσποτῶν ἡμῶν,—
as the debasing, idolatrous flattery which had become already the
diplomatic language, then expressed itself.
† Euseb. hist. eccles. l. IX. c. 1. De mort. persecutor. c. 36.

the mines in which they had been condemned to labour, crowds of thankful Christians returned to their homes ; and the public wayfares resounded with their songs of praise. The churches began to be rebuilt, and to be filled once more with worshipping assemblies. Scarcely for half a year did their joy and tranquillity remain undisturbed. As was to be expected, the restoration of the Christian churches, and the great number of those who now freely and publicly joined in the religious services, excited afresh the fanatic rage of the heathens, which could once more readily find an organ for its expression in that Maximinus, who, at heart, had never ceased to cherish his blind zeal for the old idolatry, and his hatred of Christianity.

At first they could not bear to see the enthusiasm which the memory of the martyrs enkindled in the Christians who assembled at their graves: It was very easy, too, in pretending fear lest some disturbance might happen to the public peace, to find a reason for prohibiting the Christians from assembling at their places of burial—the cemeteries. The religious views of the emperor being well known, the heathen priests, conjurors, and magistrates, in various cities both of his old and of his new province, where from the earliest times the pagan worship stood in high repute, and certain forms of it in particular were exhibited with much antique display (as at Antioch, Tyre, and Nicomedia in Bithynia), instigated their fellow-citizens to beg it as a favour of the emperor that no enemy to the gods of their fathers might be permitted to dwell or practise his own rites of worship within their walls. In part it was fanatical intolerance, and in part a spirit of servile flattery, more anxious to obtain the favour of the prince than to promote the honour of the gods, which dictated these petitions. Christian authors, it is true, affirm that the emperor himself secretly encouraged these persons to present such petitions, that he might have a fair pretext for persecuting the Christians.* But it is plain that they do not here report a fact which was known to themselves, but only represent as a fact the inference which they thought themselves warranted

* Thus, De mortib. persecut. c. 36: Subornatis legationibus civitatum, quæ peterent ne intra civitates suas Christianis conventicula extruere liceret, ut quàsi coactus et impulsus facere videratur, quod erat sponte facturus; and Euseb. IX. 2: Αὐτὸς ἑαυτῷ καθ' ἡμῶν πρεσβεύεται.

to draw from the manner in which Maximinus received such petitions, and from his known disposition. The reception which these petitions met with from the emperor was, at all events, without any further action on his part, a sufficient encouragement to repeat them. True, when he first took possession of the Asiatic provinces, which had belonged to the empire of Galerius, and when, on his arrival at Nicomedia, many of the citizens appeared before him with the images of their gods, and presented him, in the name of the city, a petition of this sort, he was still just enough—unless we may suppose he was restrained for the present by reasons of policy—to refuse granting their petition immediately. He caused himself, in the first place, to be informed of the true state of things; and on finding that there were many Christians in the city, he told the deputies that he would have been pleased to grant their request, but he understood that it was not the wish of all the citizens, and he desired to leave every man at liberty to follow his own convictions.* When, however, similar petitions came to him from other cities, testifying great zeal for the worship of the gods; when, moreover, pious frauds, so called, were employed to operate on the mind of the superstitious and credulous prince—as at Antioch, where it was said a voice had issued from a wonder-working statue of Jupiter-Philios, lately set up, and the god required that his enemies should be driven from the city and its territory,†—Maximin could no longer maintain that tone of impartiality which was so foreign from his nature. He thought it due to the honour of the gods, as he expressed it in the later edict, those gods to whom the state owed its preservation, that he should not reject a request which aimed at nothing but the promotion of that honour. He not only granted such petitions, but expressed to those who presented them his particular approbation of their pious disposition. At Tyre he caused to be publicly fixed up, in answer to a proposal of this sort, and as an encouraging token of his satisfaction with its pious spirit, a laudatory writing, composed in the pompous, declamatory

---

* This is stated by Maximin himself, in the edict which he subsequently published in favour of the Christians, and which Eusebius, after his usual manner, has translated in very obscure language from the Latin original; or else it was composed in a very barbarous diplomatic style.

† Euseb. IX. 3.

style of the rhetorical schools of that period, by some master or pupil of the same. Among other things it was here said, "That highest and greatest Jupiter who presides over your famous city, who saved the gods of your fathers, your wives, children, hearths, and homes, from every pestilent infection, he it was who inspired your souls with this wholesome purpose, revealing to you how noble and salutary it is to approach the worship of the immortal gods with becoming reverence." Next is set forth, in swollen expressions, how, by the renewed worship of the gods, men had been delivered from the distresses of famine and of war, from contagious pestilence, and other public calamities, which formerly had been brought on by the guilt of the Christians:—"For these things happened in consequence of the pernicious error of those reckless men, when it had taken possession of their souls, and covered almost the whole world with disgrace." It is then said of the Christians, "If they persist in their accursed folly, let them be banished, as you demand, far from your city and its territory." And that they themselves might know with what good-will the emperor received their proposition, they were invited to ask for some special favour, which should be granted them at once, as a memorial to their children and children's children of their piety towards the immortal gods.*

In every way Maximin sought to restore the splendour of paganism, and, by giving new power and new consequence to its zealous votaries, to supplant the Christians, without publishing any new edict against them. The appointment to sacerdotal offices in the provinces had hitherto been lodged with the senatorial colleges (the collegio decurionum, curialium), who chose to such posts those of their own number who had been already tried in various municipal employments. But Maximin now reserved the appointment to such places in his own hands, that he might be sure to have promoted to them the most distinguished men of the senate, and those from whom he could expect the most zealous and influential exertions to reanimate paganism. To the highest posts of the sacerdotal colleges he chose, in fact, men who had already filled the higher civil offices; and, to procure for them greater respect, he gave them the mantle of glistening white, in-

---

* The edict, in a Greek translation, is in Eusebius, IX. 7.

wrought with gold, which before was the distinguishing badge
of the court offices.*

Trials before Pilate (acta Pilati) were now forged, full of
blasphemies against Christ.† These fabricated documents were
distributed through the city and country schools, in order that
hatred to Christianity might be seasonably instilled into the
minds of the children,—a well-chosen means, no doubt, for
giving currency to convictions such as men wished to have
them.

The declamatory notice above cited, that public calamities
were warded off by the worship of the gods, was soon refuted by
experience. There was a failure of harvest, and a famine;
pestilential disorders raged. Meanwhile the Christians chose
the best way to manifest the spirit of their faith, and to show
the heathens the groundlessness of their accusations. They
collected the whole multitude of the starving population in
the city (probably Nicomedia) into one place, and distributed
bread to them. Thus it might be that more was accomplished
by this work of faith than could have been effected by any
demonstration of words; that, as Eusebius says,‡ the heathens
praised the Christians' God, and pronounced the Christians
themselves to be the only truly pious and God-fearing men.
But there is always a fanaticism which the strongest facts can
neither confute nor embarrass.

Although no new edicts of a sanguinary character were
issued, yet it could not fail to be the case, under the impulse
of freshly excited passions, the outbreaks of which were rather

---

* Euseb. IX. 4. De mortib. p. c. 36.
† Euseb. IX. 5. Still earlier than this there may have been various
recensions of the acta Pilati by Christians and pagans; and so this new
device of malice may have sprung out of some older root. Perhaps,
also, it is inexact, when it is said that those *acta* were then forged for
the first time; perhaps the fanatical hate of the pagans had already
devised some contrivance of this sort in the earlier times of the Dioclesian persecution, and special pains were now taken to put it in circulation. This we are obliged to suppose, if these *acta* are altogether
the same with those to which a pagan priest, in some earlier year of the
Dioclesian persecution, appealed before a tribunal as testimony against
the divinity of Christ. Acta Tarachi, Probi, et Andronici, c. 9. His
words to the Christians are, Μῶρι, τοῦτο οὐκ οἶδας, ὅτι, ὃν ἐπικαλῇ,
ἄνθρωπόν τινα γεγενημένον κακοῦργον, ὑπὸ ἐξουσίᾳ δὲ Πιλάτου τινὸς ἡγεμόνος
ἀνηρτῆσθαι σταυρῷ, ὃν καὶ ὑπομνήκατα κατακεῖνται.
‡ L. IX. c. 8.

favoured than checked by the supreme power of the state, that in various scattered spots the blood of the martyrs would flow copiously. Individuals who, by their zeal for the spread of the faith, and by the authority in which they stood among their fellow-believers, had drawn particularly upon themselves the hatred of the governors or of the emperor, suffered martyrdom. Instances of this kind occurred at Emesa in Phœnicia, at Alexandria, and at Antioch.* This was the last martyr's blood which flowed in consequence of the Dioclesian persecution. From the West began a train of events which placed the whole Christian church in a different relation to the civil power in the Roman state ; and the influence of these events soon extended, at least indirectly, to the Eastern portion of the empire.

Constantine, the son of Constantius Chlorus, was the individual by whom this change was brought about. The manner in which it took place had an important influence on the entire shaping of the church within the bounds of the Roman empire during the period commencing with this epoch. In order to a correct understanding of the whole matter, it is certainly much to be desired that we possessed better means of information respecting the early religious education of the person from whom all this proceeded. But, as often happens, the facts which have reached us concerning the mental development of the author of a great outward change in the history of the world are scanty and meagre ; and it only remains for us to gather our conclusions from a few scattered hints.

His father, Constantius Chlorus, was, as we have already remarked in another place, friendly to the Christians, and probably a follower of that species of religious eclecticism which united Christ along with the gods of Rome. His mother, Helena, the first wife of Constantius, becomes known, at a somewhat later period, as a zealous Christian according to the measure of her religious knowledge—devoted and punctilious in the performance of all the external duties of religion. There are no existing grounds for supposing that she came to this conviction suddenly, or that she was led to embrace it, in her later years, by the example of her son. Nothing forbids

* Euseb. IX. c. 6.

us to suppose that she was, in the earlier period of her life, if
not a Christian, at least inclined to Christianity.* Possibly
it was through her influence that this direction had been given
to the mind of her husband: since it not unfrequently happened that the husband came to the knowledge of Christianity
through means of the wife. Slight as must have been the immediate influence of his parents on the education of Constantine, who was so early removed from their side, yet it may
well be supposed that the religious principles of the parents
would not fail to make some impression on the mind of their
son. The Christians being at that time so numerous and
so widely dispersed, Constantine would, without doubt, frequently come in contact with them; and, as we may readily
suppose, they would neglect no opportunity which offered of
making the prince favourably disposed towards their religion
and their party. While a youth he resided at the court of
Dioclesian, and afterwards at that of Galerius. He witnessed
at Nicomedia the outburst of the persecution against the
Christians.† This example of bloodthirsty fanaticism could
have no other effect than to revolt his youthful, and, in
respect to such proceedings, unprejudiced mind. When he
compared the religious tolerance of his father with the spirit

---

* Nothing certain is known with regard to the relations between
Helena and her son as to this matter. Theodoret, it is true, says
expressly (H. E. l. I. c. 18) that Constantine received his first impressions of Christianity from her; but we cannot be sure that his authority
for this statement is deserving of confidence. Eusebius might have been
more correctly informed; and he says (De vita Constant. I. III. c. 47)
it was by means of Constantine that his mother first became a Christian,
—Θεοσιβῆ καταστησάντα, οὐκ οὖσαν πρότερον. But we should remark that
Eusebius was strongly inclined to turn everything to the advantage of
his hero; and that it is in nowise inconsistent with this statement to
suppose that Helena, while professing to be on the side of heathenism,
still cherished a certain veneration for Christ, as a divine being, and
was disposed to favour Christianity.

† See the religious discourse which the Christian emperor is said to
have pronounced before a Christian assembly,—Oratio ad sanctorum
cœtum,—appended to the life of this emperor by Eusebius, c. 25. Though
it assuredly cannot be supposed that the discourse was delivered by the
emperor precisely as it stands here, yet the substance of it is nevertheless
not wholly unlike what we might naturally expect from him. Compare
also what Constantine says concerning the persecution of Dioclesian, in
his proclamation issued in the East, after the victory over Licinius.
Euseb. de vita Constantin. I. II. c. 49.

which he here saw displayed, it was no difficult task for him to decide which way of thinking would best contribute to promote the tranquillity and well-being of the state. He witnessed here, too, such proofs of the power of Christian faith as might well make an impression on him. He saw there was something in Christianity which was not to be subdued by fire and sword.

In the next following years, after Constantine, as his father's successor, had been proclaimed Augustus, in 306, by the legions in Britain, he appears to have been still·attached to the pagan forms of worship. When, in the year 308, after the successful termination of the war with that Maximianus Herculius who had a second time set himself up as emperor, he received the unexpected intelligence that the Franks, against whom he was just commencing a campaign, had ceased from their hostile demonstrations, he gave public· thanks in a celebrated temple of Apollo, probably at Autun (Augustodunum), and presented a magnificent offering to the god.* From this circumstance we may gather, not only that Constantine still professed an attachment to the old heathen ceremonies, but also that he did not belong to the class of warriors and princes who make no account of the religious interest, and who, strangers to all emotions and impulses of that nature, have an eye only to the human means of prosecuting their undertakings. He believed himself to be indebted for his good fortune to the protection of a god.

It was not until after his victory over the tyrant Maxentius† that Constantine publicly declared in favour of the Christians. The question here presents itself, whether, as we must suppose according to one of the traditions, it was this victory itself, in connection with the extraordinary circumstances preceding it, which gave this new and decided direction, not to the public conduct only, but also to the religious opinions of this emperor.

* Eumeuii Panegyricus Constantini, c. 21.

† Maxentius, son of Maximianus Herculius, had seized upon the sovereignty in Italy and in North Africa, and by his abandoned and voluptuous life, his oppressions, and his despotic acts in every way, had rendered himself alike odious to heathens and to Christians; though at Rome he had in the outset showed himself favourable to the Christians, with a view to secure on his side the interest of their party. Euseb. H. E. l. VIII. c. 14.

According to Eusebius,* the way in which this important change was brought about was as follows:—Maxentius, in making his preparations for the war, had scrupulously observed all the customary ceremonies of paganism, and was relying for success on the agency of supernatural powers. Hence Constantine was the more strongly persuaded that he ought not to place his whole confidence in an arm of flesh. He revolved in his mind to what god it would be suitable for him to apply for aid. The misfortunes of the last emperors, who had been so zealously devoted to the cause of paganism, and the example of his father, who had trusted in the one true and almighty God alone, admonished him that he also should place confidence in no other. To this God, therefore, he applied, praying that he would reveal himself to him, and lend him the protection of his arm in the approaching contest. While thus praying, a short time after noon,† he beheld, spread on the face of the heavens, a glittering cross, and above it the inscription, "By this conquer."‡ The emperor and his whole army, now just about to commence their march towards Italy, were seized with awe. While Constantine was still pondering the import of this sign, night came on; and in a dream Christ appeared to him, with the same symbol which he had seen in the heavens, and directed him to cause a banner to be prepared after the same pattern, and to use it as his protection against the power of the enemy. The emperor obeyed; he caused to be made, after the pattern he had seen, the resplendent banner of the cross (called the Labarum), on the shaft of which was affixed, with the symbol of the cross, the monogram of the name of Christ. He then sent for Christian teachers, of whom he inquired concerning the God that had appeared to him, and the import of the symbol. This gave them an opportunity of instructing him in the knowledge of Christianity.

Taking the account of Eusebius as literally true, we should have to recognise in this occurrence a real miracle. We

---

* De vita Constant. c. I. 27.

† The obscure language of Eusebius—$\dot{\alpha}\mu\phi\grave{\iota}$ $\mu\epsilon\sigma\eta\mu\beta\rho\iota\nu\grave{\alpha}\varsigma$ $\ddot{\omega}\rho\alpha\varsigma$, $\ddot{\eta}\delta\eta$ $\tau\tilde{\eta}\varsigma$ $\dot{\eta}\mu\acute{\iota}\rho\alpha\varsigma$ $\dot{\alpha}\pi\sigma\kappa\tau\iota\nuo\acute{\upsilon}\sigma\eta\varsigma$—is, I think, most naturally interpreted by supposing the last clause to contain a limitation of the first.

‡ $To\acute{\upsilon}\tau\dot{\omega}$ $\nu\acute{\iota}\kappa\alpha$,—undoubtedly, in the native language of the emperor and of the Roman soldiers, Hoc vince.

should be the less tempted to separate the fact at bottom from the subjective conception and representation of it by the narrator, and thus to reduce it from the form of a supernatural to that of a natural phenomenon, because the pagan army, which Constantine was leading from Gaul, and which, according to the pagan rhetorician Libanius, conquered, praying to the gods,* is said also to have beheld the words inscribed in the heavens. But the supposition of a miracle here is one which has in itself nothing to recommend it, especially when we consider, that the *conversion, as it is called, of the Roman emperor*, such as it really was, could in nowise possess the same significance in the sight of God, who respecteth not the person, but looks upon the heart alone as an acceptable sacrifice, as it had in the eyes of men dazzled and deceived by outward show. In this particular way it is scarcely possible to conceive that a change of heart, which is the only change that deserves to be called a conversion, could have been wrought. Much rather might we presume that in this way the emperor would be misled to combine pagan superstition with a mere colouring of Christianity. And were we to judge of the end which this miracle was designed to subserve by the general consequences of the emperor's conversion on the Christian church within the Roman empire, it might be questioned whether these consequences were really so benign in their influence on the progress of the kingdom of God, as they were imagined to be by those persons who, dazzled by outward show, saw in the external power and splendour of the Christian church a triumph of Christianity.

But, aside from all this, in order to suppose a real miracle, we need better testimony to the truth of the facts, as they are stated by Eusebius. The only witness is Constantine himself, who, many years after the event, had related the circumstances to this writer.† But, in the case of Constantine himself, it

---

* Liban. ὑπὲρ τῶν ἱερῶν, ed. Reiske, vol. II. p. 160, καθαιρεῖ μὲν τὸν περιυβρισάντα τὴν ῥώμην ὁ γαλατῶν ἐπ᾽ αὐτὸν ἀγαγὼν στρατόπεδον, οἳ θεοῖς ἐπῆλθον πρότερον εὐξάμενοι.

† As Eusebius does not mention this in his Church History, and yet we can hardly suppose that, when he composed this history, he did not know *something* about it through the popular tradition of the Christians, we must explain the circumstance by supposing that what he then *knew* about it seemed to him either not well authenticated, or else not important enough for his purpose; for it was then his opinion that Constantine,

might easily happen that what was in itself a natural phenomenon would, by his own subjective apprehension of it, by
the power of fancy, the length of the intervening time, the
wish to be regarded by the bishops as a person peculiarly
favoured of God, gradually assume to itself the shape of a
miracle.   Add to this, that Eusebius himself, in the character
of a rhetorical panegyrist, might indulge in some exaggeration.

His story is not wholly consistent with itself; but contains,
besides the miraculous part of it, much that seems altogether
improbable.   Constantine must have received some knowledge
of the God of the Christians from his father; yet he inquires
who he is.   It seems that he needed to be informed what was
meant by the symbol of the cross; but the import of this sign,
which appeared in the daily life of every Christian, and concerning the supernatural influence of which so much was said,
could at that time hardly remain unknown to any one who
was in the habit of associating with Christians.   The very
style of the narration, then, as drawn up by Eusebius, would
lead us of itself to be cautious how we take everything it contains as literally true; and to conjecture that a natural phenomenon was the basis of what he has represented as a supernatural event.   Now we do actually find other accounts which
may, perhaps, be traced back to a still older and purer source,
—to an account given by Constantine, or by Christians who
were with him, soon after the event,—and which point more
directly to a natural incident.   According to Rufinus, he sees,
in a dream, towards the East, the flaming sign of a cross; and,
waking in a fright, beholds at his side an angel, who exclaims,
" By this conquer."* The work, "*De mortibus persecutorum*,"
reports that he was directed in a vision to cause the sign of
the Christian's God to be placed on the shields of his soldiers.†
These statements point to a psychological explanation.   Yet
we must admit that what then transpired in the mind of Con-
tantine would have an important influence on his way of thinking and on his conduct in regard to matters of religion.

following the example of his father, was already a Christian, and marched
against Maxentius, calling on God and Christ to assist him.
   * Rufin. hist. eccles. l. IX. c. 9.
   † De m. p. c. 44. Commonitus est in quiete Constantinus ut cœleste
signum Dei (the monogram of Christ) notaret in scutis atque ita prœlium
committeret.

But it may be doubted whether we have sufficient warrant for adopting this hypothesis. It is possible that the whole story may have sprung up after the event. In the eyes of both pagans and Christians, the victory over Maxentius was an event of the utmost importance. Pagans and Christians were at that time inclined, each party in their own way, to introduce, under such circumstances, the aid of higher powers; and the rhetorical panegyrists especially contributed to the propagation of such legends. Pagans saw, in this case, the gods of the eternal city engaged to deliver them from the disgraceful yoke. Among them, accordingly, was circulated the legend of a heavenly army seen in the air, and sent by the gods to the succour of Constantine.* Among the Christians, on the other hand, the story was propagated of an appearance of the cross. Constantine having been observed, in the later years of his life, to show a peculiar veneration for the cross, men would fain trace this habit to the fact that it was by the aid of the cross he had obtained his victory; and by an anachronistic combination of events which is of no unfrequent occurrence, they referred many things which belonged to a later period of the reign of Constantine—as, for instance, the erection of the banner of the cross—back to the present time. In the later part of his life Constantine may have acknowledged this account of the popular tradition, to give himself importance in the eyes of the Christians; perhaps, by degrees, persuading himself that the event had actually so happened. This, we must admit, is possible. But, in this case, we should have to trace those regulations of Constantine in favour of the Christian church, which immediately ensued, to some other cause. It is altogether inadmissible, however, to explain these regulations as resulting from the policy of Constantine. In gaining over the Christian party to his side, he lost ground with the heathen; and yet the heathen party, if not the most numerous, was for the most part still in possession of the power. Many things, moreover, are to be observed in the

---

* Nazarii Panegyricus in Constantin. c. 14. In ore denique est omnium Galliarum, exercitus visos, qui se divinitus missos præ se ferebant. The words are even put into their mouth, Constantinum petimus, Constantino imus auxilio. And the pitiable flattery adds to this, Habent profecto et divina jactantiam et cœlestia quoque tangit ambitio. Illi, divinitus *missi, gloriabantur* quod *tibi* militabant.

proceedings of Constantine after this time, which assuredly do not admit of being explained from any plan of policy, but only on the ground of a peculiar religious interest. From what has been said above, however, respecting the early education of Constantine, we might very easily account for the fact, even without resorting to the vision of the cross, that, like Alexander Severus and Philip the Arabian, he had become convinced that the God of the Christians was a powerful Divine Being, who was to be worshipped along with the ancient gods of the nation ; and that he was led, after the defeat of Maxentius, when his power was increased, and he had obtained the sovereignty over those lands where Christianity had become more widely diffused, to express, in his public and civil acts, a conviction which he had already long entertained.

But although the origin of this legend might be thus explained, and although we are not driven to a fact of this sort in order to account for the conduct of Constantine towards the Christian church, yet we ought not, without weighty reasons, to reject the legend altogether; nor should we, without weighty reasons, charge Constantine with a partly intentional fraud; especially as he himself here furnishes us with a key to explain his way of thinking and acting in matters of religion, which is in every respect exceedingly well suited to that end, and which in many ways is proved to be the right one. We have already observed that Constantine in his wars was in the habit of looking to the gods for assistance.* Christian and pagan historians are agreed that Maxentius, whose superstition, as it frequently happens, was equal to his crimes, offered many sacrifices to secure the victory on his side ; and that he relied more upon supernatural powers than upon the might of his arms.† Even in the later period of Constantine's life we meet with many things which show that he dreaded the effects of the pagan rites. Supposing this to be the case, we may readily conceive that he, too, would wish to have some superior power on his own side; and that with this feeling, in accordance with the pagan mode of thinking, which, for the most part, still

* Comp. with the above remark the coins of Constantine with the inscription *Soli invicto comiti.* Eckhel, doctrina nummorum veterum, vol. VIII. p. 75.

† Vid. Zosim. l. II. c. 16.

clung to him, his attention would be directed to watch for signs in the heavens, from which he could gather an omen.* In his intercourse with the Christians he had heard of the miraculous power of the cross ; he already believed in the God of the Christians as a powerful being. Now it is very possible that, either of himself, or at the suggestion of Christians about his person, he imagined he perceived, in the shape of the clouds, or in some other object, a sign of the cross—the Christians being disposed to trace their favourite symbol in almost every object of nature. The vision in his sleep, which perhaps immediately followed, admits itself also, in this case, of an easy explanation. Thus, then, Constantine was led to conceive the hope that, by the power of the God of the Christians and the sacred symbol of the cross, he should conquer.† He obtained the victory, and now felt that he was indebted for it to the God of the Christians. The sign of the cross became his amulet, of which fact we find many and various indications in the ensuing life of Constantine. After the victory he caused to be erected in the Forum at Rome his own statue, holding in the right hand a standard, in the shape of a cross, with the following inscription beneath it : " By this salutary sign, the true symbol of valour, I freed your city from the yoke of the tyrant."‡ He was afterwards in the frequent

---

* We may compare the Θεοσημεία in Eusebius, vita Const. l. xxviii., with a διοσημειον.

† Although the remark is certainly just in itself, that the Christian historians were very ready to imagine they saw the sign of the cross where there was nothing of the kind, yet there are no existing grounds for applying this remark, with Eckhel and Manso, to all the monuments belonging to the time of Constantine, and for regarding the Labarum as no more than an ordinary Roman banner; still less is there any good reason for seeking in the Attic antiquities an explanation of the monogram of Christ, the meaning of which is so obvious.

‡ Euseb. hist. eccles. IX. 9; de v. C. II. 40. Τούτῳ τῷ σωτηριώδει σημείῳ, τῷ ἀληθινῷ ἐλέγχῳ τῆς ἀνδρίας, τὴν πόλιν ὑμῶν ἀπὸ ζύγου τοῦ τυράννου διασωθεῖσαν ἐλευθερῶσα. Rufinus has it, Hoc singulari signo : he seems, however, not to have had before him the original Latin words, but, in his usual way, to give an arbitrary translation of the Greek words in Eusebius. As Eusebius lays a particular stress on the word σωτηριώδης, we may conclude that in the Latin there was something exactly corresponding to it, as " salutari." Now unquestionably it may be said that the emperor had perhaps caused himself to be represented simply with a Roman basta (δόρυ σταυροῦ σχήματι, says Eusebius), and that it was only the word " salutare," and some accidental peculiarity

habit of making this sign (to which he ascribed a supernatural power of protection) on the most ordinary occasions.
and was often observed to draw the cross upon his
forehead.*

This hypothesis is rendered probable by similar examples
belonging to the same period, where superstition became the
way to faith, and men who imagined they perceived supernatural effects to proceed from the sign of the cross in the
common occurrences of life were thereby first led to repose
faith in the God of the Christians.† Examples of this sort
occur also at other periods, as, for instance, in the conversion
of warlike princes, such as Clovis and Olof Trygwæson.

In this way we may best explain how in Constantine's mind
there was at first only a mixture of heathen with Christian
views,—how at first he could worship the God of the Christians along with the gods of paganism, until, gradually led on
by the conviction that this his patron God had procured him
the victory over all his enemies, and made him master of the
whole Roman empire, in order that His own worship might
by his means become universally diffused, he came at length to
believe that this God was the Almighty Being who alone
deserved to be worshipped, and that the gods of the heathen
were malignant spirits, opposed to the only true God—spirits
whose kingdom was, through his instrumentality, to be

in the shape of the spear, coupled with what was known respecting
Constantine in his later life, which led to the explanation of that symbol
as the cross ; but the truth is, we have not the least warrant for accusing
Eusebius of any such misapprehension, especially when we consider that
in his Church History, where this circumstance is already related,
nothing as yet occurs respecting the supernatural appearance of the
cross.   The language certainly applies more naturally to the symbol of
the cross than to an ordinary spear; yet we should remember that, in
the language of Constantine, Roman and Christian notions flow together.

  * Euseb. III. 2. Τὸ πρόσωπον τῷ σωτηρίῳ κατασφραγιζόμενος σημείῳ.

  † In the poem of Severus, belonging to the fifth century, which may
be taken as a picture drawn from real life, the pagan shepherd is led to
embrace the faith, from observing, as he supposes, that the fold of the
Christian shepherd is preserved by the sign of the cross from the contagious murrain which fell on the other folds. He concludes,—

> Nam cur addubitem, quin homini quoque
> Signum prosit idem perpeti sæculo,
> Quo vis morbida vincitur?

In the same manner, a warrior, from observing, as he supposes, the power
of the sign of the cross in battle, becomes more inclined to the faith.

destroyed. In the first instance, *his religious convictions* moved him, in conformity with his eclecticism, simply to grant equal toleration and freedom to all the religions existing in the Roman empire; and this, certainly, was the course best suited, under the existing circumstances, to secure tranquillity to the state. His peculiar veneration for the God of the Christians moved him to give special distinction to the Christian worship, without prejudice to the old Roman religion. The paganism of Greece and Rome was, in fact, as the religion of the state, already in possession of the privileges; the Christian worship, hitherto oppressed, had yet to be elevated to the same rank with the other.

The first law relating to matters of religion which Constantine enacted in common with Licinius has not come down to us. The nature of its contents, therefore, can be gathered only from the character of the second law, published in the following year, in which the first is said to be amended. But this latter rescript has also come down to us in a form which renders the attempt to do this both difficult and unsafe.* It is most probable that, in the first rescript, all the religious parties then existing in the Roman empire—including the Christian party, with its various sects—were mentioned by name, and then the free exercise of their religion accorded to all the members of these different religious parties. This, however, was so expressed that it might at least be interpreted to mean that each individual was allowed indeed to follow, with unlimited freedom, the principles of that religious party with which he happened to be connected when this rescript appeared; but could not be permitted to leave the religious party with which he then happened to be con-

* We have this rescript in an abbreviated form, in the book de mort. persecut. chap. 48. Conditions are here spoken of, by which the free exercise of the Christian worship seemed to have been limited in the first rescript: the nature of these conditions, however, is not mentioned. In the next place, we have the same, after a Greek translation, in the Church History of Eusebius (x. 5), but somewhat obscurely expressed, as such translations from the Latin in Eusebius usually are (and perhaps distorted from the true sense by various misapprehensions of the Latin original). Yet we may infer, even from a comparison of Eusebius with the passage in the book de mortibus, that the translation was made from a somewhat different form of the rescript than that which is found in the book de mortibus.

nected, in order to unite himself with another.*   This addition must have been felt to be a great constraint, especially by the Christians; for it may be conceived that, under a new government so favourable to the Christians, many who had

* In the book de mortibus it says, in the second rescript, *amotis omnibus omnino conditionibus*, quæ (in) prius scriptis ad officium tuum datis super Christianorum nomine videbantur. If we chose to take the word αἵρεσις in the expression of Eusebius, ἀφαιρεθείσων παντελῶς τῶν αἱρέσιων, as synonymous with conditio, then Eusebius would agree word for word with the book de mortibus; but to take the word αἵρεσις as meaning simply the same thing with conditio is what neither the general usage of the Greek language, nor the way in which Eusebius uniformly employs this word in the rescript, will permit. It always retains in Eusebius the significations, choice, choice arising from free conviction, the religious sect which one embraces from conviction,—hence sect in general. If the word αἵρεσις in this rescript occurred nowhere else in Eusebius, it might be said that the translator had misunderstood the Latin word conditiones; as, in fact, it seems quite evident that in one passage of the rescript an error of translation has arisen out of a misunderstanding of the Latin, where the question relates to the indemnity which those were to receive who gave up to the churches the landed estates they had been deprived of, and where in the book de mortibus the rescript runs thus: Si putaverint, de nostra benevolentia aliquid vicarium postulent (if they think good to do so, they may ask of our benevolence some indemnity), and where the translator in Eusebius understands the word vicarium as a masculine noun, designating the name of an office, hence reads the passage as if it stood thus: aliquid Vicarium postulent (may demand something from the Vicarius of the province), and translates, προσίλθωσι τῷ ἐπὶ τόπων Ἐπάρχῳ δικαζόντι. But since the same word occurs several times in a similar connection in Eusebius, and since, moreover, as we have remarked, the form of the original document as known to Eusebius, and the form of the rescript in the book de mortibus, seem not to have been in all respects the same, we are not warranted to suppose here a misconstruction of words, but must rather endeavour to gather the nature of the *conditions*, which are not clearly stated in the book de mortibus. from the rescript in its more detailed form, as it appears in Eusebius. The connection in Eusebius is as follows: as in the first rescript many sects of different kinds seem to have been expressly added, the case was perhaps, that many belonging to the above-named sects, soon after the appearance of this rescript, abandoned their previous religion (ἀπὸ τῆς τοιαυτῆς παραφυλάξιως ἀνεχρούοντο). These now seemed by that rescript, which extended religious freedom expressly to the then members of the respective sects, to be hindered from passing over to any other religious party; hence in the second edict it was determined, ὅπως μηδένι παντελῶς ἐξουσία ἀρνητία ᾖ τοῦ ἀκολουθεῖν καὶ αἱρείσθαι τὴν τῶν χριστιανῶν παραφυλάξιν ἢ θρησκείαν, ἑκάστῳ τὶ ἐξουσία δοθείη τοῦ διδόναι ἑαυτοῦ τὴν διάνοιαν ἐν ἐκείνῃ τῇ θρησκείᾳ ἣν αὐτὸς ἑαυτῷ ἁρμόζειν νομίζῃ.

heretofore been held back by fear would wish to go over to the Christian church. The attention of the emperor having been directed to the injurious consequences of the first law, he published at Milan, in the year 313, in common with Licinius, a second edict, in which it was declared, without mentioning by name any of the different religious parties, that, in general, every one might be permitted to adopt the principles of the religious party which he held to be right; and, in particular, every one without exception to profess Christianity. This rescript contained, in fact, far more than the first edict of toleration published by the emperor Gallienus; since, by the latter, Christianity was merely received into the class of the *religiones licitæ* of the Roman empire; while this new law implied the introduction of a universal and unconditional religious freedom and liberty of conscience; a thing, in fact, wholly new, and in direct contradiction with the political and religious mode of thinking which had hitherto prevailed, grounded on the dominant *state* religion ;—a principle which, without the indirect influence of Christianity, would hardly have been brought to light, although the ground on which this general toleration was established, in the present instance, is by no means the purely Christian position. The emperors expressly declared it to be their intention that the interest of no religion whatever should seem to be injured by them :*
and for this they assign political and religious motives; first, that it would be conducive to the tranquillity of the times; and, secondly, that it might conciliate the good will of whatever there was possessed of a divine and heavenly nature to the emperor and his subjects. †

While under the influence of this eclectic liberality, it was really of great importance to Constantine that he should be accurately informed respecting the different religious sects in the Roman empire, and especially respecting those which were little known and much decried (as, for example, the Manichean sect) in order to see whether he might not, consistently with

---

* Ὅπως μηδεμία τιμῇ μηδὲ θρησκείᾳ τινι μεμειῶσθαι φι ὑφ' ἡμῶν δοκοίη.

† Ὅπως ὅτι ποτε ἔστι θειότης καὶ οὐρανίου πράγματος, ἡμῖν καὶ πᾶσι τοῖς ὑπὸ τὴν ἡμετέραν ἐξουσίαν διάγουσιν, εὐμενὲς εἶναι δυνήθη. In the book de mortibus: quod quidem (should perhaps be quid quid est), divinitas (perhaps divinitatis) in sede cœlesti nobis atque omnibus, qui sub potestate nostra sunt constituti, placatum ac propitium possit existere.

the welfare of the state, extend the above-mentioned toleration to these sects also. He made it the special duty of Strategius, a man well fitted for this business by his education and learning, to examine fully into the character of the different sects, particularly of the Manicheans, and to draw up for him a report on the whole matter.*

He at the same time directed, with regard to the Christians, that the places of assembly and other estates which belonged to the Christian church, but which had been publicly confiscated in the Dioclesian persecution, should be restored to the original proprietors. But he did this with a just provision for the indemnification of those private individuals who had purchased these estates, or received them as presents. In this case, too, he assigned as the reason of his conduct, "that the public tranquillity would thereby be promoted, since, by this method of proceeding, the care of the divine Providence, which we have already experienced in many things, will remain secure to us through all time."

This union of two Augustuses to promote the interests of the Christians would necessarily have a favourable influence upon their situation in the other provinces. As the two emperors transmitted their laws also to Maximinus, who then stood on good terms with them, the latter, from special considerations, would be unwilling alone to exasperate the Christians against himself. He wished to introduce a change in his conduct towards that class of his subjects, without appearing to contradict his previous regulations, and to accommodate himself to influences from another quarter; but to do this he was obliged to resort to various shifts and evasions. In a rescript addressed to Sabinus, his prætorian prefect, he declared it to be generally known that Dioclesian and Maximian, when they observed *how almost all were forsaking the worship of the gods and joining themselves to the Christian party,* had rightly decreed that whoever forsook the worship of the immortal gods should be brought back again to the same by

---

* Ammian. Marcelliu. l. XV. c. 13. Constantinus cum limatius superstitionum quæreret sectas, Manichæorum et similium, nec interpres inveniretur idoneus, hunc sibi commendatum ut sufficientem elegit. Having fulfilled this duty to the satisfaction of the emperor, he was afterwards called by him Musonianus, rose to a still higher post, and finally became præfectus prætorio in the East.

open punishments. But when he first came to the East,* and found that very many such people, who might be serviceable to the state, had on this ground been banished by the judges to certain places, he had given directions to the several judges that they should no longer use forcible measures with the inhabitants of the provinces, but rather endeavour to bring them back to the worship of the gods by friendly per-suasion and admonition. Now, so long as the judges had acted agreeably to these directions, no one in the Eastern pro-vinces had been exiled or otherwise treated with violence; but for the very reason that no forcible measures were employed against them, they had been reclaimed to the worship of the gods. The emperor proceeds to explain how he had been afterwards induced to yield to the petitions of certain heathen cities, who were unwilling to tolerate any Christians within their walls. He next renewed the ordinance which secured the Christians against all oppressive measures, and forbade other means to be employed than those of kindness for bring-ing his subjects to acknowledge the providence of the gods. If any individual was led, out of his own free conviction, to profess veneration for the gods, he should be joyfully received; but every other one was to be left to his own inclination, and no reproachful and oppressive conduct was to be allowed in any man. This will of the emperor was everywhere to be made publicly known. But although this was done, yet the Christians had so little confidence in the disposition of the man who had deceived them once already—the rescript itself wore so plainly the marks of constraint, and gave them so little security, inasmuch as the public and common exercise of their religious worship was nowhere distinctly permitted, that they could have no encouragement to avail themselves of this more favourable declaration. It was the misfortune of the emperor which procured for them what they could hardly have expected from his free inclination.

After Maximin had with the greatest difficulty barely saved himself out of the war with Licinius in the year 313, which was so unfortunate for him, he proceeded to arm himself for a new conflict with the enemy, who was pursuing him and laying

---

* This took place in fact after he had already, in his older possessions, followed in some measure the edict of Galerius. (See above.)

waste his provinces.   In this difficult situation the exaspera-
tion of so considerable a party as the Christians already
formed could not be regarded by him as a matter of indifference : perhaps, too, he had been led by his misfortunes to
believe that the God of the Christians might, after all, be a
powerful being, whose vengeance he was now made to experience.   He therefore published another rescript, in which he
declared, that a misconception in some of the judges had
betrayed his subjects into a distrust of his ordinances.   In
order, therefore, that all ambiguity and all suspicion might
thenceforth be removed, it should be made publicly known
that all who were disposed to profess the religion of the
Christians were left free to engage in the public exercise of
this religion in whatever way they chose.   The Christians
were expressly permitted to found churches, and the houses
and estates of which they had been deprived were to be restored
back to them.   Shortly afterwards, he met with a terrible
death at Tarsus.   Constantine and Licinius, who had heretofore both shown themselves favourable to the Christians,
became, by the death of this last persecutor of the Christian
church, sole masters of the Roman empire.

Ambition, love of power, and the strife for absolute sovereignty in the Roman empire, particularly on the part of
Constantine, would not allow them to remain long peaceful
neighbours to each other.   By the battle of Cibalia in lower
Pannonia, in the year 314, the war was decided in favour
of Constantine.   It ended, it is true, in a treaty between
the two princes ; but their respective interests still continued
to conflict with each other.   Licinius, who perhaps was but
little interested in the affairs of religion in themselves considered, had been only moved by his connection with Constantine, and perhaps also by the influence of his wife Constantia,
the sister of Constantine, whom he had married in the year
313, to participate in the favourable proceedings begun towards
the Christians.   The former reason for favouring them was
now removed.   On the other hand, the Christians, as the
friends of Constantine, especially the bishops, to whom Constantine paid so much honour, would become objects of suspicion to him.*   Perhaps many of the bishops gave occasion

* Probably Sozomen represents the matter most correctly (i. 7), when

for this by the public manner in which they avowed their friendship for Constantine.*   The pagans would naturally avail themselves of this state of feeling in Licinius,—would endeavour to confirm him in his hostile sentiments against the Christians, and to inspire him with the hope that he was destined by the gods to re-establish their worship, and prostrate the power of their enemies.   His ordinances against the Christians proceeded in part from his political suspicions ; and partly it was their design to present the Christians, and especially their bishops, in an unfavourable light.   He forbade the latter to assemble together : no bishop was allowed to pass over the limits of his own diocese ; where, however, to allow to the pagan emperor what is justly his due, we should notice that, as is evident from the synodal laws of the fourth century, worldly-minded bishops, instead of caring for the salvation of their flocks, were often but too much inclined to travel about, and entangle themselves in worldly concerns. Whether, however, in the case of Licinius, any well-grounded occasion existed for these proceedings, aside from his excessive suspicion and unwarranted hostility, we are unable to determine with certainty, as the only accounts we have respecting these matters come from prejudiced Christian writers.   He moreover directed that the seats of the men and the women should be separate (a custom which afterwards the ecclesiastical authorities themselves thought proper to retain) ; that no bishop should instruct a female in Christianity, but the women should be instructed only by women.   The same remark which we have just made applies also to these regulations : it is impossible to decide whether the hostile disposition of Licinius led him to adopt all these measures on false pretences, merely with a view to degrade the Christians in the eyes of the people, or whether he was led to them by individual examples of abuse and criminality.   He commanded the Christians at his residence at Nicomedia to hold their assemblies, not in the churches, but in the open fields without the city, under the sarcastic pretence that the fresh air was more healthful in such multitudinous assemblies.   He caused the churches in Pontus to be closed, and others to be demolished ;

he states that Licinius first altered his conduct towards the Christians after his unfortunate war with Constantine.
    * Euseb: de v. C. I. 56.

accusing the Christians that they had prayed, not for his welfare, but for that of the emperor Constantine. He removed the Christians, who refused to offer, from his palace, also from all the high civil and military posts, and from the service of the military police in the cities. There were not wanting those who would have been willing to surrender even more than their earthly means of subsistence and their honours as a sacrifice to their faith; but there were also to be found those who, being Christians rather from habit than from any inward reason, or who, having become Christians only from outward motives, were hence ready again, from similar motives, to change their religion.* Others stood firm, it is true, at first, but afterwards the love of the world overcame their love of religion; they denied the highest and only true good for an empty name, and gave bribes and good words into the bargain, so they might but be restored to their offices.† Licinius published no edict authorising sanguinary measures; even the canons of the Nicene council represent this persecution as one which was attended with no effusion of blood. Yet it may have been the case that, in consequence of the popular fury, and the malice of individual magistrates in many districts, and the opportunity which presented itself in the execution of the imperial laws themselves, the Christians suffered from occasional acts of violence and bloodshed. But on this point we are left without any sufficiently distinct and credible information.‡

---

* Against such the eleventh canon of the Nicene council is directed: Περὶ τῶν παραβάντων χωρὶς ἀνάγκης ἢ χωρὶς ἀφαιρέσεως ὑπαρχόντων ἢ χωρὶς κινδύνου ἤ τινος τοιούτου. ὁ γέγονεν ἐπὶ τῆς τυραννίδος Λικινίου.

† Against such the twelfth canon of the Nicene council is directed: Οἱ προσκληθέντες μὲν ἀπὸ τῆς χάριτος καὶ τὴν πρώτην ὁρμὴν ἐνδειξάμενοι καὶ ἀποθέμενοι τάς ζώνας (the cingulum utriusque militiæ, palatinæ et militaris), μετὰ δὲ ταῦτα ἐπὶ τόν οἰκεῖον ἔμετον ἀναδραμόντες ὡς κύνες, ὧν τινάς καὶ ἀργύρια προϊσθαι καὶ βενεφικίοις κατορθῶσαι τὸ ἀναστρατεύσασθαι.

‡ Particularly famous in the ancient church were the forty soldiers at Sebaste in Armenia, whom their commander endeavoured to compel to offer incense, by exposing them naked to the most extreme cold, of whom thirty-nine are said to have remained steadfast, and were brought to the stake almost frozen. By the rhetorical descriptions of the ancient Homilists, Basil of Cæsarea, Gregory of Nyssa, Chrysostom, Gaudentius of Brescia, Ephraem Syrus, this story has been variously embellished; but we are in want of credible historical accounts, such as would enable us to determine what degree of truth lies at the bottom of this tale.

Finally, in the year 323, the second war broke out between Constantine and Licinius. This war was, it is true, very far from being a religious war, inasmuch as on both sides the grounds of contention were merely political, and not religious. But yet it may notwithstanding be truly affirmed that the triumph of the pagan or Christian party was hanging on the issue. This, too, was well understood on both sides; and it is therefore natural to suppose that the pagan and the Christian parties would embark in the war each with the feeling of their different interests, and that the two emperors also, in different ways, according to the difference of their religious convictions, would place their hopes of success in religion. A characteristic fact to denote the state of feeling among the Christians in the provinces of Licinius is contained in the tradition cited by Eusebius,[*] that, even before the commencement of the war, men believed they saw several legions of Constantine marching victoriously through the streets at mid-day.[†]

Augurs, haruspices, pagan soothsayers of all sorts, fired the hopes of Licinius. Before proceeding to the war he conducted the heads of his prætorians, and the most distinguished officers of his court, into a grove consecrated to the gods, where their images had been set up, and wax candles placed burning before them.[‡] After having sacrificed to the gods, he spoke as follows: "Here stand the images of the gods, whose worship we have received from our fathers. But our enemy, who has impiously abandoned the sanctuaries of his country, worships a foreign god, who has come from I know not whence, and dishonours his army by the disgraceful sign of his god. Placing his confidence upon this, he carries on the war, not so much with ourselves as with the gods whom he has forsaken. The issue of this war must settle the question between his God and our gods. If that foreign thing which we now deride come off victorious, we too shall be obliged to acknowledge and worship it, and we must dismiss the gods to whom we vainly kindle these lights. But if our

* De v. C. II. 6.
† It is well known that similar legends respecting such visions occur also in the case of other wars.
‡ Eusebius relates this after the report of eye-witnesses (de v. C. II. 5) and there is no existing reason for doubting the essential part of the narrative.

gods conquer, as we doubt not they will, we will turn ourselves, after this victory, to the war against their enemies."

Constantine, on the other hand, relied upon the God whose
symbol accompanied his army. He caused the Labarum to
be borne in turn by fifty of his choicest soldiers, who constantly
surrounded it. He had observed, as he supposed, that victory
everywhere accompanied the appearance of this sign, operating
with supernatural power, and that those divisions of his army
which had already begun to give way were often rallied by
its means; an observation which, especially if the emperor
had a considerable number of Christians in his army, might
doubtless be correct, and which may be easily explained from
natural causes. Constantine imagined that, among other
instances, he had met with a proof of the magical power of
the sign of the cross in an incident which he afterward
related to the bishop Eusebius, and which we may cite as
furnishing a characteristic trait of Constantine's religious way
of thinking.* A soldier who bore the ensign of the cross, suddenly overcome with fear, gave it over to another, meaning to
save himself by flight. Soon after he was transfixed by an
arrow; while he who bore the ensign, although many arrows
were shot at him, and the staff of the ensign was struck, was
yet unharmed himself, and came out of the battle without
receiving a wound.

The defeat of Licinius, whom Constantine dishonourably and
faithlessly allowed to be killed, made the latter sole master of
the Roman empire; and certainly, this fortunate accomplishment of his political plans had also an important influence
upon his religious convictions, and the manner in which he
exhibited them. Before we pass to these matters, we may
take a retrospective glance of the manner in which he conducted himself in relation to matters of religion, from the
time of the above-cited edict until this decisive epoch. To
form a correct judgment of his conduct during this period, we
must make the following remarks.

Constantine had indeed gradually abandoned his system of
religious eclecticism, and gone over to monotheism; but yet
the belief in the power of the heathen ceremonies (sacra),
which had taken so deep root in his soul, could not at once be
entirely removed, especially as his superstition had in many

* Euseb. v. C. II. 9.

respects but altered its dress, in exchanging the pagan for a Christian form; and it was natural that the influence of heathens who were about him, of the philosophers and rhetoricians, such as Sopatros, who still retained much of their ancient authority, as well as other circumstances, would again call forth the superstition that had been suppressed. In the next place, although Constantine already looked upon the pagan deities as evil spirits, yet, on this very account, he might still attribute a supernatural power to the magical arts of paganism, and regard them with dread. To this we must add the political motives that forbade him to destroy at once the ancient religion of the state, which still had a considerable party in its favour; while it may be observed in general, that, by his naturally unbiassed judgment, by the experience which he had already obtained in the persecution of Dioclesian, and by his earlier eclecticism, Constantine was for the most part inclined to toleration, except when his mind had been thrown in an opposite direction through some paramount foreign influence.

Although Constantine had manifested in many ways, before that first edict,* a dispostion to promote the Christian form of worship, yet, even down to the year 317, we find marks of the pagan state-religion upon the imperial coins.† Laws of the year 319 presuppose the prohibition of sacrifices in private dwellings. No haruspex was allowed to pass the threshold of another's house. Whoever transgressed this law should be burned; whoever had called an haruspex into his house should be banished, after the confiscation of his goods. Haruspices, priests, and other ministers of the pagan worship, were not allowed to go into the private dwelling of another, even under the plea of friendship. These rigid ordinances are still insufficient of themselves to prove that Constantine meant to suppress the heathen worship out of religious motives. His motives may have been merely political. He may have feared that the consultation of the haruspices and the use of the heathen rites (sacra) might be taken advantage of to form conspiracies against his government and against his life, the suspicions of men being at that time constantly awake on these matters; and *he* might be the more fearful of all this,

---

* See onward, the section concerning the relation of the church to the state.   † Vid. Eckhel doctrina numism. Vol. VIII. p. 78.

since he was by no means free as yet from all faith in the power of the pagan magic.[*]

How far he was, at the same time, from wishing to suppress the public rites of heathenism by force is sufficiently manifest from what he declares in the two cited laws of the year 319 : [†] " They who are desirous of being slaves to their superstition have liberty for the public exercise of their worship ;" [‡] and " You, who consider this profitable to yourselves, continue to visit the public altars and temples, and to observe the solemnities of your usage ; for we do not forbid the rites of an antiquated usage to be performed in the open light." [§] In this concession we see only a wise toleration, the consciousness of the natural limits of civil power, and a knowledge of that human nature whose cravings are but the more strongly excited for that which has been forbidden. By the manner in which the emperor speaks of the heathen worship,—when he calls it a superstition, a *præterita usurpatio,*—he lets it be sufficiently seen that he was no longer held by any religious interest in favour of paganism. With this, however, a law of the year 321 seems to conflict, in which Constantine not only repeats that permission in respect to the institution of the *haruspicia,* but expressly ordains that, " whenever lightning should strike the imperial palace or any other public building, the haruspices, according to ancient usage, should be consulted

---

* Libanius says of Constantine, praising his gentleness in other respects, χαλιπώτατος δὲ ἦν τοῖς ὀριγομένοις βασιλείαν καὶ τὰ τοιαῦτα ἐπιβουλεύουσι, καὶ οὐ τούτοις δὲ μόνοις, ἀλλὰ καὶ ὅσοι μάντισιν ὑπὲρ τοῦ ποῖ χωρήσει τὰ ἐκείνων διελίγοντο, καὶ οὐδεμία τίχνη τόν γὲ τοιοῦτον ἐξείλιτ' ἂν τοῦ πυρός· π. θιοδόσ. πιρὶ στάσιως. II. vol. I. ed. Reiske, p. 635. Eunapius, whose testimony to be sure in such things is not wholly to be relied on, being a zealous pagan, relates that Constantine, at the delay of the provision fleet from Alexandria, whereby Constantine was exposed to the danger of a famine, ordered Sopatros, who had stood high in his favour, to be executed, because the people accused Sopatros of being the cause of this delay, alleging that he had bound the winds by the power of the heathen magic. See Eunapius, vit. Ædes. vol. I. p. 23, ed. Boissonade. Similar accusations are said to have been brought even against the bishop Athanasius. Ammian. Marcellin. hist. l. XV. c. 7.

† Cod. Theodos. l. IX. Tit. 16, c. I et 2.

‡ Superstitioni suæ servire cupientes poterunt publice ritum proprium exercere.

§ Qui vero id vobis existimatis conducere, adite aras publicas atque delubra, et consuetudinis vestræ celebrate solemnia. Nec enim probibemus præteritæ usurpationis officia libera luce tractari.

as to what it might signify, and a careful report of the answer
should be drawn up for his use." * It is, indeed, possible that
he gave this direction, simply because he knew the power
of this kind of superstition, of the belief in omens and similar
things, which continued for so long a time over the minds of
the Roman people; and because he feared that, if the haruspices and their consultors were left wholly to themselves, or if
none but indefinite reports of their interpretations went abroad,
the thing might be followed by still more dangerous consequences. On the other hand, he might hope to be able to dissipate more easily the public anxieties, if he reserved to himself,
as the Pontifex Maximus, the supreme control of the whole.
In this manner might we defend Constantine against the
reproach of having fallen back into pagan superstition, and
explain the whole as proceeding from a Roman policy, by
which he seemed to confirm the pagan superstition ; although
we must admit that such a course can never be justified in a
Christian prince. Yet the other hypothesis, namely, that
Constantine had actually fallen back into heathen superstition, may undoubtedly be regarded as the more natural. By
a law of the same year he declares also the employment of
heathen magic, for good ends, as for the prevention or healing
of diseases, for the protection of harvests, for the prevention of
rain and of hail, to be permitted, and in such expressions too
as certainly betray a faith in the efficacy of these pretended
· supernatural means, unless the whole is to be ascribed simply
to the legal forms of paganism. †

* Cod. Theodos. l. X. Tit. 10, c. 1. Altogether in the technical language : Si quid de palatio nostro aut cæteris operibus publicis degustatum
fulgore esse constiterit, retento more veteris observantiæ, quid portendat,
ab haruspicibus requiratur.

† L. c. c. 3. Nullis vero criminationibus implicanda sunt remedia
humanis quæsita corporibus, aut in agrestibus locis, ne maturis · vin-
demiis metuerentur imbres aut ruentis grandinis lapidatione quaterentur
innocenter adhibita suffragia, quibus non cujusque salus aut existimatio
lædentur; sed quorum proficerent actus, ne divina munera et labores
hominum sternerentur. So that what the devotedly pagan, and on this
point extremely prejudiced historian, Zosimus, says of Constautine (II.
120),—ἐχρῆτο δὲ ἔτι καὶ τοῖς πατρίοις ἱεροῖς, οὐ τιμῆς ἕνεκα μᾶλλον ἢ χρείας,
ἢ καὶ μάντεσιν ἐπείθετο, πιπειραμένος, ὡς ἀληθῆ προειπούσιν ἐπὶ πᾶσι τοῖς
κατωρθωμένοις, αὐτῷ,—may be true so far as this, namely, that, at a time
when Constantine would no longer be consciously a pagan, he was still
involuntarily governed by pagan superstition.

As Constantine, by the defeat of Licinius, had now become master of the whole Roman empire, he expresses everywhere, in his proclamation issued to his new subjects in the East, the conviction that the only true and Almighty God had, by his undeniable interpositions, given him the victory over all the powers of darkness, in order that his own worship might by his means be universally diffused. Thus, in one of the proclamations of this sort issued to the inhabitants of the Eastern provinces of the Roman empire, he says, "Thee the Supreme God, I invoke ; be gracious to all thy citizens of the Eastern provinces, who have been worn down by long-continued distress, bestowing on them, through me thy servant, salvation. And well may I ask this of thee, Lord of the universe, holy God ; for by the leading of thy hand have I undertaken and accomplished salutary things. Everywhere, preceded by *thy sign*,* have I led on a victorious army. And if anywhere the public affairs demand it, I go against the enemy, following the same symbol of thy power. † For this reason I have consecrated to thee my soul, deeply imbued with love and with fear ; for I sincerely love thy name, I venerate thy power, *which thou hast revealed to me by so many proofs, and by which thou hast confirmed my faith*." ‡ And in a letter to the bishop Eusebius of Cæsarea he says, "Freedom being once more restored, and, by the providence of the great God and my own ministry, that dragon driven from the administration of the state, I trust that the divine power has become manifest even to all ; and that they who through fear or unbelief have fallen into many crimes will come to the knowledge of the true God,§ and to the true and right ordering of their lives." What Constantine expresses in this written declaration he represented visibly under an emblem which he caused to be publicly exhibited before the palace in his new residence at Constantinople, consisting of a group of wax figures, in which the emperor was seen with the sign of the

---

* Τὴν σὴν σφραγῖδα (the symbol of the cross) πανταχοῦ προβαλλόμενος.

† Τοῖς αὐτοῖς τῆς σῆς ἀρετῆς ἑπόμενος συνθήμασιν, ἐπὶ τοὺς πολεμίους πρόειμι·

‡ Euseb. de v. C. II. 54.

§ Τὸ ὄντως ὄν, after the Platonic form of expression. The language of the imperial court inclined sometimes to the doctrinal and biblical style of the church, at others to that of the Greek philosophy.

cross over his head, treading under foot a dragon transfixed by an arrow.[*]

It would be a very unjust thing to suppose that all these public declarations and exhibitions amounted to nothing but mere Christian cant, or deliberate and intentional hypocrisy. Constantine's language and conduct admit of a far more natural explanation when we consider them as in part the expression of his real convictions. We have already remarked that he was not lacking in susceptibility to certain religious impressions; he acknowledged the peculiar providence of God in the manner in which he had been delivered from dangers, made victorious over all his pagan adversaries, and finally rendered master of the Roman world. It flattered his vanity to be considered the favourite of God, and his destined instrument to destroy the empire of the evil spirits (the heathen deities). The Christians belonging to his court were certainly not wanting on their part to confirm him in this persuasion, having many of them come to the same conclusion themselves, dazzled by the outward splendour which surrounded the emperor, and which passed over from him to the visible church, and by looking at what the imperial power, which nothing any longer withstood, could secure for the outward interests of the church.

Constantine must indeed have been conscious that he was striving not so much for the cause of God as for the gratification of his own ambition and love of power; and that such acts of perfidy, mean revenge, or despotic jealousy, as occurred in his political course, did not well befit an instrument and servant of God, such as he claimed to be considered; but there was here the same lamentable self-deception, the same

* Euseb. de v. C. III. 3. Quite like the coins which Eckhel represents, l. c. p. 88: a serpent lying beneath the Labarum—above it, the monogram of Christ, symbol of the spes publica. Although many coins of Constantine are not to be found which allude to the victory by means of the cross, yet this cannot be considered as any proof that the above legend has no true foundation. Else we might also argue, from the general fact of so few coins of Constantine being found with Christian symbols, against the undeniable public measures adopted by that emperor in favour of the Christian church. It may be questioned also whether there are any sufficient grounds for pronouncing the coins to be not genuine, which in Eckhel (l. c. 84, col. II.) present an exhibition of the whole event, as Constantine related it to Eusebius.

imposition upon one's own conscience, which is so often to be
seen in the mighty of the earth, who wear religion as their
motto, and which, in their case, so easily insinuates itself, and
gains the mastery, because it is so difficult for truth to find its
way through the trappings of pomp which surround them;
because they are approached by so many who, blinded themselves, dazzled by this splendour, blind them still more in
return, and because no one has ever got access to them who
had the impartiality or the courage to discover to them the
cheat, and teach them how to distinguish between outward
show and truth. Thus was it with Constantine. And what
wonder that he should proceed under such a delusion, when
even Eusebius, one of the best among the bishops at his court,
is so dazzled by what the emperor had achieved for the outward extension and splendour of the church as to be capable
of tracing to the purest motives of a servant of God all the
acts which a love of power that would not brook a rival had,
at the expense of truth and humanity, put into the heart of the
emperor in the war against Licinius; and of even going so far
as to represent him giving out the orders of battle by a special
divine inspiration, bestowed in answer to his prayers, in a war
that beyond all question had been undertaken on no other
grounds than those of a selfish policy? although we must
allow that, waged as it was against a persecutor of the Christians, it would naturally be regarded by Eusebius as a contest in behalf of the cause of God.* Bishops in immediate
attendance on the emperor so far forgot indeed to what master
they belonged, that, at the celebration of the third decennium
of his reign (the tricennalia), one of them congratulated him
as constituted by God the ruler over all in the present world,
and destined to reign with the Son of God in the world to
come. The feelings of Constantine himself were shocked at
such a parallel. He admonished the bishop that he should not
venture to use such language as that, but should rather pray
for him, that he might be deemed worthy to be a servant of
God both in this world and in the next.†

It was now the wish of Constantine that all his subjects
might be united in the worship of the same God. This wish

---

* De v. C. II. 12. Θεοφανίας ἐτύγχανεν, θειοτέρα κινηθεὶς ἐμπνεύσει.
† Euseb. v. C. I. IV. 48.

he expressed publicly, and gladly employed every means in his power to bring it about; but he was determined not to resort to any forcible measures. He still continued to express publicly the principles of toleration and of universal freedom of conscience, and distinctly contradicted the report, which had arisen from very natural causes, that he intended to suppress paganism by force. Thus he declares in the proclamation, already cited, to the people of the East,—" Let the followers of error enjoy the liberty of sharing in the same peace and tranquillity with the faithful: this very restoration of common intercourse among men * may lead these people to the way of truth. Let no one molest his neighbour, but let each act according to the inclination of his own soul. The well-disposed must be convinced that they alone will live in holiness and purity whom Thou thyself dost call to find rest in thy holy laws. But let those who remain strangers to them retain, since they wish it, the temples of falsehood: we have the resplendent house of thy truth, which thou hast given us in answer to the cravings of our nature. We could wish that they too might share with us the joy of a common harmony. Yet let no one trouble his neighbour by that which is his own conviction. With the knowledge which he has gained let him, if possible, profit his neighbour. If it is not possible, he should allow his neighbour to go on in his own way; for it is one thing to enter voluntarily into the contest for eternal life, and another to force one to it against his will. I have entered more fully into the exposition of these matters, because I was unwilling to keep concealed my own belief in the truth; and especially because, as I hear, certain persons affirm † that the temple-worship and the power of darkness are abolished. I would avow this as my counsel to all men, if the mighty

* Αὔτη γὰρ ἡ τῆς κοινωνίας ἐπανόρθωσις (perhaps ipsa hæc commercii restitutio). The indefinite words may also mean "the improving influence of intercourse." The connection, however, favours the first interpretation.

† These "certain persons" may have been fearful pagans, or Christians triumphing in a false zeal—more naturally the latter, especially as the emperor made use of expressions which only a Christian could employ. At all events, it is clear how important it was considered by Constantine to repress the zeal of the Christians, which might easily lead to violent proceedings, and to inspire confidence in the anxious pagans.

dominion of error were not too firmly rooted in the souls of some to permit the restoration of the common happiness." *

In the particular instances in which Constantine first caused temples to be destroyed, and ancient forms of worship to be suppressed by force, the criminal excesses sanctioned under the name of religion, or the fraudulent tricks resorted to for the maintenance of heathen superstition among the credulous multitude, gave him special and just occasion for these proceedings; as, for example, when he caused to be demolished the temple and sacred grove of Venus at Aphaca in Phœnicia,† where from the remotest times the most abominable licentiousness was practised under the name of religion; and when he suppressed the like abominable rites at Heliopolis in Phœnicia. At the same time he sent to the inhabitants of this ancient heathen city a letter, in which he represented to them the hatefulness of these rites, and exhorted them to embrace Christianity. He founded here a church, with a complete body of clergymen and a bishop;—somewhat too early, indeed, since there were as yet no Christians in the place. He bestowed on this church *large sums for the support of the poor;* so that *the conversion of the heathen might be promoted by doing good to their bodies*—a measure, doubtless, which was calculated rather to mislead these people into hypocrisy than to conduct them to the faith. ‡ Again, there was at Ægæ in Cilicia a temple of Æsculapius of ancient fame, where the priests availed themselves of their knowledge of certain powers of nature, perhaps of magnetism (the incubationes), for the healing of diseases; and these cures were ascribed to the power of the god who appeared there, and employed as a means to promote the declining paganism. The temple was filled with the consecrated gifts and the inscriptions of those who supposed themselves indebted to it for their recovery. Far-famed in particular were the remedies which, as it was pretended, the god

---

* Euseb. de v. C. II. 56 and 60.   † Euseb. de v. C. III. 55.

‡ Eusebius (l. c. III. 58) says that the views of Constantine on this matter were precisely like those of the Apostle Paul, Philippians i. 18: "Notwithstanding, every way, whether in pretence or in truth, Christ is preached." This, however, is manifestly a wrong application of that passage, which has been often enough repeated. Paul is speaking of a preaching of the gospel from motives not altogether pure, and not of a hypocritical conversion.

himself prescribed in dreams to the sick who slept in the temple. Not only the populace, but many even of the better class, men of learning, and self-styled philosophers, lauded these wonderful cures. With a view to put an end to the knavery at a single blow, Constantine ordered the temple to be destroyed.* How important a prop of heathenism, which needed such means for its support, was taken away by the destruction of this temple, appears from the complaints which a man like Libanius utters over this impiety and its attendant consequences: "The sick now," he says, "in vain make their pilgrimages to Cilicia." † By dismantling and publicly exhibiting those images of the gods to which miraculous powers had been ascribed, many a trick of the priests was exposed, and what had been venerated by the deluded populace became the objects of their sport. Magnificent temples and statues of the gods were despoiled of their treasures, and stripped of all their costly materials; and then were either turned to the public use, or bestowed as presents on private individuals. Many objects of art taken from the temples were used for the decoration of the imperial residence.‡

For the rest, this method of proceeding against the heathen cultus did not everywhere produce upon the heathen themselves the same effect, owing to the differences of character. The fanatical heathen, especially the educated, who had constructed for themselves a mystical heathenism spiritualized by Platonic ideas, and reasoned themselves into an artificial system composed of heterogeneous elements, could not be disturbed by any exposure of facts, and only felt exasperated by that desecration of their venerated sanctuaries which they were obliged patiently to endure. There were others who

---

* Euseb. de v. C. III. 56.

† Liban. de templis, vol. II. 187. Καὶ νῦν οὓς ἄγει μὲν εἰς Κιλικίαν νοσήματα, τῆς τοῦ Ἀσκληπιοῦ χρήζοντα χειρὸς, αἱ δὲ περὶ τὸν τόπον ὕβρεις, ἀπράκτους ἀποπέμπουσι. And quoting from the eulogy of a pagan rhetorician, in the time of the emperor Julian, probably in reference to the destruction of this temple: Νῦν μὲν σὴν τοῦ θείου δύναμιν δεικνύς ἐκ τῶν ἐπιγραμμάτων, ἃ ἦν τῶν ὑγιανόντων, νῦν δὲ τραγῳδῶν τὸν τῶν ἀθέων κατὰ τὸν νέω πόλεμον, ἀδικουμένους ἱκέτας, οὐκ ἐῶ μένους ἀπαλλαγῆναι κάκων. Liban. ep. 607.

‡ De v. C. III. 54, Liban. ed. Reiske, III. 436, concerning Constantine, Ἐγύμνωσε τοῦ πλούτου τοὺς θεούς. He calls him plainly the σεσυληκώς. Pro templis, vol. II. p. 183.

were under the dominion of no such fanaticism, and whose superstition therefore, when it was stripped of its pompous array, might be more easily exposed in its emptiness. These might, by such sudden impressions, be brought to a sense of their error, and by degrees made capable of receiving a knowledge of the gospel. Others made sport of that which they had formerly believed, without receiving the true faith in place of their superstition. They fell into total scepticism, or contented themselves with a general system of Deism.* It is a fact worthy of remark, and a proof of the already diminished power of heathenism over the popular mind, that officers, commissioned with full powers by the emperor, could venture, without any protection of an armed force, to pass through immense crowds of people, and plunder famous temples, bearing off their venerated treasures. † What fierce commotions, on the other hand, were excited at a later period by the seizure of the *Christian* images in the Byzantine empire!

Again, Constantine endeavoured to place Christians in the highest offices of state, and to appoint them governors in the provinces. Since, however, it was difficult at that time to carry this plan into execution, and wholly exclude the pagans from the public service of the state, and since, moreover, he was unwilling to pass any law of this kind, he contented himself with forbidding the holders of office to sacrifice—a practice which the previous importance of paganism, as the religion of the state, had made a duty incumbent upon them in the execution of many kinds of public business. At length the erection of idolatrous images, and the performance of religious sacrifices, were universally forbidden. But as many pagans still occupied important civil stations, and as Constantine, moreover, was not inclined to resort in this case to arbitrary force, it naturally followed that these laws were but little observed. Hence the succeeding emperor, Constantius, was under the necessity of re-enforcing this ordinance.‡

---

* Euseb. de v. C. III. 57.   † Euseb. III. 54.

‡ This prohibition of the emperor, Eusebius cites in his work, De v. C. II. 44, 45; IV. 23; and Sozomen, I. 8, who seems, however, here merely to copy from Eusebius, and that not accurately. The surest proof that Constantine did actually enact such a law lies in the fact that Constantius, by renewing the prohibition in the year 341, presupposed this law as already existing. If Libanius, on the contrary, in

It was a religious interest which actuated Constantine in his attempts to introduce the Christian form of worship ; but he never employed forcible measures for its extension : he never compelled any person whatever to act in matters of religion against the dictates of his own conscience.　To those of his soldiers who were Christians he gave full liberty to attend church on Sunday.　Upon those of them who were not Christians he did not enforce a Christian form of prayer, nor did he compel them to unite in any of the Christian forms, as the pagan emperors had endeavoured to force Christians to join in the pagan ceremonies.　He simply required the pagans among his soldiers to assemble before the city, in the open fields, and here, at a given signal, to repeat, in the Latin language, the following form of prayer : " Thee alone we acknowledge as the true God ; thee we acknowledge as ruler ; thee we invoke for help ; from thee have we received the victory ; through thee have we conquered our enemies ; to thee are we indebted for our present blessings ; from thee also we hope for future favours ; to thee we all direct our prayer. We beseech thee that thou wouldst preserve our emperor Constantine, and his pious sons, in health and prosperity through the longest life." *　The same thing indeed becomes clearly apparent here, which we have observed on various other occasions, that the emperor had no just conception of the true nature of divine worship and of prayer, and that he laid an undue stress on outward religious forms ; for it was hardly possible surely, that, in repeating, at the word of command, a prayer committed to memory, and that in a language which to a part of the soldiers was not their own, there could be any of that devotion which alone gives to prayer its significance ; but yet it is worthy of remark how the emperor respected the religious convictions of his soldiers.　He avoided in this prayer everything peculiar to Christianity, and nothing

his discourse defending the temple (vol. II. 162), says of Constantine, Τῆς κατὰ νόμους ἱερατίας ἐκίνησεν οὐδὲ ἕν, and 183, ὡς οὐκ ἐπὶ τὰς θυσίας προῆλθε, we remember not only that Libanius was interested here to represent what had been done by the first Christian emperor for the suppression of paganism as of the least possible account, but also that he confounded what was done at different times, and that he was looking at the effects of those laws, which it must be allowed were insignificant.
　* Euseb. de v. C. IV. 18, 19.

in it but the monotheism would be incompatible with the
pagan religion. As it respects this, Constantine perhaps
regarded the belief in one God as that which the contemplation of the universe would teach every man, and the necessary
acknowledgment of which might be presupposed in every man :*
besides, the heathen soldiers, who were not so scrupulous in
regard to every word, might easily interpret the whole as an
address to their own Jupiter.

But, if Constantine was unwilling to employ any forcible
measures for the extension of Christianity, it by no means
follows that he rejected *all outward* means for this end, and
that he had come to understand how Christianity, disdaining
all outward means of persuasion and outward supports, would
make its own way, simply by the power with which it operates
upon the inner convictions and in the life of men.   We have
from himself a remarkable declaration concerning the means
which he supposed necessary to promote the spread of Christianity.   At the council of Nice he exhorted the bishops not
to be envious of each other on account of the applause bestowed on their discourses and the reputation of oratorical
gifts ; not to lay the foundations of schisms by their mutual
jealousies, lest they should give occasion to the heathen of
blaspheming the Christian religion.   The heathen, he said,
would be most easily led to salvation, if the condition of the
Christians were made to appear to them in *all respects* enviable.
They should consider *that the advantage to be derived from
preaching could not belong to all.   Some,* he said, *might be
drawn to the faith by being seasonably supplied with the
means of subsistence; others were accustomed to repair to that
quarter where they found protection and intercession* (alluding
to the *intercessions* of the bishops, see below) ; *others would
be won by an affable reception; others, by being honoured
with presents.   There were but few who honestly loved the
exhibitions of religious doctrine ; but few who were the friends
of truth* (therefore few sincere conversions).†   For this

---

* See his declaration in Euseb. II. 58.
 † Euseb. III. 21.   I place the passage here, which, as it seems to me,
has been corrupted by a transposition of the words, in the way in which
I suppose it ought to be corrected, by restoring the words to their proper
order : ῏Ων μάλιστα σωθῆναι δυναμένων, εἰ πάντα τὰ καθ᾽ ἡμᾶς αὐτοῖς ζηλωτὰ
φαίνοιντο, μὴ δεῖν ἀμφιγνοεῖν, ὡς οὐ τοῖς ζᾶσιν ἢ ἐκ λόγων ὠφέλεια συντελεῖ.

reason they should accommodate themselves to the characters of all, and, like skilful physicians, give to each man that which might contribute to his cure, so that in every way the saving doctrine might be glorified in all. A course of proceeding upon such principles must naturally have thrown open a wide door for all manner of hypocrisy. Even Eusebius, the panegyrist of Constantine, blinded as he was by the splendour which the latter had cast over the outward church, although he would gladly say nothing but good of his hero, yet even he is obliged to reckon among the grievous evils of this period, of which he was an eye-witness, the *indescribable hypocrisy* of those who gave themselves out as Christians merely for temporal advantage, and who, by their outward show of zeal for the faith, contrived to win the confidence of the emperor, which he suffered them to abuse.*

It must appear surprising that Constantine, although he exhibited so much zeal for all the concerns of the church, although he took part in the transactions of a council assembled to discuss matters of controversy, had never as yet received baptism; that he continued to remain without the pale of the community of believers; that he could still assist at no complete form of worship, no complete celebration of a festival. He continued to remain in the first class of catechumens (not catechumens in the stricter sense of the word, see below), though already sixty-four years of age. Thus far he had enjoyed sound and uninterrupted health. He now, for the first time, began to feel the infirmities of age; and illness induced him to leave Constantinople, and repair to the neighbouring city of Helenopolis in Bithynia, Asia Minor, recently founded by his mother, in order to enjoy the benefit of the warm springs in that place. When his malady grew worse, and he felt a presentiment of the approach of death, he repaired, for the purpose of prayer, to the church consecrated to the memory of the martyr Lucian. Here first he made the con-

---

οἱ μὲν γὰρ ὡς πρὸς τροφὴν χαίρουσιν ἐπικουρούμενοι· οἱ δὲ τῆς προστασίας (ταῖς προστασίαις or τὰς) ὑποτρέχειν εἰώθασιν· ἄλλοι τοὺς δεξιώσεσι φιλοφρονουμένους ἀσπάζονται, καὶ ξενίοις τιμώμενοι ἀγαπῶσιν ἕτεροι· βραχεῖς δ' οἱ λόγων ἀληθεῖς ἐρασταὶ καὶ σπάνιος αὖ ὁ τῆς ἀληθείας φίλος.

* See c. IV. 53. Εἰρωνείαν ἄλεκτον τῶν τὴν ἐκκλησίαν ὑποδυομένων καὶ τὸ χριστιανῶν ἐπιπλάστως σχηματιζομένων ὄνομα, οἷς ἑαυτὸν καταπιστεύων τάχα ἄν ποτε καὶ τοῖς μὴ πρέπουσιν ἐνεπίρετο.

fession which was customary before entering into the class of the catechumens, so called in the stricter sense ; and the bishops gave him the blessing.* He next repaired to a castle near the city of Nicomedia, where he called together an assembly of the bishops, and, surrounded by them, received baptism from Eusebius bishop of Nicomedia. This took place shortly before his death, in the year 337. Now, for the first time, he could profess it to be his purpose that, if God spared his life, he would join in the assembly of God's people, and join with all the faithful in all the prayers of the church.†

Doubtless we should consider here that it was not the custom in this period for all to receive baptism immediately after embracing the faith ; but many, especially in the East, deferred it until some special occasion, inward or outward, brought about in them a new crisis of life.‡ But still it must ever seem strange that an emperor who took such interest in the concerns of the Christian church should remain without baptism till his sixty-fourth year. We may indeed give credit to what he says, and suppose—what was quite in character with his religious notions—that he entertained the design to receive baptism in the Jordan, whose water Christ had first consecrated by his own baptism.§ This does not suffice, however, to explain his long delay. It is most probable that, carrying his heathen superstition into Christianity, he looked upon baptism as a sort of rite for the magical removal of sin, and so delayed it, in the confidence that, although he had not lived an exemplary life, he might yet in the end be enabled to enter into bliss, purified from all his sins. He was doubtless sincere, therefore, when, on receiving baptism, he said, as Eusebius reports, that from thenceforth, if God spared him his life, he would devote himself to God's worthy laws of life.|| This remark leads us to notice a report, which circulated among the heathen of this period, respecting the cause of Constantine's conversion ; for the mode of thinking which

---

* He received for the first time the χειροθεσία, and was thus taken among the γονυκλινόντες.

† Euseb. IV. 62. Οὕτως ἐμὲ συναγελάζεσθαι λοιπὸν τῷ τοῦ θεοῦ λαῷ καὶ ταῖς εὐχαῖς ὁμοῦ τοῖς πᾶσιν ἐκκλησιάζοντα κοινωνεῖν ἅπαξ ὥρισται.

‡ See below, under the history of worship.

§ Euseb. v. C. IV. 62.

|| Θεσμοὺς ἤδη βίου θεῷ πρέποντας ἐμαυτῷ διατιτάξομαι.

betrays itself in his notion of baptism furnishes us also with a key to the right interpretation of this story.

Constantine, instigated by the calumnious representations of his second wife, Fausta, had, in a paroxysm of anger, caused his son, the Cæsar Crispus, step-son of Fausta, to be put to death. Reproached for this act by his mother Helena, and convinced afterwards himself that he had been falsely informed, he had added another crime to this by a cruel revenge on Fausta, whom he caused to be thrown into the glowing furnace of a bath. Suspicious jealousy had misled him to order the execution of his nephew, a hopeful prince, the son of the unfortunate Licinius ; and several others, connected with the court, are said to have fallen victims to his anger or his suspicion. When at length he began to feel the reproaches of conscience, he inquired of the Platonic philosopher Sopatros, or, according to others, of heathen priests, what he could do to atone for these crimes. It was replied to him that there *was* no lustration for such atrocious conduct. At that time an Egyptian bishop from Spain (probably Hosius of Cordova is meant) became known at the palace, through the ladies of the court. He said to the emperor that in the Christian faith he could find a remedy for every sin ; and this promise, which soothed the conscience of Constantine, first led him to declare decidedly in favour of Christianity.* Certain it is that any *true* herald of the gospel, if he found the emperor suffering under these misgivings of conscience, would not have begun with calming his fears ; but he would have endeavoured first of all to bring him to the full conviction of the corruption within, of which these gross and striking outbreaks of sin were but individual manifestations ; he would also have discovered to him the vanity of those seeming virtues by which he had often sought to gloss over this inward corruption ; he would have shown him that in general no opus operatum by outward lustrations could have any effect to cleanse the inner man from sin ;—and then, after having cleared the wounded conscience of all those deceitful and soothing hopes which serve only as a prop for sin, and shown him what true repentance is, he would have presented before him Christ, as the Redeemer of the truly penitent and believing sinner ; constantly warning him against the seeming faith which leads men to

* Zosim. II. 29 ; Sozom. I. 5.

seek in Christ only a deliverer from that outward suffering which a violated conscience holds up to their fears, and a stay for the sinfulness of their nature.   But we may well suppose that, among the bishops of the court, there was none who would have spoken to the emperor in this manner.   As it would be quite in character for Constantine, when suffering under the reproaches of conscience, to seek after some magical expiation, so we may easily suppose that a bishop who possessed little of the simple temper of the gospel and of pure Christian knowledge, and who was moreover blinded by the splendour of the court, might point the emperor to such a means of expiation in the rite of baptism, or in an empty profession of faith, and thus poison for him the very fountain of salvation.   But the testimony of pagans, inimical to Christianity and the emperor, furnishes no sufficient evidence *for the truth* of a story which they could have so easily invented; while, on the other hand, the silence of Christian historians, whose prejudices were all on one side, furnishes no evidence *against its truth.*   That this account cannot, however, be literally true appears, as Sozomenus has justly remarked, from the gross anachronism which it contains; for, long before Constantine had committed these crimes,* he had taken his decided stand in favour of Christianity.   The whole story, therefore, may have no other foundation than the fact that Constantine strove to quiet his sins by relying on the opus operatum of outward means of justification, especially upon the justifying power of outward baptism, which he reserved against the time of his death, and upon the merit of what he had done to promote the outward splendour of the church; and it may be that the bishops of the court, instead of teaching him better, confirmed him in this destructive error.†   This doubt-

---

* The execution of Crispus took place at the same time with the vicennalia of Constantine, or the celebration of the twentieth anniversary of his assuming the dignity of Augustus, that is, in 326; and it was in the preceding year that Constantine displayed, at the council of Nice, so decided a zeal in favour of the Christian faith.

† Eusebius of Cæsarea was a man conversant with still higher things than mere worldly interests, and cannot be reckoned among the number of the ordinary court bishops of this period; yet mark how he describes a banquet which the emperor gave to the bishops at the breaking up of the Nicene council, in celebration of the *vicennalia* of his entrance upon the dignity of Cæsar: "When the emperor held a banquet with

less would be observed by the pagans, who would not be slow in taking advantage of it to misrepresent Christianity.*

If the reign of Constantine *bears witness that the state which seeks to advance Christianity by the worldly means at its command may be the occasion of more injury to this holy cause than the earthly power which opposes it with whatever virulence*, this truth is still more clearly demonstrated by the reign of his successor Constantius.

Constantius, in the outset, shared the government with his two brothers, Constantine the younger and Constans, to whose portion fell the dominion of the West. The younger Constantine having, in the war against his brother Constans, lost his life, Constans made himself master of the whole Western, as Constantius was already of the whole Eastern empire; and when Constans perished, in the year 350, in the revolt of Magnentius, Constantius was left sole master of the entire Roman empire. Now, although the measures adopted for the

the bishops, among whom he had established peace, he presented it through them, as it were an offering worthy of God. No one of the bishops was excluded from the imperial table. The proceedings on this occasion were sublime beyond description. The soldiers of the emperor's body-guard were drawn up before the door of the palace with their bare swords. The men of God (the bishops) passed along undaunted between their files into the interior of the palace. Some sat at the same table with the emperor himself, the others at side-tables. One might easily imagine that one beheld the type of Christ's kingdom." Euseb. vit. Constant. I. III. c. 15. Making due allowance for the corrupt rhetorical taste of those times in passing our judgment on these expressions, still we must feel certain that a man who was capable of using such language was in no condition to speak to the emperor in the spirit of the gospel, as one charged with the care of souls.

* Thus Julian, in his satirical performance entitled "The Cæsars," makes Constantine in the lower world proclaim to all, "Whoever is a voluptuary, a murderer, whoever is a vicious man, a profligate, let him boldly come hither. Having washed him with this water, I will instantly make him pure. And should he fall into the same crimes again, let him only beat on his breast and on his head, and I will bestow on him power to become pure." Ὅστις φθορεὺς, ὅστις μιαιφόνος, ὅστις ἐναγὴς, καὶ βδελυρὸς ἴτω θαῤῥῶν. ἀποφανῶ γὰρ αὐτὸν τουτῳὶ τῷ ὕδατι λούσας, αὐτίκα καθαρόν, καὶ πάλιν ἔνοχος τοῖς αὐτοῖς γένηται, δώσω τὸ στῆθος πλήξαντι καὶ τὴν κεφαλὴν πατάξαντι, καθαρῷ γενέσθαι. And Libanius sees in the cruelty of Constantine towards his own family a punishment inflicted on him for his plundering of the temples: Τίς οὕτω μεγάλην τῶν περὶ τὰ ἱερὰ χρήματα δίδωκι δίκην τὰ μὲν αὐτὸς αὐτὸν μετίων; Pro templis, p. 184, vol. II.

suppression of paganism proceeded directly from Constantius, although they were executed in his empire with the greatest severity and rigour—despotism in the East being, as a general thing, the most oppressive—yet, on the whole, the principles upon which he proceeded were those which prevailed throughout the entire empire. Constantius, in re-enacting, in the year 341, the law of the previous reign against sacrifices, gave the following peremptory command: " Let superstition cease; let the folly of sacrifices be abolished.* Whoever, after the publication of this law, continues to sacrifice, shall be punished according to his deserts;" yet the nature of the punishment is not clearly defined.

Although this law might properly refer only to the Eastern empire, yet in a law of the year 346, enacted in common by the emperors Constantius and Constans, and therefore valid for the whole Western and Eastern empire, it is presupposed that the extirpation of the entire pagan superstition had already been commanded;† and in the same year the two emperors again conjointly directed that the temples should everywhere be closed, that access to them should be forbidden to all, and thus liberty for crime taken away from abandoned men.‡ Sacrifices were forbidden on pain of death and the confiscation of goods. When at a still later period, under the usurper Magnentius, who himself professed to be a Christian,§ the pagan cultus in the West had recovered a certain degree of freedom —whether it was that the usurper, from political reasons or want of interest in religious matters, made show of greater toleration; or whether it was that, without any interference of his own, the laws which had been passed against the pagan worship had, in the turmoils of this revolution, lost their power—yet for this cause Constantius thought it necessary, after he had suppressed the insurrection in the year 353, and became the sole ruler, to issue a new law against sacrifices by night, which had been again introduced. Three years later, in 356, he passed a law, in the name also of the Cæsar Julian, who was even then secretly inclined to paganism, by which law he made it once more capital to sacrifice and worship the

* Cod. Theodos. 1. XVI. Tit. X. c. 2. Cesset superstitio, sacrificiorum aboleatur insania.   † Omnis superstitio penitus cruenda.
  ‡ Licentiam delinquendi perditis abnegari.
  § As the ensigns of the cross on his coins prove. See Eckhel, VIII. 122.

images of the gods. The relation of things had become reversed. As in former times the observance of the pagan ceremonies, the religion of the state, had appeared in the light of a civil duty, and the profession of Christianity in that of a crime against the state, so now it was the case, not indeed that the outward profession of Christianity was commanded as a universal civil duty, for against this the spirit of Christianity too earnestly remonstrated, but that the exercise of the pagan religion was made politically dangerous. There was an inclination to regard the heathens as unsatisfied with the present order of things; and the suspicious despot Constantius feared, whenever he heard about the celebration of pagan rites, especially about augurs, haruspices, consultation of oracles and sacrifices, that conspiracies were brooding against his government and his life. It was especially the notary Paulus, widely known under his well-deserved soubriquet, the *Chain* (catena), who, in the latter times of this reign, working upon the suspicious temper of Constantius, and using him as the instrument of his own designs, ravaged the land as a cruel persecutor. It thus happened that a heathen philosopher, Demetrius Chytas of Alexandria, was convicted of having repeatedly sacrificed. Not so much for religious as for political reasons, this transgression of the laws was interpreted as a grievous crime; his judges pretending to look upon it as a magical ceremony, undertaken in a hostile spirit against the emperor.* No credit was given to his assurances that from his early youth he had been accustomed to sacrifice, simply to propitiate the favour of the gods. But when he steadfastly persisted in the same assertion under the rack, he was dismissed to his home; although, if the imperial law had been strictly carried into execution, he must have suffered the penalty of death, as a heathen who, by his own confession, had offered sacrifices. To wear heathen amulets for keeping off diseases, to consult an astrologer on any private affair whatever, might easily involve one in a crimen majestatis, leading to tortures and death.†

To the great vexation of the pagans, Constantius caused

* See Ammian. Marcellin. l. XIX. c. 12.

† Ammian. Marcellin. l. c. Liban. pro Aristophane, vol. I. p. 430. The words of Ammianus Marcellinus are particularly worthy of notice: "Prorsus ita res agebatur, quasi Clarium, Dodonæas arbores et effata Delphorum, *olim solennia* in imperatoris exitium sollicitaverint multi."

several celebrated temples to be destroyed. Some he plundered, and presented others or their treasures to Christian churches, or to his favourites among the courtiers ; and sometimes, therefore, to the most unworthy of men. The property of the temples, which might have been employed to a better purpose in the cause of religion, often became a prey to cupidity and rapine ;* and when many, who had become rich by the plundering of temples, abandoned themselves to every lust, and finally brought ruin upon themselves by their own wickedness, the pagans looked upon this as the punishment sent by their gods for robbing the temples ; and they predicted that similar punishments would follow every instance in which the temples were desecrated, as appears from the asseverations of Libanius and Julian.

The emperor, however, thought it advisable to keep under some restraint the fury for destroying temples, in order to preserve certain national antiquities which were dear to the people. By a law of the year 346 he ordained that all temples existing without the walls of the city should be preserved uninjured, since with many of them were connected national festivities, and certain of the public games and contests had derived their origin from them.† When Constantius, after his victory over Magnentius, resided in Rome, and there saw the heathen temples in their full splendour, he took no measures against them ; and heathenism, as the old religion of the Roman state, still retained so much consequence, that much that belonged to the heathen forms of worship was left unaltered in the Western empire. Thus it was with the privileges of the vestals and the priestly dignities, which were given to Romans belonging to the noblest heathen families,‡ although we must allow that these dignities had lost much of their ancient importance. Subsequently to the establishment of the law which made the offering of sacrifice a capital crime,

---

* Liban. de accusatorib. III. 436. Κατίσκαψε τοὺς ναοὺς καὶ πάντα ἱερὸν ἐξαλείψας νόμον, ἔδωκεν αὐτὸν (αὐτοὺς), οἷς ἴσμιν. Liban. Epitaph. Julian. 529 : Τὸν σῶν ἱερῶν πλοῦτον εἰς τοὺς ἀσελγεστάτους μεμερισμένον. Ammian. Marcellin. l. XXII. c. 4. Pasti quidam templorum spoliis.

† Cod. Theodos. l. XVI. Tit. X. c. 3. Nam cum ex nonnullis vel ludorum vel circensium vel agonum origo fuerit exorta, non convenit ea convelli, ex quibus populo Romano præbentur priscarum sollennitas voluptatum.

‡ See Symmach. relat. ad Valentinian. l. X. ep. 61.

Tertullus, the prefect of the city, did not hesitate, when a storm at sea hindered the provision fleet from arriving at Rome and threatened a famine, to offer public sacrifices in the temple of Castor, near the mouth of the Tiber, that the gods might calm the fury of the storm.*

Whilst falsely flattering pagan rhetoricians, such as Libanius and Themistius, publicly spoke in praise of the emperor, whom at heart they detested as the enemy of the gods, there were still among the teachers of the Christian church many bold and fearless voices, which plainly told him that he rather injured than aided Christianity when he sought to advance its interests by outward power,—voices which now presented before a professedly Christian emperor, who confounded the Christian with the political standing-ground, the principles of liberty of conscience and belief brought to light by Christianity, just as they had been presented before the pagan emperors by its first defenders. Very pertinently says Hilary to the emperor Constantius, "With the gold of the state you burdened the sanctuary of God; and what has been torn from the temples, or gained by the confiscation of goods, or extorted by punishments, that you force upon God."† Concerning the resort to violent measures for the advancement of religion, Athanasius finely remarks,‡ "It is an evidence that they want confidence in their own faith, when they use force, and constrain men against their wills. So Satan, because there is no truth in him, wherever he gains admittance, pays away with hatchet and sword. But the Saviour is so gentle that he teaches, it is true, '*Will* any one come after me, and who *will* be my disciple?' while he *forces* none to whom he comes, but only knocks at the door of the soul, and says, 'Open to me, my sister;' and if the door is opened, he goes in. But if any one is unwilling to open, he withdraws; for the truth is not preached by sword and javelin, nor by armies, but by persuasion and admonition.§ How can there be anything like persuasion where the fear of the emperor rules? How can there be anything like admonition where he who contradicts has to expect banishment and

* Ammian. Marcellin. l. XIX. c. 10.
† C. Constant. imperator. lib. c. 10. ‡ Hist. Arian. s. 3.
§ 'Ου γὰρ ξίφεσιν ἢ βέλεσιν οὐδὲ δία στρατιώτων ἡ ἀληθεία καταγγελίται, ἀλλα πειθοῖ καὶ συμβουλία.

death?" Says the same writer in another place,* " It is the character of true piety, not to force, but to convince; since our Lord himself forced no man, but left free the choice of each individual, saying to all, ' If any man *will*, let him come after me;' but to his disciples, ' *Will* ye also go away?'" The men who expressed such truths with Christian boldness were thinking indeed, in this case, not so much of the conduct of the emperor towards the pagans as of his conduct towards the contending parties of the Christian church; their own interest (for they belonged to a party which lay under the constraint of outward power) coincided in this case with what the spirit of Christianity requires; and hence they might the more readily perceive this, and be led to make it a prominent point in opposition to the prevailing sentiments of their time. It is plain that the same could have been said also concerning the emperor's conduct towards the pagans; but it may be justly questioned whether they would have been equally free to recognise and proclaim the same truths in this wider application. It is certain, at least, that many of the fathers were actuated by another spirit than this Christian one: they were concerned only for the outward suppression of paganism, without considering whether the means employed for this purpose agreed with the spirit of the gospel, and were suited to destroy paganism in the hearts of men. Julius Firmicus Maternus† thus addresses the emperors Constantius and Constans: " Take off without scruple the decorations of the temples; use all their consecrated gifts for your own profit, and that of the Lord. After destroying the temples, ye are, by the power of God, exalted higher." He paid homage to the error, so ruinous to the emperors, which led them to imagine that, by merely destroying the outward monuments of paganism, they proved themselves to be Christians, and secured the divine favour. He also describes the political success of the emperors in the usual style of exaggerated flattery, peculiar to the panegyrists of the age, and says nothing of their misfortunes. He next invites them to punish idolatry, and assures them that the divine law required them to suppress all

---

* Hist. Arian. s. 67.

† Concerning whom we shall speak further in another place, under the head of the Apologists.

paganism by force.* Forgetting the spirit which it became Christians to cherish, and by what means the Christian church had overcome all earthly powers that had opposed her and finally rendered them subservient to her own interests, he employs those passages of the Old Testament which threatened with the punishment of death those who became idolaters from among the people of God, to show how Christian emperors should deal with the same class of men. Worldly-minded bishops, who by their proceedings caused the name of the Lord to be blasphemed among the Gentiles, such as Georgius of Alexandria, raged against paganism, and stood ready to reward with everything which their powerful influence at court enabled them to procure, with the favour of the prince, and titles, and stations of honour, the hypocrisy of those who accounted earthly things of more value than divine.†

If we consider more closely the relation, as it now stood, of Christianity to paganism in the Roman empire, we cannot fail to see that a reaction of the latter, to recover itself from its depression, was already prepared. As nothing can be more hurtful to the cause of truth than attempting to support and further it by some other power than its own, thus converting truth itself into a falsehood; so nothing, on the other hand, can contribute more to promote the cause of error than raising up martyrs for it, and thus lending it the appearance of truth.

* C. 30. Ut severitas vestra idololatriæ facinus omnifariam persequatur.

† Libanius doubtless expresses what he had seized from the life of the times, when he says, speaking of a certain Aristophanes, who, even under the reign of Constantius, had continued steadfast in the profession of heathenism, " What rewards might he not have obtained from Georgius, if he had been willing to make in the church a public profession of Christianity, and to insult the gods? What prefecture of Egypt, what power with the eunuchs of the court, and with the emperor himself, would not Georgius have procured for him? Ποίαν οὐκ ἂν προοῦπιεν Αἴγυπτον ἀντὶ ταύτης τῆς κωμῳδίας; παρὰ τίσιν οὐκ ἂν εὐνούχοις τὸν ἄνθρωπον ἀπέφηνεν ἰσχυρόν; ἥττιτ' ἂν εὖ ἴσθι, καὶ τῆς Κωνσταντίου κεφαλῆς εἰ τὴν ἑαυτοῦ κεφαλὴν πρὸς Γεώργιον ἤρειδεν." Pro Aristophane, vol. I. p. 448. This agrees with the description which Athanasius gives of those who became Christians for the sake of spiritual offices, to obtain exemption from the burdens of the state, and to secure powerful connections,—men who were satisfied with any creed, provided only they could be released from state burdens, and maintain their connections with those in power: Ἕως μονὸν εἰσὶν ἀλειτουργήτοι καὶ προστασίαν ἀνθρωπίνην ἔχουσι. Athanas. hist. Arianor. ad monachos, s. 78.

It certainly had been possible for paganism, under the existing circumstances, to gain vastly more if this religious system, which consisted of the old popular superstition, coming out in a new dress from the school of pompous mystical sophists and conceited rhetoricians, had not been in itself so utterly unsubstantial and powerless; an idle gewgaw, hardly capable of imparting to any soul enthusiasm enough to become a martyr.

Many had hypocritically assumed the profession of Christianity, while at heart they were still inclined to paganism, or were ready to adopt any religion which happened to be in favour at court; others had framed a system for themselves, mixed up of paganism and Christianity, in which often there was nothing more than merely an exchange of pagan for Christian names—in which only Christian forms and ceremonies were substituted in place of the pagan, and from which, under a change of circumstances, it would not be difficult to retreat back to paganism. The passions which in controversial disputes excited the Christians to rail at each other; the impure motives which crept in on these occasions, especially through the influence of the court; the zeal for a formal orthodoxy and church ceremonial among so many who in their lives manifested a spirit so different from that of the gospel—all this must have served to give support to the false accusations against Christianity current among the pagans; as in the earlier times the effects of the gospel on the lives of its followers had tended to further its progress. Thus a heathen party had kept itself alive, which, in its fanaticism, rising under the pressure of distress, and taking advantage of all that was bad in the Christian church, flattered itself with the hope of one day seeing the worship of its gods victoriously restored.

The spirit which for the most part animated this party was by no means a purely religious fanaticism. It was a blind love for the old antiquities of Greece and Rome; for Grecian art and science, which, to these pagans, seemed, not without reason, to be closely connected with the old religion. It was their enthusiastic attachment to everything connected with the old Greek and Roman manners which filled them with hatred to Christianity,—a religion which introduced a new, spiritual, and to them unintelligible, creation. Hence it was that paganism found its most zealous promoters among the rhetoricians, philosophers, and men of learning; and that the attachment to it lingered especially in many of the ancient and noble families of Greece and Rome. The rhetoricians who made an open profession of paganism, or who, although they professed Christianity, were pagans at heart, had opportunities enough, although they did not venture publicly to attack the latter in their lectures, yet, in expounding the ancient authors, to communicate imperceptibly to the minds of the youth a direction hostile to Christianity. What we have already remarked with reference to the preceding period still continued to be true—that the religious symbolism, derived from the Neo-Platonic philosophy, was the most important means resorted to for dressing out paganism as a rival of Christianity, and for imparting an artificial life to that which was already effete. Speculative ideas and mystical intuitions were to infuse into the old insipid superstition a higher meaning. Theurgy, and the low traffic in boastful mysteries, contributed greatly also to attract and enchain, by their deceptive arts, many minds, influenced more by a vain curiosity, which would penetrate into what lies beyond the province of the human mind, than by any true religious need. Yet in art and science there was nothing truly creative which could spring any longer out of the withered trunk of paganism. All the creative power dwelt in Christianity. This alone could impart the spirit of a new life into the forms borrowed from the Grecian art and science. Those who, instead of yielding to the new creation by which everything was to be restored to the freshness of youth, mourned over the grave of the ancient world, which had long since perished, could do nothing more than form an idle patchwork out of the old fragments of rhetoric, philosophy, and literature.

From what has now been said, it is easy to see that, should a pagan emperor once more ascend the throne, this paganism would make another attempt to gain the supremacy; since for the moment everything in fact depended upon the will of the emperor, although indeed no human will had the power of actually calling back to life what was already dead. And to this very end, that a pagan emperor should once more be established on the throne, Constantius was to prove the instrument,—Constantius, who had ever been the chief cause of mischief to the Christian church, for which he displayed so much zeal.

The new emperor was Julian, the nephew of Constantius, whose desertion to paganism admits of an easy explanation, both from the peculiarity of his character, and from his course of life and education.   In fact, a very slight turn seemed all that was necessary to change the peculiar bent, manifested by the whole family of Constantines for the outward show and form of religion, from Christianity to paganism ; and this turn Julian took from his earliest youth.   Having lost, as it is said, early in life, his nearest relatives, through the jealousy of his uncle, who discarded the natural feelings of kindred, this circumstance would leave on the mind of Julian no very favourable impression of the religion which prevailed at the imperial court, and for which Constantius manifested such excessive zeal ; although, at the time this took place, he was too young to be conscious of any such impression.   Every pains was taken to keep him away, while a boy and a young man, from the infection of paganism, and to fasten him to Christianity.   This was done as well from political as from religious motives, since any connection of the prince with the pagan party might prove dangerous to the state.   But the right means were not chosen to secure this end.   What was thus forced upon him could not easily take root in a mind which naturally hated constraint. This careful surveillance would only have the natural effect to excite his longing after that which they were so anxious to keep from him.   And the men, too, whom the court employed as its instruments, were not such as would be likely to scatter in the mind of Julian the seeds of a thorough Christianity, and to leave impressions on his heart calculated to give a decided Christian direction to his inner life.   It was in a diligent attention to those outward religious forms which busy the imagination that he and his brother Gallus were chiefly exercised while pursuing their education under vigilant masters, in the solitude of Macellum, a country seat in Cappadocia. Their very sports were made to wear the colour of devotional exercises ; as when they were taught to emulate each other in erecting a chapel over the tomb of Mamas, a pretended martyr, held in special veneration throughout this district.   The boys might easily become accustomed to all this ; and, unless some mightier reaction took place in the inmost recesses of the mind, the habits thus formed might become fixed, as they actually were in the case of Gallus ; but not so, where a mightier influence than religious mechanism began to work in an opposite direction, as in the case of Julian.

Both are said to have been educated as ecclesiastics; they were consecrated as pre-lectors in the church, little as the disposition of either one of them was suited for the clerical profession. This office, which had been given to Julian when young, must have made him quite familiar with the scriptures; and the writings of Julian do actually show that he possessed a ready acquaintance with the letter of the scriptures; but of what avail could that be when his mind had taken a direction which unfitted him altogether for entering into their inward meaning, and his heart was ever wholly disinclined from submitting to the doctrines which they taught? Homer, on the other hand, was expounded to him by a man much more skilful in imparting to the imagination of the young student an enthusiasm for his author, than the clergy had proved to be in implanting a love of the divine word in his heart. This was Nicocles, a civilian, enthusiastically devoted to the Grecian literature, who, after the fashion of the Platonists of that period, contemplated Homer, through the medium of an allegorical interpretation, as the guide to a higher wisdom.[*] Probably, in his own convictions, he was a pagan,[†] although he might not openly avow this to be the case; and we may well conceive that such a person was far more fitted to disseminate imperceptibly in the mind of the young student something hostile to Christianity, than to cherish in him the Christian tendency. Besides, the light in which such an instructor must have taught him to contemplate Homer would not be likely to harmonize with Christianity. Two heterogeneous and hostile elements were here brought at once into his soul; the one penetrated deeply, the other only touched lightly upon the surface. These two elements might, it is true, rest peaceably side by side; and the more so, the less deeply Christianity took hold of the life; but a conflict between them might afterwards easily be excited by outward causes, and a religion afterwards find its way to his soul, the medium of entrance for which had been prepared by that fundamental

---

* Liban. Πρεσβευτικὸς πρὸς Ἰουλιανόν. Vol. I. p. 459. Ἐιδὼς ἵπτερ τις, τῆς Ὁμήρου γνώμης τὰ ἀπόῤῥητα.

† Otherwise Libanius would hardly have bestowed on him so much praise in the passage just referred to.

element of his education.   Thus he contracted a great fondness for the study of the ancient Greek poets and orators
generally; and this love for ancient literature next formed a
point of transition to the love of ancient paganism, as the
living spring of this literature, the two things being in fact
intimately connected in the view of the pagan party among
the learned.   It was said, indeed, that the ancient literature
had sunk with the ancient religion, and that the disgrace of
that literature had followed close after the degradation of the
temples in the time of Constantine;—a complaint which in
one respect was wholly groundless, inasmuch as this literature,
without inward life, had long carried within it the germ of its
own decay, and nothing but Christianity remained to infuse
new life into the dead bones of antiquity.*

After six years' residence at the country-seat in Cappadocia,
Julian was called in the year 350 to Constantinople, where
he occupied himself exclusively with literary pursuits.   Here
he was not allowed to avail himself of the instructions of the
rhetorician Libanius, who openly acknowledged himself a
pagan; but the rhetorician Ecebolius, a man of less elevated
mind, who accommodated his religion to the air of the court,
and who, under Constantius, was a zealous Christian and a
violent antagonist of paganism, while under Julian he became
an equally zealous pagan and antagonist of Christianity,
obtained, as the reward of his hypocrisy, the charge of the
prince's education. †   How could such an instructor imbue
the youthful mind of his pupil with the love of Christianity?

The foolish Constantius, who must be so often deceived and
led to act contrary to his own interests where he thought that
he was doing the utmost to promote them, was afraid to leave

---

* Libanius, not without reason, says to Julian, Ὅτι καὶ πρὸς τιμὴν
τῶν θεῶν ὑπ᾽ αὐτῶν ἐκινήθης τῶν λόγων. Πρὸς φωνητικ. Vol. I. p. 405,
οἰκεία καὶ συγγένη ταῦτα ἀμφότερα, ἱερὰ καὶ λόγοι. Vol. III. p. 437.

† Liban. epitaph. Julian. vol. I. p. 526, Σοφιστής τις πονηρὸς τοῦ κακῶς
ἀγορεύειν τοὺς θεοὺς μισθὸν εἶχε τὸν υἱόν. Socrates (l. III. c. I) mentions
his name.   The same writer also relates the rest which is noticed in the
text, and moreover adds, that after Julian's death he was for once more
playing the Christian, and proposed to subject himself to the penance of
the church, that he might be again admitted to its communion; that he
prostrated himself on the earth before the door of the church, and called
out to the people,—" Tread me under foot; I am the senseless salt,"
πατήσατέ μι, τὸ ἅλας τὸ ἀναίσθητον. Socrat. I. III. c. 13.

a young prince, that already began to attract a good deal of attention, behind him at Constantinople, while he himself went to the West on his expedition against Magnentius. He gave him leave, therefore, to visit Nicomedia, in Bithynia, for the purpose of prosecuting his literary pursuits at a flourishing seat of learning, where several distinguished rhetoricians were teachers. Yet there he was exposed much more to the infection of paganism than at Constantinople, where fear and worldly interest induced even those who were pagans at heart to wear the mask of Christianity. He was obliged to promise, on departing from Constantinople, that he would not attend the lectures of the pagan Libanius, who also then taught at Nicomedia. But the prohibition, as might be expected, served only to stimulate his curiosity; and he contrived to procure copies of the lectures of Libanius, which indeed, if we may judge from his writings that remain, barren as they were of ideas and sentiments, dry in their contents, and rich only in the ornaments of rhetoric, could have attractions only for a very disordered mind, unaccustomed to healthy nourishment, weaned from simplicity, and easily pleased with the glare of superficial ornament. The gratification which he found in the lectures of Libanius doubtless brought him gradually into connection with the whole pagan party. At its head stood at that time, along with the rhetoricians, *the Platonists*, who had schools in Asia Minor, particularly at Pergamos. The most renowned among these Platonists were the old Ædesius, Chrysanthius, Eusebius, Maximus. The last-mentioned was also an adroit juggler, who boasted of his power to do great things by means of supernatural agents. These Platonists maintained a close correspondence with the pagans at Nicomedia. To gain over a young man who was destined to hold so important a position in the state was naturally regarded by them as a great object, worthy of the most skilful finesse. It may easily be conceived that the mind of Julian, already perverted and made vain by his rhetorical education, and eagerly catching at the glitter and pomp of words, would be more strongly attracted by the dainty philosophico-mystical paganism which these people set forth—by their high-sounding phrases about the heavenly derivation of the soul, its debasement to matter, its bondage and its freedom, and by their pretended clearing up of the doctrine concerning

gods and demons—than by the simple gospel, even if this had
been preached to him.   But the Christianity which he actually
possessed, a Christianity that turned wholly on externals, could
easily make the transition to paganism.   They now gave him
proofs of the pagan art of divination, which surprised and
deceived him.   They showed him predictions * of an approaching triumph of the gods, and, indeed, flattered him with the
hope that he himself was the destined instrument to achieve
it.   The greatest influence over him was possessed by the
braggart Maximus, who had come over from Ephesus; for
he was precisely the man to entrap a youth like Julian.   He
took him along with him to Ionia; and there, in the society
of Neo-Platonic philosophers and hierophants, the work begun at Nicomedia was finished.   Julian was converted, from
being an outward Christian, with a secret leaning to paganism,
of which perhaps he was himself unconscious, into a decided
and zealous pagan.†

* To this Libanius alludes in ep. 701, when, under Julian's reign, he
writes :, Νῦν τῆς ἀληθείας τὸ κρατός, τὰ μὲν λογίσμοις, τὰ δὲ μαντείαις
εὑρισκομένης.

† Here especially the narratives of Libanius, who was then a
rhetorician at Nicomedia, and in part an eye-witness of the facts, are of
weight. Προσφωνητικ. πρὸς Ἰουλιανόν, vol. I. p. 408. Respecting Julian's
residence in Nicomedia, he says, Ἦν γὰρ τις σπινθὴρ μαντικῆς αὐτόθι
κρυπτόμενος, μόλις διαφυγὼν τὰς χεῖρας τῶν δυσσεβῶν (the severe persecu-
tious, by the Christian emperors, of the pagan art of divination, see
above) ὑφ' ᾧ δὴ πρῶτος τἀφανὲς ἀνιχνεύων τὸ σφοδρὸν μῖσος κατὰ τῶν θεῶν
ἐνίσχες (perhaps hopes, which were entertained by himself with regard
to what he should one day become) ; then he mentions his journey to
Ionia, where, by the δοκοῦντα καὶ ὄντα σοφόν, that is, by Maximus, he
was led to the full knowledge of the truth. Epitaph. Julian. l. c. 528,
he mentions less distinctly how Julian, during his residence in Nicomedia, having once fallen into company with Platonicians, and heard
them discourse on divine things, suddenly changed his opinions. Εἰς
Ἰουλιανον Αυτοχρατορ. ὑπατον, l. c. 376, ἐκείνην ἐγὼ τὴν ἡμέραν ἀρχὴν ἐλευθερίας
τῇ γῇ καλῶ, καὶ μακαρίζω τόπον τι ὃς τὴν μεταβολὴν ἐδέξατο καὶ τὸν τῆς
γνώμης ἰατρὸν, ὃς κινδύνον τὸν κάλλιστον αὐτός τι κινδυνεύσας, καὶ τόνδι
πείσας, μετὰ τοῦ μαθητοῦ τὰς κυανίας διέπλευσιν (the voyage to Ionia in
company with Maximus, which beyond question would have exposed
both him and Julian to great danger, if Julian's conversion to paganism
had been discovered). What Eunapius relates, particularly in the life
of Maximus (ed. Boissonade, vol. I. p. 49, ff.), cannot indeed be received
as literally true; and, besides, it is too inexact to be used in deciding
about the time when events occurred in this portion of Julian's history;
yet these accounts contain a good deal which serves to illustrate the

Although Julian had special reasons for concealing his conversion to paganism, which, if it became known to Constantius, might have cost him his life, yet he could not avoid exciting suspicions with regard to his connections in Ionia. His brother Gallus, who happened to be at that time in the neighbourhood, heard reports which troubled him. But Ætius, an ecclesiastic of Antioch, who was on friendly terms with Julian, quieted his suspicions by informing him that Julian frequented the churches, and especially the chapels of the martyrs; * and since it can hardly be supposed that Ætius invented this story merely to soothe Gallus, it may hence be gathered to what arts of dissimulation Julian descended. The assassination of Gallus (in 354); the danger in which he was himself for a long time involved through the jealousy of Constantius; the imprisonment in which he was held—all this could only serve to render the Byzantine court, and the Christianity which was here worn for a show, still more hateful to him. The ever-deluded Constantius finally gave him permission to reside for some time at Athens, the ancient flourishing seat of literary studies and Hellenism.† Pagan priests, hierophants,

characters of both Julian and Maximus. When Chrysanthius first tells the young man about the magical arts of Maximus (how by his forms of incantation he had caused the statue of Hecate to laugh, and the torches in her hands to kindle of themselves), as it is said, for the purpose of warning him against these things, so foreign from the pure spiritual philosophy, Julian exclaims—" Keep to your books; you have shown me the man whom I seek;" and he hastens from Pergamos to meet him at Ephesus. Something like this may perhaps have happened, though the time, place, and circumstances are here not correctly stated. The warning letter which Gallus wrote to Julian during the residence of the latter in Ionia, because the reports that Julian had gone over to paganism had excited his alarm, agrees with the above account; as also the remark of Julian in his proclamation to the Athenians, that he was a zealous and decided Christian until his one-and-twentieth year ; for this would coincide with the time of his residence in Nicomedia, with the year 351; though it ought to be taken into consideration that this cannot well be understood literally, and that Julian himself perhaps would not be able distinctly to recall that which had taken place in his mind by gradual and progressive changes.

* See the letter of Gallus to Julian. Julian, opp. 454.

† Gregory of Nazianzen, who just at that time was also studying at Athens, writes in his orat. XC. p. 331, Βλαβέρα τοῖς ἄλλοις Ἀθῆναι τὰ εἰς ψύχην τοῖς εὐσιβεστέροις καὶ γὰρ πλουτοῦσι τὸν κακὸν πλοῦτον τὰ εἰδωλα μᾶλλον τῆς ἄλλης ἰλλάδος, καὶ χαλιπόν μὴ συναρπασθῆναι τοῖς τούτων ἐπαινέταις καὶ συνηγόροις.

and rhetoricians, here combined their efforts to stimulate his
zeal in the cause of paganism; pagan youth were his companions; and he became the secret hope of the whole pagan
party.

While Julian, already elevated to the dignity of Cæsar,
was carrying on the war in Gaul, his fear of the jealous temper
of Constantius led him to adopt every possible expedient for
keeping his pagan way of thinking concealed; and so, on the
feast of Epiphany of the year 361, he assisted at the celebration of the Christian worship at Vienna.* He was attended
by only three men, who agreed with him in their religious
views, and joined with him in his secret observance of the
pagan cultus,—a slave who was his librarian; his physician
Oribasius,† an enterprising man, whose pretended knowledge
of magic, divination, and the interpretation of dreams, gave
him great influence with Julian; and Sallustius, a learned
civilian, whom the emperor had sent with him for the purpose
of watching his proceedings, but who, by his friendly inti-
macy with Julian, soon excited suspicion, and was removed.

Thus the religious convictions of Julian had been rendered
doubly dear to him by these measures of constraint, when, in
the year 361, he was placed himself on the imperial throne,
and found it in his power not only freely to express his true
principles, but also to aim at remodelling after them the
whole state of religion in the Roman empire.

Perhaps beyond any one of his predecessors among the Roman emperors he made account of the office of supreme pontiff.
He took special delight in offering multitudes of sacrifices and
in slaughtering the victims with his own hand, and, by the
great zeal which he manifested on these occasions, often exposed himself to the ridicule of the Christians. He laboured
to found a mystical hierarchy, fashioned after his own Neo-
Platonic ideas, leaving ample room, however, for the admission of the old superstitions of paganism; a phenomenon of

---

* Ammian. Marcellin. l. XXI. c. 2.

† Comp. Julian, ep. ad Atheniens. Eunap. vit. Oribas. Eunapius
says, indeed, that he made Julian emperor, which probably has reference
to those higher arts in which Oribasius was supposed to be a proficient.
See the letter of Julian to Oribasius in his critical situation, where he
also communicates to him a dream. Ep. XVII. Respecting Sallust,
Zosim. l. III. c. 9. Julian's consolatory address at taking leave of
Sallust, orat. VIII., and ep. ad Athenienses.

which history furnishes many examples, where it is attempted, by means of some arbitrary speculative system, to infuse artificial life into the dead form of an antiquated superstition. In his letter to a high priest Julian declares himself an enemy to all innovation, especially in whatever pertains to the gods: "The traditional laws of the country ought invariably to be observed from the beginning; for these were manifestly given by the gods, otherwise they could not have been so excellent."[*] We may learn from a set of instructions, which he probably drew up for the use of his priests, how he would attempt to restore the whole worship of images, and defend himself against the objections of the Christians : "Out of the supreme unity emanated first the pure world of intelligence,[†] embracing the gods, who are exalted above all contact with sensible things, and who live only in pure spiritual intuition : the intermediate link between these and the partly spiritual, partly sensual race of mankind, is formed by the eternal living images of those invisible gods in the heavens—viz. the divine souls veiled under the resplendent heavenly orbs, which visibly represent the former, and by which their influence is diffused down to the earth. But since these great heavenly beings are still too far removed from the sensual race of man, and since, moreover, no sensual worship, such as is adapted to man's sensual nature, can be paid to these, images of the gods have been invented on earth, in order that, by paying homage to them through these, we might thereby obtain their favour; just as those who pay homage to the emperors' images obtain thereby the favour of the emperors, not because the emperors stand in need of such homage, but because, by showing our willingness in whatever it is possible for us to do, we evince the true piety of our dispositions. But whoever, neglecting that which lies in his power, pretends to strive after what transcends his powers, only neglects the former, without really being in earnest about the latter. If we are to offer God no sensible worship, because he is the self-sufficint Being, it would also follow that we must not praise him by words, nor honour him by our actions. Accuse us not of holding the gods to be wood, stone, and brass. When

* Ep. LXIII. ad Theodos. Φεύγω τὴν καινοτομίαν ἐν ἅπασι μὲν, ὡς ἔπος εἰπεῖν, ἰδίᾳ δὲ ἐν τοῖς πρὸς τοὺς θεούς.

† The κόσμος νοητός.

we look at the images of the gods, we ought not to see in them stone and wood ; but neither ought we to suppose that we see the gods themselves. We should not think of calling the *images* of the *emperors* stone, wood, and brass, nor the emperors themselves, but we should call them images of the emperors. Now, whoever loves the emperor is pleased at beholding his image—whoever loves his child is pleased at beholding the image of his child. So whoever loves the gods looks with pleasure on their images, penetrated with awe towards those invisible beings that look down upon him."* But what good could that man's heart, whose necessities impelled him to seek after the fountain of salvation, and to whom religion was something more than a mere play of idle speculations or an entertainment of rhetoric or poetry, derive from all these fine-spun explanations? How great the difference between *this religion*, which, flattering man's sensual nature, offers him the most beautiful forms, only that he may never come to the consciousness of what he is and of what he needs, and the religion which deprives man of every sensual prop to which he would fain cling in order to evade this sacrifice and self-renunciation, so that he may rise through faith in the only Redeemer, who has come down to him in order to raise · him up to himself, to heaven, to that life which is hid in God, to the worship of God in spirit and in truth! And of what advantage were Julian's explanations to the rude populace, who did not understand them? They, at least, saw *their* gods in the images of wood, stone, and brass. The emperor, therefore, is right indeed, when, from his own point of view, he says that the Christians could not derive from the destruction of the idols and of the temples under the former reigns any evidence against them, since everything that is transient and temporal must share the fate of the temporal. " Let no one," says he, " refuse to believe in the gods, because he has seen or heard that some have committed sacrilege on the images of the gods and on the temples." But against the *popular superstition* this evidence was after all by no means so feeble. And of this Julian himself seems to be aware— hence he is so indignant on the subject.† He proceeds next

---

* See opp. Julian. fol. 293 seq.

† He appeals to the fact that at this time all the insults on the sanctuaries had met with due punishment. An argument which, we

to deduce the whole sensual pagan worship out of those general ideas: "We are bound," he says, "to pay religious worship, not only to the images of the gods, but also to the temples,—to the sacred groves and the altars. It is right, moreover, to honour the priests, as ministers of the gods, the mediators between us and the gods, who help to procure for us those blessings which flow to us from the gods, since it is they who sacrifice and pray for all." Here indeed Julian needed only to transfer the ideas of the priesthood which he might have derived from his Christian education back again to the pagan soil which was most congenial to them. Very consistently, he required that even in unworthy priests the objected dignity of the priesthood should be honoured: "So long as he sacrifices for us, and stands before the gods as our representative, we are bound to look upon him with reverence and awe, as an organ of the gods most worthy of all honour. If the priest were only spirit, not soul and body together, he might uniformly maintain the same tenor of life. But since this is not so, the life which he devotes to his sacred functions must be distinguished from the rest. During the whole of that time he must live like a super-earthly being, be constantly in the temple, occupied with holy contemplations; he may not go into any private house, visit any public place, nor even see a public magistrate elsewhere than in the temple. In performing the functions of his office he should also wear *the most costly apparel.*" The divine, therefore, was to be represented by earthly pomp—quite in accordance with the *pagan* way of thinking.

The species of intellectual and moral culture which Julian would give to his priests had been, until now, foreign from the mechanical ritual of paganism. The priest was to live a life worthy of the gods,—he was never to hear or to use any

---

must allow, was often employed in like manner by the Christians; and which in no case proves anything, since God's judgments are unsearchable to men. In many cases, without doubt, the divine judgments, so far as they had their ground in the uniform law of moral order in the world, could be very justly pointed out; and Julian was mistaken only in his interpretation of them. The depraved men who, under the reign of Constantine, had enriched themselves at the expense of the temples, met with the punishment of their wickedness; and sometimes Julian himself did his own part to bring about these pretended punishments of the gods.

unbecoming language, nor to read any improper poet. It behoved him especially to occupy himself wholly with philosophy, and particularly with that which begins from the gods, as the philosophy of Pythagoras, of Plato and Aristotle, of Chrysippus and Zeno. The priest should restrict himself to those doctrines of philosophy which lead to piety; and these, we must allow, make up a very meagre list: "First, that the gods exist; next, that they take an interest in the affairs of this world; and next, that they bring no evil on men, that they are free from jealousy, not the enemies of mankind." The last, he says, ought to have been taught by the Grecian poets, and by the prophets whom the Galileans admire. Thus to Julian, who had very superficial notions respecting the nature of God's holiness, and of sin, which is opposed to it, everything said in the Old Testament of God's vindictive justice seemed jealousy and enmity to mankind. "Of Epicurus, of Pyrrho, the priest should read nothing; indeed, it had been so ordered by the gods for the general good, that of the writings of these men the greatest part had already perished." *

Julian was obliged to borrow much from the Christian church, in order to bring about, by means of his spiritualized paganism, a reaction against Christianity;—a thing which could not last, however, but which must eventually turn to the advantage of Christianity. He wished to introduce the didactic element from the Christian church into his pagan forms of worship. Garlanded priests appeared upon the tribune, clothed in a purple mantle; it being the wish of Julian that, in performing the functions of their office, they should wear sumptuous vestments, and thereby command respect. † Here, in pompous language, they gave allegorical

---

* In like manner as when Christian ecclesiastics were forbidden to read the writings of pagan authors or of the heretics.

† Gregory of Nazianzen pertinently remarks on the conduct of these pagans in this particular, "I have often observed that they study after what is dignified and imposing, what surpasses the ordinary experience; as if the common things of every day were easily despised, while the pompous and seemingly sublime inspired faith." Πολλαχοῦ τὸ σέμνον ἔγνων αὐτοῖς σπουδαζομένον, καὶ τὸ ὑπεράνω τοῦ ἰδιώτου, ὡς τοῦ μὲν κοίνου καὶ πέζου τὸ εὐκαταφρονήτον ἰχόντος, τοῦ δὲ ὑπερόγκου καὶ δυσαφίκτου τὸ ἀξιοπίστον. Gregor. Nazianz. orat. steliteut. I. vel orat. III. opp. I. p. 103.

expositions of the pagan fables, expositions which the populace did not understand, or which at least could not affect
their hearts.

Julian would not admit that there was anything of divine
power in Christianity: he sought, therefore, to explain and
to account for its spread by outward causes; and he endeavoured to make these available for the promotion of his own
new pagan hierarchy, without duly considering that these
outward means were closely connected with the peculiar spirit
of Christianity. In his letter to Arsacius,* supreme pontiff
of Galatia, he says, what has especially contributed to the
spread of atheism is philanthropy towards strangers, care for
the burial of the dead, and an affected dignity of life (things,
evidently, which had sprung of their own accord out of the
peculiar influence of Christianity on the minds of men);
Christian brotherly love, that tenderness of feeling which
showed itself in honouring the memory of the dead, and the
moral sobriety which was so opposed to pagan licentiousness.†
" All these things the pagans should make matters of earnest
study. And let it not be thought enough if Arsacius himself
leads a *worthy* life; ‡ he must prevail upon the priests gene-

* Eph. 49.

† So also in the fragment of the Instruction for a high priest, opp.
305. The Galileans, having observed that the poor were neglected by
the priests, had taken care to pay special attention to these acts of
philanthropy, and had thus enticed men to their ruin. In the same
manner as men coax children with cakes, so they had commenced at
once with the agapæ, with the liberal reception of strangers, and with
the office of deacons—ἀρξάμενοι διὰ τῆς λεγομένης παρ' αὐτοῖς ἀγάπης καὶ
ὑποδοχῆς καὶ διακονίας τραπεζῶν—alluding to the oldest institutions and
arrangements of the church. From this point should begin the cure.
In other words, then, Julian was in hopes *to bring over* many to paganism
by the *distribution* of *money;* and doubtless, where there were so many
whose highest object was the satisfaction of their earthly wants, he may
not have calculated wrong. Constantine had in fact pursued a similar
course (see above). To be sure, this method of conversion accords
badly with Julian's declamation—that the gods had respect only to the
disposition of the heart. But there was a similar contradiction also
between Constantine's proclamations and his conduct.

‡ That, however, no great stress was laid on the moral character of
those who were thought to assist towards restoring the pagan worship,
and that sometimes the moral principles of those persons were extremely
lax, may be shown from a passage in Libanius. He applauds it as a
proof of the chastity of his Aristophanes, that he had never been guilty
of adultery,—ἀλλ' ἐν ταῖς ἀφειμέναις εἰς Ἀφροδίτης ἐξουσίαν τὰς ἧς φύσεως

rally in Galatia to pursue the same course, or depose them from the priestly office, if they would not, *with their wives, children, and slaves, devote themselves* to the honour of the gods; if they would suffer their wives, servants, or sons to unite themselves with the Galileans. Their priests were not to visit the theatre nor the shops; they were not to engage in any unsuitable occupation.* In every city houses were to be established for the reception of strangers (ξενοδοχεῖα),† where not only pagans, *but all others who needed assistance, might find entertainment.* ‡ To meet the expense of these establishments, he caused to be distributed among the priests thirty thousand measures of grain: and whatever was left, after they had provided for their own support, was to be distributed among the strangers and paupers; since it was shameful, he said, that no Jew ever begged, and that the godless Galileans, besides their own poor, supported those of the pagans, while the pagan poor obtained no assistance from their own people. He should also accustom the pagans themselves to such acts of kindness, and the pagan villagers to offer their first fruits to the gods. § The governors he should seldom see in his house; for the most part he should only write to them. Whenever they made their entrance into the city, no priest should go out to meet them; but if they came to the temple, the priest might go out to meet them as far as the court. In that case, no guard should accompany them; *for as soon as he crossed the threshold of the sanctuary, the magistrate became a private man;* the priest was supreme in the interior of the temple."

This last principle Julian applied to his own person, and not without reason, at that time; since he could not fail to remark that in the temples many paid more attention to the

---

ἐκούφιζεν ἀνάγκας. And yet he says, Ἐγὼ μὲν γὰρ οὐδ' ἱερὰ τῶν κειμένων ἀνοικοδομεῖν ὑπὸ ταῖς τοῦδε φροντίσι, φαίην ἂν πλημμελές, ὁρῶ γὰρ οὐκ ὀλίγων τῶν νῦν ἐπ' ἐκείνῳ τεταγμένων τόνδε σωφρονέστερον, vol. I. p. 446.

* Imitation of the laws of the church respecting the clergy.

† Imitation of the Christian ξενοδοχεία and πτωχοτροφία.

‡ It is easy to see Julian's design in this.

§ Imitation of the church collects and of the oblations among the Christians. To this imitation of the ecclesiastical regulations of the Christians in the founding of schools, in the institutions of charity, in the epistolis formatis for travellers, and in the system of penance, Gregory of Nazianzen very justly refers in orat. III. p. 102.

emperor than to the gods. Thus he was not pleased with the general salutation, "Long live the emperor!" which broke forth when on a certain occasion he unexpectedly (as he supposed, although, perhaps, the assembled crowd had been long waiting only for him) appeared in the temple of Fortune at Constantinople; and he therefore issued the following rescript to the people of that city : " Whenever I appear unexpectedly in the theatre, you are permitted to salute me with acclamations. But when I come unexpectedly into the temple, preserve quiet, and transfer your praises to the gods, or rather the gods require no praise."*

The objective dignity of the priesthood Julian sought zealously to maintain. For example, an officer, whose duties were in some way or another connected with the administration of the pagan cultus, had caused a pagan priest to be beaten, and on this ground was accused before the emperor by the high priest of his province. Julian severely reprimanded him for not respecting the priesthood, even in its unworthy representative, if such he were; and for having dared to expose to such violent treatment the priest before whom he was bound to rise even from his chair of office. Having observed probably that many, to please him, represented themselves as cherishing different opinions from what they really entertained, he added, " Perhaps the bishops and presbyters of the Galileans sit with you, if not publicly out of regard to me, yet secretly in your house." The individual here addressed was punished by being excluded for three months from all business which stood connected with the functions of the pagan priesthood.†

* Published by Muratori, anecdoto Græca. Patav. 1709, p. 332. Εἰ μὲν εἰς τὸ θέατρον λάθων εἰσῆλθον, εὐφημεῖτε, εἰ δὲ εἰς τὰ ἱερά, τὴν ἡσυχίαν ἄγετε καὶ μετενίγκατε ὑμῶν τὰς εὐφημίας εἰς τοὺς θεούς, μᾶλλον δὲ οἱ θεοὶ τῶν εὐφημιῶν οὐ χρῃζοῦσιν. Muratori was of opinion that the οὐ, which the manuscript has here, originated in a misconception; but the negation is required by the δὲ, by the whole construction of the passage, and by the sense. It is moreover altogether in Julian's manner to conclude with a dignified philosophical sentence of this sort, in whatever contradiction it might stand with his superstition.

† Julian. ep. LXII. It is difficult to determine to whom this letter was addressed. From the condemning sentence, τῶν εἰς ἱερία μηδὲν ἐνοχλεῖν, it might be conjectured that the matter related to a priest; yet the whole contents of the letter contradict this supposition. The lan-

As Constantine caused the churches which had been destroyed in the Dioclesian persecution to be rebuilt, and restored to them the estates of which they had been deprived, so Julian undertook to pursue a similar course in regard to the temples which had been destroyed and plundered in the preceding reign. Many of the governors prosecuted this business with great zeal ; some, led on by their own interest in the cause ; others, because they knew that by so doing they would in the surest and easiest way gain favour with the emperor. The images of the gods, which had been rescued from the hands of the Christians, were conveyed back to the temples in the midst of festive processions.*

But, in rebuilding the temples, Julian did not proceed in the same upright and honourable manner as Constantine had done in restoring the churches. The latter, as we have remarked, had caused these to be rebuilt at his own expense ; and he had indemnified those who had legally come into possession of the buildings belonging to the churches, or of the grounds upon which they stood. But Julian compelled the Christians who had taken any share in the destruction of the temples during the preceding reign, or who perhaps were only accused of this by popular rumour, to be at the expense of rebuilding them. To those who were required to give up property of this sort he allowed no indemnification ; thus giving occasion to many acts of oppression and violence, resorted to against individual Christians under the pretence of

---

guage, moreover, does not lead us to suppose that a mere excommunication from the pagan ceremonies (sacris) is here meant. Hence I have represented the matter as it stands in the text.

* See respecting the festivities at the restoration of an image of Artemis, which had been torn down by the Christians, Liban. ep. 622, etc. The emperor himself was informed by the governor of the province how great expense had been made at this festival, and how many sacrifices had been offered, ep. 624. Libanius writes to a certain Seleucus, who probably held civil office, " At present we behold altars, temples, sacred groves, and images of the gods, which have been decorated by you, but which will also decorate you and your posterity. Since you have so great allies, count the arrows of the godless race to be pointless (he should give himself no concern about the enmity of the Christians). Make them to weep, who have long time made merry with the better cause. You are bound to give thanks to the gods that they have caused you to become a father ; which thanks you must render to them, by helping to erect their prostrate temples," ep. 680.

restoring the temples*—which oppressions sometimes fell on those who in the former reign had been distinguished for their gentleness and forbearance, and the moderate use of the power which was in their hands. The letters of Libanius the rhetorician to Antioch, in which he intercedes with the pagan governors and priests in behalf of those who are said to have suffered under such acts of injustice, furnish indubitable evidence of this, while they redound to the honour of the man, in spite of his many foibles, who, zealous pagan as he was, so earnestly remonstrated against the injustice done to the Christians.†

* See Sozomen, Hist. v. 5. The edict was made known at Alexandria on the X. Mechir (4th of February), 362:—"Reddi idolis et neocoris et publicæ rationi, quæ preteritis temporibus illis sublata." See the anonymous biography of Athanasius, p. 69.

† Thus to Hesychius, a priest at Antioch (ep. 636); "That I am no less desirous than you priests that the temples should be preserved in their beauty, you are aware of more than others. Yet I should be unwilling to have that done by the destruction of houses, which might be done if they remained standing; since I prefer that what already exists should remain, and what has been prostrated should be restored; and not that we should beautify the cities in one respect, while we deform them in another. True it is easy to bring a complaint against the house of Theodulus; but it deserves to be spared, since it is beautiful and spacious, and makes our city more beautiful than other cities. In the next place for this reason —because Theodulus did not plunder the temple with arrogance and. impiety, but purchased it from the sellers, paying the price for it, which was a privilege allowed to all those who could buy." In like manner he intercedes with Bacchius, one of those who had it in charge to restore the temple worship, as he was about to re-erect a demolished temple of the Graces, and intended to collect the necessary money in ready cash from a certain Christian, named Basiliscus, who had perhaps had a hand in the destruction of the temple, or had in some way come into possession of its treasures, thus throwing the latter into great embarrassment. Libanius petitions for this individual, that he might be required to pay only half the sum at once, and permitted to discharge the remainder of the demand at a future time. He entreats Bacchius to have some regard to Æmylianus, the father or relative of this Christian, who, although the power was in his hands, yet under the former reign had conducted himself towards the pagans with so much moderation: Οὐ γὰρ ἦν τῶν ὑβριζόντων, καὶ ταῦτα ἰνὸν, εἴπερ ἐβούλετο. This noble feeling deserved to be rewarded. "Show your care for the sanctuaries, by increasing the multitude of sacrifices, by seeing that the sacred rites are accurately performed, and by restoring the prostrate temples; for you must be devout to the gods, must *show yourself compliant to the will of the emperor* (τῷ βασιλεῖ χαρίζεσθαι), and embellish your native city." Ep. 669. Thus he intercedes with a certain Belæus, who, from a rhetorician had become

It was a topic on which Julian often declaimed that the
gods regard only the disposition of their worshippers. He
declared that no godless person ought to take part in the holy
sacrifices, until he had purified his soul by prayer to the gods,
and his body by the prescribed lustrations.* Yet he was quite
satisfied if he could but induce goodly numbers to sacrifice,
without troubling himself any further about their disposition ;
and to promote this object he spared neither money nor places

a judge at Antioch, in behalf of a certain Orion, who in the preceding
reign had distinguished himself in a public office by his moderation, but
who now was charged with having robbed the temples of their treasures,
and, although he was quite poor, was called upon to pay large sums of
money, and, as he found himself unable to do this, was to be compelled to
it by bodily punishment. In his first letter to Belæus, ep. 673, he says,
"Orion proved himself, under the preceding reign, to be a mild and gene-
rous man ; he did not imitate those who made a bad use of their power,
but, on the contrary, blamed them. But I have also heard from the
citizens of Bostra that he neither made war against our worship, nor persecuted priests ; and that he saved many from misery by the mild administration of his office. This man I have now seen cast down and full of
distress. And shedding a flood of tears before he could give utterance to
his words, he said, ' I have but just escaped from the hands of those to
whom I have shown kindness. Though I have done evil to no man when
I had the power to do so, I have notwithstanding been almost torn in pieces.'
And he added to this, the flight of his brother, the breaking up and
scattering of his whole family, and the plundering of his furniture ; all
which, as I know, is not according to the will of the emperor. But the .
emperor says, that, if he has any of the property which belongs to the
temples, let him be called upon to give it up ; but if he has not, then let
him neither be insulted nor abused. Yet it is manifest, that *those men
are coveting the goods of others, while they pretend to be desirous of helping
the gods.*" In the second letter he writes, "Although he differs from
us in his religious persuasion, it redounds to his own injury that he has
deceived himself ; but he ought not in justice to be persecuted by his
acquaintance. I could wish that those very persons who now oppress
him would only recollect the cases in which he has so often assisted
them, and would prefer rather to show him their gratitude than seek
to bury their benefactor alive. Having long since persecuted and plundered his relations, they seized at last upon the person of this man,
as if they would thereby fulfil the wishes of the gods, while in truth
they are very far from honouring the gods by any such conduct as this.
But it can be no matter of surprise that the multitude allowed themselves to be hurried along without reflection, and follow their impulses,
instead of that which is right. He says, he made no robbery. But
granting that he did, how is it that you now hope, when the whole
has been consumed, to find mines of gold in his skin ?" Ep. 731.

    * Ep. 52 ad Bostrenos.

of honour ; though we must admit that the Christian emperors
had done the same thing, and in a manner still less becoming,
with regard to Christianity.* In this way, as a matter of
course, many would be gained over, who, in the preceding
reign, had been induced, by similar motives, to profess Christianity ; men who, as a father of this period (Asterius of
Amasea, in Pontus), remarks, changed their religion as easily
as their dress.† In a discourse preached in the reign of one
of the next succeeding emperors, the same contemporaneous
writer describes this class of people as follows : " How many
abandoned the church, and ran to the altars? How many
allowed themselves to be enticed to apostacy by the bait of
honourable offices? Branded with disgrace, and despised,
they wander about the cities, and are pointed at by the finger
of scorn, as those who also have betrayed Christ for a few
pieces of silver."‡ As Julian attached a superstitious value
to sacrifices, he laboured, for nine months, to prevail upon the
soldiers of the army which he was preparing against the Persians to offer to the gods. When the arts of persuasion had
been tried in vain, he employed gold and silver for the purpose of buying over the soldiers to his views.§

His hatred of Christianity and of the Christians might of
itself, it is true, have rendered Julian more favourably disposed towards Judaism and the Jews ; but, as in everything
he was glad to take the contrary course from that which had
been pursued in the previous reign, it was agreeable, both to

* Gregor. Nazianz. orat. funeb. in Cæsar. orat. X. fol. 167. Τοὺς μὲν
χρήμασι, τοὺς δὲ ἀξιώμασι, τοὺς δὲ ὑποσχέσεσι, τοὺς δὲ παντοίαις τιμαῖς
ὑφελκόμενος.

† Adv. Avaritiam, ed. Rulben. Antverp. 1615, p. 43. Ὅσπερ ἱμάτιον
ταχέως τὴν θεοσκείαν μετιμφιεσάντο.

‡ See l. c. Modestus, an officer of state, who had for a long time
supported the party of the emperor Constantine in opposition to Julian,
probably in order to acquire the favour of the latter, embraced paganism,
and obtained for this not only pardon, but the præfecture of Constantinople, although Libanius writes to him, Πρὸς τῶν θεῶν, οὓς πάλαι
θαυμάζων νῦν ὡμολόγησας. Ep. 714.

§ This Libanius narrates in praise of the emperor, Epitaph. in Julian.
vol. I. p. 578. He says on this occasion, " By means of a small gain,
the soldier obtained a greater one ; by gold, the friendship of the gods,
on whom depends the fortune of war." Such was the religion of these
persons, who, in contrast with the Christians, assumed the air of
enlightened men!

his inclination and his principles of government, to patronize
the Jews, who had been oppressed under Constantius. It
must be added, however, that he was more favourable to
Judaism than to Christianity, for the same reasons that had
influenced the pagans before him. He saw in that religion,
at least, a national ritual addressed to the senses, from which
he conceived it possible to prove an affinity between Judaism
and paganism. Said he to the Christians, " I am a true wor-
shipper of the God of Abraham, who is a great and mighty
God ; but you have no concern with him. For I worshipped
him as Abraham worshipped him; but you do not follow
Abraham. You erect no altars to God, nor do you worship
him, as Abraham did, with sacrifices." * In his opinion the
worship of the God of Abraham might blend harmoniously
with the worship of the Grecian gods ; he blamed only the
exclusive, intolerant character of Judaism. So very imperfectly did he understand the nature of pure Theism, which,
wherever it exists, will have absolute supremacy, and must
strive to destroy, as an ungodly element, everything which
claims authority along with it, that the jealous God of the
Old Testament, who, to all the ungodly, is a consuming fire,
appeared to him as an envious God, subject to human passions.
He supposed there could be only two possible cases : either
that the God whom the Jews worshipped was the universal
Architect of the world, the δημιουργός to whom the other particular divinities were subordinated ; in which case it was only
his prophets who had been unworthy of him ; men who, because their minds had not been purified by scientific culture,
had transferred to him their own false notions, and represented
him as so selfish and intolerant ; or else, that they had in
reality had only a limited national God, whom they regarded,
however, as that Supreme Being ; just as the Gnostics maintained that the Jews had confounded their Demiurge with the
Supreme Deity.† He seems to have inclined, for the most part,
to the former view,—that the God of the Old Testament was,
in truth, the great Architect and Ruler of the whole visible
world, whom the pagans also worship under other names.‡

* Julian. ap. Cyrill. c. Julian. l. X. p. 354.
† L. c. l. IV. f. 48, 155, where he calls the doctrine of a θεὸς
ζηλώτης a βλασφημία.
‡ Ep. 63, p. 454, fragment. Epist. ad sacerdot. p. 295. Τὸν μὲν

Since, then, he entertained a high respect for the Jewish worship, as an ancient national institution, he conceived the wish to restore the Temple at Jerusalem, as a splendid memorial of his reign ; in doing which he perhaps hoped, also, that he should be able to defeat the prophecy of Jesus, although this had already been fully accomplished. He expended vast sums upon this object; but the work which had been undertaken with so much labour did not succeed. Volumes of fire, bursting forth from the subterranean vaults which had been opened, destroyed the unfinished labours, and frightened the workmen.* Although this may have proceeded from natural causes, yet might it be a warning rebuke to the emperor that no human will could rebuild what had once been destroyed by a divine judgment.† But he did not, on this account, as yet relinquish his plan.‡ Having relieved the Jews from the heavy impositions by which they hitherto had been oppressed, he invited them now, with minds free from anxiety, to implore their great God, who could turn everything to the advantage of his government, that, after having brought the Persian war to a successful termination, he might be enabled, with them,

---

θίον εἶναι μιγάν, οὐ μὴν σπουδαίων προφήτων οὐδὲ ἐξηγήτων τυχεῖν, αἰτοῦν δὲ ὅτι τὴν ἑαυτὴν ψύχην οὐ παρέσχον ἀποκαθᾶραι τοῖς ἐγκυκλίοις μαθήμασιν. F. 306, Cyrill. c. Julian. l. IX.

* The historian Ammianus Marcellinus, who was not a Christian, gives the simplest and most impartial account of this event, I. XXIII. c. 1: Metuendi globi flammorum prope fundamenta crebris assultibus erumpentes, fecere locum deustis aliquoties operantibus inaccessum: hocque modo elemento destinatius repellente cessavit inceptum. The exaggerating legend added a great deal more about fire falling from heaven, fiery shapes of the cross on the clothes of the workmen, &c.

† It is noticeable how lightly he himself touches on the subject. Fragm. epist. p. 295: Τί πιρὶ τοῦ νιὼ φησούσι, τοῦ παρ' αὐτοῖς τριτὸν ἀνατραπίντος, ἰγιιρομίνου δὲ οὐδὲ νῦν. Pagi places the command for the rebuilding of the temple in the year 3C3, in which fell the celebration of the Decennualia in honour of Julian's accession to the Cæsarean dignity; and the position which Ammianus Marcellinus gives to this event might seem to favour this view. But as the above-cited letter of Julian must have been written after the frustration of the plan for rebuilding of the temple, and that letter cannot be placed in so late a period, this circumstance would stand opposed to such a determination of the chronological date.

‡ That is, in case the letter mentioned in what follows in the text was written after the frustrated attempt to rebuild the temple, which is indeed possible, although the contrary is generally assumed to be the fact.

to dwell and worship the Almighty in the holy city Jerusalem, rebuilt by his labours.*

As it respects Julian's conduct towards the Christians, he was not inclined by nature to cruel and violent measures. Besides, he was fond of assuming an air of philosophical tole-ration, and, in this particular respect, wished to present a direct contrast to the character of Constantius, who had occa-sioned so much evil by his fanatical and despotic spirit of persecution. Moreover, the Christian party was already so powerful, that violent measures might easily prove dangerous to the public peace, which he sought to preserve. And Julian was wise enough to learn from the oft-repeated trials that persecution would but tend to increase the spread of Chris-tianity. There were, moreover, examples, under his own reign, of individual Christians who, after having been exposed to ill-treatment, on account of their faith, from a fanatical pagan populace or cruel governors, and exhibited constancy under all their sufferings, became objects of universal reverence among the Christian population, and obtained the greatest influence; as was remarkably shown in the case of Marcus bishop of Arethusa in Syria. When, therefore, Libanius, in the letter which we have just cited, would restrain a governor from indulging in the cruel persecution of a Christian who had been accused of robbing the temples, he warned him thus: "If he is to die, then, in his chains, look well before you, and consider what will be the result. Take heed lest you bring upon us many others like Marcus. This Marcus was hung up, scourged, plucked in the beard, and bore all with constancy. He is now honoured as a god, and, wherever he appears, everybody is eager to take him by the hand. As the emperor is aware of this, *he has not allowed the man to be exe-cuted*, much as he is grieved at the destruction of the temple. Let the preservation of Marcus be a law for us." †

* See ep. 25, f. 397.
† See Liban. ep. 731. The same Libanius says. in his Epitaph. in Julian, p. 562, that the Christians, in the beginning of Julian's reign, expected to suffer similar persecutions as they did under the earlier pagan emperors. But Julian, he observes, censured those measures, by which. after all, they could not attain their end. " For men may indeed bind the bodily sick in order to heal them, but a false opinion respecting the gods cannot be expelled by the knife and cautery. Though the hand may offer incense, the soul is still dissatisfied with it, and there is only a

It may, indeed, be questioned, whether rational grounds, wise purposes, and humane feelings, would have availed anything against a fanaticism made up of such heterogeneous elements,—a fanaticism which is ever the most easily inclined to persecution,—whether they could have checked his natural disposition, which impelled him to violence wherever he met with opposition. Yet deep within his soul there existed another principle, which prompted him' to bring back the erring to their own good, to the way of truth, though at first it might be against their will. This he undesignedly illustrates in a rescript, issued by him in a state of mind very much excited by opposition, where he says, " It were right that these persons, like madmen, should be cured in spite of themselves. Yet to all who are suffering under this sort of disease indulgence must be shown; for I am of the opinion that we ought to instruct, and not punish, the unreasonable." * How easily might it happen, under some particular outward excitement, that the principle to which the voice of reason and the feelings of humanity were still opposed should finally become the ruling one!

At first, however, Julian was best pleased when, by covert attacks, in which indeed he often forgot what honesty and justice required even in an opponent, and what became the dignity of an emperor, he could injure the church, and undermine its interests, by means which betrayed no hostile design. To this class of measures belongs that edict, well conceived for this purpose, by which, at the very beginning of his reign, *he recalled all the bishops and clergy who had been banished in the reign of Constantius, and granted equal freedom to all parties of the Christian church.* He might have found sufficient inducement for enacting such a law in the relation he stood in to the Christian church; for it was impossible for him to take the same interest in the controversies of the Christians which Constantius had done. Although some among the Christian sects may have come nearer to his own views, in the character of their doctrinal opinions, than others—as

seeming change. Some afterwards obtained pardon (those who, yielding to force, had offered, and were afterwards restored to the fellowship of the church). But those who died for their convictions were honoured as gods." Yet it is very evident that these truths were rather worn for a show than consistenly carried out.   * Ep. 42.

indeed he himself allowed,*—yet all the Christian parties
were exposed to his hatred, on account of their opposition to
paganism.† He was desirous also, at the same time, to place
the mildness of his own government, in this respect, in direct
contrast with the severity of Constantius. " I believed," he
says in a letter to the inhabitants of Bostra,‡ " the leading
men of the Galileans would feel themselves more indebted to
me than to my predecessors in the government; for it happened under the latter that many of them were banished, persecuted, deprived of their property ; and, indeed, whole masses
of heretics, as they are called, were swept off at a stroke ; so
that, in Samosata, Cyzicus, Paphlagonia, Bithynia, Galatia,
and among many other races of people, entire villages were
made utterly desolate. But under my government the fact
has been the very reverse; for the banished have been permitted to return, and their property is restored back by our
laws to those whose estates had been confiscated." But
Julian certainly entertained the hope,—a fact respecting
which both Christian and pagan historians are generally
agreed,—that the different parties of the Christians, who persecuted each other with so much fury, would in this way
each destroy the other. In this hope he was doomed to be
disappointed ; and from the very nature of the case it could
not be otherwise. Party passion among the Christians would,
undoubtedly, never have risen to so high a pitch, had it not
been for the interference of the state. As this disturbing and
circumscribing influence of a foreign power now fell away of
itself, and the church was left to follow out naturally its own
development from within itself, the right relations were everywhere more easily restored. No patronage of the Christian
church by the civil power could have been so advantageous to

* Thus, for instance, he praises Photinus, because his representation
of Christ's person was more rational than the prevailing doctrine of the
church. See the fragment of Julian's letter to Photinus in Facund.
Hermian. defensio trium capitulor. I. IV. p. 379. Sirmond. opp. t. II. f.
376, ed. Venet. 1728. The special honour which he showed to the Arian
Ætius was owing, not so much to his doctrinal opinions as to his earlier
personal connection with the emperor. See ep. 31, Julian.

† Thus, in another passage, to be found in Cyrill. c. Julian. VII. f. 262,
he places Photinus in one and the same class with the other Christian
dogmatists, and says he did not concern himself with their doctrinal disputes, ἀφίημι δῆτα τὴν μάχην ὑμῖν.   ‡ Ep. 52.

it, under the then circumstances, as this indifference of the state towards all that transpired within its pale.

The edict by which Julian recalled the bishops from their banishment may, without doubt, have been very indistinctly expressed;* so that it could be understood to refer merely to their return into their country, or also to their return to their posts. As Julian allowed to all religious parties the free exercise of their religion, it was understood, as a matter of course, that the bishops of all Christian parties could enter freely into the administration of their offices. But the emperor might have expressed himself indistinctly on purpose; or he might some time afterwards have given the law this construction of indistinctness, in order to provide himself with liberty to act against those bishops whose influence seemed to him too powerful a counterpoise to his own designs. To this class belonged the zealous and energetic bishop Athanasius of Alexandria.

After this bishop had again administered his office for eight months,† earnestly labouring for the interests of the Christian church, there appeared an edict of the emperor, addressed to the Alexandrians, in which it was charged upon him as a grievous crime, that, after having been banished by many rescripts of many emperors,‡ that is, of Constantine and Constantius, he had not waited for a single imperial edict authorising him to return back again to his church; § for the emperor had given permission to those who had been banished by Constantius to return home, not to their churches, but only to their country. Yet Athanasius, it was alleged, hurried on by his usual pride, had arrogated to himself what

---

* The edict arrived at Alexandria on the XIV. Machir (the 8th of February, according to Ideler's tables) of the year 362, and was published on the day following: "Episcopos omnes factionibus antehac circumventos et exiliatos reverti ad suas civitates et provincias." Thus it is stated in the life of Athanasius, which was composed by an anonymous contemporary writer, and of which a fragment in an ancient Latin translation has been published by Maffei, Osservazioni letterarie. Verona, 1738. Tom. III. p. 69.

† See the above-cited Life.

‡ Where Julian might take advantage of the fact that various charges were brought against Athanasius, which did not relate barely to doctrine, passion at that time mixing everything up together.

§ Yet Gerontius, the prefect of Egypt, had thought himself authorized to recall Athanasius to his bishopric. (See l. c.)

among them was called the episcopal throne. But this was not a little displeasing to that God-fearing people the Alexandrians. By this God-fearing people Julian meant, of course, only the pagans, to whom, indeed, it could be no otherwise than in the highest degree unpleasant that Athanasius should be bishop. As soon as this letter* arrived at Alexandria, Athanasius was commanded to leave the city, under the threat of far severer punishments. Sorely vexed must have been Julian when he found that the diseased portion, as he expressed it, of the Alexandrians (the Christians), showed no disposition to follow the healthy portion (the pagans); but the diseased part, who in fact constituted by far the majority, ventured to call themselves the city, and, in the name of the whole city of Alexandria, to send him a petition, in which the community besought him that their bishop might be spared to them. In a declamatory letter† he not only rejected their request, but immediately banished Athanasius from the whole province of Egypt. His remarks to the Alexandrians on this occasion show how little he knew what the heart of man, thirsting after righteousness, requires, and what religion is designed to bestow on man,—how accustomed he was to confound worldly and spiritual things. "Tell me," says he to them, "what good have they ever done to your city, who have now introduced among you this new proclamation? Your founder was Alexander the Macedonian, who, indeed, ought not to be brought into comparison with any of these; nay, not even with the Hebrews, who were far superior to these." He then goes on to rebuke them severely for refusing to worship the god visible to all, the Sun, whose powerful and benign influence they must all experience; and for thinking themselves bound to receive Jesus, whom neither they nor their fathers had seen, as the God-Logos. He descends to rude and vulgar language, equally unbecoming a philosopher and an emperor, in speaking of the great man whom he ridiculed,‡ without a sense to appreciate the spirit which actuated him; and yet the anger he shows towards him proves how much he dreaded his influence. In this letter he assigns, it is true,

---

* See ep. 26. † Ep. 51.

‡ He styles him a man who deserved not to be called a man, a miserable little man—ἀνθρωπίσκος εὐτελής—alluding probably to his bodily stature.

political reasons as his motives for banishing Athanasius:
"It was a dangerous thing for so cunning and restless a man
to be at the head of the people." Yet, in his letter to the
prefect of Egypt, he betrays the true cause of his displeasure
against the man, expressing his vexation that, through the
influence of Athanasius, all the gods should be despised; and
declaring that nothing would give him greater joy than to hear
that Athanasius, the godless wretch who had dared *under his
reign to baptize noble Grecian women,* was banished from
every district of Egypt.*

Julian descended to many an unworthy trick for the purpose of bringing men, without a resort to forcible measures, to
join against their will in the ceremonies of the pagan religion.
He caused his statues, which were set up in the public places,
to be surrounded with emblems taken from the pagan religion.
A Jupiter over his head reached down to him the purple
mantle and the crown, while Mercury and Mars looked on
with an approving smile. Whoever now paid obeisance, as
was customary at that time, to the emperor's image, must at
the same time testify respect to the gods; and whoever
declined to do so was liable to be accused as a violator of the
imperial authority.† It might here be said that Julian,
according to his own religious principles, was compelled
to regard all the affairs of state as standing in this connection
with religion; and was without any design, in this case, of
injuring the conscience of the Christians. But, judging from
the spirit which he evinces on other occasions, we may well
believe him capable of such banter: and, at all events, if he
understood the rights of conscience, he ought to have been
more indulgent to the religious convictions of a majority of
his subjects. In like manner, when he distributed from the
imperial throne a donative among the soldiers, he had placed
beside him a censer, with a dish of incense. He who would
receive the donative from his hands must first cast some of the
incense into the censer. This was to signify that he offered
incense to the gods, whose images, perhaps, were standing
somewhere near by. If Julian looked upon it as so important
a thing, when, by the distribution of money, he could prevail
upon his soldiers to sacrifice, it would doubtless gratify him,
even when he could do no more than bring them to the me-

* Ep. 6.   † Sozom. v. 17.

chanical act of scattering incense; and he might hope, by
accustoming them to such a mechanism, and by the golden
bait, to carry them a step farther. When they had once become aware that by such conduct they had violated the obligations of the Christian faith, and that the love of earthly
gain had overpowered the voice of conscience, one step in sin
would easily lead them to another. But many were really
not aware of what they had done; and when they afterwards
learned that they had been betrayed into an act of idolatrous
worship, they became despondent, publicly declared before the
emperor that they were Christians, and begged him to take
back the money, if it was to be the price of their denial of the
faith. A particular case of this sort is related, in which a
number of soldiers were first made aware of what they had
done at a festival which followed the distribution of the donative, when, drinking to their comrades, as was customary on
such occasions, in the name of Christ, they were reminded
that they had just denied him whose name they now invoked.*

Among the artifices by which Julian hoped to undermine
the Christian church without resorting to sanguinary persecutions, was also his forbidding the Christians to set up schools
of rhetoric and grammar, and to explain the ancient authors.
He supposed that Christianity could not dispense with these
foreign supports; that, unless it had appropriated to its own
purposes the scientific culture of the Greeks, it would not
have spread so far; and that the scriptures, which the Christians called divine, did not afford a sufficient fountain in itself
of human cultivation, but that this must be derived by them
from the creations of the gods whom they denied, from the
literature of the Greeks. In his work against Christianity,
says Julian to the Christians, " Why waste your energies
on the literature of the heathens, if the reading of your own
scriptures content you? Certainly you ought to be more
solicitous to keep men from the former, than from eating the
meat of the sacrifices ; for, according to Paul himself, the latter
can harm no one; but, by those sciences, every noble spirit
that nature has produced among you has been led to renounce

* See Sozom. v. 17.   Gregor. Naz. orat. III. steliteut. i. fol. 85.
According to the latter's description, it took place when, at the conclusion of the meal, the cup of cold water was handed round, and each, before he drank, made over it the sign of the cross in the name of Christ.

your godless doctrine." A very bold asssertion, directly in the face of plain facts ; such, for example, as that the most zealous students of the ancient writers were precisely those who had become the most distinguished teachers of the church. But, if Julian really believed his own assertion, he must have vastly preferred that the Christians should teach the ancient classics than that they should explain the Bible to their youth. " Let them," said he, " try the experiment of instructing a boy from the first in nothing but the Bible, and see if he would turn out anything better than a slave." *

The truth is, however, that it was not the design of these scriptures to serve as a means of *human cultivation*, but rather to impart the element of a divine life, without which no human cultivation can truly thrive,—an element whereby the human education becomes ennobled to a divine one. And what the spirit of these scriptures, wherever received in its purity, can accomplish, independent of any means of human culture, is taught by the history of the effects of Christianity among the laity at all times—effects of which even Julian might have found examples, if he had only inquired into what took place in the retirement of private life. Christianity, indeed, as Julian understood it,—a Christianity which consisted merely in a certain mechanical routine of outward actions, or in a system of formal and lifeless notions—was incapable of producing such effects.

Ancient art and literature appeared to Julian, as we have already remarked, closely connected with the worship of the gods ; but it was unjust, and a manifest tyranny over conscience, to force these, his own subjective opinions, on all his subjects. It was a policy which unprejudiced pagans themselves—as, for example, Ammianus Marcellinus † — openly condemned. We see to what result this system of religion, at once sophistic and fanatical, could lead. " How scandalous," he declares in his law relating to this matter, " that they should expressly teach that which they hold to be most detestable ; that they should entice away by their flatteries those to whom they would inculcate their own bad opinions ! All teachers, in whatever department they teach, should be honest men, and *cherish in their soul no opinions at variance*

---

* C. Christian. l. VII. p. 229.   † L. XXV. c. 4.

with those which are publicly recognised.* But they, beyond
all others, should be such who, as expounders of the ancient
authors, exert an influence upon the education of the youth,
whether they be rhetoricians, or grammarians, or, above all,
sophists; † for they will be teachers not of words only, but
also of morals." They might either avoid teaching what
they themselves considered not good; or else, by their own
act, first convince their pupils that none of the authors whom
they explained erred and blasphemed in religion, as they had
hitherto been accustomed to say. But in attempting to gain
their subsistence in so dishonourable a manner, by means of
the writings of those authors, they must confess themselves the
most covetous of men, and ready to commit any meanness for
a few drachms.

Julian would have had good cause for this accusation, if
Christians had consented to become pagan priests, and, under
this outward appearance, made sport of the pagan religion. But
the case was different when they gave instruction in such matters
as in their own opinion stood in no connection whatever with
religion, and at the same time openly avowed their Christianity; so that it was at the pleasure of heathen parents, if they
feared the influence of these teachers upon their children, to
keep them away from such schools. We see here a most unjustifiable instance of arguing consequences, which all others
must be obliged to adopt, because they seemed just as regarded from the emperor's own religious point of view; but
in this we must allow that Julian was by no means alone. He
goes on to say, " If they believe those men to be in error on
the most important subjects, then let them go into the
churches of the Galileans, and expound Matthew and Luke."
At the same time, however, he permitted the Christian youth
to attend the schools of pagan teachers,‡—a permission of

---

* Καὶ μὴ μαχομένα τοῖς δημοσία τὰ ἐν τῇ ψύχη φέρειν δοξάσματα,—a
principle which, avowed with some consistency on the ground assumed
by Julian, who was for establishing a pagan state-religion, was often
very inconsistently expressed by Christian magistrates, on the ground
of Christianity, which should never be a state-religion.

† The sophists, in the stricter sense of the word, who were to diffuse
an influence into the *whole* literary and intellectual culture, were then
distinguished from the *rhetoricians* in the more restricted sense of the
word.

‡ Without troubling ourselves about manifestly exaggerated and

which he would of course be gratified to have them avail
themselves, as he might hope they would be gained over by
pagan teachers to embrace their religion.*

Two celebrated men of that age are known to us, who re-
linquished their stations as rhetorical teachers for the sake of
their faith; Proæresius, a distinguished rhetorician at Athens,†
and Fabius Marius Victorinus at Rome. The latter had
shortly before embraced Christianity in his old age. He had
been a diligent student of the Greek philosophy, and had
translated several of the works of Plato into Latin. He was
probably attached to the Neo-Platonic Hellenism, and was
esteemed one of the most important pillars of the old religion. But in his old age he became conscious of a craving
after some more certain and stable ground of faith. He went
to the study of the Bible, and examined it carefully. He was
convinced of the truth of the divine doctrine; and in confidence informed the presbyter Simplicianus of Milan that
he was at heart a Christian. The latter replied to him that
he would not believe it until he saw him within a Christian church. " What! then," rejoined Victorinus, "do walls
make Christians?" The truth was, however, that his heart
still clung too strongly to the world,—he was not willing to
sacrifice everything to the Lord; and it was this which prevented him from making a public profession. He was afraid
of those zealous pagans, the noble Romans who were his disciples, and with whom he stood in the highest consideration.
But as the word entered more deeply into his heart, his own
conscience forced him to a public profession; and he demanded that it should be made in the most public manner,
when, to spare his feelings, the presbyters of the church proposed to omit some part of the usual ceremony. After this it
cost him no struggle to lay aside his rhetorical office.‡

The two learned Christians from Syria, Apollinaris, father

inaccurate accounts, we confine ourselves simply to the words of Julian
and to the narrative of the impartial Ammianus.

* I suppose that in the passage above referred to, Ep. 42, the reading should be οὐδὲ φόβῳ καὶ. . . . Otherwise the second οὐδὲ required
here would be wanting, and the appropriate reference would be wanting
to the following antithesis. Besides in Julian, τὰ πατρία is always used
to designate the national pagan sacra.

† See Eunap. vit. Proæres. T. I. p. 92.

‡ Augustin. Confession. l. VIII. c. 2 et seq.

and son, as a compensation to the Christian youth for that
which they had been deprived of, were in the habit of writing
historical and doctrinal portions of scripture in all the forms
of Greek verse. This, however, would prove but a sorry
substitute for that which the study of classical antiquity
was designed to furnish, in order to that natural development of the human mind which Christianity presupposes.
As the church historian Socrates very justly remarks, in
stating this fact, " Divine Providence was mightier than
the painstaking of these two men, and than the will of the
emperor." *

Julian hated especially the bishops, who were so active in
propagating the faith ; and these would most easily have become the objects of persecution, if his fanaticism had but
once proved too strong for his feelings of humanity and principles of civil polity. Like the pagan emperors before him,
he saw in those who presided over the instruction and government of the Christian communities the chief supports of
Atheism (ἀθεότης). He imagined that by a crafty policy he
could easily gain over the misguided people, if he was not
counteracted by the bishops. And for the reasons just mentioned, hated above all others by him were those bishops who
had been zealous students of the Greek literature, and who
applied this literature itself to the service of Christianity and
the subversion of paganism ; for instance, those men with
whom, when a youth, he had studied at Athens, the two
friends, Basilius bishop of Cæsarea, and Gregory of Nazianzen ; and those who, under his reign, dared to employ Grecian science in combating paganism and in defending Christianity, such as Apollinaris of Laodicea, and Diodorus bishop
of Tarsus in Cicilia.†

* The remarks of Socrates on this occasion, respecting the necessity of
the study of ancient literature, in order to the progressive culture of the
Christian church, are very correct. L III. c. 16.
† Well worthy of notice are the fierce declamations of Julian against
this latter, in his letter to Photinus, of which Facundus of Hermiane has
preserved to us the fragment already mentioned, in a bad Latin translation, Defens. trium capitulor. I. IV. 379. He reproaches him with
having attended the school at Athens ; there studied philosophy, music,
and rhetoric ; and thereby armed his tongue to fight against the gods.
Hence he was punished by the gods with consumption ; for his sunken
features, full of wrinkles, and his emaciated body, were not, as those

In a very unworthy manner did he conduct himself towards Titus bishop of Bostra in Arabia. When he had made him responsible for the preservation of the public peace and order in that city, where, on account of the excited state of feeling between pagans and Christians, the slightest cause might lead to scenes of violence, the bishop, in a memorial drawn up in the name of the whole body of the clergy, and intended for their defence, declared to him, " Although the Christians, on account of their numbers, might bid defiance to the pagans, yet they were restrained from disorders by the admonitions of the clergy." Upon this Julian despatched a letter to the inhabitants of Bostra, in which he exhorted both parties, Christians and pagans, to maintain quiet and use forbearance towards each other ; and then proceeds to describe the clergy (whose conduct, indeed, in many countries, had, under former reigns, well deserved this reproach) as being the authors of all the disturbances. " It is," says he, " because they look back with longing to their former authority, because they are not permitted to hold tribunals, to dictate wills,* to seize upon the possessions of others, and appropriate the whole to their own uses, that they throw everything into confusion." He next quotes to the Christian communities the above-cited declaration from the bishop's letter, wrested out of its proper connection, for the purpose of representing him as their accuser, and of holding him up to their detestation. They ought, he said, to rise of their own accord against such an accusing bishop, and drive him from the city, and the masses should be united together. This latter hint, certainly, did not agree well with his general exhortation to quiet ; but it is easy to see that Julian hoped, if he could get them into a

whom he deceived would have it appear, the effects of his rigidly ascetic life (of his πολιτεία φιλοσοφικὴ), but the just punishment of the gods. Quod non est philosophicæ conversationis judicio, sicut videri vult a se deceptis; sed justitiæ pro certo deorumque pœnæ, qua percutitur competenti ratione usque ad novissimum vitæ suæ finem asperam et amaram vitam vivens et faciem pallore confectam. Assuredly we can more easily pardon such judgments in pagans than in Christian teachers and writers of this period, the altogether similar way in which, unmindful of the book of Job, and of the words of our Saviour, John ix. 3, they interpret attacks of disease and other calamities which befel heretics.

* See below, in the section concerning the constitution of the church.

G 2

quarrel with their bishop, to make them unite more easily with the pagans.*

Sometimes the bishops forgot the duties which, according to the Christian doctrine, they owed to the supreme magistrate, even though a pagan, and gave the emperor just cause for persecuting them; yet, in such cases, he did not do everything which in strict justice he might have done. In general he was more apt to be excited where anything was attempted in his reign against the Gods and their worship, than where the honour due to his person was attacked. Gregory bishop of Nazianzus, the old father of the celebrated Gregory, had allowed public prayers to be offered in the church against the emperor, as a godless man. The occasion of this, without much doubt, was, that the governor of the province had sent soldiers to tear down the church; but, opposed by the firmness of the old man, who failed, indeed, to unite to this quality the gentleness becoming the Christian and his own spiritual office, they did not venture to make the attempt.† The bishop Maris of Chalcedon, an old man almost blind, who had to be led about by the hand, seeing the emperor offering a sacrifice in the temple of Fortune at Constantinople, went in, and, hurried on by his over-passionate zeal, publicly called him a renegade and an infidel. Julian forbore, it is true, from punishing such a violation of the duty of a subject, as he might justly have done; but he forgot, too, his own dignity, by indulging in vulgar sarcasms after his usual way; and, bantering the old man on his blindness, said, "Will not thy Galilean God, then, heal thee too?"‡

It could not fail to be the case, however, that, even without any instigation from Julian, in those cities where there still existed a considerable pagan party, and this party had not, till now, given loose to its pent-up fury, and where they had been exasperated by the violent proceedings of the bishops under the previous government, sanguinary tumults would sometimes arise. Thus it happened at Alexandria, soon after

* Julian, ep. 52. It should be remarked, however, that Julian wrote this letter to Antioch in an excited state of mind.

† Gregor. Nazianz. orat. XIX. f. 308.

‡ This Sozomen (V. 4) cites as a flying story; but many a bishop at that time might venture to do this, and Julian's conduct on the occasion is not unlike him; so that the story may perhaps be true.

Julian's accession to the throne. The bishop Georgius, a worldly man, of a violent and headstrong temper, who had been thrust by an armed force upon the community devoted to the bishop Athanasius, had administered his office after the same manner with its commencement; and by his persecuting spirit towards all who thought differently from himself, by acting as a spy and an informer to the emperor Constantius, by misusing his influence at court for the gratification of his own passions, had made himself hateful to all parties except his own.* He had drawn upon himself the anger of the pagans, by destroying splendid temples, by exposing the sanctuary of the Mithras worship to universal derision, and, finally, because he had been heard to say to his attendants, when passing by a temple at Tychæ, "How much longer shall this tomb stand?" Scarcely had Julian's accession to the throne become known at Alexandria, when the pagan populace seized upon Georgius; upon the knight Dracontius, director of the mint; and upon a third, who had also rendered himself hateful to the pagans; and threw them into prison. After they had been kept in prison twenty-four days, the multitude poured together again. All three were murdered; the body of Georgius was carried through the city upon a camel, and, after being exposed to every indignity, was towards evening burnt.† Probably it was not pagans alone who engaged in this riot: at all events, the affair could never have been carried to such an extreme if Georgius had not made himself so universally hated. In consequence of these riotous proceedings, Julian addressed to the Alexandrians one of his declamatory rescripts, censuring their conduct in most emphatic language; but he punished no one. So, too, in other similar cases, the emperor went no farther than words, which, however, were of little use, especially as men were aware how much the emperor was pleased by any manifestation of zeal for the gods. He seems, in fact, in many cases, to have approved rather than rebuked the outbreaks of popular fury against those who had been guilty of

---

* Ammianus Marcellinus says of him (l. XXII. c. 11), Professionis suæ oblitus, quæ nihil nisi justum suadet et lene, ad delatorum ausa feralia desciscebat.

† Sozom. V. 7; Ammian. Marcellin. XXII. 11; and the most accurate account in the above-cited anonymous life of Athanasius, p. 68.

destroying the temples, or who were unwilling to rebuild the temples which had been destroyed.

Marcus, a bishop of Arethusa, on Mount Lebanon, had in the preceding reign drawn upon himself the hatred of the pagan inhabitants, by causing the destruction of a magnificent temple, and by resorting to forcible measures to make converts. According to the law which Julian everywhere published,* he was, under these circumstances, bound to make good the value of the temple in money, or else to cause it to be rebuilt. Being in no condition to do the former, and thinking he could not conscientiously do the latter; fearing, at the same time, for his life, amidst a ferocious populace, he betook himself to flight. As others, however, were involved in danger on his account, he turned back, and voluntarily offered himself to his enemies. The fanatical multitude now fell upon him; he was dragged through the streets, treated with every sort of abuse, and at last given up to be made sport of by ungoverned schoolboys. When the old man had almost done breathing, they besmeared him with honey and other liquids, laid him in a basket, in which he was swung up in the air, and left to be preyed upon by bees and wasps. Marcus shamed his cruel enemies by the cool indifference which he exhibited under all his sufferings—an indifference, however, which seemed more that of the cynic than of the Christian. The governor, himself a pagan, is said to have represented to Julian what scandal it must occasion if they allowed themselves to be outdone by the constancy of a weak old man; and the emperor finally commanded him to be set free; for it was not his wish to give the Christians any martyrs.†

As Julian was in the habit of appointing zealous pagans to the high sacerdotal and civil offices, and as the latter were aware that nothing would serve better to ingratiate them with the emperor than zeal for the spread of paganism; as they were incited by the double stimulus of their own fanaticism, and of their wish to please the emperor; so it was a matter of course that individual instances of the oppression and perse-

---

* See above.

† See above, the letter of Libanius, who confirms the asseverations of the Christian authors, Sozomen, Socrates, Theodoretus, and Gregory of Nazianzen.

cution of Christians would easily happen, which might proceed even to cruelty.

Julian became still more embittered against the Christians in the summer of 362, during his stay at Antioch. In this city Christianity had for a long time been the prevailing religion ; insomuch that Libanius remarked on the spot, that only a few old men remained who were still familiar with the ancient pagan festivals, when Julian came to the government.* In this great capital of Asia, which, while maintaining the form of Christianity, had become the seat of mingled oriental and Roman splendour, licentiousness and corruption of manners, Julian, the emperor, was resolved to affect the ancient simplicity which was wholly abhorrent to the prevailing manners, and in such a place could only expose him to the jeers and sarcasms of the disaffected. His zeal in the pagan worship, in which he would fain set an example to his subjects, only made him ridiculous to the higher classes and hated by the people in this ancient Christian city. Frugal in his expenses for the maintenance of his court, he spared no cost in offering sacrifices of all kinds. He often slaughtered a hecatomb of cattle ; and it was his delight to bring the victims to the priests with his own hands, followed by a train of old women, who still clung to paganism. Wherever an ancient temple was to be found on the mountains around Antioch, Julian clambered to the spot, however steep and rugged the path, for the purpose of presenting an offering.†

He was seen standing at the altar, under an open sky, though the rain poured down in torrents, and all the others present sought protection under the roof of the temple, and although his attendants besought him to pay some regard to his health.‡ The greater his zeal for the pagan worship, the more confidently he had hoped that, when the heathen sanctu-

---

* Liban. de vita sua, vol. I. p. 81. Libanius plays the rhetorician here perhaps only in this respect, that he represents what might be said of Antioch as universally the case.

† Ammian. Marcellin. l. XXII. c. 12, ff. Augebantur cærimoniarum ritus immodice cum impensarum amplitudine antehac inusitata et gravi. The same writer relates that, owing to the vast multitude of sacrificial banquets, rioting and drunkenness were spread among the soldiers. Οὐδὲν οὕτω χαλιπὸν, οὐδὶ δύσβατον, ὃ μὴ λίιον ἰδόκιι νιῶν ἴχον ἢ προτιρόν γι ἰσχηκός. Liban. Monodia in Julian. vol. I. p. 513.

‡ Liban. presbeut. Julian. vol. I. p. 476.

aries, which had so long been closed, were re-opened, he should witness the same enthusiasm among the people at Antioch by which he was inspired himself; and the more painful it must have been to him to find his expectations so completely disappointed. True, multitudes of the people and of the higher classes assembled in the temples and groves which he visited; not, however, for the sake of the gods, but for the purpose of seeing the emperor, and being seen by him, as he himself must have known. He was saluted on these occasions with the loud shout of "Long live the emperor!" just as if he had made his appearance in the theatre. Hence he was led to address to the people of Antioch an admonitory discourse, complaining that they converted the temple into a theatre, to which they resorted rather for his own sake than on account of the gods.* Yet soon the voice of praise, with which he had been received out of respect for his person, was exchanged for that of mockery and disdain; for an injudicious regulation, the object of which was to force a reduction of the price of provisions to a degree disproportionate to the produce of the year, and the result of which was directly the reverse of what had been intended, made him hated both among the higher classes and the populace, and his attempts to injure Christian sanctuaries alienated the popular feeling; and he was obliged to hear men express their longing for the return of the Kappa and the Chi, that is, of the reign of Constantius and Christianity.†

One incident which made him extremely unpopular with the zealous Christians was this: In the grove of Daphne, about five miles from Antioch, but still reckoned as belonging to the suburbs of the city, stood a famous temple of Apollo; and the fountain which flowed near by was said to possess virtues which communicated the gift of divination.‡ Hence an oracle of Apollo had sprung up on this spot. But, ever since the times of the emperor Hadrian, this fountain had been neglected and had gone to decay. With a view to suppress the old pagan cultus, as well as to check the dis-

---

* Julian in Misopogon. p. 344. Liban. de vita sua, p. 82.
† Misopogon. 357.
‡ To which legend perhaps, in this and in similar cases, the exhilarating and intoxicating influence of the exhalations of some mineral spring had given occasion.

sipation which the amenity of this spot, famous as the seat of vicious pleasures, invited, Gallus, when governor of the province, had caused to be buried here the bones of the martyr Babylas, and had erected a church for the use of those who wished to perform their devotions at the tomb of the martyr. Julian caused the long-closed temple of Apollo to be reopened, and surrounded it with a new and magnificent peristyle. Setting great value upon soothsaying of all kinds, he wished to restore also the ancient oracle, and directed the fountain to be cleared out. The priests now declared that the oracle could not go into operation. The god would give no response, on account of the vicinity of the dead; besides, according to the pagan notions, no dead body could be suffered to remain in contact with the holy place. Julian construed this as referring particularly to the neighbouring bones of Babylas; for the Christian worship among the tombs, as he called it, was his special abomination, and, above all, in the present case, so near to the shrine of his own Apollo. He caused the bones to be exhumated. Multitudes of Christians, young and old, men and women, now assembled to bear away the bones of the martyr, in solemn procession, to a place about forty stadia (five miles) distant; and, through the whole of the way, they chanted choral psalms which alluded to the vanity of idolatry. The whole throng joined with one voice in the words, "Confounded be all they that serve graven images, and boast themselves in idols!"* Julian, who saw himself and his gods insulted at the same time, did not manifest on this occasion the philosophical calmness which he was so fond of exhibiting in other cases of a like nature. He commanded the prefect Salustius to search out the guiltiest of those engaged in the tumult, and punish them severely. Salust, although a pagan, yet, from motives of humanity and prudence, reluctantly executed the command. He caused a number of individuals to be seized, but subjected only one, Theodorus, a young man, to torture. The latter continued firm and unmoved, and in the midst of his sufferings sang the psalms which the day before he had sung with the others in the procession.† Salust now reminded the emperor how

---

* Ammian. Marcellin. l. XXII. c. 12, 13.   Sozom. V. 19.
† The presbyter Rufinus, who knew him when an old man at Antioch,

much the cause of the Christians gained by such constancy in
their suffering companions. This led to the release of the
young man and of all the rest.*

When Julian, for the first time after so long a period,
restored the ancient feast of Apollo Daphnicus, he hoped that
it would be celebrated by the inhabitants of Antioch with
great display. But, as he says in a sarcastic defence of
himself against the reproaches of the people of Antioch,†
" Not an individual brought oil to kindle a lamp to the god ;
not one brought incense ; not one a libation or a sacrifice."‡
But one solitary priest appeared, bringing a goose for an
offering. The emperor was greatly astonished and excited at
this result ; he severely reprimanded the noble inhabitants of
Antioch, who knew no better how to appreciate the restoration
of an ancient national festival ; just as if his religion must
necessarily be theirs. He complains of them in this writing,
that they allowed their wives to carry away everything from
the house for the support of the Galileans, or to bestow it
upon the poor ; while they themselves were unwilling to
expend the smallest trifle to sustain the worship of the gods.§

It happened afterwards that a fire broke out in this temple,
as it was said through the carelessness of Asclepiades, a pagan
philosopher, who had come on a visit to the pious, philosophical emperor. Asclepiades had left standing, with lighted
tapers before the statue of Apollo, a small silver image of the
Dea cœlestis (Venus Urania), which he carried about with
him to perform his devotions by, wherever he travelled. But
Julian attributed it to the revengeful spirit of the Christians ;
and they were accused as the authors of the conflagration.

relates that he told him that during all his sufferings he imagined he saw
a young man standing by him who wiped away his sweat and poured
over him cold water. Rufin. vers. Euseb. X. 36.
    * Sozom. V. 20.
    † The Misopogon, in allusion to the jokes on the long beard of the
emperor.
    ‡ Misopogon. p. 363.
    § Misopogon. p. 363. This passage deserves notice, inasmuch as we
may see from it that Julian was well aware of the indifference entertained by many of the higher class of the Antiochians towards the affairs
of religion ; and that he considered the females as the chief supporters of
Christianity in the families of such persons. See, below, a like assertion of Libanius.

He directed torture to be employed for the purpose of finding out the guilty, and ordered the great church of Antioch to be closed, to show his displeasure against the whole body of Christians.[*] Although judicial investigation could elicit no evidence against the Christians, yet Julian did not give up his suspicions. He complained that the senate of Antioch had not done all in their power to detect the guilty.[†] The people of Antioch feared the worst; as we see from the discourses delivered or written in their defence by Libanius. Julian exhibited on several occasions his excited state of feeling against the Christians. He said himself that, at a signal given by his own hand, the tombs of the martyrs in the neighbouring towns, together with the churches erected over them, had been destroyed; and that the people had even gone farther against the enemies of the gods than he himself designed.[‡] Before leaving Antioch he placed at the head of the judicial department in Syria a man of a passionate and naturally cruel disposition named Alexander. He is reported to have said that Alexander was not worthy of the office; but that the covetous and slanderous Antiochians deserved no better judge.[§] It is evident, from particular instances of his conduct, that the administration of justice by this Alexander corresponded entirely with the natural character of the man. He took great pains to prevail on Christians to deny their faith. Many, indeed, suffered themselves to be induced by promises, persuasions, and threats, to sacrifice; but the reproaches and tears of their wives,—among whom, at Antioch, there seems to have been more true piety than among the men,—and the silence of night, suited to lead men to the recesses of their own hearts, roused their conscience, and they returned again to Christianity. This excited Alexander even to fury; he not only persecuted these individuals, but asserted that they could not have gone so far of themselves. He thought he could trace the frustration of all his efforts to propagate the worship of the gods to the secret plots of a Christian. He was persuaded by the enemies of a certain Eusebius to believe that the whole mischief proceeded from him. This man was about to be thrown into prison and con-

[*] Ammian. Marcellin. l. XXII. c. 13.   [†] See Misopogon. p. 361.
[‡] Misopogon. p. 361.   [§] Ammian. Marcellin. l. XXIII. c. 2.

fined in chains ; but he succeeded in effecting his escape, and
took refuge with the pagan rhetorician Libanius, whose friendship he had gained by the moderation and mildness of his
conduct towards the pagans under the preceding reign.
Libanius behaved in the same noble manner as he was ever
accustomed to do in like cases. He boldly rebuked Alexander for his conduct, and assured him that he would not give
up Eusebius.*

But, although Libanius did not wish to see men persecuted
for the sake of religion, yet he was gratified when any, even
though it might be at first by mere external considerations,
were brought back to the worship of the gods. This is evident from the manner in which he endeavours to take advantage of the dread of Julian's anger, as a means of persuading
the noble Antiochians that they had better restore the worship
of the gods, *which*, he said, *was the only effectual and certain
means of appeasing the emperor.*†   In this, doubtless, he was

* In his letter to Alexander (ep. 1057) he thus expresses himself:
"It was my wish that you might be zealous indeed for the gods, and gain
over many to their law : but that you should not be surprised, however,
if many a one of those who have just offered should consider what he
has done as a very wicked thing, and praise again the refusing to offer.
For, away from home, they follow you when you advise them what is best,
and go to the altars. At home they are turned about, and withdrawn
from the altars by the wife, by tears, and by the night. But as to Eusebius, who is accused of having undone again what was accomplished by
your pains, he is manifestly calumniated, and far from that which has
been laid to his charge ; for he well understands the times, and acts uniformly with reflection rather than with foolhardiness ; and, as he knows
your wrath. he would not, were he ever so foolish, thus throw himself
upon a sheaf of swords. But he is not one of those ordinary men who easily
change with the changes of the times ; but, as one who has busied himself
with science, and cultivated his mind, he was, even in the time when he
had the power, oppressive to no one, and arrogant to no one. One might
say he foresaw the future, so moderate was he. It was this indeed which
made the man dear to me and to Nicocles (see above ; I suppose that, instead of ᾧ καὶ φίλον ἐποίησας, we should read, ὁ καὶ φίλον ἐποίησιν) ; for
while he honoured *his own* religion, he yet did not annoy those who
swore by the name of Jupiter."   In like manner Libanius warned this
Alexander, in ep. 1375, to take care lest, by the way in which he proposed to help the insulted gods, he might rather do them injury. Probably letter 1346 also has a similar reference.

† In the discourse, περὶ τῆς τοῦ βασιλιῶς ὀργῆς, which perhaps was only
written and not delivered (vol. I. p. 502), " Ye will appease the anger
of the emperor," says he to the nobles of Antioch, " by no petitions, no
clamour, no ambassadors (even though you sent your most talented

right; for when the town of Pessinus in Galatia, celebrated in earlier times on account of the worship of Cybele, petitioned the emperor for assistance, on some occasion or other, he replied that, if they wished to enjoy his favour, they must first, by a general procession of penitence, propitiate the mother of the gods, from whose worship they had fallen.*

Wherever, in his march against the Persians, Julian passed through any of the Christian cities of Syria, he took this opportunity of exhorting the senators who welcomed him to restore the worship of the gods. Thus it was, for example, when, after two days' journey, he came to Beroa in Syria. But he complained that the senators all applauded his speeches, though only a few followed his advice; indeed, none but those who seemed already to have cherished sound views in religion, but, until now, had been ashamed to express their convictions openly. His pleasure was the greater when, on the third day's journey, he came to a place † where the odour of incense breathed upon him from all sides, and he everywhere beheld sacrifices publicly offered; although he could not avoid suspecting that these public exhibitions were intended more for himself than for the gods.‡

orators), unless you desist from these tricks, and give up your city to Jupiter and the other gods,—about whom, long before the emperor, even from your childhood, Hesiod and Homer have taught you. But you seek after the honour of being cultivated, and call an acquaintance with those poets cultivation. In respect to man's highest interests, however, you follow other teachers (see above); and you fly from the temples, which are once more thrown open, when you ought to sigh that they were ever closed. In the next place, when the authority of a Plato and a Pythagoras is appealed to in your presence, *you hold out on the other hand that of your mothers and wives, of your butlers and cooks,* and the tenacity of your early convictions; thus allowing yourselves to be led by those whom you ought to lead." A great deal in this description of nominal Christians among the fashionable people of the higher ranks, who were held to Christianity by the force of custom and the *influence of their domestic associations,* is doubtless taken from the real life. He concludes thus: "Shall we not hasten to the temples, persuading some, and forcing the rest to follow us?"

* Julian. ep. 49. † Βατναι.

‡ See Julian's letter to Libanius, describing his journey (ep. 27). Sozomen (VI. 1) reports that Julian, in a menacing letter, summoned Arsaces king of Armenia, who was a Christian, to arm himself for the war against the Persians; that he announced to him the God whom he worshipped would not be able to help him; that this letter contained blasphemies against Christ. Muratori has published this letter in the

As the feelings of Julian against the Christians and against Christianity were continually more and more exasperated by the opposition which he experienced, it may be readily conjectured that, if he had returned back successfully from his Persian campaign, he would have become a violent persecutor of the church. But in this war he perished, in the year 363; and at a single blow the frail fabric erected by mere human will was dissolved; although Julian, deceived by his apparent success in making proselytes, had boasted of having produced, in a short time, a wonderful change; for in a letter, in which, indeed, he complained that the cause of Hellenism, through the fault of its professors, did not yet progress according to his wishes, he had asserted that the friends of the gods ought to be satisfied; for who, a short time before, would have ventured to predict that so great and so important a change could be produced in so brief a period?*

Had the Christians searched after the real cause of this transient victory of the heathen party, they might have derived from it many important lessons for the future.   In the beginning of Julian's reign, the wise Gregory of Nazianzen, contemplating those evils within the church, without which even this transient ascendancy of paganism could hardly have been gained, had expressed the great truth, *that the Christian church had still more to fear from its enemies within than from those without.*† The same father exhorted the Christians, *after the death of Julian*, now to show, by their actions, that they had profited by the divine discipline; to show that God had not given them up as evil-doers into the hands of the pagans, but that he had chastised them as his children; to be careful that they did not forget the storm in the time of calm,

anecdot. Græc. Patav. (see above), p. 334. All the boastful language, perhaps in imitation of oriental taste, which Sozomen refers to, is found in it; nothing, however, which would seem expressly pointed against Christ. Yet, when Julian says to the king, "You seek to keep concealed with you an enemy of the public weal," Sozomen, perhaps with reason, may have supposed this referred to Christ. At all events, in the threat expressed against the city Nisibis, which should share that misfortune of king Arsaces the gods had long since predicted against him, we perceive the hatred he entertained against this city, which for many years had been zealously Christian.

* Ep. 49. Τίς γὰρ ἐν ὀλίγῳ τοσαύτην καὶ τηλικαύτην μεταβολὴν ὀλίγῳ πρότερον ἐτόλμα;

† Gregor. Nazianz. orat I. p. 35.

after the deliverance from Egypt. " It ought not to appear,"
he said, " as if the time of suffering was better for them than
the time of rest; for so it would appear, if then they were
humble and moderate, and pointed all their hopes to heaven,
but now proud and haughty, ready to fall back again into the
same sins which brought them into all their misfortunes." He
then gave the Christians *the advice* to which he was conscious
that he should find the most difficulty in making them listen.
He advised them to take no advantage of the power which
they obtained through the change of the times, in *retaliating upon the pagans the injuries which they had received.*
" Let us show," says he, " what a difference there is between
what these men learn from their gods, and the lessons which
Christ teaches us,—Christ, who, glorified through sufferings,
obtained the victory by forbearing to use his power. Let us
pay God our united thanks; let us, by long suffering, promote the spread of the gospel; for this, let us take advantage
of the times. Let us by gentleness subdue our oppressors."*

The pagans now saw all their brilliant hopes destroyed;
and in their faith they found nothing to console them. Libanius says he supposed that the emperor, who had rebuilt the
temples and altars; who had forgotten no god and no goddess,
and sacrificed upon the altars whole herds of oxen and lambs;
who had called forth troops of priests from their hiding-places,
would need no mighty armed force, but must conquer through
the power of the gods.† Now he quarrelled with his gods,
because they had permitted Constantius to reign forty years,
but Julian only for so short a period, and then, with him,
suffered his whole work to fall to the ground.‡

Julian was immediately succeeded by Jovianus, an emperor
who professed Christianity. He had learned from the preceding times the lesson that religion could not be helped by outward force. Hence, although for his own part a zealous
Christian, yet he left to all his subjects the liberty of exer-

---

* Gregor. Nazianz. λογ. στηλιτευτ. II. orat. IV. f. 130, 131.

† Monod in Julian. t. i. 508. He had actually prophesied that the
gods themselves would smite the Persians. Ep. 649.

‡ L. c. p. 510. How strongly contrasted with this is the spirit of
Augustin, when he says " that no emperor should be a Christian in
order to procure for himself the fortune of Constantine—as each should
be a Christian *for the sake of eternal life*. God took away Jovian sooner
than he did Julian." De civitate Dei, I. V. c. 25.

cising the religion which they preferred,—a principle which he expressed in one of the laws published on his accession to the throne. He permitted the temple-worship and the sacrifices to go on unmolested; and expressly prohibited nothing, except employing the pagan rites for the purposes of magic.*

---

* That Jovian enacted a law of this import can hardly be doubted,— judging from what Themistius said to him at the consular celebration. We must admit that the accounts of persecutions against the pagans, and of measures for the suppression of paganism, under the reign of this emperor, seem to conflict with this supposition; as, for example, when Libanius, in his epitaph, in Julian, p. 619, says that, after Julian's death, those who spoke openly against the gods once more stood in authority, but the priests were unjustifiably called to an account. An indemnification was demanded for the money expended in sacrifices. The rich anticipated a judicial investigation, and paid the money down; the poor were thrown in chains. (We may conjecture that the writer is here speaking of those who were accused of having expended money which did not belong to them —whether taken from the public coffer or from elsewhere—for the offering of sacrifices.) The temples, he continues, were in part demolished, and in part stood unfinished—objects of mockery and sport to the Christians. The philosophers (i. e. all those who, in the time of Julian, had appeared in the philosopher's cloak, and thereby acquired specially great influence with him) were abused. All who had received presents from the emperor Julian were accused of theft, and subjected to every sort of torment, in order to extort from them the money they were supposed to have received. In respect to this report of Libanius, what he says as a passionate opponent of the emperor, and with rhetorical exaggeration, cannot be received as altogether credible. It may have been the case that many pagans, believing that the end sanctioned the means, stimulated by zeal for their religion, or making this a mere pretence and out of sheer cupidity, had allowed themselves, under the preceding reign, in practices which might in some measure give just occasion for judicial investigations against the heathens. But it also may have been the case that indemnification was *unjustly* required for that which had been done in a perfectly legal manner, and in compliance with supreme imperial authority—just as Julian had proceeded in respect to what had been done under his predecessor. And, finally, it would be wrong to suppose that everything which Christian governors, or those that used Christianity as a pretext, under an emperor who appeared zealous for Christianity, thought themselves entitled to do, without being authorized by his laws, ought to be laid to his charge. Jovian himself showed respect to Maximus and Priscus—the two philosophers who possessed the highest influence under the emperor Julian, and the former of whom had laboured earnestly for the support of paganism. See Eunap. vita Maximi, p. 58. But yet, without some occasion given by the emperor, it could not happen that pagan philosophers should be persecuted. This, in fact, is intimated by Themistius, although he absolves the emperor from the charge of having himself had any hand in it,—ad Valentem, de bello victis. ed. Harduin, f. 99. c.

Golden words were those which the moderate pagan Themistius addressed to Jovian, on his entrance upon the consular
office, with a view to confirm him in those principles recognising man's universal rights, and the toleration in matters of
religion connected therewith, which he had expressed immediately after coming to the throne. Having congratulated
the emperor that the first law of his reign related to religion,
he says, "You alone seem to be aware that the monarch
cannot force everything from his subjects; that there are
things which are superior to all constraint, threatenings, and
laws; as, for instance, virtue generally, and, in particular,
piety towards God. And you have very wisely considered,
that in all these matters, unless there is hypocrisy, the uncon-
strained and absolutely free will of the soul must move first.
For if it is not possible, emperor, by any *new edicts* to make
a man well disposed towards you, if he is not so at heart, how
much less is it possible, by the fear of human edicts, by transient constraint, and those weak images of terror which the
times have often produced, and as often annihilated, to make
men truly pious, and lovers of God! We play, in such cases
often, the ridiculous part of serving, not God, but the purple;
and change our religion more easily than the sea is moved by
the storm. There used to be but one Theramenes; but now
all are fickle-minded.* He who but yesterday was one of the
ten (deputies of the Athenians to the Lacedemonians) is to-
day one of the thirty (tyrants). The man who yesterday
stood by the altars, the sacrifices, and the images, stands to-

---

Socrates (l. III. c. 24) says that, under Jovian, all the temples were immediately closed; that the pagans concealed themselves; that the philosophers laid aside their cloaks; that the public sacrifices ceased. All
this, although not taken in so general a sense, may have been true—as a
natural consequence of the fears entertained by the pagans, or of their
lukewarmness entering of its own accord, when the atmosphere of the court
ceased to be favourable to paganism. Socrates himself seems to be aware
that Jovian was not disposed to oppress any party. L. III. c. 25, etc.
What Sozomen says (l. VI. c. 3), respecting a letter of the emperor addressed to all the governors, may be understood, supposing it to be
correct, as only meaning that Jovian expressed a wish to have all his
subjects come to the knowledge of the truth in Christianity, and distinguished the Christian church once more by peculiar privileges. Libanius
himself (orat. pro templis, vol. ii. p. 163) says that after Julian's death,
down to the time of Valens, μένει τινὰ το θύειν ἱεραῖα χρόνον.

* Νῦν ἁπάντις κοθόρνοι.

day by the holy tables of the Christians. Yet this, O emperor! is not what you desire. While you would now and ever be sovereign as to everything else, you command that religion should be left to the free choice of each individual. And in this you follow the example of the Deity, who has implanted the capacity for religion in the whole human nature, but has left the particular kind of worship to the will of each man. But whoever employs force here takes away the freedom which God has bestowed on every man. For this reason, the laws of a Cheops and of a Cambyses hardly lasted as long as their authors' lives. But the law of God, and your law, remains for ever unchangeable,—the law that every man's soul is free in reference to its own peculiar mode of worship. This law, no pillage of goods, no death on the cross or at the stake, has ever been able to extinguish. You may, indeed, force and kill the body; but, though the tongue may be forced to silence, the soul will rise, and carry along with it its own will, free from the constraint of authority."

The same principles, in regard to matters of religion, were followed by Valentinian, who succeeded Jovian in the year 364. As Valentinian, by his steadfast profession of Christianity, had incurred the displeasure of the emperor Julian;[*] as he hated Julian and his friends; as he was, in other respects, inclined to despotism; it is the more remarkable that he still recognised on this point the limits of human power, and perceived the folly and ruinous consequences of attempting to overstep them.[†] By laws which he issued at the very commencement of his reign, he allowed each of his subjects unlimited freedom of exercising the religion which he conceived to be true.[‡] By another law, of the year 371,

---

[*] The thing itself admits of no doubt, since pagan and Christian historians here agree. The only question relates to the particulars, which are stated in many various ways.

[†] Ammianus Marcellinus, who frankly describes the despotic acts of this emperor, says of him, l. XXX. c. 9, " Postremo hoc moderamine principatus inclaruit, quod inter religionum diversitates medius stetit, nec quemquam inquietavit, neque ut hoc coleretur imperavit aut illud, nec interdictis minacibus subjectorum cervicem ad id quod ipse coluit inclinabat, sed intemeratas reliquit has partes, ut reperit."

[‡] Unicuique, quod animo imbibisset, colendi libera facultas. This law is cited in a law of the emperor belonging to the year 371. Cod. Theod. l. IX. Tit. 16. l. 9.

he expressly declares that neither the practice of the haruspices, nor any other form of worship permitted by the fathers,
should be forbidden.*

This toleration of Valentinian was rather helpful than
injurious to the spread of Christianity. This appears from
the fact, that, under the reign of this emperor, heathenism
began first to be called by the name of the 'peasants' religion
(paganismus†); just as, in the primitive times, Christianity
was considered as the religion of shoemakers, weavers, and
slaves. To be sure, we are not to conclude, because heathenism was called distinctively the religion of the ignorant countrymen, that it had lost all its followers among the educated
and higher classes.

In the East the political suspicions of the emperor Valens
brought many a persecution upon those pagans who practised
divination and sorcery,‡ although the same tolerant laws were
recognised also in the East. The pagan rhetorician Themistius addressed the emperor Valens in terms very similar to
those which he had used before Jovian, extolling these principles of toleration.§ According to the testimony of Libanius,

* He gave this direction, perhaps, expressly because a law which he
had enacted against the nocturna sacrificia and pagan magic might be
misinterpreted; and even that first law, in consequence of the remonstrances of an influential pagan statesman, did not go into general execution—if Zosimus (IV. 3) speaks the truth.

† The name religio paganorum, applied to heathenism, first occurs in
a law of the emperor Valentinian, of the year 368. Cod. Theodos. l. XVI.
Tit. ii. l. 18. The above derivation of the name is, however, the only
tenable one, and is moreover confirmed by the testimony of Paulus Orosius. This writer, in the preface to his short history of the world, says,
Qui ex locorum agrestium compitis et pagis pagani vocantur. To this
derivation the Christian poet Prudentius also alludes, when (contra Sym-
machum, l. I. v. 620) he calls the heathens " pago implicitos."

‡ Liban. de vita sua, p. 113, vol. I. Chrysostom. hom. 38, in act.
apost. fin.

§ Orat. VI. de religionibus, which hitherto has been known to us only
in a Latin translation. Socrates (IV. 32) and Sozomen (VI. 36) cite a
discourse of similar import which Themistius is said to have delivered
before Valens, dissuading him from the persecution of *Christians entertaining other opinions* in the time of the Arian controversies. If we must
suppose that this refers to the discourse above cited, it could not be correct;
for that discourse manifestly treats of *toleration only to paganism.* But
both those authors, however, quote distinct expressions of Themistius,
which are not to be found in that discourse. Although they quote
many other thoughts which do actually occur in it, yet this is no proof

Valentinian and Valens were finally moved, by the political jealousies growing out of the frequent conspiracies, *to forbid entirely all bloody sacrifices;* though the other kinds of heathen worship continued to be permitted;[*] yet no such law of these emperors has come down to us.[†]

The emperor Gratian, who succeeded his father in the year 375, had not, like·the latter, adopted it as an absolute principle to alter nothing pertaining to the religious condition of his empire; but still he adhered to the rule of allowing a free exercise of the pagan rites. So accustomed were men to consider the pagan religion as the religion of the state, and the emperors as its chiefs, that even the Christian emperors still retained the title of supreme pontiffs, and, on ascending the throne, received, along with the other badges of the imperial dignity, the robe of the supreme pontiff; but it had now become a mere formality.

Gratian is said to have been the first who declined to receive this robe because he could not conscientiously do it as a Christian;[‡] yet he still retained the title.[§] Moreover, in the place where the Roman senate met there stood an altar dedicated to Victory, at which the pagan senators were accustomed to take their oaths, and upon which they scattered incense and made offerings. It had been first removed by Constantius, and afterwards replaced by Julian. Jovian and Valentinian had made no alteration, allowing things to remain as they were; but Gratian caused the altar to be removed again. He confiscated estates belonging to the temples. He deprived the priests and vestals of the support they had received from the

---

that they have in view the same performance; since, in the discourse also which was delivered before Jovian, a good deal is expressed in precisely the same way as in the oration before Valens. It is therefore more probable that Themistius actually delivered a discourse of this sort, of which, however, nothing has come down to our times.

[*] Orat. pro templis,.p. 163.

[†] It may be possible that Libanius did not in this case duly separate the affairs of the East and of the West; yet he was doubtless interested in that discourse to bring together everything which could be found, in the ordinances of the earlier emperors, *favourable* to paganism.

[‡] Zosim. 1. IV. c. 36.

[§] Thus, for example, Ausonius gives it to him, in his gratiarum actio pro consulatu, where he styles him "pontifex religione;" and he bears it in inscriptions. See Inscriptionum latinarum amplissima collectio, ed. Orelli, vol. I. p. 245.

public treasury, and of all their other privileges.* He took away also from the college of priests the right of receiving legacies of real estate. All this took place in the year 382. As a considerable number of pagans were then still to be found in the Roman senate, it being generally the case that the first and oldest families in Rome adhered to the old Roman religion, along with all the other old Roman customs, they chose a man out of their number, distinguished for his personal merits, Quintus Aurelius Symmachus, as their delegate, to procure from the emperor, in the name of the senate, the abrogation of these laws. But the Christian party of the senate, who claimed to be the majority,† transmitted through the Roman bishop Damasus a memorial to the emperor, complaining of this proceeding on the part of the heathens. Ambrose bishop of Milan, who possessed great influence with Gratian, presented him with this petition; and Gratian was so indignant at the demands of the pagan party as to refuse even to grant an audience to their delegate.‡ As Rome was visited in the following year, 383, by a great famine, the zealous pagans looked upon this as a punishment sent by the gods, on account of the wrong done to their religion.§

When the young Valentinian II. succeeded his brother Gratian in the government, the pagan party of the senate at-

* See the reports of Symmachus and Ambrosius to Valentinian II. directly to be quoted, and the edict of Honorius of the year 415. Cod. Theodos. l. XVI. Tit. x. l. 20. Omnia loco, quæ sacris error veterum deputavit, secundum *D. Gratiani constituta* nostræ rei jubemus sociari.

† Having here nothing but the reports of parties, we cannot determine with certainty as to that which was formally right in the case.

‡ Evil-minded men, says Symmachus in his memorial to the successors of this emperor, had brought this about; because they well knew that, if the emperor heard the deputies, he would not refuse them justice. Denegata est *ab improbis* audientia, quia non erat justitia defutura.

§ Symmachus writes, in his great extremity, to his brother, with a certain simple piety, which, with all his superstition, yet renders him far more worthy of respect than those were who embraced Christianity to honour the emperor, Dii patrii! facite gratiam neglectorum sacrorum! Miseram famem pelle. Quamprimum revocet urbs nostra, quos invita dimisit (this is ambiguous, and may refer either to the strangers banished from Rome, with a view to spare the means of subsistence, or to the gods). Quicquid humana ope majus est, Diis permitte curandum. Symmach. epistolæ, l. II. ep. 7.

tempted once more (in the year 384), through the instrumentality of Symmachus, at that time prefect of the city, to obtain from the emperor a compliance with their demands. He asks of the emperor, that he would distinguish his own private religion from the religio urbis. Taking his stand at the position of paganism, he explains that men would do better, inasmuch as they are excluded from the knowledge of divine things,* to abide by, and to follow, the authority of antiquity; in doing which their fathers for so many centuries had experienced so much prosperity. Rome is personified, and made to address the emperor in the following language: " I wish, as I am free, to live after my own manner. These rites of worship have subjected the whole world to my laws." The famine of the preceding year he represented as following in consequence of the wrong done to the pagan rites. " What was there," he says, " like this, which our fathers were ever compelled to suffer, when the ministers of religion enjoyed the honour of a public maintenance?" As Symmachus was well aware that the Christians would have the emperor make it a matter of conscience to refuse all support to the idolatrous worship, he endeavoured to quiet his scruples on this point by the distinction already alluded to between the religio urbis and the religio imperatoris. If he did but suffer that to remain which the city (urbs) could demand by ancient right, he would by so doing concede no privilege to a religion which was not his own.†

But Ambrose bishop of Milan, on hearing of this, sent to the young emperor Valentinian a letter written with dignified earnestness. He represented that this compliance on the part of the emperor would be a sanction of paganism, and a tacit denial of his own Christian convictions. The emperor ought to allow liberty of conscience to every one of his subjects; but he must also maintain the freedom of his own conscience. " Wrong is done no man," he writes, " when the Almighty God is preferred before him. To him belong your convictions. You force no one yourself to worship God against his own will; let the same right be conceded also to yourself. But if some nominal Christians advise you to such a decision, do not suffer yourself to be deceived by mere

---

* Cum ratio omnis in operto sit.   † Symmach. l. X. ep. 61.

names.* He who advises this, and he who decrees this, sacrifices. We, bishops, could not quietly tolerate this. You
might come to the church, but you would find there no priest;
or a priest who would forbid your approach. What would
you have to reply to the priest, when he says the church
wants not your gifts, since you have honoured with presents
the temples of the heathen? The altar of Christ disdains
your offerings, since you have erected an altar to idols; for
your word, your hand, your signature, are your works. The
Lord wishes not for your service, since you have become the
servant of idols; for he has said to you, ' Ye cannot serve
two masters.' "† The strong representations of Ambrose had
their effect, and Valentinian rejected the petition.

In the beginning of the reign of the emperor Theodosius,
Chrysostom composed at Antioch his noble discourse on the
martyr Babylas,‡ in which he described the divine power
wherewith Christianity had penetrated into the life of humanity, and obtained the victory over heathenism. He rightly
maintained that Christianity disdained in this warfare all
weapons which were not her own; and he predicted the
entire destruction of paganism, which was crumbling in ruins
through its own nothingness. He says, " *It is not permitted
the Christians to destroy error by violence and constraint:
they are allowed to labour for the salvation of men only by
persuasion, by rational instruction, and by acts of love.*"§
He affirms that zeal for paganism was still to be seen only in
a few cities; and that in these the pagan worship was pro-

---

* Ambrosius was afraid, as it seems, of several of the members of the
emperor's privy council, of the consistory, to whom the political interest
might be of greater account than the religious. There were several
members of the emperor's privy council also who were pagans. See
Ambros. ep. 57, ad Eugen. s. 3.

† For the rest, the question whether the emperor was obligated to
grant this, and whether he could grant it with a good conscience, admits
not of being answered from the purely religious point of view; the consideration of civil rights also enters in here, which Symmachus doubtless
alluded to, but at the same time confounded too much with the religious
question, and which, as the matter then stood, would certainly make the
decision more favourable to Ambrosius than to Symmachus.

‡ Εἰς τὸν μάρτυρα Βαβύλαν λόγος δεύτερος.

§ Οὐδὲ γὰρ θέμις χριστιανοῖς ἀνάγκῃ καὶ βίᾳ καταστρέφειν τὴν πλάνην,
ἀλλὰ καὶ πειθοῖ καὶ λόγῳ καὶ προσηνείᾳ τὴν τῶν ἀνθρώπων ἐργάζεσθαι
σωτηρίαν.

moted by the respectable and wealthy citizens, who allowed the poor to join them in their heathen and sensual festivities, and thus chained them to their interests. Chrysostom was assuredly right in this, that men might rely upon the divine power of the gospel, which would carry the work, hitherto so successful, completely to its end: but so thought not the emperors.

Theodosius, the reigning emperor in the East, but whose influence extended also to the West, went in his proceedings against paganism gradually farther in the way struck out by Gratian. At first he was content to abide by those measures against the sacrifices which had already been adopted by him in common with Gratian. Properly speaking, indeed, the employment of sacrifices for the purposes of magic and sooth-saying alone had been forbidden; and even by the new law which Theodosius gave, in the year 385, to the prætorian pre-fect Cynegius, a man extremely zealous for the extinction of paganism, soothsaying from the sacrifices only was prohibited; yet these laws were, in their execution, certainly applied, for the most part, to all the forms of sacrificial worship; as ap-pears from the plea of Libanius in defence of the temples—a discourse shortly after to be more particularly noticed, in which the writer, however, drew arguments from every quar-ter, to limit, as far as possible, the meaning of the existing laws against paganism. Undoubtedly an exception was made in favour of those capital towns where paganism still had a considerable party, and in favour of the more noble families; since Libanius could appeal to the fact, before the emperor Theodosius, that the sacrificial worship still existed at Rome and Alexandria.*

Now, these laws might easily furnish a pretext for the de-struction of the temples. The pagans were found assembled in the temples for the purpose of sacrificing, or they were accused of having sacrificed. Blind zealots, or those whose avarice prompted them to wish for the plunder of the temples, immediately seized upon this circumstance as a lawful reason for destroying them, pretending that they had caused the im-perial laws to be broken. The wild troops of monks, to whom any object which, under the name of religion, excited their passions, was welcome, undertook, especially in the country,

* Oratio pro templis, vol. II. p. 180 et seq.

these campaigns for the destruction of temples in which sacrifices were alleged to have been performed.* As the synagogues of the Jews, whose worship was protected by the laws of the state,† were not secure against the fanatical fury of blind zealots and the avarice of men who used religion as a pretext, so the temples of the pagans, against which they might act under some show of legal authority, must have been much more exposed to danger. In countries where the pagans still constituted the majority, they returned the Christians like for like, and burnt the churches, as at Gaza and Askelon in Palestine, and at Berytus in Phœnicia.‡ The emperor himself declared at first against those who were for turning the laws which forbade sacrificial worship into a means for wholly suppressing the worship of the temples.§

When the temple-destroying fury was now increasing and spreading on all sides, the pagans could not but fear that the emperor would gradually go further. Libanius addressed to

---

* What Libanius (p. 164) says of this destruction of the temples by the monks (the μιλανναιμονοῦντις) may, compared with what we otherwise know respecting the way of a part of these people, doubtless be received as true. Godofredus, meanwhile, has assuredly misconceived this passage (p. 170), when, by σωφρονισταῖς, he understands here those whose duty it was to see to the execution of the imperial laws on this point. Libanius evidently means to say that the monks had, upon their own authority, thrust themselves in as σωφρονισταῖς.

† Secta nulla lege prohibita; see the law of the emperor Theodosius, in the year 393, cited below.

‡ See Ambros. ep. ad Theodos. l. V. ep. 29.

§ By a law of the year 382 he ordered that the temple at Edessa, in which statues were to be found, deserving of estimation more on account of their artistic than of their religious worth (artis pretio quam divinitate metienda), should always stand open. The emperor was no doubt inclined, in cases where such violences were committed, to exercise justice, when his purpose was not counteracted by the powerful influence of the bishops. Thus, upon the report of the Comes orientis, in the year 388, he was in fact on the point of punishing the monks, who had destroyed a temple of the Valentinians near the castle of Callinicum in Mesopotamia, and to oblige the bishop, who by his discourses had stirred up the people there to demolish a Jewish synagogue, to cause it to be rebuilt; but the declamations of Ambrose bishop of Milan led him to change his mind. See Ambros. ep. 40 ad Theodos. ep. 42 ad sororem. Paulin. vit. Ambros. Still, in the year 393, he issued to this part of Asia a law, that those, qui sub Christianæ religionis nomine illicita quæque præsumunt, et destruere synagogas atque exspoliare conantur, should be punished congrua severitate. Cod. Theodos. l. XVI. Tit. viii. l. 9.

him his remarkable plea in defence of the temples. The immediate occasion of it seems to have been the destruction of a very magnificent ancient temple, on the borders of the Roman empire, towards Persia.* In this discourse he calls to his aid all the political and all the religious reasons which he could possibly find in defence of the temples. Together with much that is sophistical and declamatory, he made also many excellent remarks. Among these belongs what he says to refute the argument for the destruction of the temples, that paganism, by being deprived of these, would lose the chief means of its support among the people; that the people would now visit the churches instead of the temples, and thus by degrees be led to embrace Christianity. " That is," says he, " they would not embrace another kind of worship, but hypocritically pretend to embrace it. They would join, it is true, in the assemblies with the rest, and do everything like the others; but when they assumed the posture of prayer, it would be either to invoke no one, or else the gods." In the next place, he very justly appeals to the Christian doctrine itself: †
" Force is said not to be permitted, even according to the laws of your own religion; persuasion is said to be praised, but force condemned by them. Why, then, do you reek your fury against the temples, when this surely is not to persuade,‡

---

* Comparing the above-cited law of Theodosius with the description which Libanius gives of the magnificence of this temple, we might suppose that the temple at Edessa was here meant. The connection of events may be conceived to be as follows :—that Theodosius at some earlier period had been persuaded to approve of the shutting up of the temple, but had been afterwards induced by the representations of the heathen party to pass the ordinances already cited in favour of the temple. But it having been reported to him by a governor in these districts—(the Dux Osrhoëuæ), who (if Libanius does not misrepresent) was led on by his wife, as she was by the monks—that the devotional exercises in the neighbouring cloisters were disturbed by the fumes of the sacrifices diffused abroad from the temple, the emperor finally was prevailed upon to allow it to be destroyed. (The supposition, however, that this governor was the Præfectus Prætorio Cynegius, as well as the fixing of the chronological date by Godofredus on the assumption of this fact, is one which has not been duly proved.) Meanwhile this hypothesis is still not altogether certain; for there may have been many magnificent temples on the borders of Syria, as, for example, at Palmyra.
† Page 179.
‡ Instead of εἰ τὸ, the reading, as it seems to me, should be εἰ τοῦτο.

but to use force? Thus, then, it is plain you would transgress even the laws of your own religion." *

Many pagans being still to be found in high civil offices, a fact which Libanius refers to in the above-mentioned discourse as showing the favourable disposition of the emperor towards this party,† the imperial commands, of course, were still very far from being carried into rigid execution; and this experience led again to new authoritative measures.

We are by no means to suppose, however, that in these matters Theodosius always acted after the same consistent plan. On the contrary, he might, at one and the same time, publish ordinances of an opposite character, according as he allowed himself to be influenced either by those members of his privy council (the consistorium imperatoris) who, if they were not themselves pagans, yet were governed far more by the political than the religious interest, or by the exhortations of the bishops. In the year 384 or 386 ‡ he directed the prætorian prefect Cynegius, well known on account of his zeal for the spread of Christianity, to shut up all the temples, and make an end of the entire temple-worship in the East (that is, in the eastern part of the Roman empire, and in Egypt).§ And yet a law of the emperor, published about the middle of June, 386, presupposes the toleration of the temple-worship, and the recognisance of the college of priests. ‖

---

* What Libanius elsewhere says in this discourse, so recklessly to the advantage of paganism and in praise of Julian, is of a sort which he could hardly have ventured to utter before the emperor. We may conjecture that this discourse was delivered or *written* only as a specimen of rhetorical art.   † L. c. p. 293.

† The question comes up, whether Cynegius received this commission when he was appointed præfectus prætorio, or not till afterwards. The accurate determination of the chronological date is attended in this case with many difficulties. See Tillemont, hist. des empereurs Romains, Theedose, N. 15. We must either suppose that the historians have given too wide an extension to the commission intrusted to Cynegius, and that it concerned only Egypt, where the influence of a certain Theophilus had occasioned it; or that Theodosius, in the same period of time, acted in absolute contradiction to himself, or that this commission was first given to Cynegius after the passage of the above-cited law of June, 386.

§ See Zosimus, l. IV. c. 37, and Idatii Chronicon, at the death of Cynegius in 388.

‖ In consequenda achierosyna ille sit potior, qui patriæ plura præstiterit, nec tamen a *templorum cultu* observatione Christianitatis abscesserit. Cod. Theodos. l. XII. Tit. i. l. 112.

After the suppression of the public pagan worship, by the
commission given to Cynegius, had been effected, so far as that
was possible, certain events occurred which led to the adoption of still more decisive measures.   The first occasion was
given to these events by Theophilus bishop of Alexandria, a
man of an altogether worldly spirit, who had little or no
hearty interest in the cause of Christ, and whose manner of
administering the episcopal office was least of all calculated to
exert a good influence in building up the temple of the Lord
in the hearts of men.   This bishop, who was much more
interested in erecting large and splendid edifices than in the
spiritual welfare of his flock, had, in the year 389, obtained
from the emperor the gift of a temple of Bacchus, and was
busily employed in converting it into a Christian church.
The symbols of the worship of Bacchus which were found
here, and many of which were offensive to the sense of decency
and good morals,* he ordered to be carried in a procession
through the streets, and publicly exposed, so as to bring the
Grecian mysteries into universal contempt.   Since Alexandria
was considered as a central point of the Hellenic religion, a
principal seat of the mystical Neo-Platonic heathenism, where
its votaries poured together from all countries of the Roman
empire,† and since the Alexandrian pagans were, from the
most ancient times, extremely fanatical, such a transaction
could not fail to occasion the most violent excitement.   The
exasperated pagans assembled in crowds ; they made a furious
onset upon the Christians, wounded and killed many of them,
and then retired to the colossal and splendid temple of Serapis,
situated upon a hill, which was ranked among the greatest
pagan sanctuaries in these times.‡   Here, under the direction
of a certain Olympius, a fanatical pagan, who went clad in

---

* As the Phallus, Lingam, the symbol of the productive power of life
in nature.

† Eunap. vita Ædesii, p. 43. Ἡ Ἀλεξανδρεία διὰ τὸ τοῦ Σαραπίδου
ἱερὸν ἱερὰ τις ἦν οἰκουμένη, οἱ πανταχόθεν ϕοιτῶντες ἰς αὐτὴν πλῆθος ἦσαν τῷ
δήμῳ παρισουμένοι.

‡ In what high veneration this temple stood among the heathens we
may gather from the words of Libanius, who already expressed his
alarm for its fate, when, in speaking of the temple at Edessa (Orat. pro
templ. 194), he said. Ἤκουσα δὲ καὶ ἰσιζόντων τινῶν ἐν ὁποτέρῳ τὸ θαῦμα
μεῖζον, ἱερῷ τῷ μηκέτ᾿ ὄντι τούτῳ ἢ ὃ μήποτε πάθοι ταὐτὸν, ἐν ᾧπερ ὁ
Σάραπις.

the philosopher's cloak, they formed a regular camp. This man exhorted them to sacrifice even their lives for the sanctuaries of their fathers. From their stronghold they sallied out upon the Christians: those who were dragged away by them as prisoners they endeavoured to force by tortures to sacrifice; and such as remained steadfast were often put to death in the most cruel manner. After these acts of violence, having the worst to fear, desperation, united with fanaticism, drove them onward, and all the efforts of the civil and military authorities to restore order were to no purpose. The emperor Theodosius endeavoured to profit by this favourable conjuncture to effect the suppression of paganism in Egypt. Upon the report of these disturbances, there appeared from Constantinople, probably in the year 391, a rescript ordering that all the pagans who had shared in this tumult should be pardoned; and that, as an acknowledgment of the mercy which they had experienced, they might the more easily be converted to Christianity, all the heathen temples at Alexandria should, as the cause of this tumult, be destroyed.

Whilst the heathen were rejoicing at the prospect of saving their lives, and had but just recovered from their alarm, it was a favourable juncture for carrying into execution a stroke of policy, which, under the state of feeling that existed at Alexandria, might at all times be attended with great hazard. Large bodies of men assembled around the temple of Serapis, upon which the imperial command was now about to be executed.* But there prevailed among the heathen a reverential awe before the colossal statue of Serapis; and from ancient times the report had been propagated, that, when this statue was demolished, heaven and earth would fall in one common ruin. This report had some influence even upon the multitude of nominal Christians, who were still inclined to the ancient superstition. No one ventured to attack the image, until at last a believing soldier seized an axe, and, exerting all his strength, clove asunder the vast jaw-bone of the image, amidst the universal shouts of the Pagan and Christian multitude. After the first stroke had confuted the superstition, the whole image was easily demolished and consumed to ashes. And, upon this, all the temples at Alexandria, and in the

---

* The case was somewhat similar here, as it was in later times with the thunder-oak of Bouiface.

neighbouring district, taking its name from the Canopian branch of the Nile (ὁ Κάνωβος), which particularly abounded in Egyptian sanctuaries, were in part levelled with the ground, and in part converted into churches and cloisters.*

The same course was followed in other countries; sometimes not without bloody conflicts, which might have been avoided if the bishops had been more governed by the spirit of love and of wisdom. Marcellus bishop of Apamea in Syria proceeded with great zeal to destroy all the temples in the city and in the country, because he supposed that by these ancient monuments of their worship, so venerated by the people, paganism would always continue to preserve itself alive. With a train of followers little becoming the Christian bishop, an armed force of soldiers and gladiators, he advanced to destroy the largest temple. It was necessary that the temple should be forcibly wrested out of the hands of its pagan defenders. While the conflict was going on, some pagans seized upon the old bishop, who had been left behind alone, and hurried him to the stake. The sons of the bishop were desirous of punishing his murderers, but the provincial synod dissuaded them from this, calling upon them rather to thank God that their father had been deemed worthy of martyrdom.† From the present year, 391, and onward, followed many laws, forbidding every description of pagan worship, under penalty of a pecuniary mulct, and still severer punishments. As the pagan magistrates themselves encouraged the violation of these imperial laws, pecuniary fines were established against these and against all their attendants in such cases. By a law of the year 392 the offering of sacrifice was in fact placed upon the same level with the crime of high treason (crimen majestatis); and, accordingly, the offerer incurred the penalty of death.‡

Whilst these events were transpiring in the East, everything in the western part of the empire continued to remain as it was; and men belonging to ancient and noble families in

---

* Eunapii vit. Ædes. Rufin. hist. eccles. c. 23. Sozom. VII. 15. Socrates, V. 16. Marcellini Comitis Chronicon ad A. 389, ff. in Sirmond. opp. t. ii.   † See Sozom. VII. 15.
‡ Cod. Theodos. l. XVI. Tit. x. l. 12. Quodsi quispiam immolare hostiam sacrificaturus audebit, ad exemplum majestatis reus accipiat sententiam competentem.

Rome still ventured to raise their voice in behalf of the religion of the eternal city. When Theodosius, after the defeat of the usurper Maximus, was, in the year 388, holding his residence in the West, the heathen party of the Roman senate proposed to him once more, perhaps through Symmachus, their former agent, that the revenues and privileges should be restored to the temples and colleges of priests of which they had been deprived. Theodosius seems to have been very near granting them their petition; but the pointed representations which Ambrosius bishop of Milan made against this measure restrained him.* The heathen party succeeded, on the other hand, under more favourable circumstances, in obtaining from the emperor Eugenius, who, after the murder of the young Valentinian II., had, in the year 392, been raised to the imperial throne by the pagan commander Arbogast, everything which had been refused them by Gratian, Valentinian, and Theodosius. The voice of those influential pagans, upon whom Eugenius felt himself to be dependent, availed more with him than what Ambrosius, with inconsiderate boldness, wrote to him in the name of religion.†

But when Theodosius marched into Rome, after the defeat of Eugenius, in the year 394, he made a speech before the assembled senate, in which he called upon the pagans, who, under the short reign of Eugenius, had once more enjoyed the free exercise of their religion, to desist from their idolatry, and to embrace the religion in which alone they could find forgiveness of all their sins. In spite of all their representations, he took back from the pagans what Eugenius had accorded to them.‡

The successors of the emperor Theodosius, Arcadius in the East, and Honorius in the West, from the year 395 and onwards, confirmed, it is true, soon after their accession to the throne, the laws of their father against the pagan worship with new

---

* Insinuationi meæ *tandem* adsensionem detulit, says Ambrosius, ep. 57 ad Eugen. s. 4. What the pretended Prosper (de Promiss. et Prædict. Dei, pars iii. Promiss. 38) says about the disgraceful banishment of Symmachus may perhaps be a fable. † See Ambros. ep. 57.

‡ Zosimus, a zealous pagan, is in this case a suspicious witness. It cannot therefore be certainly determined how far what he reports respecting the constancy and boldness of the pagan senators is true or false.

sanctions ; but the weakness of their government, the various political disturbances, especially in the West, the corruption or pagan views of individual governors, would all favour the preservation of paganism in many districts ; and hence it was necessary that those laws should be continually re-enacted.

Whilst in Rome the public monuments of the pagan worship had already vanished, the images of the old Tyrian Hercules could still be worshipped and decorated by the pagans in Carthage. As in earlier times the popular cry in that city had demanded the destruction of the Christian churches, so now resounded there the cry of the Christian populace, demanding that all idols should be destroyed at Carthage, as they had been at Rome. The people were excited by the folly of a heathen magistrate, who had ventured to order the beard of Hercules to be gilded.* The prudent bishops were obliged to take special measures for moderating the ferocious zeal, so as to prevent acts of violence.†

Pagan landlords endeavoured to maintain the heathen worship on their estates, and, by means of sacrificial feasts and other means which their power over the peasants gave them in spite of the existing laws, to bind them to heathenism. Pious and prudent bishops like Augustin were obliged, in such cases, to exhort the Christian country people to obey God rather than men ;‡ but they were also obliged to restrain the blind zeal of the Christian populace, which was for destroying, in an illegal manner, the idols upon the estates of other men. On this point Augustin speaks thus :—" Many of the heathen have those abominations upon their estates. Shall we go about to destroy them ? No ; let us make it our first business to extirpate the idols in their hearts. When they have

---

* Quomodo Roma, sic et Carthago! exclaimed the populace.

† Augustini Sermo 24, t. v. ed. Ben.

‡ On this point he says (p. 62), "The martyrs endured the laceration of their members, and Christians stood in fear of the wrong which might be done them in Christian times. Whoever at present does you wrong does it in fear. He does not openly say. 'Come to the idols;' he does not openly say, 'Come to my altars, and feast yourself.' And if he said it, and you would not do it, he might, in presenting his complaint against you. testify this :—'He would not come to my altars—to the temples which I venerate.' Let him even say this. He dares not say it. But in a fraudulent manner he calls you to answer for something else. He will rob you of your superfluity."

become Christians they will either invite us to so good a work, or they will anticipate us in it. At present we must pray for them, not exasperate them."*

But it was not pagan landholders alone that promoted the worship to which they themselves were attached; even Christian proprietors were willing to ignore it, when their peasants brought offerings into the temples, because the imposts which were laid upon the temples were a source of profit to them.† No doubt they could effect more by instruction and zeal for the spiritual welfare of their tenants in the spirit of love than by any forcible measures. The bishop Chrysostom, in a discourse delivered at Constantinople about the year 400, justly rebukes them because they did not procure the erection of churches and the settlement of ministers who could preach the gospel upon their estates. " Is it not the duty," he says, "of the Christian proprietor first to see to it that all his tenants are Christians? Tell me, how is the countryman to become a Christian when he sees the welfare of his soul is so much a matter of indifference to you? You can perform no miracles to convert men. Well, then, convert them by those means which lie in your power; by charity, by your care for men, by a gentle disposition, by a kind address, and by whatever other means you possess. Many erect baths and forums; but none churches, or everything else sooner than these. Therefore," said the zealous preacher, whose heart glowed so warmly for the welfare of men, " I exhort you, I beseech you, I require it of you as a favour to be shown me, *or rather I lay it down as the law, that no man allow his estate to be without a church.*"‡

It being now represented to the government that the idolatrous temples and images on the country estates contributed much to the promotion of paganism among the peasantry, the emperor Honorius passed a law, in the year 399, directing *that all temples in the country should be destroyed without tumult, so that all occasion of superstition might everywhere*

* L. c. s. 17.

† Zeno bishop of Verona (l. I. Tract. xv. s. 6) complains on this subject. In prædiis vestris fumantia undique fana tunc non nostis, quæ (si vera dicenda sunt) dissimulando subtiliter custoditis. Probatio longe non est. Jus templorum ne quis vobis eripiat, quotidie litigatis.

‡ Homil. 18, act. ap.

be removed. *   This law was expressly confined to the *temples in the country*, which could not reasonably be considered as monuments of art contributing to the ornament of the country ;† for the latter were protected by new laws against the fury of destruction.‡   Yet, on the *one* hand, it is certain that in those cities in which only a comparatively small number of pagans were still to be found, and where this small number were kept together by the temples which were still remaining, the zeal of the Christian population would easily bring about the destruction also of these ;§ but, on the *other* hand, however, there can be no doubt that this law was never universally executed according to the letter.

Among the pagans in many countries an impression prevailed, in consequence of one of those predictions by which they were so often deluded, that Christianity would last for *only three hundred and sixty-five years* ; and this prediction, by a loose reckoning from the time of Christ's passion, seemed now to be near the time for its accomplishment.   Hence the destruction of the temples, which took place this year, made the greater impression upon many of the pagans.‖   Yet they were still powerful enough on many of the country estates of North Africa to commit acts of violence on the Christians, while engaged in the exercises of worship.¶

After the death of the powerful Stilicho, by whom Honorius had been governed, the latter, probably through the

---

* Si qua in agris.templa sunt, sine turba ac tumultu diruantur.   His enim dejectis atque sublatis, omnis superstitionis materia consumetur.

† Thus in the Codex canonum eccles. Africanæ (c. 58) it is said, Quæ in agris vel in locis abditis constituta nullo ornamento sunt.

‡ Cod. Theodos. l. XVI. Tit. 10. l. 18.

§ Augustin (de civitate Dei, l. XVIII. c. 54) says that in this year all the idolatrous temples and images at Carthage were destroyed, by the two comites, Gaudentius and Jovius.

‖ See Augustin. l. c.

¶ Thus sixty Christians were murdered at Suffetum in Numidia, probably in consequence of an attack on the statue of Hercules, Augustin. ep. 50.   At Calame in Numidia, A.D. 408, the pagans ventured, in defiance of the laws enacted shortly before by the emperor Honorius against all pagan festivities, to march in an indecent heathen procession before the Christian churches ; and, when the clergy remonstrated, a wild uproar arose.   The church was attacked with stones, finally set fire to, and a Christian murdered.   The bishop, who was hunted after, was obliged to conceal himself.   Augustin. ep. 90. 91. 104.

influence of some of the great who were favourably disposed
to paganism, enacted a law which contradicted the laws
hitherto issued. For, between the years 409 and 410, there
appeared in the western empire a law which ordained universal
religious freedom.* Yet this law remained in force certainly
but a very short time; and the old ones soon went once more
into operation. By an edict of the year 416† pagans were
excluded from all civil and military places of trust, yet the
necessities of the time and the weakness of the empire hardly
allowed of its being carried into strict execution.‡

The consequences which followed the emigrations of tribes
in the western empire; the political disturbances which threw
everything into confusion; the irruptions of savage and pagan
hordes, might sometimes light up a ray of hope in the small
pagan party; but it soon dwindled away again to nothing.

In many districts of the East paganism maintained itself
for a longer time; and the party of pagan Platonists, which
continued down into the sixth century, was its principal support. The emperors were moved by their political interests
to avoid destroying everything at once in those cities where
paganism predominated, lest they might destroy those interests
also. They chose rather to proceed gradually. This principle may be detected in the remarkable answer which the

---

* Ut libera voluntate quis cultum Christianitatis exciperet, cod. eccles.
Afric. c. 107. It is true, this law, as it here reads, can be understood,
according to its letter, to mean only that no one should be forced to embrace Christianity. And this was in fact a thing which, properly speaking, had as yet never been done. But it is clear that it was so interpreted,
as if the legal penalties which had been in force against those who exercised any other form of worship than that of the catholic Christians
should be done away.

† As late as the year 403 the Spanish Christian poet Prudentius had
asserted that difference in respect to religion had no influence in the be-
stowment of posts of honour, and declared this to be right. L. l. c. Sym-
machum, v. 617.

> Denique, pro meritis terrestribus æqua rependens
> Munera, sacricolis summos impertit honores
> Dux bonus, et certare sivit cum laude suorum,
> Nec pago implicitos per debita culmina mundi
> Ire viros prohibet : quoniam cœlestia nunquam
> Terrenis solitum per iter gradientibus obstant.

‡ If the account of Zosimus (l. V. c. 46) is true, the feeble Honorius,
unable to dispense with the services of one of his pagan generals, Generid,
who would serve only on this condition, was obliged immediately to
repeal this law.

emperor Arcadius gave Porphyry bishop of Gaza in Palestine,
when the latter, in the year 401, prayed for the destruction of
the idolatrous temples in this city, inhabited for the most part
by fanatical pagans.* " I am aware," says he, " that your
city is given to idolatry ; but it faithfully pays its tributes,
and brings a great deal into the public treasury. If we proceed now to disturb it thus suddenly, the inhabitants will fly
away in fear (namely, that the attempt would finally be made
to bring them over to Christianity by force), and we should
lose so much in our revenue. But we will rather oppress
them by degrees, depriving the idolaters of their dignities and
places of trust, and issuing our commands that the temples
shall be closed and oracles no longer be delivered ; for when
they are oppressed on all sides, they will come to the knowledge of the truth,"—a fine mode of conversion, to be sure !—
" for all sudden and too authoritative measures are hard for
the subjects." Yet finally the cunning of the empress Eu-
doxia prevailed—a woman who perfectly understood how
Arcadius was to be managed, by taking advantage of his
weaknesses ; and who was led to think that her zeal for the
destruction of idolatrous temples, and her many gifts to the
clergy and the monks, would make atonement for her sins.
By her influence the reasonable hesitation of the weak Arcadius
was finally overcome.

---

* The life of Porphyry bishop of Gaza, from which this story is
taken, and which was composed by his disciple the deacon Marcus,—a
work which is important as furnishing many facts illustrative of the
history of the church and of manners in this period,—has as yet been
published only in a Latin translation, whose author seems not even to
have given himself the pains of accurately deciphering the Greek text :
see Acta Sanctorum, at the 26th of February, and the Bibliotheca
Patrum, Galland, T. IX. From a promising young Danish scholar, Dr.
Clausen, we are led to expect the publication of the Greek original
work, which is still extant among the treasures of the imperial library
at Vienna. Meantime I shall insert here the passage relating to the
present subject, as it reads in the original. The words of Arcadius are,
Οἶδα, ὅτι ἡ πόλις ἐκείνη κατείδωλός ἐστιν, ἀλλ' εὐγνώμων ἐστὶ περὶ τὴν εἰσ-
φοράν τῶν δημοσίων, πόλλα συντελοῦσα. Ἐὰν οὖν ἄφνω διασοβῶμεν αὐτοὺς, τῷ
φόβῳ φύγῃ χρήσονται, καὶ ἀπολοῦμεν τοσοῦτον Κάνονα, ἀλλ' εἰ δοκεῖ, κατὰ
μέρος θλίβωμεν αὐτούς, περικειροῦντες τὰς ἀξίας τῶν εἰδωλομένων καὶ τὰ ἀλλὰ
πολιτίκα ὀφφίκια, καὶ κελεύωμεν τὰ ἱερὰ αὐτῶν κλιισθῆναι καὶ μηκέτι χρημα-
τίζειν. Ἐτὰν γὰρ θλίβωσιν εἰς πάντα στενούμενοι, ἐπιγινώσκουσι τὴν ἀλήθειαν·
τὸ γὰρ ὑπερβολὴν ἔχον αἰφνίδιον βαρὺ τοῖς ὑπηκόοις.

It is true, in a law of the year 423, it is expressed as doubtful whether any pagans still remained :* but as it was considered necessary, in confirming the ancient laws against them, to change the punishment of death, which had hitherto been established against those who sacrificed, into the confiscation of goods and banishment ; as it was considered necessary to protect the still remaining pagans, who attempted nothing contrary to the laws, against being abused and plundered by nominal Christians, who used religion as a pretext ;† it follows from all this, that there still continued to be pagans, which is proved moreover by the laws issued under this reign against those who apostatized from Christianity to paganism. Had there been good reason to doubt whether there were any more pagans, there certainly would have been no occasion for a law of this sort. But undoubtedly the fact, that few remained who openly declared themselves pagans, may be reconciled with the other, that it was necessary to devise laws of this sort, if the matter is presented in the following point of light ; namely, that many were called apostates from Christianity who had never seriously passed over to the Christian church— individuals who had submitted to baptism only as an outward form, but had ever continued to practise the pagan rites in secret. Whenever they were discovered, they were called apostates.‡

The heathens, then, were compelled, from the present time in the fifth century, to practise and propagate their religion in secret, for the purpose of avoiding persecutions ; and by this

* L. XVI. Tit. X. l. 22. Paganos qui supersunt, quanquam jam nullos esse credamus.

† L. c. l. 23 et 24. Hoc Christianis, qui vel vere sunt, vel *esse dicuntur*, specialiter demandamus, ut Judæis ac paganis, in quiete degentibus, nihilque tentantibus turbulentum legibusque contrarium, non audeant manibus inferre, religionis auctoritate abusi. Against those who, under the pretext of religion, robbed the pagans, Augustin also felt himself called upon to preach : " Perhaps, in order that Christ may not say to you, I was clothed, and thou hast robbed me, thou alterest the custom, and thinkest to rob a pagan and to clothe a Christian. Here also Christ will answer thee ; nay, he answers thee even now by his servant, whoever he may be : Here too do me no harm ; when, being a Christian, thou robbest the heathen, thou hinderest him from becoming a Christian." Sermo 179, s. 5.

‡ Qui nomen Christianitatis induti, sacrificia fecerint. Cod. Theodos. l. XVI. Tit. VIII. l. 7.

means their religion was rendered the dearer to them. The holding of the knowledge of divine things as a secret, which could be the property only of the philosophically educated; the engrafting of it upon the mythical representations, beyond which the people knew nothing ; this belonged necessarily to the system of the Neo-Platonists, and these principles made it possible for them, with all their enthusiasm for Hellenism, yet to adapt themselves to the character of the times.* A remarkable example of this is presented in the life of the pagan philosopher Proclus,† which his disciple Marinus has written.‡

---

* The art represented in the symbol of Proteus: Συνεῖναι τοῖς ἀνθρώποις οὐ θείως, ἀλλὰ πολιτικῶς. See Synes. ep. 137 ad Herculian. Of the pagans who were arrested in the exercise of the cultus forbidden by the laws, Augustin says (Enarrat. in ψ. 140, s. 20), Quis eorum comprehensus est in sacrificio, cum his legibus ista prohiberentur, et non negavit? Quis eorum comprehensus est adorare idolum, et non clamavit: non feci ; et timuit ne convinceretur ?

† Born A.D. 412, died 487.

‡ As a proof of the confidence which Heron the mathematician had in the young Proclus, it is mentioned here that he communicated to him *the whole method of his worship of God.* When he first visited the heathen Platonic philosopher Syrianus at Athens, the moon having begun to shine, the latter sought to get him out of the way, so that he might perform his devotions unobserved with another pagan, c. 11. We see from this biographical narrative, that the worship of Isis still prevailed at Philæ in Egypt (p. 47); that in Athens the worship of Esculapius was secretly practised in the temple, which, however, was soon afterwards destroyed ; and that the pagans prayed there for their sick. Proclus thought himself happy in that he occupied a dwelling near the temple, so as to be able to perform his devotions there without being observed, and invoke the aid of Esculapius in behalf of the sick, p. 73. Καὶ τοιοῦτον ἔργον διεπράξατο οὐκ ἀλλῶς· ἢ κἂν ταῦθα τοὺς πόλλους λανθάνων, καὶ οὐδεμίαν πρόφασιν τοῖς ἐπιβουλεύειν ἐθελοῦσι παρασχεῖν. Marinus extols it as a proof of the Herculean courage and spirit of Proclus, that under all the storms of this Titanic period he stedfastly and without once wavering, though not without danger, maintained himself to the end, τὸ δὲ τῆς πολιτικῆς ἀνδρείας εἶδος ἡρακλείον οὕτως ἐπεδείξατο, ἐν ζάλη γὰρ παρίλεων καὶ τρικυμία πραγμάτων τυφωνείων ἀντὶ πνεόντων τῇ ἐννομοζώη (the ancient national cultus), ἐμβριθῶς οὗτος ἄνηρ καὶ ἀστεμφῶς, εἰ καὶ παρακινδυνευτικῶς, τὸν βίον διενήξατο. Once, probably by his over-zealous observance of the pagan rites, he drew on himself a persecution from the Christians, and took refuge for some length of time in Asia Minor, p. 35. At Adrota in Lydia there was still practised among the heathens, in an ancient temple. a worship respecting the name of which they were not agreed. According to some, the temple belonged to Esculapius ; according to others, to the Dioscuræ. Remedies for the cure of

The emperor Justinian (from the year 527 and onwards), whose despotism even in spiritual things was the source of so many disorders to the Eastern church, endeavoured, soon after the commencement of his reign, to suppress the last remains of paganism by force, so far as this could be done in such a way. The persecutions were aimed particularly at men in the civil service. They were deprived of their property, tortured, executed. Many hypocritically assumed the profession of Christianity to escape the persecutions: of course, in such cases they soon took off the mask, and were once more seen attending the performance of sacrifices.* The emperor, doubtless having heard that Athens† still continued to be a seat of paganism, and that this religion was propagated by the pagan Platonists who still taught there, forbad the holding of philosophical lectures in that place.‡ These persecutions induced the pagan philosophers, among whom were Damascius and Isidorus and the renowned Simplicius,§ to take refuge with the Persian king Chosroes, respecting whose love for philosophy they had heard exaggerated accounts. This prince, it is true, received them in a friendly manner; but their expec-

---

diseases were said to be here suggested by supernatural inspiration, and miraculous cures effected. Many legends were circulated respecting it, c. 32.

* Theophanes Chronograph. ad. A. 522, i.e. according to our reckoning, 531 from the birth of Christ. See Ideler's Manual of Chronology, ii. 458. Procop. hist. arcana, p. 90, c. xi. ed. Orelli. The same author (c. 19) relates that Justinian employed the accusation of heathenism as a pretext to get into possession of the estates which his cupidity thirsted after. Comp. the chronicle of Johannes Malala, pars ii. p. 184, ed. Oxon.

† The Athenian schools had sunk so low in the beginning of the fifth century, that Synesius could write, Athens is now famous only for her Hymettian honey, and that he could compare the then Athens, in her relation to the ancient, with the hide of a slaughtered victim; so completely was philosophy banished from the place, while only those dead and silent spots, the Academy, the Stoa, the Lyceum, were shown to and wondered at by strangers. See the 136th letter of Synesius to his brother; but, after this time, Athens was somewhat restored to its bloom by the Neo-Platonic philosophy.

‡ Joh. Malala, l. c. p. 187.

§ Simplicius (in Epictet. Enchiridion, c. 13, ed. Lugd. Batav. 1640, p. 79) probably alludes to the fact that the pagans were to be forced to renounce their convictions. Τυραννικὰς βίας, μέχρι καὶ τοῦ ἀσεβεῖν αναγκαζούσας.

tations were by no means realized. Parsism was as little agreeable to them as Christianity ; and they had many a long-ing wish after the Grecian customs. Chosroes, in the treaty of peace, prevailed upon the emperor Justinian to allow them the free exercise of their religion in the Roman empire.*

B. *Of the polemical writings of the Pagans against Christi-anity ; of the charges which they brought against it gene-rally ; and of the manner in which these charges were answered by the teachers of the Christian church.*

In respect to the attacks on Christianity by pagan writers, it may be observed that it was a necessary consequence of the altered circumstances of the times, that few would venture to combat Christianity in works devoted expressly to that object. Julian, who endeavoured to supplant Christianity as an empe-ror, appeared against it also as an author ; and his work, of which considerable fragments have been preserved to our times, in the refutation of it by Cyril bishop of Alexandria, is the most important one, in this respect, belonging to the present period.† Although, as we have remarked before, much that was bad, and which had been presented to Julian under the Christian name, had, from the first, exerted its influence in giving his mind an impression unfavourable to Christianity, yet it is also true that his hatred was not confined to the corrupt and distorted representations of Christianity prevailing at that period, but was turned against Christianity itself ; that Christianity, though presented in all the purity of its essential character, could not have appeared to him, in the temper of mind which he actually cherished, otherwise than hateful. It may, indeed, be said, that many of the foreign elements which had engrafted themselves on Christianity came nearer to Julian's pagan mode of thinking than the purely Christian doctrine. He was sufficiently well acquainted with the written records of Christianity to discern the differ-ence between many of the notions which prevailed among Christians at this time and the doctrines of the New Testa-

---

* See Agathias de rebus Justiniani, I. II. c. 30, p. 69, ed. Paris. L. II. c. 30, p. 131, ed. Niebuhr.

† Julian wrote this work in the winter, during his residence at Antioch. Liban epitaph. Julian. vol. I. p. 581.

ment; between the life of the Christians of this period and the requisitions of the original doctrine of Christ. Thus, in reference to the honour paid to martyrs, concerning which nothing indeed is to be found in the New Testament, he reproached the Christians with departing from the words of Christ. Yet Julian knew too little of the spirit of Christianity, which, with all his knowledge of the letter of the New Testament, yet could not be understood by him while he cherished such inward opposition to the essence of the gospel, —he knew too little of that spirit to see *wherein* the honour paid to the martyrs conflicted with the primitive religion. To him, looking at the matter from his own pagan position, the Christian element, which lay at the root even of this superstition, was precisely the thing which appeared hateful. It was the importance which the Christian feeling attached to the remains of a body that had once been the temple of the Holy Ghost, and was destined to be so again; the new views of death, and of the sanctification and transfiguration of the earthly, of all that is peculiar to humanity, which Christianity brought with it. To him, the pagan, whatever was dead was impure and defiling: hence he tauntingly remarked against the Christians that they had filled everything with graves and monuments, and that they rolled themselves upon graves.* He accused them of practising magic in this way, and of seeking prophetic dreams by sleeping upon the graves (incubationes). The apostles, he said, had from the first instructed the faithful in these things; and among the Jews the art had long been known, for they often had been reproached with it by the prophets (Isaiah lxv.).† So, again, he rightly perceived that the

---

* He also employs arguments wholly irrelevant and out of place, for the purpose of showing them that this was an unchristian thing; as for example, from Matth. chap. 23: "How then do you call upon the same God, when Jesus says that the sepulchres are full of all uncleanness?" Again, Christ had said, "Let the dead bury their dead." Though the truth was, those who called on the martyrs looked upon them, not as the dead, but as those who were living with God.

† Cyrill. c. Julian. l. X. 335—40. Perhaps the Christians may have themselves given occasion for this charge, by their stories about appearances of the martyrs in visions by night in the chapels of the martyrs— about cures of diseases, which had been wrought by them; and by their custom of transferring a great deal from the pagan superstition of incubations to the martyrs.

persecutions against heretics and pagans, which had hitherto been resorted to, were contrary to the doctrine of Christ and of the apostles. " You destroy temples and altars," says he,[*] "and you have not only murdered those *among us* who persevere in the religion of our fathers, but also those among the heretics who are in the same error with yourselves, but who do not mourn the dead man (so he sarcastically calls the worship of Christ) in the same way that you do. But this is something which must be ascribed to your own invention; for neither Jesus nor Paul invited you to do it." Instead of acknowledging, however, that this was contrary to the spirit of the gospel, or at least to the character of Christ and the apostles, Julian maliciously gives it the following explanation. He says that Christ—which, however, is refuted by Christ's own language—and the apostles did not expect their party would ever acquire such power; and here again he repeats the old objection to Christianity, which in truth redounds to its honour, that it did not first spread among the wise and mighty of the world. " But the reason is," says he, " they never looked forward to such mighty things; for they were satisfied if they could deceive maids and slaves, and through these the women and their husbands, such as Cornelius and Sergius. You may put me down for a liar, if a single author of that period (for these events happened under Tiberius or Claudius) ever mentioned these men." How could he possibly have possessed the least sense for the godlike in the life of Christ, when he was capable of bringing up such a question as the one which follows, where, comparing Christ with great kings,[†] he says, " But Jesus, who has persuaded a few of the worst among you, has been named these three hundred years; yet what remarkable thing had he done, unless you suppose that healing the lame and the blind and exorcising demoniacs in the villages of Bethsaida and Bethany are to be ranked among the greatest works?"—when he alleges against the sovereignty of Christ, that he was one of the subjects of the emperor; that he who commanded the spirits, *who walked upon the sea,* and ejected evil spirits, could not change the will of his friends and kinsmen so as to secure their own salvation; could not bring them to believe in him? How little did he who could say this understand the nature of a moral change!

* L. c. l. vi. p. 206.   † VI. 491.

No less characteristic of the man was the credulity with which, after ridiculing the well-authenticated faith of the Christians, he received one of the absurd tales of heathenism, objecting to the Christians that they had forsaken the ancilia which had fallen from heaven, and which secured eternal protection to the city of Rome and the Roman empire; and, instead of these, worshipped the wood of the cross. * And equally characteristic is his objection to Christianity, — an objection which contains some truth, but truth which redounds to the honour of Christianity,—when he says that the Christians had let the best things of Judaism and paganism go, and blended together the worst out of both. They had, for instance, thrown away from Judaism the sacred rites, the various legal prescriptions, which required the holiest life, and from paganism the devout feeling towards all higher natures; while, on the contrary, they had taken from the Jews their intolerant monotheism, and from the pagans their freedom and indifference of living; † or, as Julian expressed it, their custom of eating everything, like the green herb. The truth here is, that Christianity delivered men from the yoke of the ceremonial law, and from a religion which cleaved to the elements of the world; and that, on other grounds, it gave a freedom of outward life, which, in outward appearance, might seem like the pagan freedom, although it came from an entirely different spirit. The relation here is precisely the same as that between the freedom of the man who has never felt the power and the burden of sin, and the freedom of him who has been actually redeemed from its bondage.

He says the Christians had given to the pagan freedom a still wider scope;—correctly, we must admit, so far as it concerned outward things;—and this they had been compelled to do as a matter of course, "because their religion was to suit all nations, all forms of human life; the innkeeper, the publican, the dancer, &c." ‡ Bating the circumstance that Julian carries the case out to the extreme of caricature, there is, undoubtedly, a foundation of truth underlying even this accusation, conformably to what has just been remarked. It was

* L. c. VI. 194.
† Τὴν ἀδιαφορίαν καὶ χυδαιότητα. Genesis ix. 3. Rom. xiv. 2.
‡ VII. 238.

precisely because Christianity started with this freedom, because it was bound to no particular outward and earthly forms
of life, because its transforming influence operated from
within, that it was capable of approaching, in like manner,
people of all nations, ranks, and relations, so as to diffuse its
sanctifying influence over them all. So, too, he glorifies the
gospel, which was given to make returning sinners holy and
happy, when he reckons it as a reproach to Christianity that it
came first of all to sinners; and when, to give the satire more
point, he cites the testimony of the apostle Paul himself, 1
Corinthians vi. 11. In this case, however, instead of dream-
ing of the justifying and sanctifying power of faith in Christ,
to which Paul alludes, he perverts the sense of the apostle's
language, as if he referred to some magical power of baptism
to destroy sin. " Dost thou see," he says, " that these were
also such? But they have been sanctified and cleansed, because they have received a water that penetrates to the soul,
by which they could be purified. Baptism cannot remove
leprosy, gout, warts, and other less or greater bodily defects;
but it was able to purge away all the sins of the soul."*

As Julian did not recognise the one image of one only God
in all humanity,—but imagined that he saw in the different
races of men only the impress of the different individualities
of their presiding deities; or rather as he carried out the
principle of the deification of nature, and his gods were
merely the different human individualities of character, ab-
stracted and deified,—a national character once in existence
appeared to him to be incapable of change. He adduces the
Western nations as a proof of this, who, although they had
been for so long a time under the Roman dominion, yet
continued to remain for the most part uncultivated: † but
history, to whose testimony he appealed, has confuted what he
says; for Christianity has been able, without destroying the
more essential national peculiarities, to develop and bring out
the spiritual and moral elements which lie at the foundation
of the human nature in all.

---

* VII. f. 245. And so indeed it must appear to a man who reads these
words with such a temper and habit of mind; because such a temper of
mind clings only to the outward. The Christians, moreover, promoted
this misapprehension by their own representations of the magical effects
of baptism.   † IV. 131.

Julian labours to show that Christianity generally had taken its shape only by degrees, through the coöperation of various outward causes; as the fact would easily seem to be to the superficial observer, and in general to every man who does not look at it from the very centre of Christian intuition; since he will not know how to distinguish in Christianity itself the unchangeable essence from the changeable form, nor that which springs out of the essence of Christianity from the foreign elements which have mixed in with it. Now, although Julian undoubtedly perceived the difference between the Christian life and the Church doctrines of his time and that which was contained in the letter of the sacred scriptures, yet he could not separate what was really foreign in the prevailing church doctrines of the Christians of his time, and had been added to the original doctrines of the New Testament, from what was merely the drapery of a particular age in which the essential Christian truth hath clothed itself; and thus he might easily be led to suppose that he found contradictions in the doctrines of the New Testament, because he was incapable of recognising the unity of the essence in the variety of its forms of representation.

Thus, for instance, he imagined that he perceived a contradiction of this sort in the case of the doctrine of Christ's divinity; and, in his remarks on this point, he does not even agree with himself. In one passage he says of Christ to the Christians of his time, * "*As you would have it*, he has created heaven and earth; for none of his disciples has said this of him, except John alone, and even he not clearly and explicitly." And in another place he says † that neither Paul nor any one of the evangelists ventured to call Jesus God; but that John, on hearing that in the cities of Greece and Italy many had already become infected with this contagion, and that the graves of Peter and Paul were secretly worshipped,‡ had first endeavoured, by stealth and artifice, to foist in the doctrine of Christ's divinity.§ And yet in another place, ‖ where he wishes to point out contradictions between

* VI. 213.   † L. X. f. 317.
‡ We see with what assurance Julian here created facts after his own imagination.
§ L. X. f. 327.
‖ L. IX. f. 291.

the Old and New Testaments,* he finds in the formula of
baptism, which he nowhere attempts to explain away as a
foreign addition to the gospels, a direction to invoke Christ,
and the doctrine of three divine essences.† He accuses the
apostle Paul of self-contradiction, of a wavering between uni-
versalism and particularism in the doctrine concerning God;
simply because, while looking himself upon the outside of the
matter, and everywhere hunting up contradictions, he was
incapable of perceiving the inner connection of the Pauline
system. " Paul," says he,‡ " changes his doctrine concerning
God, as a polypus changes colour on the rocks. At one time
he calls the Jews God's only inheritance ; at another, he per-
suades the Gentiles that God is not the God of the Jews only,
but also of the Gentiles. We might rightly ask Paul, if God
was not the God of the Jews only, but also of the Gentiles,
why did he send Moses, the prophets, and the miracles of the
fabulous legends, to the Jews alone ? "§ Yet this question
might have been easily answered, by simply unfolding the
Pauline doctrines concerning the law of God which is within
man ; concerning the divine descent of humanity ; concerning
the God in whom we live, move, and have our being, and who
has nowhere left himself without a witness ; concerning the
revelation of God in the works of creation, and in the conscience ; concerning the reaction between moral corruption and
spiritual blindness ; concerning the object of the Old Testament theocracy, as a preparatory system to the spread of
God's kingdom among all mankind ; concerning the fixed time
of God's grace to all, after all had been brought to the con-

---

* In respect to the relation of the Old Testament idea of the Messiah
to that of the New Testament, the Christian teachers here laid themselves open to his attacks, in a way which he well knew how to take
advantage of, when they professed to find the whole doctrine concerning
Christ, as it was first clearly unfolded in the New Testament, or even as
with all the later church definitions, contained already in the Old Testament.

† L. VIII. f. 262, he says that in the Old Testament no such designation of a higher nature belonging to the Messiah, as in the words
πρωτότοκος πάσης κτίσεως, is to be found ; and yet this expression belongs
to Paul, whom Julian had placed, on this subject, in such direct opposition to John.

‡ L. III. f. 106.

§ Thus he speaks who cited the fable of the Ancilia above-mentioned
as an undoubted fact.

sciousness of guilt. In like manner he accuses the apostle Paul and the Christians of that period of contradicting the doctrines of Christ himself, when they held that it was not necessary to observe the Mosaic ceremonial law, notwithstanding that Christ, in his sermon on the mount, had said that he had not come to destroy the law, but to fulfil, and had declared even the least of the commandments to be binding *—a difficulty which admitted of being easily resolved, by rightly determining the meaning and the references of our Saviour's remarks.

In the reign of Julian, some one, probably a pagan rhetorician, wrote the dialogue in imitation of Lucian, called *Philopatris.* This contains a satirical account of the church doctrine of the Trinity, and of the monks, who, as they were the emperor's most violent enemies, predicted nothing but failure of his enterprises. They are represented as men who took pleasure in the public misfortunes, as the enemies of their country; and hence the title of the dialogue.† In order

---

* L X. 351.

† The very way in which the doctrine of the Trinity is ridiculed in this dialogue (s. 12) favours the supposition that it was composed at some period subsequent to the Nicene council, and this is confirmed by the description of the persons (s. 20 and 26), who are. represented altogether after the same manner as the monks were usually depicted by the pagans of this period. The expression, οἱ κικαρμίνοι τὴν γνώμην, manifestly alludes to the monkish tonsure. The monks say, that when they have fasted ten days, and watched ten nights, singing spiritual songs, they received revelations of future events in dreams. Prophetic dreams often occur in this age, both among pagans and Christians. Not only what the friend of the emperor says respecting the entire victory over the Persians, but also what he remarks concerning the cessation of the inroads of the Scythians (ἐκδρόμαι τῶν Σκυθῶν), is in keeping with this period. And this latter passage has been wrongly adduced by Kelle, who attributes the production to Lucian (see his dissertation on this dialogue in the Commentationes theol. of Rosenmuller, Fuldner, and Maurer, Lips. 1826, T. I. p. II. p. 246), against Gessner's hypothesis, with which we agree; for, by the authors of the fourth century, the Goths were assuredly sometimes designated by the general appellation of Scythians (see, for example, Eunapii excerpta, c. 26, in Majus scriptorum veterum nova collectio, tom. II. p. 272). But there is one point in which Kelle is unquestionably right, viz. in saying that what is affirmed concerning the subjection of Egypt, a country which had then been so long time already a Roman province, cannot without force be interpreted of this period. Yet it may be questioned whether all the particular marks denoting the time in this dialogue are to be understood as historically true; whether the author did not purposely intend to

to understand the nature of the charges which the pagans brought against Christianity and the Christian church, we must not only look into their polemical works, which, for the reasons already alleged, could in this period be but few in number; but we must also endeavour to find out the current objections brought against Christianity by the pagans in the ordinary intercourse of life. The sources from which such knowledge may be obtained are partly such writings of the pagans in which they occasionally allude to Christianity or the Christians; and partly the apologetical writings of the fathers, and the homilies of Chrysostom and Augustin.

Although *many* of the objections of the pagans to Christianity, springing out of the natural relation of paganism, or of man in his corrupt state of nature, to Christianity, must ever be recurring, yet there are many also which were called forth by the particular condition of the Christian church in this period. This is the case with all such objections as arose from the confounding together of church and state, and from the mass of corruption which, under the garb of Christianity, had attached itself to the church. If, in the former period, the extension of the church, in spite of all persecution, witnessed of that which *the divine power of the gospel alone* was able to effect; *now*, on the other hand, the pagans, looking, as men are wont to do, at the present moment, and forgetting the experience of the preceding centuries, could object against the divine character of the religion, *that Christianity depended for its spread on the favour of the princes.** To refute this objection, Theodoretus must appeal to the experience of the past, and to what was transpiring in Persia † when he wrote, in the beginning of the fifth century.

In the preceding period the Christians had been accused of irreverence towards the Cæsars (irreligiositas in Cæsares),

transpose the age, and therefore purposely introduce many things which belonged in no respect to the existing period. In Gieseler's Kirchengeschichte, I. bd. 2te Auflage, s. 131, I see that the Herr Staatsrath Niebuhr makes this dialogue to have been written at Constantinople, under the emperor Nicephorus Phocas, in the year 968. But, as I am ignorant of the reasons which are supposed to recommend this hypothesis above that of Gessner, I can only mention the fact.

* Ἐκ βασιλίκης νυξησεαι δυνάμεως. Theodoret. Græc. Affect. curat. Disputat. IX. p. 935, T. IV. ed. Schultz.

† See below, persecutions in Persia.

because they refused to join in those demonstrations of respect which idolatrous pagan flattery paid to the emperors. But when the Christians now reproached the pagans with prostrating themselves before the images of the gods, the reply they sometimes received was, that they did not scruple themselves to fall down before the images of the emperor; which was the less excusable in *them*, since, according to their own doctrine, it was an honour due to God alone.* The Christian, indeed, had an answer—that this was an abuse which had sprung from paganism, and, having become deeply rooted by the length of time, could not be extirpated by Christianity; though the church did not cease to condemn it.†

Next, while in the earlier times the conduct of the Christians had been the most expressive and convincing proof of the divine power of their faith, now, on the other hand, the enormous corruption which, under the show of Christianity, manifested itself in the public relations and among the great mass of nominal Christians was seized upon by the pagans as a testimony against Christianity, and against the Christian period which had led to such results. They did not reflect that the evils which float on the surface are ever easily detected, but that it requires more penetration to discern the truly good, which loves concealment and is less obtrusive. They saw, as Augustin justly expresses himself with regard to such characters, the scum only, which swims above, but did not remark the good oil, which had its secret channels, and, silently passing through them, made increase without notice.‡

Thus it was urged as an objection to Christianity, which the bishop Augustin was required to answer,§ how it was that

---

* The pagan Apollonius, in the Consultationes Zachæi Christiani et Apollonii philosophi, 1. I. c. 28: Cur imagines hominum, vel ceris pictas, vel metallis depictas, sub regum reverentia, etiam publica adoratione veneramini, et, ut ipsi prædicatis, Deo tantum honorem debitum etiam hominibus datis? D'Achery, spicileg. T. i.

† L. c. and cons. the work De promiss. et prædict. Dei, pars V. De dimidio temporis, where, in c. vii., this transfer of pagan adulation is rebuked: Æterna cum dicitur, quæ temporalis est, utique nomen est blasphemiæ: cum mortales licet reges, in ea dicantur Divi, eisque supplices dicant: numini vestro altaribus vestris, perennitati vestræ, et cætera, quæ vanitas, non veritas tradit, atque exsecrabilia sunt.

‡ Augustin. Sermo xv. s. 9. Amurca per publicum currit, oleum autem ad sedem suam occultos transitus habet: et cum occulte transeat, in magnitudine apparet.   § See Augustin. ep. 136 ad Marcellin.

such great and manifest evils had befallen the church under Christian princes, *who for the most part were diligent obser-vers of the Christian religion.** Augustin, it is true, in his answer does not undertake (as would have been best) to dispute the position that such princes had been diligent observers of Christianity; but what he says tacitly supposes that he did not himself concede this position, and in some measure touches the merits of the case, although he does not enter deeply into it. " It were to be wished," he says, " that something, at least, had been said of the conduct of the earlier emperors: thus examples would have been adduced of a similar or even worse character under emperors who were not Christians; and it might be seen that this is the fault of the men, and not of the doctrine; or else, not of the emperors themselves, but of others, without whom the emperors could have done nothing."† The position itself he disputes in his excellent apologetical work, " *The City of God*," where he says, " If all the kings of the earth, all the nations, all the great, and all judges; if young and old together would hear and obey the doctrines of Christ, such a people would at once participate of all civil prosperity in this present life, and of eternal blessedness in the next. But," he adds, " because one man listens to these doctrines, and another despises them; and because the great mass are more attached to the vices which flatter their corruption, than to the salutary rigour of the virtues; the servants of Christ, whether they be kings or subjects, rich or poor, freemen or slaves, endure, if need be, even the worst of governments; and, by that patient endurance, contribute to prepare for themselves a place in that holiest and most exalted community of angels, in that heavenly city where the will of God is law."‡ Augustin, moreover, very justly remarks that the fountain of those evils which were improperly charged on Christianity was to be traced to a far earlier time—to the corruption of the Roman state, which had been introduced by

---

* Christianam religionem maxima de parte servantes. This was just the evil of it that the pagans heard such princes extolled as zealous Christians, that such incorrect, such meagre notions were entertained of what belonged to the observance of Christianity; that zeal for forms of belief, for the external interests of the church, for outward matters of the church, were confounded with vital Christianity.

† Ep. 138 ad Marcellin.   ‡ De civitate Dei, I. II. c. 19.

earthly prosperity, and which had been checked by no earthly counterpoise. He justly appeals here to the testimony of the older Roman authors themselves; and, convinced that the Christian religion furnished the only thorough remedy for the evil, he thanks God that he had bestowed the means of a radical cure precisely at the time of the greatest corruption, whence mankind would have ever sunk lower in ruin. " Thanks be to the Lord our God," he exclaims, " who sent us his own special assistance against those evils."*

Another objection was urged against Christianity on political grounds, which sprang, however, not from any confounding of the precepts of Christianity with the behaviour of those who called themselves Christians, but partly from a misapprehension of these precepts themselves, and partly from the necessary opposition between the more political way of thinking peculiar to antiquity and the theocratical and moral spirit of Christianity. The pagans, for instance, supposed that the Christian doctrine was irreconcilable with the fundamental principles of a state, and that no state could subsist in connection with it; since the precepts of the sermon on the mount forbade war even on the justest occasions, and thus the state must be exposed to every kind of insult and wrong from the barbarians.† To this Augustin replies that these precepts had reference to the disposition of heart, which, in Christians, should always be the same, rather than to the outward actions. They required that the heart should constantly cherish the same disposition of patience and good will, while the outward actions must differ according as the best interests of those towards whom we are thus disposed require.‡ To those who maintained that Christianity necessarily conflicted with the

---

* Augustin, in the letter above cited, (s. 171,) comparing the effects of Christianity with the civic virtues of the ancient Roman republic, finally remarks, "Thus God showed, in the example of that flourishing empire of the Romans, how much the civil virtues could effect even without the true religion, that it might appear evident that men, when this is also added, become the citizens of another state, whose king is the truth, whose laws are love, and whose duration is eternity."

† Augustin. ep. 136.

‡ Augustin. ep. 138. Ista præcepta magis ad præparationem cordis, quæ intus est, pertinere, quam ad opus, quod in aperto fit, ut teneatur in secreto animi patientia cum benevolentia, in manifesto autem id fiat, quod eis videatur prodesse posse, quibus bene velle debemus.

welfare of states, he says, " Let them give us such warriors
as the Christian doctrine requires they should be; such subjects, such husbands and wives; such fathers, sons, masters,
and servants; such kings and judges; such payers and re-
ceivers of tribute as they ought to be according to the precepts
of the Christian doctrine;—and would they still venture to
assert that this doctrine is opposed to the state? Nay, would
they not rather confess, without hesitation, that, if it were
followed, it would prove the salvation of the state?"

The pagans also laboured to show in the historical way
that it was by forsaking the national gods, to whom the Roman
empire owed its increase and prosperity, and by the spread of
Christianity, the state had been ruined. Such was the aim of
Eunapius and of Zosimus in their historical works, written in
the fifth century. The Spanish presbyter Paulus Orosius, of
Tarraco, in Spain, at the request of Augustin, wrote, in the
year 417,* his historical compend, for the purpose of refuting
this charge by facts of history; and for the same reason
Augustin himself was led to write his profound work concerning the origin, character, progress, and ultimate aim of the
city of God. †

C. *Various obstacles which hindered the Progress of Christianity among the Heathen; various means and methods
by which it was promoted; and the different kinds of Conversion.*

The obstacles which, in this particular period, hindered the
progress of Christianity among the heathen, varied among
the different classes of the heathen according to their different
tendencies of mind and feeling. Some to heathen superstition
united the consciousness of great crime, and sought in the
former an antidote against the stings of the latter. They were
unwilling to abandon the superstition in which they had been
used to find so convenient a prop; and a religion presenting
moral claims had no attractions for them, unless when unworthy priests, who made Christianity itself to be only another
paganism, had either lowered, or concealed from them, these
moral claims, for the purpose of converting avowed pagans

* Adversus Paganos historiarum libri vii.
† De civitate Dei, libri xxii.

into nominal Christians. Others, who, to the eyes of men or in their own superficial view, had led blameless lives, imagined they possessed all they needed in their own religion, and especially that they needed not a Redeemer. In this delusion they were more confirmed, when, instead of examining their hearts by the demands of the holy law in their conscience, or of comparing themselves with real and living Christians, of whom perhaps they never saw an example within the circle of their acquaintance, they contrasted themselves with the vastly great number of nominal Christians. It is of such Augustin speaks :* " You will find," he says, " many pagans refusing to embrace Christianity, because they are satisfied with their own good lives. One should live, say they, uprightly. What further precept can Christ give us? We lead good lives already : what need have we of Christ? We commit no murder, theft, nor robbery ; we covet no man's possessions, we are guilty of no breach of the matrimonial bond. Let something worthy of censure be found in our lives, and whoever can point it out may make us Christians." Comparing himself with the nominal Christians · " Why would you persuade me to become a Christian? I have been defrauded by a Christian ; I never defrauded any man ; a Christian has broken his oath to me, and I never broke my word to any man."† Others, men of profounder feelings, men who were animated by a loftier moral idea, and who perceived the contrast between this and their own life, sought for peace in doctrines which no doubt had sprung from the universal religious sense of mankind—those doctrines which formed the system of the Neo-Platonists concerning a God who would purify from the stains that adhered to them, and free from their chains the struggling and suffering souls which, derived from himself, were fettered in the bonds of a sensual nature, and sighed after their original source.‡ With this they united a theory which taught various mysterious outward methods of expiation and cleansing, whereby men could draw down upon themselves the redeeming and sanctifying powers of the deity to purify and preserve both body and soul; where, however, it was doubtless at the same time assumed that the right disposition

* In Ps. xxi. Enarrat. II. s. 2.
† In Ps. xxv. Enarrat. II. s. 14.
‡ Ζεύς ῥύσιος, καθάρσιος, μειλίχιος. See the Hymns of Synesius.

existed within.*   To many this presentiment of a redeeming
God became afterwards, when they perceived the insufficiency
of those outward means of expiation, a point of transition to
Christianity.

Again, from the rude and uncultivated mass who were
wholly sunk in blind superstition, we should distinguish the
men of education.   In particular, there were then among the
pagans in the large cities multitudes of half-educated men,
from the rhetorical schools, with whom certain rhetorical
flourishes, a certain round of fine set phrases, which they had
learned to repeat, passed for a genuine culture of mind and
heart; men whose taste, trained to effeminacy from their
youth upwards in those showy and superficial schools, had
contracted a disrelish for all vigorous and sound nourishment,
both of mind and heart.   The difficulty of approaching such
persons increased in the same proportion with their shallow
and superficial way of thinking, and their dulness of sense to
all the deeper moral and religious wants of their nature.   Such
men could put up with nothing but that which came recommended to them in beautiful phrases.   The plainness and simplicity of the sacred word was to them reason enough for despising
it.   And, although they knew very little about philosophy
themselves, yet they wanted a philosophical religion, and
reproached the Christians on account of their blind credulity.
Of such, Theodoretus says, " Some who have read the poets
and orators, some who have also had a taste of Plato's eloquence, despise the sacred scriptures, because they are not set

* E. g., Longinianus, a pagan of North Africa, writes to Augustin,
who had questioned him with regard to his own opinion on the right
way which leads to God (ep. 234), Via est in Deum melior, qua vir
bonus piis, justis, veris, castis dictis factisque probatus, et Deorum
comitatu vallatus, in Deum intentione animi mentisque ire festinat.   Via
est, quæ purgati antiquorum sacrorum piis præceptis, expiationibusque
purissimis, et abstemiis observationibus decocti, anima et corpore con-
stantes deproperant.   Also Simplicius holds that, along with the inner
spiritual purification of the soul by the rational knowledge of God and a
life in harmony with nature, the external means of purification handed
down from the gods, by which the body is sanctified as the organ of the
soul, are also necessary in order that the whole man may partake of the
θεία ἐλλάμψις.   Simplicii in Epictet. enchiridion, p. 218.   It must be
confessed that a great deal may be found here which is analogous to the
church doctrine of that period respecting the magical sanctifying effects
of the sacraments.

'out with beautiful phrases; and they are ashamed to learn the truth from fishermen. And this pride is found in men who possessed but a superficial knowledge of the Greek philosophy, —who have only scraped together, from one quarter and another, a sort of literary medley.* Of such, Augustin, in his beautiful tract, entitled, " A guide to the instruction of the different classes of pagan catechumens," says that their teachers must accustom them to hear scripture read, without despising it because its language is so simple and free from all rhetorical embellishments.† It is to such Theodoretus says,‡ " It was God's will that all men, Greeks and barbarians, learned and unlearned, shoemakers, weavers, and other mechanics, moreover slaves, beggars, women, both such as live in the abundance of all things, and such as depend on the work of their own hands, should draw from the same fountain of salvation: for this reason he employed fishermen, and one who was a shoemaker (he should have said a tent-maker, Paul), as his instruments; *and he let their language remain as it was in the beginning*, but poured through the same the clear streams of heavenly wisdom."

Chrysostom once heard a Christian, in disputing with a rhetorically educated pagan of this class, contend that, in the elegant and proper use of the Greek language, Paul was superior to Plato. He censured the Christian who so badly understood how to defend his own cause; since the very point he was chiefly concerned to make out was, that the apostles were men destitute of human learning and art, in order to show that it was not human power, but the power of God, which operated through them.§

Among the cultivated pagans the following view of religion extensively prevailed: that with the diversity of nations and the varieties of the human race was necessarily connected the diversity of religions. There was, indeed, but one original divine Essence; but the union between this highest one and

---

* Theodoret. Græc. affect. curat. Disputat. I. p. 696, T. IV.

† De catechizand. rudib. c. 9. Sunt quidam de scholis usitatissimis grammaticorum oratorumque venientes, quos neque inter idiotas numerare audeas neque inter illos doctissimos. Docendi sint scripturas audire divinas, ne sordeat eis solidum eloquium, quia non est inflatum.

‡ Disputat. VIII. p. 899.

§ Chrysostom. ep. ad Corinth. I. H. III.

the endlessly diversified forms of humanity could only be mediated through certain higher natures which had emanated from that original Essence, viz. the gods, under whose dominion the several portions of the earth were distributed. Or, again, they conceived all the different religions to be only different forms of the revelation of one and the same divine substance—to be one essence in manifold forms; and it was precisely by this manifoldness, as they supposed, that God was most highly honoured. There could not be one single way alone which conducted, exclusive of all others, to the supreme, hidden, original Essence; it was only by different ways that men could attain to the most hidden mystery of the divine Being. Accordingly, says Simplicius,* God is everywhere present, *with all* his divine powers; but limited men, who are confined to their several determinate spots of the earth, could not grasp the immense whole. The divine powers, like natural gifts, must be variously distributed. Accordingly, the Neo-Platonic pagan philosopher Proclus worshipped Greek and Oriental divinities, according to the peculiar Greek and Oriental modes of worship; it being his wont to say, that the philosoper ought not to bind himself to the observance of this or that national form of worship, but, as the common hierophant for the whole world, be familiar with every form of religion.† "The rivalship of the different religions," says Themistius to the emperor Jovian,‡ "directly contributes to stir up zeal in worship. There are different ways—some more difficult, others easier; some rougher, others more plain and even—which lead to the same goal. If you allow but one way to be good, and hedge up the others, emulation is at an end. God desires no such agreement among men. As Heraclitus says, Nature loves to hide herself, and still more than nature, the Creator of it—whom we reverence particularly on this account, because the knowledge of him does not lie on the surface, and is not to be acquired without toil. As you have various ranks and conditions among your subjects, who all in like manner depend on you, and look up to you, so, be assured, the Lord of the universe also takes pleasure in variety and in the diversities of condition. It is his will that the

* In Epictet. enchiridion, pp. 219, 220.
† See Marini vita Procli, p. 74.
‡ See the above-cited discourse, pp. 67, 68.

Syrians should worship him in one way, the Greeks in another, and the Egyptians in still another. And, again, the Syrians are not agreed among themselves, but are subdivided into different minor sects. None have precisely the same notions with the others. Why, then, should we try to force that which is impossible in the nature of things?" In like manner writes Symmachus, in the above-cited Relatio ad Valentinianum: "It is reasonable that we should hold that Being whom all worship to be one and the same. We all see the same stars; there is a common cope of heaven; the same universe contains us. What matters it in what way each finds the truth? By one way it is impossible to reach so hidden a matter." If no regard were paid to the essential opposition between Christian Theism and paganism, it might seem as if Christianity too easily admitted of being taken up into this eclecticism, and might find its place, along with the others, as one of the manifold forms of religion. But the peculiar essence of Christianity struggled against everything like this; and on this account it was exposed the more to the reproach of a stiff and uncompromising intolerance. It substituted an objective, firm, and stedfast word of God in place of the impure and barely subjective presentiment, feeling, and opinion of man, which confounded godlike and ungodlike; and it made that divine word a judge of the thoughts and feelings. Ambrosius says rightly to Symmachus, " Come and learn on the earth the walk in heaven. Here we live, and there is our walk. Let God, my Creator, teach me himself the mysteries of heaven. Let not man teach me, who knows not even himself."

It is true, the religious way of thinking we have just described possessed some truth at bottom; which truth, however, Christianity alone teaches us how to separate from the falsehood with which it is associated. That free development of the individualities of human character in religion is to be found in Christianity, as it had nowhere been seen before; but it is here subordinated to a higher, all-transforming principle; and by this it was to be gradually purged from all intermixture of the ungodlike element. To that equalization of all forms of religion, which sprang out of the principle of the deification of nature, an error of the contrary kind did, indeed, oppose itself at that time in the Christian church. This error had its ground, however, not in Christianity itself, but in human inventions, confounded with Christianity—in a narrow dogmatism, which would adhere to one fixed and determinate form of the human apprehension of Christianity, which form could, no more than anything else human, be exempt from error and adapted to all human minds and all stages of the development of Christian faith and Christian knowledge. Yet this form was to be maintained as complete, eternally valid, the only true way of apprehending Christianity; and all minds forced into this one yoke. As opposed to this *other* extreme, the erroneous, pagan way of thinking might the more easily seem to present a semblance of truth.

As the relation of the different classes of pagans to Christianity varied, so also the ways were various by which they were led to embrace the gospel; and in the great variety of these leadings was shown the manifold wisdom of God. But we must first distinguish in this period between conversion in the proper and Christian sense — an inward change of disposition wrought by Christianity—and the mere outward adoption of Christianity; that is, of its name and ceremonial observances, or an exchange of open, undisguised paganism, for a nominal Christianity covering a pagan way of thinking. It must be evident, from what has already been observed respecting the spread of Christianity under the Christian emperors, that in this period the number of conversions of the latter kind far exceeded those of the former. And this is confirmed by the testimony of those church-teachers who were right earnest in bringing about conversions of the genuine stamp. Thus Augustin, for instance, in remarking on John vi. 26, complains, " How many seek Jesus only that he may benefit them in earthly matters! One man has a lawsuit,—so he seeks the intercession of the clergy; another is oppressed by his superior,—so he takes refuge in the church. Others are seeking, one in this way, and another in that, to be interceded for in some quarter where they have but little influence themselves. The church is daily full of such persons. Seldom is Jesus sought for Jesus' sake."*

* In John. Tract. XXV. c. 10. Augustin also notices as outward reasons which led many to adopt Christianity (p. 47), Ut majorem amicum conciliet, ut ad concupitam uxorem perveniat, ut aliquam pressuram hujus seculi evadat.

Doubtless it might happen that many, whose sole intention was hypocritically to put on the profession of Christianity, would be led farther than they meant to be, by some bishop or catechist who understood his calling and its duties. Such an one first took pains to inform himself, in the way prescribed by Augustin in his excellent guide to the catechist (the tract de catechizandis rudibus), of the reasons which induced the pagan to seek baptism. If he showed that he was actuated by impure motives, such an enlightened teacher would gently repel him. Or if, which was most often the case, he answered the inquiries of the catechist in conformity with his own hypocritical disposition, still the catechist endeavoured to give his conversation such a turn as to reach the heart of the heathen man. "Often," says the bishop Augustin,—speaking here from the experience which must belong to all men of the like spirit,—"often the mercy of God so comes to the help of the catechist's ministry, that the pagan, moved by his discourse, resolves to *become that which* he meant to feign."* But if pagans of this character came to one of the great majority of those ecclesiastics, men wholly without experience in the trial of spirits, or who were only interested to multiply the number of nominal Christians, they were received at once into the same number without further question. Yet even these, after being incorporated with the visible church, might be led by what was there presented to them; by the impressions which they involuntarily received; by the society of Christians; by participating in the acts of worship; by some word of the sermon to which they might be listening with others on some great festival,—by such or other means,—to find in the church a good of a higher kind than any which they had sought for in it. Hence, Augustin remarks, "Many, who presented themselves to the church with such impure motives, were, notwithstanding, reformed after they had once come into it."†

---

* De catechiz. rudib. c. 5. Sæpe adest misericordia Dei, per ministerium cathechizantis, ut sermone commotus jam fieri velit, quod decreverat fingere. So also Cyril of Jerusalem, in the prologue to his Catechesis, s. 4, remarks, "A man may present himself for baptism to please his wife, a wife to please her husband, a servant to please his master, a friend to please his friend. And now it is incumbent on the catechist, through whatever motives the individual may have come, to lead him to find in the church something higher and better than he was seeking for."

† Augustin. s. 47. Multi etiam sic intrantes corriguntur ingressi.

But, assuredly, no one was warranted for this reason to coun-tenance such hypocrisy,—to approve the evil, that good might come out of it.   And beyond all doubt, the number was far greater of those who grew hardened in that worldly sense, by which from the first they had profaned a holy profession, and who were thus the means of introducing into the church a great mass of corruption.   Among the fruits of such mere out-ward conversions were those who were found, soon afterwards, at the altars of the false gods.   We have proof of this in the laws enacted against apostates in the reign of the emperor Theodosius (see above).*

Yet these *gross worldly motives* were not the only ones which led to hypocritical conversions ; as, indeed, there were many different stages of hypocrisy in these conversions, accord-ing as the consciousness of deception was more or less present ; according as intentional fraud or unconscious self-deception more or less predominated.   Many were first awakened by outward impressions, which might lead them to a superstition which had simply changed its colour, as well as from superstition to the faith.   Many supposed they had seen miraculous effects produced by the sign of the cross, similar to what had been witnessed, though under different circumstances, by Constan-tine ; others, who had heard of the divine power of Christ, driven in some strait to seek for assistance from the unknown God, believed they had seen him visibly manifested, and that they were thus delivered.†   To others, some occurrence of the day, which was afterwards forgotten, but which had made an impression on their souls, of which, however, they were but vaguely conscious, would reappear in the form of a dream, where they imagined they saw Christ, or some martyr, threat-ening, warning, admonishing them.   In all such cases, how-ever, it might be that the individual was seeking in Christianity only for some earthly good, although he was not hoping to obtain it from man, like the class of hypocritical professors first mentioned, but from God.   Not love, but fear, which easily creates idols, or not the love which is bent on heavenly things, but a material craving after miraculous revelations to the senses, which he hoped to find in Christianity, led him to

* See the entire Titulus VII. of the l. XVI. Cod. Theodos.   Comp. the decrees of Siricius ad Himerium, of the year 385, s. 4.

† See, *e. g.*, Paulin. Nolan. ep. 36 ad Macarium.

the church. Much depended also on the circumstance whether
he found a teacher who could point him away from sensuous
to spiritual things. According to Augustin's directions to
the catechist, it was the duty of the latter to take advantage
of such communications to impress it on the heathen's heart
how great was God's care for men; but then he should also
aim to divert his mind from such wonders and dreams, and lead
it in the more certain way, and to the surer testimonies of
Holy Scripture;—he should inform him that God would not
awaken him by such signs and dreams, if a safer way had not
been already prepared for him in Holy Scripture, where he
was not to seek for visible miracles, but accustom himself to
wait for invisible ones;—where he would be taught of God,
not in the *visions of sleep*, but while *awake*.[*] But when such
teachers in Christianity were wanting, individuals of this class
might easily be so misled as merely to substitute, in place of
the pagan superstition, another under the Christian dress.

It so happened that many had their fears excited by particular outward impressions, or by the inner excitements of
conscience.[†] They felt the need of pardon; but they had no
right conception of the forgiveness of sins, or of what must be
done on man's part in order to obtain it. They dreamed of
obtaining at once, by the opus operatum of baptism, the
magical extinction of their sins, although they still continued
in the practice of them. Now, in case such individuals came
to a bishop or catechist, of the character required in the above-
cited work of Augustin, such a teacher would avail himself of
the disturbed conscience, which had brought them to him, as
a favourable opportunity for preaching to them repentance,
and of leading them from the way of a hypocritical to an
honest conversion. But, unhappily, there were bishops whose
only wish was to make the conversion to Christianity a right
easy thing for the pagans; and whose instructions, therefore,
served much rather to confirm them in this wrong state of
mind than to draw them away from it. They merely told
them what they would have to believe in order to be Christians;
but they were silent as to the obligations to a holy life which

[*] De catechiz. rudib. c. 6.

[†] Augustin. de catechizand. rudib. c. v. Rarissime quippe accidit,
immo vero nunquam, ut quisquam veniat volens fieri Christianus, qui
non sit aliquo Dei timore perculsus.

flowed out of this faith, lest they might thus be deterred from baptism.   Hence they baptized even those who lived in open sin, and who plainly enough manifested that it was not their purpose to forsake it.   They imagined that, when these were once baptized and introduced into the fellowship of the church, it was then time enough to admonish them against sin.   These corrupt modes of procedure originated partly in the erroneous notions of worth attached to a barely outward baptism and outward church fellowship; and partly in the false notions of what constituted faith, and of the relation of the doctrines of faith and of morals in Christianity to each other.*

Against this mode of procedure, and the errors out of which it sprang, Augustin wrote his excellent work de fide et operibus.   He says here, § 9, "What more befitting time can be found for one to hear about the faith which he ought to cherish, and how he ought to live, than that time when, with a soul full of longing desire, he pants after the sacrament of faith that conducts to salvation?   What other season can be a more appropriate one for learning what manner of walk is suited to so great a sacrament, which they are longing to receive? Will it be after they have received it; even though after baptism they should be in the practice of great sins,—even though they have never as yet become new men, but remain in their former guilt?   Then, by a strange perversion of language, it would first be said to them, 'Put on the new man;' and then, after they have done so, 'Put off the old man;' whereas the apostle, observing the proper order of things, says, 'Put

* They imagined that such persons, by means of that outward baptism and the outward fellowship of the church, by means of that which *they* called faith, had at least a hope of salvation beyond that of the pagans, although, ere they could attain to it, it would be necessary for them to pass through a refining fire, ignis purgatorius.   Against such bishops, animated with this false zeal for multiplying the numbers of the Christians, Chrysostom takes ground in his tract πρὸς τὸν Δημητρίον περὶ κατα- νύξεως, T. VI. ed. Savil. f. 145.   "Our Lord utters it as a precept, Give not that which is holy unto the dogs, neither cast ye your pearls before swine.   But through foolish vanity and ambition we have subverted this command too, by admitting those corrupt, unbelieving men, who are full of evil, before they have given us any satisfactory evidence of a change of mind, to partake of the sacraments.   It is on this account many of those who were thus baptized have fallen away, and have occasioned much scandal."

off the old man, and put on the new,' Colos. iii. 9, 10 ; and the Lord himself exclaims, ' No man putteth a piece of new cloth into an old garment; neither do men put new wine into old bottles,' Matth. ix. 16, 17."

The advocates of these measures alleged in their defence, that in the letters of the apostles the doctrines of faith preceded those of morals. To this Augustin replied, " This might have some weight, if it were the fact that there are particular writings of the apostles addressed to the catechumens, and other particular epistles addressed to the baptized ; and in the former nothing but the doctrines of faith were presented ; in the latter nothing but the doctrine of morals. But the truth is, all the epistles are addressed to *Christians already baptized.* Why, then, do we find the two things combined? We must grant, both belong to the complete sum of Christian doctrine ; but that they have commonly placed the doctrines of faith before the precepts of living, because a holy life presupposes the faith out of which it springs." Next, they defended their mode of proceeding by appealing to the example of the apostle Peter, who preached nothing but faith to the three thousand who were baptized after his first discourse, and who, when they asked him what they should do, simply replied, " Repent and be baptized, every one of you, in the name of Jesus Christ, for the remission of sins," Acts ii. 38. To this Augustin replied, that in the requisition of repentance was in fact implied already the requisition to put off the old man and to put on the new ; and the remark in verse 40, that Peter with many other words testified and exhorted, saying, " Save yourselves from this untoward generation," certainly supposes that they were required to renounce every sinful practice which belonged to the character of that sinful generation.

In opposition to the practice of citing exclusively those passages of scripture which speak solely of the preaching of faith in Christ, or of Christ crucified, as Acts viii. 37, and 2 Cor. ii. 2, iii. 10, Augustin very justly remarks, " One important part of preaching faith in Christ is, to teach how the members must be constituted, which he seeks in order to be their head ; which he forms, loves, redeems, and conducts to eternal life. An important part of preaching Christ crucified is, to teach how we ought to be crucified with him to the world,—consequently everything that relates to the duty of

self-denial. By that faith in Christ which Paul makes the
foundation of the whole Christian life, he does not understand
such faith as wicked spirits also might possess, but that faith
by which Christ dwells in the heart,—that living faith which
works by love, and comprehends in itself every other grace."

Many educated pagans were conducted to the faith, not at
once, by means of some sudden excitement, but after they had
been led by particular providences, by the great multitude of
Christians around them, to entertain doubts of the pagan religion they had received from their ancestors, and to enter upon
a serious examination of the several systems of religion within
their reach.   They read the holy scriptures and the writings
of the Christian fathers; they proposed their doubts, their
difficulties to Christian friends,* and finally made up their
minds to go to the bishop.   Many came, by slow degrees,
through many intervening steps to Christianity ; and the Neo-
Platonic, religious idealism formed one stage in particular by
which they were brought nearer to *Christian ideas*, as is seen
in the examples of a Synesius and an Augustin.   This system
made them familiar with the doctrine of a Triad.   Although
this doctrine, in its speculative matter and its speculative tendency, was altogether different from the Christian doctrine,
which is in its essence practical throughout, yet they were
thereby made attentive to Christian ideas.   They were conducted still nearer to practical Christianity by the doctrine
that man needed to be redeemed and purified from the might
of the ὕλη, which not only fettered and clogged, but corrupted
that element of his soul which stands related to God.   It is
true they believed only in a general redeeming power of God,
which was imparted to individuals in proportion to their worth ;
or the communication of which was connected with various
religious institutions under different forms.   But, notwithstanding, all this was calculated gradually to pave the way
both for the speculative mind and for the heart to embrace
Christianity ; even though Christianity might be regarded at
first only as one of the manifold forms of the revelation of the
divine, as we see illustrated in the case of Synesius.

In the idea of a divine Logos or Nus, the eternal revealer

* Augustin. de catechizand. rudib. s. 12.   Tales non cadem hora. qua
Christiani fient, sed antea solent omnia diligenter inquirere, et motus
animi sui cum quibus possunt communicare atque discutere.

of God, these Platonicians would perhaps find themselves at home ; not so with regard to the faith in the historical Christ crucified. They would have been pleased to place Christ on a level with those enlightened sages by whom the divine Logos had revealed himself under different forms, and who, by the fleshly multitude, too prone to cleave to the personal being, had been misunderstood. But to abide by this historical Christ alone, to seek in him their salvation, this was requiring too much from their speculative idealism.* Augustin, in his confessions (1. VII. § 13), after having described this state of mind from his own experience, since it was from a position of this sort that he himself passed over to the simple gospel, says, " Thou hast hid these things from the wise and prudent, and revealed them unto babes, that so they who feel themselves weary and heavy laden might come unto him, and he might give them rest, because he is meek and lowly of spirit. But those who are inflated with the pride of a doctrine that styles itself sublime, hear not the call of him who says, ' Learn of me, for I am meek and lowly of spirit, and ye shall find rest to your souls.' Matth. xi. 29."

Yet when those to whom Christianity appeared at first as one peculiar revelation of the divine, co-ordinate to other forms of manifestation, and not as the absolute religion of humanity, were induced to read the holy scriptures, and to attend divine worship in Christian churches, so far as this stood free and open to the unbaptized (i.e. the reading of the scriptures and the sermon), they might by their own study of the scriptures, and through numberless immediate impressions derived from the church life, be let more deeply into the Christian truth than they had divined of it, until at last they found the redeeming God only in Christ; and the ideal Christ, by means of their own inward experience, became to them the real one. Thus Synesius, for example, came from the position above described still nearer to Christianity, when, in the year 399, having been sent to Constantinople, as a delegate from his

---

* Many of these, had they been as clear to themselves, as honest and humble, as was Jacobi, might have said what that devout and noble spirit, so full of earnest longing after the truth, said in a letter to Lavater, that Christianity met their wants, so far as it was mysticism, but that on that very account it was the more difficult for them to get along with the historical faith. See Jacobi's Auserlesenen Briefwechsel, II. B. S. 55.

native city Cyrene, driven to a great strait, where he was abandoned of all human help, he visited the church, spent much time in prayer, and in this place felt the near presence of God.   Thus he was first left to desire baptism ;—and he was doubtless brought to a still more profound acquaintance with the deep things of Christianity by the experiences of the episcopal office, which he had reluctantly been induced to assume.   Thus it happened to Augustin, who from this position came to the study of the apostle Paul, in the expectation of finding here the same things that he had found in Platonism, only in a different form ; instead of which, he found *such a spirit* as brought about the great ferment and crisis in his inner life.

II. *Spread of Christianity beyond the limits of the Roman Empire.*

Among the means which contributed to further the progress of Christianity in nations not subjected to the Roman dominion, may be mentioned, first, the commercial intercourse of nations.   Along with the goods of the earth, the highest blessings of the Spirit also were thus often transmitted to distant lands.   In the next place, many of those monks who lived in the Libyan and the Syrian deserts, on the borders of barbarian tribes, acquired, by the godly character which shone forth in their lives, and which exercised a mighty power even over those rude minds, the respect and confidence of the wandering nomadic hordes ; and they would doubtless avail themselves of the opportunity thus afforded of bringing home the gospel to their hearts.   Even that which seemed to threaten destruction to the church must contribute to its extension.   Many Christians who had been driven by the persecution of Dioclesian out of Egypt, Libya, and Syria, took refuge with the neighbouring barbarian tribes,[*] and there enjoyed that freedom in the worship of God which they could not find in the Roman empire.   The pagans murmured when they saw the idolatrous homage they had been used to pay to the " eternal city " exhibited by history in its nothingness, and the colossal creation which had sprung forth from Rome crumbling daily to ruin.   But through Christianity, to which

[*] Euseb. vit. Constant. l. II. c. 53.

they ascribed all the public misfortunes, a new and more glorious creation was to be called forth out of the ruins of the old one. Both the hostile and the peaceful relations of the Romans with the rude tribes, particularly those of German origin, which were the first, after the general migration of races, to take an important part in the grand historical events of the world, contributed to bring these tribes to their first acquaintance with the gospel. A man who lived in the early part of the fifth century, and was an eye-witness of these events,—the author of the work " de vocatione gentium" (probably Leo the Great, afterwards bishop of Rome, but then a deacon)*—remarks finely on this point, " The very weapons by which the world is upturned must serve to promote the ends of Christian grace. Many sons of the church, who had been taken captive by the enemy, made their masters the servants of the gospel of Christ, and were teachers of the faith to those whose slaves they had become by the fortune of war. But other barbarians, who aided the Romans in war, learned among our people what they could not have learned at their own homes, and returned to their native land carrying with them the instruction they had received in Christianity."

We turn first to Asia. In the former period it was re-marked that Christianity had already made progress in Persia. The number of Christians had gone on increasing among all ranks until the beginning of the present period. At the head of the Christian church in Persia stood the bishop of the royal residence and chief city of the ancient Parthian kingdom, namely, Seleucia Ctesiphon. But the Magians, the Persian sacerdotal caste, applied every means to counteract the spread of Christianity; and the Jews, who were thickly scattered over the Persian empire, joined also in these hostile machinations.

The emperor Constantine recommended the Christians to the protection of the Persian emperor Shapur (Sapor) II., taking occasion of an embassy which the latter prince sent to him.† His letter contains nothing which alludes to the ex-istence as yet of any persecution against the Christians in the Persian empire. At all events it is certain, according to the more accurate chronology of the oriental accounts, that the beginning of the most violent and harassing persecution must not be placed, as the Greek writers on church history assert,

* L. II. c. 32.   † Euseb. IV. 9.

under the reign of Constantine, but under that of his successor. But, if some oriental notices * are entitled to credit, this persecution was preceded by two others of shorter duration, in which many Christians suffered martyrdom—one in the year 330,† the other in the year 342.‡ Still it may be a question whether those documents are worthy of entire confidence, and whether their narratives are chronologically accurate. The credible records of the principal persecution above mentioned contain not a hint that others had preceded it. Moreover, the Greek church historians, notwithstanding the anachronism just mentioned, speak of but one persecution, and make no mention of any before this. They state that at the time of the commencement of that principal persecution the Christian church was in a flourishing condition.

Now, with regard to the main persecution, which broke out in the year 343,§ it is manifest that the hostile relations existing between the Roman and the Persian empires were the immediate occasion of it. It was attempted to excite the suspicions of the emperor against the Christians on political grounds, because of the correspondence which they maintained with their brethren of the same faith in the Roman empire. For this purpose advantage was taken of the respect usually paid by the emperors at Constantinople to the chief of the Persian bishops. Thus, for example, the Persian Jews represented to the emperor Sapor, that, when the Roman

* See the two Chaldee documents extracted from the history of the Persian martyrs, in Stephan. Euod. Assemani acta martyrum orientalium et occidentalium appendix, p. 215.

† In the eighteenth year of the reign of Shapur, the beginning of which should be placed, according to Ideler's chronology (see b. II. s. 558), in the year 312.

‡ In the thirtieth year of his reign. The passage in the Acts of the second persecution (Assemani, l. c. 227), where Sapor, addressing the Christians, says, "What God is better than Hormuzd, or mightier than the terrible Ahriman?" is hardly in agreement with the Persian religious ideas; for, according to these, Ahriman, the object of abhorrence, would scarcely be mentioned in such connection with Ormuzd.

§ The most important records of its history, of which we shall say more hereafter, may be found in the collection of the acta martyrum, made under the direction of the bishop Marathas, (see Assemani bibliotheca oriental. T. III. P. I. p. 73,) from which were derived also those narratives already made use of by the Greek historians of the church. These acta were published by Stephan. Euod. Assemani, in the work already cited.

emperor received from him magnificent epistles and costly presents, they were scarcely noticed, in comparison with a miserable note from the bishop of Seleucia Ctesiphon, to which the emperor paid every mark of respect.* So also Christian ecclesiastics were accused of harbouring in their houses Roman spies; of betraying to them the secrets of the empire; of writing letters themselves to the Roman emperor, informing him of everything that transpired in the East.†

The objections brought against Christianity by the Persian civil authorities mark the peculiar relation in which Parsism stood, both to Christianity generally, and to that prevailing tendency of the religious and moral spirit which obtained particularly among the Persian Christians. To those who held to the principles of the Parsic Dualism, in which the opposition between Ormuzd and Ahriman, and their respective creations, a pure and an impure one, was uniformly adhered to, the Christian monotheistic view of the universe must have appeared as a confounding of good and evil, of the godlike and the ungodlike, as a profanation of the holy essence of God; since God was made to be the creator of that which could proceed only from the evil principle. Accordingly, in the proclamation issued by the Persian commander and governor, Mihr-Nerseh, to the Christians in Armenia, about the middle of the fifth century, it is said,‡ "All that is good in heaven Ormuzd created, and all that is evil was produced by Ahriman. Hatred, calamity, unhappy wars, all these things are the working of the evil principle; but, on the other hand, good fortune, dominion, glory, health of body, beauty of person, truthfulness in language, length of years, all these things proceed from the good principle. Evil, however, is mixed with all. They who affirm that God created death, and that evil and good proceed from him, are in error: for instance, the Christians, who say that God, being angry with his servant because he had eaten a fig,§ created death,

---

* Acta martyrum, l. c. p. 20.   † L. c. f. 152.

‡ In the French version, in the Mémoires historiques et géographiques sur l'Arménie par St. Martin. T. II. Paris, 1819, p. 472.

§ The reason why the fig in particular comes to be mentioned here is, that many of the fathers of the oriental church, as, for instance, Theodorus of Mopsuestia (see his observations on the first chapters of Genesis, in the catena of Nicephorus, on the Octoteuch. Lips. 1770), supposed it might be inferred from Genesis iii. 7, that this was the forbidden fruit.

and thereby punished men." In like manner it was objected
to the Christians, that they taught that insects, serpents,
scorpions, were created by God, and not by the devil.*
Although the Parsic religion acknowledged the being of one
primal Essence, under the name of Zervan (Κρόνος = αἰών,
βυθός of the Gnostics), from whom all existence flowed, yet
this idea of the one hidden, primal Essence, from the very
nature of the case, retreated into the obscure ; and the idea
constantly predominant was that of Ormuzd, the revealer of
this hidden, divine, primal Essence ; the creator, the victorious
antagonist of Ahriman ; and, although *he* was the object of
all prayer and adoration, yet various genii and powers of a
pure, holy nature, which were supposed to have emanated
from Ormuzd, received also a certain share of worship, so far
as they represented him. The sun, fire, water, earth, as
elements of a pure nature, working with the energy of Ormuzd, were objects of worship with the Persians ; and hence
it was objected to the Christians that they worshipped only
one God, but did not pay due honour to the sun, the fire, the
water ; especially, that they profaned the water by using it
for improper lustrations. In the ritual of the Parsic religion,
however, lustrations by water were frequently used. In the
case last cited, either Christian baptism itself is represented
as a profanation of the holy element, or else it is meant that
the Christians paid no regard to the sacredness of water in
their daily use of it.† As to the holy earth, the Persians
believed, doubtless, that they saw it profaned by the burial of
the dead ; for this practice, too, was urged as an objection
against the Christians.‡ It constituted again a part of the
nature-worship of the Persians, that they looked upon many of

* Assemani. l. c. fol. 181.
† See Herodot. l. I. c. 138.
‡ The custom of burying the dead contrasted strongly with the usage
of the Persians at that period. The dead body was cast into the open
field, as a prey for dogs and ravenous birds. They regarded it as a bad
token, a sign that the deceased was an abandoned wretch and his soul
belonged to the Dews, if the body was left untouched by the beasts of
prey. The bones that were left were allowed to moulder away on the
ground. See Agathias, II. 22 and 23, p. 113, ed. Niebuhr. This historian says expressly of the Persians, Θήκη τινι ἐμβάλειν ἢ λαρνάκι τοὺς
τιθνεῶτας, ἢ καὶ τῇ γῇ καταχωννῦναι ἥκιστα θέμις αὐτοῖς. The former
practice is noticed already by Heredotus, I. 140. He says, however,
that the bones left behind were besmeared with wax and buried.

the brute animals as being specially consecrated to Ormuzd, and sacred, while others were consecrated to Ahriman;—and hence the Christians were censured for slaughtering brute animals indiscriminately. Necessarily connected with the nature-worship of the Persians, with the idea pervading the whole life of the Persians that every man should be a servant of Ormuzd in the struggle to defend his holy creation against the destructive powers of Ahriman, was the precept of their religion which required a life of activity and industry devoted to the culture of nature. All employments, even that of war against the enemies of the servants of Ormuzd, were reckoned as belonging alike to the contest for Ormuzd against Ahriman. The gifts of nature were to be enjoyed as holy gifts of Ormuzd; every fortunate event was thus made holy; riches, and especially a numerous progeny,[*] were considered as blessings conferred by Ormuzd. But at this time an ascetic spirit had become diffused among the Christians of the East; and it is easy to imagine what a contrast this must have presented to the Persian view of life. Hence it was affirmed of the Christians that they forbade men to marry and beget children; to do military service for the king; to strike any one.[†] And, in the above-cited proclamation of Mihr-Nerseh, it is said, "Believe not your leaders, whom you call Nazarenes;[‡] they are deceitful knaves, teaching one thing and doing the contrary. They say it is no sin to eat flesh, and yet they eat none. They say it is right and befitting to take a wife, and yet they refuse even to look upon a woman. According to them, whoever accumulates riches is guilty of a

---

[*] See Herod. I. 136.

[†] Assemani, l. c. 181. Thus it was required of a Christian priest, if he would save his life, to worship the sun, to partake of blood (the oriental Christians holding the ordinance mentioned in Acts xv. 29, to be still binding), and to marry. Ass. l. c. 188.

[‡] St. Martin is of opinion that this name is used here as a general appellation of the Christians: but this will not do; for the subject of discourse here is the heads and teachers of the communities; and, moreover, the other remarks here cannot be referred to all Christians. We are to conceive rather that this name (the monks being compared with the Nazarenes of the Old Testament) was in the East a common designation of the monks; and the clergy in these districts were then chosen, for the most part, from among the monks. Comp. e. g. Gregor. Nazianz. orat. p. 527, concerning the monks: Ναζαραίων χοροστασίαι, and οἱ καθ' ἡμᾶς Ναζαραῖοι, orat. 19, p. 310.

great sin. They place poverty far above wealth; they praise
poverty, and they defame the rich. They scorn the name of
good fortune, and ridicule those we stand on the pinnacle of
glory. They affect coarse garments, and they prefer common
things to the costly. They praise death, and they have a
contempt for life. They hold it an unworthy thing to beget
men, and they praise barrenness. Follow their example, and
the world would soon come to an end."

A Persian governor asks the Christians, Which is the
true religion, that which was professed by the kings, the
lords of the world, the nobles of the empire, the men of rank
and of wealth; or that which they, poor people, had preferred
to it? He reproached them as a people too indolent to apply
themselves to those useful occupations by which men obtain
wealth, and therefore so fond of praising poverty.* The doctrine, too, of the crucified Redeemer of mankind appeared to
the Persians preëminently foolish. Thus, in the proclamation
above cited, it is said, " But what they have written, still
more detestable than anything mentioned as yet, is this: that
God was crucified for men; that he died, was buried, rose
again, and finally ascended to heaven. Do such detestable
opinions really deserve an answer? Even the *Dews* (the
demons of the Persians, the creatures of Ahriman), who are bad,
cannot be imprisoned and tortured by men; and it is pretended
that this could be done to God, the Creator of all things!"

The first ordinance of the emperor probably ran as follows:
—*The Christians, unless they would consent to worship the
Persian deities, should be required to pay an inordinate tax,
levied on each individual.* This law may have been directed,
perhaps, to the bishop of Seleucia, who was expected to collect the required sum from all the Christians, and pay it over.
Simeon,† the venerable old man who then held this office,
gave a high-hearted answer, which stood out in bold and
striking contrast with the servile spirit of the Orientals;
though it is wanting in the temper of Christian humility, and
fails to mark the distinction between spiritual and political
freedom. Yet it should be borne in mind that the emperor
probably demanded of the Christians an amount of money

* Assemani, l. c. 186.
† Barsaboe, son of the leather-dresser. His father was the king's
purple-dyer.

which they could not possibly raise, thinking to compel them in this manner to abjure their religion. The Christians, Simeon declares, whom their Saviour had emancipated by his blood from the most shameful yoke, and whom he had delivered from the most oppressive of burthens, could not submit to have such a yoke imposed on them. Far was it from them to be so foolish and sinful as to exchange the liberty which Christ had bestowed on them for slavery to men. " The Lord, whom we are resolved to obey, is the upholder and director of your government. We cannot subject ourselves to an unrighteous command of our fellow-servant."—" As God is the Creator of your divinity (the sun), so they held it to be a reckless thing to place God's creature on a level with himself. They had neither gold nor silver, as the Lord had forbidden them to heap up such treasures; and Paul had said to them, ' Ye are bought with a price; be no man's servants.' " * The emperor interpreted this letter as if Simeon invited the Christians to insurrection, and commanded that he and his people should be threatened with severe punishment. To this Simeon replied that it was far from any thought of his to betray his flock for the purpose of saving his life and purchasing peace. He was ready, following the example of his Saviour, to give up his life for his flock. Sapor then declared, " Whereas Simeon scorns my authority, and obeys the Roman emperor, whose God alone he worships, but utterly despises my God, he must present himself before me and be executed." And he immediately issued another decree against the Christians :—*The clergy of the three first grades were to be immediately executed, the churches of the Christians demolished, their church utensils devoted to profane uses.*

Simeon, with two presbyters of his church, was conveyed in chains to Ledan, a city in the province of Huzitis, where the emperor then resided. Before this he had never hesitated to prostrate himself, after the oriental manner, in the king's presence,—this being a custom of the country, which in itself contained nothing idolatrous. But now, when he was called upon to renounce the sole worship of his God, he declined doing this; since it behoved him at present to avoid every act which could be interpreted as if he gave to a creature the honour due to God alone. The emperor then required him

* L. c. iv.

to do homage to the sun,—assuring him that he might thus deliver himself and his people. To this Simeon replied, that he could still less pay to the sun, a lifeless being, that homage which he had declined showing to the king, who was a rational being, and therefore far more than the sun. As neither promises nor threats had any power to move him, the emperor ordered him to be thrown into prison till the next day, to see if he would not come to his senses.

To the Christians belonged at that time the head of the imperial household, and most considerable of the eunuchs, to whose care Sapor had been intrusted when a child—the venerable Guhsciatazades. This person had been prevailed upon to do homage to the sun. When Simeon was conducted by him in chains, he fell on his knee, after the oriental manner, and saluted him. But Simeon turned away his head ; for he had denied the faith. His conscience was awakened by this silent reproof: he witnessed a bold confession before the emperor, and was sentenced to lose his head. When brought already to the place of execution, he begged of the emperor, as a reward for the services he had rendered to his whole family, that it might be publicly made known how Guhsciatazades died,—not because he had betrayed the secrets of the empire, or committed any other crime, but simply because, as a Christian, he refused to deny the God whom he professed to worship. He hoped that the example of his death in behalf of the faith which he had once denied would have the more powerful effect on others. Sapor consented, not knowing the power of faith, and expecting that the terrible example would prove a warning to many ; but he soon learned the contrary.

The aged Simeon, in his dungeon, had thanked God for the repentance and martyrdom of this brother in the faith. He rejoiced to learn that his own death would probably take place on the very day which the Persian Christians had consecrated to the memory of Christ's passion. So it happened. The next day after his arrest, and after the martyrdom of Guhsciatazades, he appeared before the emperor ; and showing that he was firm in his confession, he likewise was condemned to die. A hundred others of the clerical order, who had been condemned at the same time, were led out with him to the place of execution. Simeon and his two companions were to be reserved till the last. The whole design of the emperor was to shake his constancy, so that, through his example, he might work on the great mass of the Christians; and he hoped that the blood of so many shed before his eyes would make him waver; but he was mistaken. Simeon confirmed the band of confessors by his exhortations, and at last died himself with his two companions. It happened that one of these latter, Ananias, when it was his turn to strip himself and be bound, in order to receive the stroke of the axe, suddenly seized by the natural fear of death, trembled through his whole frame; the flesh only being weak, while the spirit was strong as before. When this was observed by Phusik, an officer of some rank, superintendent of all the workmen in the palace, who was himself a Christian, said he to him, " Never mind; shut your eyes but a moment, and partake of the light of Christ." This was immediately communicated to the king. Sapor was the more incensed at the disobedience of Phusik, because but a short time had elapsed since he had conferred on him his new honours. Phusik declared that he would gladly exchange these poor honours for the crown of martyrdom. His tongue was torn out in the most cruel manner, and thus he died.*

Still more violent was the persecution in the following year, 344. An edict appeared which commanded that all Christians should be thrown into chains and executed. Many belonging to every rank died as martyrs. Among these was a eunuch of the palace, named Azades, a man greatly prized by the king. So much was the latter affected by his death, that he commanded the punishment of death should be inflicted from thenceforth only on the leaders of the Christian sect; that is, only on persons of the clerical order. Of these a great number suffered martydom. Yet, within the space of the forty years during which this persecution lasted, it became occasionally more general and violent again, which was especially the case towards its close.

The treaty of peace which terminated the unfortunate war of the Romans with the Persians under the emperor Jovian, was unfavourable to the interests of the Christians; the ancient Christian city Nisibis, on the border of Mesopotamia, being given up to the Persians. Yet the Christian inhabitants had permission to leave the country.

* Assemani, tom. I. 35. Sozom. 1. II. c. 11.

In the early part of the fifth century, by the wise and prudent conduct of a man zealously engaged in promoting the spread of the gospel, a very favourable change was brought about in the situation of the Christians, which might have been attended with important consequences for a long time in the future, if his labours had not been defeated by the imprudent zeal of another bishop. The bishop Maruthas, of Tagrit in Mesopotamia,* consented to serve as an agent in the negotiations between the emperors Arcadius and Theodosius II. and the Persian emperor Jezdegerdes II.; and, in these negotiations, he gained the esteem and confidence of the Persian emperor. The intrigues of the Magians to effect his downfall he was enabled to defeat by his sagacity, and his reputation only rose higher. He obtained permission for the Christians to rebuild their churches, and to hold their meetings for divine worship; but the whole was made nought by the imprudent behaviour of Abdas bishop of Susa. The latter caused one of the Persian temples (a πυρεῖον), in which fire, the symbol of Ormuzd, was worshipped, to be demolished. Owing, perhaps, to the still remaining influence of the bishop Maruthas, Jezdegerdes at first showed a moderation seldom witnessed among oriental princes under the like circumstances. He summoned Abdas into his presence, mildly upbraided him for this act of violence, and simply required him to rebuild the temple. As the latter thought, however, that he could not conscientiously do this, and resolutely declined to do it, the king was greatly exasperated. He ordered the Christian churches to be destroyed, and Abdas to be executed (about the year 418).† This was the commencement of a thirty years' persecution of the Christians in Persia, which, under the reign of Varanes, the successor of Jezdegerdes, from the year 421 and onward, became far more violent. Oriental cruelty invented

* Maipheracta, Martyropolis.
† The judgment which the mild Theodoretus, who relates this, passes on the bishop's conduct, is worthy of notice (h. eccles. l. V. c. 39): "I affirm, indeed, that the wrong time was chosen for the destruction of the fire-temple; for the apostle Paul himself, when he came to Athens and found the whole city given to idolatry, destroyed none of the altars which they reverenced, but by instruction refuted their ignorance, and showed them the truth. But that the bishop preferred rather to die than to rebuild the temple commands my admiration; for to me it seems the same thing to worship fire, and to rebuild the temple for such worship."

against the Christians the most painful modes of death ; and men of all ranks, even the highest, suffered martyrdom. Jacobus, a man belonging to one of the most distinguished families, had already been moved by his benefactor, the king Jezdegerdes, to deny the faith. But through the remonstrances of his mother and his wife, filled with remorse, he repented, and after this remained steadfast under protracted tortures, one limb being severed from his body after another. Once only, when his thigh was dismembered, a cry of anguish was heard from him : " Lord Jesus, help and deliver me, for the bands of death are about me." * Another noble Persian, Hormisdas, who was ordered by the king to deny his faith, answered, " You bid me do what is in itself a sin, and what you yourself cannot approve ; for he who can consent to deny the Amighty God will still more easily deny his king, who is a mortal man." The king thereupon deprived him of all his honours, confiscated his estate, and condemned him, naked, with only a girdle about his loins, to drive the camels in the rear of the army. But some days after, observing him, from his palace windows, in this pitiable condition, scorched by the sun and covered with dust, he was seized with compunction. Summoning him to his presence, he ordered him to be clothed in a linen robe, and called on him anew to renounce his faith. But Hormisdas rent the linen robe in twain, saying, " If you suppose I shall renounce my faith for this, keep the gift by which you would bribe me to deny God." Of another Christian, by the name of Suenes, the master of a thousand slaves, Jezdegerdes demanded, after he had refused to deny his faith, which was the worst of his slaves, and immediately made the latter lord over the whole, including his old master.

Among other incidents, it so happened that a certain deacon, named Benjamin, was cast into prison. He pined away two years in his dungeon, until the arrival of an ambassador sent on other business from the Roman empire. The latter petitioned the king for the release of Benjamin ; and it was accorded to him, on condition that he would never preach Christianity to any adherent of the Persian system of religion. The ambassador assented to this condition without consulting with Benjamin. But, on communicating it to the latter, he declined it altogether, saying, " It is impossible for me not to impart to

* See Assemani, acta Martyrum, l. c. p. 243.

others the light that I have received myself; for the gospel
history teaches us to what sorer punishment he justly exposes
himself who hides his talent." Notwithstanding he obtained
his freedom, under the presumption that after all he would
comply with the condition. He continued to preach the gospel; and, having laboured a year in this way, he was accused
before the king, who required him to deny the faith. Upon
this, he asked the king to what punishment he would sentence
the man who deserted his government, and swore allegiance
to another. The king replied that he should sentence him to
death. " Then," said Benjamin, " what punishment might
not that person justly suffer, who should disown his Creator,
and give the honour due to God alone to one of his fellow-
servants?" He was executed with cruel torments.* The
bishop Theodoretus of Cyros, on the Euphrates, wrote on this
occasion to Eusebius bishop of Persian Armenia a letter of
exhortation, breathing the genuine Christian spirit, in which
he admonishes him to be not only steadfast in maintaining his
own conflict, but forbearing and kindly provident towards the
weak—an exhortation which perhaps was not unnecessary to
the Persian Christians, who were somewhat inclined, as it
would seem, to a fanatical pride. " Let us be watchful," he
writes,† " and fight for the sheep of our Lord. Their master
is at hand; he will surely appear, will scatter the wolves, and
bestow honour on the shepherds. ' For the Lord is good
unto them that wait for him, to the soul that seeketh him.'—
Lam. iii. 25. Let us not murmur at this storm which has
arisen; for the Lord knows what is best. On this account he
did not grant the request even of his apostle, who besought
him to deliver him from his trials; but said to him, ' My
grace is sufficient for thee, for my strength is made perfect in
weakness.' But I beseech you, let not our only care be
for ourselves; but let us bestow still greater care on the
others; for the precept has come down to us from the apostles,
to ' comfort the feeble-minded, and support the weak.'—
1 Thess. v. 14. Let us reach forth our hand also to the fallen;

---

* Theodoret. V. c. 39. The same Theodoretus speaks of the steadfastness of the Persian Christians under all their tortures, de Græc. affect.
curat. disput. ix. pag. 935, t. iv. He finely remarks, " They mutilate
and destroy the body, but cannot get at the treasury of faith."

† Epist. 78.

let us heal their wounds, that we may put them also in battle array against the wicked spirit. The Lord loves men; he receives the sinner's repentance;—let us hear his own words: ' As I live, saith the Lord God, I have no pleasure in the death of the wicked, but that the wicked turn from his way and live.'—Ezek. xxxiii. 11. For this reason he has even confirmed his words by an oath, although he forbids the oath to others, in order to convince us that he longs after our repentance and our salvation. But the God of peace will shortly cause Satan to be trodden under your feet, and rejoice your ears with the tidings of your peace, when he shall say to the raging sea, ' Peace, be still.' "*

As many were inclined to save themselves by fleeing from the Persian dominion into the Roman empire, command was given to all the garrisons on the frontiers, and to the chiefs of the nomadic hordes in the Persian service, who kept watch over the boundaries of the empire, to arrest all Christians who might attempt to leave the kingdom.† Many, nevertheless, succeeded in effecting their escape, and sought aid, through Atticus bishop of Constantinople, from the Roman emperor. On the other hand, the Persian king demanded the surrender of the fugitives. This being refused, led, in conjunction with various other difficulties, to the war between the two empires, which again operated unfavourably on the situation of the Persian Christians. But with the restoration of peace their prospects once more grew better. In particular, the charitable and Christian conduct of a pious bishop could not fail to make a favourable impression on the Persians. The Roman soldiers had carried off seven thousand Persian prisoners, whom nothing would prevail upon them to release, and who, deprived of all the necessary means of subsistence, were in the most pitiable condition. Then Acacius bishop of Amida in Mesopotamia called together his clergy, and said to them, " Our God needs neither dishes nor drinking-vessels, since he is all-sufficient in himself. Now, as the church, through the love of its children, possesses many utensils of gold and silver, we must dispose of these to ransom

* Ep. 78.
† Vit. Enthym. c. 18. Coteler. Ecclesiæ Græcæ Monumenta, t. II. If this account is quite accurate, the order was issued already under the reign of Jezdegerdes—unless he is confounded with Varanes.

and to refresh the prisoners." No sooner said than done: the prisoners were not only redeemed, but, after being provided with the means of subsistence, and with money to defray their travelling expenses, were sent back to their homes. This work of charity is said to have affected so deeply the heart of the emperor, embittered as it was against the Christians, that he desired an interview with the bishop.[*]

As doctrinal controversies in the Roman church, in the course of the fifth century, led to a schism between the Christian church of the Persian and that of the Roman empire (concerning which we shall speak in the fourth section), the political cause of the persecutions in Persia would thus be removed, and this circumstance would operate favourably on the situation of the Persian Christians.

By means of Persia, Syria, and other bordering provinces of the Roman empire, many seeds of Christianity would early find their way to *Armenia ;* but the fanatical spirit of the Persico-Parthian religion was here for a long time an insurmountable obstacle to the spread of the gospel. The Armenian *Gregory,* who on account of his apostolical activity obtained the cognomen of " the Enlightener" (δ $\phi\omega\tau\iota\sigma\tau\eta\varsigma$), first led the way, by his active zeal, to a more general diffusion of Christianity in his native country, from the commencement of the fourth century and onwards; and it was by his means also that the Armenian king Tiridates was converted.[†] The old religion, notwithstanding this event, still continued to maintain itself in many of the Armenian provinces. In the beginning of the fifth century, Miesrob, who had once been the royal secretary, having devoted himself wholly to the service of religion, disseminated Christianity still more widely in countries to which it had not yet penetrated, by taking up his abode in those regions as a hermit. Up to this time the Syrian version of the Bible, the authority of which was recognised in the Persian church, had been used in Armenia; and hence an interpreter was always needed to translate into the vernacular tongue the portions of scripture read at the public worship. Miesrob first gave his people an alphabet, and translated the Bible into their language.[‡] Thus was the pre-

---

[*] Sozom. l. VII. c. 21, 22.
[†] See Moses Chorenens. hist. Armen. l. II. c. 77 and c. 88.
[‡] Moses Chorenens. l. III. c. 47 and 52.

servation of Christianity among this people made sure, even while the country was subjected to such dynasties as were devoted to the Zoroastrian or to the Mohammedan religion, and sought to supplant Christianity ;—and a Christian literature proceeded from this time forward to form itself in Armenia. Miesrob was a successful and well-deserving labourer also among the neighbouring kindred populations.

A party devoted to the ancient cultus, who continued to maintain themselves in some districts of Armenia, were encouraged and supported by those who held the same faith in Persia. The Persian kings were striving continually to extend their dominion over Armenia. Where they were victorious, they persecuted Christianity, and sought to restore the old religion. The Persian commander and governor, Mihr-Nerseh, about the middle of the fifth century, addressed a proclamation to all the Armenians, in which he affirmed that all who did not adopt the religion of Mazdejesnan (the Zoroastrian faith) must be mentally blind, and deceived by the wicked spirits (the *Dews*).* The Armenian governors and chiefs are said either to have answered in a written document the objections here made to Christianity, or to have appeared before a great tribunal, which was to decide the question on the affairs of religion. On this occasion the Armenian nobles, whom the patriarch Joseph had assembled, A.D. 450, in the city of Ardaschad, declared that they preferred to die as martyrs rather than to deny their faith. After the Persian king, however, had summoned them to his court, and threatened them with a cruel death, they were prevailed upon to give in their denial. But the attempt of the Persians to extirpate Christianity by force, and to introduce the Zoroastrian religion, brought about a universal popular movement, and a religious war, a thing of frequent occurrence in those regions.† It was amidst the distractions in which the Persian church, as well as the whole country, was then involved, that the Armenian *Moses* of *Chorene* wrote the history of his native land, which he concludes with sorrow and complaint.

The conversion of the race of *Iberians*, bordering on the

* See the proclamation, which has been already cited, in the Mémoires historiques et géographiques sur l'Arménie par St. Martin. Paris, 1819. T. II. p. 472.

† See the Mémoires sur l'Arménie, cited above, T. I. p. 323.

north, (within the present *Georgia* and *Grusinia*,) proceeded
from a very remarkable, insignificant beginning.*

Under the reign of the emperor Constantine, a Christian
female, perhaps a nun, was carried off captive by the Iberians,
and became the slave of one of the natives of the country.
Here her rigidly ascetic and devotional life attracted the
attention of the people, and she acquired their confidence and
respect.   It happened that a child who had fallen sick was,
after the manner of the tribe, conveyed from house to house,
that any person who knew of a remedy against the disease
might prescribe for it.   The child, whom no one could help,
having been brought to the Christian woman, she said that
she knew of no remedy, but that Christ, her God, could help
even where *human* help was found to be unavailing.   She
prayed for the child, and it recovered.   The recovery was
ascribed to the prayer; this made a great impression, and the
matter finally reached the ear of the queen.   The latter afterwards fell severely sick, and sent for this Christian female.
Having no wish to be considered a worker of miracles, she
declined the call.   Upon this, the queen caused herself to be
conveyed to her; and *she* also recovered from her sickness.
through the prayers of this female.   The king, on hearing of
the fact, was about to send her a rich present; but his wife
informed him that the Christian woman despised all earthly
goods, and that the only thing she would consider as her
reward was when others joined her in worshipping her God.
This, at the moment, made no farther impression on him.
But some time afterwards, being overtaken, while hunting,
with gloomy weather, by which he was separated from his
companions, and finally lost his way, he called to mind what
had been told him concerning the almighty power of the God
of the Christians, and addressed him with a vow that, if he
found his way out of the desert, he would devote himself
entirely to his worship.   Soon after the sky cleared up, and
the king safely found his way back.   His mind was now well
disposed to be affected by the preaching of the Christian
female.   Afterwards he himself engaged in instructing the

* Among this people, too, the prevailing religion was probably some
modification of the Persian cultus, adapted to their rude manners.   They
worshipped an image of Ormuzd, notwithstanding that the genuine Zoroastrian religion allowed of no images.   See Moses Chorenensis. l. II. c. 83.

men, while his queen instructed the women of his people. Next they sent in quest of teachers of the gospel and clergymen from the Roman empire; and this was the beginning of Christianity among a people * where it has been preserved, though mixed with superstition, down to the present times.†

From this tribe the knowledge of Christianity may have been extended also to the neighbouring populations. About the year 520,‡ Tzathus, prince of the Lazians, one of the tribes of this country, came on a visit to the emperor Justin. He received baptism, and Justin stood as his godfather. He returned back to his people with a noble Greek lady, whom he had married, richly loaded with presents from the emperor, who acknowledged him as a king. In the time of the emperor Justinian, the assassination of a prince of this tribe, by a Roman general, produced among them a great excitement; and some individuals took advantage of this state of feeling to persuade them to drop their connection with the Roman people, and attach themselves to the Persian empire. But the fear lest a connection with the Persians would endanger their Christian faith is said to have contributed especially to deter

---

* Betwixt the years 320 and 330.

† One of the original sources of this story is Rufinus, from whom the Greek church historians have borrowed it. Rufinus had it from the mouth of the Iberian chieftain Bacurius, who had risen to the dignity of a Comes Domesticorum in the Roman empire, and, at the time Rufinus knew him, had become Dux over the borders of Palestine (see Rufin. h. e. c. 10). The simple tale bears within itself the marks of truth: and, indeed, the spread of Christianity has often received an impulse from similar occurrences. The second, perhaps independent, channel is the history of Moses of Chorene (l. II. c. 83). It is possible, indeed, that this historian took his account indirectly from the Greek writers, who were indebted for it to Rufinus. But, considering the vicinity of the country, it may be conceived, too, that he derived his account immediately from the spot. In favour of this latter supposition would be the slight discrepancies in the two several accounts, though these, too, might be accounted for by the story's being given in an Armenian dress. According to this writer, the name of the Christian woman was Nunia, and that of the prince Miraus. The Christian woman was an Armenian; and the application for teachers of Christianity was made, not to the church of the Roman empire, but to the Armenian bishop Gregory, who has been already mentioned. It may be a question, however, whether this modification of the story was not invented in favour of the Armenian church, to which the Iberian became subsequently united.

‡ 512 according to the era of Theophanes.

M 2

them from following this advice.* Another tribe also, belonging to this district, bordering on Mount Caucasus, namely,
the *Abasgians*, were converted under the reign of the emperor
Justinian. Until this time groves and lofty trees (after the
manner of the ancient Germans) had been the objects of their
worship. The emperor Justinian sent them ecclesiastics, and
founded among them a church. He produced a favourable
disposition towards Christianity among the people, by forbidding their rulers to engage in the scandalous traffic in cas-
trated slaves, to which many of the male children of the people
were sacrificed.†

What we had to say respecting the vagueness of the accounts relative to the spread of Christianity in the earliest
times in India applies also to many of the accounts belonging
to the earlier times of *this* period. The same cause of the
obscurity still continued to exist; namely, the unsettled use of
the name India, by which was understood sometimes Ethiopia,
sometimes Arabia, and sometimes East India proper. At the
same time, however, it should be borne in mind, that there was
at this time a constant intercourse between all these countries
by commercial connections and colonies, which also might
serve as a channel for communicating Christianity from one of
these districts to the other. The various passages, therefore,
in which Chrysostom names the *Indian* among the different
languages into which the holy scriptures had been translated,
can settle nothing definitely; and even if it could be made
probable, by the accompanying descriptions, that Chrysostom
had really East India proper before his mind, still such rhetorical representations could not properly be considered as evidence to be relied upon, especially as he himself might possibly
have been deceived by the vague meaning of the name. Of
more importance, on this point, is what the Arian historian
Philostorgius relates concerning the missionary Theophilus,
who bore the cognomen of Indicus (ὁ Ἰνδός). This Theophilus had been sent by his countrymen, the inhabitants of
the island Diu,‡ in the reign of the emperor Constantine, as
a hostage to Constantinople. He was there educated, and
trained for the spiritual office; afterwards consecrated as deacon, and still later made a bishop, that he might be prepared

* See Agathias III. 12, p. 165, ed. Niebuhr.
† See Procop. de bello Gothico, l. IV. c. 3.   ‡ Διβοῦς.

to preach the gospel to his countrymen and to the Arabians. According to the representation of Philostorgius, in the extracts made by Photius, we should conceive, it is true, no other country to be meant here than Arabia. But the name *Diu* reminds us rather of East India proper, and, in particular, of the place by this name near the entrance of the Persian Gulf; the situation of which harmonizes, moreover, with Theophilus' journey from Arabia. Theophilus, it is said, went from Arabia to Diu, his native land; and from thence visited the other countries of India. Here he found still existing the Christianity which had been already planted in that region at an earlier period.* Perfectly certain and distinct accounts of the diffusion of Christianity in India we meet with first in Cosmas, who, on account of his travels in India, received the name *Indicopleustes*.† He found Christians in three different places in India; first, on the island *Taprobane*, called by the inhabitants Sieledibu (the present Ceylon). Here he found a church, which had been planted by Persian merchants residing on the spot, and which was presided over by a presbyter who had been ordained in Persia. This island carried on a brisk commerce with Persia and Ethiopia. Maritime commerce was the channel by which Christianity had reached this spot from Persia. Again, he met with Christians, and an ordained clergy, at *Male*, "where the pepper grows" (perhaps the present Malabar); next at Calliana (perhaps Calcutta), where there was a Persian bishop.‡ From the accounts of Cosmas it is by no means to be gathered that Christianity had spread among the native population of these countries: it is only clear that commercial colonies of the Persians here practised the rites of Christian worship. These

---

* When the Arian Philostorgius says the inhabitants of this country needed no correction of their doctrine, *i. e.* their doctrine did not at all coincide with the Nicene creed,—they had preserved the ἑτεροούσιον⁴ unaltered from the beginning, this can only be understood to mean that they had the older, more simple form of church doctrine, the subordination system, before it had undergone any further change by the dialectic process, — that form which would have satisfied the Arians. See Philostorg. III. 14.

. † He had made these journeys first as a merchant, and afterwards communicated the geographical and ethnographical facts which he had collected in the τοπογραφία χριστιανική, which he wrote when a monk, in the year 585, published by Montfaucon in the collectio nova patrum et scriptorum Græc. T. II.

‡ See Cosmas. I. III. p. 178, in Montfaucon, and l. XI. p. 336.

Persian Christians are the progenitors of the Christian colonies still existing on the coast of Malabar.*

We observed, it is true, that, perhaps already in the previous period, isolated attempts had been made to disseminate Christianity even in those parts of *Arabia* which were not subject to the Roman dominion; but concerning the success and issue of those attempts we have no accurate information. The nomadic life, which prevailed over the largest portion of Arabia, ever presented a powerful hindrance to the spread of Christianity. For it is certain that Christianity could strike its root deeply and firmly only where it entered as a forming power into the whole life of the people. The extensive commercial intercourse between a part of Arabia and the Roman empire induced the emperor Constantine to send an embassy, with numerous presents, to one of the powerful Arabian chiefs, the king of the ancient and mighty nation of the *Hamyares* (Homerites), or Sabæans, in Yemen, Arabia Felix. He was at pains to select for this mission the above-mentioned Theophilus of Diu, who, by reason of the old commercial connections between his country and Arabia, and perhaps of his descent from some ancient Arabian colony,† might claim affinity with the race with whose language he was acquainted. This Theophilus, it is said, obtained permission from the Arabian chieftain to found a church, at the emperor's expense, in which Christian worship might be held for the benefit of the Roman merchants. The labours of Theophilus were attended with the happiest effects. He converted the prince of the country, who founded, at his own cost, three churches: one in the principal town of the nation, which was called *Zaphar*; another at the Roman port and commercial depot, *Aden*; and the third at *Hormuz*, the Persian place of trade on the Persian Gulf.‡ Theophilus, from the first, encountered the fiercest

---

* The deciphering of the ancient documents of these Christians will perhaps throw more light on the subject of the spread of Christianity in India. See Tychsen's Dissertation de inscriptionibus Indicis in the Commentationes Soc. Reg. Gotting. recentiores, T. V.

† See Arabia in Ritter's Geography; and, in particular, b. II. p. 292; and Hartmann's Aufklärungen über Asien, b. II. s. 125, u. d. f.

‡ See Philostorg. II. s. 6; III. s. 4. As Theophilus was an Arian, we cannot think it strange that the other Greek writers of church history, who belonged to the orthodox party, make no mention of these meritorious labours of an Arian.

opposition from the Jews, whose influence in this country was great. The same party succeeded afterwards to supplant the Christian communities which had been able to maintain themselves here. See below.

Monks who lived in the deserts bordering on Arabia, and who came in contact with the wandering hordes of nomadic Arabians, acquired the respect and confidence of these rude men, and could take advantage of it to preach the gospel to them. Eusebius of Cæsarea relates that, in his time, Christian churches were planted in the deserts of the Saracens.* Bands of Saracens came, with their wives and children, to the monk Hilarion, and besought his blessing. He availed himself of these opportunities of exhorting them to the worship of the true God, and to faith in Christ.† Still later, about the year 372, it happened that a Saracenian queen, Mavia or Mauvia, who was at war with the Romans, heard much of a Saracenian monk in the neighbouring desert, by the name of *Moses*. She made it one of the conditions of peace that this Moses should be given to her people as their bishop, which was granted.‡

In the first half of the fifth century Simeon the Syrian monk (and Stylite), who spent several years standing on a pillar thirty-six ells in height, by this extraordinary spectacle, and the complete subjection which he seemed to exercise over his body, drew upon himself, as might have been expected, the attention of the nomadic Saracens. They looked upon him as a super-earthly being, and placed great confidence in blessings which they obtained from him, as well as in his prayers. Hundreds and thousands came to him and were moved by his exhortations to receive baptism. Theodoretus relates this as an eye-witness.§

Among the examples of conversion most deserving of notice belongs the following :—The chief of a Saracenic tribe, whose name, according to the Greeks, was *Ashebethos*, was, at the beginning of the fifth century, attached to the service of the Persian empire ; and the business assigned to him was to

---

* Commentar. in Jesaiam, in Montfaucon's collectio nova patrum, T. II. f. 521. Ἐκκλησίων Χριστοῦ καὶ ἐν ταῖς ἐρήμοις τῶν Σαρακήνων, καθ' ἡμᾶς αὐτοὺς ἱδρυμίνων.

† See Hieronymi vita Hilarionis, T. IV. ed. Martianay, p. II. f. 82.

‡ Socrat. IV. 36. Sozom. VI. 38. Rufin. II. 6. Theodoret. IV. 23.

§ Hist. religios. c. 26, T. III. p. 1274.

watch over the boundaries. Now, the Christians in the Persian empire were at this time suffering persecution, and the Saracenic commander was ordered to seize and confine every Christian fugitive who attempted to pass the limits. But he was touched with pity towards them, and allowed them to pass free. Thus having brought persecution on himself, he fled to the Romans. He became head of an Arabian tribe in alliance with the latter. Some time afterwards, believing himself indebted for the cure of his son, *Terebon*, to the prayer of the venerable monk Euthymius, he caused himself and his son to be baptized by the latter; and many of his tribe followed his example. He encamped in the neighbourhood of Euthymius, and many other Saracens also pitched their tents near by. Euthymius had great influence over their minds. Finally, Terebon, having now arrived at mature age, became the chief of his tribe, and Ashebethos, who had taken the baptismal name of Peter, was made bishop of the several Saracenic bands. He was called the first Saracenic camp-bishop* in Palestine.† Somewhat later, in the beginning of the *sixth* century, occurred the conversion of a Saracenic skeikh (φύλαρχος), *Almundar;* perhaps not without some connection with the facts above related.‡

We pass from Asia to Africa. The most important event in the present period, connected with the conversion of this quarter of the world, was the founding of the Christian church among the Abyssinians, in a population among whom it has preserved itself down to the present time as the dominant religion, amidst surrounding Pagan and Mahommedan tribes, and which is perhaps destined to be an instrument in the hands of Providence for the benefit of this entire quarter of the world. In this case, also, the great work proceeded from an inconsiderable beginning. A learned Greek of Tyre, named Meropius, had, in the reign of the emperor Constantine, undertaken a voyage of scientific discovery. Already on the point of returning, he landed on the coast of Ethiopia or Abyssinia, to procure fresh water, where he was attacked, robbed, and himself and crew murdered, by the warlike

---

* 'Επίσκοπος τῶν παρεμβολῶν.

† See vita Euthymii in Cotelerii monumenta ecclesiæ Græcæ, T. II. c. 1819, 38, 39.

‡ See Theodoret. lector. l. II. fol. 564, ed. Mogunt. 1679.

natives, who were at that time in a state of hostility with the Roman empire. Two young men, his companions, Frumentius and Ædesius, alone were spared, out of pity for their tender age. These two youths were taken into the service of the prince of the tribe, and made themselves beloved. Ædesius became his cup-bearer; Frumentius, who was distinguished for intelligence and sagacity, was appointed his secretary and accountant. After the death of the prince, the education of *Æizanes*, the young heir, was intrusted to them; and Frumentius obtained great influence as administrator of the government. He made use of this influence already in behalf of Christianity. He sought the acquaintance of the Roman merchants visiting those parts, who were Christians; assisted them in founding a church, and united with them in the Christian worship of God. Finally, they obtained liberty to return home to their country. Ædesius repaired to Tyre, where he was made a presbyter. Here Rufinus became acquainted with him, and learned all the particulars of the story from his own mouth.* But Frumentius felt himself called to a higher work. He felt bound to see to it that the people with whom he had spent the greater part of his youth, and from whom he had received so many favours, should be made to share in the highest blessing of mankind. He travelled, therefore, to Alexandria, where the great Athanasius had recently been made bishop (A.D. 326). Athanasius entered at once with ready sympathy into the plan of Frumentius. But he found, very justly, that no one could be a more suitable agent for the prosecution of this work than Frumentius himself; and he consecrated him bishop of Auxuma (Axum), the chief city of the Abyssinians, and a famous commercial town. Frumentius returned back to this place, and laboured there with great success. Subsequently Theophilus of Arabia, who has already been mentioned, visited the same country and repaired to the principal town, Auxuma (Axum). Theophilus being an Arian, and Frumentius, the friend of Athanasius, professing in all probability the doctrines of the council of Nice, it is possible a dispute may have arisen in their announcement here of their respective doctrines, which would necessarily be attended with unfavourable effects on the nascent church; but perhaps,

* Rufin. hist. eccles. I. c. 9.

too, Frumentius, who had not received a theological education, did not enter so deeply into theological questions. Still the emperor Constantius considered it necessary to persecute the disciples of the hated Athanasius, even in these remote regions. After Athanasius had been banished from Alexandria, in the year 356, Constantius required the princes of the Abyssinian people to send Frumentius to Alexandria, in order that the Arian bishop Georgius, who had been set up in place of Athanasius, might inquire into his orthodoxy, and into the regularity of his ordination.*

The fate of the Christian church among the Homerites in Arabia Felix afforded an opportunity for the Abyssinians, under the reigns of the emperors Justin and Justinian, to show their zeal in behalf of the cause of the Christians. The prince of that Arabian population, Dunaan, or Dsunovas, was a zealous adherent of Judaism ; and, under pretext of avenging the oppressions which his fellow-believers were obliged to suffer in the Roman empire, he caused the Christian merchants who came from that quarter and visited Arabia for the purposes of trade, or passed through the country to Abyssinia, to be murdered.   Elesbaan,† the Christian king of Abyssinia, made

* See the letter of Constantius, in the Apologia Athanasii ad Constantium, s. 31.   The princes of the Abyssinians are here called Αιζανας and Σαζανας.   A Greek inscription, which proceeded from the former of these while he was still a pagan (he is here called 'Αειζανας), has recently been discovered by the English in Abyssinia, and is given in Salt's Voyage to Abyssinia, p. 411.   In this inscription, 'Αειζανας alone is called *king*.   Σαιαζανας, on the other hand, together with Δηφας, is named his brother.   But the fact may have been, that, when Constantius wrote his letter, the first of these had become co-regent.   It is singular, however, that Constantius expresses himself as if Frumentius had then visited Auxuma for the first time.   This might lead us to infer that there is some chronological inaccuracy in the narrative of Rufinus ; as he places the ordination of Frumentius in the beginning of the episcopal presidency of Athanasius.

† Theophanes is certainly mistaken when, at the year 524, he relates that these events first led the Jewish king of Ethiopia to embrace Christianity, and to obtain a bishop from the emperor Justinian.   Nor have we any good reason to presume, on the authority of this historian, that Christianity in Abyssinia had become extinct again, and was restored in consequence of these events.   Much rather, the zeal of the Abyssinian monarch in the cause of the Christians, together with his own commercial interests and his connection with the Roman empire, was a sufficient reason why he should espouse the cause of the persecuted Christians in the neighbouring country.   Nor would it be difficult to show

this a cause for declaring war on the Arabian prince. He, conquered Dsunovas, deprived him of the government, and set up a Christian, by the name of Abraham, as king in his stead. But at the death of the latter, which happened soon after, Dsunovas again made himself master of the throne; and it was a natural consequence of what he had suffered, that he now became a fiercer and more cruel persecutor than he was before. Against the native Christians he raged with fire and sword. Many died as martyrs, especially in a town called Negran, inhabited for the most part by Christians. Upon this, Elesbaan interfered once more, under the reign of the emperor Justinian, who stimulated him to the undertaking. He made a second expedition to Arabia Felix, and was again victorious. Dsunovas lost his life in this war; the Abyssinian prince put an end to the ancient, independent empire of the Homerites, and established a new government favourable to the Christians.[*]

The Cosmas already mentioned, who composed his description of the earth in the time of the emperor Justinian, was aware that Christian churches, bishops, and monks, were then existing in Homeria, and the country of the Auxumites, or Ethiopia.[†] We learn also from him that many Christians, and persons of the clerical order, resided in the island of Socotora (νῆσος Διοσκορίδους). The latter had been ordained in Persia, and it seems that Christianity had been conveyed there by means of the commercial connections with Persia.[‡]

We now return to *Europe*. But we shall reserve many of the most important facts of this section—the greatest part of that which relates to the diffusion of Christianity and the

that it was the effort to ascribe great effects to the zeal of the emperor Justinian in behalf of the Christian church which led to this false report; as it was moreover ignorance respecting the precise time of the Abyssinian conversions which led to the natural effort at explaining what was unknown by the method of combination. Procopius, a contemporary, calls the Ethiopian king, whose name with him is Ἑλλισθιαιος, a zealous Christian, de bello Pers. l. I. c. 20.

[*] F. Walch has undertaken to collect and compare all the conflicting oriental and Grecian notices of these events—respecting which every particular fact cannot be certainly determined—in the two dissertations on this subject, in the 4th volume of the novi commentarii soc. reg. Gotting. 1774.

[†] L. III. f. 179, l. c.   [‡] See l. c.

planting of the Christian church among the populations of *German* descent, who established themselves, after the migration of the nations, on the ruins of the Roman empire—to the following period, so as not to separate what strictly belongs together, and that we may be enabled to survey, at a single glance, the whole missionary work among these populations. We shall notice here, therefore, only those matters which may be separately considered, and which may most easily be connected with the history of the church in the Roman empire.

Christianity had long since extended itself, as we remarked already in the previous period, among the Britons, the ancient inhabitants of England; while as yet the natives of Scotland and Ireland, the Picts and Scots, had heard nothing of the gospel. The incursions of these tribes into the province of the Britons often spread terror and devastation; and in these forages they frequently carried away with them, as slaves, large numbers of prisoners.

It was by an altogether peculiar combination of circumstances that, in the first half of the fifth century, the man was trained and prepared for his work who was the means of first planting the Christian church in Ireland. This was Patricius (or, as he was called in his native country, *Succath*). The place of his birth was *Bonnaven*, which lay between the Scottish towns Dumbarton and Glasgow, and was then reckoned to the province of Britain. This village, in memory of Patricius, received the name of Kil-Patrick, or Kirk-Patrick.* His father, a deacon in the village church, gave him a careful education. He was instructed, indeed, in the doctrines of Christianity; but he did not come to know what he possessed in this knowledge until the experience of great trials brought him to the consciousness of it. At the age of sixteen he, with many others of his countrymen, was carried off by Scottish pirates to the northern part of the island *Hibernia* (Ireland). He was sold to a chieftain of the people, who made him the overseer of his flocks. This employment compelled him to spend much time in the open air; and solitude became pleasant to him. Abandoned of al.

---

* The collection of old traditions in User. Britannicarum ecclesiarum antiquitates, f. 429.

human aid, he found protection, help, and solace in God, and found his chief delight in prayer and pious meditation. He speaks of all this himself, in his confessions * ' I was sixteen years old, and I knew not the true God; but, in a strange land, the Lord brought me to the sense of my unbelief, so that, although late, I minded me of my sins, and turned with my whole heart to the Lord my God; who looked down on my lowliness, had pity on my youth and my ignorance, who preserved me ere I knew him, and who protected and comforted me, as a father does his son, ere I knew how to distinguish between good and evil."

He had spent six years in this bondage, when twice in dreams he thought he heard a voice bidding him fly in a certain direction to the sea-coast, where he would find a ship ready to take him, and convey him back to his country. He obeyed; and, after various remarkable experiences of a guiding Providence, he found his way back to his friends.

Ten years afterwards he was a second time taken captive by Scottish freebooters, and conveyed to Gaul, where, by means of Christian merchants, he obtained his freedom. He then returned back to his country, and his friends were greatly rejoiced to have him once more among them. He might now have lived quietly with his friends; but he felt within him an irrepressible desire to carry the blessing of the gospel to those pagans with whom he had spent a great part of his youth. He thought he was called upon, by nightly visions, to visit Ireland, and there consecrate his life to Him who had given his own life for his ransom. The remonstrances and entreaties of kindred and friends could not prevent him from obeying this call. " It was not in my own power," says Patricius, " but it was God who conquered in me, and withstood them all." It seems that he now betook himself first to France,† for the purpose of fitting himself still better for his work in the society of pious monks and clergymen.

* This work bears in its simple, rude style, an impress that corresponds entirely to Patricius' stage of culture. There are to be found in it none of the traditions which perhaps proceeded only from English monks —nothing wonderful, except what may be very easily explained on pyschological principles. All this vouches for the authenticity of the piece.

† His biographer, Jocelin, a writer in the 12th century, makes his journey to France follow after his return to Ireland; and this harmonizes,

As the old legends relate, he next made a journey to Rome, in order to receive full powers and consecration to his office from the Roman bishop. The news of the death of the arch-deacon Palladius,[*] who had been sent from Rome as a missionary to Ireland, but had accomplished very little on account of his ignorance of the language, having just arrived there (in the year 432), the Roman bishop, Sixtus III., did not hesitate to appoint Patrick in his place. We cannot, it is true, pronounce this tradition at once to be false; yet we shall be struck with many difficulties upon examining it. If Patrick came to Ireland as a deputy from Rome, it might naturally be expected that in the Irish church a certain sense of dependence would always have been preserved towards the mother church at Rome. But we find, on the contrary, in the Irish church afterwards, a spirit of church freedom similar to that shown by the ancient British church, which struggled against the yoke of Roman ordinances. We find subsequently among the Irish a much greater agreement with the ancient British than with Roman ecclesiastical usages. This goes to prove that the origin of this church was independent of Rome, and must be traced solely to the people of Britain. Moreover, Patrick could not have held it so necessary as this tradition supposes he did, either as a Briton or according to the

moreover, with the confessions of Patrick; although it is possible that, immediately after his release, since this took place in France itself, he entered on his travels to visit the more celebrated cloisters of this country. That he maintained an intimate correspondence with the pious men of southern France may be gathered from his confessions, where he says that he would be glad to visit once more, not only his native country, but also Gaul: Eram usque Gallias, visitare fratres, et ut viderem faciem sanctorum Domini mei.

[*] From the notices of Prosper Aquitanicus, it appears that the bishop Cœlestinus of Rome had ordained Palladius as a bishop for the Scots, by whom perhaps may have been intended the Irish; and, according to these accounts, he must have accomplished a good deal. But Prosper may perhaps have received at his distance from Rome exaggerated stories. He says in his Chronicle, under the year 431, Ad Scotos *in Christum credentes* ordinatus a Papa Cœlestino Palladius, et primus episcopus mittitur; and in the liber contra Collatorem, c. 21, s. 2, Ordinato Scotis episcopo, fecit etiam barbaram (insulam) Christianam. The tradition of the mission of Palladius to Ireland seems, according to the citations of Jocelin, to have been preserved in that country for a long period; but also the tradition that the conversion of the nation was not due to his labours, but was reserved for those of Patrick

principles of the Gallic church, to obtain first from the Roman bishop full powers and consecration for such a work.
Again, no indication of his connection with the Roman
church is to be found in his confession; rather everything
seems to favour the supposition that he was ordained bishop
in Britain itself, and in his forty-fifth year.* And it may be
easily explained how the tendency of later monks to trace
the founding of new churches to Rome, might, among so
many other fabulous legends, give rise also to this.

Arrived in Ireland, he possessed a great advantage in prosecuting his work from his knowledge of the customs and the
language of the country. He assembled around him in the
open fields, at the beat of a drum, a concourse of people; where
he related to them the story of Christ, which relation manifested its divine power on their rude minds. It is true the
people were excited against him by those powerful priests
the Druids; but he did not allow himself to be frightened on
this account. As the chief men had it in their power to do
him the most injury while they remained under the dominion
of these Druids, he laboured especially to gain access to them.
Perhaps numbers were already prepared for the faith in the
gospel, like that Cormac, an Irish prince, belonging to the
last times of the fourth century, who, after having abdicated
his government and given himself up to silent reflection and
religious contemplation in solitude, is said to have come to the
conviction of the vanity of the Druidical doctrines concerning
the gods.†

A proof of the power exercised by Patrick over the youthful

---

* Patrick intimates in his confession, c. 3, that some respectable clergymen in Britain opposed his consecration to the episcopal office. He intimates that his enemies turned against him the confession of a sin, committed thirty years before, which confession he had made before he was
chosen deacon. And from what follows it is quite evident that this has
reference to something he had done when a boy of *fifteen*. It would
follow from this then that he was ordained bishop in his forty-fifth year,
and so probably commenced his labours in Ireland in the same year of
his life. Now if we could also determine with accuracy the year of his
birth, we might fix precisely the year of his episcopal ordination and his
missionary journey. But this is a point with regard to which nothing
can be considered as settled; the chronological data of the traditions,
both in Usher and in Jocelin, being, to say the least, extremely uncertain.

† See the History of Ireland. by F. Warner, Vol. I. p. 247.

mind is seen in the way in which he is said to have drawn to him those who were to be his successors in the guidance of the Irish church. He came into the house of a person of rank, taught there, and baptized the family. The young son of the house was so attracted by the impression of the looks and words of Patrick, that he could never afterwards be separated from him. He followed him and kept close to him amid all his dangers and sufferings. Patrick is said to have named him Benignus, on account of his kindly nature. He is said also to have converted one of the chief bards, called Dubrach Mac Valubair; and the minstrel, who had been used to rehearse the Druidical doctrine of the gods, now composed songs in praise of Christianity*—a circumstance which would have no inconsiderable influence on a people naturally inclined to poetry and music.

The lands which he received as presents from converted chieftains Patrick applied to the founding of cloisters, having contracted in France a predilection for the monastic life. The cloisters were designed to serve as nursing schools for teachers of the people, and from them was to proceed the civilization of the country. Although Patrick was qualified himself to impart but little scientific instruction to his monks, yet he infused into them the love of learning, which impelled them subsequently to seek for more information, and for books, in Britain and France. Yet he gave them the first means of all culture, in inventing an alphabet for the Irish language.† He had much to bear continually from the opposition of the pagan chiefs. He was once, with his attendants, fallen upon by one of these chiefs, robbed, and detained fourteen days in captivity.‡ Often he sought to purchase quiet for himself and his friends by presents. And it was not with Irish pagans alone that he had to contend. A piratical British chieftain, named Corotic, from the district of Wallia (Wales), fell upon a number who had been recently baptized by Patrick, carried off a part of them captives, and sold them as slaves to heathen Picts and Scots. To this man, who professed out-

* Jocelin, c. V. s. 38.   Mensis Mart. d. 17.
† Of the zeal for the monastic life which he inspired, Patrick speaks himself in his confessions: Filii Scotorum et filiæ regulorum monachi et virgines Christi esse videntur. Opuscula Patricii, ed. J. Waræi, pag. 16.
‡ L. c. Waræus, p. 20.

wardly to be a Christian, Patrick wrote an emphatically threatening letter, which has been preserved, and excommunicated him from the church. Glad as he would have been to visit his old friends in Britain and France, yet he could not think it right to leave the new church. "I pray God," he said, after a long residence among this people, "that he would grant me perseverance to enable me to approve myself a faithful witness, for the sake of my God, to the end. And if I have ever laboured to accomplish anything good for the sake of my God, whom I love, may He grant that, with those converts and captives of mine, I may pour out my blood for his name!"

The *Goths* belonging to the stocks of *Germanic* descent, first had opportunity of coming to the knowledge of Christianity by means of their wars with the Roman empire, probably as early as the second half of the preceding period. During those incursions which, in the time of the emperor Valerian, they made into Cappadocia and the bordering countries, they are said to have carried away captive many Christians, and, among the rest, persons of the clerical order. These remained with the Goths, propagated themselves among them, and laboured for the diffusion of Christianity.[*] Accordingly we find already, among the bishops who subscribed their names to the decisions of the Nicene council, a certain *Theophilus*, who is called bishop of the Goths.[†]

From one of these Christian families of Roman origin, which had thus continued to propagate itself among the Goths, *Ulphilas*, who is entitled to the credit of having done most for the spread of Christianity and Christian culture among the Goths, is said to have sprung.[‡] Ulphilas did the Goths important service in their negotiations with the Roman emperors, a business for which he was eminently fitted on account of his relationship with both nations. He thus won their love and

---

[*] Philostorg. II. 5.

[†] Socrat. hist. eccles. l. II. c. 41.

[‡] As Philostorgius, himself a Cappadocian, distinctly mentions the village to which the family of Ulphilas originally belonged, we have the less right to call in question his statement. The manifestly German name Wolf, Wölfel, furnishes no proof to the contrary; for their residence among the Goths might unquestionably have induced the members of this family to give themselves German names. Moreover, Basil of Cæsarea (ep. 165) says that the Goths received the first seeds of Christianity from Cappadocia.

confidence, of which he could avail himself to promote the spread of Christianity.   He was consecrated bishop of the Goths, and secured the means for a permanent propagation of Christianity among them, particularly by inventing an alpha-bet for them, and by translating the holy scriptures into their language.   He is said, however, to have omitted in this trans-lation the books of the Kings, to which the books of Samuel, also, were then reckoned, that nothing might be presented which was calculated to foster the warlike spirit of the Goths.*

Certain as these facts are in general, yet it is difficult to fix with precision the time when Ulphilas first made his appear-ance as a teacher amongst his people, and when he was em-ployed in the negotiations with the Roman empire; for on these points there are many contradictory statements in the historians of the church.†   These, however, admit of being

---

* Philostorg. II. 5.

† According to Philostorgius, Ulphilas was employed in negotiations with the emperor Constantine, who had a high respect for him, and was used to call him the *Moses* of his time.   Constantine permitted the Goths to settle down in the district of Mœsia.   At this time Ulphilas was con-secrated bishop of the Goths by Eusebius of Nicomedia.   According to Socrates, ii. 41, Ulphilas subscribed, in the first place, the Arian creed, drawn up at Constantinople, in the year 360, under the emperor Constan-tius.   Before this he was an adherent of the Nicene doctrine; for he followed the teaching of the Gothic bishop Theophilus, who had been one of the signers of the Nicene creed.   Next, the same church historian re-lates, iv. 33, that the assistance and support which the emperor Valens afforded to that portion of the Goths to which Ulphilas belonged, induced many of them at that time to embrace Christianity, but at the same time also to espouse the Arian doctrine then prevailing in the Roman empire. He places the origin of Ulphilas' version of the Scriptures as late as the time just referred to. Sozomen (IV. 24 and VI. 37) agrees in the main with Socrates, and only adds that Ulphilas was at first a follower of the doc-trines of the Nicene council; that, in the time of the emperor Constan-tius, he had, indeed, imprudently become intimate with certain bishops of the Roman empire who professed Arianism, yet continued to maintain his fellowship with the orthodox bishops according to the Nicene council. But, having come to Constantinople on occasion of certain negotiations with the emperor Valens, he was moved by the persuasions of the domi-nant Arian bishops, and by their promises to give him their support with the emperor, to embrace Arianism.   Theodoretus, IV. 37, reports that the Goths were devoted to the true faith until the time of the emperor Valens; but that, under this emperor, the Arian dominant bishop at court, Eudoxius, represented to them that agreement in religious doc-trine would render the union between them and the Romans more secure. But he was able to effect nothing with them until he applied himself to

reconciled with each other by supposing that Ulphilas first began his labours, as a bishop among the Goths, in the time of Constantine ; and that he continued to prosecute them until near the close of the reign of the emperor Valens ; that he repeatedly conducted the negotiations between the Goths and the Roman empire, and in this way ever rose higher in the confidence of the former.

Athanasius, in a work which he wrote while a deacon, previous to the time of the Nicene council, speaks of the diffusion of Christianity among the Goths, and alludes to the fact that the ameliorating influence of this religion had already begun to manifest itself on that people.[*] He says, with regard to the effects of Christianity among these rude tribes, " Who is

their influential bishop, Ulphilas, and succeeded, by persuasive speeches and by money, to win him over. He so represented the matter as if the dispute between the two parties related only to unimportant differences, and was made so important merely through their obstinacy and love of dispute.

If we compare together these accounts, we find that Philostorgius departs from all the other church historians in placing the whole period of Ulphilas' labours within the reign of the emperor Constantine, and making no mention whatever of the negotiations in the time of Valens, which were the most important. But as the accounts of the others presuppose also that the Goths had long been Christians ; as Socrates and Sozomen assume that Ulphilas was already bishop in the reign of Constantius, the account of Philostorgius may certainly be brought into agreement with these reports. If it may only be supposed—against which supposition there is no reasonable ground of objection—that Ulphilas lived to a very old age, it may be assumed that he began his labours as a bishop among the Goths as early as the time of Constantine ; for it is very possible, certainly, that he may have exercised the functions of the episcopal office through a period of *fifty* years.

In the next place, it must be remarked that Philostorgius, being an Arian, had an interest in making it appear that Ulphilas was an Arian from the first ; while, on the other hand, the other church historians, as opponents of Arianism, were interested to represent the fact as if Ulphilas was in the first place orthodox, and to trace his defection from the orthodox doctrines to outward influences and causes, and hence to fix the time of this defection under the reign of an emperor who was zealously devoted to Arianism. It is very possible that Ulphilas had received the simple form of the doctrine of Christ's divinity from the older Roman church ; that in the beginning he held simply to this, without taking any part in the dialectic doctrinal controversies, until, by coming in contact, in various ways, with the Arian bishops, he was led to embrace the Arian system.

[*] Athanas. de incarnatione verbi, s. 51 et 52.

it that has wrought this; that has united in the bonds of peace those who once hated one another;—who else than the beloved Son of the Father, the common Saviour of all, Jesus Christ, who, through love to us, suffered everything for our salvation? For already of old the *peace* that should go out from him had been the subject of prophecy, since the holy scriptures say, Isa. ii. 4, ' Then they shall beat their swords into plough-shares, and their spears into pruning-hooks; nation shall not lift up sword against nation, neither shall they learn war any more.' And this is nothing incredible; since even now the barbarians, to whom savagery of manners is a nature so long as they worship dumb idols, rage against each other, and cannot remain one moment without the sword; but, when they hear the doctrine of Christ, immediately they turn away from war to agriculture; instead of arming their hands with the sword, they lift them up in prayer; and, in a word, from henceforth, instead of carrying on war with each other, arm themselves against Satan, striving to conquer him by the bravery of the soul. And the wonder is, that even they despise death, and become martyrs, for the sake of Christ."

The division of the Goths among whom Ulphilas appeared were the Thervingians, under king Fritiger—the West Goths; and these were at war with the Greuthingians, whose king was Athanarich—the East Goths.* When, therefore, Ulphilas laboured to diffuse Christianity also among the Greuthingians, his efforts met with opposition; Christianity was persecuted by them, and many died as martyrs.† The martyrs certainly contributed greatly among the Goths also to the spread of the gospel.‡

The historian Eunapius relates that the Goths, in the time of the emperor Valens, while they contrived to maintain in

---

* See the passages above cited from Socrates and Sozomen, and Ammian. Marcellin. XXXI. 4, &c.

† It is interesting to observe that Socrates, IV. 33, recognised even among the Goths, although they were Arians, the genuine spirit of martyrdom. For he says, although the barbarians erred through their simplicity, yet they despised the earthly life for the sake of the faith in Christ: Ἁπλότητι τὸν χριστιανισμὸν δεξάμενοι, ὑπὲρ τῆς εἰς Χριστὸν πίστεως τῆς ἐνταῦθα ζωῆς κατεφρόνησαν.

‡ Comp. Basil. Cæsareens. ep. 155, 164, 165, in which letters, of about the year 374, mention is made of the martyrs among the Goths. Basil procured relics of the martyrs who died there.

great secrecy the ancient rites of their national religion, often assumed the outward show of Christianity, and carried about with them pretended bishops in their waggons, for the purpose of gaining thereby the favour and confidence of the Byzantine court; which they could the more easily deceive, as they had among them people who wore the monkish dress, and whom they pretended to call monks, because they understood in what high esteem this class of men stood among the Christians.* It is true the mere assertion of this violent enemy of the Christians is no sufficient authority for a fact of this sort. At all events, he expresses himself in too general terms. Yet very possibly the Goths were shrewd enough to discern that in this way they could most easily deceive the Byzantine court; and it may be that, in some particular cases, they resorted to this means of deception; although, in the main, there can be no question with regard to the reality of the conversion of the Goths to Christianity.

The great Chrysostom, while patriarch of Constantinople, and during his exile after he was expelled from Constantinople, laboured earnestly for the establishment of missions among the Goths. He set apart a particular church at Constantinople for the religious worship of the Goths; where the Bible was read in the Gothic translation, and discourses were preached by Gothic clergymen in the language of their country. He adopted the wise plan of here training up missionaries for the people from among the people themselves. On a certain Sunday in the year 398 or 399, after causing divine worship to be celebrated, the Bible to be read, and a discourse to be preached, by Gothic ecclesiastics, in the Gothic tongue, to the great surprise, no doubt, of the refined Byzantians in the assembly, who looked down upon the Goths as barbarians, he took advantage of this remarkable scene to point out to them in the example before their own eyes the transforming and plastic power of Christianity over the entire

---

* See Eunapii Excerpta, in Maii scriptorum veterum nova collectio, T. II. Romæ, 1827, pp. 277, 278. ῏Ην δὲ καὶ τῶν καλουμένων μονάχων παρ' αὐτοῖς, γίνος κατὰ μίμησιν τῶν παρὰ τοῖς πολεμίοις ἐπιτετηδευμένων, οὐδὲν ἐχουσῆς τῆς μιμησέως πραγματῶδες καὶ δύσκολον, ἀλλ' ἐξηρκεῖ φαία ἱμάτια συροῦσι χιτῶνια, πονήροις τε εἶναι καὶ πιτινίσθαι, which the fierce enemy of Christian monasticism could not deny himself the gratification of adding.

human nature, and to enlist their sympathies in the cause of the mission. He delivered a discourse, which has come down to us, full of a divine eloquence, on the might of the gospel, and the plan of God in the education of mankind.*   Among other things he remarks, quoting the passage in Isa. lxv. 25, " ' The wolf and the lamb shall feed together, and the lion shall eat straw like the bullock.'   The prophet is not speaking here of lions and lambs, but predicting to us that, subdued by the power of the divine doctrine, the brutal sense of rude men should be transformed to such gentleness of spirit, that they should unite together in one and the same community with the mildest. And this have you witnessed today—the most savage race of men standing together with the lambs of the church—one pasture, one fold for all—one table set before all."   Which may refer either to the common participation in the sacred word, which had been presented first in the Gothic and then in the Greek language, or to the common participation in the communion.

The Gothic clergy began already to busy themselves with the study of the Bible.   The learned Jerome was surprised, while residing at Bethlehem (in 403), by receiving a letter from two Goths, Sunnia and Fretela, making inquiries about several discrepancies which they had observed between the vulgar Latin and the Alexandrian version of the Psalms ; and Jerome begins his answer † in the following words: " Who would have believed that the barbarian tongue of the Goths would inquire respecting the pure sense of the Hebrew original ; and that, while the Greeks were sleeping, or rather disputing with each other " (according to another reading— " despising it "), " Germany itself would be investigating the divine word?"‡   Jerome could say that the red and yellow haired Goths carried the church about with them in tents ; and perhaps, for this reason, battled with equal fortune against the Romans, because they trusted in the same religion.§

* The 8th Homily, among those first published by Montfaucon, tom. XII. opp. Chrysostom.

† Ep. 106, in the edition of Vallarsi ; in other editions. ep. 98.

‡ Quis hoc crederet, ut barbara Getarum lingua Hebraicam quæreret veritatem ; et dormitantibus, immo contendentibus (or contemnentibus) Græcis, ipsa Germania Spiritus Sancti eloquia scrutaretur ?

§ Ep. 107 ad Letam, s. 2.   Getarum rutilus et flavus exercitus ecclesiarum circumfert tentoria.

The influence of Christianity was, perhaps, seen also in those who as yet made no profession of it, when Alaric, the leader of the West-Gothic army, captured Rome, and spread consternation all around. The churches of St. Peter and St. Paul, and the chapels of the martyrs, became the universal places of refuge; and they remained with all their treasures, and all the men who had fled to them, respected and spared amid all the havoc of devastation. Not a man of the barbarians touched these spots; nay, they conveyed thither themselves many unhappy individuals who had excited their pity, as to a place of safety. Pagans, who had ascribed to Christianity all the calamities of the period, and Christians, united here in giving thanks to God. "He who does not see," exclaims Augustin, speaking of this fact,* "that the thanks for this are due to the name of Christ, to the Christian period, must be blind; he who does see it, and praises not God, is an ingrate; he who would hinder them that praise God is a madman. Far be it from any intelligent man to ascribe this to the rudeness of barbarians. He bridled and tempered the savage nature of the barbarians in a miraculous manner who had said long before, ' Then will I visit their transgression with the rod, and their iniquity with stripes. Nevertheless, my lovingkindness will I not utterly take from them.' "—Ps. lxxxix. 32, 33.

* De civitate Dei, l. I. c. 7.

SECTION SECOND.

HISTORY OF THE CHURCH CONSTITUTION. CHURCH DISCIPLINE. SCHISMS OF THE CHURCH.

I. History of the Church Constitution.

1. *Relation of Church to State.*

In the relation of the church to the state there occurred, with the commencement of this period, a most important change, the consequences of which extended to all parts of the church constitution, and which had an influence in various ways on the whole course and shaping of the church development. In the preceding period the church stood to the state in the relation of an independent, self-included whole, and was to the state, for the most part, an object of hostility. At all events, the utmost which she could expect from the state was bare *toleration*. The important consequence of this was, that the church was left *free* to develop itself outwardly from its own inward principle ; that no foreign might could introduce its disturbing influence ; and that the church itself could not be exposed to the temptation of employing an alien power for the prosecution of its ends, and of thus entering into a province that did not belong to it. But, on the other hand, the church had no immediate influence on civil society and its different relations. In this there was much which stood in contradiction with the spirit that animated the church ; the transforming influence which Christianity necessarily exercises on all with which it comes in contact could not as yet here manifest itself. Only in an indirect manner —and, in this respect, we must allow, although in a very slow, yet in the safest and purest way—could the church exert an influence on the state, by ever drawing over more of its members into itself, and communicating to them the spirit by whose influence everything must be made better. Yet this,

however, could not take place in all the members of the
church at once ; but only in those who, while they belonged
to the visible church, belonged at the same time also, by the
disposition of their minds, to the invisible church. From such
only could proceed the new creation which the spirit of Christianity produces, as they alone had experienced this creation
in their own hearts. But, with the commencement of this
period, the church entered into an entirely different relation
to the state. It did not merely become a whole, recognised
as legal, and tolerated by the state,—which it had been
already from the reign of Gallien down to the Dioclesian persecution,—but the state itself declared its principles to be those
to which everything must be subordinated. Christianity became by degrees the dominant state religion, though not
entirely in the same sense as paganism had been before.
Church and state constituted henceforth two wholes, one
interpenetrating the other, and standing in a relation of
mutual action and reaction. The advantageous influence of
this was, that the church could now exert its transforming
power also on the relations of the state ; but the measure and
the character of this power depended on the state of the inner
life in the church itself. The healthful influence of the church
is indeed to be perceived in many particular cases ; though it
was very far from being so mighty as it must have been had
everything proceeded from the spirit of genuine Christianity,
and had the state *actually* subordinated itself to this spirit.
But, on the other hand, the church had now to struggle under
a great disadvantage ; for, instead of being left *free*, as it was
before, to pursue its own course of development, it was subjected to the influence of a foreign, secular power, which in
various ways would operate to check and disturb it ; and the
danger, in this case, increased in the same proportion as the
political life with which the church came in contact was corrupt, and a lawless, despotic will ruled supreme,—a will
which acknowledged no restraints, and which therefore, whenever it intermeddled with the church development, was prone
to act after the same arbitrary manner as it did elsewhere.
So it actually happened in the East Roman empire. Without
doubt, it belongs to the essential character of Christianity
that it can propagate itself even under the most depressing of
earthly relations, and by the surpassing energy of its spirit

break through every species of temporal bondage. This was seen under the empire of pagan Rome, and in the Persian empire. Despotism, arrayed in open hostility to Christianity, only served to call forth, in still greater strength, the Christian sense of freedom rising superior to all earthly constraint. But despotism in outward alliance with the church, proved a more dangerous enemy. It was now necessary that one of two things should happen;—either the spirit of Christianity, as it became more widely diffused, must—not by a sudden and glaring revolution, but by its power in the heart, which is far mightier than any arm of flesh—gradually introduce the order of law in the place of arbitrary despotism; or the corruption of the state would introduce itself into the church, as it actually did in the Byzantine empire. Furthermore, the church was now exposed to the temptation of appropriating a foreign might for the prosecution of its ends; a temptation ever ready to assail man the moment the spirit is no longer sovereign alone, but the flesh intermeddles with its proper work. Looking only at the holy end which he fancies himself in pursuit of, any means that can subserve it seem good to him. He does not consider that the *truth itself*, forced on man otherwise than by its own inward power, *becomes false-hood*. How easily might the bishops in their zeal,—more or less unwise, more or less directed by selfish views,—be tempted to invite those emperors who professed to belong to the Catholic church to assist in securing the victory for that which *they* deemed the pure doctrine, and in crushing its adversaries, when in fact the Syrian bishops, in the previous period, had already sought after the aid of a pagan emperor, Aurelian, in a similar case! And in cases of this sort, how invariably did the wrong proceeding bring along its own punishment! In forgetting and denying its own essential character, on the simple preservation of which its true power depends,—in consenting to make use of a foreign might for the furtherance of its ends, the church succumbed to that might. Such is the lesson taught by the history of the church of the Roman empire in the East.

The great change of which we speak, in the relation of the church to the state, must be ascribed to the *transition of the Roman emperors to the side of Christianity*. The supreme magistrates now considered themselves as members of the church, and took a personal share in its concerns; but it was no easy matter for them to fix the proper limits to this participation, and, by so doing, to give up their relation as emperors to subjects. They would be strongly inclined to transfer the relation they had stood in as pagans to the pagan state-religion, over to their relation to the Christian church. Yet they were here met by that independent spirit of the church which in the course of three centuries had been developing itself and acquiring a determinate shape; and which would make them see that Christianity could not, like paganism, be subordinated to the political interest. There had in fact arisen in the church, as we observed in the previous period, a false theocratical theory, originating, not in the essence of the gospel, but in the confusion of the religious constitutions of the Old and New Testament, which, grounding itself on the idea of a visible priesthood belonging to the essence of the church, and governing the church, brought along with it an unchristian opposition of the spiritual to the secular power, and which might easily result in the formation of a sacerdotal state, subordinating the secular to itself in a false and outward way. The emperors did in fact entertain precisely that view of the church which was presented to them by tradition; or rather, since—if we except Valentinian II., who seems to have consistently carried through one determinate theory—they had no judgment of their own, they were involuntarily borne along by the dominant spirit. The entire church constitution, as it then stood, appeared to them, equally with Christianity, a divine institution, built on the foundation of Christ and the apostles, in which nothing could be altered by arbitrary human will. Add to this, that the same church constitution had acquired its form in a time when the church was an independent society by itself, under the government of the bishops.

This theocratical theory was already the prevailing one in the time of Constantine; and, had not the bishops voluntarily made themselves dependent on him by their disputes, and by their determination to make use of the power of the state for the furtherance of their aims, it lay in their power, by consistently and uniformly availing themselves of this theory, to obtain a great deal from him. Thus, for example, in a rescript of the year 314, when an appeal was made from an episcopal tribunal to the imperial decision, he declared, " The sentence of the bishops must be regarded as the sentence of Christ himself."* But, on the other hand, it flattered Constantine so to regard the matter as if God had made *him* master of the whole Roman empire, to the end that, through his instrumentality, the worship of the true God might be everywhere extended and promoted. When, in a jesting tone, he once observed to the bishops, at a banquet, that he too was a bishop in his own way,—namely, a bishop over whatever lay without the church,—he meant by this, that God had made him overseer of that which was without the church, *i.e.* the political relations, for the purpose of ordering these according to the will of God; of giving the whole such a direction as that his subjects might be led to pious living.† The disputes among the bishops on doctrinal matters led him, on the matter of his relation to the church, to derive from this, his supposed vocation, many consequences which, at the beginning, had never entered into his thoughts. He exhorted them to unanimity; and, when his exhortations were unheeded, he resorted to such means for uniting the opposite parties as his sovereignty over the whole Roman state put into his hands. He convoked an assembly of bishops from all parts of the empire, in order to give a decision for all the Christians under his government.‡

---

* Sacerdotum judicium ita debet haberi, ut si ipse Dominus residens judicet. See Optav. Milev. de schismate Donatistar. f. 184.

† This remark of Constantine, which Eusebius quotes (de vita Coustantini, IV. 24), as he heard it at table from the emperor's lips, has not so great importance in itself considered; for in truth it was a mere pun, from which no theory about church rights could be drawn—a sportive allusion to the ambiguity of the Greek word ἐπίσκοπος, which may be used to denote either a particular ecclesiastical officer, or an overseer generally: Ὡς ἄρα εἴη καὶ αὐτὸς ἐπίσκοπος, ἀλλ' ὑμεῖς μὲν τῶν εἴσω τῆς ἐκκλησίας, ἐγὼ δὲ τῶν ἐκτὸς ὑπὸ θεοῦ καθισταμένος ἐπίσκοπος ἂν εἴην. Eusebius, who could best know in what sense Constantine meant this to be taken, understands by ἐκτὸς τῆς ἐκκλησίας, simply the state, so far as Coustantine exercised such oversight over his subjects as to lead them, to the best of his ability, in the way of pious living: Ἀκόλουθα δ' οὖν τῷ λόγῳ διανοούμενος, τοὺς ἀρχομένους ἅπαντας ἐπισκόπει, προὔτρεπέ τε ὅση πὲρ ἂν δύναμις τὸν εὐσεβῆ μεταδιώκειν βίον. And, in fact, he expresses himself in precisely the same way in other public declarations respecting the office intrusted to him by God. See the 1st section.

‡ Eusebius of Cæsarea, the court bishop,—whose views of the case cannot be considered, however, as the prevailing one at that time,—derives this authority from the fact that God had intrusted the general

The decrees of these synods were published under the imperial authority, and thus obtained a political importance. Those only who adopted them could enjoy all the privileges of catholic Christians favoured by the state; and, in the end, civil penalties were threatened against those who refused to acknowledge them.

The coöperation of the emperors having once become so necessary in order to the assembling of these councils and the carrying out of their decisions, it could, of course, no longer remain a matter of indifference to them which of the contending parties they should sustain with their power. However emphatically they might declare in theory that the bishops alone were entitled to decide in matters of doctrine, still *human passions proved mightier than theoretical forms.* Although these councils were to serve as organs to express the decision of the divine Spirit, yet the Byzantine court had already prejudged the question as to which party ought to be considered pious and which impious wherever it could be contrived to gain over the court in favour of any particular doctrinal interest;[*] —or in case the court persecuted *one* of the contending doctrinal parties merely out of dislike to the man who stood at the head of it, then the doctrinal question must be turned into a means of gratifying personal grudges.[†] The emperors were under no necessity of employing force against the bishops: by indirect means they could sufficiently influence the minds of all those with whom worldly interests stood for more than the cause of truth, or who were not yet superior to the fear of man. It was nothing but the influence of the emperor Constantine which induced the Eastern bishops, at the council of Nice, to suffer the imposition of a doctrinal formula which

oversight of the whole church to the emperor, just as the oversight of their particular dioceses belonged to the bishops—a sort of universal episcopate in relation to the several individual bishoprics: Οἷα τις κοίνος ἐπίσκοπος ἐκ θεοῦ καθεστάμενος, συνόδους τῶν τοῦ θεοῦ λειτουργῶν συνεκρότει. De vita Constantini, l. I. c. 44.

[*] As it had been contrived, before the assembling of the Council of Nice, to persuade the emperor Constantine that the Arian doctrine contained a blasphemy against the divinity of Christ, and that the ὁμοούσιον was absolutely required in order to maintain the dignity of Christ's person.

[†] As at the first council of Ephesus, where the revenge of Pulcheria, who governed the imperial court, turned the doctrinal controversy into a means of removing the patriarch Nestorius from Constantinople.

they detested, and from which, indeed, they sought immediately
to rid themselves.   The emperor Theodosius II. declared to
the first council of Ephesus that no person who was not a
bishop should interfere with the ecclesiastical proceedings ;*
and in this declaration he himself may have been in earnest :
but he was borne along by the current of a powerful court
party, which itself had combined with a party of the bishops,
and to this party he must serve as the instrument.   The pious
and free-hearted abbot, Isidore, of Pelusium, wrote to the
emperor that no remedy existed for the evil in the church,
unless he placed some check *on the dogmatizing spirit of his
courtiers ;*†—and the sequel proved how entirely he was in the
right.

It is true, powerful voices were heard simply protesting
against this confusion of political and spiritual interests ;‡ as,
for example, Hilary of Poitiers, who remarked well and beautifully to the emperor Constantius, " It is for this purpose
you govern and watch, that all may enjoy sweet liberty.   The
peace of the church can no otherwise be restored, its distractions can in no other way be healed, than by permitting every
man to live wholly according to his own convictions, free from
all slavery of opinion.   Even though such force should be
employed for the support of the true faith, yet the bishops
would come before you and say, God is the Lord of the
universe ; he requires not an obedience which is constrained,
a profession which is forced.   He does not want hypocrisy,
but sincere worship."§   But these isolated voices could accomplish nothing in opposition to the great mass ; and they proceeded mainly from those who were themselves made sore by
oppression.   Now, as so much depended on the fact whether
a party had the emperor's vote on its side, consequently every
art was employed to secure this ; all that was corrupt in the
Byzantine court found its way into the bosom of the church,
—court parties became doctrinal parties, and the reverse.

* Ἀθέμιτον, τὸν μὴ τοῦ καταλόγου τῶν ἁγιωτάτων ἐπισκόπων τυγχάνοντα
τοῖς ἐκκλησιαστικοῖς σκέμμασιν ἐπιμιγνῦσθαι.   See the Sacra Theodos. II. in
the acts of this council.
  † Isidor. Pelusiot. l. I. ep. 311.   Παρέξεις τούτοις θεραπείαν, εἰ παύσιας
τῶν δογματισμῶν τοὺς σοὺς διακόνους.
  ‡ Comp. the examples cited in the 1st section, pp. 35, 36.
  § Ad Constantium, l. I

Imperial chamberlains (cubicularii), eunuchs, directors of the princes' kitchen,* disputed on formulas of faith, and affected to set themselves up as judges in theological disputes. That which must pass current for sound doctrine in the church was subjected to the same fluctuations with the parties at court. At length, in 476, the usurper Basiliscus, who enjoyed a brief authority, set an example wholly in accordance with the spirit of the Byzantine court of effecting changes in the ruling doctrines of the church by imperial decrees, and of settling dogmatic controversies by a resort to the same expedient;—and this example was soon after but too eagerly followed by other emperors, such as Zeno and Justinian. These attempts to rule over the conscience by imperial mandates opened a new source of disturbances and disorders in the Greek church. It is true, that which had been obtruded upon it from without, and which was alien from the whole course of the development of the church at that time, could gain no substantial existence within it; but then a violent crisis was always necessary to throw it off again. The proof of what has been asserted will be furnished in the history of the disputes on doctrine. The Greek church presents here a warning example for all ages. The church of the West developed itself, in the main, with more independence; because the theocratic principle, of which we have spoken, obtained more power in it; because the predominant authority of the Roman bishops formed a certain counterpoise to the interference of the state; and because the more rigid and less versatile spirit of the Western church gave less frequent occasion for the interposition of a foreign power.

We shall now proceed to consider the relations of the church to the state more in detail.

The state at present took some part in providing for the support of the churches. More was effected in this respect by one law of Constantine than by all other means put together. This was a law which expressly secured to the churches a right which, perhaps, they had already now and then tacitly exercised,† namely, the right of receiving legacies; which, in

---

* As, for example, that chief cook who was sent as a deputy from the court of the emperor Valens to persuade Basil of Cæsarea not to show any opposition to doctrines of the court. See Gregor. Naz. orat. 20, f. 348. Theodoret. hist. eccles. IV. c. 19.

† For, during the persecutions in the third century, we find it inti-

the Roman empire, no corporation whatever was entitled to exercise, unless it had been expressly authorized to do so by the state. Such a law Constantine enacted in 321, assigning as the reason for it, not the interests of the church, but the *inviolable sacredness of the last will.**

In part zeal for the cause of the church, but partly also the delusive notion that such gifts, as meritorious works, were particularly acceptable in the sight of God, and that it was possible thereby to atone for a multitude of sins, *or both together*, procured for the churches, especially in large towns,† very considerable and very numerous donations. But it was undoubtedly the case, too, that the wealth of the church often led the bishops of the large towns to forget the nature of their calling; and dishonourable means were not seldom employed by worldly-minded ecclesiastics to increase the bequests in favour of the churches. It was on this account the emperor Valentinian I. restricted this right by various limitations; and distinguished church-teachers complained, not so much of

mated that attempts were made to deprive the churches of their estates, which evidently they could have come in possession of in no other way. Consult the edict of Gallien. And Alexander Severus had already conceded to the Christians a public place as legally belonging to them. See Ælii Lampridii Vita, c. 49.

* Cod. Theodos. l. XVI. Tit. II. s. 4.

† Ammianus Marcellinus (l. XXVII. c. 3) speaks of the great wealth which the Roman bishops owed to the donations of the matrons. His description shows to what an extent the bishops of the great capital of the world had, amidst the wealth and in the splendour of their church, forgotten or forfeited their spiritual character. He says it ought not to be wondered at that the candidates for the Roman episcopate were ready to sacrifice everything to obtain it: Cum, id adepti, futuri sint ita securi, ut ditentur oblationibus matronarum procedantque vehiculis insidentes, circumspecte vestiti, epulas curantes profusas, adeo ut eorum convivia regales superent mensas. He says it had been happy for them if they had followed the example of many of the provincial bishops, who, by their frugal and simple mode of life, commended themselves in the sight of God and all his true worshippers as pure men. So speaks the pagan. In like manner Gregory of Naziauzen describes the state which the bishops of Constantinople were used to affect—how, at their tables and in the pomp and train of their attendants with which they appeared in public, they vied with the first men of the state (orat. xxxii. f. 526). Hence it was too, that men who were disposed to live as it became bishops, such for example as Gregory of Nazianzen and Chrysostom, were far from being agreeable to the taste of many in Constantinople.

these limitations, as of the fact that the clergy had rendered them necessary.*

But in this case, too, as in all the appearances of the church at this period, the lights and shades should be compared together. We see, on the other hand, pious bishops giving up from Christian motives their title to bequests which, according to the civil law, they might have received. A citizen of Carthage made over all his property, in the expectation that he should have no children, to the church, reserving to himself only the use of it while he lived. But afterwards, when he had children, Aurelius, contrary to the legator's expectations, gave back the whole: "For, according to the *civil law*," says Augustin, who relates the case,† "he might have retained it, but not according to the *law of heaven*." And Augustin himself, who, indeed, was found fault with by many because he had done so little to enrich the church, declared "That he who would disinherit his son to make the church his legatee might look for some other one to receive the inheritance besides Augustin; nay, he hoped and prayed that he might look in vain for any one."‡

* See Hieronym. in the celebrated letter to Nepotianus, ep. 52, in which he places the corruption of the clergy in contrast with the end of their calling: Nec de lege conqueror; sed doleo cur meruerimus hanc legem. Jerome doubtless had floating before his mind, when he spoke of the corruption of the clergy, what he had seen particularly at Rome (see ep. 22 ad Eustochium, s. 28), where he presents a sad picture of the clergy, running about to the houses of the rich matrons, and seeking only to press donations out of them. Si pulvillum viderit, si mantile elegans, si aliquid domesticæ suppellectilis, laudat, miratur, attrectat, et se his indigere conquerens; non tam impetrat quam extorquet, quia singulæ metuunt veredarium urbis offendere.

† Sermo 356, s. 5.

‡ So a certain Bonifacius, belonging to the guild of the navicularii, whose employment was to convey grain in their vessels to Rome, Constantinople, or Alexandria, made the church at Hippo his legatee; but Augustin declined the bequest, because, in case of shipwreck, the church would either be obliged, by a judicial process and the application of torture against the crew, to prove that the mishap was unavoidable, or to make good the loss to the state exchequer. In respect to the first alternative, it did not befit the church, in the opinion of Augustin, to subject mariners who had been rescued from the waves to the pains of torture. As to the second, the church might not be possessed of the means. "For," says Augustin, "it is not befitting the bishop to be amassing money, and to push back the hand of the beggar." Possidius states, in the life of Augustin, c. 24, that the latter would never receive a bequest

And if it was often the case, especially in the larger towns, that bishops might be found who applied the great incomes of their churches to diffuse around them an air of state and splendour, there were, on the other hand, shining examples of other bishops who, living frugally themselves, applied all they had to spare for the support of charitable institutions. Beyond question, it lay in the power of the bishops to make use of the largest revenues for good and benevolent purposes; for they not only had to provide for the expense of preserving the churches, of maintaining divine service, of supporting the clergy, of supplying the means of subsistence for the poor, who, in the great cities, such as Constantinople, were very numerous and but too often suffered to live in indolence, but also, as a general thing, the establishments for the reception of strangers (ξενῶνες *), the almshouses (πτωχοτροφεῖα †), the institutions for the support of helpless aged persons (γηροκομεῖα), the hospitals and orphan-houses (the νοσοκομεῖα and ὀρφανοτροφεῖα), originated in the churches, and the churches had to provide the means for their support. A celebrated establishment of this kind was the one founded by Basil bishop of Cæsarea, and which existed in the third and fourth century—the *Basilias*—an institution designed for the reception of strangers, and to provide medical attendance and nursing for the sick of whatever disease. Here everything was brought together that could contribute to the welfare and comfort of the patients. The physicians of the establishment resided within its walls, and workshops were provided for all the artizans and labourers

which injured in any way the relations of the individual by whom the gift was made. A respectable citizen of Hippo had made over to the church an estate, merely reserving to himself the use of it while he lived. Afterwards he repented of what he had done, and requested that the papers might be returned to him, sending in lieu of them a sum of money. But Augustin sent back both, declaring that the church would not receive forced gifts, but those only which were made with a free will.

* With regard to the ξενών: Ἔστι κοίνον οἴκημα, ὑπὸ τῆς ἐκκλησίας ἀφωρισμένον. Chrysostom, in act. ap. hom. 45, near the end. Of this institution, as an ancient one in the church, though the name was new, see Augustin. Tractat. 97, in Joh. s. 4. *Xenedochia* postea sunt appellata novis nominibus, res tamen ipsæ et ante nomina sua erant, et religionis veritate firmantur.

† These institutions for the poor were under the supervision of clergymen, also of monks, οἱ κλήρικοι τῶν πτοχείων. Conc. Chalc. canon. 8.

whose services were needed ;* so that Gregory of Nazianzen, in his funeral discourse at the death of Basil,† could call this institution a city in miniature. Basil had also caused similar almshouses to be established in the country, one in each provincial diocese (συμμορία), placed under the care of a country bishop, who had the supervision of its concerns.‡ Theodoret bishop of Cyros, who had a diocese which was poor on account of its location, was, notwithstanding, able to save enough to erect porticos for the use of the city, to build two large bridges, to construct a canal from the Euphrates to the town, which had before suffered for the want of water, and to repair and improve the public bath, which was so important a means of health to the inhabitants of those hot districts.§

Among the favours bestowed by the state to further the ends of the church, belonged the exemption of the clerical order from certain public services (munera publica, λειτουργίαι). Such pertained partly to certain classes of citizens, and in part they were attached to the possession of a certain amount of property. Now, with these state burdens stood connected for the most part the undertaking of certain kinds of business and employments which were incompatible with the nature of the spiritual calling. For this reason, in the previous period, when no calculation could be made on the disposition of the state to accommodate the clerical order, a law had been passed that no person who was liable to any civil imposition (seculo obstrictus) should be ordained to the spiritual office.‖ But the church having now been freed by Constantine from these restrictions, it might be hoped that the like privileges would be accorded to the clergy as were allowed to pagan priests, physicians, and rhetoricians. In fact, Constantine ordered by a law of the year 319, after having already conceded to the clergy previous to 313 a certain degree of exemption, that they should be freed from all *burdens of the state.*¶ This unconditional exemption of the clergy from those civil duties

---

* See Basil. Cæsareens. ep. 94, and Sozomen. VI. 34.
† See his orat. 30 and 27.   ‡ Basil. ep. 142, 143.
§ See Theodoret. ep. 81.
‖ When, for instance, Tertullian alleges against the heretics (præscript. c. 41), that they ordained seculo obstrictos, it may be gathered from this that the practice was forbidden in the dominant church.
¶ Cod. Theodos. l. XVI. Tit. II. l. 2.

was destined to prove, however, the source of many evils both
to church and to state ; since it was the natural consequence that
numbers, without any inward call to the spiritual office, and
without any fitness for it whatever, now got themselves
ordained as ecclesiastics for the sake of enjoying this exemption ;—whereby many of the worst class came to the
administration of the most sacred calling,* while at the same
time the state was deprived of much useful service.   The
emperor Constantine, in this collision of interests, sought to
secure only those of the state.   That the true interests of the
church could not have been foremost in his thoughts is the
more evident, since he shows by this law itself how imperfectly
he understood them.   By a law of the year 320, which presupposes the existence of a still earlier one, he ordered that for
the future no person belong to the *families of Decurions*, no
one provided with sufficient means of living, no one who was
fitted for the performance of those civil duties, should take
refuge in the spiritual order ; that, as a general thing, new
clergymen should be chosen only to supply the places of those
who had deceased,† and these should be persons of small
means, and such as were not bound to take upon them any of
those burdens of the state.   They who were obligated to any
of those duties, if they had crept into the clerical order, were
to be forcibly thrust back to their former condition,—for which
regulation Constantine gave this singular reason : " The rich
must bear the burdens of the world, the poor must be main-

---

* Comp. what Athanasius (hist. Arianorum ad Monachos, s. 78) says
of the pagans who passed over from the senatorial families to Christianity for the purpose of obtaining as ecclesiastics the ταλαίπωρος
ἀλιτουργησία.   Basil. Cæsar. ep. 54, respecting such as got themselves
ordained to the inferior ecclesiastical offices in the country, merely for
the sake of eluding the obligation to do military service : Τῶν πλείστων
φόβῳ τῆς στρατολογίας εἰσποιούντων ἑαυτοὺς τῇ ὑπηρεσίᾳ.   Comp. also the
acts of the process against the bishop Antonius of Ephesus, in Palladius'
life of Chrysostom. opp. ed. Montfauc. T. XIII., where it comes out that
that metropolitan bishop sold episcopal dignities to such as were merely
seeking by episcopal ordination to be released from the burdensome
curial duties.

† But what had prompted this certainly excessive multiplication of
ecclesiastics was partly the number and magnitude of the external advantages, whereby the spiritual order now became attractive to so many
who were not spiritually minded, and in part the existence of so many
church offices which required for their discharge merely outward liturgical services.

tained by the wealth of the church ;"* as if this were the object of church property and of the church offices! But this restriction was not less unjust than the reason alleged for it was false ; for it well might be that the very men who felt the inward call, and possessed the best qualifications for the spiritual office, were to be found among the higher ranks in the provinces ; while by such a law these were excluded. Yet with the powerful influence of the spiritual order at court, under the Christian emperors, it must often happen as a matter of course that such laws would be evaded, and not unfrequently to the injury of the church. Some wavering and uncertainty too soon began to show itself in the execution of the law ; expedients were devised to avoid injuring the interests either of the state or of the church ; and, finally, the law was enacted that those who were under obligation to render such civil services should, upon entering the ecclesiastical order, give up their property to others who could discharge those services in their stead. It was very justly given as a reason for this regulation, that, if they were really in earnest in what they proposed, they must despise earthly things. But it was certainly far from being the case that this law could be strictly kept.†

The state allowed to the church a particular jurisdiction, when it recognised in a legal form what had already obtained in the church before. It was the rule from the first, in the Christian communities, that disputes between their members should not be brought before heathen tribunals, but settled within their own body. This was befitting the mutual brotherly relation subsisting between Christians ; and it had been the course adopted already in the Jewish synagogues. Paul had, in fact, expressly required this method of procedure, while he regretted that such differences should exist at all among Christians. When the episcopal form of church government became matured, it was made a part of the function of the episcopal office to decide these disputes. Yet, hitherto, the sentence of the bishop stood valid only so far as both parties had voluntarily agreed to submit to it. Constantine made the sentence of the bishops legally binding whenever the two

---

* See Cod. Theodos. l. XVI., Tit. II. l. 6. Opulentos enim sæculi subire necessitates oportet, pauperes ecclesiarum divitiis sustentari.

† See the laws of the year 383, in the Titulus de Decurionibus.

parties had once agreed to repair to their tribunal, so that no farther appeal could be made from it.* Thus a great deal of business of a foreign nature came upon the episcopal office. Bishops more spiritually disposed made it a matter of complaint that so much of the time which they were prompted, by the inclination of their hearts, to bestow on the things of God, must be employed for the purpose of immersing themselves in the investigation of secular affairs.† At the same time they had to suffer no little vexation; for, however impartially they might decide, they still exposed themselves to many an accusation on the part of those who were looking merely at their *own* advantage, and who, when the decision of the bishop was adverse to their interests, could not pardon it in them that they must submit without any right of appeal from an unfavourable sentence.‡ Yet, from love to their communities, they bore this burthen attached to their calling, grievous as it was to them, with the self-denial which an Augustin evinces when from a full heart he exclaims in the language of the 119th Psalm, ver. 115 (as it is found in the Alexandrian version), " Depart from me, ye evil doers, for I

---

* Sozomen, 1. I. c. 9.

† When certain theological labours had been committed by two African councils to the care of the bishop Augustin, who was now advanced in years, he agreed with his community, that, for the purpose of executing these, he should be spared from attending to their business during five days in the week. A formal protocol or bill (gesta ecclesiastica) was drawn up, specifying what the church had conceded to him; but he was soon besieged again, so that he was compelled to say, Ante meridiem et post meridiem occupationibus hominum implicor. (See the gesta ecclesiastica Augusti. ep. 213.) In the Greek church the case may have been, however, that bishops, whether for the purpose of devoting themselves with greater blessing to other kinds of labour, or whether it was simply out of indolence, turned over these matters of business to certain members of their clergy, whom they invested with full powers for transacting them. At least, Socrates incidentally relates this of a certain Silvanus bishop of Troas, a man inclined to ascetic retirement, belonging to the first times of the fifth century, without remarking that it was anything unusual. But when this good bishop observed that the clergy to whom he had intrusted this business were endeavouring to make gain of it without regard to right, he committed the investigation to a justice-loving layman. Socrat. VII. 37.

‡ See Augustin. in ψ. 25, s. 13, t. IV. f. 115. Etsi jam effringi non potest, quia tenetur jure forte non ecclesiastico, sed principum seculi, qui tantum detulerunt ecclesiæ, ut quidquid in ea judicatum fuerit, dissolvi non possit.

would study the commandments of my God;" and when he proceeds to say, "Wicked men exercise us *in observing the commandments of God;* but they call us away *from exploring them* (from the study of holy scripture), not only when they would persecute us or contend with us, but even when they obey us and honour us, and yet compel us to busy ourselves in lending support to their sinful and contentious desires; and when they require of us that we should sacrifice our time to them; or when at least they oppress the weak, and force them to bring their affairs before us. To these we dare not say, Man, who has made me a judge or a divider of inheritance over you? For the apostle has instituted ecclesiastical judges for such affairs, in forbidding Christians to bring suits before the civil tribunals." Such bishops might undoubtedly avail themselves also of this opportunity of becoming better acquainted with the members of their flock, of diffusing among them the spirit of unanimity, and of opportunely dropping many a practical admonition. But to worldly-minded bishops it furnished a welcome occasion for devoting themselves to any foreign and secular affairs, rather than to the appropriate business of their spiritual calling; and the same class might also allow themselves to be governed by impure motives in the settlement of these disputes.

In many cases it was apparent that the gradually forming hierarchy furnished a salutary counterpoise against political despotism. The bishops acquired a great deal of influence in this respect, owing to the point of view in which the external church and its representatives appeared to the men of this period, and gradually also through the habits and customs of the people; since the prevailing ideas passed over into life, before anything came to be determined by the laws.

To this kind of influence belongs that which the bishops obtained by their intercessions (intercessiones). It was then not unusual for persons who enjoyed some reputation as men of learning, as rhetoricians, to avail themselves of this for the purpose of interceding with the great, who affected to patronize science, in behalf of the unfortunate. But that this custom should pass over especially to the bishops was a natural consequence of the new direction which Christianity gave to the mode of contemplating the forms of social life. New ideas of the equality of all men in the sight of God; of the equal accountableness of all; of mercy, love, and compassion, were diffused abroad by Christianity. Christian judges and magistrates were uncertain how they should unite the discharge of their official duties with what was required of them by the precepts of Christ. In the previous period *one* party of Christians, in fact, held the administration of such offices to be incompatible with the nature of the Christian calling. The council of Elvira (in 305) directed that the supreme magistrates in the municipal towns, the *Duumviri* (though these were not called upon to pronounce sentence of death), should not enter the church during the year of their office.* The council of Arles, in 314, directed indeed that the *presidents* in the provinces, and others who were incumbents of any civil office, should continue to remain in the communion of the church,† yet charged the bishops in the places where they exercised their civil functions with a special oversight of them; and, when they began to act inconsistently with their Christian duties,‡ they were then to be cut off from the church fellowship. Thus, then, it came about that conscientious Christians who occupied official stations, whenever they were beset with doubts from the above-mentioned causes, had recourse to the bishops for instruction and for the quieting of their scruples. For example, a certain functionary, by the name of Studius, betook himself, in a case of this sort, to Ambrosius bishop of Milan. The latter told him that according to Romans xiii. he was authorized to employ the sword for the punishment of crime, yet proposed for his imitation the pattern of Christ in his conduct towards the woman taken in adultery (John, c. viii.).§ If the transgressor had never been baptized, he might still be converted, and obtain the forgiveness of sin: if he had been already baptized, he could yet repent and reform. Ambrosius says on this occasion that those who pass sentence of death would not, indeed, be excluded from the communion of the church, since they are

* C. 56. Magistratum uno anno, quo agit duumviratum, prohibendum placuit, ut se ab ecclesia cohibeat.
† Literas accipiant ecclesiasticas communicatorias, c. 7.
‡ Cum cœperint contra disciplinam agere.
§ An example, indeed, which did not wholly apply in the present case; for it was one where the question was not a juridical, but a religious and moral one. But Ambrose was for ennobling the juridical position by that of morality and religion.

justified, by the above-cited declaration of the apostle, to pass such a sentence; but that the majority, however, did abstain from the communion, and that their conduct in this respect was to be approved.*

In this way it came about that the bishops gradually obtained the right of exercising a sort of moral superintendence over the discharge of their official duties by the governors, the judges, the proprietors, who belonged to their communities †—an authority which was not always, indeed, alike respected;—that they were empowered, in the name of religion, to intercede with governors, with the nobles of the empire, and even with the emperors, in-behalf of the unfortunate, the persecuted, the oppressed; in behalf of individuals, entire cities and provinces, who sighed under grievous burdens, laid on them by reckless, arbitrary caprice, or who trembled in fear of heavy punishments amidst civil disturbances. Where the fear of man made all others mute, it was not seldom they alone who spoke out in the name of religion and of the church, who ventured to utter themseves with freedom; and their voice might sometimes penetrate to the consciences of those who were intoxicated by the feeling of their absolute power, and surrounded by servile flatterers.

Some examples will render this clear. When the separation of the province of Cappadocia into two provinces (Cappadocia prima et secunda), under the emperor Valens, in the year 371, had reduced the inhabitants, who thus lost much of their gain and were oppressed by a double weight of civil burdens, to

---

* According to the old editions, ep. ad Studium, l. VII. ep. 58.

† By a law of the year 409, which directed the judges on all Sundays to interrogate prisoners whether they had experienced humane treatment, it was at the same time presupposed that the bishops felt it incumbent ou them to exhort the judges to humane treatment of their prisoners: Nec deerit antistitum Christianæ religionis cura laudabilis quæ ad observationem constituti judicis hanc ingerat monitionem. Cod. Theodos. l. XI. Tit. III. l. 7. By a law of the emperor Justinian, of the year 529, it was devolved on the bishop, on Thursday and Friday (probably on these days in particular, on account of the memory of Christ's passion), to visit the prisons, to inquire into the crimes for which each person was confined, and accurately inform himself with regard to the treatment he met with, and point out to the higher authorities everything that was done contrary to good order. They were also to see to it that no one should be held in confinement elsewhere than in the public prisons. See Codex Justinian. l. I. Tit. IV. l. 22 and 23.

great distress, it was the bishop Basil of Cæsarea who interceded—to no purpose indeed—with the great, and, through
them, with the emperor, in behalf of the whole province.
Among other things, he thus wrote to one of the nobles : " He
could boldly tell the court that they were not to imagine they
should have two provinces instead of one ; for they would not
have secured another province from some other world, but
have done just the same as if the owner of a horse or of an ox
should cut him in halves, and suppose that by so doing he
obtained two instead of one."* When, in the year 387, a
popular movement at Antioch, which had been brought about
by the oppression of excessive taxes, gave reason to fear a
severe retribution from the emperor Theodosius, who might
easily be hurried, in a momentary paroxysm of passion, to the
extremest measures, and all was in a state of the utmost confusion, the aged and sick bishop Flavianus proceeded himself
to Constantinople. Said he to the emperor, " I am come, as
the deputy of our common Master, to address this word to
your heart : ' If ye forgive men their trespasses, then will your
heavenly Father also forgive you your trespasses.' " These
words, to which he gave a still more pointed emphasis by
alluding to the import of the approaching festival of Easter,
so profoundly affected the heart of an emperor easily susceptible of religious impressions, that he exclaimed, " How could
it be a great thing for me, who am but a man, to remit my
anger towards men, when the Lord of the world himself, who
for our sakes took the form of a servant, and was crucified by
those to whom he was doing good, interceded with his Father
in behalf of his crucifiers, saying, ' Forgive them, since they
know not what they do ' ? "   All that had been done he promised should be forgotten, and Flaviau should hasten back to
convey the glad tidings to his community before the commencement of the Easter.†

* Ep. 74 ad Martinian.
† See Chrysostom. orat. 20, de statuis, near the end. In the same
manner Theodoret interceded with great men and with the imperial
princess Pulcheria in behalf of the inhabitants of his poor church diocese,
who were calumniated at the court and oppressed by heavy tributes.
(See ep. 42, and the following.) So Augustin used the most earnest remonstrances with a rich landholder, by the name of *Romulus*, who was in
the practice of unjustly oppressing the poor people of the country, and
who had avoided speaking with Augustin himself; and he closed with

It cannot be denied, indeed, that while pious and prudent bishops effected much good by a discreet resort to these intercessions, others, by a haughty abuse of them, by hierarchical arrogance, by a confusion of the Christian and the juridical point of view, to which they obstinately clung, might seriously interfere with the civil order.* Yet the injury which thence resulted in the case of particular individuals is certainly not to be compared with the benefits which accrued, in various ways, from the intercessions of the bishops in behalf of the innocent who were oppressed, and of the weak who were abandoned to the caprices of passion and arbitrary power.† The bishops were considered particularly as the protectors of widows and orphans. The dying, who left orphan children behind them, commended them, in that period of despotic authority, to the protection of the bishops. The property of widows and orphans, which there was cause to fear might fall a prey to the rapacity of the powerful, was placed under the guardianship of the churches and the bishops.‡ Ambrosius bishop of Milan reminds his

these words : " Fear God, unless you wish to deceive yourself: I call him to witness on your soul, that, while saying this, I fear more for you than for those in behalf of whom I may seem to intercede. If you believe, let God be thanked. If you do not believe, I comfort myself in what the Lord says, Matth. x. 13." Augustin. ep. 247.

* Respecting such haughtiness of the bishops, a certain judge, by the name of Macedonius, complains in a letter to Augustin (ep. 152), to whom he states his doubts about the reasonableness of intercessions. He denounces those who complained of wrong when their intercessions, however unreasonable, met with no hearing; from whom, however, he altogether distinguishes such men as Augustin. The latter, in reply, explains at large his deliberate judgment respecting the end, the right and the wrong use of the episcopal *intercessiones*, ep. 153. To guard against such abuses, it was ordered by a law of the year 398 that the monks and the clergy should not be permitted to snatch condemned malefactors from their merited punishment: yet they were allowed, even by this law, to resort to a legal intercession, as a sort of reparation for this infringement on their rights. Cod. Theodos. l. IX. Tit. 40, l. 16.

† How common it was for those whose life or freedom was suddenly endangered by powerful enemies, or for their relatives and friends, to enter the church and apply to the bishop for his speedy assistance, is seen from Augustin. p. 161, s. 4, p. 368, s. 3. Videtis, si cujus vita præsentis seculi periclitetur, quomodo amici ejus currunt pro eo, quomodo curritur ad ecclesiam, rogatur episcopus, ut intermittat, si quas habet actiones, currat, festinet.

‡ See Augustin. ep. 252; according to other editions, 217. Sermo 176, s. 2.

clergy of the fact how often he had withstood the attacks of the imperial power in defending the property of the widow; nay, of all;—and he says to those clergy that they would thereby magnify their office, if the attacks of the powerful, under which the widow and the orphan must succumb, were warded off by the protection of the church; if they showed that the precept of the Lord had more weight with them than the favour of the rich.*

It was the same with another right which the churches gradually obtained by traditional usage. As the pagan temples had been already considered asylums for such as fled to them for refuge, and as the images of the emperor served the same purpose, so now this use passed over to the Christian churches. It is evident, from what has been said, how salutary a thing this might prove under the circumstances of those times; since taking refuge in the asylum of the church, particularly at the altar, afforded time for the bishops to intercede for the unfortunate, before any injury could be done them. They who were persecuted by a victorious party, in times of civil disturbance, could, in the first instance, here find protection against the sword; and the bishops, meanwhile, gain time to apply to the powerful for their pardon. Many examples of this kind are furnished in the labours of Ambrose during the Western revolutions of his period. Slaves could here find protection, for the first moment, against the cruel rage of their masters, and subsequently, by the interposition of the bishops, appease their anger. Such as were by misfortune involved in debt, and persecuted by their creditors, could here gain shelter for the first moment; and pious bishops could, in the mean time, find means, either by a collection in their communities, or by an advance of money from the church funds, of cancelling their debt, or of effecting a compromise between them and their creditors.† It is true, this right of the churches, which, under the circumstances of those times, could be applied to such salutary purposes, might also be abused by the hierarchical arrogance of some bishops.‡   This

* Ambrosius de officiis, I. II. c. 29.
† See Augustin. ep. 268 ad plebem; according to other editions, 215.
‡ An example in Augustin. ep. 250. Certain individuals guilty of perjury having taken refuge in the church, the Comes Classicianus, accompanied by a few men, went to Auxilius the bishop, for the purpose of

right was at first not conceded to the churches by a law, but had its ground simply in the universal belief; and hence it happened, too, that it was often violated by rude, tyrannical men. Pious bishops here had an opportunity of evincing their steadfast courage in protecting the unfortunate who had taken refuge with them, against the rage of powerful enemies who would not suffer themselves to be restrained by any respect for the asylum.* The first imperial law which appeared with reference to the asylum was in fact directed against it. The case happened thus:—Chrysostom, the venerable bishop of Constantinople, had defended a number of unfortunate individuals against the arbitrary violence of the unprincipled, but for a time powerful, Eutropius; in consequence of which, the latter procured the enactment of an express law, in 398,

making such representations to him as would prevent him from receiving them. But though the guilty persons voluntarily left the church, the haughty bishop, notwithstanding, pronounced *excommunication* on the entire family of the Comes. Augustin, on the other hand, received the Comes into his own communion, telling him that he had nothing to fear from an unjust excommunication; and he wrote to the bishop, "Believe not that we may not be hurried on by an unjust anger because we are bishops; but let us rather think that we live in the greatest danger of being caught in the snares of temptation, because we are men."

* Here follow two examples. A man of some consequence and influence, owing to his connection with the vicar-general of Pontus, with whom he acted as assessor judge, wished to compel a noble widow to marry him. She fled to the asylum of the church at Cæsarea. That governor, who was besides an enemy of the bishop Basil, gladly availed himself of this opportunity to make him feel his power. But Basil refused to deliver up the widow. The vicar caused him to be arraigned before his tribunal; but the people were excited by this course of proceeding to such violent agitation, that the governor, struck with fear, finally himself implored Basil to use his influence in soothing them. See Gregor. Naz. orat. 20, p. 353. In like manner, the bishop Synesius of Ptolemais, in the early part of the fifth century, had to contend with a governor, Andronicus, who dealt in an arbitrary manner with the lives and property of the citizens, sacrificing everything to his avarice and his passions. He caused an edict to be posted up on the doors of the church, in which he threatened every ecclesiastic who should give protection to his unhappy victims. He declared that not one should escape his hand, even though he clasped the feet of Christ. No asylum could afford shelter against such a man. The only course that was left for Synesius was to pronounce on him the sentence of excommunication, ep. 58. Yet Andronicus, who fell into disgrace with the court, and was plunged in misfortune, was forced himself to seek protection from the church, and Synesius received him. Ep. 90 ad Theophilum.

restricting this right of the church, which had grown out of common usage and custom.* So much the stronger, therefore, must have been the impression made on the popular mind when, in the following year, Eutropius himself, having fallen from the summit of earthly fortune to the lowest infamy, was obliged to seek shelter, at the altar of the church, from the fury of the exasperated Gothic troops to which the weak Arcadius was willing to abandon him; and it was Chrysostom who defended him there. A great effect was also produced by an incident which occurred in Constantinople itself, under the reign of Theodosius II. Certain slaves of one of the chief men of the city took refuge, from the harsh treatment of their cruel master, in the sanctuary of the principal church. There, for several days in succession, they disturbed the divine service; and when at length resort was had to force against them, they killed one of the ecclesiastics, wounded another, and then put an end to their own lives.† This and similar occurrences led finally to the enactment of the *first law* for the asylum of the church, in the year 431. It was here settled that not only the altar, but whatever formed any part of the church buildings, should be an inviolable place of refuge.‡ It was forbidden, on pain of death, forcibly to remove those who fled thither unarmed. Resort might be had to force only against such as took refuge in those places with weapons in their hands, and who refused to give them up at the repeated solicitations of the clergy.§ In a law, passed in the following year, it was ordered that, whenever a servant fled unarmed to the church, the clergy should delay giving information of it to the master, or to the person whose vengeance he was endeavour-

---

* See Cod. Theodos. 1. IX. Tit. 45, 1. 3; which law, to be sure, is not expressed in general terms, but is properly directed only against those who were bound under some obligation to the state or to private persons, which they were wishing to evade. Yet the law, in the form in which it stood, might easily be farther made use of also against the asylum.

† Socrates, VII. 33.

‡ The reason alleged probably had some reference to the fact that those cases in which the violators of the asylum were subsequently visited by some great calamity, which was generally regarded as a divine punishment, particularly contributed to promote the feeling of reverence for the asylum: Ne in detrahendos eos conetur quisquam sacrilegas manus immittere; ne, qui hoc ausus sit, cum discrimen suum videat, ad expetendam opem ipse quoque confugiat.

§ Cod. Theodos. 1. IX. Tit. 45, 1. 4.

ing to escape, no longer than a day ; and that the latter, out
of regard to him to whom the fugitive had fled for refuge,
should grant him full forgiveness, and receive him back without the infliction of any further punishment.

2. *Internal Organization of the Church.*

Two things had a special influence in modifying the development of the church constitution in this period ; first, that
confounding of the Old and the New Testament view of the
theocracy which had prevailed and proved so influential in the
previous period ; secondly,—what became accessory to this in
the period before us,—the union of the church with the state ;
which union, although really in conflict with the theocratic
principle above mentioned, was, notwithstanding, indirectly
promoted by it. For the more the church strove after outward dominion, the more was she liable to go astray, and to
forget, in this outward power, her own intrinsic essence as a
church of the spirit, and the more easy it became for outward
power to obtain dominion over her; as it was true, on the
other hand, that the more clearly she retained the consciousness of her own intrinsic essence as a church of the spirit, and
the less she was tempted to strive after dominion otherwise
than through the spirit, through the power of the gospel, the
purer she was enabled to maintain herself from all corrupt
intermixture of the worldly principle.

The central point of the theocratic church system was the
idea of a visible, outward priesthood, serving as the medium
of connection between Christ and the church ; of a sacerdotal
caste distinctively consecrated to God, and requisite for the
life of the church,—through which order alone the influences
of the Holy Spirit could be diffused among the laity. This
idea had, in the previous period, become already a dominant
idea in the church, and had exerted the greatest influence in
changing and modifying all ecclesiastical relations. Though
this idea was employed by such church teachers as Chrysostom
and Augustin only for the purpose of setting in its true light
the religious and moral dignity of the spiritual order, and of
bringing it home to the hearts of such as were intending to
form themselves for this order, and though such men meant
by no means to disparage thereby the dignity of the universal

Christian calling, yet thus the germ of many other errors came to be once introduced. Hence the false antithesis now set up between spiritual and secular, which had so injurious an influence on the whole Christian life, and by which the lofty character of the universal Christian calling was so much lowered. Hence the delusive notion that the clergy, as super-earthly beings, must withdraw themselves from all contact with the things of sense ; and hence the erroneous notion that the priestly dignity was desecrated, was too much drawn down to the earth, by the married life. It would be doing wrong to this period to assert that such an opinion was purposely invented, or set afloat, with a view to enhance thereby the dignity of the spiritual order. Ideas of this sort, which reign supreme over an age, are, in general, not the contrivance of a few ; and what has been thus purposely contrived can never acquire such vast influence in shaping human relations. As that idea of the priesthood had originated, as we have seen, in a declension from the primitive Christian mode of thinking ; the same was true also of this opinion, which naturally grew out of the idea of the priesthood,—the opinion that the clergy, as mediators between God and men, as the channels through whom alone the influences of the Holy Spirit must flow to the rest of mankind, enchained to the world of sense, must hence, in their whole life, be elevated above that world,—must keep themselves free from all earthly ties and family relations. It is plain, indeed, that in many nations not Christian the idea of such a priesthood led to the same conclusion of the necessity of celibacy in the priests ; and already, in the previous period, we observed a tendency of the same kind among the Montanists.

This idea could not penetrate at once everywhere alike ; the primitive Christian spirit still offered considerable resistance to it. The council of Elvira in Spain, which met in the year 305, and was governed by the ascetic and hierarchical spirit that prevailed particularly in the Spanish and North-African churches, was the first to announce the law, that the clergy of the three first grades should abstain from all marriage intercourse, or be deposed.* Men of the same bent of spirit were

---

* Placuit in totum prohiberi episcopis, presbyteris et diaconibus, vel omnibus clericis positis in ministerio, abstinere a conjugibus suis.

for making this a general law of the church at the council of Nice; but a bishop, whose opinion may have had the more weight because it was unbiassed, as he had himself led a strictly ascetic life from his youth upward,—the bishop and confessor Paphnutius,—opposed this motion, declaring that wedlock was also a holy estate, as Paul affirmed; and that the clergy who held that relation might lead, notwithstanding, a holy life. No yoke ought to be imposed on men which the weakness of human nature could not bear; and it would be well to use caution, lest the church might be injured by excessive severity.* Yet even Paphnutius, plainly as he saw the mischief which must accrue from such an ordinance universally imposed, was too much governed by the spirit of his time to speak generally against the practice of binding the spiritual order to celibacy. The old order of things was simply retained, that ecclesiastics of the first three grades, when once ordained, should no longer be permitted to marry; and the rest was left to the free choice of each individual. And this was not a thing altogether new: the council of Neocæsarea, in the year 314,† had already decreed that the presbyter who married should forfeit his standing; and the council of Ancyra, in the same year,‡ that the deacons who, at the time of their ordination, should declare that they could not tolerate the life of celibacy, might subsequently be allowed to marry; while those who said nothing on this point at their ordination, yet afterwards married, should be deposed from their office. How much the ascetic spirit of the moral system which prevailed in many portions of the Eastern church, first giving rise to monasticism, and then receiving support from the same system, contributed to spread the erroneous notion of the necessity of celibacy to the sacred character of the priesthood, is made evident by the decisions of the council of Gangra in Paphlagonia, somewhere about the middle of the fourth century; which council, at the same time, deserves notice, as being opposed to this spiritual tendency and to this delusion. Its fourth canon pronounces sentence of condemnation *on those who would not hold communion with married ecclesiastics.* The practice became continually more prevalent, it is true, in the Eastern church, for the bishops at least, if they were married, to abandon the marriage relation: yet we

* Socrat. I. II.   † Canon 1.   ‡ Canon 10.

still find exceptions, even in the fifth century ; as in the case
of Synesius, who, when about to be made bishop of Ptolemais
in Pentapolis, signified to Theophilus patriarch of Alexandria
his intention of living in the same relations with the wife to
whom he himself had joined him ; and yet he was ordained
bishop.*   It was different with the Western church, where
the law which Paphnutius had turned aside at the council
of Nice succeeded, nevertheless, to establish itself.   It had
hitherto been nothing more than a fundamental principle in
the usages of the church, when the Roman bishop Siricius decreed the first ecclesiastical law on the subject.   The occasion
of it was this :—Spanish presbyters and deacons resisted the
unmarried life ; and, as the whole idea of the church priests
and sacrifices was derived from the Old Testament, they
appealed in their defence to the fact that the Old-Testament
priests lived in the state of wedlock.   Himerius bishop of
Taraco, in a letter to the Roman bishop Damasus, which
treated of various other ecclesiastical affairs, had also mentioned this circumstance, and asked for advice.   Siricius, who
in the mean time had succeeded Damasus in the episcopal
office, replied in a letter of the year 385, in which, by a singular perversion of holy writ, he endeavoured to prove the
necessity of celibacy in priests ; and in which letter, moreover,
the connection of this error with the unevangelical idea of the
priesthood and the unevangelical idea of what constitutes holiness is very clearly brought to view.   The requisition to be
holy (Levit. xx. 7) is here confined solely to the priests, and
referred simply to abstinence from marriage intercourse ; and
the bishop appeals for proof to the fact that the priests of the
Old Testament, during the period of their service in the temple,
were obliged to dwell there, and to abstain from all marriage
intercourse ;—that Paul (Rom. viii. 8, 9) says, they that are
in the flesh cannot please God.   And he adds, " Could the
Spirit of God dwell, indeed, in any other than holy bodies ? "
as though true holiness accordingly were incompatible with the
marriage estate, and the clergy were the only ones in whom

---

* Jerome may perhaps have expressed himself, in his zeal. too generally, when he says, in the beginning of his book against Vigilantius,
Quid facient orientis ecclesiæ, quid Ægypti et sedis apostolicæ, quæ aut
virgines Clericos accipiunt, aut continentes, aut si uxores habuerint,
mariti esse desistunt.

the Spirit of God resided. It was indeed true that a considerable time elapsed before the principle, established in theory,
could be generally adopted also in practice. There arose, even
in the last times of the fourth century, many men superior to
the prejudices of their age, such as Jovinian, and perhaps also
Vigilantius, who combated the doctrine of celibacy in the spiritual order. Jovinian rightly appeals to the fact that the
apostle Paul allowed one to be chosen a bishop who had a wife
and children. And Jerome names bishops among the friends
of Vigilantius, who, because they feared the pernicious consequences to morals of a constrained celibacy, *would ordain no
others as deacons but those who were married.**

This idea of the priesthood was bad, also, in its influence on
the prevailing notions with regard to the training necessary for
those who were preparing for the spiritual order. As many
placed implicit confidence in the magical effects of the priestly
ordination, whereby the supernatural powers, of which the
priest was to be the channel, were communicated at once ; as
they held the outward acts of the church, by which the priest
was supposed to set in motion the higher energies communicated to him, to be the principal thing in the administration of
his office ; they were, for this very reason, led to suppose that
no special previous culture was necessary for this office.† It
is rue the more eminent teachers of the church—such men as
Gregory of Nazianzus, Chrysostom,‡ and Augustin§—combated this delusion, and laid down many wholesome and judicious
rules for the education of the spiritual order ; yet these in-
junctions, proceeding from individuals, could produce no ade-
quate effects, as they were not sufficiently sanctioned and upheld

* See Hieronym. adv. Vigilant. at the beginning. The frequent complaints about the συνείσακτοι of the clergy,—against whom canon 3 of the
Nicene council is directed (vol. I., s. 2, p. 467),—prove the bad effects
which the rules of celibacy had on *morals.*

† Gregory of Nazianz. sarcastically denounces this erroneous notion
in his satirical poem against the bishops, V. 503: Ἔιποι τάχ' αὖ τις ὡς
ἐπισκόπων χεῖρες | τότ' ἐν μέσῳ κήρυγμα (the public proclamation of the
choice made in the church); λούτρου τίς χάρις (the ordination, a second
baptism) ἅς τ' ἐκβοῶμεν, ὡς ἂν ἄξιοι μίσας | φωνάς, διδόντες τὴν καθάρσιν
τῆ κλίσει (prayer over the candidate who was kneeling) | καὶ τῷ τυραννη-
σάντι δῆθεν πνεύματι (as if the Holy Ghost at the ordination wrought with
irresistible power) | κρίσει δικαίων καὶ σόφων ἐπισκόπων.

‡ In his work περὶ ἱερωσύνης.

§ In his work de doctrina Christiana.

by the decrees of councils.* There was, moreover, a great want of institutions for the theological education of the spiritual order. The school at Alexandria was at first the only one. This became distinguished under the superintendence of the learned Didymus, who, although blind from his youth, was one of the most accomplished church-teachers of his time. Then arose, at the end of the fourth century, the theological school of Antioch, the formation of which had been already prepared, a century earlier, by the learned presbyters of that church. This school rendered itself particularly distinguished by diffusing a taste among the clergy for the thorough study of the scriptures.† From this, as the mother, several others sprang up in the Syrian church, whose salutary influence on that church continued long to be felt. In the Greek church it was the practice, as we may see in the examples of Basil of Cæsarea and Gregory of Nazianzus, for such young men as were destined, by the wish of their familes, to consecrate themselves to the service of the church, to visit the schools of general education, then flourishing at Athens, Alexandria, Constantinople, Cæsarea in Cappadocia, and Cæsarea in Palestine. Next, they passed some time in pursuing the study of the ancient

---

* In an old collection of ecclesiastical laws, belonging to the fifth century, falsely called the decisions of the fourth synod at Carthage, c. I., we find the only decree of this sort, which is itself, however, very generally expressed: Qui episcopus ordinandus est, antea examinetur, si sit literatus, si in lege Domini instructus, si in scripturarum sensibus cautus, si in dogmatibus ecclesiasticis exercitatus. See Mansi Concil. III. 949.

† Hence the Nestorian seminaries for the clergy were at the beginning particularly distinguished; as, for example, their school at Nisibis in Mesopotamia, which had a settled course of studies, and was divided into several classes. The teachers and students enjoyed special privileges in the Nestorian churches (see Assemani Bibl. Vat. t. III. p. 2, f .927). The North-African bishop Junilius, about the middle of the sixth century, describes this school, in the preface to his work de partibus divinæ legis, as one " where the holy scriptures were expounded by teachers publicly appointed, in the same manner as grammar and rhetoric were among the Romans." The well-known East-Gothic statesman and scholar Cassiodorus, who was troubled to find that in the West there were no public teachers of the right method of scriptural exposition, as there were of the right method of understanding the ancient authors, entered into an understanding with the Roman bishop Agapetus that such a school should be founded at Rome; but the stormy times prevented the execution of that plan. See præfat. l. I. de institutione div. Script.

literature, either with particular reference to their own improvement, or as rhetorical teachers in their native towns; until, by the course of their own meditations, or by some impression from without, a new direction, of more decided Christian seriousness, was given to their life. In this case, it now became their settled plan to consecrate their entire life to the service of the faith and of the church; whether it was that they entered immediately into some one of the subordinate grades of the spiritual order, or that they preferred, in the first place, in silent retirement, by sober collection of thought, by the study of the holy scriptures, and of the older church-fathers, either in solitude or in some society of monks, to prepare themselves for the spiritual office. That previous discipline in general literature had, in one respect, a beneficial influence; inasmuch as it gave a scientific direction to their minds in theology, and thus fitted them also for more eminent usefulness as church-teachers; as becomes evident when we compare the bishops so educated with others. But, on the other hand, the habits of style thus contracted, the vanity and fondness for display which were nourished in those rhetorical schools, had on many an influence unfavourable to the simplicity of the gospel, as may be seen, for example, after a manner not to be mistaken, in the case of Gregory of Nazianzus.

The cloisters, moreover, are to be reckoned, in the Greek church, among the seminaries for educating the clergy; and, indeed, among those of a healthful influence; in so far as a practical Christian bent, a rich fund of Christian experience, and an intimate acquaintance with holy scripture, was to be acquired in them; but, on the other hand, it is true, also, that a certain narrowness of theological spirit was engendered in the cloisters, injurious in its influence on the education of church-teachers, as may be perceived in the case of an Epiphanius; and those that received their education there were often at a loss how to adapt themselves to wider spheres of spiritual activity, especially when they were transferred at once to the great capital towns, as the example of Nestorius shows. The awkwardness of their movements, amid the intricate relations into which they were thrown, operated not seldom to hinder and disturb them in their labours.

An excellent seminary for the ecclesiastics, not merely of a single church, but of an entire province, was often the *clerus*

of a pious and well-informed bishop. Young men in this case
were first admitted into the body as church readers or copyists
(lectores or excerptores); they were trained up under his eye,
formed after his example, his counsels, his guidance; they
availed themselves of his experience, and were thus introduced,
under the most favourable auspices, into the field of practical
labour.   Many pious bishops, such as Augustin and Eusebius
of Vercelli, endeavoured, by drawing still closer the bond of
union among their clergy, and inducing them to live together
in common, to carry still farther this disciplinary influence of
theirs on the younger members of their order—the first germ
of the *canonical* life, afterwards so called.

We have already observed that, by the temporal advantages
connected with the spiritual profession, many who had neither
the inward call nor any other qualifications for this order
were led to aspire after church offices; so that, in fact, numbers became Christians solely with a view of obtaining some
post in the church, and enjoying the emoluments therewith
connected.   Several synods of these times endeavoured to
suppress this abuse.   Already the Nicene council, in its
second canon, ordered that no one, after being instructed for a
short time, and then baptized, should for the future, as had
been done before, be ordained a presbyter or a bishop; for
some time was necessary for the probation of a catechumen,
and a still longer trial was requisite after baptism; and the
council of Sardica, in its tenth canon, directed that, if a person of wealth, or from the arena of the forum, wished to become
a bishop, he should not attain to that office until he had gone
through the functions of a reader, deacon, and presbyter, and
spent sufficient time in each of these offices to make proof of
his faith and temper.   Yet these and similar laws availed but
little to diminish the evil; as it ever proves true that abuses
grounded in the wrong character of general relations are not
to be fundamentally cured by single prohibitory laws, but only
by the improvement of these general relations themselves.
The confounding of spiritual and worldly things was the
source of these abuses.   Hence it happened that the spiritual
offices presented so many attractions to those who would have
been the last men to be drawn by the essential character of
the spiritual calling itself; and hence, in the choice of candidates to spiritual offices, especially the most elevated, more

attention was paid to every one of the others than to the spiritual qualifications. Men considered what they had to expect, not so much from the spiritual qualifications of the candidate to care for the good of souls, as from his political influence to promote the external splendour of the church, the temporal well-being of the community.* As the source of these abuses continued ever to remain the same, these ecclesiastical laws were often enough violated; and in the Eastern church the evil was increased by the disorders growing out of disputes on matters of doctrine. Greater strictness on this point prevailed, in the main, with individual exceptions, in the church of the West, where the Roman bishops took ground decidedly against the practice by which laymen were elevated at once from worldly professions of an altogether different character to the highest stations in the church.†

This method of appointment to spiritual offices was not only attended with the mischievous consequence that, by these means, when such offices came thus to be filled by men altogether unworthy of them, every sort of corruption was introduced into the church; but also, in the most favourable cases, when men having the inward call for the spiritual standing were chosen at once, from some entirely foreign circle of action, to spiritual offices, without any preparatory training, it was natural that such persons, owing to their want of an independent theological education, instead of guiding, by a clear theological consciousness, the existing ecclesiastical

* The abuses in the appointment to episcopal offices, the methods by which men of the most alien occupations and modes of life found their way into them, are set forth by Gregory of Nazianzus in the caricature description of his carmen de episcopis, V. 150. He names *collectors of the tribute*, seamen, people who came from the plough and from the army. Although it is his object in this poem to expose the faults of the Eastern church in the most vivid light, yet his picture is assuredly not without truth. And the same writer says, in his remarkable farewell discourse before the church assembly at Constantinople, in the year 381 (orat. 32, f. 526), "People at present are on the look-out, not for priests, but for rhetoricians; not for those who understand the cure of souls, but for those who are skilled in the management of funds; not for those who offer with a pure heart, but for powerful intercessors."

† Thus the Roman bishop Siricius, in his letter ad Gallos episcopos, declares himself very emphatically against the practice of elevating to episcopal offices, by the favor popularis, those qui, secularem adepti potestatem, jus seculi exercuerunt.

spirit of their time, instead of separating the true from the
false in the existing church tradition, rather suffered themselves to be unconsciously borne along by the spirit of the
church for the time being; and thus contributed, by their instruction and by their course of procedure, to confirm and give
wider spread to those errors which had been transmitted from
earlier times.

As regards the participation of the laity in the election to
church offices, traces are still to be found in this period of the
share which the communities had once taken in this proceeding.   It continued to be the prevailing form that the bishop
in the first place named to the community the persons whom
he proposed as candidates to fill the vacant offices, and demanded if any one had aught to object to the choice ; and,
the acquiescence of the church being publicly expressed, an
official instrument (gesta ecclesiastica) was drawn up accordingly. Through the preponderating influence of the bishops,
this, it is true, might often be no more than a mere formality ;
but it was precisely in the case of appointments to the highest
offices of the church that this influence still often proved to
be greatest.   Before the provincial bishops could introduce a
regular choice according to the ecclesiastical laws, it sometimes happened that, by the voice of the whole community,
or of a powerful party in it, some individual standing high in
their confidence was proclaimed bishop.   But as, in the then
existing state of the church, the most pious, and they who
had a right conception of the essence of the spiritual office,
and who had at heart the spiritual interests of the community, did not constitute the majority and the most powerful
party, but rather, particularly in the more considerable towns,
it was often those very persons with whom impure motives
and a worldly interest mainly predominated who, as the most
reputable of the citizens, possessed the greatest influence ;
the elections, accordingly, which were made after this manner,
were not always the best ; and cases are to be met with in
which bishops and ecclesiastics who had at heart the true interests of the church, were brought into conflict with the bois-
terous demands of some popular party, governed by a bad
influence.* This abuse of the influence of the communities in

* Thus in the year 361 the popular party at Cæsarea in Cappadocia,

the choice of church officers furnished some good reason for restricting it.

Worldly interest, ambition, and the love of rule, frequently led bishops of the provincial towns, in the Eastern church, to aspire after the vacant bishoprics of the chief cities. Mischievous quarrels and disputes must often have arisen from this source, and the erroneous notion obtained, which was justly denounced by the emperor Constantine, that the large cities had greater claims than others to a bishop who was solicitous for the cure of souls.* Soon after the church in the East had become the dominant church of the state, it was deemed necessary to find some preventive against these abuses; but whatever measures were adopted, these, for the reasons already mentioned, like all similar precautionary legal measures against abuses springing out of the circumstances of the times, proved of little avail. The council of Nice, in its fifteenth canon, forbade the transfer, not only of bishops, but of presbyters and deacons, from one church to another, on account of the many disorders and schisms resulting from this

supported by the garrison of the place, insisted on having for their bishop one of the civil magistrates, Eusebius, who had as yet not been baptized; and the provincial bishops, many of whom perhaps had a better man in mind, allowed themselves to be forced to ordain him. A similar schism arose again on the demise of Eusebius, in choosing his successor. Basilius possessed, without doubt, so far as spiritual qualifications were concerned, the best claims to the office; but he was opposed by a party to whom his spiritual strictness and his purely spiritual mode of thinking were not acceptable. As Gregory of Nazianzus affirms (orat. 20, f. 342), the most considerable persons of the province were against him, and these had the worst men of the city on their side. Gregory says (orat. 19, f. 310), on this occasion, that the election ought to proceed particularly from the clergy and from the monks; but not from the most wealthy and powerful, or the blind impetuosity of the populace. In the negative part of his remark he is undoubtedly in the right; but, with regard to the positive part, it may be questioned whether, if the whole choice was made to depend on the classes mentioned, other impure motives might not equally enter in. In the letter which Gregory of Nazianzus wrote, in the name of his father, to the collective inhabitants of Cæsarea, he spoke against those elections which were decided by combinations and clanships (κατὰ φρατρίας καὶ συγγενείας). As the ill health of Basil had been made use of as an objection to his appointment, he wrote to them that it became them to consider they were not choosing an *athlete*, but a spiritual teacher. See Gregor. Naz. ep. 18 et 19.

* See vit. Constant. III. 60.

practice, which, contrary to the laws of the church, prevailed
in some districts.   But although this law, which, in reference
to the bishops, was sanctioned anew by the twentieth canon of
the Antiochian council, A.D. 341, was adhered to in all cases
where there was a particular interest that it should be, yet it
was often enough violated in the Eastern church, and treated
in the same way, in fact, as if it had no existence; as, indeed,
we find that Gregory of Nazianzus, about the year 382, could
reckon it among the laws *which had long been defunct.**   In
the same period, on the other hand, the Roman bishop Damasus declared it—and, on the principles held by the Western church, very justly—a law of the fathers which had always
been in force, that no officer ought to be transferred from one
church to another, because it gave occasion for disputes and
divisions.†   True, it was for the most part ambition that led
to the violation of this law of the church; but there were
cases too where this measure might conduce to the best interests of the church; as, for example, when the peculiar gifts of
an eminent individual, whose place of labour in some smaller
town might be easily made good, were peculiarly needed in
some wider field of action.

We remarked above that the bishops were often under the
necessity of interceding at the court in behalf of oppressed
cities or individuals; but this description of labour would
often furnish a pretext for worldly-minded men, who preferred
residing at court rather than with their flocks, and who more
willingly busied themselves with secular than with spiritual
matters, to absent themselves from their communities.   This
restless and meddlesome activity of the bishops beyond the
limits of their calling proved the source of many disorders in
the Eastern church.   To counteract the evil, the council of
Antioch, in the year 341 (canon 11), ordained that every
bishop, or ecclesiastic generally, who, without permission and
a recommendatory letter on the part of the provincial bishops,
and particularly of his metropolitan, presumed to visit the
emperor, should be excommunicated from the church and
deposed from his office.   Hosius bishop of Cordova complained at
the council of Sardica, because the bishops repaired to the court
so frequently and often so unseasonably with demands having

---

* Πάλαι τιθνηκότας νόμους.
† See Damasi epistola 9 ad Acholium Thessalonicensium episcopum.

no connection with their calling; leaving their dioceses, not, as it became them, to plead the cause of the poor and the widows, but for the purpose of securing places of honour and profit for this or that individual, and to manage for them their worldly concerns;—a practice which injured not a little the good name of the bishops, and which hindered them from speaking out with the same boldness where necessity called for it. Upon his motion it was resolved that in future no bishop, unless he had been specially summoned by the emperor, should visit the court; but, as it was the case that persons deserving compassion, who had been condemned for some offence to exile, to transportation, or to some other punishment, often took refuge in the church, and the latter must not refuse its aid to such individuals, it was on his motion resolved that the bishops, in such cases, should transmit the petition of such offenders by the hands of a deacon, and that the metropolitan should assist him by letters of recommendation.

The foundation having been already laid in the preceding period for distinguishing the bishops above the presbyters, and for gradually maturing the monarchical power of the episcopacy, this relation was carried out still farther, according to the same principles, in the present period. Men were accustomed, indeed, already, to consider the bishops as the successors of the apostles, as the necessary intermediate links of connection between the church and the original apostolic foundation, through whom the influences of the Holy Spirit were to be transmitted to all the other grades of the *clerus*, the latter being organs for their wider diffusion. It followed as a natural consequence from this idea, that the bishops alone could impart spiritual ordination. Again, it was in the Western church considered as the distinctive mark of the bishops, that they alone were empowered to administer the rite of *confirmation* (σφραγίς, signaculum)—(see vol. i., section 2). Hence at certain periods they visited the different parts of their dioceses for the purpose of imparting this seal to those who had been baptized by their presbyters.* It was held that they alone could consecrate the holy oil used

* See Hieronym. adv. Lucif. T. IV. f. 295, ed. Martianay. Qui in castellis aut in remotioribus locis per presbyteros et diaconos baptizati ante dormierunt, *quam ab episcopis inviserentur.*

in the rite of baptism; and that the presbyters could not,
unless empowered by them, even bestow absolution.* Yet
a Chrysostom and a Jerome still asserted the primitive
equal dignity of the presbyters and the bishops; very justly
believing that they found authority for this in the New Testament.†

As, from the idea of the bishops considered as the successors
of the apostles, everything else pertaining to the primacy of
these over the presbyters followed as a matter of course; so
from the idea of the priesthood necessarily proceeded the distinction of the presbyters above the deacons. The deacons
continued, in the main, to be the same as they were in the
preceding period; they attended on the bishops and the presbyters, while performing their official functions, and they had
various liturgical services of their own. It devolved on them
to recite the church prayers, and to give the signal for the
commencement of the different portions of divine service.
In the Western churches the gospels, as containing our Lord's
discourses, were distinguished from the other selections of
Scripture, in that they were read, not by the prelectors, but
by the deacons, at the public worship.‡ The office of deacons
having been rightly derived from those seven deacons appointed by the apostles at Jerusalem, it was held, through
a superstitious notion of the unchangeableness of the form, that
even in large churches there should be but seven deacons;
and hence, in large cities, the great number of presbyters singu-
larly contrasted with the small number of deacons. § Later it
came about in large cities that the original number was greatly

---

* Ut, sine chrismate et episcopi jussione, neque presbyter neque
diaconus jus habeant baptizandi. Comp. Innocentii epistola ad Decentium, s. 6, codex canonum ecclesiæ Africanæ, canon. 6 et 7. Chrismatis
confectio et puellarum consecratio a presbyteris non fiat, vel reconciliare
quemquam in publica missa presbytero non licere.

† See Chrysostom, hom. 11 on Timoth., at the beginning. Jerome, in
his commentary on the epistle of Titus, and ep. 101 ad Evangelum.
Quid facit, excepta ordinatione, episcopus, quod presbyter non faciat:
where perhaps he only had in mind the usage of the East.

‡ See Hieronym. ep. 93 ad Sabinian. vol. IV. f. 758. Concil. 2,
Vasense (at Vaison) 529, canon 2.

§ See Euseb. VI. 43. Hieronymus, ep. 146 or 101 ad Evangelum;
diaconos paucitas honorabiles facit. The order of the council of Neo-
cæsarea, c. 15, that even in large towns not more than seven deacons
should be appointed.

exceeded, so that in the sixth century, in the time of the emperor Justinian, the principal church in Constantinople could count a *hundred deacons;* * and it was now attempted to obviate the objection that this was a deviation from the apostolic usage, by maintaining that the deacons of this period ought not to be compared with those of the apostolic institution. The latter were only a temporary order, designed for the dispensation of alms to the poor;—and, in support of this view, an argument, on an insufficient basis, was drawn from the changes which, since those times, had taken place in the business of the deacons and in the management of the church funds.†

Although the *deacons,* according to the original institution, were to occupy a position far below that of the presbyters, yet it so happened in many districts that they sought to exalt themselves above the latter,‡ and it became necessary for the synods to make laws by which they should be once more confined within the appropriate bounds of their order.§ The reason of this, in the opinion of Jerome,‖ was not that the deacons, being fewer in number, were, like other rare things, more highly esteemed, but rather because, owing to their closer connection with the bishops, they enjoyed special regard as the confidential agents of the latter. Hence, this was particularly the case with the *archdeacons,* who stood at the head of the order, just as the arch-presbyters stood at the head of the presbyters ; for, as the former were often employed by the bishops as their deputies and plenipotentiaries, they thus obtained a predominant influence, which, doubtless, under weak bishops, they sometimes abused.¶

The institution of *deaconesses* had, as we remarked in speaking of the origin of this office in the preceding period, its special

---

* See Justinian. Novell. 1. I. N. 3.

† See Chrysostom, h. 14, act. ap. and Concil. Trullan. 2, can. 16.

‡ Jerome, for instance, complains of this, particularly in reference to the Roman church, ep. 145 ad Evangelum.

§ Concil. Nic. c. 18, and Concil. Laodicen. c. 25.   ‖ L. c.

¶ Thus Isidorus of Pelusium objects to a certain Lucius of Pelusium, au archdeacon, that by his wicked arts he kept the bishop, who blindly followed him (τὸν πιθόμινόν σοι ἀκρίτως ἱπίσκοπον), in the dark ; that he made traffic of ordination. He calls here the deacons ὀφθαλμοὺς ἱπίσκοπου ; the archdeacon should therefore ὅλος ὀφθαλμὸς ὑπάρχειν.. Isidor. Pelusiot. l. IV. ep. 188.

reason in the circumstances of those times.   When these circumstances changed, the office would also lose its significance.
Originally the deaconesses were looked upon as the female part
of the clerus ; and ordination was given them for the purpose
of consecrating them to their office, in the same sense as it was
given to the other clergy.*   The Nicene council seems still
to have recognised this also to be right.†   But now, when
exaggerated notions about the magical effects of ordination
and the dignity of the clerical order became continually more
predominant, men began to conceive something offensive in
the practice of ordaining deaconesses, and associating them
with the *clerus*—which practice was, perhaps, already forbidden by the council of Laodicea in their eleventh canon.‡   The

---

* We see this from Tertullian. ad uxorem, 1. I. c. 7, viduam *allegi
in ordinem.* Also the apostolic constitutions still know of no difference
between the ordination of deaconesses and other clerical ordinations.
The ordinary prayer of the bishop should, according to the same authority, run thus : " Eternal God, Father of our Lord Jesus Christ,
Creator of man and of woman : thou who didst fill with thy spirit
Miriam, Deborah, Hannah, and Huldah ; thou who didst vouchsafe to a
woman the birth of thy only-begotten Son ; thou who didst, in the
tabernacle and in the temple, place female keepers of thy holy gates ;—
look down now also upon this thy handmaid, and bestow on her the
Holy Ghost. that she may worthily perform the work committed to her,
to thy honour, and to the glory of Christ."

† Connected with this matter is the obscure passage in the 19th
canon, where, moreover, the reading is disputed.   The subject of discourse in this canon relates to the *Samosatenean* clergy, who, if they
joined the Catholic church and were found qualified and able, were to
be permitted to retain their places ; and it is then added, according to
the common reading, " The same rule shall hold good with regard to
the *deaconesses ;*" and it is accordingly presupposed that the latter
belonged to the spiritual order.   Shortly afterwards, from the proper
deaconesses are distinguished the (*abusivè*) so-called widows, who, *as
they had not received the* χειροθεσία, *belonged generally to the laity.*
According to this, the proper deaconesses received clerical ordination.
Following the other reading, it would in the first place run as follows :
" The same rule shall hold good with respect to the *deacons.*"   And in
this case, what comes after would relate to the proper deaconesses, and
it would follow from this that they had received no ordination whatever,
and were reckoned with the laity.   The whole connection, however,
seems chiefly to favour the first reading ; for it is difficult to see any
reason why, after the whole body of the clergy had been mentioned in
general, anything should now be said with regard to the deacons in
particular.

‡ This canon is likewise of doubtful interpretation: Μὴ δεῖν τὰς

Western church, in particular, declared very strongly against this custom.* Western synods of the fifth and six centuries forbade generally the appointment of deaconesses. Where ordained deaconesses were still to be found, it was ordered that they should receive in future the blessing of the bishop along with the laity ;—another proof that before this they were reckoned as belonging to the clergy.† Those prohibitions came, however, only from French synods ; and it cannot be inferred from them that the appointment of deaconesses in the Western church ceased at once, and in all the districts alike. In the East the deaconesses maintained a certain kind of authority for a longer period. We find among them widows possessed of property, who devoted their substance to pious works and institutions ; like Olympias, known on account of her connection with Chrysostom. They there had it in charge

λεγομένας πρεσβύτιδας ήτοι προκαθημένας ἐν ἐκκλεσία καθιστᾶσθαι. It may be, that the canon had no reference whatever to deaconesses generally, but only to the oldest of them, who, according to Epiphanius (hæres. 79), were styled distinctively πρεσβύτιδες. The phrase ἐν ἐκκλησία might then be connected either with the preceding or with the following word, and the passage explained thus : " As the oldest of the deaconesses have arrogated to themselves a special authority over the female portion of the church, the synod forbids the appointment of such." But since it was required generally, according to the ancient rule, that the deaconesses should be sixty years old, and since they were the presiding officers over the female part of the community, nothing forbids us to suppose that the name stands for the *deaconesses generally.* Now, if we suppose, what to be sure is not impossible, that the synod forbade the appointment of deaconesses generally, then this would conflict with the usage of the Greek church during this whole period. Or we might lay a particular emphasis on the phrase ἐν ἐκκλησία, and, connecting it with the word that follows, understand the sense to be, that *ecclesiastical consecration* or *ordination* only was forbidden to the deaconesses. The *article* in the passage would favour this last explanation.

* Hilarius (called the Ambrosiast) says of the Montanists, Etiam ipsas diaconas ordinari debere vana præsumptione defendunt. But the Montanists adhered in this case simply to the ancient usage of the church; for, as to the rest, they too followed the general rule which excluded women from speaking publicly before the church.

† The first council of Orange (Arausicanum, in the year 441), c. 26. Diaconæ omnimodis non ordinandæ: si quæ jam sunt, benedictioni, quæ populo impenditur, capita submittant. So, too, the council of Epaon, in the year 517, c. 27 ; the second council of Orleans, in the year 583, c. 18. Yet this council attributed to such an ordination a certain validity ; since, in its 17th canon, it directed that the ordained deaconesses who had remarried should be excluded from the fellowship of the church.

also, by private instruction, to prepare the women in the country for baptism, and to be present at their baptism.[*] It was considered the privilege of the wives of bishops, who, by common understanding, separated from their husbands after the latter had bound themselves to a life of celibacy, that, if found worthy, they might be consecrated as deaconesses;[†] and thus the female church-office continued to be preserved in the East down into the twelfth century.

Without any change in the grades of the clerical order hitherto existing to the church-offices already established, many new ones, of greater or less importance, were added, which had been rendered necessary in part by the great increase of ecclesiastical business in large towns. As the chief wealth of the churches consisted in landed estates, and the care of improving and farming these estates required much labour and attention, the management of these matters was specially intrusted to one of the clergy, under the name of "steward" (οἰκονόμος),[‡] and this officer obtained by degrees the supervision generally over the income and expenditures of the church. This method of procedure was not, however, everywhere followed alike; and, for this reason, the council of Chalcedon directed, in its 25th canon, that all bishops should appoint such "stewards," who, intrusted under their authority with the management of the church revenues, could be witnesses of the manner in which they were administered. Thus the malappropriation of the property of the churches by the bishops, as well as the suspicion of any such thing, was to be provided against. But, inasmuch as the management of property and the protection of the poor who were supported by the church might sometimes lead to lawsuits; and inasmuch as the conducting of such suits did not seem compatible with the standing of the clergy, and they

---

[*] See Pelagius on Romans xvi. 1. This custom must have existed also in other places besides the East; for in a collection of *Western*, perhaps North-African church ordinances, which are wrongly quoted as coming from a fourth council of Carthage, a canon (c. 12) occurs: Viduæ vel sanctimoniales, quæ ad ministerium baptizandarum mulierum eliguntur, tam instructæ sint ad officium, ut possint et sano sermone docere imperitas et rusticas mulieres, tempore, quo baptizandæ sunt, qualiter baptizatori interrogatæ respondeant et qualiter accepto baptismate vivant.

[†] Concil. Trull. II. 691. canon 48.

[‡] Vid. Basil. Cæsar. ep. 285 and 237.

were wanting, moreover, in the requisite legal knowledge; the expedient was finally adopted that the church, like other corporations, should have, for the management of its affairs, a person skilled in the law, who should always stand prepared to defend its rights. This individual was called the ἔκδικος, defensor.*

Again, the drawing up of the protocols, or reports, of the public acts of the church (the gesta ecclesiastica), which were prepared with great exactness, rendered necessary the appointment of trust-worthy secretaries, familiar with short-hand writing, out of the body of the clergy (the notarii, exceptores). The choice in this case, as in that of the prelectors, was made, by many of the churches, out of the class of young men who were to be trained up for the service of the church.†

As we observed, in the preceding period the spirit of Christian charity and tenderness was shown, from the first, in the care of providing for the sick, and in the attention bestowed on the burial of the dead. Yet perhaps no particular church-offices were, till now, instituted with reference to these objects; it had been a voluntary work of Christian love.‡ But, as in this period general hospitals had been established under the direction of the churches, it became necessary that particular individuals should be appointed in the churches to take care of the sick. They were called *Parabolani*.§ At Alexandria,

* The council of Carthage, of the year 401, resolved to petition the emperor, that persons might be assigned to the churches, with the approbation of the bishops, who should be prepared to defend the poor against the oppressions of the rich. See canon 10, in the Cod. canon. eccles. Afr. c. 75; the council of Carthage, in the year 407, c. 3, Cod. Afr. c. 97, ut dent facultatem defensores constituendi scholasticos (advocates). Which was granted: see Cod. Theodos. l. XVI. Tit. II. l. 38, comp. Possid. vit. Augustin. c. 12. Different from these defensores were the stewards and agents of the bishops, occurring under the same name in the Roman church. These latter the bishops chose from their clergy; and they are frequently mentioned in the letters of Gregory the Great.

† Epiphanius, afterwards bishop of Ticinum (Pavia), in the fifth century, after having been prelector when eight years of age, was admitted, as soon as he had made some proficiency in the art of short-hand writing, among the exceptores of the church. See his life by Eunodius.

‡ In respect to burial, comp. Cyprian's behaviour during the pestilence, vol. I. s. 1.

§ Παραβόλανοι, from the Greek παραβαλλίσθαι τὴν ζώην, ψύχην, since these people, in cases of contagious disease, exposed their lives to danger.

they formed, in the fifth century, a distinct order or guild, which might legally consist of *six hundred* members. But, it must be admitted, the same abuse seems to have crept in here which infected so many of the institutions of the churches in the principal cities. Wealthy citizens, who of course kept aloof from actual attendance on the sick, obtained admittance into this guild, merely for the sake of enjoying the exemptions to which it was entitled; and the ambitious prelates of Alexandria sought, by the multitude of these *Parabolani*, to form around them a body of men devoted to their interests, whom they could employ for purposes which were not always the purest. Hence it became necessary to provide by civil statutes against the abuses to which this institution was liable.[*]

The burial of the dead was also committed to the care of a particular class of men, retained in the service of the church (the κοπιάται, copiatæ, fossores).[†]

In respect to the constitution of the episcopal dioceses, the country bishops (χωρεπίσκοποι) (see vol. i.), who probably had their origin in very early times, first appear in conflict with the city bishops in the fourth century. The former name was borne by such as presided over the church of a principal village, and to whom a certain number of village churches, which had their own presbyters or pastors, were subjected.[‡] As the episcopal system connected with the city churches had at so early a period become already matured, this system would now, as a matter of course, be extended also to the relation of the churches subordinated to the rural or chor-bishops; and these latter themselves provoked the restriction of their power by the abuse which they made of it.[§] By synods

---

[*] Cod. Theodos. l. XVI. Tit. II. I. XLII. et XLIII.

[†] Vid. Hieronymi, ep. 17 ad Innocent. Clerici, quibus id officii erat, cruentum, linteo cadaver obvolvunt (of one who had been executed), &c. Cod. Theodos. l. XIII. Tit. I. l. I. and l. XVI. Tit. II. l. XV.

[‡] Such a circle of village churches under a chor-bishop was called a συμμορία. Οἱ προστησάμινοι τῆς συμμορίας. Basil. ep. 290, and ep. 142. The several places subordinate to the episcopal main village were denominated ἀγροὶ ὑποκείμινοι, or ὑποτελοῦντες τῷ . . . Basil. ep. 138, or canonica I. canon 10.

[§] Basil of Cæsarea learned that his chor-bishops had received into the service of the church many unworthy men, who were only seeking to escape the military service by procuring themselves to be ordained as ecclesiastics. For this reason he required them to send him an accurate list of all the ecclesiastics in their dioceses, and directed them to ordain

of the fourth century it was settled that the chor-bishops should only have power to nominate and ordain, without consulting the city bishop, ecclesiastics of the lower grade.[*]

The council of Sardica, and the council of Laodicea, at length forbade wholly the *appointment of chor-bishops.* The former, indeed, prohibited the appointment of bishops in those smaller towns where one presbyter would suffice as presiding officer over the church. The reason given for this ordinance was one which grew out of a perverted hierarchical pride —namely, *that the name and the authority of the bishops should not be degraded.*[†] The council of Laodicea ordained, moreover, that in place of the country bishops, *visitors* (περιοδευταί) should be appointed; that is, probably, that the bishops should nominate certain presbyters of their own clergy to make visitations of the country churches in their name; and thus, in respect to general oversight and other business, to supply the place of the chor-bishops.[‡] Yet,

no one for the future without informing and consulting him. He. asserted, however, that this had been the ancient usage. Basil. ep. 54.

[*] See the thirteenth canon of the council of Ancyra. Concil. Antio-chen. canon 9. The council of Laodicea directed, indeed, in its fifty-seventh canon, that they should have power to do nothing without consulting the city bishop.

[†] Concil. Laodicen. c. 57. Concil. Sardic. c. 6.

[‡] The word περιοδεύειν is employed to denote those tours of visitation which the bishops, accompanied by a number of clergy and laity, made through the several parts of their dioceses. Athanas. Apolog. c. Arianos, s. 74, according to ed. Patav. T. I. p. 1. f. 151, a. We might accordingly suppose that those presbyters whom the bishops empowered, in their stead, to make such tours of visitation in particular portions of their dioceses, would be designated with the name περιοδευταί. Accordingly, such occur in the times of the Dioclesian persecution, who, during the absence of the captured Egyptian bishops, were invested with full powers to make the visitations in their dioceses. The bishops say, Multi euntes et redeuntes ad nos, qui poterant visitare. See the letter of the Egyptian bishops to Miletius, in Maffei Osservazioni letterarie, T. III. p. 15. At the same time, the notion of a person travelling about as a visitor, is by no means necessarily implied in the term περιοδευτης. It might also signify simply an *inspector*, who, the name only being changed, was the same as the chor-bishop before him; for περιοδεύειν, περιοδευτης are terms which sometimes occur in the sense to attend upon, to heal, physician. See the Homily, erroneously ascribed to Athanasius, in cœcum, s. 9 and s. 12. The former signification is, however, the more probable one. The predicate περιοδευτης is given to a presbyter: Σεργιος πρεσβυτερος και περιοδευτης, in the acts of the council under the Patriarch Mennas, at Constantinople, in the year 536, actio 1.

Q 2

chor-bishops are still to be met with, at later periods, in the churches of Syria and in the West.

But the practice became continually more general of substituting, in the place of the chor-bishops, presbyters placed by the city bishops over the country churches, which presbyters stood in a relation of more immediate dependence on the latter.[*]

In respect to the city churches, it was absolutely necessary, it is true, in this period, that, besides the old episcopal and principal church, other churches should be founded; in which, since all could not be conveniently accommodated with room in the principal church, the portions of the community dwelling at a distance might hold their assemblies on Sundays and feast-days. Still it was by no means as yet a general regulation that in the cities, as in the country, separate filial communities arose under the supervision of the episcopal headchurch. Epiphanius cites it as a peculiarity of the Alexandrian church, that there, on account of the wants of the inhabitants, different churches under particular presbyters, as parish clergymen, were founded, to which the residents in adjacent streets belonged.[†] At Constantinople, each church had also its own particular clergy. The founders of churches determined, at the same time, the number of clergy for them, and the proportional amount of revenue. The three filial churches of the mother church at Constantinople formed here the only exception; these had no separate body of clergy; but a certain number, taken interchangeably, according to a certain routine, from the clerus of the principal church, were sent on Sundays and feast-days to conduct the public worship in these churches. We are not warranted, however, from this fact, to determine anything as to the regulations of the

---

[*] The term $\pi\alpha\rho\omicron\iota\kappa\iota\alpha$ denoted originally each church: Ἐκκλησία ἡ παροικοῦσα, Euseb. III. 28, subsequently the greater divisions of the church, which in the political phraseology were denominated διοικήσεις, Basil. ep. 66; so also a smaller ecclesiastical whole, the city church, with its filial country communities; and finally the country communities in particular, Basil. ep. 206 and 240. Hence the Latin Parœcia, Parochia, Presbyter regens parochiam, Sulpic. Sever. dial. l. I. c. 8. And hence Parochus.

[†] Hæres. 29, Arian. Ὅσαι ἐκκλησίαι τῆς καθολίκης ἐκκλησίας ἐν Ἀλεξανδρίᾳ ὑπὸ ἵνα ἀρχιεπίσκοπον οὖσαι, καὶ κατ᾽ ἰδίαν ταύταις ἐπιτεταγμένοι εἰσι πρεσβύτεροι διὰ τὰς ἐκκλησιαστίκας χρείας τῶν οἰκητέρων, πλησίων ἑκάστης αὐτῶν καὶ ἀμφόδων ἤτοι λάβρων ἐπιχωρίως καλουμίνων.

other churches in this great capital.* At Rome, the relation of *all* the other churches to the episcopal head-church seems to have been very nearly like the relation of those three filial churches to the head-church at Constantinople; but perhaps with this difference, that though all the clergy were incorporated with the clerus of the episcopal head-church, yet they did not conduct the public worship in the other churches by turns; but its own particular presbyter was constantly assigned to each one of these churches (tituli).† The Roman presbyters who conducted the public worship in the filial churches had not, however, the right of consecrating the holy supper; but bread which had been consecrated by the bishop was sent to them from the principal church : this they simply distributed,‡ —the holy symbol serving at the same time to denote the unbroken ecclesiastical bond between them and the bishop of the principal church.

The *metropolitan constitution*, which we saw growing up in the preceding period, became in this more generally diffused and more perfectly matured and consolidated. On the one. hand, to the metropolitans was conceded the superintendence over all ecclesiastical affairs of the province to which their metropolis belonged; it was decided that they should convoke the assemblies of provincial bishops, and preside over their deliberations; but, on the other hand, their relation to the entire *collegium* of the provincial bishops, and to the indi-

---

* Justinian. I. T. III. Novell. III. Οὐκ ἰδιαζόντται κληρίκους, οὐδὲ εἴς τουτῶν ἔχει τῶν τρίων οἴκων, κοίνοι δὲ εἴσι τῆς τὲ ἁγιοτάτης μιγάλης ἐκκλησίας καὶ αὐτῶν, καὶ τούτους ἁπάντες περινοστούντες κατὰ τίνα περίοδον καὶ κύκλον, τὰς λειτουργίας ἐν αὐτοῖς ποιούνται.

† That the presbyters of the filial churches at Rome did not quit their connection with the clerus of the principal church, seems to follow from the words of the Roman bishop Innocent, in his letter to the bishop Decentius, of the year 416, s. 8, Quarum (ecclesiarum) presbyteri, quia *die ipso*, propter plebem sibi creditam, nobiscum convenire non possunt (where seems to be understood the words,—sicuti cæteris diebus nobis—cum conveniunt), as also the words—ut se a nostra communione, maxime illo die, non judicent separatos. But that the presbyters were usually appointed, in the case of these filial churches, to minister for some considerable length of time, seems evident from the designation of a church of this sort at Rome : Ἔνθα Θίτων ὁ πρισβύτερος συνήγεν (the church where he was accustomed to conduct the worship). Athanas. apolog. c. Arian. s. 20.

‡ In the above-cited passages from the letter of Innocent, Fermentum a nobis confectum per acolythos accipiunt.

viduals composing it, were also more strictly defined, so as to
prevent any arbitrary extension of their power, and to establish on a secure footing the independence of all the other
bishops in the exercise of their functions.   For this reason,
the provincial synods, which were bound to assemble twice in
each year, as the highest ecclesiastical tribunal for the whole
province, were to assist the metropolitans in determining all
questions relating to the general affairs of the church; and
without their participation, the former were to be held incom-
petent to undertake any business relating to these matters of
general concern.   Each bishop was to be independent in the
administration of his own particular diocese, although he could
be arraigned before the tribunal of the provincial synods for
ecclesiastical or moral delinquencies.   No choice of a bishop
could possess validity without the concurrence of the metropolitan ; he was to conduct the ordination ; yet not alone, but
with the assistance of at least *two* other bishops ; and all the
bishops of the province were to be present at the ordination of
the metropolitan.

We noticed already, in the preceding period, that the
churches in some of the larger capital towns of entire great
divisions of the Roman empire, from which towns also Christianity had extended itself in wider circles, had attained to a
certain pre-eminence and peculiar dignity in the estimation of
Christians.   This, by force of custom, passed over also into
the present period ; yet without any distinct expression at first
of the views of the church on that point.   The council of
Nice, in its sixth canon, which, by its vague, indeterminate
language, gave occasion for many disputes, was the first to
attempt to settle some definite rule on this point, particularly
with reference to the *Alexandrian* church ; having been led
to do this, perhaps, by occasion of the Meletian controversies
in Egypt.   It is here said: " Let the ancient custom which
has prevailed in Egypt, Libya, and Pentapolis, that the
bishop of Alexandria should have authority over all these
places, be still maintained, since this is the custom also with
the Roman bishop.   In like manner, at Antioch, and in the
other provinces, the churches shall retain their ancient pre-
rogatives."[*]   Afterwards this canon goes on to speak of the

---

[*] Τὰ ἀρχαῖα ἔθη κρατείτω τὰ ἐν Αἰγύπτῳ καὶ Λιβύῃ καὶ Πενταπόλει,
ὥστε τὸν ἐν Ἀλεξανδρείᾳ ἐπίσκοπον πάντων τούτων ἔχειν τὴν ἐξουσίαν, ἐπειδὴ

rights of the metropolitans generally ; from which, however, we are not to infer that the bishops first named were placed in the same class with all the other metropolitans: on the con‑ trary, they are cited as metropolitans of higher rank, though nothing was definitely said respecting their precise relation to the other metropolitans. As in the provinces here named, which were to be subordinate to the Alexandrian church, there were also particular metropolitans, it is plainly evident that some higher rank must have been intended, in this case, than that which was attributed to the ordinary metropolitan. The whole relation having been in the first place of political origin, it was designated at first by a name borrowed from the political administration of the empire. As the magistrates that presided over the political administration in these main divisions of the Roman empire were denominated *Exarchs* (ἐξάρχοι), this appellation was transferred also to those who presided over the ecclesiastical government.* Subsequently, choice was made of the more ecclesiastical name of *Patriarchs*.†

Originally, it was the churches of the three great capital cities

καὶ τῷ ἐν τῇ Ρώμῃ ἐπισκόπῳ τοῦτο συνῆθες ἔστιν· ὁμοίως δὲ καὶ κατὰ τὴν 'Αντιοχείαν καὶ ἐν ταῖς ἄλλαις ἐπαρχίαις, τὰ πρεσβεῖα σωζίσθαι ταῖς ἐκκλησίαις.

* See Concil. Chalc. canon 8 : 'Ο ἐξάρχος τῆς διοικησέως, and canon 16. Doubtless many eminent bishops were then still reckoned among the exarchs, who subsequently were not recognized as patriarchs.

† This name occurs first at the council of Constantinople in the year 381, in an application somewhat different from that which it afterwards received. When, in consequence of the preceding controversies con‑ cerning doctrines, many schisms arose in the Eastern church, and it became necessary to correct various disorders, it was determined, for the sake of restoring unanimity and order in the church, to appoint—besides the bishops of Alexandria, Antioch, and Constantinople, who were already, through their churches, possessed of a peculiar precedence of rank—certain individual bishops that had acquired this distinction by virtue of their personal character; and these were intrusted with a supervisory power over the several dioceses and provinces of the Roman empire—as Asia Minor, Pontus, and Cappadocia—under the name of *Patriarchs*. In particular it was decided that none but such as stood on terms of church fellowship with these individuals should share in the common rites of the Catholic church (see Cod. Theodos. 1. XVI. Tit. II. I. III. Socrat. hist. V. 8). To this arrangement, and the quarrel among the bishops which sprung out of it, Gregory of Nazianzus alludes, in his Carmen de Episcopis, V. 798, where he says to the bishops, Θρόνους μὲν ἔχοιτε καὶ τυραννίδας | ὑμεῖς, ἔπει καὶ πρῶτα ταῦθ' ὑμῖν δόκει | χαιροίτε, ὑβρίζοίτε, πατριαρχίας | κληροῦσθε· κόσμος ὑμῖν εἰκέτω μέγας.

of the Roman empire, Rome, Alexandria, and Antioch, which
held this prominent rank. In these churches, which were
regarded, moreover, as ecclesiæ apostolicæ, ecclesiastical and
political considerations were conjoined. But to these there
was now added another church, which had in its favour neither
antiquity of political nor of ecclesiastical dignity; while many
churches which were subordinated to it, as, for instance, the
church of Ephesus, had precedence over it, as by ecclesiastical
character, so by its political relation in the ancient constitution
of the Roman empire. When the city of Byzantium, which
in earlier times was itself subordinate to the metropolis at
Heraclea in Thrace, became, under the name of Constantinople, the seat of government for the whole of the Roman
empire in the East, and the second capital of the entire Roman
world, it was necessary that its church also should be distinguished as the church of the second imperial residence, and
should receive the rank of a patriarchate. Accordingly, the
second ecumenical council of Constantinople directed already
in 381, in its second canon, that the bishop of Constantinople
should take rank next after the Roman bishop, since Constantinople was New Rome;* and the council of Chalcedon
(A.D. 451), in its last canon but one, confirmed this decree
with the following noticeable comparison between the church
of the ancient and that of the new Rome: "*The fathers
rightly conceded that rank to the episcopate of ancient Rome,
because Rome was the mistress city;*" and following out the
same principle, the fathers of this council of Constantinople
attributed equal rank to the episcopate of the new Rome,
because they rightly judged that the city which was the seat
of the imperial government and of the senate, enjoyed equal
dignity with ancient Rome, had the same precedence in ecclesiastical affairs, and must take the second place after the latter;
so that the bishop of Constantinople ought to ordain the metropolitans of the dioceses of Pontus, Asia Minor, and Thrace,
and also the collective bishops of the barbarian tribes within
those dioceses. Finally, after many disputes with the church
of Antioch, there was added still the fifth patriarchate, of a
church distinguished simply in a spiritual respect, enjoying

---

* Ἔχειν τὰ πρισβεῖα τῆς τιμῆς μετὰ τὸν τῆς Ῥώμης ἐπίσκοπον, διὰ τὸ
εἶναι αὐτὴν νέαν Ῥώμην.

originally not even the rank of a metropolis, the patriarchate of Jerusalem.*

The division of the whole Romish church jurisdiction into four or five patriarchates, intimately connected as it was, in part, with the political constitution of the Roman empire, would naturally have respect, in the first place, to those churches only which lay within the bounds of the Roman empire ; although it naturally exerted some indirect influence also on those churches without the empire, which had been planted by the churches within it. But it did not apply in the same sense, and in the same way, even to all those parts which belonged to the empire. A peculiar spirit of freedom distinguished, from the earliest times, the church of North Africa. The church at Carthage had, it is true, enjoyed by custom particular consideration as the church of the principal city of North Africa ; her bishop presided in all the general assemblies of the North-African church ;† yet he by no means stood in the same relation to the bishops of the other five North-African churches, as the patriarchs did to the bishops of their greater church dioceses ; and even the bishop of Rome did not properly possess the authority of a patriarch in the North-African church. This church, in a council at Hippo-regius (now Bona, in the district of Algiers), A.D. 393, protested expressly against such a title as the patriarchs bore in other countries, and would recognize the validity of no other title than that of bishop of the first church.‡

Since the patriarchal constitution formed a still more universal bond of unity for the church than that of the metropolitan bishops, and since the patriarchs stood related to the metropolitans in the same manner as the latter to the bishops, it is possible that, by this means, greater unity and order were introduced into the management of all the ecclesiastical affairs of the Roman church : but it may be questioned if the outward unity which was brought about by this system of constraint, proved salutary in its influence on the church development. The bond of outward constraint could never

, * Concil. Chalc. act. VII.

† Concilia plenaria Africæ.

‡ Canon 39 in Cod. Canon. Eccles. Afr. Ut primæ sedis episcopus non appelletur princeps sacerdotum, aut summus sacerdos (ἐξάρχος τῶν ἱρέων), aut aliquid hujusmodi : sed tantum primæ sedis episcopus.

rightly adjust itself to the spirit of Christianity, which requires a free outward development of the individuality of character from within.   The history of the church in the fifth century, in particular, teaches how oppressive the des-potism of the patriarchs at Alexandria and at Antioch some-times became.   And if, on the one hand, four principal por-tions of the Romish church were in this manner brought into closer unity ; yet, on the other, oppositions so much the more violent were thereby engendered between the patriarchal churches of the East,—the sources of numberless schisms and disorders.   The history of the church in these centuries shows how much of impure, worldly interest became diffused in the church, through the eager thirst and strife of the bishops for precedence of rank ; what mischievous disputes sprang out of the mutual jealousies of the patriarchs, — particularly the jealousies of the patriarchs of Alexandria towards the patri-archs of Constantinople,—and how this state of things contri-buted to check the oppositions of the different tendencies of the dogmatic spirit in their free evolution, and to intermingle with them worldly and party passions ; so that, by the impure motives which made use of the doctrinal interest as a pretext, this interest itself was smothered.   Very justly could Gregory of Nazianzus say, as he did at Constantinople in 380, when lamenting over the evils of the church, which he had learned from his own experience : " Would to heaven there were no primacy, no eminence of place, and no tyrannical precedence of rank ; that we might be known by eminence of virtue alone ! But, as the case now stands, the distinction of a seat at the right hand or the left, or in the middle ; at a higher or a lower p ace ; of going before or aside of each other, has given rise to many disorders among us to no salutary purpose whatever, and plunged multitudes in ruin." *

In proceeding to speak, then, of the Roman bishop in par-ticular, regard must be had to two different points of view : *the Roman bishop, considered as one of those four patriarchs,* in his relation to the more extended church jurisdiction, which was subordinate to the Roman church in especial ; *and the Roman bishop in his relation to the entire church,* or *particu-larly to that of the West.*   As it respects the first ;—it is to this, the above-cited sixth canon of the Nicene council has

* Orat. XXVIII. f. 484.

reference; and probably Rufinus* gives, in this case, the most correct explanation of the matter, when he expounds this canon as implying that the diocese of the Roman bishop embraced the whole circle or district which belonged to the administration of the vicarius urbis Romæ (the provincias suburbicarias, i.e., the major part of middle Italy; all lower Italy, Sicily, Sardinia, and Corsica†). Add to this, that the Roman church had become possessed, by donations and legacies, of many landed estates lying without these limits, which gave her opportunity of knitting firmly to her interests many influential connections. Again, as the whole constitution of the church in the Roman empire hung closely connected with the political constitution, the Roman church necessarily possessed this advantage over all the patriarchal churches, that it was the church of the ancient capital of the Roman empire. This politico-ecclesiastical point of view was always made of prominent importance by the Orientals, as is shown in the above-cited decrees of the Constantinopolitan and of the Chalcedonian councils. Theodoretus, bishop of Cyprus, says, in a letter in which he solicited the aid of the Roman bishop, Leo the Great,‡ that everything conspired to give the church of Rome the primacy: those advantages which, in other cases, were found distributed among different churches, and whatever distinguishes a city, either in a political or in a spiritual respect, were here conjoined;—and he then proceeds to notice first the political superiority. Rome was the largest, the most splendid, the most populous city: from her proceeded the existing magisterial power; from her the whole empire took its name. Finally, the great distinction of the Roman church, in respect to religion, was, that she had been honoured by the martyrdom of the apostles Peter and Paul, and possessed their tombs, which were objects of reverence also to the East. §

* Rufin. I. 5, ut suburbicariarum ecclesiarum sollicitudinem gerat.
† See Notitia Dignitatum Imperii Romani, sectio 45, and the letter of the council of Sardica to the Roman bishop Julius, s. 5. Ut per tua scripta qui in *Sicilia*, qui in *Sardinia*, et in *Italia*, sunt fratres nostri, quæ acta sunt cognoscant.
‡ Ep. 113.
§ Theodoretus, in the letter above referred to, expresses himself on this subject as follows, Ἔχει καὶ τῶν κοίνων πατέρων καὶ διδασκάλων τῆς ἀληθείας, Πέτρου καὶ Παύλου, τὰς θήκας, τῶν πιστῶν τὰς ψύχας φωτιζούσας. So an illuminating influence, which issued from their proximity.

All this taken together might create, even among the Orientals, a peculiar veneration for the Roman church.

With the people of the West all this was made to rest on such dogmatic grounds as converted it into something entirely different. We observed already, in the preceding period, how from confounding the ideas of the visible and the invisible church, from the notion of a necessary outward unity of the church, the idea had there sprung up of an uninterrupted outward representation of this unity, necessarily existing at all times; and how this idea had been transferred to the cathedra Petri in the Roman church. This idea, handed down, in its yet vague and unsettled shape, to the present period in connection with its root, the false and grossly conceived Old Testament view of the Theocracy, contains within it the entire germ of the papacy, which needed nothing more than to unfold itself, under favourable circumstances, in the congenial soil of the spirit of an age in which the confusion of the outward form with the inner essence became continually more inveterate.

We saw this idea carried out to some extent in the preceding period, particularly in the North-African church:—not that this tendency of the Christian mind prevailed more than elsewhere in the North-African church; but rather, because here was the dogmatic spirit which apprehended this tendency with the clearest consciousness,—and in this church it appears again, during the present period, with peculiar prominence. Optatus of Mileve, who wrote in the last half of the fourth century, represents the apostle Peter as the head of the apostles, —as the representative of the unity of the church and of the apostolic power, who had received the keys of the kingdom of heaven for the purpose of giving them to the others. He finds it worthy of remark, that Peter, notwithstanding that he had denied Christ, yet continued to hold this relation to the rest of the apostles, so that the objective side of the unity of the church, which was thus incapable of being invalidated by any human fault, appears in its unchangeable constancy. In the Roman church he perceives the indestructible cathedra Petri. This stands in the same relation to the other episcopal churches as the apostle Peter stood to the rest of the apostles. The Roman church represents the one visible church, the one episcopate.* There was one apostolic power

* See Optatus Milevitan. l. VII. c. 3. Bono unitatis Petrus satis erat,

in Peter, from which the apostolic powers of the others issued forth, as it were like so many different streams; and, in like manner, there is one episcopal power in the Roman church, from which the other episcopal powers are but so many different streams. How much might be derived out of this idea so apprehended? Far more than the individual who thus expressed himself was aware of. Augustin would be led by his thoroughly Christian character; by the prevailing tendency in his inner life and in his system of faith to the objectively godlike; by that spirit of protestation against all deification of man which actuated him,—and by which no inconsiderable opposition was, in the next succeeding centuries, actually excited against the Catholic element, although, in the case of Augustin himself, this religious element had become completely fused with the Catholic; by all these inward causes Augustin would be led to more correct views of the words of our Lord in their reference to Peter. He rightly perceived that not Peter, but Christ himself is the Rock on which the church has been founded; that this word of our Lord, therefore, has reference only to that faith in Christ in the person of Peter, through which he was the man of rock; and that consequently the whole church, which rests on this faith, is represented by Peter. " He was," says Augustin, " in this case, the image of the whole church, which in the present world is shaken by divers trials, as by floods and storms; and yet does not fall, because it is founded on the rock from which Peter received his name. For the rock is not so called after Peter, but Peter is so called after the rock; just as Christ is not so denominated after the Christian, but the Christian after Christ; for it is on this account our Lord declares, On this rock I will found my church, because Peter had said : Thou art the Christ, the Son

si post quod negavit, solam veniam consequeretur, et præferri apostolis omnibus meruit et claves regni cœlorum communicandas cæteris, solus accepit. Thus men confounded the faith which Peter expressed in the spirit of all believers, and to which alone Christ's words referred, with the person of Peter as a man; instead of drawing the conclusion from this very circumstance of Peter's denial, that *his person* could, as little as that of any other man, furnish the rock on which the kingdom of Christ was to be built. And l. II. c. 2: In urbe Roma a Petro primo cathedram episcopalem esse collatam, in qua sederit omnium apostolorum caput Petrus, in qua una cathedra unitas ab omnibus servaretur, ne cæteri apostoli singulas sibi quisque defenderent.

of the living God.   On this rock, which thou hast confessed,
he declares I will build my church ;* for Christ was the Rock
on whose foundation Peter himself was built ; for other foundation hath no man laid than that which is laid, which is
Christ Jesus." †   Had Augustin made himself clearly conscious of what he here expressed, and prosecuted it to the
end, he would have arrived at the conception of the church
as the community of the believers in Christ, and so—as this
faith is an inward invisible fact—to the conception of the
invisible church ; and consequently this passage would no
longer have retained with him the sense which men would
fain give it in reference to the visible church, to the episcopal
power, and to the relation of the Roman church in particular
to the church universal.   Having once been led, however, by
the whole course of his religious and theological training, into
the habit of confounding together the visible and the invisible
church, and having allowed this error to become firmly rooted
in his doctrinal system, his views became thereby narrowed ;
and instead of holding fast by the purely spiritual conception
of the church which must have here presented itself to him,
he involuntarily substituted for it the conception of the visible
church, which had already been firmly established in his
system ; and so it may have happened that even in his mind
too, with the notion of Peter as a representative of the church,
there came to be associated the idea of a permanent representation in the Roman church.‡   But, without question, the

---

* This exposition is certainly correct as to its spirit, but not exactly
according to the letter ; as these words refer literally not to Christ himself, but to Peter personally,—but at the same time only in so far as he
had borne witness of this faith.

† Ecclesia non cadit, quoniam fundata est super petram, unde Petrus
nomen accepit.   Non enim a Petro petra, sed Petrus a petra ; sicut non
Christus a Christiano, sed Christianus a Christo vocatur.   Ideo quippe
ait Dominus, Super hanc petram ædificabo ecclesiam meam, quia dixerat
Petrus : Tu es Christus, Filius Dei vivi.   Super hanc ergo petram quam
confessus, ædificabo ecclesiam meam.   Petra enim erat Christus, super
quod fundamentum etiam ipse ædificatus est Petrus, 1 Cor. iii. 11.
Ecclesia ergo, quæ fundatur in Christo.   In Johann. Evang. Tractat.
124, s. 5.   The other exposition of this passage, by which it is referred
only to the person of Peter, Augustin himself had presented in his work
contra epistolam Donati, which has not come down to us.

‡ In the book de utilitate credendi, s. 35, he traces the development of
the church as a divine institution, endowed with divine authority, ab

spirit of ecclesiastical freedom among the North Africans was the farthest possible removed, as we shall see hereafter, from any inclination to concede all the consequences which there was a disposition already in the Roman church to derive from these notions.

In the minds of the Roman bishops we perceive the idea beginning already to develope itself more clearly and distinctly, that to them, *as the successors and representatives of the apostle Peter,* belonged the sovereign guidance of the whole church. Although it may be observed, doubtless, here and there, in occasional instances, that the idea of universal dominion, associated with Rome, was transferred from its political meaning, and clothed in a spiritual dress;* yet nothing was to them more offensive than that confusion of the political and spiritual provinces which they believed they discovered, whenever their higher dignity and authority, instead of being suffered to rest on the foundation of the divine institution, was attempted to be derived from the political superiority of Rome. The delegates of the Roman bishop, Leo the Great, protested emphatically against the above-mentioned decree of the council of Chalcedon, which

apostolica sede per successiones episcoporum. This book he wrote, to be sure, before he had come to deviate, as he did afterwards, from the ordinary exposition of this passage, as it was understood at Rome and in North Africa; but the fact is explained in the way above described, that, by this change of views as to the exegetical meaning, nothing was changed in Augustin's doctrinal system. He distinguishes, in the place above referred to, a threefold relation of Peter;—the same person being considered in respect to his individual nature as a man, in respect to his nature by divine grace as a Christian, and at the same time as abundantiore gratia primus apostolorum. Those words, it is true, ought properly to refer to the second relation of Peter, inasmuch as he represented the person of all Christians; but it is easy to see, that, in substituting the notion of the church in the place of Christians, he might be led to confound the second and the third together. Thus Peter was distinguished as the first of the apostles by the very circumstance that he was to represent the visible church in his own person, and that its development was to proceed forth from him. And what was considered true of Peter, was transferred to the church of Rome.

* In the remarkable work, de vocatione gentium, which was probably written by Leo the Great while he was still a deacon, l. II. c. 6, it is said: Roma, quæ tamen per apostolici sacerdotii principatum amplior facta est arce religionis quam solio potestatis; and Leo M. p. 80: Civitas sacerdotalis et regia, per sacram b. Petri sedem caput orbis effecta, latius præsidens religione divina, quam dominatione terrena.

on this ground attributed to the bishopric of Constantinople
the same rights as to the episcopate of Rome.   When this
decree came to be made known to Leo, he despatched various
letters to the emperor, to Anatolius the patriarch of Constantinople, and to the whole council, in which he strongly declared his disapprobation of what he pronounced to be a
usurpation.   In the letter to the emperor he says,* "The
case is quite different with worldly relations, and with those
that concern the things of God ; and without that rock which
our Lord has wonderfully laid as the foundation, no structure
can stand firm.   Let it satisfy Anatolius that, by your assistance, and by my ready assent,† he has attained to the bishopric
of so great a city.   Let not the imperial city be too small for
him, which yet he cannot convert into an apostolic see" (sedes
apostolica).   Leo appealed to the inviolable authority of the
Nicene council : he alluded very probably to the above-cited
sixth canon of that council, which really stood in necessary
contradiction with this new arrangement, only on the principle
that the dignity of the church stood wholly independent of
political relations.   He contended for the rights of the Alexandrian and of the Antiochian churches, which would be im-
paired in case that the church at Constantinople claimed to
itself the primacy over the entire East ; he contended for the
rights of the metropolitan bishops, which would be jeopardized
by the patriarchate which Anatolius assumed over Asia Minor,
Pontus, and Thrace.   And he contrived, in the end, to trace
back the higher inviolable dignity of the Alexandrian and
Antiochian churches also to the apostle Peter ; of the former,
namely, to Mark, the disciple of the apostle Peter ; and of the
second, immediately to Peter himself, since he was the first to
preach the gospel in that place.   Anatolius having appealed
to the authority of the second ecumenical council, which had
adjudged this rank to the church of Constantinople, Leo replied, that no assembly of bishops, whether large or small,
could decide any thing against the authority of the Nicene

* Ep. 78.

† Which refers to Leo's approval of the choice of Anatolius, which
had been sought after in consequence of certain disputes as to matters of
doctrine. The Roman bishops well understood, however, how to take
advantage of every occasion which could be interpreted into the recognition of a right conceded to them.

council. He speaks on this occasion with singular contempt of a council which was afterwards generally reckoned, both in the Western and in the Eastern church, among the number of ecumenical councils. The canon drawn up by that body he declared to be null and void; and would allow it no validity, if for no other reason, because it had never been communicated to the Roman church.*

It is impossible to doubt as to what the popes, even as early as the fifth century, believed themselves to be, or would fain be, in relation to the rest of the church, after having once listened to the language which they themselves hold on this subject. When a North-African council at Carthage had sent a report of their conclusions, in the decision of a controverted point of doctrine, to the Roman bishop Innocent, and demanded his assent to these conclusions; in his answer of the year 417, he first praised them because they had considered themselves bound to submit the matter to his judgment, since they were aware what was due to the apostolical chair; since all who occupied this seat strove to follow in the steps of that apostle from whom the episcopal dignity itself, and the entire authority of this name, had emanated. With good right had they held sacred the institutions of the fathers, who had decided, not according to human, but according to the divine counsels, that whatever was transacted in provinces, let them be ever so remote, should not be considered as ratified until it had come to the knowledge of the apostolic chair; so that, by its entire authority, every just decision might be confirmed, and the other churches (as the pure streams should be distributed from the original, undisturbed source, through the different countries of the whole world) † might learn from *this*

---

* Ep. 80, c. 5. Persuasioni tuæ in nullo penitus suffragatur quorumdam episcoporum ante sexaginta (ut jactas) annos facta conscriptio, nunquamque a prædecessoribus tuis ad apostolicæ sedis transmissa notitiam, sui ab initio cui caducæ dudumque collapsæ sera nunc et inutilia subjicere fundamenta voluisti. It hardly answers the purpose to attempt, as has been done, to make out that the authority of this council was recognized by Leo, and thus to bring the latter into agreement with the opinion of the later Roman church, by referring this disparaging judgment of Leo, without any regard to the natural sense of the passage, simply to this single canon of the council.

† The thought is plainly implied, that all the churches could hold fast to the pure doctrine only by remaining steadfast in their connection with the Roman, as the mother church—the original, invincible foun-

church what they had to ordain, whom they had to pronounce innocent, and whom to reject as irreclaimably wrong. Leo the Great declares, in a letter to the Illyrian bishops, in which, after the example of the Roman bishop Siricius, he names the bishop of Thessalonica the representative of the apostolic power (vicarius apostolicus), "that on him, as the successor of the apostle Peter, on whom, as the reward of his faith, the Lord had conferred the primacy of apostolic rank, and on whom he had firmly grounded the universal church, was devolved the care of all the churches, to participate in which he invited his colleagues, the other bishops." *

The favourable situation of the Roman church in its relation to the Eastern churches, brought along with it many circumstances which might be turned in support of this assumption of the Roman bishops. As we have already had occasion to observe, the Eastern church stood in far greater dependence on political influences than the Western; and what, in some respects, stood connected with this fact, there was in the former no church possessed of such decided external preponderance as the Roman church enjoyed in relation to the West. On the contrary, the oppositions and jealousies among the patriarchal churches, as we have said, were the source of many disputes; and the higher authority of the recently promoted Byzantine church, in particular, was, at all times, a thing extremely offensive to the ancient patriarchal church of Alexandria. Again, the Western church, by reason of its predominant Roman spirit, so unbending and practical, and by reason of its characteristic life, which was not so restlessly scientific, preserved greater tranquillity in the course of its doctrinal development. On the other hand, the more excitable and actively scientific spirit of the Greeks, the speculative bent of mind, the manifold spiritual elements which here came in contact with each other,—all this was a source of manifold disputes in the Greek church, which, through the

tain-head of the transmitted, divine doctrine, as well as of all spiritual power.

* Quia per omnes ecclesias cura nostra distenditur, exigente hoc a nobis Domino, qui apostolicæ dignitatis beatissimo apostolo Petro primatum fidei suæ remuneratione commisit, universalem ecclesiam in fundamento ipsius soliditate constituens, necessitatem sollicitudinis, quam habemus, cum his, qui nobis collegii, caritate juncti sunt, sociamus. Leo. ep. 5, ad Metropolitanos Illyr.

disturbing interference of the state, were still further promoted, and at the same time rendered more intricate and per-
plexing. Now, while in the Western church the greatest
tranquillity prevailed, contrasted with this agitated condition
of the Greek church, it came about that the contending parties
of the latter, and especially those who had against them the
dominant power, sought to obtain on their side the voice of
the Western church, and especially of the Roman as the most
influential, and the one which gave the tone to all the rest;
and that those who were persecuted by the dominant party
took refuge at Rome. Now, as it was of the utmost importance to such persons to gain in their favour the voice of the
Roman church, so this interest influenced them in the choice of
their expressions; and to show their respect for the Roman
church, they made use of such expressions as they would not
have employed under other circumstances. But the Roman
bishops, who were already in the habit of passing judgment on
all the relations of the church from that once established and
settled point of view which we have just described, found
accordingly in such expressions, looking as they did at nothing
but the letter, an acknowledgment of that point of view without concerning themselves to inquire what the persons who
used these expressions really had in their minds. Protestations
undoubtedly sometimes followed from the dominant party of
the East, when the decisions of the Roman bishops ran contrary to their interests. Thus, for example, when the Roman
bishop Julius, instead of concurring with the dominant party
of the Eastern church, which had deposed from his office the
bishop Athanasius of Alexandria, had invited both parties to
present the matter, by their delegates, before an assembly of
the Western church; the Eastern bishops, convened at Antioch, declared that it did not belong to him, a foreign bishop,
to set himself up as a judge in the affairs of the Eastern
church; that every synod was independent in its decisions;
that he, as bishop of a larger city, was no more than the other
bishops; that it had, in truth, just as little entered into the
minds of his predecessors to interfere in the interior affairs of
the Eastern church, to set themselves up as judges over the
decisions of the Eastern synods in the Samosatenian disputes,
as it had occurred to the older bishops of the East to constitute themselves judges in the controversies of the West; as,

for example, the Novatian.* But the party in whose favour
the Roman bishops had decided, finally obtained the victory;
and they could accordingly, taking advantage of this fact,
declare that protestation to be null, and maintain the validity
of their own judicial sentence. Under such favourable circumstances they received many public testimonials of their
supreme juridical authority, which in the sequel became of importance to them. To this class belong the *three* following
decrees of the council of Sardica:† "I. When a bishop is
condemned in a matter, and he believes that injustice has been
done him, the synod which judged him shall write to the
Roman bishop Julius; so that, if necessary, the investigation
may be renewed by the bishops of the neighbouring province,
and he himself name the judges. II. That, in such a case,
no other person shall be nominated to fill the place of the
deposed bishop until the Roman bishop shall have received
notice of it, and decided on the point. III. If, in such a case,
the deposed bishop appeal to the bishop of Rome, and the
latter considers a new investigation to be advisable, he may
commit such investigation to the bishops of the neighbouring
province, and may also send to it presbyters out of the body
of his clergy to assist in the inquiry." Thus this synod, no
doubt, assigned to the Roman bishop a certain supreme power
of jurisdiction, a right of revision in the affairs of the bishops.
But it admits also of being easily explained how they came to
do this. Besides the Western bishops, those only from the
East were present at this council who had been condemned
and deposed there by the party hostile to them. It was the
interest of the dominant party in this council, that the judgment of the Eastern synods with regard to Athanasius should
be reversed, and the latter restored to his place again. The
council of Sardica was intended, it is true, in its first arrangement, to be an œcumenical one. But as the Orientals had in
a great measure separated from it, it could lay no just claims
to this character; and it seems that its canons, in the next
succeeding times, stood in no very high authority even in the
Western church itself. But, very naturally, these canons
must have been highly acceptable to the Roman church; and

---

* Vid. Julii epist. 1 adv. Eusebianos, ss. 4 et 5. Socrat. l. II. c. 15.
Hilarii opus historicum Fragmentum, III. s. 26.
† Canon. III. IV. et V.

in this church, therefore, they could not be forgotten. So much the more easily might it here happen that these canons, to which a peculiar importance must have been attached, would be unconsciously confounded and given out for the same with those of the Nicene council. A second declaration, by which, in the year 378 or 381, a certain supreme authority of jurisdiction in ecclesiastical affairs was conceded to the Roman bishop Damasus, proceeded, however, only from an emperor, Gratian; and had reference simply to a schism which had arisen in Rome, in which the Roman bishop was particularly interested. (See, below, History of Schisms.)

A third case was this: The bishop Hilarius of Arles, whose zeal in discharging the duties of his spiritual office, whose life of strict piety and active benevolence, commanded universal respect, had proceeded, on a certain occasion, while visiting the churches as metropolitan bishop of this part of Gaul (Gallia Narbonnensis)—which authority the bishops of Arles had exercised for a long time, though not without its being disputed,—to depose from his office, with the consent of a synod, a certain bishop by the name of Celidonius.* The latter, however, applied to Rome, and succeeded in persuading Leo that injustice had been done him. Hilarius himself hastened to Rome, and openly defended his cause. But when he perceived that Leo was already committed on the side of Celidonius, and determined to take his part, he judged it advisable to leave Rome again. At this proceeding, Leo was still more exasperated: it appeared to him a very punishable act of disobedience, that Hilarius ventured to withdraw himself from his ecclesiastical jurisdiction. He, without further ado, reinstated Celidonius in his office; though, even according to the decrees of Sardica, it simply belonged to him to direct that a new investigation of the matter should be instituted in the province itself, by the neighbouring bishops, in which he himself might participate by means of his delegates. He went so far as to declare that, as the metropolitan authority had been conferred by his predecessors on the bishop of Arles only by a special grant, Hilarius had forfeited this power by his abuse of it, and that it should

---

* It is disputed, whether this bishop belonged to the metropolitan diocese of Hilarius, or whether zeal for church discipline, or passion, led him to the wrong step of stretching his power beyond the limits of that diocese, and thus to violate ecclesiastical forms.

again be transferred to the bishop of Vienna. His unspiritual
mode of apprehending the idea of the church, and the hierarchical arrogance so easily combined therewith, carried him to
such an extreme that he could say : " He who thinks himself
called upon to dispute the primacy of the apostle Peter, will
find himself in nowise able to lessen that dignity ; but, puffed
up by the spirit of his own pride, will plunge himself into
hell."* Thus, whoever refused to subject himself to the usurped
spiritual domination of a man, was to be excluded from the
kingdom of heaven.   It had been well for Leo, if he had
applied to himself what he addressed to the Gallic bishops ;
" That the fellowship of the church was not to be forbidden to
any Christian by the arbitrary will of an angry priest ; that a
soul for which Christ has shed his blood, must not be excluded
from the privilege of church communion on account of some
insignificant word."   The young emperor, Valentinian III.,
who was at the beck of the Roman bishop, issued thereupon a
law in the year 445, in which he says : " The primacy of the
apostolic seat having been established by the merit of the apostle
Peter, by the dignity of the city of Rome, and by the authority
of a holy synod,† no pretended power shall arrogate to itself
anything against the authority of that seat.   For peace can be
universally preserved only when the whole church acknowledges
its ruler."   Resistance to the authority of the Roman bishop
is declared to be an offence against the Roman state.   It is
established as a settled ordinance for all times, that as well the
Gallic bishops, as the bishops of all the other provinces, could
not properly undertake anything without authority from the
Pope of the eternal city (Papa urbis æternæ).   What the
authority of the apostolic seat ordained, should be law for all,
so that every bishop who, when summoned before the tribunal
of the Roman bishop, declined to appear, should be forced to
do so by the governor of the province.

The emperor, by whom the spiritual and the political points
of view were here confounded together, willed that the *church*
of his empire, just as the *latter itself*, should have one acknowledged principal head ; but the whole previous constitution of
the church could not possibly be overthrown by an imperial
edict.   Hilarius seems, notwithstanding, to have remained in

* Vid. ep. 9. 10.
† The council of Nice, or of Sardica.

possession of his metropolitan dignity; he maintained the rights of his church, although he sought by a respectful deportment to become reconciled with the Roman bishop.*

The North-African church, which most distinctly expressed the principle from which these consequences were derived, was, however, the farthest removed from conceding these latter. That spirit of ecclesiastical freedom which had already, in the time of Cyprian, opposed itself to the Roman assumptions, was here ever predominant. As cases were frequently occurring in which members of the clerical body that had been deposed on account of their offences, took refuge with the Roman church, and were there received; the councils of Carthage, in the years 407 and 418, ordained† that whoever thereafter, instead of appealing to the jurisdiction of the North-African church itself, appealed to one beyond the sea, should be excluded from the fellowship of the church. Yet it subsequently happened that a deposed presbyter, Apiarius, appealed to the Roman bishop Zosimus. The latter was disposed to bring the matter before his tribunal; and when this met with some resistance, he fell back for support on the recited canons of the council of Sardica; which, however, he caused to be presented by his delegates at the council of Carthage in the year 419, as Nicene canons. To the Africans it appeared extremely strange that these canons, which were wholly unknown to them, were nowhere to be found in their collection of the doings of the Nicene council. They resolved that they would assume them for the present to be valid; yet cause inquiry to be made by consulting the genuine ancient manuscripts of the doings of the Nicene council, preserved in the Eastern churches at Constantinople, Alexandria, and Antioch, for the purpose of ascertaining whether they really belonged to them. This they gave notice of to the Roman bishop Bonifacius, who had meanwhile succeeded Zosimus. They invited him also to make inquiries of

---

* It is to be regretted, that there are no remaining records of these transactions between Hilary and Leo. The words which the city præfect, (præfectus urbis,) Auxiliaris, who sought to make himself mediator, addressed to Hilary, are worthy of notice: Impatienter ferunt homines, si sic loquamur, quomodo nobis conscii sumus. Aures præterea Romanorum quadam teneritudine plus trabuntur, in quam si se Sanctitas tua demittat, plurimum tu nihil perditurus acquiris.

† Cod. Afr. c. 28.

the like nature; but at the same time they declared that, even
according to these laws, the affairs of other ecclesiastics besides
bishops must be settled only within their own provinces. "Now
although these laws were observed in Italy, yet they should
not be compelled to submit to such intolerable encroachments.
Yet they hoped that under his ecclesiastical rule they would
not have to suffer from such arrogance.* Amid the doctrinal
disputes of the fifth and sixth centuries, the Pelagian controversy and that concerning the edict *de tribus capitulis*, we see
often the Africans maintaining their doctrinal principles even
when in contradiction with the Roman; and we see, in fact,
the Roman bishop Zosimus finally yielding to the decisions of
the Africans.

We must accordingly hold fast to this as the result of the
church development of this period,—that the idea of an external church theocracy under one sovereign head was already
present in the minds of the Roman bishops; and although a
spirit of ecclesiastical independence, which flowed from the
earliest Christian antiquity, still presented many obstacles to the
realization of this idea, and the Eastern church ever remained
disinclined to acknowledge it, yet important germs of such a
realization were already existing in the Western churches,
which, under favourable circumstances, in later times, would
doubtless be taken advantage of.

To represent the outward unity of the church, another important institution came in during this period, which, it is true,
originated also in that general, fundamental idea of the external
visible church; yet, if the Christian doctrine had not first
evolved itself into precisely this form of a universal monarchy,
could not so easily have shaped itself in the way it did;—we
mean the *general assemblies of the church*, concilia universalia,
συνόδοι οἰκουμενίκαι (by οἰκουμένη was understood, originally,
the Roman empire). Men being accustomed already to regard
the provincial synods as the highest legislative and judicial
tribunals for the churches of the several provinces, it was
natural, when disputes arose which occupied the largest portion
of the Christendom of the Roman empire, that the thought
should occur of forming, after some analogous manner, a like
tribunal for the Christendom of the whole Roman empire; and

---

* Non sumus jam istum typhum passuri.

this was soon transferred, generally, to the entire church universal. The provincial synods then being customarily regarded as organs of the Holy Spirit for the guidance of the churches of a certain district, so now this was applied to the relation of universal councils to the whole church. These universal councils had a twofold aim, to decide disputes concerning doctrines, and to determine the constitution, the forms of worship, and the discipline of the church; to which latter the canons of these assemblies had reference.

It was not possible, at these councils, to arrive at a calm understanding of disputed points of doctrine. Each party was fettered to its system already made out, and judged everything by it without entering at all into the examination of the notions entertained by others. It was a strife of party passions; and the result of the proceedings was already predetermined by the relation of the contending parties to the dominant power. Gregory of Nazianzus, who expressed the result of a large and various experience, gives the following remarkable account of the mode of proceeding at such assemblies:*—"I am so constituted," he writes, "that, to speak the truth, I dread every assembly of Bishops; for I have never yet seen a good end of any one,—never been at a synod which did more for the suppression than it did for the increase of evils; for an indescribable thirst for contention and for rule prevails in them, and a man will be far more likely to draw upon himself the reproach of wishing to set himself up as a judge of other men's wickedness, than he will be to succeed in any attempts of his to remove it."

Yet, despite of the many impure human motives which intruded themselves into these councils, men regarded them as the organs by which the Holy Ghost guided the progressive movement of the church,—as the voice by which the Holy Ghost determined what had before been doubtful, and to which every man was bound, therefore, to submit his own fallible, subjective judgment. The *theory* of Augustin on this subject was, that "the decision of controverted questions does not proceed in the first instance and directly from the transactions of these councils; but that these transactions, rather, are prepared by the theological investigations which have preceded them. The decisions of councils simply give the expression of

* Ep. ad Procop. 55.

public authority to the result at which the church, in its development thus far, has arrived.   Hence it may happen that a
controverted matter, at a particular time, cannot as yet be
decided, even by a general council ; because the previous investigations have not as yet sufficiently prepared the way for
a definitive, a settled result." According to this theory, general
councils should express and settle firmly the universal Christian
consciousness, up to that point of its development which, under
the guidance of the Holy Spirit, who is the actuating principle
of the whole life of the church, it has reached at a certain
period of time.   The universal Christian consciousness is thus
merely fixed in a determinate expression,—the sum and contents of Christian truth more clearly and distinctly evolved in
opposition to the latest errors.   Hence an enlightened church-
teacher may, at a particular period, be in error on some one
important point, without therefore falling into heresy ; since,
in respect to this one point, there may as yet have been no
general decision of the Christian consciousness.   But when, by
continual investigation, the evolution of the universal Christian
consciousness has reached this point, and expressed itself on
the matter in question through the voice of a general council,
a proper humility requires it of the individual, that he should
submit his own subjective judgment to that general decision
guided by the Holy Ghost.   It is only the pride of self-will
that revolts against lawful authority ; it is, in truth, a principle
grounded in nature, that the part should subordinate itself to
the whole.   According to the theory of Augustin, however,
the earlier councils might be corrected and improved by
later ones ; since each council gives only that decision which
answers to the stage of development which the church has
arrived at in each several period.   Yet it may be a question
whether Augustin really supposed that a council could express
positive errors ; or whether his opinion was simply like that
soon afterwards expressed by Vincentius of Sirinum, in his
Commonitorium, a work written somewhere about the year
434 ; namely, that a later council should correct the decisions
of the earlier, only so far as to define what the other had left
undetermined, just as the more advanced development of the
church might require in its opposition to new forms of error.*

* Augustin. de baptismo contra Donatistas, I. II. c. 3. Ipsa plenaria
concilia sæpe priora posterioribus emendari, cum aliquo experimento

Thus the freedom of the spiritual evolution of Christianity among mankind was to find an impassable barrier in the decisive authority of general councils.* We see here, fully developed already, the germs of that system of restriction which grew out of the habit of confounding together the visible and the invisible church, and which reigned supreme, until by the work of God in the Reformation, was produced that *free* life of the spirit which has its ground in the essence of the gospel, and uniformly accompanies it where it is preached in its purity.

The essence of Christianity struggles against the demand of a blind submission to human authority; it requires no other obedience than that which answers to the true nature and dignity of man's spirit; and it stands in no sort of contradiction with true freedom, but rather is the only thing that can produce it. All that it requires is, that man's spirit, having become conscious of its true wants, should submit to the teachings of God's eternal spirit, who alone can communicate that which will satisfy all its longings. The spirit speaks, through the divine word, to each individual, in the inner recesses of his heart, according to the measure of his recipiency; and it is only what each one knows from this source and through this revelation, in the inner recesses of his heart, that he can vitally believe, and from his inmost consciousness acknowledge to be true. Facundus of Hermiane says :† " To his priests, assembled in his name, Christ can never be wanting; because he, being almighty truth, can in no way prove false to his promise." But the condition here presupposed, without which the fulfilment of that promise could not be realized, was in fact precisely the thing so often wanting in these assemblies. Al-

---

rerum aperitur quod clausum erat et cognoscitur quod latebat, sine ullo typho sacrilegæ superbiæ, sine ulla inflata cervice arrogantiæ, sine ulla contentione lividæ invidiæ, cum sancta humilitate, cum pace catholica, cum caritate Christiana. But where did ever such a spirit prevail in a council? Compare with this the above-cited words of Gregory of Nazianz.

* Thus the excellent bishop Facundus of Hermiane—a man who shows great freedom within certain limits—says. about the middle of the sixth century (defens. trium capitulorum, l. V. c. 5): Neque enim est alia conciliorum faciendorum utilitas, quam ut quod intellectu non capimus, ex auctoritate credamus.

† In the VIII. vol. of his work, Defens. trium capitulorum, c. 7.

most anything else might, in many cases, be affirmed of them, than that they were assembled in the name of Christ. What warrant had men to believe that they who had not brought with them the temper which was required in order to hear the voice of the Divine Spirit, ought to be considered as its organs for the rest of the church? In things spiritual and divine, it cannot hold good that the individual must subordinate himself to the whole ; for the individual spirit may, in truth, by its freedom, and by the purity of its will, outrun, in its own course of development, the whole multitude chained to that spirit of the age which is not the spirit of truth. The individual may have fought his way to freedom, where the multitude are in bondage. Errors are often propagated without design, when they have made good their dominion over the consciousness of men. Individuals who surrender themselves to the spirit of truth, which speaks not barely to the masses, but also to each individual according to the recipient temper of his mind, attain by clear consciousness to the separation of the true from the false ; and how could they possibly be under any obligation to subject themselves to the dominant spirit of untruth? But even in case the spirit of truth had been spoken by a general council, still this expression could be binding only on him who, by the same spirit of truth, had recognized the same as true from the divine word. Thus there was substituted here a cringing to human authority and consequent servility of spirit, in place of that true humility which gives all the honour to God, the Spirit of absolute truth alone ; and which, there-fore, in freeing men from bondage to human opinions, makes them free indeed.

As the decisions of general councils had respect not only to matters of doctrine, but also to matters connected with the outward life of the church, to the church constitution, and to church usages, another evil ensued ; namely, that by means of them the forms of training, which by their own nature are multiform and variable, were subjected to an unchangeable law of dead uniformity.

Again, since the general councils constituted a legislative tribunal for the entire church, the material was now at hand for a universal ecclesiastical legislation. The Roman abbot, Dionysius Exiguus, presented to the Western church, in the early times of the sixth century, a book of ecclesiastical laws ;

consisting of a collection which he had made from the written decisions (decretales) of the Roman bishops—in answer to ecclesiastical questions addressed to them—from the time of Siricius, or from the year 385 and onward, and from decrees (canones) of the general, and of the more important provincial councils. This work soon obtained paramount authority ; and it had an important influence in shaping out the papal monarchy in the Western church, that he had assigned so prominent a place to the papal decrees.

II. The Discipline of the Church.

The principle was transmitted from the preceding to the present times, that those who had by gross transgressions violated their baptismal vows, should be excluded from the fellowship of the church and from participating in the communion ; and not till they had given satisfactory proofs of repentance were they to receive absolution from the bishop, and to be admitted again to church fellowship. During the Novatian controversies of the preceding period, men had agreed on certain common principles respecting the nature of penitence. It was agreed that to no one, of whatever offence he might have been guilty, provided that by his conduct thus far he had shown the marks of sincere repentance, should be refused the communion in the hour of death.* Gradually the penitents came to be distributed into different classes, after the same manner as the catechumens, according to their different degrees of fitness for being restored back to the fellowship of the church. The first class was formed of those who were not yet allowed to enter the church.† They were bound to stand without the doors of the church, and to implore with weeping the intercession of the members of the community as they entered ; at the same time prostrating themselves to the earth, hence they were called προσκλαιόντες. Next followed those who were permitted to listen with all the unbaptized in the outer area of the church (the νάρθηξ, the ferula) to the sermon and to the reading of the scriptures. Then followed those in

---

* See Concil. Nic. canon 13. If such a person subsequently recovered, he was to be placed back once more in the fourth class of pœnitentes.

† Ἀπειργόμενοι τῆς ἐκκλησίας they are called, in Gregory Nyssen. epistola canonica ad Letojum.

whose behalf a special prayer of the church was offered ; on
which occasion they fell on their knees, and hence were called
ὑποπίπτοντες, substrati. Finally, those who were allowed to
be present at all the prayers and transactions of the church,
but yet could not themselves bring a gift to the altar, or participate in the communion (χωρὶς προσφορὰς κοινωνοῦντες τῶν
προσευχῶν.*

Entering under obligations to do penance for particular sins
within a determinate time, was a practice which had no existence in this period. The only cases which could occur were,
either that the bishop excluded from church fellowship those
whose transgressions had become sufficiently notorious, and
granted to them the privilege of readmission only on condition
of subjecting themselves to a church penance fixed upon by
himself in some proportion to their crime; or else that they
voluntarily made confession of their sins to the bishop, which
act was considered in itself a token of repentance, and therefore
had some influence in mitigating the penance of the church.†

Still, in carrying out the principles which had been established on the subject of admission to the communion and of
penance, the church, since it no longer constituted, as in the
preceding period, a body subsisting by itself and independent
of all others, found many difficulties which could not exist in
the foregoing period, at least in the same degree.‡ Cases occurred in which the bishop, by rigidly carrying out these
principles, must necessarily fear that a schism would be produced in the church. The Donatists, of whom we shall presently
speak, maintained that, in such cases, in order to keep the

---

* Basil. ep. canonica, III. Ambros. de pœnitentia, l. II. c. 10.

† It is uncertain what is meant in the seventeenth canon of the
council of Ancyra by εἰς τοὺς χειμαζομένους εὐχίσθαι—whether it denotes
those among the first class of catechumens without the doors of the
church, where they were exposed to all weathers, or whether it stands
for those in the class vexed by evil spirits, in the same place with
Energumens. The first is the more probable.

‡ Chrysostom says of those who came to the communion as impenitent
sinners : Τοὺς μὲν δήλους ἡμῖν αὐτοὶ πάντως ἀπείρξομεν, τοὺς δὲ ἀγνώστους
ἡμῖν τῷ θεῷ καταλείψωμεν, τῷ τὰ ἀπόρρητα τῆς ἑκάστου διανοίας εἰδότι.
See the Homily on the feast of Epiphany, Savil. T. V. fol. 528. The
same holds the deacons accountable if they should admit to the communion a person whom they knew to be guilty of any sin which was
punishable with exclusion from the fellowship of the church. Hom.
82, Matth. near the end.

church pure, no regard should be paid to consequences; although even their own bishops, it was alleged, could not always proceed in exact accordance with this principle. Others, on the contrary—as, for instance, Augustin—maintained that men should be content simply to rebuke many of the evils which were widely spread. Much, they said, must be reserved to the judgment of God. At the same time it was necessary to proceed with wisdom and patience, so as to avoid a worse evil, and not to root up the good fruit with the tares.* The second difficulty was, to carry out these principles in their application to the great men of this world, who, even in the church, could not be forgetful of their worldly rank. It was everywhere an acknowledged principle that here, before the tribunal of God's word, no respect to persons ought to be admitted. Chrysostom, in requiring the deacons to debar the unworthy from participating in the Lord's supper, says: "Though the commander of an army or the governor of a province, though one decked with the imperial crown, should approach, yet, if he is unworthy, refuse him."† But there must also have been men, like Chrysostom, who spoke thus and acted accordingly; who did not fear to sacrifice everything temporal, in rigidly carrying out what they owned to be their duty as shepherds of the flock. In the western church the example of an Ambrose of Milan, who declared to several emperors, that if they proceeded to execute a purpose which appeared to him in violation of the duty of a Christian emperor, he could not admit them to the communion, showed how much could be effected in these times of despotism by the firmness of a bishop deeply penetrated with a sense of the elevation and responsibleness of his calling. The emperor Theodosius I., incensed at a seditious tumult which broke out in the year 390 at Thessalonica, abandoned thousands, the innocent with the guilty, to the blind fury of his soldiers. When the emperor came afterwards to Milan, Ambrose, who had taken advantage of a sickness to retire into the country, at first avoided an interview with him, supposing that passion left in his soul no room as yet for the lessons of religion. He thought that a letter which the emperor might find time to peruse silently by himself, might make a more salutary impression on him. He

* See Augustin, c. Parmenian. l. III. c. 13, et seqq.
† Hom. 82, Matth. near the end.

placed before him the example of the penitent King David, and wrote : "Sin can be removed only by tears and repentance. No angel or archangel can forgive sin ; and the Lord himself, who only was able to say to us, *I* am with you, when we sin, forgives the sins of those only who come to him with repentance. Add not to the sin already committed still another—that of presuming to partake of the holy supper unworthily, which has redounded to the ruin of many. I have no occasion to be obstinate with you ; but I have cause to fear for you. I dare not distribute the holy elements, if you mean to be present and receive them. Shall I venture to do that which I should not presume to do if the blood of *one* innocent individual had been shed, where the blood of so many innocent persons has been shed ?"* These words of Ambrose made such an impression on the heart of Theodosius, that, penetrated with the deepest anguish, he subjected himself to the public penance of the church, having first laid aside his imperial robes ; and as Ambrose says, not a day of his life passed afterwards in which he did not remember with pain that cruel transaction.† Ambrose, it is said, did not give him absolution until, to prevent the like effect of his irascible disposition for the future, he had renewed the law of the emperor Gratian, which forbade any sentence of death pronounced by the emperor to be executed short of an interval of thirty days ; so that the sentence might be recalled, if, after the subsiding of passion, he found occasion to repent of it. The excellent bishop Facundus of Hermiane observed subsequently to the emperor Justinian, who was distracting the church by his despotic conduct : " Would God

---

* Paulinus in his life of Ambrose. Theodoretus and Rufinus speak, it is true, of a personal interview of Ambrose with the emperor, whom he met at the threshold of the church. In this case we must suppose that the emperor, notwithstanding the written representations in this letter, still ventured to come to the communion ; which is not probable. And as those writers make no mention at all of Ambrose's letter, but make Ambrose say orally to the emperor nearly the same things which are written in this letter, it is quite probable, that what was contained in the letter came to be transferred to an oral interview which never took place. How is it conceivable, that the emperor, as Paulinus states, should have adduced in his defence on this occasion, that very example of king David which Ambrose, in the letter, had already used against him !

† Ambrose, in his funeral discourse over this emperor: Stravit omne, quo utebatur, insigne regium, deflevit in ecclesia publice peccatum suum, neque ullus postea dies fuit, quo non illum doleret errorem.

but raise up another Ambrose, there would be no want of another Theodosius."*

When powerful individuals bade defiance to all the tribunals of the church, one means still remained in the hands of the bishops, that of solemnly excluding them from the church by the anathema, and making this, together with the crimes committed by such individual, known to all their colleagues in a circular letter. These means were employed by Synesius against Andronicus, the worthless governor of Pentapolis, who had oppressed the poor in the most cruel manner; and the means were attended with a happy result.

In the large cities, especially within the Greek church, a special presbyter was appointed, for the purpose of attending to the duty of confession, and of determining for the penitents their due proportion of church penance. But when the patriarch Nectarius of Constantinople was led, by the scandal created by the crime of an ecclesiastic thus made publicly known, to rescind this office (about the year 390), the consequence of this was, that the whole system of confession and penance, as it had till now existed in the Greek church, came to an end; and it was left free to each individual, according to his conscience, to partake in the communion.† Still bishops—even the Greek church, as examples of the next succeeding times teach us—ever reserved to themselves the right of refusing the communion to vicious men. That abolition, however, of the ancient system of church penance had, if we may believe the church historian Sozomene, an injurious influence on the general state of morals.

III. History of the Schisms of the Church.

As in the preceding period, so also in this, we have concluded to separate the history of church schisms from that of the disputes concerning doctrine; the former standing closely connected with the history of the development of the idea of

---

* Quia si nunc Deus aliquem Ambrosium suscitaret, etiam Theodosius non deesset. Pro defens. trium capitulorum, 1. XII. c. 5.

† Socrates, v. 19. Sozom. VII. 16. Comp. Morin. de Pœnitentia, l. VI. 22. The homilies of Chrysostom, which still presuppose the ancient usage, were preached by him at Antioch.

the church, and the history of the church constitution, and hence finding here its most natural place.

I. *The Donatist Schism.*

The most important and influential church division which we have to mention in this period is the Donatist, which had its seat in North Africa. This schism may be compared, in many respects, with that of Novatian in the preceding period. In this, too, we see the conflict, for example, of Separatism with Catholicism ; and it is therefore important, in so far as it tended to settle and establish the notion of the visible, outward unity of the church, and of the objective element in the things of religion and of the church. That which distinguishes the present case is, the reaction, proceeding out of the essence of the Christian church, and called forth, in this instance, by a peculiar occasion, against the confounding of the ecclesiastical and political elements ; on which occasion, for the first time, the ideas which Christianity, as opposed to the papal religion of the state, had first made men distinctly conscious of, became an object of contention within the Christian church itself,— the ideas concerning universal, inalienable human rights ; concerning liberty of conscience ; concerning the rights of free religious conviction. The more immediate and local occasion of these disputes lay in a certain spirit of fanaticism, which, ever since the spread of Montanism, had prevailed in North Africa, and also in various circumstances superinduced by the Dioclesian persecution.

We observed already, in our account of the persecution under Dioclesian, that as there were many at that time who had been induced, by force or by fear, to deliver up the sacred writings in their possession (the traditores), so, too, there were many accused of this, against whom the accusation could by no means be proved. Such a charge might easily be converted into a weapon for the gratification of personal malice : the propensity to mistake inferences for facts rendered it no difficult matter to prove the accusations. When, for example, an individual who had been arrested by the pagan magistrates, found means, through some favourable circumstances or other, to deliver himself without denying ; yet men were prone to draw the conclusion that if he had remained true to the faith, he would assuredly, like other true confessors, have suffered martyrdom,—he could have escaped only by denying. Again, as we have also remarked already in the history of that persecution, the same principles were not held by all with regard to the proper mode of conduct on these occasions. Two parties stood opposed to each other ; a prudent and a fanatical one. At the head of the prudent party was the bishop Mensurius of Carthage ; and as it was common, especially in the Western church, for the archdeacons to be the confidants of the bishops, and to take pains that the regulations ordained by them should be carried into effect, and that the discipline or the church should be maintained ; so it happened that his archdeacon, Cæcilianus, stood in this relation to Mensurius. The two seem to have been united in a mutual understanding to oppose superstition and fanaticism.

There were many who, with broken credit, having become weary of life, and anxious to get rid of it, hoped in martyrdom to find a death honourable among the Christians and meritorious in the sight of God ; or who, persecuted by the consciousness of guilt, hoped in this way to free themselves at once from all their sins ; or who were eager to be thrown into prison as confessors, that they might there be loaded with honour, kind treatment, and presents of all kinds by their fellow-Christians. Mensurius could not endure that such persons should be confirmed in their knavery or their delusion, and that other Christians should be deceived and abused by them. He was desirous also of preventing the scandal which would thus be given to the pagans. He therefore endeavoured to put a stop to the expressions of honour and respect which were paid to such men in their prisons, as well as to the reverence shown them as martyrs after their death. In general, this prudent man was unwilling to allow that fanatics who, without being accused or called for, surrendered themselves to the pagan authorities, and, though unasked, yet publicly declared they had Bibles in their houses, but that they would not deliver them up—that such enthusiasts should be reverenced as martyrs. Since the Christians, moreover, without reflection or prudence, thronged in crowds to their dungeons, and uneasiness and alarm might in this way be easily excited among the pagans, he directed his archdeacon to take precautions against such results. As Mensurius disapproved of everything like fanatical imprudence, so he considered it his duty to do everything for the preservation of his own life, and for the external quiet of his community, which could be done without directly or indirectly denying the faith. When he heard that a church at Carthage was to be searched by the pagans, he caused all the manuscripts of the Bible to be removed from it to a place of safety, and writings of heretics to be substituted in their stead, which the inquisitors were satisfied to find there, and asked no further questions.* Mensurius, as a natural consequence, made all with whose superstition and fanaticism, or with whose selfish interests, his own prudence and firmness came in conflict, his fiercest enemies ; and these persons took pains to propagate the most infamous stories of his conduct. Whether in this matter he and Cæcilianus were *wholly* innocent, or whether, misled by a well-meant but over-earnest zeal against fanaticism, they allowed themselves to be drawn into various acts of violence which might furnish grounds for just crimination, cannot, for the want of impartial sources of information, be certainly known. Suffice it to say, that the antagonists of Mensurius accused him of concealing the truth, and of asserting that none but writings of heretics were surrendered to the pagans, for the purpose of clearing himself from the charge of giving up the sacred scriptures. And even if the pretence were well-grounded, yet, declared they, it was not allowable for a Christian to use such deception. Again, they accused him of having caused the most harsh and violent measures to be adopted by Cæcilian for the purpose of hindering the Christians generally from testifying their love and their sympathy for the imprisoned confessors.†

* Vid. Augustin. breviculus collationis cum Donatistis diei III. c. 13, N. 25, and the monumenta vetera ad Donatistarum historiam pertinentia in Optat. Milevitan. de schismate Donatistarum, p. 174.

† See the representation of this matter by a Donatist, in the collection of Du Pin, above referred to, f. 155 et 156. The fanatical, fact-perverting hatred of the Donatists, the language of unbridled passion, which is not to be mistaken even in this representation itself, inspire the reader with but little hope of finding here any historical truth. Thus among other things it is said: Et cædebantur a Cæciliano passim, qui ad alendos martyres veniebant, sitientibus intus in vinculis confessoribus, pocula frangebantur ante carceris limina, cibi passim lacerandi canibus spargebantur, jacebant ante carceris fores martyrum patres matresque sanctissimæ, et ab extremo conspectu liberorum excussi, graves nocte dieque vigilias ad ostium carceris exercebant. Erat fletus horribilis, et acerba omnium,

The fanatical party was patronized by the then primate of Numidia, Secundus, bishop of Tigisis. In a letter to Mensurius, he disapproved the manner in which that bishop had censured the fanatical confessors ; and declared that all those who had suffered martyrdom rather than deliver up their Bibles, deserved to be honoured as martyrs. Following the prevailing style of allegorical exposition peculiar to that age and country, he appealed to the example of Rahab, who refused to surrender up the two spies ; for these were a symbol of the Old and New Testaments. " When the soldiers of the police," as he reported, " came also to him and demanded copies of the Bible, he said to them—I am a Christian and a bishop ; I am no *traditor*. And when they asked only for a few useless pieces as a show (such as writings of heretics), he refused to give them even these ;—imitating the example of the Maccabee Eleazar, who would not consent even to appear as if he partook of the swine's flesh, lest he might set an example of apostacy to others."*

It is certain that the opinion was still prevailing with many in the North-African church, which had maintained its ground from the time of Cyprian,† that the validity of all sacerdotal acts depended on the subjective character of the persons who performed them, and that therefore they were valid only in case they were performed by members of the true Catholic church ;—that consequently a sacerdotal act executed by an excommunicated person was wholly without force. When, therefore, in the year 305, the Numidian provincial bishops, under the presidency of the above-named Secundus, assembled at Cirta in Numidia, for the purpose of ordaining a new bishop for this city, the president opened the meeting by declaring that they ought first to examine themselves, and make sure that there was no traditor among them, since a person of this description, excluded by the fact itself from the communion of the church, was unfit for the performance of any sacramental act. Several among the existing bishops were accused

qui aderant, lamentatio, prohibere pios martyrum complexus et divelli a pietatis officio Christianos, Cæciliano sæviente tyranno et crudeli carnifice.

* Augustin. breviculus collat. cum Donatistis. d. III. c. 13, s. 25. Monumenta in Du Pin, l. c. f. 174.

† See above, the disputes concerning baptism by heretics, vol. I. s. 2.

by rumour; several could excuse themselves on the ground of
having given up other writings (*e. g.* on medicine) instead of the
Bible; one, who plainly had no such excuse to offer, but, though
he had surrendered a copy of the Bible, yet remained stedfast
in the confession of the faith, said to the bishop Secundus:
" You know how long Florus (the police-officer) persecuted
me, to induce me to scatter incense, and God delivered me
from his hands, my brother; but since God has forgiven me,
do you also leave me to the judgment of God?" Hereupon
Secundus, in a way characteristic of his fanatic, spiritual
pride, exclaimed: " What are we to do, then, with the *martyrs?* Because they did not give up their Bibles, was the
very reason for which they have been crowned." The accused
said: " Leave me till I appear before the judgment-seat of
God; there I will render my account." A certain bishop,
Purpurius, of irascible temperament—against whom a far
weightier charge was pending, which doubtless required to be
more carefully looked into—instead of speaking in his own
defence, cast suspicion on Secundus himself: " How could it
be believed that when he had been seized, and had declared
that he possessed copies of the Bible, and yet did not deliver
them up, the officers of police would quietly receive such a
declaration, and allow him to go free, while so many others
who had declined to surrender their Bibles, were compelled to
suffer severe tortures and death?" Since, however, the conduct of the Pagan authorities varied so much according to
their different tempers, and since so many particular circumstances might procure for one a better lot than fell to the
others, this conclusion, which was intended to bring suspicion
on Secundus, was at least a very unsafe one. Another
Secundus among the assembled bishops, nephew of the one
first mentioned, begged the latter to consider what danger
threatened the peace of the church if men should be disposed
to push the matter further. All the accused would in the end
unite against him; and, consequently, a schism was inevitable.
Therefore it was finally resolved, for the preservation of the
quiet of the church, to leave all that was past to the judgment
of God.*

* See the transactions of this assembly in Augustin. contra Cresconium,
I. III. c. 17, s. 30, and the monumenta in Du Pin, f. 175. The Donatists declared, it is true, at the religious conference in Carthage, A.D. 411,

We have brought together these characteristic traits out of the times that preceded the Donatist schism, because it is in the excitement of temper which here betrays itself, and in the hostile relations betwixt the prudent party of Mensurius of Carthage, and the opposite fanatical party of the Numidian bishops, we must look for the original causes of this schism.

The bishop Mensurius died soon after the Dioclesian persecution was ended, in the year 311, by the edict of Galerius. Having been called on some special business to appear before the emperor Maxentius at Rome, he died on the way when he was returning home. It was frequently the case, on the demise of a bishop, that his archdeacon was chosen to fill the vacancy; because, having possessed the confidence and been often vested with the full powers of the bishop, he had already acquired the greatest influence in the church. But inasmuch as the archdeacon was inferior in rank to the presbyters, this practice would easily become an occasion of jealousies and

that these documents were interpolated (vid. Augustin. brevicul. collat. d. III. c. 17, and l. c. Du Pin, fol. 321); but their assertions can be regarded no otherwise than as very suspicious, as they were inclined to deny everything that conflicted with the interests of their party; and the reasons alleged by them against the genuineness of these writings have no decisive weight whatever. *One* reason was, the definite statement of the date and of the consuls, which common practice in civil transactions was contrary to the ecclesiastical custom. Without doubt this was censured, too, by Athanasius, as an unchurchlike thing, in the Sirmian formulas of faith; yet it was in the instance where he censured it, an entirely different affair—it related there to a determination of doctrines, which could not be so bound to a particular time; but here, on the other hand, it related to a judicial investigation, and an external act of the church, where dates were of more importance. At all events, enough has not been left us of the older synodal transactions to render it possible to decide whether this was really so unprecedented. The other party could, however, adduce an example to the contrary. To the Donatists, who pushed their opposition to the confounding of ecclesiastical and political matters to the extreme of fanaticism, such a determinate date was in itself a hateful thing, because it looked like such confusion. It is worthy of remark, that they even required an example of such an ecclesiastical determination of date from the Holy Scriptures—a proof of the very narrow character of their criticism. The *second* reason was, that at the time of the persecution no such assembly could have been held. This reason, Marcellinus, the president of the religious conference, who rejected the first as amounting to nothing, declared to be more weighty. But the bishops of the other party could easily cite examples out of the history of the persecutions, by which the possibility of such an assembly, even under these circumstances, might be proved.

divisions. Cæcilian had particularly against him that party in the Carthaginian community and in the Numidian church who disputed the *principles* of Mensurius. At the head of his enemies in Carthage stood a bigoted widow by the name of Lucilla, a person of wealth, and, by means of her wealth, of power. This individual attached great importance to certain fragments of human bones which she had obtained from some quarter or other, and which she gave out to be relics. These pretended relics she was in the habit of kissing every morning previously to partaking, as was customary in this country,* of the consecrated bread.† She usually took them along with her also to the early morning service, and here too kissed her relics previously to partaking of the communion. The archdeacon, whose duty it was to look after the order of the church, reprimanded her for this superstitious custom, and threatened her, in case she did not desist from it, with ecclesiastical censures. It was undoubtedly necessary that some check should be given to the spreading superstition with regard to relics, and perhaps Cæcilian found it particularly offensive that she seemed to attribute a higher sanctifying power to her relics than to the sacrament of the supper.‡ Many indications go to show that the Numidian bishops anticipated the choice of Cæcilian, and immediately after Mensurius' death endeavoured to secure for themselves a party in the community, and to oppose this party to Cæcilian. Donatus, bishop of Casæ Nigræ in Numidia, is said to have been busy even at this early stage.§ Secundus of Tigisis, primate

---

* See vol. I. sect. 2, respecting the daily communion in the church of North Africa.

† See Optatus Milevit. de schismate Donatistar. l. I. c. 16. In this place it is said: ante spiritalem cibum et potum; which cannot refer to the domestic communion alone, for in this the second had no place. Probably Lucilla observed the same custom in the church communion which she had been in the practice of at home, and thus her superstitious observances became known to Cæcilian. The opinion of Aubespin (Albaspineus), that she had been led by the custom of the mutual kiss of brotherly love preceding the communion, to transfer this form to her relics, for the purpose of maintaining thereby the communion with her patron saint, is not sufficiently well-grounded, since the practice of kissing relics, especially with females, existed elsewhere also.

‡ Optatus: cum *præponeret* calici salutari os, etc.—although the *præponeret* may be referred also simply to time.

§ By the investigations of the tribunal which sat subsequently at

of Numidia, the zealous antagonist of the Cæcilian party, sent certain ecclesiastics to Carthage, who held separate assemblies in the house of Lucilla, and placed a provisionary superintendent, under the customary title of visitor, ($\pi\epsilon\rho\iota o\delta\epsilon\upsilon\tau\acute\eta\varsigma$,) over the entire affairs of the church.* The more resistance the party of Cæcilian had to fear against his choice, the more urgent reason had they for hastening the whole thing to a conclusion. But, without doubt, it was difficult here to hit upon the right course for preserving unanimity and quiet; for if they waited until the arrival of the Numidian provincial bishops, who were in the practice of assisting at the ordination of the bishop of Carthage, it was to be foreseen that these would oppose the election. Should the ordination be completed before their arrival, new cause would be given them for dissatisfaction and complaint; but still they could not pronounce the episcopal consecration, after it had once been solemnized, null and void; since, although the Numidian provincial bishops might often be invited to assist on these occasions, yet nothing had been expressly settled on this point in the ecclesiastical laws.† The election and ordina-

---

Rome, under the Roman bishop Melchiades, it is said to have been proved : Donatum a Casis Nigris adhuc diacono Cæciliano schisma fecisse Carthagine. See Augustin. breviculus, l. c. apud Du Pin, f. 319.

* Thus says Augustin, Sermo 46, s. 39, T. v. ed. Benedict. Paris, f. 146, D. The assertion of Augustin, a violent opponent of the Donatists, is testimony, indeed, which cannot be wholly relied on. Yet the thing is in itself not improbable ; and all these preceding circumstances place the origin of the Donatist schism in a clearer light.

† The opponents of the Donatist party, at the religious conference in Carthage, affirmed that it was by no means a common custom for the bishop of Carthage to be ordained by a Numidian Metropolitan bishop, cum aliud habeat ecclesiæ Catholicæ consuetudo, ut non Numidiæ, sed propinquiores episcopi episcopum ecclesiæ Carthaginis ordinent, sicut nec Romanæ ecclesiæ ordinat aliquis episcopus metropolitanus; sed de proximo Ostiensis episcopus. Augustin, breviculus d. III. in Du Pin monumenta, f. 321. According to Optatus, I. 18, there were two individuals, Botrus and Celestius, probably presbyters in the Carthaginian church, who hastened the election in the hopes that the choice might fall on one of themselves. The fact that so many reasons were hunted up from one quarter and another to invalidate that objection of the Donatist party, renders it probable, that the ordination of the bishop of Carthage was, according to the more common practice, solemnized in the presence and with the co-operation of the Numidian bishops. Optatus, however, introduces that remark of his only as a report (dicitur). Perhaps the truth at bottom was simply this, that those two presbyters aspired after

tion were therefore hastened to a completion, and the latter office was performed by a neighbouring bishop, Felix of Aptungis.* Against the new bishop, the powerful Lucilla, with her party, now took her stand; and to this party belonged the elders of the Carthaginian church.†

The primate of Numidia came afterwards, with his bishops, to Carthage, either without being sent for, or, as the other party alleged, at the invitation of Lucilla and those connected with her. They met from the latter with a very friendly reception; and they manifested, from the first, hostile feelings towards Cæcilian, whom they refused to acknowledge as a bishop. Cæcilian now challenged his adversaries to produce their charges, if they had any against him: but they began by accusing as a traditor the bishop who had ordained him; and, in conformity with that old principle of the North-African church, they refused to recognize as valid an ordination which had been performed by a traditor. Cæcilian went still farther: he offered to resign his office, and return to his former post as a deacon, so that he could be ordained anew by the Numidian bishops.‡ But the latter were too far com-

the episcopal dignity, and, having been disappointed, were for this reason led to foster the division.

* The name of this town is written variously: Aptugnensis, Aptungitanus, Autumuitanus.

† The seniores plebis, according to the system of organization which prevailed in the North-African church (see vol. I. s. 1). The adversaries of the Donatists explain this as follows: when the bishop Mensurius, uncertain as to the issue of his business, left Carthage, he entrusted the precious movables of the church to the care of these elders, with the charge to deliver them over, in case he died before his return, to his successor in the bishopric. But, as these seniores wished to retain the whole in their own possession, it grieved them to be obliged to deliver them over into the hands of Cæcilian, and this was the cause of their enmity to him. Optatus, I. 19: Qui faucibus avaritiæ commendatam ebiberant prædam. Cum reddere cogerentur, subduxerunt communioni pedem. But how was this known to be the fact? For these persons certainly could not decline giving up what had been entrusted to them; and, at all events, must have been obliged to give up the whole to the *new* bishop, whoever he might be. It is quite evident that, as often happens in similar cases, such motives, the existence of which could not possibly be proved, were falsely imputed to these persons—after they became hated as the promoters of Donatism.

‡ Optat. I. 19. Cæcilian would hardly have been induced to consent to this, had he not at that time conceded the principle, that an ordination performed by a traditor was invalid.

mitted against him to enter into any such compromise. They now proceeded to accuse Cæcilian himself; and, as they did not acknowledge him to be a regular bishop, they chose in his stead the reader Majorinus, a favourite of Lucilla. An assembly of seventy Numidian bishops at Carthage excommunicated Cæcilian, because he had allowed himself to be ordained by a traditor.* The fanaticism which prevailed already at this assembly is characteristically shown by the following expression of one of its members: "As unfruitful weeds are mown down and cast away, so the thurificati and traditores,† and those who are schismatically ordained by traditors, cannot remain in the church of God, except they acknowledge their error, and become reconciled with the church by the tears of repentance." ‡

Thus was laid the foundation of the schism in the North-African church. According to the usual mode of proceeding in such cases, each of the two parties now endeavoured to secure for itself the recognition of other churches; and thus the breach would necessarily be extended. The emperor Constantine, who just at the present juncture had obtained the sovereignty over this part of the Roman empire, must have been prejudiced from the beginning against the party of Majorinus; for, in the very first laws by which he bestowed various privileges on the Catholic church in this quarter of the world, he expressly excluded the party from all share in them, and declared himself decidedly opposed to it; although this proceeding was in direct contradiction to those principles of universal toleration which Constantine had avowed in the laws enacted about the same time. The fanaticism which we find prevailing in this party at its very origin, may doubtless have furnished occasion enough for representing it to the emperor as composed of dangerous men, without his knowing anything more about the character of these disputes.§ The party of Majorinus, which saw itself condemned without a hearing, presented to the emperor, then residing in Gaul, a

* Augustin. breviculus d. III. c. 14, s. 26.
† See vol. I. s. 1.
‡ Liber c. Fulgentium Donatistam, c. 26. Du Pin monumenta, p. 176.
§ In a rescript issued in the beginning of the year 313, addressed to Cæcilianus, bishop of Carthage, and cited in Eusebius, X. 6, the adherents of the other party are styled μὴ καθεστώσης διανοίας ἄνθρωποι; mention is made of their μανία.

petition, entreating him, by his love of justice, to name judges
in that country itself for the purpose of inquiring into the
nature of the controversy which had arisen in the North-
African church.*   They probably chose to have their judges
from Gaul, because these would be least liable to suspicion;
inasmuch as this country had escaped the last persecutions of
the Christian church, and therefore no traditors were to be
found there as in the other churches.   The emperor thereupon
directed that Melchiades (Miltiades), bishop of Rome, with
five other Gallic bishops, should inquire into the affair; that
Cæcilian should appear before them, with ten bishops who
were to present the charges against him, and ten other bishops
who were to defend him.   The trial was holden in the year
313; and Melchiades came, attended with fifteen other Italian
bishops.   The bishop Donatus of Casæ Nigræ in Numidia,
with whom, as we remarked above, the germ of the schism
began, now also stood at the head of Cæcilian's accusers; as
indeed he seems generally to have been at that time the soul
of the whole party.   His charges against the latter were found
to be unsustained; but he himself was declared guilty of
various acts contrary to the laws of the church.   The party of
Majorinus having declared, as was to be expected, that injustice had been done them by this decision, Constantine
directed, in the year 314, that the charges against the ordainer
of Cæcilian, the above-named bishop Felix, should be examined
according to the usual judicial form at Carthage, where access
could be had to all the records and witnesses that might be
needed in the trial; and that an ecclesiastical convention at
Arles should hear delegates from the two parties, and so enter
into a new investigation of the whole matter.   The result of
the first inquiry was, that Felix was declared innocent.   The
council of Arles decided likewise against the party of Majorinus, and established at the same time three canons, which in
part were opposed to the conduct of this party, and partly
were designed to prevent the occurrence of similar divisions for
the future.   As the charge of denying the faith in the Dioclesian persecution had been one of the principal occasions
which led to this schism, and such accusations, repeated over
merely on the ground of vague report, might often result in
similar consequences, it was decided in the thirteenth canon

* The petition is to be found in Optatus, I. s. 22.

that those only *who could be convicted by public documents* of having delivered up copies of the holy scriptures or property of the church, or of having informed against other Christians before the tribunals, should be deposed from their spiritual offices. No other accusation but those which could be thus substantiated, should be received. As, moreover, the party of Majorinus held fast to the ancient principle of the North-African church, that the validity of a sacramental act depended on the fact that the performer of it was a member of the Catholic church, it. was established as a rule, in reference to ordination, that, although this ceremony had been performed by a person who could be legally convicted of those transgressions, it should still remain valid in case nothing else was to be objected against it. The same principle of the objectivity of sacramental acts was, moreover, in the eighth canon, so defined—probably with reference to the proceedings of the North-African schismatics—that baptism was always to be considered valid if it had been performed in the name of the Father, Son, and Holy Ghost.* For the rest, it may well be inferred, from the passionate tone of the report drawn up by this council, and sent to the Roman bishop Silvester, that the spirit which prevailed in it was not calculated to dispose the other party for peace. The party of Majorinus appealed from this decision to the judgment of the emperor himself. We have observed before, how very strange it then appeared to Constantine, that an appeal should be made from an episcopal decision on ecclesiastical matters to his own tribunal. In his reply to the bishops, he manifests his displeasure against the party of Majorinus by the most violent expressions.† Yet he accepted the appeal, and listened himself to the delegates of the two parties at Milan, in the year 316; his decision also went in favour of Cæcilian. From this time the whole matter took another turn; laws of the state now appeared against the party of Majorinus; they were deprived of their churches, and the places where they assembled were confis-

---

* According to one reading, this canon would be pointed, not against these North Africans, but against the Arians. But the other is most probably the original reading. What possible occasion could there be at that time, especially in the Western church, for the expression of any such opposition to the Arians?

† See this letter in Du Pin, acta, f. 184.

cated.* They were treated as transgressors of the imperial laws. The force by which it was sought to destroy them proved, as usually happens, only the means of giving them a new impulse, and pushed the spirit of enthusiasm, already existing among them in the bud, into full development. Majorinus, indeed, died in the year 315; but with him the schism, which had struck deeper root, by no means ceased. Besides, he had rather served to give an outward name to the party, than really constituted the head and soul of it. The latter had till now been Donatus, bishop of Casæ Nigræ in Numidia, who stood in the same relation to Majorinus as, under similar circumstances, Novatus had done to Novatian at the beginning of the Novatian schism. But Donatus, the successor of Majorinus, was himself the head and soul of the sect. And he was well suited to stand at the head of a party, being a man of fiery untutored eloquence, of great firmness of principle, and of great energy of action. The excessive admiration of his party converted him into a worker of miracles, and gave him the title of *the Great*.† From him, too, they received their name, *the Donatists;* and by this name we shall henceforth call them.‡

---

* Aug. ep. 88, s. 3. Contra lit. Petiliani, c. 92, s. 205.

† It went to such a pass that they were in the habit of swearing per canos Donati. August. Enarrat. in Ps. X. s. 5.

‡ One might be doubtful, whether the names pars Donati, Donatistæ, Donatiani, were derived originally from Donatus a Casis Nigris, or from Donatus Magnus. The explanation given by Donatists themselves points, it is true, quite distinctly, to the latter derivation (see the words of Petilianus, bishop of Cirta in Numidia, which will presently be quoted, collat. c. Donatist. fol. 296, s. 32). But it may be that although this name was taken originally from Donatus a Casis Nigris, yet this person was afterwards forgotten among his party, in consequence of the far greater influence of the second Donatus. The title pars Donati actually occurs already in the petition of the Donatist party addressed to the emperor Constantine, in the year 313 (in Optatus, l. I. s. 22); and if this citation is perfectly correct, no further doubt could exist about the correctness of the derivation of the name from Donatus a Casis Nigris. But it is certain that Optatus does not give us the original title of this petition, but has modified it by the name which the Donatist party then bore. The original title we find rather in the relatio Anulini proconsulis Africæ, where it is said, libellus traditur a parte Majorini. Thus the party was styled, till the time when the name of Majorinus became wholly eclipsed by that of Donatus Magnus. Yet there is one other possible supposition —that Donatus a Casis Nigris and Donatus Magnus were one and the same individual; that the former, on account of having so greatly dis-

The Donatists, in their public declarations, must, of course, apply to themselves some appropriate title, in order to distinguish their own sect from the party of their opponents, and from the dominant church in North Africa. They therefore called themselves by a name wholly inoffensive in itself, the "pars Donati," as the most convenient way of making themselves known in their relation to another determinate human party. This other party, it is true, following the unjustifiable practice of imputing inferences of their own as facts against their adversaries, argued from this party name that they were for being something else than the church of Christ and the Catholic church; that they thus set themselves off as a mere human party; just as in after times a similar licence of imputation was often indulged in by the *church dominant* against *church parties* which had seceded from it. The Donatists by no means admitted the thing which was assumed in these accusations; they declared that they called themselves after the name of Donatus, not as the founder of a new church, but as one of the bishops of the ancient church derived from Christ.[*] And not without reason could they say that they might rightly call their adversaries, precisely after the same manner, Mensurists and Cæcilianists.[†] The name Donatists, which was

tinguished himself by his activity in behalf of the interests of his party had, after the death of Majorinus, obtained the first bishopric of his party. In favour of this would be the fact, that Optatus of Mileve seems to have knowledge of only one Donatus; but against it is the fact, that the Donatists expressly distinguished one of these two Donatuses from the other—(see Augustin. breviculus collat. c. Donatistis d. III. Du Pin, f. 323, c. 20); and, moreover, the Catholic bishops recognized, at the religious conference in Carthage, this distinction as a correct one; and Augustin—who at an earlier period, as he says in his Retractions, had confounded together the two Donati—expressly distinguishes them, c. Cresconium Donatistam, I. II. s. 2. Again: the translation of bishops, forbidden by the laws of the church, was by no means so common in the Western church as it was in the Eastern; and, had Donatus M. incurred the charge of an act so contrary to the laws of the church, his adversaries could hardly have failed to make use of such an advantage against him.

[*] The words of the Donatist Cresconius are : Quod Donatus non auctor et institutor ecclesiæ, quæ antea non fuerat, sed a Christo deductæ et antiquæ unus ex episcopis fuerit. In Augustin. c. Cresconius Donatistam, l. IV. s. 7.

[†] The words of the Donatist bishop Petilianus at the conference in Carthage : Ego eos dicere possum, immo palam aperteque designo Mensuristas et Cæcilianistas, l. c. f. 296, N. 30.

applied to them by their opponents, may, in its intended meaning, perhaps, have implied from the beginning something that was offensive: they themselves would never acknowledge it.*

Ursacius, a count of the empire, had been directed to carry the laws against the Donatists into effect; and a person of this description, accustomed to military despotism, was certainly not calculated to proceed in an affair of this kind with that spirit of kindness and forbearance, without which the enthusiastic spirit, already in existence, might easily be fanned into a fiercer flame. The forcible measures to which Ursacius resorted,† for the purpose of compelling the Donatists to unite with the dominant church, produced the most violent ferment of spirits. There existed in North Africa a band of fanatical ascetics, who, despising all labour, wandered about the country among the huts of the peasants (whence they were called by their adversaries *circumcelliones*), and supported themselves by begging. They styled themselves the Christian champions, *agonistici*. These people could easily be excited to any species of fanaticism: whilst the pagans were still in power, parties of these circumcelliones had often, to no useful purpose, demolished the idols on their estates, and thus exposed themselves—which was in fact their object—to martyrdom.‡ It is no more than natural that these persons, stimulated perhaps by the discourses of their bishops, and roused by the per-

* The Donatist grammarian Cresconius affirmed that, according to the Latin grammatical use, they ought at least to be called, not Donatistæ, but Donatiani. l. II. c. 1, s. 2.

† The Donatists were persuaded that the death of this man, who was killed some time afterwards in an affray with the barbarians, was a divine judgment in punishment for his crimes. But the logic of fanaticism, as usual, argued from one or two cases to all, and hence the Donatist bishop Petilianus said: Periit Macarius, periit Ursacius, cunctique comites vestri Dei pariter vindicta perierunt. Augustin. c. literas Petiliani, l. II. s. 208.

‡ That it was by their opponents alone these people were called *circumcelliones*, while they gave themselves the name of *agonistici*, is clear from Augustin. enarrat. in ψ. 132, s. 6. They sprang from the ancient ascetics, and hence were opposed to the more recent monasticism. Augustin describes them as follows: Genus hominum, *ab utilibus operibus otiosum*, crudelissimum in mortibus alienis, vilissimum in suis (fanatical contempt of life) *maxime in agris territans, ab agris vacans, et victus sui causa cellas circumiens rusticorum*, unde et *circumcelliones* nomen accepit. c. Gaudentium Donatistam, l. I. s. 32.

secutions against the Donatist party, should be easily hurried on to every species of fanaticism and violence.

The emperor Constantine was perhaps cool and prudent enough to have learned, from what had fallen under his own sad experience, the disastrous consequences of persecutions; or he may have been guided by the counsels of some one of the wiser bishops. For, as early as the year 317, he sent a rescript to the North-African bishops and communities, in which he exhorted them to forbear retaliating with wrong the wrong which they suffered from the Circumcellions. They ought not, with foolish hands, to intermeddle with the vengeance which God had reserved to himself; especially in a case where what they suffered from the rage of such men would, in the sight of God, be equivalent to martyrdom. If they adhered to this principle, they would soon see the fanaticism perish of its own accord.* When now the Donatists, in addition to what they had done already, transmitted to the emperor, in the year 321, a petition, in which they declared that nothing would induce them to enter into church fellowship with that scoundrel, his bishop;† that they would rather suffer everything he might choose to inflict on them;‡ Constantine became convinced, doubtless, still more than ever, by the tone of this document, of the dangerous consequences which must follow, if violent measures for the restoration of the peace of the church were pursued any farther. Experience led him to act according to the principles which, in obedience to the voice of reason and the spirit of Christianity, he ought to have pursued from the beginning. In a rescript addressed to the Vicar Verinus in North Africa, § he granted to the Donatists full liberty to act according to *their own* convictions, declaring that this was a matter which belonged to the judgment of God. ‖

To these principles Constantine remained firm to the end. When the Circumcellions, with force of arms, demolished

---

* See Constantine's rescript in the *Monumenta*. Du Pin, f. 138.

† Nullo modo se communicaturos antistiti ipsius nebuloni.

‡ In Augustin. breviculus collationis diei III. c. 21, n. 39.

§ Epistola Constantini, qua libertatem agendi tribuit Donatistis. Index Collationis, III. cap. 549.

‖ In expressions, it must be allowed, which were wounding to the Donatists, since he does not avoid such terms as *eorum, furor*.

a church which he had caused to be erected for the Catholics in the town of Constantina, the emperor ordered it to be rebuilt at his own expense, and demanded no indemnification of the Donatists.* If men had only remained true to these doctrines of toleration, and simply punished the acts of violence committed on both sides, according to the laws; had the emperor always spoken and acted on this principle of the Christian politician (which consists precisely in acknowledging the just limits of all civil power), a principle which is capable of exhibiting itself in the province of religion only on the negative side; the North-African church doubtless would not have been exposed to any of those disorders which subsequently ensued, although the Donatists might have long subsisted as a distinct party in the church. But disastrous was the result whenever an emperor was disposed to pursue any other than a negative course in relation to religious disputes.

The Western emperor, Constans, to whom North Africa fell after the death of his father, was not at first inclined to resort to any forcible measures for uniting the Donatists once more to the dominant church. He simply employed those means which were then frequently resorted to on the part of the court, for the purpose of making proselytes.† He directed his two commissaries, Ursacius and Leontius, in the year 340, to endeavour, by the distribution of money under the name of alms, to win over the Donatist churches.‡ As the

---

* The rescript in Du Pin, 189, composed, it must be admitted, in too theological a style for an emperor.

† See above, in the cases of Constantine and Julian.

‡ Optatus represents this as having been done *first* by Macarius. He mentions, indeed, the preceding persecutions by Leontius, Ursacius, and Gregorius; but, as he gives no precise dates, it is nevertheless quite possible that the whole ought to be referred to the first persecution under the emperor Constantine: and consequently the persecution under the emperor Constans would have first commenced after the death of the bishop Cæcilian of Carthage, and under the new bishop Gratus. But the discourse (sermo) in memory of the two martyrs, Donatus et Advocatus, first published by Du Pin in the collection of *monumenta* (l. c. fol. 190), represents the persecution as having begun already, under Leontius and Ursacius, in the attempt to win over the Donatist churches by means of the distribution of money. It is here said (c. 3): "Mittit (viz. diabolous, salutis inimicis) pecunias, quibus vel fidem caperet, vel professione legis occasionem faceret avaritiæ (foster avarice under the pretext that nothing more was intended than a profession of divine truth— the *professio* being in this case nothing more nor less than a means of

emperor Constans issued at the same time an edict whereby he called upon the North-African Christians to return back to the unity of the church which Christ loved,* it was the less possible that the object of these measures should remain concealed from the Donatist bishops. This covert attack served only to exasperate them; they excited their communities to the • most determined resistance. More forcible measures soon succeeded;—the Donatists were to be deprived of their churches;—they were fallen upon by armed troops while assembled for the worship of God. Such acts could not be committed without the effusion of blood; those that fell victims to the per-

receiving money from the emperor)." But this hardly agrees with the first beginning of the persecution under the emperor Constantine; for then the Donatists were attacked at once with severe measures as violators of the imperial decree. The question now arises, whether we ought rather to follow the representation of the case in the *sermo*, or that of Optatus; or whether we should seek to unite them both together. In the first case, it might be assumed that everything said by Optatus, relative to the distribution of money and the measures taken by Donatus against it, should be transferred to an earlier time than that which he assigns—namely to the first part of the reign of Constans; that what he relates of Macarius should be ascribed to Leontius and Ursacius; and that in place of the bishop, *Gratus* of Carthage, should be substituted his predecessor, *Cæcilian*. Thus Optatus must have wholly confounded the times—as indeed he is not remarkably exact in such matters. At the same time, however, we cannot be certain that we are justified in attributing to the unknown author of the "Discourse," although it is highly probable that he did not live at a period far remote from the time of these events, so much higher authority as an historical witness. It may furthermore be supposed, on the other side, that the author of the "Discourse" might himself have confounded times and names; and that thus the persecution under the emperor Constans began first with Macarius, in the year 347. But still it is not probable that the bishops of the Catholic party would have quietly observed, for so long a time, the toleration with which the Donatists were treated, without making any attempt to draw from the emperor Constans some new measures for the suppression of the schism. The reports of the "Discourse" and of Optatus may perhaps be reconciled by supposing that three separate attempts were made in the reign of Constans—the first by Leontius and Ursacius, the second by Gregorius, and the last by Macarius. In the case of the first and of the second of these attempts, the beginning may have been made by the distribution of money. It cannot assuredly be affirmed to be improbable, that Constans would have resorted twice in succession to the same means with such unhappy results; since we are but too well aware how slow the Byzantine emperors were to grow wise by experience.

* Christus amator unitatis est, unitas igitur fiat. l. c. Passio Donati et Advocati, s. 3.

secution were honoured by their party as martyrs;* and the annual celebration of the days of their death furnished new means for enkindling the enthusiasm of the Donatist party.

The second attempt was made by a count of the empire, named Gregorius. The bishop Donatus wrote to him in a wild, insurrectionary spirit,† with abusive language little becoming the character of a bishop. But the most furious persecution began in the year 347. The imperial commissaries, Paul and Macarius, traversed, in the first place, the whole of Northern Africa, distributed money to the poor in the name of the emperor, presented costly church utensils to individual communities, and, at the same time, exhorted all to offer no resistance to the unity of the church. In this connection, the object of these presents was perfectly clear to every one. The bishop Donatus of Carthage repelled the advances of the imperial officer with the remark : " What has the emperor to do with the church?"‡ He sent admonitions to all the Donatist churches, charging them to receive none of the money. Judging from the character of Donatus, it may well be presumed that he betrayed a great want of Christian reflection and prudence—qualities most needful at this time to prevent the worst excesses of fanaticism, when parties of enthusiastic Circumcellions were wandering about through the country.

The principle expressed in those words of Donatus, that church and state should be kept wholly distinct from each other, had at that time, through the reaction which began to manifest itself against the dominant church party, become universally recognised among the Donatists. In their sermons, the Donatist bishops spoke of the corruption of the church, which had originated in the confusion of the church and the state. " The evil spirit, before openly combated in the church," said they, " was now a still more dangerous enemy in its covert attacks, since it made a pretext of religion itself, and strove to insinuate itself into men's hearts by flattery.§ Those

---

* Thus it was with Honoratus, bishop of Siciliba, whose life is related in the tract above referred to.

† Gregori, macula senatus et dedecus præfectorum ; words quoted by Optatus, I. III. c. 3.

‡ Quid est imperatori cum ecclesia ? Optat. I. III. c. 3.

§ In the Donatist sermon, quoted in Du Pin, f. 191 : Blandæ decep-

whom it seduced to apostacy, (the traditors,) and who, by humbling themselves, might have been able to regain the divine favour, it now endeavoured to make secure by flattering them that they could still be Christians, and, in truth, bishops, and by tempting their ambition and their avarice with the favour of princes and worldly gifts." What impression must these and the like discourses have produced on the minds of the Circumcellions, inclined already to every fanatical extravagance! Accustomed to trace all corruption among the Christians to the influence of earthly power and grandeur, and to the abundance of worldly goods, this ruling idea mounted with them to a fanatical spirit, that breathed hatred against all who possessed power, rank, or wealth. They roved about the country, pretending to be the protectors of the oppressed and suffering—a sacred band who were fighting for the rights of God. Perhaps they rightly perceived that there was a great deal in the relation between the proprietors and their oftentimes heavily oppressed boors,* between masters and slaves, that was at variance with the spirit and doctrines of Christianity. But in the way in which *they* were disposed to better the matter, all civil order must be turned into confusion. They took the part of all debtors against their creditors: their chiefs, Fasir and Axid, who styled themselves the leaders of the sons of the Holy One,† sent threatening letters to all creditors, in which they were ordered to give up the obligations of their debtors. Whoever refused to obey was attacked on his own estate by the furious company, and might congratulate himself if he could purchase back his life by the remission of the debt. Whenever they met a master with his slave, they obliged the former to take the place of the latter. They compelled venerable heads of families to perform the most menial services. All slaves who complained of their masters, whether justly or unjustly, were sure of finding with them assistance and the means of revenge.‡ Several of the Donatist bishops,

tiouis insidiæ, quæ sub obtextu religionis animas fraudulenta circumventione subvertunt.

* Of which oppressions the bishops by their *intercessiones* and Libanius frequently testify.

† The phrase: Deo laudes! constituted the watch-word of their fanaticism. Vid. Augustin. c. Petilian. l. II. s. 146.

‡ See, among others, Augustin. ep. 185, ad. Bonifac. s. 18.

desirous of clearing their party from the reproach of being the
abettors or advocates of such atrocities, when they found themselves unable to produce any effect by their representations on
the fanatics, are said to have besought themselves the interposition of the civil power against men who refused to be
governed and set right by the church;* and this gave the first
occasion for resorting to force for the purpose of checking the
outrages of the Circumcellions. Now came in those exhortations of Donatus, and other like-minded bishops, to excite the
Circumcellions to revolt. Their ferocious deeds furnished a
welcome pretext for resorting to other persecuting measures.
It was determined that the unity of the church should be
forcibly restored; the Donatists were to be deprived of their
churches, and compelled to worship with the Catholics. It
cannot be exactly determined, how much, in all that was
done, proceeded from imperial edicts, and how much from the
despotism, the passion, or the cruelty of individual commanders.
Force continually excited the fanatic spirit still more; the
report spread that the emperor's image was set up after the
pagan manner in the churches, and the worship paid to it
which is due only to God. Many Donatist bishops and clergymen, many Circumcellions, fell victims to the persecution. It
is natural to suppose that the reporters of the facts on the
Catholic side would seek to curtail, and those on the other
side to exaggerate, the truth; hence an accurate statement is
out of the question. Certain it is, that many Circumcellions
sought only the glory of martyrdom. Finally it came to that
pass, that they threw themselves from precipices, cast themselves into the fire, and hired others to kill them.† The most
eminent bishops of the Donatist party, such as Donatus of
Carthage, were exiled; and thus it was imagined a final check
had been given to the resistance of the Donatists. So much
the more violent was the reaction when a change of political
relations took place, and the party hitherto oppressed thereby
recovered once more its freedom. This came about under the
reign of the emperor Julian, in the year 361. The Donatists,
in conformity with their peculiar principles, were quite satisfied that Christianity should cease, under the pagan ruler, to

* According to Optatus, III. 4, this appears to have taken place before
the attempt of Macarius to restore union.
† Vid. Optat. III. 4 and 12.

be the dominant religion of the state. Their bishops transmitted to him a petition, in which they besought a ruler who regarded only justice, to rescind the unjust decrees that had been issued against them. There could be no difficulty in obtaining a favourable answer, since the petition perfectly agreed with the principles of this emperor (see section i. p. 73). He therefore issued an edict by which everything which under the preceding reign had been unlawfully undertaken against them, was to be annulled. As they were now reinstated in possession of the churches which had been taken from them, their separatist fanaticism displayed itself in the wildest freaks. They regarded those churches, and the church furniture, as having been stained and polluted by the use which the profane had made of them while they were in their possession; they dashed the utensils of the church to pieces; they painted over the walls of the churches; they polished down the altars, or removed them entirely from the churches.*

Under the succeeding emperors, the situation of the Donatists again became worse; and they themselves did the most injury to their cause by their wild fanaticism. The passionate temper of their bishops naturally led to new divisions among themselves. A Donatist deacon in Carthage, by the name of Maximian, who had fallen into a quarrel with Primianus, the Donatist bishop of that city, and who had been excommunicated by the latter, finding followers, set up a separate party, which stood in precisely the same relation to the main body of the Donatists as the Donatists themselves did to the Catholic church. In this controversy, the Donatists were driven into many inconsistencies, of which their adversaries were not slow to take advantage.

The deplorable effects of this long-continued schism on the peace and prosperity of the African church,† and also, as it must be allowed, the prevailing conviction that there was no way of salvation out of the Catholic church, fired the zeal of the North-African bishops to use every effort in order to heal the division. Particularly deserving of mention here as a dis-

---

* See Optat. Milevit. II. 25, and l. VI.

† The fanatical intolerance went so far, that when the Donatists were the dominant party at Hippo, none of them would venture to bake bread for the Catholics, who were in the minority. See Augustin. c. lit. Petiliani, I. II. s. 184.

tinguished theological polemic, is Augustin, a presbyter, and subsequently a bishop, of Hipporegius in Numidia. His confidence in the validity of his logical and dogmatic principles made him feel perfectly sure, that, if the Donatist bishops could only be induced to enter into a calm investigation of arguments, they might easily be led to an acknowledgment of their errors.* But, not to mention that a fundamental error in the notion entertained on both sides concerning the church, presented a great difficulty in the way of a mutual understanding between the two parties, the chief obstacle of all, which prevented any hearty and permanent union, the prejudices of party spirit and passion did not admit of being banished from the dispositions of men by any power of logic; but, on the contrary, it was far more natural that disputation would serve only to excite the passions to a fiercer flame, and to cause the differences to appear still greater on both sides. It was an excellent plan which Augustin proposed to the aged bishop Fortunius—both of them men distinguished, in their respective parties, for Christian love and moderation—that each of them, with ten others, lovers of peace, and agreeing with them in doctrine, should come together in some villa, where there was no church of either party, and where members of both parties dwelt; that each should prepare himself, by silent prayer to the God of peace, for the common investigation;† and that they should agree not to separate till they had come to the wished-for union. But where would it have been possible to find ten such men of both parties, who would be able constantly to maintain, even in the heat of dispute, that tone of mind which Augustin required? Since the Donatists contended as the oppressed party with the dominant one, they had reasons, not

---

* The Donatist Cresconius was not so much out of the way, when he censured the confidence of Augustin, who professed to be able to dispose so easily of a controversy, on which, for so long a time, so many things had been said on both sides; Hoc velle finire post tot annos, post judices atque arbitros, quod apud principes tot disceptantibus litteratis ab utriusque partis episcopis finiri non potuit. See Augustin. c. Cresconium Donatistam, l. I. s. 4. He ought indeed to have learned something from so long experience: but the only difficulty on the part of Augustin was not surely, as Cresconius complains, an intoleranda arrogantia, but the natural confidence of one who was firmly rooted, with all his habits of thinking, in a dogmatic system.

† See Augustin. ep. 44, A.D. 398.

without some foundation, for mistrust with regard to any proposal coming from that quarter; and, besides this, they feared and hated the superior logic of Augustin.*

At the general African council held at Carthage, A.D. 403, a form was drawn up, whereby all the Donatist bishops were to be invited to choose delegates out of their own body, prepared to discuss the contested points with chosen men from the Catholic party. The forms of this invitation were conceived, it is true, in the spirit of love; yet it contained a good deal which was calculated to irritate the minds of the Donatists. The Catholic bishops could not consent to forget that *they* spoke, in the secure possession of the truth, with men who were *in error*, and whose errors it was *their* business to correct.† It was to be expected that the Donatists would refuse to comply with any such proposal. And when now, in addition to this, Augustin, in the name of the church, wrote a letter to the Donatist churches,‡ in which he exposed the inconsistencies of their party, and interpreted the conduct of their bishops in declining the invitation held out to them, as a token of distrust in the goodness of their cause, the effect could only be to increase their indignation. Hence it happened that the Circumcellions were stirred up to new fury, and that those ecclesiastics who had taken a zealous part in the disputation with the Donatists became the special objects of it. Such occurrences would furnish occasion for new penal statutes against the Donatist party; though influential voices already protested against the practice of applying to the emperors for the passage of such laws.

In respect to Augustin, he, at least, who through so many

---

* The Donatist Cresconius objects to Augustin, that dialectics "non congruat Christianæ veritati," and that the Donatist teachers would therefore much sooner avoid than refute him, as a homo dialecticus (c. Cresconium. l. I. s. 16). In reply to this, Augustin says: Hanc artem, quam dialecticam vocant, quæ nihil quam consequentia demonstrare, seu vera veris seu falsa falsis, nunquam doctrina Christiano formidat. He refers to the fact that Paul did not avoid a disputation with the Dialectic Stoics: that Christ repelled the entrapping questions of the Pharisees, Matth. xxii. 17, with a syllogism; and he says of these latter, "They had not learned from you to revile; else perhaps they would have chosen, with more bitterness, to call him a *dialectitian* rather than a *Samaritan.*"

† De vestra correctione gaudere cupientes. Cod. canon. eccles. Afr. c. 92.   ‡ Ep. 76.

devious ways and severe struggles had come to the knowledge
of the truth in which he found rest, must doubtless have been,
on this very account, more mildly disposed towards those who,
in his opinion, were in error.   He may have learned from his
own experience, that errors were not to be expelled by force;
that it required something else besides human wisdom to guide
the development and purification of a human soul.   The more
deeply penetrated he was with the truth that grace alone could
truly enlighten and sanctify men, the less would he be inclined
to attempt producing religious conviction by outward means.
In fact, Augustin, before his habits of thinking became fixed,
and particularly before they had attained to a systematic harmony around *a single point*, was far from indulging any wish
to subject to outward constraint that which only can proceed,
under the guidance of the Divine Spirit, out of the free development of the inner man.

In the meeting above alluded to with the Donatist bishop
Fortunius, it came about that the latter, as the Donatists were
frequently in the habit of doing, urged against the Catholic
church the violent measures of which it had been the occasion.
Augustin, feeling compelled to say something in vindication
of his party, was so far misled as to appeal to the example of
Elijah, who slew, with his own hand, the prophets of Baal.
But when Fortunius replied that a distinction was to be made
in such matters between the times of the Old and of the New
Testament, Augustin acknowledged that he was right.*   Somewhat later, he published a work against the party of Donatus,
in the first book of which he decidedly condemns all the measures which had been employed to force back the Donatists to
the ruling church.†   And when, at the council of the North-
African church, held at Carthage, A.D. 404, the question was
agitated about requiring the emperor to pass new penal laws

* Ep. 44. Hic revera vidit, quod videndum erat, talia tum licuisse
justis. Hæc enim *prophetico* spiritu auctoritate Dei faciebant, qui procul
dubio novit, cui etiam prosit occidi.

† This work, contra partem Donati, has not come down to us; but its
tendency has been thus described by Augustin, in Retractation, l. II. c. 5.
He says in this place, he had then so conceived it because he had not as
yet learned by experience how much sin the Donatists were bold enough
to commit, while they went unpunished, or how much a severe course of
conduct would contribute to their improvement. But *one* wrong can
never justify another, nor the end sanctify the means.

against the Donatists, by which numbers might be the more easily brought back to the Catholic church, Augustin, with several others of the younger bishops, declared against it. He said men must go forward simply with the word of truth, must seek to conquer by arguments, unless, instead of open and avowed heretics, they would have hypocritical Catholic Christians. Hence the council ought not to be satisfied with merely providing for the safety of those who, by defending the cause of the Catholic church, exposed themselves to the fury of the Circumcellions.* This opinion was adopted in part by the council. It was proposed to the emperor Honorius by the deputies of the North-African church, that the fixed pecuniary mulct of ten pounds of gold, which had been laid by his father Theodosius against the clergy of the heretics, or the owners of those places where they held their assemblies for worship, should be assessed only against those Donatist bishops and clergy, within whose dioceses acts of violence against the Catholic clergy should be perpetrated. Yet the attempt is said to have been made, at the same time, to procure that the law whereby heretics were excluded from the right of receiving donations and legacies, and of leaving legacies in their wills, should be expressly extended to the Donatists, who would not consent to be reckoned among the heretics.† When, moreover, to the proposal of the North-African council were added the complaints of individuals who had been abused by the Circumcellions, there were enacted, in the year 405, against the entire Donatist party, as a heretical one, various laws

---

* Ep. 93. Augustini ad Vincentium, s. 17, and epist. 185, ad Bonifacium, s. 25.

† Cod. Afr. canon 93. If we compare these minutes of the proceedings of the council with the report of them drawn up by Augustin, in the letter already referred to, addressed to Boniface, we shall doubtless see that this report is not strictly correct; perhaps because the whole matter was no longer present to Augustin's memory; for this council certainly required, as is evident from the appendix, a penal law against the Donatists generally, as such, but one by no means so severe; and such a spirit of mildness and liberality as is described by Augustin in the two letters above referred to, as peculiar to his earlier mode of thinking, by no means expresses itself in those minutes. Moreover, it may be gathered from many of the works against the Donatists which Augustin had at that time already written, and which we shall hereafter cite, that he had then actually made the transition from his earlier liberal principles, to more strict and rigid ones.

which were still more severe than the council itself had required.

The North-African bishops, of whom Augustin was the soul, laboured incessantly to bring about a religious conference with the Donatists, where they might be brought over to the true faith by the force of arguments. The Donatists, generally, sought every means of avoiding so useless an experiment. But it so happened, in the year 410, that certain Donatist bishops who had been summoned before the higher civil authorities were, by some means or other, perhaps by some objection which was brought against them, led to assert, for the first time, that they would doubtless be able to prove the truth of their cause, were they but allowed a patient hearing.* They were immediately taken at their word; and the Catholic bishops, urgently renewing their request that a religious conference might be appointed, appealed to the fact that the Donatists themselves were ready to acquiesce in that movement. And the emperor Honorius ordered a religious conference to be held between the two parties at Cathage, A.D. 411. If the Donatist bishops, after being three times invited, still declined taking any share in the religious conference, their conduct should be interpreted to signify a consciousness of being unable to defend their cause, and their communities should therefore be compelled to unite with the Catholic church. On the other hand, any who might comply with the invitation, should at some future time receive again the churches of which they were deprived. The imperial tribune and notary, Flavius Marcellinus, Augustin's friend, was appointed to preside over this religious conference as the emperor's commissioner, and to act as judge.

The Catholic bishops made such overtures to the Donatists as were calculated to give them confidence. They declared themselves ready to resign their bishoprics, and to surrender them into the hands of the Donatist bishops alone, in case the latter gained the victory in the conference. Such a pro-

---

* In the letters missive of this conference, the fact was appealed to, that the Donatists themselves had demanded it (sic ante brevissimum tempus Donatistarum episcopos in judicio illustrium potestatum collationem postulasse non dubium est. Gesta collationis in Du Pin, f. 247), although the Donatists denied all knowledge of having demanded any such thing.

position, it may be granted, required but little self-denial, since, beyond all doubt, they were well convinced that the case supposed could never happen. There was more in the other proposal, that if the cause of the Donatists was lost, and if their bishops would come over to the Catholic church, they should be recognized in their episcopal character, and stand on the same level with the Catholic bishops in the exercise of their functions. But if the communities were not satisfied with this, both should resign their dignities, and the Donatists and Catholics, now united, choose a new bishop. " Be brothers with us in the Lord's inheritance," said Augustin ; " let us not, for the sake of preserving our own stations, hinder the peace of Christ."* Augustin preached in Carthage before the commencement of the conference two discourses, in which he endeavoured to inspire the Catholics there with love and gentleness towards the Donatists, and called on them sedulously to avoid everything which might be calculated to give offence to their excitable feelings, or to arouse their passions. " Their eyes are inflamed," said he : " they must be treated prudently and with forbearance. Let no one enter into controversy with the other—let no one at this moment even defend his faith by disputation, lest some spark from the controversy kindle into a great fire, lest occasion of offence be given to those who seek occasion for it. Do you hear reviling language, endure it ; be willing not to have heard it ; be silent. Do you say, he brings charges against my bishop, and shall I be silent? Yes ; be silent at those charges ; not that you are to allow them, but to bear them. You best subserve the interests of your bishop at the present moment, when you forbear meddling with his cause. Repay not revilings with revilings, but pray for him."†

There met together at Carthage, A.D. 411, two hundred and eighty-six bishops of the Catholic, and two hundred seventy-nine of the Donatist party. The Donatists had evidently come to the conference with reluctance, and full of distrust: this was shown on all occasions. The tribune Marcellinus, in conformity with the imperial edict, made known to them the proposal, that, in case they wanted confidence in him, they were at liberty to choose another person of equal or of superior rank to preside along with him. The Donatist bishop Pe-

* Augustin. ep. 128, Sermo 358, f. 4.   † P. 357, s. 4.

tilianus thereupon declared—"It is none of our concern to ask for another judge, since in fact *we* did not ask for the *first*. The business belongs to those who have been the contrivers of this whole affair."*

Amid such vast numbers on both sides, the transactions could hardly be conducted in a quiet and orderly manner. Marcellinus demanded, in compliance with the imperial letters missive, that, according to the common mode of judicial proceedings, deputies should be chosen from each of the two parties, seven in number, to advocate the cause of their respective sides in the name of the rest. But the distrustful Donatists, prejudiced against the whole business, at first positively refused to enter into such an arrangement. They declared that the judicial mode of proceeding was not applicable to this spiritual concern. Amid wearisome, fruitless disputes about this and other matters relating to the form of transacting business, the time of the meeting during the greater part of the first day was spent. At length the Donatists were obliged to yield, and to choose seven bishops. Augustin was the ablest speaker on the one side, Petilianus on the other.

When, on the second day of the assembly, the seven deputies of each party entered the hall, the imperial commissioner invited them to take their seats as he took his own. The Catholic bishops followed the invitation; but Petilianus said, in the name of the Donatists—"We do not sit in the absence of our fathers, (the other bishops, who could not assist at the conference,) especially as the divine law, Ps. xxvi. 4, forbids us to sit down with such adversaries." Marcellinus thereupon declared, that respect for the character of the bishops forbade that he should remain seated, if they chose to stand; and he ordered his chair to be removed.

The matters brought forward at this religious conference related to two disputed questions; the one, as to the fact whether Felix of Aptunga, and Cæcilian, were traditors; the other was a question of doctrine, viz. what belonged to the essence of the Catholic church,—whether the church, by communion with unworthy members, lost the predicate of the genuine Christian Catholic church. The controversy on the first point can have no farther interest for us: in respect to the controversy on the second point, we shall treat upon it

* Gesta collat. f. 248.

connectedly, when we come to survey the whole matter of dispute between the two parties.

The imperial commissioner decided, as was to be expected, in favour of the Catholic church. The decision was followed by severer laws, by which all the Donatist clergy were banished from their country, and the laity of the party were condemned to pecuniary fines. The fanaticism of the oppressed party was thereby excited to new and more violent outbreaks. When, in the year 420, the imperial tribune Dulcitius signified his intention to carry the laws against the Donatists into execution, Gaudentius, bishop of Thamugade, who had been one of the seven speakers on the side of the Donatists at the conference of Carthage, declared that, if force were used to take away his church, he would burn himself up in it, together with his community. The tribune having written to him that such a proceeding would not be in conformity with the doctrine of Christ; that, according to this, he must rather seek safety in flight; Gaudentius defended his premeditated suicide, and appealed, among other arguments, to the example of Razis, 2 Maccab. xiv. This was the occasion of Augustin's writing his work against Gaudentius; a treatise important on account of its bearing on the question of suicide, and on other points connected with the history of Christian morals (see the fourth Section). When the Vandals, in the fifth century, made themselves masters of this country, the Donatists, as such, had to suffer no persecutions from them. It was only as adherents of the Nicene creed that they were persecuted in common with other confessors of the same system. They continued to survive as a distinct party down to the sixth century, as may be seen from the letters of the Roman bishop Gregory the Great.

We now pass to consider the theological points of dispute between the two parties. The first point related to the doctrine concerning the church. The same remarks which we made on this subject, in speaking of the Novatian controversies in the preceding period, apply also to the Donatist disputes. Both parties were involved in the same grand mistake with regard to the conception of the church, by their habit of confounding the notions of the invisible and of the visible church with each other. Proceeding on this fundamental error, the Catholic fathers maintained that, separate from the communion

of the one visible Catholic church, derived, through the succession of the bishops, from the apostles, there is no way of
participating in the influences of the Holy Spirit and of
obtaining salvation; and hence it could not seem otherwise
than a matter of the highest importance to those of them who
were actuated by a pure zeal of Christian charity, to bring the
Donatists to acknowledge this universal visible church, although
they were not separated from them by any difference of creed.
On the other hand the Donatists, owing to this same confusion
of notions, held that every church which tolerated unworthy
members in its bosom was itself polluted by the communion
with them; it thus ceased to deserve the predicates of purity
and holiness, and consequently ceased to be a true Christian
church, since such a church could not subsist without these
predicates.

As it concerns Augustin, the principal manager of this controversy, it is easy to explain, from the course of his religious
and theological development, how this notion of the church
came to be considered by him of so much importance; and
the foundation on which this notion was established by his
logical, systematizing mind, exerted a great influence on all
succeeding times. Augustin had been carefully educated by
his pious mother, Monica, in the faith, early implanted in his
soul, that the way to heaven was to be found only in the
Catholic church. From the years of his youth and upward,
he had fallen into many errors of theory and practice, and into
a series of violent conflicts. He passed, finally, from Manicheism, which had disappointed the expectations of many
years, to Scepticism. Whilst he was in this state of scepticism,
and whilst an inward impulse of his intellect and his heart
compelled him still to believe in some objective truth, the
thought took possession of his soul: Must not God have
instituted an authority, capable of being known by sure and
certain marks, to conduct the restless doubting spirit of man
to the truth which he needs? From scepticism, the transition
was here formed in his case,—which was a case often repeated
in history,—to the faith in the authority of a visible church,
proved to be of divine origin by evidences not to be mistaken.
Again, although the belief in the truth and divinity of the
doctrines of Christ, which had attended him from his childhood, and never forsaken him, even when he embraced Mani-

cheism, asserted its power in his soul more strongly as he grew older; yet he was in doubt as to the question where these doctrines of Christ were to be found, since each one of the sects claimed to be itself in possession of them. He wanted that knowledge of the right hermeneutical, exegetical, and critical principles, which would have enabled him to answer this question, as to what were the true doctrines of Christ, out of the sacred scriptures alone. The hermeneutical and critical principles of the Manicheans had completely unsettled him: he wanted a stable authority, which could show him where the pure doctrines of Christ, the unfalsified collection of religious records, and the correct doctrinal exposition of them, were already present. This authority he believed he found in the tradition of the universal church. When Augustin considered that this church had come forth victorious out of all her conflicts with the powers that had assailed her from without, and with the manifold corruptions of Christianity in erroneous forms of doctrine; when he perceived what a revolution in the whole mode of human thought, and in the entire life of man, had been effected by means of this church, how the loftiest truths of religion had passed into the common consciousness of humanity where this church had become dominant; he confounded, in this case, what the church had effected through Christianity, and what Christianity had effected through the church, as the instrument and vessel for its diffusion and propagation, with what the church had done in and of itself as a visible, outward institution, in this determinate earthly form. What he might justly regard as a witness for the divine, world-transforming power of the gospel, appeared to him as a witness for the divine authority of the visible, universal church; and he did not consider that the gospel truth would have been able to bring about effects equally great, by its inherent divine power, in some other vessel in which it could have been diffused among mankind; nay, that it would have been able to produce still purer and mightier effects, had it not been in many ways disturbed and checked in its operation by the impure and confining vehicle of its transmission.*

* The authorities for this delineation are furnished by Augustin's confessions, by the works which he composed during the great crisis of his inner life until the first years of his spiritual office, and especially

As Augustin, at the time of his controversy with the Donatists, had already incorporated into his life, and woven into the very texture of his thoughts, this confused mixture of conceptions necessarily distinct; as this error then universally prevailing in the Western, and particularly in the North-African church, had thus passed over into his inmost habits of thinking, it is easy to see of what weight this point must have seemed to him in the present dispute. Hence he could say :* " No one attains to salvation, and to eternal life, who has not Christ for his Head. But no one can have Christ for a Head, who does not belong to his Body, which is the Church."† Hence the error, growing out of this confounding and mixing together of distinct notions, that the union of believers with Christ was brought about through the union with this visible church. And hence, in following out this principle, he asserts : " The entire Christ is the Head and the Body ;—the Head is the only begotten Son of God, and the Body is the Church. He who agrees not with scripture in the doctrine concerning the Head, although he may stand in external communion with the church, notwithstanding belongs not to her. But, moreover, he who holds fast to all that scripture teaches respecting the Head, and yet cleaves not to the unity of the church, belongs not to her."‡

It is a fact particularly worthy of notice in the polemical writings of Augustin, that, whenever the Donatists made appeals to miracles, answers to prayer, visions, and to the holy lives of their bishops, as evidences that the true church was with them, he, on the other hand, will allow the validity of no other evidence than the objective testimony of the divine word. " Let them not try to prove the genuineness of their church," says he,§ " by the councils of their bishops, by deceitful miraculous signs, since we have been warned and put on our guard against such proofs by the word of the Lord (Matth. xxiv. 25), but let them do it by the law and prophets, and by the word of the only Shepherd.‖ Neither do we ourselves

---

the works de ordine, de moribus ecclesiæ catholicæ et moribus Manichæorum, de vera religione, and de utilitate credendi.

   * De unitate ecclesiæ, c. 49.

   † Habere caput Christum nemo poterit, nisi qui in ejus corpore fuerit, quod est ecclesia.

   ‡ De unitate ecclesiæ, s. 7.   § L. c. s. 47.   ‖ L. c. s. 50.

affirm that men ought to believe us in maintaining that we are in the Catholic church, because this Church is recommended by an Optatus of Mileve, or by an Ambrose of Milan, or other numberless bishops of our communion; or because it has been approved by the assemblies of our colleagues; or because such wonderful instances of answers to prayer, or of the healing of the sick, have been witnessed on sacred spots in the whole world, which have been visited by the members of our communion; or because this person has had a vision, and that other has heard in a trance, that he should not unite himself with the Donatist party, or that he should forsake it." It must be admitted, however, that Augustin is inconsistent with himself, and moves round in a circle, when, in disputing with the Donatists, he allows validity to no evidence but that of the scriptures, in favour of the Catholic church; while, in his controversy with the Manicheans, he makes the authority of the holy scriptures themselves to depend on that of the church which referred to them, and from which we have received the sacred canon.*

The Donatists maintained that the church should cast out from its body those who were known, by open and manifest sins, to be unworthy members. To prove this, they adduced the fifth chapter of Paul's first Epistle to the Corinthians, where the apostle has given certain rules for the practice of church discipline. "When the Church did not act in accordance with these rules," said they, "but tolerated such unworthy members in her communion, she lost the predicates of purity and holiness." All those passages of holy writ which bid us avoid the company of the wicked, they referred—confounding inward disposition with outward conduct—to the avoiding of external companionship with them. Augustin, taking the position of the Catholic church, replied that, it was true, church discipline should, by all means, be vigorously

* The well-known and remarkable words, contra epistolam Manichæi, s. 6 : Ego vero evangelio non crederem, nisi me catholicæ ecclesiæ commoveret auctoritas; while, on the other hand, what he says against the Donatists would admit, perhaps, of being expressed by reversing the proposition : Ego vero catholicæ ecclesiæ non crederem, nisi me evangelii commoveret auctoritas. But if tradition conducts, through the church, to the scriptures, it by no means follows that they are believed on the ground of its authority. We see here that confusion of ideas, the cause of which is so easily accounted for by what has been said above.

maintained; but that still such a complete separation from the rest even of manifest transgressors, was, in the existing state of the church, impracticable; that the evil must be patiently endured, to avoid a still greater one, and to give opportunity for reformation to such as could be reformed, especially in those cases where the wickedness which was to be corrected by church discipline, was shared by too many. The Apostle Paul, he attempts to show, by what we must allow to be a rather forced interpretation,* was speaking only of *individuals*, whose vices were not common to many, and whose vices were universally known; so that the sentence of excommunication pronounced against such persons must have been acknowledged as just by all. But when the same disease had infected many, nothing was left to the good but pain and grief, that so by the mark revealed to Ezekiel (Ezek. ix. 4), they might be preserved from the destruction with which all were threatened. Where the infection of sin had seized on the many, the severity of a divine chastisement was required; for the counsels of human separation were vain and mischievous; they proceeded from pride; they rather disturbed the weak among the good, than exerted any power of reformation on the boldly wicked. Let man then punish, what he may punish, in the spirit of love. Where he may not, let him suffer patiently, sigh and mourn with love, until either chastisement and reformation come from above, or, at the general harvest, the tares be rooted out, and the chaff sifted away. Thus the good and faithful Christians, certain of their own salvation, may persevere to dwell in unity among the corrupt, whom it is beyond their power to punish, seeking to extirpate the sin which is in their own heart.†
The Catholic party appealed to those parables of our Lord which treat of the separation of the good and bad, reserved unto the final judgment; the parables of the tares, of the good fruit, of the draught of fishes. The Donatists replied, either that these passages referred simply to the mixing together of the good and the bad in the *world*, and not within the church; that by the *field*, the *net*, was to be understood, not the church, but the world; or they maintained that those passages referred

---

* In the phrase, "si quis," he maintained, was implied one among many differently disposed; and in the words, "fratres nominantur," that his offence was generally known.

† Augustin. c. epist. Parmenian, l. III. s. 12, et seqq.

simply to the mixing in of secret sinners with the saints; since even *they* allowed that a complete separation was in this life impossible, and demanded only the exclusion of those who were manifestly vicious.* As it respects the first of these positions, we may remark here a noticeable dispute between the Donatists and their antagonists, relative to the use of the term " world," in the sacred scriptures; where it becomes evident, how the same fundamental error in confounding *the notions of the invisible and of the visible church*, in which both parties were involved, prevented their coming to a mutual under-standing. The Donatists appealed to the fact, that Christ himself, in explaining this parable, taught that the *field* is the *world*. Augustin, on the other hand, replied, that in this passage, Christ used the term, " world," in place of the church.†
This was perhaps correct; but the question comes up, In what particular point of view was this notion of the church employed? That portion of the visible church which belongs at the same time to the invisible, could, however, only form an antithesis to that portion which the New Testament calls, in a peculiar sense, the *world*. But of the external visible church, in so far as it is not *one* with the invisible, it may with propriety be said that it belongs to the world in the sense of the Bible. Precisely because the Donatist bishop Emeritus failed to mark this distinction of ideas, he uttered—as Augustin expressed it —that petulant exclamation. He then proceeded directly to quote those passages from John, where the *world* expresses that which is opposed to the kingdom of God; and demanded whether that could be said of the church?—for example, the world knows not God, therefore the church knows not God. But of one portion of the *visible* church all this may with propriety be said; and the Donatist himself could have no hesitation in applying all this to the secret unworthy members who yet belonged to the visible church. Pity that he had not

---

* As it respects the second position, the Donatists explained; Hoc de *reis latentibus* dictum, quoniam reticulum in mari positum quid habeat a piscatoribus, id est a sacerdotibus, ignoratur, donec extractum ad littus ad purgationem boui seu mali prodantur. Ita et latentes et in ecclesia constituti et a *sacerdotibus ignorati*, in divino judicio proditi, tanquam pisces mali a sanctorum consortio separantur. See Collat. Carthag. d. III. ed. Du Pin, fol. 314, and the breviculus of Augustin concerning this day.

† Mundum ipsum appellatum esse pro ecclesiæ nomine.

made himself distinctly conscious of this! Augustin answered, that the holy scriptures used the term, "world," sometimes in a good, and sometimes in a bad sense. In the former, for example, when it is said, the world believes in Christ, is redeemed by him; but he ought to have considered, that the invisible church receives its members out of the world; that they who once belonged to the world, in that biblical sense, do, by becoming incorporated, by faith and participation in the redemption, into the invisible church, cease belonging to it any longer. Augustin says, one need only distinguish the different senses of the term "world," and one would no longer find any contradiction here in the scriptures. But he would have advanced farther, and been still more free from prejudice, in his interpretation of the Bible, if he had duly distinguished the different significations of the word "church." He says: "Behold the world in the bad sense, all who cleave to earthly things among all the nations:—behold, on the other hand, the world in the good sense, all who believe and have hope of eternal life among all nations."* But are not the last mentioned precisely the members of the genuine church of Christ, of the *invisible* church, among all the nations where the gospel has found its way,—among all the different earthly forms of appearance of the visible church?

It is remarkable, but also very natural, that the Donatists, to show the necessity of a severe sifting in the church, and to prove that the church was corrupt where such a sifting had not been made, drew their arguments, for the most part, from the Old Testament, and from such passages of the Old Testament as treat of the external purity of the people of God.† They ought, however, in this case, to have paid some regard to that necessary distinction between the positions of the Old and of the New Testament, which they were not slow to insist on, in other cases, against their opponents.

According to *the Catholic point of view*, to the essence of the genuine Catholic church belonged its *general spread through the medium of the episcopal succession down from the apostles*. From the conception of the Catholic church in this sense was then first derived the predicates of purity and holiness. On the other hand, according to the Donatist point of

* L. c. f. 317.   † Collat. l. c. fol. 313, 314.

view, the predicate of Catholic ought to be subordinate to
those of purity and holiness.   When the church, however
widely extended,—they inferred,—became corrupted by intercourse with unworthy members, then that church, in whatever
nook or corner of the earth it might be, which had no manifestly vicious members within its pale, is the genuinely Catholic one.*   They appealed, not without reason, from the pre-
judgment grounded on numbers and universality, to the passages of scripture where the little band of genuine confessors
were distinguished from the great mass of apostates, or of
those belonging to the kingdom of God merely in outward
appearance; as, for example, the seven thousand that had not
bowed the knee to Baal,—where the few, who went in the
strait way towards heaven, were opposed to the multitude of
those who went in the broad way to destruction.   They maintained that when Christ represented it as so doubtful (Luke
xviii. 8), whether at his reappearance he should find faith on
the earth, this indicated that the faithful, in the true sense,
would not be thus diffused in one mass over the whole earth.†
But although they were right here, in distinguishing those
who in the visible church constituted the church proper, the
invisible one, from the great mass of those who made up the
appearance of the visible church; yet they were wrong in this
respect, that, confounding once more, on another side, notions
distinct in themselves, they persisted in forming this genuine
church only according to the dictates of a separatist pride.
They imagined the saying was here confirmed, that the last
should be first; the holy, pure church was at present in
Africa; while the East, where Christianity commenced its
progress, had fallen from purity;—and although in Africa
(i.e. North Africa) no church was to be found which was of
apostolic origin.   They protested here, therefore, against the
claims of the sedes apostolicæ, and against those who were for

* The Donatist bishop Emeritus says, in opposing the assumption of
the other party, who always preceded on the supposition that they were
the Catholic church according to the principle of universality : Quicun-
que justis legitimisque ex causis Christianus fuerit approbatus, ille meus
est Catholicus.   And the bishop Gaudentius : Catholicum nomen non ad
provincias vel gentes referendum : cum hoc sit quod sacramentis plenum,
quod perfectum. quod immaculatum.   Collat. d. III. f. 301 et 2.
    † Augustin. de unitate ecclesiæ, s. 33, et seqq.

uniformly attaching to the outward fellowship with these the predicate of a Catholic church.*

Midway between both parties stood the Donatist grammarian, Tichonius, approving neither of the intolerant, proud spirit of separatism, nor of Catholicism, which was for forcing men into an external unity. He allowed that his party was wrong in holding themselves to be the alone pure church; and in making the fulfilment of the divine promise, as to the blessing which should be dispensed through the posterity of Abraham to all mankind,—the blessing of a preached gospel which should reach the whole world,—to depend on a subjective human purity which nowhere existed. He could not agree that, by communion with unworthy members which it did not expel from itself, the church could lose its character, which rested on an objective, divine foundation.† He doubtless made his own party mark their inconsistency in the fact, that the Donatists might perceive a great deal of the same impurity in their own communities which they so sharply reproved in the Catholic church as a profanation of its character. What was holy or not holy must be determined by their own caprice.‡ Augustin, however, accused Tichonius himself of inconsistency,§ because he did not, in accordance with these principles, abandon his party, and acknowledge those who stood in church fellowship with the Christendom extending throughout the entire world, as the Catholic church. This inconsistency, however, he could find in Tichonius, only by supposing in his mind the same confusion of the invisible with the visible church in which he himself was involved, and the same principles of a necessary visible unity of the church. But on this very point he was mistaken. Tichonius distinguished two parts of the body of Christ (corpus Domini bipartitum), i. e. of that which exhibits itself in manifestation as the body of Christ, as the church; one part, the individuals scattered

* De unitate ecclesiæ, s. 37.

† See Augustin. c. epistolam Parmeniani, l. I. c. 1 et 2; l. III. s. 17. Comp. also the hermeneutic rules of Tichonius, reg. I., where, probably in opposition to the other Donatists, he remarks: Non enim sicut quidam dicunt, in *contumeliam regni Dei invictæque hæreditatis Christi*. quod non sine dolore dico, Dominus totum mundum potestate et non sui corporis plenitudine occupavit. Bibl. patr. Lugd. t. VI. f. 50.

‡ Quod volumus sanctum est. Augustin. c. epist. Parmeniani, I. II. s. 31

§ C. epist. Parmeniani, l. I. c. 1.

through the whole world, who, by faith and temper of mind, really belong to Christ's spiritual body, who are truly one with him as the Head of the spiritual body; in whom he is daily born and grows up into the holy temple of God;[*] to whom the description applies which Paul gives in Ephesians v. 27, inasmuch as they are purified in the faith by the blood of Christ—therefore the true community of the saints;— another part, those scattered throughout the world, who belong indeed, as to visible appearance, to the same body of Christ, and draw nigh to God with their lips, but in heart are far from him.[†] Accordingly, Tichonius could say that the two portions of the manifested body of Christ remained connected with each other throughout the whole world; and the important question was, to which of these two portions did each individual belong, by the temper of his mind. Owing to this intermediate relation to both parties, he could of course make his cause good to neither; in addition to which it must be remarked that he seems to have been somewhat obscure in his mode of expressing himself.[‡]

That separatist pride of the Donatists, which attributed so much weight to the subjectively human element, as their principle compelled them to do, often expressed itself, in the heat of controversy, in an extremely harsh and unchristian manner. On the other hand, Augustin not unfrequently explains his own views in a very beautiful style, and in the genuinely Christian sense, respecting the might and validity of the objectively divine element; respecting the relation of the human element to the same, as a mere organ; and respecting the vanity and emptiness of the human element, whenever it aspires to be anything more than this.

When the Donatist bishop Petilian pressed Augustin to declare explicitly whether he acknowledged Cæcilian as his

[*] Reg. I. God as the fountain of divine life in human nature through Christ. Deus in corpore suo filius est hominis, qui quotidie nascendo (the spiritual *becoming* of the divine life) venit et crescit in templum sanctum Dei.

[†] Reg. II. Qui ejusdem corporis sunt visibiliter, et Deo labiis quidem adpropinquant, corde tamen separati sunt.

[‡] Augustin doubtless perceived much that was anti-catholic in the hermeneutical rules of Tichonius relative to the significations of the body of Christ. These he calls Donatist views: Quæ sicut Donatista hæreticus loquitur: he could not, however, exactly specify what they were. De doctrina Christiana, I. III. s. 43.

father, in which case the cause of the Catholic church would
be made to depend wholly on the guilt or innocence of this
latter individual, Augustin at length declared: " I have *one*
Head, but this is Christ; whose apostle I hear saying: ' All
is yours, but ye are Christ's, and Christ is God's.' For even
in the case where the apostle called himself a father, he added,
that we might beware of attributing to his paternity any *weak
human* foundation, ' I have begotten you *through the gospel.*'
To the gospel, then, I trace my parentage. It is one thing,
when, from motives of respect, we call the more aged or the
more deserving, our fathers; and it is quite another, when the
question is put to us, whom have we for our father as it respects eternal salvation,—as it respects the communion of the
church, and the participation in the divine promises as it concerns eternal salvation,—I beg pardon of the apostle, or rather
it is he that bids me so speak,—the apostle is not my father
in respect to that;—he who tells me: ' I have planted, and
Apollos watered, but God gave the increase. So, then, neither
is he that planteth anything, neither he that watereth; but
God that giveth the increase.' In respect to my salvation, I
acknowledge no other father than God; of whom our Lord
says: ' Ye shall call no man father on the earth, for one is
your Father, who is in heaven,' and to whom we daily say:
' Our Father which art in heaven.' "* When Petilian made
use of the strongest expressions to show that all religious acts
possessed their true significance only in their (the Donatists')
alone pure and holy church, that none but a clergyman without spot or blame could duly administer the sacraments; when
Petilian expressed himself to this purport, that everything depended on the conscience of him who imparted baptism, since
it was through him the conscience of the recipient was to be
cleansed; Augustin replied: " Often the conscience of man
is unknown to me, but I am certain of the mercy of Christ."
When Petilian said: " Whoever receives the faith from an
unbeliever, receives not faith, but guilt."† Augustin answered:
" But Christ is faithful, from whom I receive faith, and not
guilt." When Petilian said: " The character of every thing
depends strictly on its origin and its root (consequently here
on the character of the person administering the sacraments)

* Collat. c. Donatist. l. c. f. 312.
† Qui fidem a perfido sumserit, non fidem percipit, sed reatum.

—a genuine new birth can proceed only from good seed," Augustin replied: " My origin is Christ, my root is Christ, my Head is Christ. The seed, from which I am regenerated, is the word of God, which my Lord exhorts me obediently to follow, although he through whom I hear it may not himself practise what he teaches." To the remark of Petilian : " How absurd to suppose that he who is guilty through his own transgressions, can absolve others from guilt !" he replied : " He alone makes me free from guilt who died for our sins, and rose again for our justification ; for I believe not in the minister by whom I am baptized, but in Him who justifies the sinner, so that my faith is accounted unto me for righteousness."*

As Petilian, in his pastoral letters against the Catholic church, had brought many charges against Augustin himself, the latter replied to these charges in his third book against Petilian, confining himself wholly to the interests of the cause. " Let no man," he says, " glory in man. If you see anything praiseworthy in us, let Him be praised from whom cometh down every good and perfect gift. And in all which you acknowledge to be good in us, be followers of us, if we also are followers of Christ. But if ye surmise, believe, or seek after things that are bad in us, hold fast to the word of the Lord, and, throwing yourselves on that, forsake not his church on account of the wickedness of men, Matt. xxiii. 3. Observe, do what we bid you ; but, where ye believe or know that we do wrong, do not after our works ; for at present it is not the time for me to justify myself before you, since I have undertaken to recommend to you the cause of truth and salvation without regard to my own personal concerns, that none may glory in a man. For cursed is he that putteth his trust in man. If this word of the Lord is kept and observed, even though I may fall, so far as it concerns my own personal interests, yet the cause I serve will come off victorious."†

Since the Catholics, in their controversy with the Donatists, distinguished the church on earth, in which genuine and spurious members are mixed together, from the church of heaven, purified from its spurious members, they might easily have been led, by pursuing this distinction still further, to distinguish the conceptions of the visible and of the invisible church. In this way they furnished occasion to the Donatists of charg-

* Augustin. c. Petilian. l. i. s. 8.　　　† Contra Petilian. I. III. s. 4.

ing them with supposing the existence of *two churches;* but they were extremely uneasy under this accusation, and would allow of no other distinction than that of two different conditions of one and the same church, inasmuch as it was at present a mortal church, but would hereafter be an immortal one.* And Augustin, in his book, "de unitate ecclesiæ," says: "Many stand, in the communion of the sacraments, *with* the church, and are still not *in* the church."† But what means this: They are *not in the church*, and they yet stand in communion with the church? In the outward, apparent church they are certainly; but in the inner, invisible church, to which none can belong otherwise than by the temper of the heart, they are not. And with what church can they stand in communion by a bare outward participation of the sacraments alone? Certainly with no other but with that which is itself merely an outward and visible one; from which, inasmuch as it *is* the bare form of manifestation, destitute of the inner life, no true life can proceed. Augustin would, therefore, if he had made himself distinctly conscious of what was implied in his own conceptions, have properly said: "Many stand in outward communion with the visible church, who are yet, by the temper of their hearts, by no means members of the invisible church." And he himself does in fact intimate, in another place, that there is a church, which is the body of Christ, something other than the bare appearance of a church, or the bare visible church—a church with which they who did not belong to it by the temper of their hearts, stood in no sort of connection,—when he says of such: "We ought not to believe that they are in the body of Christ, which is the church, because, in a bodily manner, they participate in its sacraments. But they are not in that communion of the church, which, in the members of Christ by mutual union, makes increase to that measure of its growth which God has appointed; for that church is founded on a rock, as the Lord says: On this rock will I build my church. But such persons build on the sand."‡ To what results would

---

* Collat. fol. 318. Eandem ipsam unam et sanctam ecclesiam nunc esse aliter, tunc autem aliter futuram.

† s. 74. Multi sunt in sacramentorum communione cum ecclesia, et tamen jam non sunt in ecclesia.

‡ C. Petilian. I. II. s. 247. and de doctrina Christiana, I. III. s. 45. He

Augustin have arrived, if he had made clear to himself the distinction of ideas which lies at the bottom of these words?

Another more important point of dispute related to the employment of force in matters of religion. The Donatists bore their testimony on this point with emphasis in favour of that course which the example of Christ and the apostles, which the spirit of the gospel, and the sense of man's universal rights, called forth by the latter, required. The point of view first set forth in a clear light by Christianity, when it made religion the common good of all mankind and raised it above all narrow political restrictions, was by the Donatists manfully asserted, in opposition to a theory of ecclesiastical rights at variance with the spirit of the gospel, and which had sprung up out of a new mixture of ecclesiastical with political interests. They could not succeed so well in unfolding the relation of the church to the state, for here they easily passed from one extreme over to the other. If their opponents erred on the side of confounding too much the church with the state, they, on the other hand, were too much inclined to represent the opposition between the two, which was grounded in the early relation of the church to a pagan state, as a relation that must ever continue to exist.

The Donatist bishop Petilian says: "Did the apostles ever persecute any one, or did Christ ever deliver any one over to the secular power? Christ commands us to flee persecutors, Matt. x. 23. Thou who callest thyself a disciple of Christ oughtest not to imitate the evil deeds of the heathens. Think you thus to serve God,—by destroying us with your own hand? Ye err, ye err, poor mortals, if ye believe this; for God has not executioners for his priests. Christ persecutes no one; for he was for inviting, not forcing, men to the faith; and when the apostles complained to him of the founders of separate parties, Luke ix. 50, he said to them: 'He who is not against us, is for us;' and so too Paul, in Philippians i. 18.* Our Lord Christ says: 'No man can come unto me,

himself, in censuring the expression of Tichonius, bipartitum corpus Domini, distinguishes the *corpus Christi verum* atque *simulatum*.

* Petilian would say, that to Christians every one should be welcome who preached Christ; but this the Catholics could not see, since to them the faith in Christ was nothing without faith in the visible church. And even the Donatists, in recognizing nothing as genuinely Christian beyond

unless the Father, who hath sent me, draw him.' But why do you not permit every man to follow his own free will, since God, the Lord himself, has bestowed this free will on man? He has simply pointed out to man the way to righteousness, that none might be lost through ignorance. Christ, in dying for men, has given Christians the example to die, but not to kill. Christ teaches us to suffer wrong, not to requite it. The apostle tells us of what he had endured, not of what he had done to others. But what have you to do with the princes of this world, in whom the Christian cause has ever found only its enemies?" He cites examples from the Old and the New Testament; he supposes he finds mention made of princes hostile to the church in I Corinth. ii. 6. Yet he adds: "This may have been said, however, of the ancient pagan princes; but you suffer not the emperors of this world, who would be Christians, to be such, since you mislead them, by your false representations, to turn the weapons prepared against the enemies of the state, against Christians." The Donatist bishop Gaudentius says: "God created man free, *after his own image.* How am I to be deprived of that by human lordship which God has bestowed on me? What sacrilege, that human arrogance should take away what God has bestowed, and idly boast of doing this in God's behalf! It is a great offence against God, when he is defended by men. What must *he think* of God, who would defend him with outward force? Is it that God is unable to punish offences against himself? Hear what the Lord says: 'Peace I leave with you, my peace I give unto you; not as the world giveth, give I unto you.' The peace of the world must be introduced among contending nations by arms. The peace of Christ invites the willing with wholesome mildness; it never forces men against their wills. The almighty God employed prophets to convert the people of Israel; he enjoined it not on princes; the Saviour of souls, the Lord Christ, sent fishermen, and not soldiers, to preach his faith."

Augustin, in attacking these arguments of the Donatists, now appeared as the advocate of a theory of ecclesiastical

the pale of their own spotless church, did not act consistently according to this principle; with which inconsistency Augustin took care to reproach them. Vid. Augustin. contra literas Petiliani. I. II. s. 178 et 180.

rights, of which he himself, as we have already remarked, was at an earlier period the opponent. He was, in this case, carried along by the spirit of the times; and this spirit had found a point of union for such errors in his habit of confounding the visible and the invisible church. He who possesses at all times a clear consciousness that the true and real church of Christ is an invisible one, is also constantly aware that it cannot be built up and advanced by any outward human mechanism, but only by that which penetrates into the inmost recesses of the mind, and begets a free conviction. But he who overvalues the vehicle of the outward church, will also deem it a matter of high importance that men should, in the first place, be introduced into this—and that indeed can be effected by a great variety of outward, human means.

As early as the year 400, Augustin had changed his principles on this subject; for already he defended against the Donatist bishop Parmenianus, the resort to force against the Donatists, though, in his advice given at the same time before 'a council in Carthage (see above), he did not yet allow himself to be determined by these principles. But, even at a still subsequent period, we find examples to show that he suffered himself to be guided in his mode of action by a milder Christian spirit than that was which could give birth to such principles.* Pity it was that errors which grew first out of practice should, by the application of Augustin's logic,—so adroit in combining things true, half true, and false, into a plausible whole,—be wrought into a systematic theory, and thereby become the more firmly rooted in the ecclesiastical polity. Augustin did indeed know too well what constituted the essence of inward Christianity,—the Christianity of faith and of temper,—to be capable of entertaining the opinion that faith could be brought into the heart by outward arrangements;—penetrated as he was with the conviction that man's conversion can only be a work of divine grace operating on the soul. Moreover, he

* He demanded that even deeds of violence, which had been committed by furious Circumcellions on the clergy, should be punished, not according to the strictness of the laws, but according to the spirit of Christian gentleness; and if he could accomplish his end in no other way, he was determined himself to make application to the emperors. See Augustin. ep. 139 ad Marcellinum.

never lost sight of the truth, that mere external communion with the church, which alone was capable of being forcibly brought about by means of fear and punishment, can make no one a member of the kingdom of God. But he maintained that man may nevertheless be prepared in various ways, by outward means, by suffering, for faith and conversion. He appealed to the highest example, that of God, who by suffering educates men, brings them to a consciousness of themselves, and conducts them to faith;—to the example of the parent who corrects the son for his profit. "Who doubts but what it is better to be led to God by instruction, than by fear of punishment or affliction? But because the former, who will be guided only by instruction, are better, the others are still not to be neglected. Show me the man who, in real faith and true consciousness, says with the whole strength of his soul: ' My soul thirsteth after God;' and I will allow that, for such a person, not only the fear of temporal punishments or imperial laws, but even the fear of hell, is unnecessary : whatever separates him from his highest good, is punishment enough for him. But many, like bad servants, must often be reclaimed to their master by the rod of temporal suffering, ere they can attain to this highest stage of religious development."* We are shown here how seductive may be a comparison of two relations altogether differing in kind. Augustin forgot to inquire into the *natural limits of the civil power*, and of all outward human might, in conformity with what the sacredness of man's universal rights, grounded in God's creation, requires. He failed to consider that, owing to the natural limits fixed and determined by these universal rights of man, the government of a state can be compared, neither with the divine government of the world, nor even with the course of training to which the parent subjects his son in the years of his pupilage. What, according to this principle set up by Augustin, might not despotism hold to be allowable, for the sake of the pretended holy end, the general good; as soon as the question, which is the only one here, *What is right?* came once to be subordinated to the question, What is expedient and salutary?

Very justly Augustin observes : " The state is as far from

* See c. Petilian, I. II. ep. 185 ad Bonifacium.

being able, by punishment, to exert an influence on the moral disposition, as on inward piety. Goodness, too, comes only from free will."* But he wrongly infers from this, that, as the state is authorized and bound to restrain the outward sallies of wickedness by punishment, the same holds good also of the outward sallies of heresy or schism. Here again he compares things wholly differing in kind. Not everything that exhibits itself outwardly, becomes subject thereby to the jurisdiction of the state. Much evil reveals itself outwardly in actions, and nevertheless cannot on that account be brought under the jurisdiction of the state. This latter extends only to that evil which can be judged on principles of political law and equity, and which violates the outward order of the civil community. But with this, the individual or common expression and the individual or common profession of religious convictions, of whatever sort they may be, do not of themselves come in conflict. It might be agreeable to the spirit of paganism, but it was in contradiction with the spirit of the gospel, to subject the individual or common expressions of religious faith to maxims of civil jurisprudence.

On these false premises, Augustin goes on to affirm, from the principle that the state has no concern with the piety of its subjects, because this must spring solely out of free conviction, "that the state must here leave everything to the freedom of each individual; from this principle it would follow that the state must also leave full freedom to its subjects for every crime. Or ought murder, adultery, and all other crimes to be punished, and sacrilege alone be left to go unpunished?"† He descended to the sophistic reasoning: " Divisions and sects are derived by Paul, Gal. v. 19, like all other transgressions, from one and the same fountain of inward corruption, the flesh — hence classed in the same category. If, then, the state is not authorized to employ punishment against some fruits of the flesh, neither can it be authorized to employ it against others;"—where he makes no account whatever of the consideration that the religious-moral point of view, from which Paul here regards the matter, is

* C. lit. Petiliani, l. II. 184.
† C. Gaudent. Donatist. l. I. s. 20. Puniantur homicidia, puniantur adulteria, puniantur cætera quantalibet sceleris sive libidinis facinora seu flagitia, sola sacrilegia volumus a regnantium legibus impunita.

altogether different from the civil and judicial, from which alone the state can regard it.*

With good right, it is true, Augustin asserts, in opposition to the Donatists, that even kings are bound as Christians to serve their particular vocation in a Christian spirit; that as each must serve God in his own peculiar way, according to *his particular vocation*, so they, too, must serve God in a peculiar way, in the fulfilment of the duties of their office.† But he erred only in deriving, from this correct position, consequences which he was in no way authorized to derive from it. The question arose, in the first place, in what does a government in the Christian sense consist; and how far does the province of kingly power, or of civil power generally, in human affairs, reach? To make use of their power against heretics, cost the emperors no sacrifice of self-denial. On the contrary, it flattered the consciousness of the sovereign's rights; and he might believe that in this way, which was so easy for him, he could atone for many transgressions. But if he allowed himself to be actuated, in his whole conduct as emperor, by the spirit of Christian self-denial, he would assuredly have far better subserved the cause of Christianity than he could have served it by the demolition of every idol, which work Augustin so highly extols as the prerogative of imperial power.‡

But we may allow that Augustin was perhaps authorized to avail himself, in defending the church, of a principle which at this time had already become universally predominant in church practice, and of which this theory of church rights already lay at the foundation. " Who," says Augustin, " will not give his approbation to the laws by which the emperors forbid sacrifices even on penalty of death? Will not the Donatists themselves agree with us here?" If they did so, it

---

* Augustin. against the Donatists : Cum in veneficos vigorem legum exerceri juste fateantur; in hæreticos autem atque impias dissensiones nolint fateri, cum in iisdem iniquitatis fructibus auctoritate apostolica numerentur? C. epist. Parmeniani, l. I. s. 16.

† C. lit. Petiliani, l. II. s. 210. Habent reges excepta humani generis societate, eo ipso quo reges sunt, unde sic Domino serviant, quomodo non possunt, qui reges non sunt.

‡ Non enim auferenda idola de terra posset quisquam jubere privatus. Augustin. l. c.

must be allowed that they were defeated by their own inconsistency.*

It was the case with Augustin here, as in many other
instances, that, owing to his ignorance of the rules of a right
interpretation of scripture, he imagined he had found, in some
detached and misapprehended passages of the Bible, a false
theory, which, in his systematizing mind, he had framed to
himself independently of holy writ; and thus, by his means,
the wrong apprehension of such a passage of scripture was
established as the classical foundation of an error that prevailed for centuries. Thus, in his exposition of the parable of
the supper, Luke xiv., paying no regard to the rule which
requires that the point of comparison should be ascertained
and held fast, and affixing too literal a sense to the word
αναγκάζειν, v. 23, he supposed he found the theory expressed
here, that men were authorized and bound to employ force,
and compel men to participate in the supper;—that is, to enter
into communion with the universal visible church, out of whose
pale salvation was not to be obtained. Thus he laid the
foundation of the theory, " Coge," or " compelle intrare in
ecclesiam." †

True, Augustin continually explains, that everything must
flow from the temper of love; but of what use was this principle in a theory which gave full sway to arbitrary will? How
often was not the holy name of love abused by fanaticism and
the love of power? It was by Augustin, then, that a theory
was proposed and founded, which, tempered though it was, in
its practical application, by his own pious, philanthropic spirit,
nevertheless contained the germ of that whole system of

* This inconsistency could not, perhaps, be laid to the charge of all the
Donatists. In the passage referred to above against Parmenian, Augustin speaks doubtfully on this point: Quid istis videatur, ut crimen idololatriæ putent juste ab imperatoribus vindicari aut si nec hoc volunt, etc.;
and he says here, that many Donatists would, in general, allow only of a
vindicta spiritalis by excommunication in religious matters. On the
other hand, ep. 93, directed to the Donatist Vincentius, he says, s. 10:
Quis vestrum non laudat leges ab imperatoribus datas adversus sacrificia
Paganorum?

† Vid. ep. 93 ad Vincent. ep. 185 ad Bonifacium. Hi qui inveniuntur
in viis et sepibus, id est, in hæresibus et schismatibus, coguntur intrare.
In illis qui leniter primo adducti sunt, completa est prior obedientia: in
istis autem qui coguntur, inobedientia coërcetur.

spiritual despotism, of intolerance and persecution, which ended in the tribunals of the inquisition.

2. *The Meletian Schism in Egypt.*

The second schism which deserves notice in this period was the *Meletian*, which originated in Egypt. The causes which led to it were in many respects similar to those that gave occasion to the Novatian and to the Donatist schisms. In the very place where the spirit of peace and of love should have most prevailed, in the prison cells, where many bishops, companions of the same sufferings, were together, arose a dispute about the different principles of proceeding with those who had fallen away during the Dioclesian persecution. There existed among the prisoners a more rigid party, who maintained, on the same principle which Cyprian had once advocated under the persecution of Decius, that all who should have violated, in any way, their fidelity to the Christian faith, ought to be excluded from the fellowship of the church until the perfect restoration of peace; and that if, up to that time, they had manifested a spirit of sincere contrition, they should then first obtain forgiveness, according to the measure of their guilt. At the head of this more rigid party stood Meletius, bishop of Lycopolis in the Thebaid. The bishop of this city, being a metropolitan, possessed the highest rank next after the bishop of Alexandria, and frequently stood on the same level with him in administering the general concerns of the church.*

Peter, bishop of Alexandria, on the other hand, who, as it seems, had, like Cyprian, in the Decian persecution, for special reasons withdrawn himself awhile from his community, agreed in his principles with the milder party. The pastoral letter on church penance, which, in the year 306, this bishop addressed to the Egyptian church, breathes a spirit of Christian love and wisdom.† He displayed in it a more cor-

* Epiphan. hœres. Meletian. 68. Τῶν κατὰ τὴν Αἴγυπτον προήκων καὶ δευτερεύων τῷ Πέτρῳ κατὰ τὴν ἀρχιεπισκοπὴν ὡς δι' ἀντιλήψεως αὐτοῦ χάριν. It is also highly probable that the *sixth* canon of the Nicene council had its origin in this relation; and its object was to secure as incontestable, to the bishop of Alexandria, his general primacy over the entire Egyptian church, which was not to be encroached upon by the rank of the church of Lycopolis.

† This letter was received by the Greek church into the number of

rect appreciation of penitence as a moral duty than generally prevailed; attaching more importance to the temper than to the external conduct, and judging with less severity those who, yielding solely to physical weakness, had been forced, by the anguish of torture, to a momentary denial of the faith, which they afterwards deeply regretted.* Many Christians had been mean enough to force their Christian slaves to offer, instead of themselves, under the delusive notion that God's tribunal could be deceived like a human one. The bishop Peter showed in this case his correct moral judgment, in treating the slaves with more lenity than the masters. Inasmuch as the former had been in a sense constrained by force and fear, their church penance was therefore to last only a year; and they were thus to learn, for the future, to do the will of Christ and to fear only him. But the masters were to be subjected to three years of penance, as hypocrites, and because they had forced their fellow-servants to offer, not having learned from the apostle Paul that servants and masters have one Lord in heaven. " But if we all have one Lord, with whom there is no respect of persons, as Christ is all in all among barbarians, Scythians, bond, and free, they should consider what they had done, when they would fain deliver their own souls, but compelled their fellow-servants to the worship of idols." His correct judgment was seen again in the severity which he showed to those of the clergy who, instead of caring solely for the salvation of the communities entrusted to them, and waiting, in their appointed sphere of labour, the will of the Lord, had, in the pride of fanaticism, abandoned their communities,† and voluntarily given themselves up to martyrdom, and then —what was frequently the punishment of fanatical presumption—shrunk back and denied in the immediate prospect of death.

the letters incorporated into the ecclesiastical code of laws, under the title of ἐπιστολαὶ κανονικαί.

* Προδιδόμενοι ὑπὸ τῆς ἀσθενίας τῆς σάρκος.

† Touching this point he says, c. 10: "So did no one of the apostles; for the apostle Paul, who had gone through many conflicts, and who knew that it was better to depart and be with Christ, added, 'Nevertheless, to abide in the flesh is more needful for you.' Since he did not seek his own profit, but what would be for the good of many, that they should be saved, he held it to be more necessary than his own rest, to abide with the brethren and care for them."

Meletius, at a subsequent period, obtained his freedom; while those bishops who held other and milder principles of penitence, remained still in the prison. He exercised his authority as the second metropolitan in Egypt, during the absence of the bishop Peter, whom, being a confessor, he thought himself entitled, perhaps, to despise, on account of his flight; he travelled through the whole diocese of the Alexandrian patriarch, within which, relying on the authority just described, he undertook to ordain, and to excommunicate, according to his own pleasure. He did not recognize the official power of those to whose charge, as *Periodeutæ*, or visitors, the bishop Peter of Alexandria had committed the destitute communities. Their different views respecting the proper mode of treating those who had fallen, or who had become suspected of denying God in some way or other, was here, too, probably made a subject of discussion, or at least used as a pretext; since the Meletians boasted of representing the pure church of the martyrs. Four Egyptian bishops, among the imprisoned confessors, declared themselves firmly against the arbitrary proceedings of Meletius, who, however, took no notice of this protestation. The bishop Peter of Alexandria issued a writing to the Alexandrian church, wherein he bade all to avoid fellowship with him until the matter could be more closely investigated in connection with other bishops; and at length he excluded him—probably after his own return—from the functions of the episcopal office, and from the fellowship of his church, as a disturber of the peace of the communities.* Also, subsequently to the martyrdom

* Among the sources which treat of the origin of the Meletian schism, there is found a good deal of contradiction. The first place among these sources is certainly due to the documents published by Maffei, from a manuscript of the chapter of the cathedral of Verona (in the osservazioni letterarie, t. III. Verona, 1738), which, therefore, we must make the point of departure in inquiring into these contradictions. First, a letter of four imprisoned confessors from Egypt, the bishops Hesychius, Pachomius, Theodorus, and Phileas, who subsequently died as martyrs (according to Euseb. h. e. VIII. 13), addressed to the bishop Meletius. In this letter it is urged against Meletius, whom still they call dilectus et comminister in Domino, that in violation of the rights of foreign bishops, and particularly of Peter of Alexandria, he is reported to have undertaken to ordain in foreign dioceses; which, nevertheless, was altogether at variance with the ancient laws of the church. It is worthy of remark, that among the grounds of excuse here mentioned, to which Meletius might perhaps appeal, that borrowed from the difference in the principles of penitence is

of the bishop Peter, A. D. 311, and in the time of the bishop Alexander, under whom the Arian controversies broke out, this schism still continued to exist.

The council of Nice endeavoured to get rid of this schism by milder regulations. The council directed that Meletius, since no confidence could be placed in his restless character,

not cited at all, as if no dispute had as yet arisen on that point. Next follows the *story*, that, when Meletius had received this letter, he did not answer it, did not even repair to the bishops in prison, nor seek for the bishop Peter; but after those bishops had already perished by martyrdom, that he came to Alexandria, and there entered into a combination with two restless men, who were anxious to obtrude themselves on the communities as teachers, of whom Arius was one (see the section relating to doctrinal controversies). These discovered to him two presbyters, nominated by Peter as church visitors, who had concealed themselves. The text now reads: Commendans eis occasionem Meletius separavit eos (in the Greek probably ἀφωρίζειν). The sense of the obscure passage is probably this: Meletius accused these presbyters of having shown inconstancy to the faith, or cowardice under the persecutions; he excluded them for a season from the fellowship of the church, or suspended them from their offices, recommending to them to improve the opportunity furnished them by the persecution, of restoring themselves to their good standing, by showing steadfastness in confessing the faith. He himself ordained two as presbyters, one of whom was in prison, and the other had been condemned to work in the mines as a reward of their constancy.

From this narrative it is apparent, that the disputes which Meletius excited were, beyond all doubt, connected with his severe principles as to the proper mode of conduct during the persecutions; although no mention is made of this in the preceding letters. The *third* document is the letter of the bishop Peter to the Alexandrian community, in which he bids them, on account of the difficulties with Meletius, to hold no communion with him. With the account of the origin of the Meletian controversies which is to be gathered from these documents, the report of Epiphanius for the most part agrees. He represents the separation, which had its ground in the difference of views as to the principles of penance, to have taken place already in the prison. Of this the letters above cited do indeed say nothing. The zealous Meletian author whom Epiphanius makes use of, may perhaps also have represented the affair in an exaggerated light; still it is quite possible that a dispute of this sort may have already occurred, although it had as yet led to no open rupture. The narrative, which is the second of those documents of Maffei, intimates this. According to Epiphanius, Meletius, when he left the common prison, had been condemned to labour in the mines. On his journey to the place of his punishment, he is represented as having undertaken to ordain according to his own pleasure. This story is perhaps false—perhaps it is a rumour which gradually arose and spread among the Meletian party in order to shield him against some evil suspicion. The documents of Maffei seem to presuppose that Meletius had then obtained his entire

should reside, simply as a titular bishop, without active jurisdiction, at Lycopolis ; and for the future refrain altogether
from bestowing ordination, whether in the city or in the country.
Yet the clergy who had been already ordained by him, should
remain in possession of their offices, only taking rank after
the others who had received ordination from the bishop of

freedom.   What Epiphanius relates is, on the other hand, in accordance
with the narrative of Maffei, that as the party of Peter had styled themselves the Catholic church, so the party of Meletius styled itself the church
of the martyrs; for it is clear, in fact, from that narrative, that Meletius
was fond of making confessors ecclesiastics.   In the church history of
Socrates, I. 24, *one* account is especially deserving of notice, that while
the bishop Peter, who afterwards died as a martyr, had taken refuge in
flight ($\varphi\varepsilon\dot{\nu}\gamma o\nu\tau o\varsigma$ $\delta\iota\grave{a}$ $\tau\grave{o}\nu$ $\tau\acute{o}\tau\varepsilon$ $\delta\iota\omega\gamma\mu\acute{o}\nu$) Meletius usurped the right of ordaining
in his diocese.   If this account were correct, the origin of the schism
would be still more clear.   Meletius had, perhaps, remonstrated against
his flight with Peter himself; and imagined himself to be the more warranted, on that account, to interfere with his authority.   The narrative of
Epiphanius does indeed conflict with this view ; but anachronisms are no
uncommon thing in this author.   From the documents edited by Maffei,
the absence of Peter from Alexandria at this time is clearly made out
indeed, but not his imprisonment.   The bishops who style themselves
prisoners say nothing, however, of the imprisonment of Peter ; neither
does he mention it himself in his letter.   Moreover, Eusebius, ix. 6, reports that under the persecution renewed by Maximinus, in 411, the
bishop Peter was suddenly seized and beheaded, without making mention
of any earlier imprisonment of his.   On the contrary, from the last words
of Peter, which, to be sure, in the Latin translation, in which they are
preserved to us, sound somewhat obscure, it might be inferred that he
was in a state of freedom, and was intending soon to appoint an ecclesiastical trial in Alexandria itself: Ne ei communicetis, donec occurram illi
cum sapientibus viris et videam quæ sunt, quæ cogitavit.

With these narratives, however, the story of Athanasius, Apolog. c.
Arianos, s. 59 (which Socrates follows), in part conflicts; that the bishop
Petrus (Μιλετίον) ἐπὶ πόλλοις ἐλιγχθέντα παρανομίαις καὶ θυσία ἐν κοινῇ
συνόδῳ τῶν ἐπισκόπων καθ' εἵλιν.   As it concerns the παρανομίαι, this
coincides with the reports above cited; for by them would of course be
understood these very arbitrary ordinations.   In respect to the second
matter, however, the passionate opponents of the Meletians are not to be
wholly believed.   It might perhaps be, that this charge was conjured up
at a later period by enemies of Meletius.   They inferred from the fact
that Meletius had been released from the same imprisonment in which
the others had experienced martyrdom, according to the same licentious
mode of drawing conclusions we have already noticed, that he must
have procured his freedom by consenting to offer.   For the rest, this
story of Athanasius, too, seems to go in favour of the supposition that
the bishop Peter was still in a state of freedom, that he subsequently
returned to Alexandria, and there convoked a synod against Meletius.

Alexandria. But if these, should be removed by death before them, then they might take their places, in case they should, by the vote of the communities, be found worthy; and this was confirmed by the bishop of Alexandria.* But the Meletian schism, which, moreover, found fresh sources of nourishment amid the Arian disputes, continued to propagate itself till into the fifth century.

3. *Schism between Damasus and Ursinus, at Rome.*

In this schism, we observe the corrupting influence of worldly prosperity and abundance, and of the confusion of spiritual things with secular, on the spirit of the Roman church.† We see what a mighty interest of profane passions was already existing there. The particular occasion which led to the breaking out of this schism, lay in the immediate circumstances of the times. The Roman bishop Liberius had, in 356, been deposed from his place, and sent into exile, by the emperor Constantius, because he would not consent to the condemnation of Athanasius.‡ The archdeacon Felix, who acceded to the emperor's wishes, was elevated to the place of Liberius. But, when the latter subsequently consented to subscribe a creed drawn up at Sirmium by the Arian party, Constantius permitted him, in the year 358, to return to Rome; and he was again at liberty to resume his bishopric. Meanwhile a distinct party had been formed in the church by a certain presbyter, named Eusebius; which party held their conventicle in a private house, and avoided all fellowship with those who were favoured by the party at court.§ Now this party refused to recognize Liberius as bishop, on account of his recantation, and hence continued to hold their separate assemblies. Felix was banished; and he is reported, at least by the enemies of Liberius,‖ to have subsequently repented of his transition to Arianism, and, for this reason, to have led a life of penance at

* See the letter of the Nicene council, in Socrates I. 9.

† As Ammianus Marcellinus very justly remarks on occasion of this controversy, l. xxvii. c. 3.

‡ See below, under the head of doctrinal controversies.

§ See the history of the sufferings of this Eusebius, which, it must be allowed, as it comes from an enthusiastic admirer, is not entitled to full belief. Published by Baluz, Miscellan. l. II. pag. 141.

‖ See vita Eusebii, l. c.

the villa to which he had withdrawn himself. The meetings of the Eusebian party were forcibly broken up; Eusebius was kept confined in a room of his own house, where the meetings had been held.

In this ferment of the Roman communities, schisms might easily be occasioned by the new election of a bishop in the place of Liberius, after his death, in 366. The real course which matters took, as we have two opposite reports, which proceed from the opposite parties, cannot be certainly traced. According to the account of one party, Damasus was, in the first place, regularly chosen and ordained bishop; but afterwards a deacon, Ursinus or Ursicinus, who had aspired to the episcopal dignity, with his party, took possession of the church, which was called after its builder, or the presbyter who conducted divine worship in it, the *church of Sicininus*,* and caused himself here to be ordained bishop.† According to the other report,‡ the party which had always continued to be faithfully devoted to the bishop Liberius, immediately after his death made choice of Ursicinus. But Damasus, who belonged to those who, during the banishment of Liberius, had attached themselves to Felix, and who had ever aspired after the episcopate, was nominated bishop by the party of Felix. Thus it cannot be determined which one of the two competitors had the principal share in the disturbances and deeds of violence. Although the truth is, that, whenever any matter became an object of zealous contention among the lower classes of the passionate and restless Roman people, many things might be done which the heads of both parties would gladly have avoided; yet it is most probable that neither of the two, in this case, could be wholly exempted from blame. Damasus appears, moreover, on other occasions, to have been a proud man.§ Bishops, who should be ministers of peace, and surrender up everything sooner than allow any strife to go on for their own honour, suffered the matter to take such

* Basilica Sicinini.

† See the accounts in the chronicle of Jerome, in Socrates and Sozomen.

‡ The introduction to the petition of Marcellinus and of Faustinus, two presbyters belonging to the party of Ursicinus, and of Lucifer of Calaris, to the emperors Theodosius and Arcadius. Published by Sirmond. opp. t. I.

§ See Basil. Cæsar, ep. 239, s. 2.

a course, that a bloody struggle must decide the question, which of the two was the regular bishop. On one day there were found, in the church occupied by Ursicinus, which was stormed by the party of Damasus, the dead bodies of a hundred and thirty-seven men.* Damasus at last conquered, and Ursicinus was banished. But the division continued to exist longer ; and, moreover, other foreign bishops were drawn into it. To suppress this schism, and the quarrels that grew out of it, the emperor Gratian issued, in the year 378 or 381, the law which we have noticed already in a cursory manner, and to which he was moved by the petition of a Roman council. By this law, he conferred on the Roman bishop the right of deciding, in the last instance, on the affairs of the bishops who were implicated in this schism ;† providing, however, that they should not encroach, by so doing, on the authority of the metropolitans in the provinces.

REMARK.—The schisms of Lucifer of Calaris and of Meletius of Antioch, on account of the intimate connection in which they stand with the history of doctrinal controversies, are reserved for the fourth section.

* Ammian. Marcellin. l. xxvii. c. 3.
† By this schism, occasion was given for the law, although its expressions are general.

SECTION THIRD.

CHRISTIAN LIFE AND CHRISTIAN WORSHIP.

I. Christian Life.

1. *Its general Character in this Period.*

From the changes which, in the preceding sections, we saw taking place in the relations and circumstances of the church, it would be easy to form some probable conjecture as to what would be the new shaping of the whole Christian life in the present period. The vast numbers who, from external considerations, without any inward call, joined themselves to the Christian communities, served to introduce into the church all the corruptions of the heathen world. Pagan vices, pagan delusions, pagan superstition, took the garb and name of Christianity, and were thus enabled to exert a more corrupting influence on the Christian life. Such were those who, without any real interest whatever in the concerns of religion, living half in Paganism and half in an outward show of Christianity, composed the crowds that thronged the churches on the festivals of the Christians, and the theatres on the festivals of the Pagans.* Such were those who accounted themselves Christians, if they but attended church once or twice in a year;† while, without a thought of any higher life, they abandoned themselves to every species of worldly pursuit and pleasure. There were multitudes, especially in the large towns of the East, who, although no longer Pagans, and although they were denominated, in the most general sense of the word, believers, yet kept back, during the greatest part, or even the whole of their lives, from the communion of the church; and only when admonished by the actual or apprehended approach of

---

* Augustin. de catechizandis rudib. s. 48. Illæ turbæ implent ecclesias per dies festos Christianorum, quæ implent theatra per dies solennes Paganorum.

† Ἅπαξ ἢ δεύτερον μόλις τοῦ παντὸς ἐνιαυτοῦ. Chrysostom. in baptism. Christi, T. V. f. 523, Savil.

death, in sudden attacks of sickness, in earthquakes, or the unforeseen calamities of war, took refuge in baptism. Others, who had received baptism, thought themselves religious enough, if they attended church on all the festivals,—a practice denounced, therefore, by Chrysostom, as a mere form,—wholly without influence on the inner life;—custom, but not piety.*

The greater the number of these nominal Christians, the more mischievous became the errors which made them feel secure in this outward Christianity, which confirmed them in the delusive notion that they could live in sin, and yet obtain salvation. Of this kind were those many corruptions of purely Christian ideas which we have already had occasion to notice in the preceding period;—false notions of what constitutes faith; the confounding of the inward thing with the outward sign; that reliance on externals in religion, which grew out of this very habit of overlooking what belongs to faith and to the life of faith, and of confounding the divine realities which faith apprehends, with the outward, earthly forms which were designed merely to symbolize them. To sum up the whole here at once,—which it will be our object afterwards to explain more fully in detail,—the mischief presents itself in the delusive persuasion that any man, no matter what his life, could make sure of being delivered from divine punishment, and introduced into the community of the blessed, by the charm of outward baptism; which mistaken confidence in the magical cleansing and atoning efficacy of baptism encouraged numbers to persevere to the last in the indulgence of their lusts, hoping to avail themselves of this as a final remedy. It presents itself again in the delusive persuasion respecting the sanctifying effects of the communion, even when received without suitable preparation, and only on the principal festivals; in the delusive persuasion respecting the merit of an outward attendance on church, of pilgrimages to certain spots consecrated by religious remembrances, of donations to churches, of alms-giving, especially to ecclesiastics and monks, —no respect being paid to the manner in which what was thus bestowed had been acquired, nor to the disposition with which it was given. Instead of bearing the cross in their hearts, men relied on the magical power of the outward sign.

---

* Συνήθειας ἐστιν, οὐκ εὐλάβειας. In Annam, H. V. T. V. f. 73.

Instead of soberly carrying out the doctrines of the gospel in their lives, they folded up the scroll on which it was written, to wear about the neck as an amulet.*

Mischievous was the influence resulting from the doctrinal controversies, inasmuch as they were conducted with an inconsiderate zeal, inasmuch as the leaders of the contending parties sacrificed everything else to the one interest of a formal, orthodox theory ; inasmuch as the attention of men was directed away from the true essence and from the demands of practical Christianity.   Mischievous was the influence, also, of the unevangelical notion, which continually gained ground, of a distinct outward priesthood, confined to a single class of men,—whereby the original idea of the priestly character belonging in common to all Christians, ever became more completely obscured and suppressed.   That which should be the concern of all Christians, and which should be required of them all as spiritually-minded men, was supposed to belong exclusively to the spiritual order and to monks ; and whoever was exhorted to lead a more sober and holy life, was ever ready to reply : " I am of the world ; and secular men, if they are believers, if they abide in the communion of the church, and do not lead an extremely vicious life, will doubtless reach heaven ; though they may not attain to those higher seats which are reserved for the saints.   I have not left the world.   I am no clergyman, no monk.   Of such alone these loftier virtues can be required."

At the same time, however, it would be wrong to judge, from the great mass of nominal Christians, the character of the whole church.   The many examples of individual church-teachers, who were truly penetrated with the gospel spirit, and earnestly laboured to promote it, may rightly be considered as testifying to what was within the church itself; for, without the Christian spirit under which they had been trained and educated, they assuredly never could have become what

* Jerome, after having spoken of the Pharisees : Hæc in corde portanda sunt, non in corpore. Hoc apud nos superstitiosæ mulierculæ in parvulis evangeliis et in crucis ligno et istiusmodi rebus usque hodie factitant. In c. 23, Matth. 1. IV. ed. Martianay, IV. fol. 109. Chrysostom, ad pop. Antiochen. H. XIX. s. 4, T. II. ed. Montfaucon, f. 197, Ἀί γυναῖκες καὶ τὰ μικρὰ παιδία ἀντὶ φυλακῆς μεγάλης εὐαγγέλια ἐξαρτῶσι τοῦ τραχήλου.

they were. So, too, in many of the appearances of Monasticism, notwithstanding all its aberrations, there was still expressed a warm Christian spirit, which must have come originally from the church.

It was natural, however, that the *bad element, which had outwardly assumed the Christian garb,* should push itself more prominently to notice in public life. Hence it was more sure to attract the common gaze, while the genuinely Christian temper loved retirement, and created less sensation; except in those cases, which were not unfrequent in this period, where opposition elicited the hidden Christian life, and made it appear brighter in the conflict. "Watch the oilpress," said Augustin to those who saw nothing but the evil swimming on the surface; "watch it a little more narrowly, and do not look at the scum alone that floats on the top. Only seek, and you will find something."*

At the present time, the relation of *vital Christianity* to the *Christianity of mere form* resembled that which, in the preceding period, existed between the Christianity of those to whom religion was a serious concern, and Paganism, which constituted the prevailing rule of life. As, in the earlier times, the life of genuine Christians had stood out in strong contrast with the life of the pagan world; so now the life of such as were Christians not merely by outward profession, but also in the temper of their hearts, presented a strong contrast with the careless and abandoned life of the ordinary nominal Christians. By these latter, the others, to whom Christianity was a serious concern, and who placed it neither in a formal orthodoxy, nor in a round of outward ceremonies, were regarded in the same light as, in the earlier times, the Christians had been regarded by the Pagans. They also were reproached by these nominal Christians, just as the Christians generally had been taunted before by the Pagans, with *seeking to be righteous overmuch.* Such is the picture which Augustin has drawn from the life of these times. "As the Pagan who would be a Christian, hears rude words from the Pagans; so he, among the Christians, who would live a better and more conscientious life, hears himself abused by the Christians themselves. He who would be sober among the intemperate, chaste among the incontinent; he who would honestly serve

* Enarrat. ψ. 80, s. 1.

God among those who consult astrologers; he who would go
nowhere but to church among those who flock to the silly
shows, must hear rude language from Christians themselves,
who will say: 'You are really a very great and righteous
man, a second Elijah or Peter;—you must have descended
from heaven.'" *   In another place, he says: † "As soon as
a man begins to live for God, to despise the world, to abstain
from revenging injuries, from seeking after riches, or any
earthly goods; to look down upon all these things, and to
think of nothing but God, and to walk faithfully in the way
of Christ,—not only the Pagans say of him, 'He is mad;' but
what should give us greater concern, because it shows that,
even in the church, many sleep and will not be awakened, he
must expect to hear Christians themselves remark : 'What is
the man about?   What can have entered into his head?'"‡
Such individuals of the laity as were distinguished by their
piety from the great mass of nominal Christians, and from the
worldly-minded members of the clergy, often excited the jealousy of these latter, and had to suffer their persecutions.§
Such examples were too troublesome; they were too severe
censors of morals.

We have already observed, in describing the spread of
Christianity, where we adduced the testimony of Pagans themselves, as unimpeachable evidence of the fact, that pious Christian females, presenting patterns of genuine wives and mothers,
often furnished a beautiful contrast to the prevailing depravation of manners and reckless pursuit of earthly things, to be
found in the families of Pagans, or of mere nominal Christians.
From such wives and mothers, the true religious instruction
of the husband, or at least the pious education of the children,
often proceeded.   By them the first seeds of Christianity were
planted in the souls of those who afterwards produced great
effects as teachers of the church.   The pious Nonna, by her
prayers and the silent influence of the religion which shone

---

* In ψ. 90, T. I. s. 4.
† In ψ. 48, T. II. s. 4.   ‡ In ψ. 48, T. II. s. 4.
§ So says Jerome, Vere nunc est cernere, in plerisque urbibus episcopos sive presbyteros, si laicos viderint hospitales, amatores bonorum,
invidere, fremere, quasi non liceat facere quod episcopus non faciat, et
tales esse laicos damnatio sacerdotum sit.   Graves itaque eos habent, et
quasi cervicibus suis impositos; ut a bono abducant opere, variis perse-
cutionibus inquietant.   In ep. ad Tit. c. l. T. IV. f. 417.

through her life, gradually won over to the gospel her husband Gregory, who had belonged to an unchristian sect, and he became a devoted bishop. Their first-born son, whom they had long yearned after, was carried, soon after his birth, to the altar of the church, where they placed a volume of the gospels in his hands, and dedicated him to the service of the Lord. The example of a pious education, and this early consecration, first received from his mother, of which he was often reminded, made a deep impression on the son; and he compares his mother with Hannah who consecrated Samuel to God. This impression abode upon him, while exposed during the years of his youth, which he spent at Athens, to the contagion of the Paganism which there prevailed. · This son, the distinguished church-teacher Gregory of Nazianzum, says of his mother, that her emotions, when dwelling on the historical facts connected with her faith, overcame all sense of pain from her own sufferings: hence, on festival days, she was never known to be sorrowful, and death surprised her while praying before the altar.* The pious Anthusa of Antioch retired from the bustle of the great world, to which she belonged by her condition, into the still retreat of domestic life. Having lost her husband at the age of twenty, from regard to his memory, and a desire to devote herself wholly to the education of her son, she chose to remain a widow; and it was owing in part to this early, pious, and careful education, that the boy became afterwards so well known as the great church-teacher, John Chrysostom. Similar was the influence exerted on the education of her son by the mother of Theodoret. In like manner, Monica, by her submissive, amiable, and gentle spirit, softened the temper of a violently passionate husband; and, while she had much to suffer from him, scattered the seeds of Christianity in the young soul of her son Augustin, which, after many stormy passages of life, brought forth their fruit in him abundantly. To make their children early acquainted with the holy scriptures, was considered by such mothers as a task which belonged peculiarly to them.†

* Gregor. Nazianz. orat. 19, f. 292, and the epigrams of Gregory. Nazianzen, in Muratori anecdota Græca, Patav. 1709, p. 92.

† Daughters also were early made familiar with such portions of the holy scriptures as were deemed to be especially suited to the capacity of childhood. They were taught to commit Psalms to memory.

2. *Ascetic Tendency, and the Monastic life which proceeded from it.*

In the preceding period, we saw that the tendency to asceticism was promoted, in the more earnest Christian minds, by the opposition to the *pagan* depravation of manners. Now, as it was the case in the present period, that, owing to the great multitude who outwardly professed Christianity, especially in the large cities, this depravation obtruded itself on these more earnest souls, even under the external forms of Christianity; and as within the outward church itself so marked a contrast had arisen between those who were Christians in spirit and disposition, and those whose Christianity consisted only in profession and ceremonial performances, the necessary consequence was, that, by pushing this opposition, apprehended in too outward a manner, to an undue extreme, this ascetic separation from the world was carried to a still greater extent: as indeed it is quite evident that the first appearances of this sort manifested themselves in the vicinity of large cities, which were seats of corruption.

In the preceding period, the ascetics were accustomed to live singly, each according to his own inclination, without any specific form of union, within the precincts of the church to which he belonged. In Egypt it was customary for the ascetics to settle down singly in the country, at no great distance from some village, where they supported themselves by the labour of their own hands, and devoted the surplus to charitable purposes.* It was first in this present period, when the previously existing germs of all tendencies of life attained to a more settled and definite mode of growth, that

See Gregor. Nysseni vita Macrinæ opp. tom. II. f. 179. What was generally supposed to constitute the pattern of a Christian woman may be seen from the description which Nilus gives of Peristera: constant study of the Holy Scriptures ($\mu\epsilon\lambda\acute{\epsilon}\tau\eta$ $\tau\tilde{\omega}\nu$ $\theta\epsilon\acute{\iota}\omega\nu$ $\lambda o\gamma\acute{\iota}\omega\nu$ $\delta\iota\eta\nu\epsilon\varkappa\acute{\eta}\varsigma$), fervent prayer proceeding from a broken heart, liberal support of the poor, care for the burial of the dead who were poor or strangers, active pity for all in distress, reverence for the pious, care for the monks, providing for their support to the satisfaction of all their bodily wants, so that they might devote themselves to their calling without disturbance. Vid. Nil. Perister. c. III.

* Athanas. vita S. Anton. ῞Εκαστος τῶν βουλομένων ἑαυτῷ προσέχειν, οὐ μακράν τῆς ἰδίας κώμης κατὰ μόνας ἠσκεῖτο.

the freer form of the ascetic life shaped itself into Monasticism
—a phenomenon of great importance, as well on account of
the influence which it had already in this period, on the evolution of Christianity, and of the Christian and church life in
the East, as on account of the vast influence which it had in
later times on the culture of the Western nations.

As it is true of this whole ascetic tendency, that, although
it might find some foothold in a partial and one-sided apprehension of Christianity, yet in cannot be regarded as a phenomenon peculiarly Christian ; so is it also true that this particular product of the ascetic tendency cannot, in itself considered, be regarded as a phenomenon peculiar to Christianity,
and springing simply out of the spirit of this religion. Something like it is in fact to be found in other religions (as for
example in Buddhaism) ; and particularly in those countries
of the East where Monasticism first devoloped itself, the way
was already prepared for it in the circumstances of the climate,
and in the prevailing habits of feeling, which were in some
measure due to these circumstances. In Egypt, the birth-
place of Monasticism, something like it had, in fact, already
appeared among the Jews, in the sect of the Therapeutæ ; and
in Palestine, where Monasticism early found its way, the
Essenes, with many other societies of a similar kind, had preceded it. Monasticism, on the contrary, was at variance with
the pure spirit of Christianity ; inasmuch as it impelled men,
instead of remaining as a salt to the corrupt world in which
they lived, outwardly to withdraw from it, and to bury the
talent which otherwise they might have used for the benefit of
many. But though Monasticism was not a form of life that
sprang originally and purely out of Christianity, yet there can
be no doubt that by Christianity a new spirit was infused into
this foreign mode of life, whereby with many it became ennobled, and converted into an instrument of effecting much
which could not otherwise have been effected by any such
mode of living.

In the fourth century, men were not agreed on the question
as to who was to be considered the founder of Monasticism,
whether Paul or Anthony. If by this was to be understood
the individual from whom the *spread* of this mode of life proceeded, the name was unquestionably due to the latter ; for if
Paul was the first Christian hermit, yet he must have remained

unknown to the rest of the Christian world, and, without the influence of Anthony, would have found no followers.* Before Anthony there may have been many who, by inclination or by peculiar outward circumstances, were led to adopt this mode of life; but they remained, at least, unknown. The first whom tradition—which, in this case, it must be confessed, is entitled to little confidence, and much distorted by fable— cites by name, is the above-mentioned Paul.† He is said to have been moved by the Decian persecution, which, no doubt, raged with peculiar violence in his native land, the Thebaid in Upper Egypt, to withdraw himself, when a young man, to a grotto in a remote mountain. By degrees he became attached to the mode of life he had adopted at first out of necessity. Nourishment and clothing were supplied to him by a palm-tree that had sprung up near the grotto. Whether everything in this legend, or, if not everything, what part of it, is historically true, it is impossible to determine. According to the tradition, Anthony, of whom we shall presently give a more detailed account, having heard of Paul, visited him, and made him known to others. But as Athanasius, in his life of Anthony, is wholly silent as to this matter, which he certainly would have deemed an important circumstance,— though he states that Anthony visited all ascetics who were experienced in the spiritual life,—the story must be dismissed as unworthy of credit.

Anthony, whom we may regard, therefore, as the father of Monasticism, sprang from a respectable and wealthy family in the village of Coma, in the province of Heracleopolis (magna), a city of the Heptanome, bordering on the Thebaid.‡ He was born about the year 251. He received a simple, pious education, but no literary training; a thing, indeed, hardly known in the old Coptic families, into which the influence of the Alexandrian Hellenism had not penetrated. *The Coptic language* was his vernacular tongue; he would have been

* Jerome, in his account of the life of Paul, says very justly of Anthony, Non tam ipse ante omnes fuit, quam ab eo omnium incitata sunt studia.

† Jerome himself speaks of the absurd fables which were circulated about Paul; but even his own biography of him is not free from them, and it gives no distinct picture of the man.

‡ Sozom. l. I. c. 13.

obliged to learn the Greek in order to make himself master of the Greek culture: and, as often happens with such men, in whom the contemplative bent of mind predominates, he had no disposition to learn a foreign language. He would have béen under the necessity, moreover, of resorting to the school in which instruction in the Greek language was given; but, owing to the more serious, retiring disposition for which he was early distinguished, he avoided the society of noisy boys.*
From the first, too, he took little interest in matters of worldly learning; but a deep religious feeling, and a craving after the intuition of divine things, were the predominant characteristics of the youth as he grew up to maturity. He was a constant attendant at church, and what he read himself in the Bible, as well as what he heard read in the scripture lessons at church, became deeply imprinted on his soul: it was to him matter for spiritual nourishment, which he constantly carried with him, so that in his subsequent years he could wholly dispense

* Athanasius says of him, in the account of his life, s. 1, Γράμματα μάθειν οὐκ ἠνέσχετο. We might take this to mean that Anthony did not learn how to read at all. Thus Augustin understood it, who, in the prologue to his work, de doctrina Christiana, s. 4, says of Anthony, that without knowing how to read, he committed the Bible to memory by merely hearing it read. But this is inconsistent with what Athanasius says of him in the same paragraph. Τοῖς ἀναγνώσμασι προσίχων, τὴν ἰξ αὐτῶν ὠφιλείαν ἰν ἰαυτῷ διετήρει. This might, perhaps, still be understood as referring solely to those portions of scripture which he heard read in the church. But afterwards too, where he is speaking of Anthony's ascetic life, he says of him, Καὶ γὰρ προσεῖχεν οὕτως τῇ ἀναγνώσει. It would be possible, indeed, still to understand Athanasius, not as speaking in this passage of Anthony's private exercises, but only explaining why it was that to him the invitation of scripture, to pray without ceasing, was so constantly present, namely, because he had everything which he had heard read from the scriptures so deeply imprinted on his memory. If the passage is so explained, it might be understood here also as speaking simply of the public reading at church, and it would be unnecessary to suppose that Anthony knew how to read. This interpretation, however, is at any rate not the most simple. But even supposing that Anthony had first read the Bible himself in the Coptic translation, yet it follows, from the narrative of Athanasius, that at a later period he could dispense entirely with the written scripture, because its words were so deeply impressed on his memory as to be constantly present to him: Καὶ λοιπόν αὐτῷ τὴν μνήμην ἀντὶ βιβλίων γίνεσθαι. Thus the statement of Augustin, and what we shall afterwards cite from a conversation between Anthony and a man of learning, may be reconciled with the above account.

with the written scriptures. Between his eighteenth and
twentieth years he lost his parents ; and on him alone devolved
the care of a young sister, left with himself an orphan, and of
all the affairs of the family. These cares may, perhaps, have
proved irksome to him, unsuited to his peculiar temperament.
Once, as he was walking in the church,—which, for the purpose of elevating his heart to God in silent devotion, he frequently visited, even at seasons when there was no service,—
his imagination set vividly before him the contrast between
a man perplexed with the care of earthly matters, and the
primitive apostolical community, in which, as it was usually
conceived, no one possessed any earthly property of his own.
Occupied with such thoughts, he once attended a meeting of
the church ; and it so happened that the gospel concerning
the rich young man was read before the assembly. Anthony
considered these words of the Saviour to the rich young man,
which he heard in this particular state of mind, as words particularly addressed from heaven to himself. And as the
language was understood by him, in common with many of
his time, in a sense which Clement of Alexandria had already
shown to be incorrect (see vol. i., sec. ii., p. 387), as if it had
reference, not to the inward disposition alone, but to the outward deed ; he persuaded himself that he was thus called to
make an outward renunciation of all his earthly goods and
possessions. The considerable landed estates which belonged
to him, he gave to the inhabitants of his village, under the
condition that, for the future, they would trouble neither him
nor his sister with demands for the payment of the public
taxes and other claims of that kind.* He sold everything
that was moveable, and distributed the avails to the poor,
reserving only the smallest portion of it for his sister. While
listening a second time, during divine service, to those words
of our Lord which bid us take no care for the morrow, taking
the language once more in too literal and outward a sense,
and not according to the spirit and connection of the whole,
he now gave away to the poor the small remainder of his property which he had reserved particularly for the maintenance
of his sister, that he might free himself entirely from all cares
about earthly things. He placed his sister to be educated

* Vita, s. 2 : 'Ἰνὰ εἰς μηδ' ὅτιουν ἐχλησώσιν αὐτῷ τε καὶ τῇ ἀδελφῇ.

with a society of pious virgins,* and, settling down near his paternal mansion, began a life of rigid asceticism. He heard of a venerable old man, who was living as an ascetic on the border of a neighbouring village. He sought him out, and made him his pattern, fixing his own residence in the vicinity of the village; and, whenever he chanced to hear of approved ascetics living anywhere in those districts, he visited them, abode with them for a season, and then returned to his former place. He supported himself by the labour of his own hands, and distributed what he did not need for himself to the poor.

Anthony wanted a right conception of the Christian renunciation of property. He failed of the right conception of supreme love to God, which, instead of destroying man's natural feelings, would include them in itself, would refine, sanctify, and ennoble them. Starting with these wrong views, he struggled forcibly to suppress the thoughts and feelings of love which drew him to his sister and other members of his family. He wanted to forget everything that bound him to the earth; but nature claimed her rights: these feelings and thoughts would intrude upon him, in spite of himself, and disturb him in his meditations. In feelings which God himself planted in man's heart, he imagined that he saw a temptation of the adversary, when he should rather have perceived in his own self-will and presumption, which aspired to rise above the natural feelings of humanity, a perversion of the pure divine impulse, and a temptation of the ungodly spirit, which vitiated and disturbed in him the pure longing after holiness. Moreover, the lower impulses and energies of nature were excited to greater activity, the less they were employed. Hence, in his solitude, he had to endure many conflicts with sense, which in some active vocation, demanding the exertion of all his powers, might perhaps have been avoided. The temptations he had to battle with were so much the more numerous and powerful, as he was given to idle self-meditation, as he busied himself in fighting down the impure images that were constantly rising up from the abyss of corruption within his heart, instead of despising them, and forgetting himself in worthier employments, or in looking away to the everlasting source of purity and holiness. At a later period, Anthony, with a conviction grounded on long years of experience, ac-

* Παρθενῶνι.

knowledged this, and said to his monks: "Let us not busy
our imaginations in painting spectres of evil spirits; let us not
trouble our minds as if we were lost. Let us rather be cheerful
and comforted at all times, as those who have been redeemed ;
and let us be mindful, that the Lord is with us, who has
conquered them and made them nothing. Let us ever remember that, if the Lord is with us, the enemy can do us no harm.
The spirits of evil appear different to us, according to the
different moods of mind in which they find us. If they find
that we are weak-hearted and cowardly, they increase our fears
by the frightful images they excite in us, and then the unhappy
soul torments itself with these. But if they find us joyful in
the Lord, occupied in the contemplation of future blessedness,
and of the things of the Lord, reflecting that everything is in
the Lord's hand, and that no evil spirit can do any harm to
the Christian, they turn away in confusion from the soul which
they see preserved by such good thoughts.*

At that time he was for overcoming the evil spirits, in whom
he beheld the enemies of his holy endeavours, by still stricter
regimen of life. He betook himself to a certain grotto in the
rock at some distance from the village, which served the
purpose of a tomb (called in the East a mausoleum). Here,
as it is probable, by excessive fasting, and by exhaustion from
his inward conflicts in this unnatural place of abode, he brought
himself into states of an over-excited imagination and nervous
derangement, in which he fancied he had received bodily harm
from the spirits of darkness. He fell at last into a swoon, and
was conveyed back to the village in a state of unconsciousness.
At a later period, he retired to a still more distant mountain,
where he passed twenty years amidst the ruins of a dilapidated
castle. After this, he yielded to the entreaties of those who
desired to have him for their guide in the spiritual life. He
gave himself up to the men who sought him out. Many joined
themselves to him, and, under his guidance, trained themselves
to the abstemious life of hermits. The deserts of Egypt became
filled with the cells of these eremites. Many flocked to him,
from different countries, partly to see the wonderful man,
partly for advice and consolation, and to obtain the cure of
diseases (particularly of those fits which men were in the custom of tracing to the influence of malignant spirits) by the

* Athanas. vit. Anton. s. 42.

virtue of his prayers. Parties in strife submitted their matters of dispute to his arbitration. He exhorted all to sacrifice everything to the love of Christ; striving to make them feel the love of God, who spared not his only-begotten Son, but gave him up for all.

To escape the wonder of the multitude, and deliver himself from the throng of men, of all conditions, that disturbed him in his prayers and meditations, Anthony betook himself to a more distant solitude among the mountains. Certain Nomadic Saracens, who wandered over this district, were seized with reverence at the impression of his appearance and brought him bread. This, together with the fruit of some date trees which he found on the spot, sufficed for his nourishment. But as soon as the monks whom he had left behind him, discovered the place of his retreat, they provided him with bread. Yet Anthony was resolved to save them this labour. He procured some implements of agriculture, sought out a spot near the mountain, capable of tillage, and well watered and sowed it with grain from which he harvested what sufficed for his support. As he was afterwards visited here, too, by strangers, he raised a supply of vegetables, that he might have wherewith to refresh those who had made the long and wearisome journey to find him. He wove baskets, and exchanged these for such articles of nourishment as were brought to him.

He could easily acquire the fame of being a worker of miracles ; since many, particularly of those who were thought to be possessed of evil spirits, were indebted to his prayers, and to the impression of tranquillity and peace which went forth from him for the soothing of the tumultuous powers which had agitated their inner being. But he pointed those who applied to him for help, or had been indebted to him for it, away from himself to God and Christ. Thus to a military officer who applied to him for the healing of his daughter, he said : " I also am a man like thyself. If thou believest in the Christ whom I serve, only depart and pray to God in thy faith, and it shall be done."* Usually he exhorted the suffering to patience. They were to know that the power of healing belonged neither to him, nor to any other man, but was the work of God alone, who wrought it when and for whom he pleased. Thus those who left him without having obtained the bodily

* Vit. Anton. s. 48.

relief they expected, learned from him a lesson more valuable
than any deliverance from bodily ills,—submission to the
divine will.* He exhorted his monks not to attribute too great
worth to miraculous gifts and wonderful cures: and not to
estimate by these, the degree of progress in the Christian life,
but to esteem holiness of living still higher. "To do wonders," he told them, "is not our work, but the Saviour's."
Hence he said to his disciples: "Rejoice not that the spirits
are subject to you, but rather rejoice that your names are
written in heaven: for that our names are written in heaven
is a witness of our virtue, and of our life; but to expel evil
spirits is the grace of the Saviour, which he has bestowed on
us."†

It was only on extraordinary occasions that Anthony made
his appearance at Alexandria; and then his appearance always
produced a great effect. Thus it was, when, in the year 311,
the emperor Maximin renewed the persecution in Egypt.
True, Anthony did not think it proper to give himself up as
a victim; but neither did he fear danger, in firing the courage
of other Christians to unwavering confession, in manifesting
love to the confessors in the prisons and the mines. His example and his words did so much, that, to hinder them, the
governor issued a command for all monks to leave the city.
Other monks, who, on this occasion, had also come into the
city, concealed themselves; but Anthony appeared in public,
yet no one dared to touch him.

A second time, in the year 352, when he was a hundred
years old, he made his appearance in Alexandria, to counteract the spread of Arianism, which was then supported there
by the power of the state. His appearance made, at that
time, so great a sensation, that pagans themselves and even
their priests, came to church for the purpose of seeing the
man of God, as they themselves called him.‡ People belonging to the Pagan ranks pressed forward with the rest, to

---

* L. c. s. 56.   † L. c. s. 38.

‡ What Athanasius relates, s. 70, is confirmed by the reverence which
a Synesius, while yet a pagan, shows towards Anthony. He names him
among the rarer men, who, by virtue of their greatness of mind, could
dispense with scholastic culture, whose flashes of spirit might serve
instead of syllogisms, and places him by the side of Hermes and Zo-
roaster. In his Dion. ed. Petav. f. 51.

touch the garments of Anthony, in hopes of being healed, if they could only do that. It is said more pagans were converted to Christianity during the few days of his residence in Alexandria, than during a year at other times.

Many sayings of this remarkable man, which have come down through the oral tradition of his disciples, lead us, indeed, to recognize in him a great soul. The favour of princes, by which so many, in other respects distinguished men of the church, have still allowed themselves to be corrupted, could not touch the mind of Anthony. When the emperor Constantine and his sons wrote to him as their spiritual father, and begged of him an answer, it made no impression on him. He said to his monks: " Wonder not that the emperor writes to us, for he is a man ; but wonder much rather at this, that God has written his law for men, and spoken to them by his own Son." At first it was with some difficulty he could be prevailed on to receive the letter, since he knew not how to answer a letter of that sort. But when the other monks represented to him that they were Christian princes, and that they might look upon his neglect as a mark of contempt, and thereby take offence, he allowed the letter to be read. In his answer, he first congratulated them that they were Christians, and next told them what he considered would be most conducive to their welfare; that they ought not to look upon their earthly power and glory as a great thing, but rather to think of the future judgment; that they ought to know that Christ is the only true and eternal King. He exhorted them to philanthropy, to justice, and to care for the poor.*

Once there came to him a learned man of the pagans and made merry with him because he could not read. He asked him how he could endure to live without books. Anthony thereupon asked him which was first, " spirit or letter." The learned man replied: " Spirit is the first." " Well," said Anthony, " the healthy spirit, then, needs not letters. My book is the whole creation ; this book lies open there before me, and I can read in it when I please—the word of God."†

* L. c. s. 31.

† Vit. Anton. s. 73. Socrates, hist. eccles. IV. 23. Perhaps this story was floating before the mind of Synesius, and he merely confounded Ammun with Anthony, when he said of the former, Οὐκ ἐξεῦρεν, ἀλλ' ἐκρίνε χρείαν γραμμάτων, τοσοῦτον αὐτῷ τοῦ νοῦ περίην, f. 48.

When others were ridiculing the faith of the Christians, Anthouy asked them which, from the very nature of the case, went first in the knowledge of all things, and especially in the knowledge of God, and which gave the more assured conviction, " the conclusions of reason, or the faith which comes from immediate contact."* When they said the last, he rejoined: " You are right; for faith proceeds from a state of the soul (a certain determination of the whole inner life).†
What *we know* by faith, that *you seek to prove* by argument; and oftentimes you cannot even express that which we behold in the spirit."

Anthony, who, in the early years of his monastic life, had tormented himself so much with temptations, and been able to find no rest in constant self-contemplation, observed afterwards, from his own experience: " This is man's great work, to take his guilt upon himself before God, and expect temptations till his latest breath. Without temptation no one can enter into the kingdom of heaven." To an abbot, who asked him what he ought to do, he replied: " Trust not in your own righteousness, and regret not what is already past."‡

Severe to himself, Anthony was mild to all others. A monk, for some offence, had been expelled from his cloister, and his brethren were unwilling to receive him back. Anthony sent him back again to his cloister, with these words to the monks: " A ship stranded, lost her cargo, and was with difficulty drawn to the shore; but ye are for sinking again at sea what has been safely brought into harbour."§ To Didymus, the learned superintendent of the catechetical school at Alexandria, who from his youth up was blind, he said, on meeting with him during his last residence in Alexandria : " Let it not trouble you that you are in want of eyes, with which even flies and gnats can see; but rejoice that you have the eyes with which angels see, by which, too, God is beheld, and his light received."‖ At the age of a hundred and five years, feeling the approach of death, and, with entire consciousness,

---

* 'Η δι' ἐνεργείας πίστις.

† 'Η μὲν γὰρ πίστις ἀπὸ διαθέσεως ψυχῆς γίνεται.

‡ He would probably say, men should not spend so much time in reflecting on their sins, instead of getting free from themselves, and striving continually forward in the work of holiness. (See Apophthegm. patr. s. 4. Coteler. monument. eccles. Græc.)

§ L. c. s. 21.   ‖ Socrat. l. c.

calmly and cheerfully awaiting the end of his earthly career, he was solicitous that the exaggerated reverence of the Egyptians towards him should not convert his remains into an object of superstition. It was their custom, after the ancient manner, to embalm the bodies, especially of those who were venerated as saints, as mummies, take them into their houses, and place them there on small couches. The superstitious veneration of reliques might here easily find a foothold. To guard against this, Anthony urgently recommended to his monks to keep the place of his burial concealed, lest his body might be dug up by others, and preserved in the manner above described; for he wished not to be more highly honoured than the patriarchs, and Christ himself, who had all been buried.

Anthony gave to his age a pattern, which was seized with love and enthusiasm by many hearts that longed after Christian perfection, and which excited many to emulate it. Disciples of Anthony, belonging to Greek and to old Egyptian families, spread Monachism throughout every part of Egypt; and the deserts of this country, to the borders of Libya, were sprinkled with numerous monkish societies and monkish cells. From hence Monachism spread to Palestine and Syria, where the climate was most favourable to such a mode of life, and where, too, even at an earlier period,—among the Jews,*—much that was analogous had already existed. Anthony, indeed, was visited, not only by monks belonging to Egypt, but also by monks from Jerusalem.† The person who most contributed to the promotion of Monachism in Palestine was Hilarion. Born in the village of Thabatha, or Thanatha, in Palestine, four miles south of Gaza, he resided, while a youth, for the purpose of study, at Alexandria, when the fame of Anthony

* We might refer here to the example of the Essenes, of a Banus. Joseph. de vita sua, s. 2. At this time Nilus speaks of Jewish monks, in the Tractatus ad Magnam, c. 39, opuscula, Romæ, 1673, f. 279. Ἰουδαίων τινὲς μὴ ἀπαιτούμενοι ἀκτημοσύνην παρὰ τοῦ νόμου, ἑκουσίως ταύτην ἠσπάσαντο, ἐν σκήναις κατοικήσαντες. It may be, as Nilus seems to suppose, that this was at that time a new appearance among them, and perhaps had arisen from an emulation of the Christian monks; but may also have been a mode of life which had come down from ancient times, and which was incorrectly thought to be something new.

† See Palladii Lausiaca, c. 26, biblioth. patrum Parisiensis, T. XIII. f. 939.

moved him to seek out the great anachoret; and, after having spent several months in Anthony's society, he returned to his native country, with the intention of pursuing there the same mode of life.* Anthony, *without any conscious design of his own*, had become the founder of a new mode of living in common; for it had, in truth, happened of its accord, without any special efforts of his, that persons of similar disposition had attached themselves to him, and, building their cells around his, made him their spiritual guide and governor. Thus arose the first societies of Anachorets, who lived scattered, in single cells or huts, united together under one superior. But, independent of Anthony, an individual made his appearance in Egypt, who brought together the monks in one large connected building, and gave to the entire monastic life a more regular and systematic shaping. This was Pachomius, the founder of the cloister life. The societies of the Anachorets, who lived in a certain union with each other in single cells, were called Λαῦραι (lauræ); a term which, derived from the ancient Greek adjective λαῦρος, denoted properly a large open place, a street; the connected buildings, in which monks dwelt together, under a common superior, were called κοινόβια (cœnobia), μοναστήρια (monasteria), φροντιστήρια.† Pachomius, at the beginning of the fourth century, when a young man, after having obtained his release from the military service, into which he had been forced, attached himself to an aged hermit, with whom he passed twelve years of his life. Here he felt the impulse of Christian love, which taught him that he ought not live merely so as to promote his own growth to perfection, but to seek also the salvation of his

* Hieronymi vita Hilarionis. Sozomen III. 14.
† Thus Evagrius, hist. eccles. l. I. c. 21, distinguishes φροντιστήρια καὶ τὰς καλούμενας λαύρας: and in the life of the abbot Sabas, which Cyril of Scythopolis composed, we find a distinction made between λαῦραι and κοινόβια, s. 58, in Coteler. ecclesiæ Græcæ monumenta, T. III. The name μοναστήρια appears here as uniting the meaning of both. Anthony himself, in the ancient life of Pachomius, s. 77, names the latter as the founder of the more closely connected societies of monks: Κατὰ τὴν ἀρχήν, ὅτε μοναχὸς γέγονα, οὐκ ἦν κοινόβιον, ἀλλ᾽ ἕκαστος τῶν ἀρχαίων μοναχῶν μετὰ τὸν διωγμὸν κατὰ μονάς ἤσκεῖτο, καὶ μετὰ ταῦτα ὁ πάτηρ ἡμῶν ἐποίησε τοῦτο τὸ ἀγαθὸν παρὰ κυρίου. Even before Pachomius, a person by the name of Aotas (Ἀώτας) made an attempt, but without success, to found some similar institution. Acta Sanctorum mens. Maj. T. III. in the appendix, s. 77.

brethren. He supposed—unless this is a decoration of the legend—that, in a vision, he heard the voice of an angel giving utterance to the call in his own breast,—it was the divine will that he should be an instrument for the good of his brethren, by reconciling them to God.* On Tabennæ, an island of the Nile, in Upper Egypt, betwixt the Nomes of Tenthyra and Thebes, he founded a society of monks, which, during the lifetime of Pachomius himself, numbered three thousand, and afterwards seven thousand members; and thus went on increasing, until, in the first half of the fifth century, it could reckon within its rules fifty thousand monks.† This whole association was called a κοινόβιον, cœnobium—a term which, originally designating the entire whole of a monkish society, although distributed through several buildings, was afterwards transferred to single cloisters; of which, too, it was usually the case that each one embraced a distinct society. The entire body of monks stood under the guidance of Pachomius; and afterwards his successors, the abbots of the cloister in which the institution had its origin, continued to be the heads of the whole order.‡ He was regarded as the superior of the whole cœnobium, the abbot or abbas-general (the Hebrew and Syriac word for father); or, as he was styled in Greek, the *archimandrite*;§ and, at certain seasons, he made visitations to the several cloisters. The entire monkish society was distributed, according to the various degrees of progress which its members had attained in the spiritual life, into several classes, twenty-four in all, after the number of letters in the alphabet; and each of these classes had its own presiding officer, as to each also was assigned its particular labours. They employed themselves in the ordinary monkish avocations; such as weaving baskets, for which they made use of the rushes of the Nile, fabricating mats or coverings (ψίαθοι), not neglecting, however, other kinds of business, such as agriculture, and ship-building. At the end of the fourth century, each cloister possessed a vessel of its own, built by

* Vit. Pachom. s. 15.

† Pallad. Lausiaca, c. 6, l. c. 909, also c. 38, f. 957. Hieronymi præfat. in regulam Pachomii, s. 7.

‡ The first example of a like rule, which was introduced into the later congregations and orders of monks.

§ From the word μάνδρα, the fold, flock. Vid. Nilus, l. II. ep. 52, μοναστήριον = μάνδρα.

the monks themselves. Palladius, who visited the Egyptian cloisters about this time, found, in the cloister of Panopolis, —which also belonged to this association of monks, and contained within it three hundred members,—fifteen tailors, seven smiths, four carpenters, twelve camel-drivers, and fifteen tanners.[*] Each cloister had its *steward* (οἰκονόμος), who provided for the bodily wants of all, and with whom the fabrics, when finished, were deposited ; and all these stewards were placed under a general steward of the whole association (μέγας οἰκονόμος), who was stationed at the principal cloister. The latter had the oversight of the income and expenditure of the entire cœnobium ; to him were given over all the products of monkish labour. He shipped them to Alexandria, where they were sold, to provide means for purchasing such stores as the cloisters needed; and whatever remained, after these wants were supplied, was distributed among the poor, the sick, and the decrepit, of this populous, though impoverished country. A part also was sent to the prisons.[†] Twice in the year, on the feast of Easter and in the month *Mesori* (about the season of our August), all the superiors of the single cloisters met together in the principal cloister. At the last meeting, they brought in reports of the administration of their office. It was at this time, the reconciliation of all with God and with each other was celebrated.[‡]

No person who wished to be taken into the society of the monks was admitted at once ; but he was first asked, whether he had not committed a crime, and was not seeking refuge, among the monks, from civil penalties ; whether he was his own master, and therefore warranted to decide on his mode of life ; whether he deemed himself capable of renouncing his property, and everything he called his own. He must, in the next place, submit to a period of probation, before he could be received into the number of regular monks.[§] He was adopted on pledging himself to live according to the monastic rules.[||] Pachomius also founded, at this early period, cloisters of nuns,

---

[*] Lausiac. c. 39.

[†] Vit. Pachom. l. c. s. 19, s. 73, s. 85. Hieronymi præfat. in regul. Pachom. Lausiaca, f. 957.

[‡] Vit. Pachom. s. 52. Hieronym. l. c. s. 8.

[§] A novitiate, according to the earlier practice of the Essenes. ¶

[||] The ὁμολόγησις, called afterwards the votum, *vow*, s. 66, Hieronym. præfat. s. 49.

which received the means of support from the cloisters of the\ monks.*

The enthusiasm for the monastic life having spread with such violence, and vast numbers of men, possessing different dispositions, and utterly without the inward strength and tranquillity necessary to endure the solitary, contemplative habits of the cloister, having withdrawn into the deserts, it could not be otherwise, than that the sudden and uncalled for adoption of the anachoret mode of life, the extravagances of asceticism, and its accompanying pride, should give birth to many wild sallies of the fanatical spirit, and many mental disorders. We find examples of anachorets, who were so persecuted by their tormenting thoughts, as to end their lives by suicide.† We hear of many who, after having pushed their abstinence and

---

* Lausiaca, f. 300.

† Examples of temptation to suicide among the monks amid their inward conflicts, occurred frequently. See that of Stagirius, to whom Chrysostom addressed his beautiful letter of consolation; a young man of a noble family, who, feeling the emptiness of life in the high world, was so much the more strongly attracted by the ideal of the monastic order; but through the sudden change of life, which his mind was not mature enough to bear, was thrown into violent fits of mental disease, and so led to imagine himself tempted of Satan to commit suicide. Nilus, l. II. ep. 140, f. 182, says that many monks who could find no escape from the inward temptations which assailed them in their solitude, filled with desperation, plunged the knife into their bodies, or threw themselves headlong from precipices. Many fancied that in this way they should die martyrs. See Gregor. Nazianz. Carmen 47, ad Hellenium opp. T. II. f. 107:

Θνήσκουσιν πολλοῖς προφρονίως θανάτοις,
Αὐτοὶ ὑπὸ σφετέρης παλάμης καὶ γάστρος ἀνάγκη,
(They died by voluntary starvation.)

Οἱ δὲ κατὰ σκοπέλων βένθεσί τ' ἢ βρόχοις
Μάρτυρες ἀτρεκίης· πολέμου δ' ἀπὸ καὶ στονόεντος
Χαιροῦσιν βιότου τοῦ δ' ἀπανιστάμενοι.

(They rejoice to be redeemed from this inward conflict and this melancholy life.)

For the purpose of warning them against such dangers from the inward conflicts of the soul, the abbot Pachomius said to his monks: "If suggestions to blaspheme God present themselves to one who wants a truly prudent and collected spirit, they will soon plunge him to destruction. Hence, many have destroyed themselves; some, bereft of their senses, have cast themselves from precipices, others laid open their bowels, others killed themselves in different ways; for it is something very bad, if one who understands the evil does not point it out to such persons ere it becomes rooted." Vit. Pachom. s. 61.

self-castigation to the utmost extreme, imagined they had reached the summit of Christian perfection, and might now soon dispense altogether with those means of grace which other weak Christians needed. They despised assembling with others for devotional purposes, and even for the communion. Finally, they imagined that they were honoured with special visions and revelations. The end of it all was, that they fell into a state of complete insanity; or else what had hitherto inspired them appeared at once to be self-delusion. From the temptation to seek an entire estrangement from the ordinary feelings of humanity, into which they had forcibly wrought themselves, they sunk back to entire abandonment and vulgarity. The sensual impulses, which, in the intoxication of pride, they had succeeded, for a short time, wholly to suppress, broke forth with still greater violence.* They not only rushed back to their ordinary earthly pursuits, but now went to the opposite extreme of giving themselves up to every sensual enjoyment. Sometimes, after having been tossed to and fro from one extreme to the other, they at length arrived, out of these hard trials, to the knowledge of themselves, and to a discreet piety.† We see a mark of true wisdom in the practice of endeavouring to heal those who, through the pride of asceticism, had fallen, or were in danger of falling, into insanity, by forbidding them to engage in such efforts any longer, and obliging them to live after the manner of ordinary men.

The history of incipient Monachism is rich in remarkable phenomena, conveying the most important instruction on the subject of the development of religious morality, and on the manifold states of the inner life. We will here introduce a few examples to illustrate the remarks which have just been made.

A monk, by the name of Valens, belonging to a monastic order in Palestine, had become proud of his great ascetic

---

* Hence Nilus, who was a man of large inward experience, gave to one who asked him why many of the monks had so sadly fallen, the following answer: "Priding themselves on their ascetic perfection, they lost by their presumption the protection of good spirits, and the evil ones became their masters." Καταβάλλουσι τὸν πεφυσιωμένον εἰς πορνείαν ἢ κλόπην ἢ φονοκτονίαν ἢ μοιχείαν. Nil. I. I. ep. 326.

† Which, in spiritual therapeutics, was designated by the name διάκρισις (discretio): Διὰ τῶν πειρασμῶν δοκιμασθεὶς, ἐρχίται πρὸς τὴν πασῶν τῶν ἀρετῶν ὑψηλοτέραν διακρίσιν.

efforts. Some friends, perhaps according to a usual custom, having made a present of certain articles of food to the monks, the presbyter Macarius, who presided over the society, sent a portion to each in his cell. But Valens, with scornful language, bade the bearer carry it back to Macarius. The latter perceived the danger which threatened the sanity of Valens' mind. The next day he went to him, endeavoured to bring him to a sense of his dangerous self-delusion, and entreated him to pray God that he might be healed. As he refused to listen to all advice, his case continually grew worse. He had visions, and imagined the Saviour himself had appeared to him, in a form of light, testifying his approbation of so holy a life. When, on the next day, the monks assembled to unite in participation of the holy supper, Valens refused to unite with them. "I need not the supper," said he, "for I have this day seen the Lord Christ himself." The monks found it necessary to bind the insane man. For the space of a year they had recourse to prayer, and to a tranquil mode of life, directly opposed to his previous ascetic habits, for his recovery; proceeding on the principle, that one extreme must be cured by resorting to the other.[*]

Another, by the name of Heron, belonging to Alexandria, who was a member of the monastic society in the desert of Nitria, had carried the mortification of his senses to such extent, that he could travel thirty miles into the desert, under the scorching rays of the sun, without food or drink, repeating constantly, as he went, certain passages of the Bible from memory; and that he often lived, for three months, on nothing but the bread of the eucharist, and wild herbs. This man became so proud as to fancy himself superior to all others. He would be advised by no one; affirming that, as Christ had said, "Let no man on earth be called your master," it was men's duty to acknowledge no earthly superior. He also came, at length, to consider it beneath his dignity to take any part in the communion. Finally, he felt within him such a fire, such a restless fever, that he could no longer endure to remain in his cell.[†] He fled from the desert to Alexandria, and there

---

[*] Ἐυχαις καὶ ποικίλη ἀδιαφορήσει καὶ ἀπραγωτέρῳ βίῳ τὸ οἴημα αὐτοῦ καθελόντις, καθώς λιγίται· τὰ ἐναντία τοῖς ἐναντίοις ἰάματα. Laus. c. 31.

[†] This, too, was no unfrequent occurrence, that the monks to escape their inward temptations, forsook their cells, and ran about from one

plunged into a directly opposite mode of life. He was a frequent visitor at the theatre, the circus, and the houses of entertainment; he ran into all sorts of extravagance: these threw him into a severe sickness, in which he came to his senses, and was seized once more with the craving after the higher life he had lost. Afterwards he found a calm and cheerful death.[*]

Another, by the name of Ptolemy, settled down by himself on a spot lying beyond the Scetic desert in Egypt, known under the name of the "Ladder," (κλίμαξ,) where no man had ever dared to dwell, because the only spring which could provide water for this spot in the parched wilderness, lay fourteen miles distant. There he persevered to dwell alone, for fifteen years, collecting, in earthen vessels, during the months of December and January, the dew, which at this season plentifully covered the rocks in this country, and, with the moisture thus preserved, quenching his thirst. This unnatural mode of life was too much for his nature. The attempt at a proud estrangement from all human passions was the means of its own punishment. In striving to deny his human nature, he lost all firm hold of real existence; he grew sceptical about his own, about the existence of God, and of all things else;— everything appeared to him like a phantasm. The thought seized him, that the world had sprung into existence of itself, without any Creator; that it moved in a constant show, without any substantial ground of existing things. In desperate insanity, he forsook the desert, wandered about dumb from one city to another, frequented the places of public resort, and gave himself up to all manner of gluttony.[†]

Besides these individual examples of monks, whose spiritual pride led them into such self-delusion that they imagined themselves superior to the ordinary means of grace, and, by virtue of the extraordinary revelations and visions which they received, enabled to dispense with all human instruction and help from others, we see this spirit of fanatical pride carried to the pitch of self-deification, extending itself with Mona-

place to another. Nilus says of a person of this description: He will change his place, but not the anguish of his heart. He will rather nourish and increase his temptations. L. I. ep. 295.

[*] L. c. c. 39.

[†] Lausiac. l. c. c. 33. Similar cases must have often occurred, as we may see from Laus. c. 95.

chism in a widening circle, like a contagious disease, through Mesopotamia, Syria, and as far as to Pamphylia. Thus arose a sect which, according to the expressed reports of the ancients, had its origin in the Syrian Monachism, and which, moreover, wears on its front the undeniable marks of its origin. This sect propagated itself from the second half of the fourth century down into the sixth, and, in its after effects, reached perhaps still further; that is, if we may suppose this sect stood in any outward connection with later appearances which bear, in many respects, a strong affinity to it.* They were called sometimes after the name of those who at different times were their leaders, Lampetians, Adelphians, Eustathians, and Marcianists; sometimes after various peculiarities supposed to be observed in them; Euchites (εὐχῖται), Messalians,† on account of their theory about constant inward prayer; also Choreutes (χορευταί), from their mystic dances;‡ Enthusiasts (ἐνθουσιασταί), on account of the pretended communications which they received from the Holy Spirit.§

* In case the Euchites of the fourth century stood in any immediate connection with the Euchites of the eleventh century, and the so-called Bogomiles of the twelfth. Without question, the affinity may also be accounted for from an inward analogy, which is found to exist between mystic sects of this sort. It is to be observed, however, that Theodoretus already describes the εὐχῖτας ἐν μοναχικῷ προσχήματι τὰ μανιχαίων νοσοῦντας. Hist. religios. c. 3. ed. Halens. T. III. p. 1146. To be sure, Theodoretus may also have held, on no good grounds, analogous doctrines of this monkish mysticism to be Manichean or Gnostic; or he may have, through mistake, confounded Manicheans who concealed themselves under the monkish garb, with the ordinary Euchites. The fact that the monks had their imaginations constantly busied with the images of evil spirits persecuting them, may have furnished ground for the introduction of the Manichean, as it did really give rise to the Euchitian doctrines. See, respecting the spread of Manicheism among the monks, Vita Euthymii, s. 33. Coteler. monumenta ecclesiæ Græcæ, T. II. p. 227.

† Signifying the same, according to the Chaldee מְצַלִּין.

‡ Comp. vol. I. the Therapeutæ.

§ All these different names are found in Timotheus de receptione hæreticorum, in Coteler. monumenta ecclesiæ Græcæ, T. III. The name μαρκιανίσται is from Marcian, an exchanger, under the emperors Justin and Justinian. The name *Eustathians* is worthy of notice. It might lead us to think of Eustathius of Sebaste, from whom, in fact, a fanatical monkish bent derived its origin; and the more, as Photius, Cod. 52, who had old synodal acts for his authority, calls this Eustathius, from whom they bore the name αἰδέσιμος.

Most probably it was in the first place a practical error, without any tendency to theoretical heresies. They were monks who fancied themselves to have reached the summit of ascetic perfection; and, as they now enjoyed such intimate communion with the Holy Spirit, such complete dominion over sense, as to be no longer under the necessity of making the same efforts as before, supposed that, delivered from the yoke of law, they needed only to follow the impulse of the Spirit, without rule or discipline. They would allow nothing to disturb them in the purely contemplative repose, the state of inward prayer, which they represented as being the highest of attainments. They discarded all the occupations of common life,—all manual labour, by which the monks were used to provide for their own support and for the relief of others, but which *they* regarded as a degradation of the higher life of the spirit. They were for living by alms alone, and were *the first* mendicant friars.* From this practical error proceeded, by degrees, all the principles and doctrines peculiar to the Euchites.

Their fundamental principle was this, that every man, by virtue of his origin from the first fallen man, brings with him into this world an evil spirit, under whose dominion he lives. Here we recognise again the monkish theory about evil spirits that awaken in men the sensual desires. All ascetic discipline, all the means of grace in the church, are without power to

---

* Epiphanius says distinctly, h. 86, that it was the monkish spirit carried to excess. a misconception of what the gospel means by renunciation of the world, in fact, the false notion lying at the bottom of the whole system of Monachism, pushed to the utmost extreme, which led to this error of the Euchites. "Εσχον δὲ τὸ βλαβίρον τοῦτο φρονήμα ἀπὸ τῆς ἀμιτρίας τῶν τιιῶν ἀδίλφων ἀφιλσίας. This direction of the monkish spirit is attacked also by Nilus, in the Tractatus ad Magnam, s. 21 and 22. He there very justly remarks that the faculties of sense, in men in the full vigour of age, being employed on nothing, they must operate so much the more powerfully to disturb and confuse the higher life; that consequently the prayer, which they used as a pretext, must in their case suffer the greatest interruption. He derives this false tendency from Adelphius of Mesopotamia (the Euchite who has already been mentioned), and from Alexander, who had been the author of disturbances for some time in Constantinople (perhaps that Alexander who was the founder of a monkish order in which prayer and singing were kept up without intermission, day and night, the members of the order continually relieving each other. They were called Acœmetes (ἀκοιμηται).

deliver the soul from the tyranny of this evil spirit. These can only avail to check the single outbreaks of sin, while the man still remains under its dominion. He is, therefore, under the necessity of a continual struggle with sin; and stands trembling before it, under the discipline of the law. They combated the prevailing notions about a magical transformation by virtue of baptism, adhering, however, to the ordinary view in another respect. "Baptism," said they, "like shears, may, indeed, clip away the earlier sins (procure the forgiveness of past transgressions), but the root of the evil still remains behind, from which, therefore, new sins will continually germinate; for the evil spirit still retains, in fact, his dominion over the soul."* But what could not be brought about by any outward means, or by any ascetic discipline, might be effected, however, by the true inward prayer. Whoever attained to this, would thereby be delivered from the power of the evil spirit that had governed him from his birth, whose departure would be sensibly perceived; and he would enter, in a way sensibly manifest to his own feelings, into communion with the divine Spirit. He would put on the divine raiment, and at once become inaccessible to all temptations of sin. That freedom from the affections of sense, to the attainment of which others sought to fight their way through a course of severe ascetic discipline, *he* would *immediately* reach by this inward prayer. Hence, too, such a man was no longer under the necessity of fasting or of self-mortification. Freed from the law, he might abandon himself with confidence to all those exposures which others must avoid through the fear of temptation. Owing to the immediate divine revelation which he would now enjoy, such a person stood exempted from all further need of instruction from others, all further need of human guidance.† By this doctrine the essence of the monastic life of that period, which was founded upon obedience

---

* Timoth. l. c. 2. Ὅτι τὸ ἅγιον βάπτισμα οὐδὲν συμβάλλεται εἰς τὴν τοῦ δαίμονος τούτου δίωξιν, οὐδὲ γὰρ ἔστιν ἱκανὸν, τὰς ῥίζας τῶν ἁμαρτίων τὰς συνουσιωμένας ἀρχῆθεν τοῖς ἀνθρώποις ἐκτέμειν. Theodoret. hæret. fab. IV. 11. Ξυροῦ δίκην ἀφαιρεῖται τῶν ἁμαρτημάτων τὰ προτέρα, τὴν δὲ ῥίζαν οὐκ ἐκκόπτει τῆς ἁμαρτίας. By this we must supply what is wanting in the less accurate account of Theodoretus, hist. eccles. IV. 10.

† Theodoret. IV. 10, h. e. Timoth. de receptione hæreticor. s. 9. Joh. Damascen. hæres. s. 9.

and subordination, would necessarily be destroyed. For, of course, to the Euchites, their prayer supplied the place of all other modes of devotion and means of grace; and they looked upon themselves as exalted far above other Christians, who were still in bondage to sense, and under the yoke of the law. They were persuaded that the true spiritual sacrament of the supper was only among themselves; the outward ordinance of the church they represented to be a matter of indifference. Although they believed that they could derive no benefit from it, yet they joined in the celebration of it, in order that they might still be considered members of the Catholic church. They also discarded, in particular, sacred music, as their mystic tendency would naturally lead them to do.* That they sought after revelations in dreams we may easily believe, according to the unanimous testimony of their opponents; since many indications of the tendency to that enthusiasm which looked for divine suggestions in dreams, is elsewhere to be found also in this period. Their adversaries, moreover, report of them that they were, for this reason, much given to sleep; which is possibly an exaggeration, but it may also be true;† for it is easy to see that such a monotonous direction of the soul, so much at variance with the essential constitution of human nature, must have often passed off into sleep and dreams.

The mystical bent of this sect led to various other errors, which are often found connected with similar appearances. In various ways we see, connected with such appearances, the habit of confounding sensual with spiritual feelings, particularly sensual with spiritual love,—a habit which has often been attended with the most pernicious consequences. Thus, too, the Euchites compared the spiritual marriage of the soul

---

* This is seen from a fragment of the tract of the monophysite Severus, written against the work of the Euchite Lampetios, which was entitled the *Testament*. We gather from the opposite position taken by the former, that the Euchites approved only of a ὕμνειν ἐν καρδία. See Wolf. anecdota Græca, T. III. p. 182; and this inference is confirmed by the acts of a synod held in opposition to the Euchites, cited by Photius, c. 52. Of this Lampetios, it is here said, ʽΟτὶ τοὺς τὰς ὥρας ψάλλοντας ἐξεμυκτηρίζε καὶ διέσυρεν, ὡς ὑπὸ νόμον ἔτι τυγχανόντας.

† Cases at least occur elsewhere of monks who, in despair from not being able to escape temptations in singing and prayer, sought relief in immoderate sleep. See Nil. III. ep. 224.

to its heavenly bridegroom, in a grossly sensual manner, with an earthly union.*

The pride of the mystical sects, and the tendency of idealism to reduce everything to a subjective form, led frequently to a pantheistic self-deification. This seems to have been the case also with the Euchites. They asserted that they had become partakers of the divine nature. The Deity was able to assume all possible forms, and did actually assume all forms, particularly for the purpose of communicating himself to such souls as were fitted to receive him. "The three hypostasies of the Triad," they taught, "are nothing but different forms of revelation of the one divine Essence,—the Trinity resolves again into Unity."† Thus they were led to look upon the appearances of the angels in the Old Testament, upon the patriarchs and prophets, and upon Christ himself, as only different forms of the manifestation and revelation of the one divine Essence ; and they were persuaded that, by virtue of their own spiritual perfection, all was concentrated in them. If angel, patriarch, prophet, Christ himself, were named to such a person, his reply, in each case, was, "That am I myself."‡ Perhaps they were likewise, by their mystical idealism, led to deny the reality of Christ's miracles, to explain them as only symbolical; since such facts in the sensible world seem to have been regarded by them as wholly unimportant to the religion of the spirit.§

It should be mentioned also, as among their peculiar opinions, that they considered fire as the creative principle of the universe, an opinion of which we find may traces also in other theosophic sects.

* Timoth. IV. Τοιαυτῆς αἰσθάνεται ἡ ψύχη κοινωνίας γινομένης αὐτῇ παρὰ τοῦ οὐρανίου νυμφίου, οἵας αἰσθανεται ἡ γύνη ἐν τῇ συνουσίᾳ τοῦ ἄνδρος.

† Timoth. s. 6. Λεγουσιν ὅτι τρεῖς ὑποστάσεις εἰς μίαν ὑπόστασιν ἀναλύονται καὶ μεταβαλλόντωι, καὶ ὅτι ἡ θεία φύσις τρέπεται καὶ μεταβάλλεται. εἰς ὅπερ ἂν ἐθίλη ἵνα συγκράθη ταῖς ἑαυτῆς ἀξίαις ψύχαις, c. 11. Ἡ ψύχη τοῦ πνευματίκου μεταβάλλεται εἰς τὴν θείαν φύσιν. The Euchites having propagated themselves for a long period, and mysticism being in its own nature an inconstant thing, it is quite possible that different parties may have arisen among them; and thus the party which asserted these things of the Trinity, may not have been the same with the one which taught that those who were enlightened by their prayer had a sensuous intuition of the Trinity. ‡ Epiphan. l. c.

§ Yet this cannot be certainly inferred from the opposite position of Severus. Wolf. anecdota, T. III. p. 17.

It was sometimes objected to the Euchites, that they pushed their Antinomianism and their mistaken freedom to such an excess as even to permit those who were called perfect to abandon themselves to every vice. True, we ought not to give too much credit here to the report of adversaries; yet it must be allowed that this practical error did not at least lie so very remote from their principles and their spirit. Their presumptuous self-confidence, their defiance of the frailties of human nature, might thus, perhaps, meet with its own punishment; and we have, in fact, noticed above, in the case of the monks, many examples of transition from the extreme of ascetic severity to an unbridled licentiousness of morals.

As it was a principle held by the Euchites, in common with many similar sects, that the end sanctifies the means, and that it was right to conceal from common men, who were enslaved to their senses, the higher truths, which they were not yet prepared to receive, and to affect an assent to their opinions; it was on this account difficult to discover the members of this sect, and to seize upon any clue to their doctrines. Flavianus, bishop of Antioch (after the year 381), condescended to act according to the same principle, with a view to find them out, punish, and expel them. He managed to enter into a conference with their superior, Adelphius, as if he were entirely of the same opinion with him, and thus enticed him to a confession, which he then made use of against Adelphius himself, and his whole sect.*

A similar spirit of ascetic fanaticism threatened to spread far and wide, when, after the middle of the fourth century, the zeal for monastic life was diffused by Eustathius, afterwards bishop of Sebaste in Armenia, through Paphlagonia, and the districts of Pontus; and there are indeed many indications which serve to show that some outward connection existed between the Euchites and the Eustathians,—a fact which the name *Eustathians*, given also to the Euchites, seems to confirm. The synodal writings, and the canons of the council of Gangra, the metropolis of Paphlagonia,† which was as-

---

* Theodoret. h. e. IV. 12.

† There are, in relation to this matter, two disputed points, viz. the question whether the Eustathians (οἱ περὶ Εὐστάθιον), against whom this council was directed, really sprung from Eustathius of Sebaste, and to what time the meeting of this council is to be assigned. The first

sembled for the purpose of opposing these errors, furnish us the best means of informing ourselves with regard to their character; while they present, at the same time, a remarkable memorial of the healthful spirit of Christian morals, which set itself to oppose this one-sided tendency of asceticism. Wives forsook their husbands and children, husbands their wives, servants their masters, to devote themselves to the ascetic life.* Several who had placed too great confidence in themselves fell into immoral practices. They despised marriage and the domestic life. Those who wore the ascetic garb, fancied that at once they had become perfect Christians, and looked down with contempt on others who went about in their ordinary apparel. They refused to take any part in the sacrament of the supper, where married priests had consecrated the elements. Where, in the country, no churches had as yet been erected, and divine worship was held in private houses, they refused to join either in prayer or in the communion, because they held that no dwelling was holy enough for such purposes,

question admits of being more easily settled than the last. All the facts are in favour of an affirmative answer to this question. Not only is the testimony of Socrates, II. 43, and of Sozomen, III. 14, to this effect, but the whole is in perfect accordance with the character of Eustathius, who was a zealous ascetic, and the first preacher of the ascetic life in the countries round the Pontus, and had formed a whole school. See Basilii Cæsareens. ep. 223, (Here we find mentioned, in fact, the ascetic dress, to which the Eustathians, according to the report of the council of Gangra, ascribed a peculiar sanctity — the ξίνα ἀμφιάσματα, that is, according to the letter of Basilius, τὸ παχὺ ἱματίον, καὶ ἡ ζώνη καὶ τῆς ἀδιψήτου βύρσης τὰ ὑποδήματα), and ep. 119. Epiphanius, hæres. 75. We perceive also, in the letters of Basilius, a trace of opposition to the new monastic spirit in the districts of the Pontus. At least at Neocæsarea, where the attachment to old usages prevailed, the spreading of the ascetic life among men and virgins was brought up as an objection against Basilius of Cæsarea. See ep. 207 ad Neocæsareens. s. 2.

But the second question is among the most difficult of decision. If we suppose with Pagi, who follows Socrates and Sozomen, the council to have been held A.D. 360, then there is something strange in the manner in which the council name Eustathius, since he was then bishop; unless we suppose that the council did not consider Eustathius, who by a party had been deposed, as really a bishop, and thought themselves justified to treat him contemptuously. But, if we assume that the council was held at some earlier date, it is singular again that no allusion to it is to be found in the letters of Basil. Still the case may have been, that Basil, on account of the relation in which he stood with the party by whom this council was held, did not recognise it as a legal one.

* The same was the case among the Euchites. Joh. Damasc. p. 997.

the owners of which lived in wedlock. They celebrated their private worship in separate assemblies, ascribing to that worship a sacredness which was wanting to the church assemblies.*

As these fanatical tendencies, which grew out of the ascetic enthusiasm, threatened to be the cause of so much disturbance to the church life, it became necessary to devise some means of protecting it against this danger, and of guiding the ascetic life, which was highly prized in a course of development which would be salutary to the church, and consistent with good order. For this purpose, in the first place, particular encouragement was given to the regular institution of the cenobitic life; and next, it was attempted to bring this into closer connection with the whole body of the church, and into a condition of greater dependence on the episcopal supervision in each diocese.† In the cenobitic life everything was subjected to one guidance, after a regular plan; to each individual was assigned his particular place and sphere of action; obedience and humility, the unconditional submission of the will of the individual to that of the superior, who should be obeyed, even to the utter sacrifice of one's own inclinations,— these stood in the highest rank of monkish virtues. Every extravagance was to be immediately checked, and reduced within proper limits, by the guidance of the superior. Whoever felt himself in any way restless and uneasy, was not only required not to conceal it from his leaders, but to disclose to them his whole heart, that through their experience and wisdom he might receive advice and consolation, lest the evil concealed in his own breast should spread wider, and at last become incurable. It must be admitted that, in the monastic life, the essence of true humility, which has its foundation within, in a temper proceeding from the sense of dependence on God, was often misconceived, and *outward* humiliation before *men* sub-

---

* The same was true among the Euchites. Joh. Damasc. p. 37.

† The examples of such men as Basil of Cæsarea and Chrysostom teach this. The life of Basil of Cæsarea, of Gregory of Nazianzum, and the doctrinal controversies of the fourth and fifth centuries, show what divisions in the churches could grow out of the influence of the monks. The council of Chalcedon decreed, in its fourth canon, that no person should be allowed to found a cloister without permission of the bishop, and that the monks in town and country should be obedient to the bishop.

stituted in the place of *inward* humiliation before God. A servile spirit grew out of this confusion of ideas. But it is not to be denied that order, strict discipline, subjection of the individuals to the laws of the whole and wise guidance were absolutely necessary to keep in the right course a multitude of men, of different humours, and often rude and uncultivated. Good and pertinent are the remarks of Basil of Cæsarea, respecting the advantages of the common life of the Cenobites over the solitary life of the Anachorets; while at the same time, they furnish one example of a truly evangelical judgment on the subject of Monachism :—" The eremetical life conflicts with the essential character of Christian love, since here each individual is concerned only for what pertains to his own good; while the essence of Christian love prompts each to seek, not alone what serves for his own advantage, but also the good of others. Neither will such a person find it easy to come to the knowledge of his failings and deficiencies; since he has no one to correct him with love and gentleness. What is written in Ecclesiastes iv. 10, applies to the case of such a person : " Woe to him that is alone when he falleth; for he hath not another to help him up." In a society many can work together so as to fulfil the divine commands on different sides. But he who lives alone is ever confined to one single work; and while this is being done other works must be neglected. Next, if all Christians constitute together one body, under one Head, and stand related to each other as the members of one body; how can any such relation subsist, when they live thus separated from one another, each striving to be enough for himself? But if they do not find themselves standing in the right relation to each other as members of the same body, neither can they stand in the right relation to their common Head. In one society, the influence of the Holy Spirit in each individual passes over to all; the gifts of grace imparted to each become a common possession of all, and the gracious gifts of all redound to the advantage of each individual. But he who lives for himself alone has, perhaps, a gracious gift; but he makes it unprofitable, since he buries it in his own bosom; and whoever is acquainted with the parable of the talents, must know how great a responsibility is thus incurred.*

* See Basil. regula fus. vii. ii. 346. It is finely remarked also by

A struggle now arose between the Cenobites and the *ascetics* who traced their origin back to an earlier period; inasmuch as the latter were unwilling to submit to the new rules of the monks, but wished to maintain their ancient independence. They were in the habit of living two or three together; and they built their cells, for the most part, in cities, or in the larger villages. They supported themselves, like other monks, by the labour of their own hands; and their very opponents, the adherents of the new order of the Cenobites, were constrained to acknowledge that they were diligent and industrious. The latter, who alone have left behind any accounts of these classes of ascetics (known in Egypt under the name of Sarabaites, in Syria under that of Remoboth), give, it is true, a very unfavourable description of them; and, as they could be no otherwise than hostilely disposed towards these adversaries of the new form of the monastic life,* what they have to say on this subject is of itself liable to suspicion; and many of their objections show at once that they originated in hatred, and were without any just foundation. Cassian, for example, accuses them of misappropriating to purposes of sensual indulgence, or covetously hoarding up the surplus of their earnings.† Or even supposing this was managed by them in the best possible manner, still it was impossible for them to attain to the virtue of the monks. For the monks practised daily the same self-denial; but to the ascetics their very bounty to the poor was an occasion of pride, which daily received nourishment. Now we see here at once what Cassian himself was unable to conceal, that the first of these charges could not, in so sweeping a manner, be laid against the Sarabaites; and, as it concerns the second, it

Nilus, against the exaggerated estimate of the hermit life, iii. 73: "Whoever says, 'I become an anachoret, that I may have no one to excite my anger,' is not essentially different from an irrational brute, for we see such also quiet when a man does not excite them to anger." And he quotes, as opposed to the anachoret life, the text in Ephes. v. 21; Pet. iv. 10; Pet. ii. 13; Philipp. ii. 4.

* In the rule of the Benedictines, c. i. it is also plainly evident, that they were particularly accused of a spirit of freedom unbecoming in monks (sine pastore et lege vivere), and to this same spirit everything bad in them was attributed. In this very place, it is conceded that they were of a far better kind than the degenerate monks that strolled about through the country (the Gyrovagi).

† Collat. 18, c. vii.

is evidently a mere inference in the writer's own mind, from
the false assumption that, without the outward and unconditional submission to another's will, without the servile obedience of the monks, there is no true humility. Bad qualities
and good were no doubt to be found among these people, as
among the Cenobites; but their enemies of course held up to
notice the worst side. Jerome charges them with *hypocrisy*,[*]
of which there was no lack indeed among many of the
monks. He says of them, that they availed themselves of
the outward show of sanctity, which they affected, to dispose
of their wares at a higher rate than others; which might be
no less true of the monks.[†] He accuses them of *speaking
against the clergy*. It may well be that, as laymen, they were
inclined to boast of their superiority to the clergy, on the
score of their ascetic mode of life. It may be that they opposed the pride of asceticism to that of the hierarchy; but it
may also be, that among these people many pious laymen
were led, by their zeal for the cause of religion, to attack the
vices of a worldly-minded clergy. There may have been
some grounds for the opinion that most of the objections
brought against them, as well as the quarrels of which they
were the occasion, would have ceased or never existed, had
they subjected themselves to the same strict oversight which
prevailed among the Cenobites.

We shall now proceed to contemplate Monachism in its
various relations, during this period, to the Eastern church.
As it commonly happens with historical phenomena of this
kind, deeply grounded in the life of an age and pervading all
its manifestations, that the best and worst qualities, springing
from the Christian and the unchristian spirit, meet together,
and are found in closest contact, so it happened in the case of
Monachism. Some care, therefore, must be exercised here,
in separating the opposite elements, if we would neither
unjustly condemn, nor, through the influence of party feelings,
without regard to historical facts, approve the phenomenon
here presented; as, in truth, we may find abundant examples,
in this very period, of both these equally partial and erroneous
ways of passing judgment on Monachism.

[*] Ep. 22 ad Eustochium.
[†] Nilus himself objects to a class of the monks, that πᾶσαν σοριστίκην
μετέρχεσθαι τέχνην. Ad Magnam, c. 30.

And here, in the first place, it is necessary to distinguish the Anachorets from the Cenobites. To the former it was objected in this period itself, that they lived solely for themselves; were wanting in active charity;*—in defending them against which objection, Augustin observes, that those who brought against them such complaints, did not reflect how useful those might be in a spiritual sense, who were not personally visible, by means of their prayers, and the example of their life.† Chrysostom, however, says that it were certainly better, if the Anachorets also could live together in a society, so as to manifest, in an outward manner, the bond of charity. Yet, in either case, he observed, the essential requisite of love might be present in the disposition; for love, assuredly, is not restricted to the limits of space. They had, in truth, many admirers; and these would cease to *admire,* if they did not *love* them; and, on the other hand, they *prayed for the whole world,* which is the greatest evidence of love.‡ Even those among the Anachorets who lived entirely secluded and separate from the world, were not therefore, by any means, excluded from all exercise of influence upon others. The greater the reverence they inspired by their strict eremetic life, the more they were sought out, in their grottoes or cells, on their rocks or in their deserts, by men of every rank, from the emperor's palace to the lowest hovel, who visited them for counsel and consolation.§ Men who, in the crowd of earthly affairs, in the dazzling glitter of the world, were not easily brought to think of any higher concerns, would approach one of these recluses in a state of mind which rendered them at once susceptible for higher impressions. A word spoken to them in that state of feeling, sustained by the whole venerable aspect of the recluse, might produce greater effects than long discourses under other circumstances.‖ Oftentimes these hermits, after having remained for years hidden from the eye of the world, appeared publicly, on the occurrence of great and general calamities, or

---

* Videntur nonnullis res humanas plus quam oportet deseruisse. Augustin. de moribus ecclesiæ catholicæ, l. I. s. 66.

† Augustin. l. c. non intelligentibus, quantum nobis eorum animus in orationibus prosit et vita ad exemplum, quorum corpora videre non sinimur.

‡ Chrysostom. H. 78, in Joannem, s. 4, opp. ed. Montf. T. VIII. f. 464.

§ See the II. book of Chrysostom contra oppugnatores vitæ monasticæ.

‖ To such experiences Nilus refers, l. II. ep. 310.

as protectors of entire cities and provinces, who were dreading the heavy vengeance of some exasperated emperor. A spirit which, living by faith, was conscious of being free from the bondage of the world and independent of earthly things, gave *them* courage and power to speak boldly, where no other man dared to do so: their independence and their reverence for a higher power, which even the mightiest of the earth acknowledged, procured for them a hearing. When, after the insurrection at Antioch, A.D. 387, the emperor Theodosius, under the impulse of violent anger, threatened the whole city with destruction, the monk Macedonius, who for many years had not suffered himself to be seen in the world, came forth from his seclusion, hurried to Antioch, and put himself in the way of the two imperial commissioners, who had been sent for the purpose of holding the judicial trials. They dismounted respectfully from their horses, and embraced his hands and knees. He bid them tell the emperor, that he ought to remember he was a man, and possessed of the same nature with those who had done the wrong. "The emperor is thus angry," said he, "because the imperial images have been destroyed, which, however, may easily be restored; and he was intending, for this reason, to destroy men who are the living images of God, and one hair of whose head it was beyond his power to restore.* The monks were frequently visited by the sick, who, when they failed of relief from medical skill, hoped to obtain a cure through the intercessions of these pious men. Those, especially, who were suffering under mental disorders, and supposed to be possessed of evil spirits, frequently applied to them; and it may be easily conceived that, in such states of mind, the immediate impression of a life so exalted above the world might produce extraordinary effects. Pious monks, rich in inward experience, might avail themselves of such opportunities, even where it was beyond their power to bestow what the unfortunate patients came in quest of, to leave on their minds, and on those of the attendants or friends who brought them, some salutary lesson. Women came to them to ask for their intercession with God, that he would send them children. Mothers brought their children that they might bestow on them their blessing, and, at the same time, scatter in their youthful minds some seed of religious truth; as in the case of

* Theodoret. religios. hist. c. 13.

Theodoret, who often recurs to a salutary impression of this
sort, which he had received in his childhood.* Monks were
also called to pray in families, and could avail themselves of
this opportunity of doing good.† Especially did the societies
of monks form a striking contrast in the more or less remote
neighbourhood of such large cities as Antioch, which were
seats of wealth, splendour, and luxury, and of dissolute manners. What an impression must it have produced, when,
either from curiosity or for the purpose of receiving the
counsel and consolation or obtaining the intercession of these
men, the citizens visited them from the midst of their busy
pursuits, and, in a mode of life destitute of every sensual
enjoyment and comfort, witnessed, amidst all these deprivations, a tranquillity of soul of which they had not even formed
a conception! Easily may it be explained why so many of
the youth, of both sexes, should feel themselves constrained to
exchange their affluence for this poverty! To the monks,
those persons, in the Greek empire, often betook themselves,
who, after an agitated and restless public life, through many
political storms and reverses, either disgusted at the vain pursuits of the world and craving for repose, or driven by necessity to escape from some threatening danger, sought here a
still retreat, where they might end their days; as in the case
of that venerable monk Nilus, who, having retired from a
station of trust and dignity in Constantinople to Mount Sinai,
in the beginning of the fifth century, could write as follows:‡
"So great grace has God bestowed on the monks, even in
anticipation of the future world, that they wish for no honours
from men, and feel no longing after the greatness of this world;
but, on the contrary, often seek rather to remain concealed from
men: while, on the other hand, many of the great, who possess
all the glory of the world, either of their own accord, or compelled by misfortune, take refuge with the lowly monks, and,
delivered from fatal dangers, obtain at once a temporal and an
eternal salvation." And in the monastic profession, might they
now find a new inner life, and turn the treasure of experience
they had acquired to their own benefit and that of others.

As to the difference between the solitary life of the Anachorets and the common life of the Cenobites, it is to be

* Theodoret. hist. relig. page 1188 et 1214, T. III:
† Nil. l. II. ep. 46.   ‡ Lib. I. ep. i.

observed, that the same objection cannot be made against the ascetic mode of *living in common* which might be brought against the insulated life of the Anachorets, viz., that the spirit of active charity was here wanting; for, as we have already remarked, judged on the principle of Christian love, the Cenobitic mode of life had the advantage over the other. The *cœnobiæ* formed, in fact, little communities, in which every kind of Christian activity and virtue found room for exercise, with the exception only of such as are strictly connected with the ties of family. Chrysostom says of this class, that they had fled from amidst the bickerings of the world, for the purpose of cultivating charity with less disturbance.* People of all ranks might here associate together, and find a suitable occupation, sanctified by the spirit of Christian fellowship. Every kind of employment not interfering with tranquillity and the other relations of the monastic life, was here pursued, and prosecuted with the feelings which ought to animate every Christian calling. Prayer, reading of the scriptures, sacred music, here alternated with, and accompanied, bodily labour.† The bond of Christian fellowship here united together what was separated by the relations of the world. Slaves, on whom their masters had bestowed freedom that they might enter a cloister, here joined in brotherly fellowship with those who had sprung from the noblest families; and here they were trained for a higher life.

* ᾿Επειδὴ γὰρ ἡ τῶν πραγμάτων φιλονεικία πόλλας ποιει τὰς ἐρίδας· διὰ τοῦτο ἐκ μέσου γενόμενοι, τὴν ἀγάπην γεωργοῦσι μετ᾿ ἀκριβείας πόλλης. H. 78, in Evangel. Joh. s. 4.

† In the greater monastic rule of Basilius, those occupations are permitted and recommended to the monks which did not compel them to be too much separated from one another, as well in the labours themselves, as in the sale of the products of their industry; such occupations as subserved the necessary purposes of life, and not unseemly or hurtful passions; as, for example, the occupation of the weaver, of the shoemaker, so far as these trades did not administer to luxury. Architecture, the carpenter's trade, the smith, the cultivator of the soil, were not to be rejected on their own account, provided only they created no disturbance, and did not interrupt the life of the community. In this case, such occupations, agriculture especially, were to be preferred to many other employments. The views on this subject were not everywhere precisely the same. They differed according as the barely contemplative or the practical point of view in the monastic life predominated. Nilus, who proceeded on the former, is against the employment of monks in agriculture. See Nil. de monastica exercitatione, c. 21.

2 A 2

It was the spirit of Monachism which gave special prominence to that Christian point of view, from which all men were regarded as originally equal in the sight of God ; which opposed the consciousness of God's image in human nature, to the grades and distinctions flowing out of the relations of the state. Hence this spirit, where it was pure, not recognizing the distance which the earthly relations had fixed between slaves and freemen, plebeians and nobles, invited and admitted all, without distinction, to the fellowship of that higher life which had respect only to the universal interests of humanity. The spirit of contempt for earthly show, the spirit of universal philanthropy, revealed itself in the *pure* appearances of Monachism, and in much that proceeded from it. Nilus says : " In raising recruits for the military service of this world, slaves are rejected ; but into the ranks of the soldiers for piety, slaves enter with joy and confidence." * The same writer, citing the example of Job, chap. xxxi., gives special prominence to compassion for the race of slaves, whom a mastership of violence, destroying the fellowship of nature, had converted into tools.† Among the works of Christian piety, he names the redeeming of slaves from bondage to cruel masters.‡ Slaves, who were oppressed, fled for protection to pious monks ; and the latter interceded for those in trouble with their masters. The abbot Isidore of Pelusium, writing in behalf of one of these to his master, observes : " I did not suppose that a man who loves Christ, who knows the grace which has made all men free, could still hold a slave;" § and to another he said : " The noble disposition frees those whom violence has made slaves ; wherever this blameless disposition was found, Paul knew no difference between bond and free." ‖

The cloisters, moreover, were institutions of education, and as such were the more distinguished on account of the care they bestowed on religious and moral culture, because educa-

---

* Nil. IV. 4.

† Nil. Perister. sect. 10, c. vi. f. 165. Τὴν περὶ τὸ οἰκετίκον γένος συμπάθειαν, ὅπερ κατεδουλώσατο τιμοῦσα τὴν φύσιν ἡ δυναστεία.

‡ The question to the rich man who came to meet death without having used his property in accordance with the impulses of Christianity. Τίνα δεσπότων ὀδυρόμενον ὠμότητα τῆς σκληρᾶς δουλείας ἀπηλλάξας ; l. c. sect. ix. c. 1. f. 134.

§ Οὐ γὰρ οἶμαι οἰκέτην ἔχειν τὸν φιλόχριστον, εἰδότα τὴν χάριν τὴν πάντας ἐλευθερώσασαν. Epp. l. I. ep. 142.   ‖ I. 306.

tion generally, in this period, as may be gathered from the complaints of Libanius and Chrysostom, had fallen into neglect. Vanity and the love of display were among the first lessons learned in the schools of the sophists; and, in the large cities, corruptions of all sorts threatened the tender age. Basil of Cæsarea, in his rules for the education of the cloister, gives the following directions: "Inasmuch as our Lord has said, 'Suffer little children to come unto me,' and the apostle praises those who from their youth had been taught the holy scriptures, and exhorts men to bring up their children in the nurture and admonition of the Lord, let it be understood that the earliest age is particularly well suited for being received into the cloisters. Orphan children should be received *gratuitously;* and those who have parents should be admitted, when brought by them, in the presence of many witnesses. They should receive a pious education, as children belonging in common to the whole society of brethren. Separate buildings should be specially appropriated to their use; a particular diet and mode of living, carefully adapted to their age, should be appointed for them; the superintendence of their education should be entrusted to a person of years, experience, and well-tried patience, who understood how to manage them with parental tenderness. Every fault should be so punished, that the punishment might prove at the same time an exercise of discipline over the temper which had led to its commission. For example, if one indulged angry passions towards another, the fault should be punished by causing him to serve the other, according to the nature of the offence: greediness should be punished by fasting. From the beginning, they should obtain a familiar acquaintance with the holy scriptures; instead of the fables of the poets they should commit to memory the narratives of the miracles; instead of the Gnomes, passages from the Proverbs of Solomon. Only at the stated hours of social prayer, should the grown people and the children come together. As many handicrafts must be learned early, the boys should, in such cases, be allowed to spend the day with the master-workmen, but should sleep and eat with the others. They should not be permitted to take the monastic vow until grown up, and then only when they showed an inclination and aptitude for the monastic life: in the opposite case, they should not be bound to do so."*

* Basil. reg. fus. s. 15.

The cloisters were distinguished for their hospitality and benevolence to the poor. The cloisters of Egypt, for example, provided means of subsistence for the unfruitful districts of Libya ; they sent ships, laden with grain and articles of clothing, to Alexandria, for distribution among the poor.*

In the cloisters on the mountain of Nitria, there were seven bake-houses, which provided the Anachorets of the bordering Libyan desert with bread. Travellers who, after a weary. pilgrimage, arrived here from the wilderness, were suddenly surprised by the sight of a large body of men at labour amidst prayer and spiritual songs; and they found among them a brotherly, hospitable reception ; they were refreshed in body and mind. These monks were not prevented, by any ascetic scruples, from providing themselves with wine, for the refreshment of their guests. Every stranger might tarry with them as long as he pleased ; but, if he remained longer than a week, they did not allow him to be idle, but required him either to join in the manual labours, or to occupy himself with a book.†

But, on the other hand, it cannot be denied that many evils resulted from the monastic institution ; which is to be attributed partly to its having degenerated, a necessary consequence of the excessive multiplication of the monks ; partly to the tendency itself so alien from the pure spirit of the gospel, which had first led to this form of Christian life, and which was then still more promoted by it. In respect to the first of these causes, the same thing happened here which so frequently occurs in connection with phenomena entering deeply into the life of a period, that numbers, without any special inner call, were hurried into the current by the general enthusiasm or the love of imitation ; or, by some momentary shock which served to deceive them as to their own character, were impelled to withdraw from the world, without being in the least degree fitted for the tranquil uniform life of Monachism. Others

---

* See Cassian. institut. cœnob. l. X. c. 22. Hist. Laus. c. 76. In this last place, it is also narrated, that a certain abbot and presbyter, named Serapion, under whose direction stood many cloisters and ten thousand monks. obtained and could distribute annually at the harvest, in the Nomos of Arsenoe in Egypt, such a quantity of grain, that not only no poor person in the whole country suffered want, but he found it in his power also to support the poor in Alexandria.

† Hist. Laus. c. vi.

chose this mode of life on account of the imposing show of
holiness with which it was invested, induced by the opportunity, which it promised them, of indolently gratifying their
desires and passions under the mask of religion. People of
the lower classes renounced no earthly enjoyment by entering
upon the monastic life, but, under the appearance of renouncing the world, secured earthly goods, on which they never
could have reckoned.* What must have been the result, when
rude people of the lowest class set themselves up all at once as
leaders of monkish societies? Yet Nilus complains, that a
man who was but yesterday a water-carrier at an inn, might
to-day make himself pass as an abbot; and Isidore of Pelusium that shepherds and runaway slaves founded cloisters,†—
for all which, indeed, the bishops were answerable, since it
showed a want of oversight over the whole diocese of the
church; unless the truth was, that the swarms of monks had
now become too powerful even for the bishops. Uneducated
men, of rude and savage character,‡ who brought their restless
spirit with them into the seats of quiet, were eager to seize on
every occasion which gave employment to their passions.
Hence the troops of wild zealots, who raved against pagans
and heretics, demolished and plundered temples; who often
took so mischievous a part in doctrinal controversies; who
were eager to be employed as tools of fanaticism, and of the
ambition of those who stood leaders of the church party. Add
to this, that to such men, who constantly moved in one narrow
circle of intuitions and feelings, and who were in no sense in
a condition to step beyond this narrow range, that to such,
every deviation from their own accustomed modes of thought
and expression easily appeared as a departure from the essentials of Christianity itself. It was persons of this class who
led the heathens, men like Libanius and Rutilius,§ to draw
up such unfavourable pictures of the monastic institution,
about which they formed their judgment from such spurious

---

* Nil. Tractat. ad Magnam, page 297. Οὐτὶ καταλιπόντες τὶ καὶ ἅ
μὴ εἴχον κτησαμίνοι, ὥσπερ ἐμπορίας οὐ φιλοσοφίας ὑποθέσιν τὸν μονάδικον βίον
πεποιήμενοι.

† Nilus de monastica exercitat. c. 22. Isidor. Pelus. l. I. ep. 262.

‡ As Isidorus of Pelusium writes: Στίφη καὶ φάλαγγες οὐ μοναχῶν,
ἀλλὰ μᾶλλον μαχητῶν.

§ See his poetical description of his travels.

off-shoots. Distinguished, on the other hand, for moderation
and love of truth, is the judgment which Synesius, while yet
a pagan, pronounces on Monachism, when he says: "Such
men as Amus of Egypt, with whom intellectual intuition supplied the place of scientific culture, might be allowed to
discourse of divine things, without scientific preparation ; but
the case was different with the great crowd of those who
wished to pass judgment on spiritual matters without the
spiritual sense, especially with such as had not been led to
adopt this mode of life by any original inclination of nature,
but, sprung from different classes of society, had seized upon
it merely on account of the peculiar consideration in which it
was held,—people whom their necessities alone had brought
together.*

Out of Monachism sprang the most heterogeneous tendencies of the religious spirit. It was the case with many, that
the incessant struggles with their own nature, and the large
and various inward experience thus acquired, opened to them
a profound knowledge of themselves, as well as of the remedy
which alone can secure to man the healing of his moral evil,
and gave him inward peace and repose. They became satisfied
from their own experience, of the vanity of the righteousness
which is founded on works ; while, in reliance on the grace of
redemption, in child-like submission to God, they found a
spring of comfort, of peace and power, which they could never
have found in all the discipline of asceticism. Thus there occasionally sprung up out of Monachism, a warm and living
Christianity, having its seat in the heart, and exerting its
influence there ;—a Christianity directly opposed to the opus
operatum of asceticism. We see this in the example of Chrysostom, who was trained up under the influence of the monastic
life ; in that of Nilus, who, in his letters, on trusting in works
which cannot stand, often points away from this, to trust in
the Redeemer alone ;† and in the example of their contempo-

* Synesii Dion. Οὕς οὐχ ἡ πρώτη φύσις ἐπὶ τόνδε τὸν βίον ἐξώρμησεν·
ὥσπερ δὲ ἄλλο τι τῶν εὐδοκιμούντων, τὴν γενναίαν αἵρεσιν ἐζηλώκασι παντοδάποι
τὶ ὄντες τὰ γένη καὶ κατὰ χρείαν ἕκαστοι συνιστάμενοι.

† For instance, in his beautiful exposition of Rom. ii. 15, I. III. ep.
284. "We shall be our own accusers in the day of judgment, if our
own conscience condemns us. What other defence or help shall we then
find, in that state of anxiety, besides reliance on our most compassionate
Lord Christ alone ? Like a benevolent, peace-bringing, friendly angel,

rary, Marcus.* Nor were *all* those who exercised themselves
in subduing the power of sense by the severest abstinence,
therefore governed by the delusive notion that the essence of
Christian perfection consisted in such works of renunciation
and mortification of self, and that it was possible, in this way,
to obtain especial merit in the sight of God. The monk Mar-
cianus, who lived towards the close of the fourth century, in a
desert of Syria, and was famed for the rigid austerity of his
life, furnishes a remarkable example to the contrary. Attracted by his universal renown, Avitus, an aged monk, came
from another desert to visit him. Marcian, out of his scanty
means, had provided himself with the best meal which could
be procured. Having conversed awhile with each other, and
united in prayer about the third hour after noon, the hermit
served up his meal in a dish, and invited Avitus to partake of
it. But the latter declined, saying that it was not his custom to
eat before evening, and that he often fasted two and even three
days together. "Well then," said Marcian, "to oblige me,
deviate a little to-day from your usual habits; for I am ill, and
cannot wait till evening." As this representation of the case,
however, made no difference with his guest, who was determined not to relax in the least from his austere rule, Marcian
said: "I am very sorry you have come so far in the expectation of seeing a man of strict self-control, and that you must
be disappointed of your hopes, since, instead of that, you have
found in me a person who indulges himself." At hearing this
Avitus was troubled, and declared he would prefer rather to
eat flesh, than allow any such thing to be said. Then said
Marcian: "I also lead the same life as you do, and am accus-

---

the remembrance of Christ, our dearly beloved Master, presents itself to
us in the midst of our despondency, and the deep-rooted, unshaken faith in
him has banished trembling and shame, filled the heart with joy, and
brought back the wanderer from God to union and fellowship with him.

   * See, e. g. in his smaller tracts, the section περὶ τῶν οἰομένων ἐξ ἔργων
δικαιοῦσθαι. Bibl. patr. Galland. T. VIII. f. 13. He says, for example:
"Some suppose they possess true faith, without keeping the commandments; but others, who keep them, expect the kingdom of God as a
reward, which God is bound to bestow on them: both are far from the
kingdom of heaven. If Christ died for us according to the Scriptures,
and we live not to ourselves, but to him who died for us and rose again,
we are assuredly pledged to serve him, even till death. How can we,
then, look upon our adoption by God as a reward which he is bound to
confer on us?"

tomed to eat only when night approaches. But we know that love is better than fasting; for the former is a divine law, while the latter, on the contrary, is a rule which we impose on ourselves of free choice."*

But on the other hand, there also sprang up, out of Monachism, the spirit of self-righteousness on the ground of works; a legal morality separated from all connection with the inward essence of the gospel, and tending especially to keep back the consciousness of the need of redemption; the spirit of a slavish self-mortification, at war with the essence of Christian liberty; the spirit of a pharisaical, ascetic pride. Many who felt the ungodly impulses in human nature, were persecuted the more by impure thoughts, the more they gave heed to them, instead of employing their minds on other subjects capable of tasking their utmost powers. Many, who would violently suppress the purely human impulses of their nature, as if they were a hindrance to the striving after moral perfection,† and yet could not wholly stifle the voice of nature, as we saw above in the example of Anthony,—many of these tormented themselves in vain; they devised the strangest expedients for the crucifixion of self and the mortification of their nature; yet without advancing a step in true inward holiness. The legal, slavish spirit of Pharisaism; fear of malignant fiends and of the evil one; fear of the dreadful images of divine wrath, came in place of the child-like, free, cheerful, God-trusting spirit of Christian love. We are here presented with appearances which remind us rather of the spirit of the self-torturing

---

* Theodoret. religios. hist. c. 3.

† Even those who were influenced more by the spirit of pure Christianity, yet suffered themselves to be so far misled, by the false notions of the monks respecting estrangement from the world, by seeking after likeness to God in the renunciation of their own human nature, as to mistake altogether, on this point, the essential character of Christianity, which would adopt into itself all the pure feelings of humanity, aiming simply to inspire into them a new life, to sanctify and ennoble them. Thus Nilus himself requires of a monk, that he should suppress within him all remembrance of earthly relationships, reckoning this a part of the duty of becoming dead to the world; so entirely did he misapprehend the nature of Christian renunciation of the world, which has reference to the world only as opposed to God and his kingdom; to that which is ungodly. In like manner, he requires of the monk, that he should show acts of kindness to his necessitous relatives, in precisely the same way as to the poor who are entirely strangers. See Nil. l. III. ep. 290.

Saniahs of India striving to unman themselves, than of the temper of child-like love, resignation, and cheerfulness, which the gospel brings with it. A few examples will illustrate this.

Eusebius, a monk in Syria, employed another, by the name of Ammianus, to read to him from the gospels. But certain countrymen who happened to be ploughing in a neighbouring field drew off his attention, so that a portion which he had not distinctly understood must be read over a second time. To punish himself for this, he took a vow that he would never go in any other way or direction than one narrow path that led to the church. And, to compel himself always to look to the earth, he fastened about his loins an iron girdle, riveted to his neck a heavy iron collar, and by a chain connected this collar to his girdle, thus bringing himself into such a bending posture, that he must always look to the earth. Being asked for what useful purpose he was submitting to so painful a constraint, which allowed him neither to look up to heaven nor around on the fields, he replied: it was a stratagem he was employing against Satan; thus confining his conflict with Satan to such trifling matters, where he had but little to lose nor Satan much to gain, and where, if the latter was overcome, still the victory would appear to be not worth the contest. This, to be sure, was reducing the struggle against sin, and the work of sanctification, from the interior of the heart to a mere outward play with mechanics! Another, who had invented a refined species of torture for the castigation of himself, assigned as a reason for it, that, conscious of his sins and the punishment they deserved, he was seeking, by means of these self-inflicted pains, to lessen the severer punishment which threatened him in hell.* Here, in the obscuration of the Christian consciousness of redemption, we find the germ of the whole unevangelical theory respecting penance, as a voluntary satisfaction paid to divine justice: out of which grew the doctrine of indulgences, and many other superstitious notions.

In this way arose the class called the Stylites, who spent whole years standing on lofty pillars. Thus Simeon, for example, who was the first of this order, and lived about the beginning of the fifth century, finally established himself on a

* Hist. religios. c. 28.

column which measured six and thirty ells, or sixty feet from the ground. We have already spoken of the impression produced by this extraordinary spectacle, and of its effects in leading to the conversion of rude pagan tribes.* Simeon is said to have been the instrument of much good, also, by the exhortations to repentance which he gave from his pillar, and by settling disputes and restoring peace between enemies. To these benevolent labours of the man, Theodoret appeals, in endeavouring to defend him from the reproach with which he might, not without reason, be charged, for expending the energies of his will upon so frivolous a thing. Divine grace—so he supposes—had thus operated through him, in order to arrest, by such an extraordinary phenomenon, the attention of men who were not to be instructed except through their senses, and to bring them by this means to the divine doctrine itself. His language deserves notice: "As princes, after certain periods, change the emblems on their coins, choosing sometimes the lion, at others stars or angels, for the die, and endeavouring to give a higher value to the gold by the striking character of the impression; so God has made piety assume these novel and varied forms of life, like so many new characters to awaken the admiration, not only of the disciples of the faith, but also of the unbelieving world." † Doubtless he was right in supposing that the spirit of Christian piety, although ever one and the same, is yet capable of exhibiting itself in manifold forms of life, as these vary with the changing forms of culture; yet this spirit, nevertheless, cannot take such forms as contradict, and threaten to suppress or to render indistinct, its own essential character. Christian piety needed not to be stamped with a form so foreign to its own nature, and adapted to excite the wonder of rude men, in order to prepare the way for exerting its appropriate influence. The divine power within it operates by its own energy, though not always in so sudden and surprising a manner, yet the more deeply and thoroughly, just because it operates, not on the senses and the imagination, but on that which affines to God in human nature. Had Simeon planted himself down among those rude men, and laboured among them, by preaching the gospel in words and works, by a life animated by the spirit of self-sacrificing love, he would not perhaps have so speedily

* See p. 167.   † Hist. religios. c. 25, T. III. pag. 1274.

induced thousands to submit to baptism; but, what is far more, he would have gradually introduced the power of the gospel into their hearts, and, by its means, brought about a new creation. On the other hand, after so sudden an impression, which was in all respects agreeable to the taste of the natural man, who looks after the godlike in outward appearances, men were easily led to form their conception of Christianity accordingly, as a religion designed to communicate to their previous modes of feeling and thinking — as we so often find it in the case of conversions produced after this manner — a different form, much rather than a different spirit. The natural man, under which scriptural name we include alike the rude and the wrongly educated, is, beyond question, more easily impressed by that which strikes the eye as something superhuman, than by the appearance of the truly godlike, which lies concealed under the cover of the purely human form; but that impression, too, will be far more likely to lead men to deify that which has produced such an effect on the senses, than to worship Him who alone is to be worshipped. And of this we have an example in the present case; for the images of this Simeon were regarded with a sort of superstitious veneration, and the figure of him, as Theodoret informs us, presented under the form of a protecting spirit, was set up, as a species of amulet, at the entrance of the shops in Rome.

Many a person might, doubtless, be prompted by ambition to subdue and bring under his sensuous nature, even to as great an extent as this Simeon did, and still be very far from presenting the vastly more difficult offering of inward self-denial, which was not to be done by such artificial modes of discipline.* That truly devout and pious monk, Nilus,

---

* The story perhaps may be true, although there was nothing supernatural in it, but only what may be very naturally explained, that Simeon had a vision, which at first he was tempted to consider as real, — a vision which presented before the much-admired man the reflected effervescence of his own spiritual pride, and which he subsequently recognized as an outward temptation of the devil, but which he might in a more salutary way have recognized as a temptation arising out of inward corruption. He once imagined he saw an angel appear before him with a chariot of fire, who wanted to transport him to heaven like Elijah, because the angels and blessed spirits were longing after him; and he was already on the point of mounting into the chariot with his right foot, which was

rightly directs the attention of one of these Stylites to the very point where he failed, to the radical evil within, which, in this partial victory itself over the flesh, found such means of nourishment. " Whoever exalts himself," he writes to him, " shall be abased. You have done nothing worthy of praise, in having stationed yourself on a lofty pillar; and yet you wish to obtain the greatest praise. But look to it, lest for the moment you be extravagantly praised here by mortals, but be obliged hereafter, contrary to your hopes, to appear wretched before the eternal God ; because you were intoxicated here by the undeserved praise of men." *

There were, in fact, monks who carried dehumanization to such an extreme, as to divest themselves of every attribute which gives dignity to humanity, and to become mere brutes. As if without consciousness, and as if deprived of their senses in broad day, they wandered about, like wild animals, in deserts and on mountains, supporting their wretched existence on the herbs with which nature supplied them.†

While Monachism must be regarded as an institution which properly originated in the Eastern church, and which corresponded particularly to the climate, no less than to the spirit of the East; it was, on the other hand, an institution which found little to favour it in the ruder and more variable climate, and in the more active spirit, of the West. Hence, too, it was a longer time before this product of the East could find its way from that quarter into the Western districts ; and, in the first instance, it met here with a more strenuous resistance than in the East. Athanasius was the first who, during his residence, at different times when banished from the East, among the Western people, introduced among them a better knowledge of the Oriental Monachism. His biographical

---

therefore sprained, when, as he made the sign of the cross, the phantom of Satan vanished. See acta sanctorum mens. Januar. T. I. f. 271. If this is not a true story, yet the inner truth at least reflected itself in this legend.

* L. II. 114.—The same writer warns one of these Stylites, l. c. ep. 115, to take heed lest while he raised his body aloft, his soul should grovel on the earth, and with its thoughts be far removed from heavenly things. Before, he had conversed with men, whom admiration had drawn around him ; now he addressed himself particularly to women.

† According to an apt similitude, the monks that grazed like animals, the βόσκοι. See Sozomen, VI. 33.

account of the monk Anthony, which was early translated into the Latin, had a great influence in this matter. Besides, respectable bishops of the West, who had been banished to the East during the Arian controversies, brought back with them, on their return, the enthusiasm for the monastic life; as for instance, Eusebius of Vercelli. Men possessing such great influence as Ambrose of Milan, Martin of Tours, the Presbyter Jerome, contributed subsequently, in the course of the fourth century, still further to awaken and diffuse this tendency of the Christian spirit in Italy and in Gaul. Men and women of the highest rank in Rome were impelled by the ascetic spirit, which was spread by Jerome during his residence in that city, to retire from the great world in which they had shone, and devote themselves, in Palestine or elsewhere, to the monastic life. But Jerome created for himself, by this very influence, a multitude of enemies at Rome, whose attacks induced him to leave that city; and we need not doubt, that the extravagances into which this man was so easily hurried with regard to everything which he undertook to advocate, contributed rather to injure than advance the cause of Monachism which he espoused. Augustin, who softened the exaggerations of Jerome, endeavoured to diffuse Monachism in North Africa. He opposed it to the licentious spirit of the strolling, wildly fanatical Donatist ascetics (the Circumcelliones); and, beyond question, it had here become quite evident that the ascetic spirit, which had continued to prevail in these districts ever since the spread of Montanism by Tertullian, needed a more rigid discipline and restraint, to keep it from breaking out in those sallies of wild fanaticism, into which it was so apt to be betrayed when left to itself. In the mind of Augustin, Monachism was associated with the ideal, which even before his conversion had floated before a soul so smitten with the craving after the divine; and first, in a form which adapted itself to the Platonism to which he was then devoted. While living, during that memorable period of his life in which the great crisis with him was preparing, in high intellectual society with his friends at Milan, he was seized with the idea of an association of like-minded men, who, united by one spirit, renouncing the cares of the world, and throwing up all worldly property, should live together in the common striving after the contemplation and knowledge of

divine things (in the συμφιλοσόφειν); all the means of the
individuals being thrown into a common fund, out of which
the common wants should be supplied.　In his then existing
state of mind, this ideal, with which the passions and desires
that still governed him were in conflict, could serve no other
purpose than to bring him to the consciousness of his own
moral impotency.　But when afterwards he obtained through
the gospel the power of bringing his ideal nearer to a realization,
the image of that Platonic association was supplanted in his
mind by the idea of that primitive apostolical community at
Jerusalem, which he strove after, and which, when he became
acquainted with Monachism, he supposed he found there once
more restored.　From this starting point was unfolded in his
mind the idea of a spiritual seminary, which he founded.
After this model he planned, when he afterwards became
bishop, the canonical community of his clergy.

But he was aware, also, of the corruptions which grew out
of the monastic life, and sought to counteract them, and to
purify Monachism from the bad influences which were connected with it.　To this end, he wrote his work on the obligation of the monks to labour (de opere monachorum), which
he dedicated to Aurelius, bishop of Carthage; hoping, through
his authority and influence, to effect a change for the better.
Augustin observes that, in these countries, the majority of the
monks consisted of persons from the lower ranks of society ;—
slaves, to whom their masters had for this object either given,
or been willing to give, their freedom,* or persons who came
from the cultivation of the soil, or from the workshops.†　It
would be a grievous sin, in his opinion, not to admit such persons; for from the ranks of such many truly great men had
proceeded ; since it is by that which is inconsiderable and vile
in the estimation of the world, that God is used to produce
the greatest effects, 1 Corinth. i. 27.　But he rightly feared·
the danger of idleness and too great freedom, in the case of
men who had been accustomed to severe corporeal labour and
to rigid restraint.　Many were there, who would be right well

---

* See above.
† Nunc autem veniunt plerumque ad hanc professionem et ex con-
ditione servili, vel etiam liberti, vel propter hoc a dominis liberati sive
liberandi, et ex vita rusticana et ex opificum exercitatione et plebeio
labore.

disposed to exchange a needy, sorrowful, and laborious life, for one free from all care, exempt from labour, and, at the same time, looked up to with universal respect. They who discarded the obligation to manual labour, ventured, in defending their principles, to pervert many passages of the New Testament. When that precept of the apostle Paul, in 2 Thessal. iii. 12, was objected to them, they appealed, on the other hand, to those misconceived passages in the sermon on the mount, in which all care for the wants of the morrow, hence all labour to acquire the means of sustenance for the morrow, were forbidden. Christian perfection was made to consist in this,— that men should expect, without labouring for their support, to be provided for by the hand of God, like the fowls of the air. This precept of Christ, they contended, Paul could not mean to contradict; the labouring, accordingly, as well as the eating, in those words of Paul, must be understood, not in the literal, but in a spiritual sense—as referring to the obligation of communicating the nourishment of the divine word, which men had themselves received, to others also — an example of the perversion of scripture, worthy to be noticed.

Augustin, in this work, also describes the mischievous consequences which had arisen from the abuse of their liberty, and from idle habits among the monks in the West. In the monkish garb which made them respected, they were accustomed to stroll about in the provinces trading in reliques, which were something trumped up for the occasion, or pretending that they had parents or relatives in this or that country, whom they were going to visit: they everywhere took advantage of the outward impression of their sanctity to extort money, and oftentimes their hypocrisy was exposed by the vices in the indulgence of which they were surprised.*

In the early times of the fifth century, John Cassianus. who became president of a cloister in Massillia (Marseilles), introduced the monastic institutions of the East into the South of France, where he made them known by his works on the rules of the cloisters (institutiones cœnobiales), and his sketches of the spiritual conversations of the Oriental monks.† The cloisters of Southern France became the seats of a practical Christian spirit, which, amid the distractions and devastations which

---

* s. 36.　　　　† Collationes.

came over this country during the marauding incursions of
barbarous tribes, proved a great blessing to the people ; as for
instance, the cloister on the island of Lerina (Lerins), in Pro-
vence in particular. These cloisters became also spiritual seminaries, which sent forth the bishops most distinguished for their
self-sacrificing and pious labours ; such as Faustus of Riez
(Rhegium, Rheji), and Cæsarius of Arles. Yet Monachism
would perhaps have been unable to withstand the destructive
influences which, in this and the next following times, were
spreading far and wide, and the irregularities prevailing in
the spiritual order would have become more widely diffused in
Monachism, which had a still laxer constitution, had not a
remarkable man introduced into the monastic life a more settled order and a more rigid discipline, and given it that shaping
and direction by which it became so influential an instrument,
particularly for the conversion and the culture of rude nations
by Christianity. This remarkable man was *Benedict.* And
since he contributed so much, by the spirit and form which he
gave Monachism, to the Christian education of the western
nations, we must endeavour to become better acquainted with
the history of the formation of his character, and with the
work which proceeded from him, in its earliest development.

It is to be lamented, however, that we possess so little that
is trustworthy and precise relative to the education, the life,
and labours of this individual ; the oldest source of information
—namely, the narrative of the Roman bishop, Gregory the
Great, though derived, according to his account, from disciples of Benedict—being so distorted by exaggerations, and
the effort to give the whole story a miraculous air, that the
facts at bottom do not, in many cases, admit of being any
longer ascertained ; and in the general type of the wonder-
working saint, as seized and delineated in the colours of that
age, it is the less possible to find out what in fact were the
peculiar characteristics of the man.

Benedict, born A.D. 480, sprang from a respectable family
in the Italian province of Nursia. His parents sent him to
Rome, for the purpose of obtaining a literary education ; but
well might the ingenuous disposition of the young man be
only shocked at the dissolute morals by which, at that time,
he must have found himself surrounded at Rome. He had
probably heard and read about the lives of the Anachorets of

the East; and these holy examples possessed so much the more attraction for him, as they were contrasted with the impure exhibitions of character which he saw everywhere around him. He longed for solitude, and left Rome, accompanied, for the first twenty-four miles from that city, by the nurse whom his parents had sent with him as an attendant to Rome, and who, from affection, was unwilling to leave him. But Benedict, following his ascetic bent, deserted her also; and, proceeding eight miles further, finally came to a deserted country lying on a lake, which hence bore the name of Sublacus (Subiaco). Here he fell in with a monk, named Romanus, to whom he made known his purpose. Struck with admiration at the glowing zeal of the young man, Romanus promised him his assistance and protection. To this person alone Benedict discovered the grotto in which he had taken up his residence. The cloister of Romanus was near by, and he could therefore provide the young hermit, who was here destitute of all means [of subsistence, with bread, by sparing what he brought him from his own daily allowance. A steep rock lying between the cloister and the grotto of Benedict, he had agreed with the latter, that he should let down the bread from the top of the rock, by means of a long rope. To the rope was attached a bell, by the sound of which Benedict might be directed to the spot where the rope was let down.

After having spent three years in this grotto, he was discovered by some shepherds who were pasturing their flocks in this region; and the story soon spread abroad about the hermit who had here been found. He was shortly held in great veneration through the whole country around, and numbers eagerly pressed forward to supply him with the means of support. His fame became at once so great, that, the place of abbot having fallen vacant in a neighbouring convent, the monks conferred the office on him. He told them, it is true, beforehand, that he would not be able to endure their savage manners. Yet he suffered himself to be over-persuaded. The degenerate monks, displeased with his severity, sought to take his life: he told them they might choose themselves an abbot that suited their own disposition, and retired again to his former solitude. But he continually became an object of more general attention, both on account of his contests with the wild monks, and on account of his deliverance from the

2 B 2

dangers which threatened him, which tradition afterwards magnified into a miracle. The disturbance of all existing earthly relations, which followed as one of the consequences resulting from the migration of the nations, would at that period impel men to seek the more, and cling firmly to that which was independent of and superior to all earthly vicissitudes, and could secure them peace and shelter amid the storms of the world. Hence multitudes thronged *to him*, for the purpose of training themselves under his guidance to the way of life which promised such a refuge, which taught men how to adopt from choice and to love these deprivations, to which many were driven by the necessity of the times. Men of consideration at Rome placed their sons with him, that he might educate and train them for the spiritual life. He was enabled to found twelve cloisters; and to each he distributed twelve monks under a superior. Some he retained under his own guidance. Even *Goths* of the lower ranks came to him: he employed them in such labours as were adapted to their physical powers and stage of culture, as agriculture, and the removal of the wild vegetable growth where gardens were to be planted.*

To get rid of the disputes with Florentius, a neighbouring priest, Benedict left this district also, after he had distributed his monks into different cloisters under suitable superiors. He himself, accompanied by a few of his followers, retired to the ruins of an ancient castle, which lay on a high mountain, called Castrum Cassinum, where he laid the foundation of one of the most famous of monastic establishments, out of which sprang afterwards the rich abbey of Monte Cassino. Amid the revolutions of these times, Paganism had still been able to maintain itself here among the country people, or to spring up and extend itself anew. He found standing here a grove and temple dedicated to Apollo, in which the peasants made their offerings. He conducted the people, by his preaching, to the faith of the gospel, and induced them to cut down the grove and demolish the temple. In place of the latter, he erected a chapel, consecrated to St. Martin. Even Totila, the king of the Ostro-Goths, evinced his respect for Benedict; and the latter spoke to him with freedom. The labours of this man were a foretype of the labours of his successors, who,

* Vita Benedicti, c. vi.

like'himself, were occupied mainly in preaching the faith, destroying Paganism, educating the youth, and cultivating the land, and by these means were enabled to accomplish so much. But the monastic rules of which he was the author, are particularly worthy of notice, as an enduring monument of his own spirit, and of the new shaping which, through his instrumentality, was given to the Monachism of the West.

Benedict aimed to counteract the licentious life of the irregular monks, who roamed about the country, and spread a corrupting influence both on manners and on religion, by the introduction of a severer discipline and spirit of order. The abbot should appear to the monks as the representative of Christ; to his will, every other will should be subjected; all were to follow his direction and guidance unconditionally, and with entire resignation. No one was received into the number of the monks until after a year's noviciate, during which he had often been reminded of the strict obligations of the monastic rule, and had withstood many trials. Then he was obliged to place himself under a solemn vow, which moreover was recorded by himself in writing, that he would remain constantly in the cloister,* live in all respects according to the rules, and obey the abbot. But the rules admonished the abbot to temper the severity necessary for discipline by the spirit of love. He was to let mercy prevail over rigid justice, that he might himself find mercy. He should love the brethren, while he hated their faults. Where he was obliged to punish, he should do it with prudence, and beware of going to excess. His own fallibility should be ever present to his mind, and he should remember that the bruised reed ought not to be broken. Not that he should give countenance and encouragement to vice, but that he should endeavour to extirpate it with prudence and love, just as he should see it would be salutary for each individual; and he should strive rather to be loved than to be feared. He should not be restless and over-anxious. In no affair whatever should he be inclined to extremes and obstinate. He should not be jealous, nor too suspicious; since otherwise he never could find peace. In his commands, even where they related to worldly employments and labours, he should proceed with foresight and reflection. He should discriminate and moderate the labours

---

* The votum stabilitatis, as opposed to the Gyrovagi.

which he imposed on each individual. He should take for
his pattern the example of prudence presented in the words of
the patriarch Jacob, Gen. xxxiii. 13, " If men should over-
drive them one day, all the flock will die." With that discre-
tion which is the mother of the virtues, he should so order all
things as to give full employment to the enterprise of the
strong, without discouraging the weak.   True, humility was
too much confounded with slavish fear, and too much importance was attached to the outward demeanour.   The monk
was to let his humility be seen in the postures of his body ;
his head should be constantly bowed down with his eyes directed
to the earth, and he should hourly accuse himself for his
sins ; he should ever be in the same state of mind as if he
were momently to appear before the dread judgment-seat
of God.   But all this, however, Benedict represented to be
only a means of culture, whereby the monks were to attain
to the highest end of love, that makes men free ; respecting
the nature of which, he thus beautifully expresses himself:
" When the monk has passed through all these stages of humility, he will soon attain to that love of God, which being
perfect, casteth out fear, and through which he will begin to
practise naturally and from custom, without anxiety or pains,
all those rules which he before observed not without fear.
He will no longer act from any fear of hell, but from love to
Christ, from the energy of right habits, and joy in that which
is good."

Benedict was doubtless aware, that the ascetic severity of
many of the monastic orders in the East was unsuited to the
rude men of the West, and also to the more unfriendly climate.
Hence he did not require of his monks many of the mortifications which were sometimes imposed upon those of the East,
and allowed them in several indulgences, which were there
sometimes forbidden ; as, for example, the use of wine in a
prescribed quantity.* As the monks, in addition to their
devotional exercises and spiritual studies, were also to be employed at hard labour in the field or in their different trades,

---

* C. 40. Licet legamus, vinum omnino monachorum non esse, sed
quia nostris temporibus id monachis persuaderi non potest ; and c. 73, he
explains himself that his rule was to lead only ad honestatem morum et
initium conversationis, not ad perfectionem conversationis—that the latter
must be learned from the rules of the fathers.

and in some seasons of the year, particularly seed-time and harvest, might be exposed to severe toil, the prudent Benedict* was careful not to prescribe any particular measure of food or drink, which was never to be exceeded. The abbot was at liberty to deviate from the general rule, according to the labours which devolved on the monks, and according to the season of the year. In like manner, it was strictly enjoined on the abbot, that he should have respect to the necessities of the sick and the feeble, of old men and of children, in the regulation of their diet, and of their occupations. He doubtless foresaw that the monks might settle down in rough and savage countries, as they afterwards often did, where they would not find even that measure of food and drink which he had allowed them. Reckoning on this, he exhorted them to submission : even *then* they should praise God and not murmur.† Worthy of notice, too, is the pains he took to avoid all appearance of the love of gain ; laying it down as a rule, that the monks should always sell the products of their industry at a somewhat lower price than was given for other worldly fabrics, so that in all things God might be praised.‡

The same circumstances of the times by which so many were induced to apply to Benedict for the purpose of being formed and disciplined under his guidance for the spiritual life, tended also to promote the enthusiasm for the monastic life which proceeded from Benedict's disciples, and to further the rapid spread of this form of it by means of his disciples, such as Placidus and Maurus, in Sicily and in Gaul.

3. The different Tendencies of the Religious Spirit in their relation to the Monastic Life and to Asceticism.

We will now once more cast a glance at the relation of Monachism to the different tendencies of the religious spirit in this period. There was a very narrow and bigoted enthusiasm for the monastic life, proceeding from the same narrow ascetic tendency which first gave birth to Monachism, and which was greatly promoted by it ;—a tendency which, while aiming to exhibit Christian perfection in the monastic life, caused the dignity and elevation of the universal Christian

---

* Who seems to have possessed himself the donum discretionis.
† C. 40. Benedicant Deum et non murmurent. ‡ C. 57.

calling to be misapprehended, and contributed very much to lower the standard of piety in the subordinate positions of the ordinary Christian life. This distinction betwixt Christian perfection in Monachism,* and the ordinary Christianity of the world and of social life, was taken advantage of by many worldly men, particularly in large towns, who excused their want of Christian earnestness and zeal, and the many stains of their lives, with the plea that they were no monks, but persons living in the midst of the world.

But, along with the fanatical enthusiasm in favour of Monachism, there arose also a blind zeal of another kind in *opposition* to it. Certainly it cannot be denied that the many worthless individuals, who only abused Monasticism to cover up their own wickedness under the show of sanctity, and, under this deceptive veil, to gratify their own worldly passions, mainly contributed to bring the monastic life into hatred and contempt. True, Salvianus, who lived about the middle of the fifth century, brings as a proof of the rude and trifling worldly taste which prevailed at that time in Carthage, that, when monks visited that place from the cloisters of Egypt or Jerusalem, they were received in the streets with jeers and curses ;†—and there may have been some ground for his complaint. But Nilus, the monk and the zealous friend of Monachism, himself accuses the worthless monks, who roamed about in the cities, pestered families by their impudent mendicancy, and, hiding all wickedness under the mask of their seeming holiness, often robbed their hospitable entertainers. It was owing to such men, that the once universally respected mode of life had become an abomination, and even the true virtue of the monk looked upon as no better than hypocrisy ;‡—that those who were once regarded as the censors of manners, were expelled from the cities as introducers of corruption ;§—that

---

* The φιλοσοφία, as it was commonly denominated.

† Salvian. de gubernatione Dei, l. 8, pag. 194, ed. Baluz. Si quando aliquis Dei servus aut de Ægyptiorum cœnobiis aut de sacros Hierusalem locis aut de sanctis eremi venerandisque secretis ad urbem illam officio divini operis accessit, simul ut populo apparuit, contumelias, sacrilegia et maledictiones accipit.

‡ Nilus de monastica exercitatione, c. 9. Ὁ περιπόθητος βίος ἐγίνετο βδελύκτος καὶ ἡ τῶν ἀληθῶς κατ' ἀρέτην βιούντων κτῆσις (it should read perhaps ἀσκήσις) ἀπάτη νενομίσται.

§ L. c. Ὡς λυμιῶνες ἀπελαύνονται τῶν πολίων οἱ ποτὶ σωφρονισταί.

the monks—which doubtless is an exaggeration—were objects of universal ridicule.*

Yet there were many who, instead of detesting this degenerate species of Monachism, rather took advantage of the monstrous births in which this degeneracy was seen, to bring into disrepute this whole mode of life; and who hated, in Monachism, not those excesses which ran in the direction alien from the spirit of Christianity, but precisely those qualities which were most truly and profoundly Christian in this mode of life;—who, with no friendly feelings, felt themselves rebuked and disturbed in their frivolous pursuit after pleasure by such Christian seriousness and strictness of Christian life. The blind zeal of this party for their convenient, worldly Christianity flamed out with the most violence on those occasions when the view of the monastic life, or the influence of pious monks in noble families themselves, had served to awaken there a more earnest and elevated sense of religion; when they witnessed in these cases a change of life extending itself which was entirely opposed to their inclinations.† Especially when young men of noble birth were induced by sudden impressions, exciting them to a more serious turn of life, or through the influence of pious mothers, to pass over to the monks, not only was the opposition between worldly-minded husbands and their Christian wives, on such occasions, often more strongly expressed, but kinsmen and friends took a lively interest in the matter; they considered it a disgrace to the noble family, that young men who might one day rise to the most splendid posts, should betake themselves to the mountains and the deserts, go about in the squalid dress of the monks, weave baskets, cultivate the soil, water gardens, and employ themselves in other such menial occupations.‡ The whole party who detested Monachism, but with it also every

---

* C. 22. Παρὰ πάντων χλευάζονται.

† Thus, in the times of cardinal Richelieu and Louis the Fourteenth in France, it was assuredly not the free spirit of the gospel, but the frivolous, worldly temper, the Christianity of politics, the ceremonial religion of Jesuitism, which is doubtless reconcilable with them both, which set itself to oppose the effects which flowed from the glowing ascetic zeal of an abbé St. Cyran and his followers.

‡ See Chrysostomus adversus oppugnatores vitæ monasticæ, l. I. s. 2. Ἀνθρώπους ἐλευθέρους καὶ εὐγενεῖς καὶ δυναμένους ἐν τρύφῃ ζῆν, ἐπὶ τὸν σκληρὸν τοῦτον ἀγομένους βίον.

form of earnest Christian life, was roused to activity on such
occasions. When the emperor Valens, in 365, promulgated
a law which, perhaps not without good grounds, was aimed
against those who, under the pretext of religion, but really
for the sake of indulging their indolent propensities and rid-
ding themselves of the burdens of the state, had withdrawn
themselves into the monkish' fraternities;* the party above-
mentioned availed themselves of this opportunity to institute
persecutions against the monks. Chrysostom, who was at
that time himself a zealous monk, felt himself called upon, on
this occasion, to write his three books on Monachism.

But between these two extremes there was a more moderate
party, which, while they recognized all that was truly of worth
in Monachism, opposed on evangelical grounds the one-sided
over-valuation of this, and the under-valuation of every other,
form of life which should equally be pervaded with the Christian spirit. This tendency is apparent in the council of Gangra, already mentioned. Here the ascetic and unmarried life
was admitted to be, in itself considered, and so far as it proceeded from a pious disposition, a good thing; but the married
life also, and life in the ordinary civil and social relations,
together with the use of earthly goods, were represented as
capable of being sanctified by a right temper; and sentence of
condemnation was pronounced on the proud ascetic spirit that
despised the common relations of life. This tendency particularly characterizes Chrysostom. Although himself greatly
indebted to Monachism for the character of his inner life;
although everywhere inclined to place a very high value on
the victorious power of the will over the sensuous nature, where
it was enlivened by the spirit of love; although enthusiastically
alive to the ideal of holy temper and holy living in Monachism;
yet he was too deeply penetrated by the essence of the gospel,
not to be aware that the latter should pervade *all the relations
of life.* And his large experience, gained at Antioch and at
Constantinople, had led him to see how mischievous the delusive notion that men could not strive after the ideal of the

---

* Cod. Theodos. l. XII. Tit. I. l. 63. Quidam ignaviæ sectatores de-
sertis civitatum muneribus captant solitudines ac secreta, et specie religionis cum cœtibus monazontôn congregantur,—they should be drawn
forth from their lurking-places, and compelled to take on them the
burdens of the state; or they should, like the clergy, give up their property to others.

Christian life amid ordinary earthly relations, must be, and had actually been, to practical Christianity. This delusion, therefore, he sought in every way to counteract. After having described, in one of his discourses, the various means of grace which Christianity furnishes, he supposes the objection to be raised: "Why say you this to us, who are no monks?" And he answers, "Do you put this question to me? Ask Paul, when he says, 'Watch with all perseverance and supplication,' Ephes. vi. 18, and 'Put ye on the Lord Jesus Christ,' Rom. xiii. 14; for surely he wrote these words, not for monks only, but for all inhabitants of cities. Except in relation to marriage, there ought to be no distinction between the secular and the monk; everything else the former is bound to do equally with the latter. And Christ, in the sermon on the mount, confines not his benediction to the monk. Enjoy the marriage estate with due moderation, and you shall be first in the kingdom of heaven, and entitled to all its blessings."* And in another place, where he is speaking of the prophetic visions of Isaiah :† "Would you know how the prophet saw God? Be yourself, too, a prophet. And how is this possible, do you ask, since I have a wife, and must provide for the bringing up of my children? It is possible, if you do but will it; for the prophet also had a wife, and was the father of two children; but none of these things was a hindrance to him." In expounding the first words of salutation in the epistle to the Ephesians, he lays particular stress on the circumstance that to men who had wives, children, and servants, Paul nevertheless applies the appellation of saints. Although Chrysostom —which may easily be accounted for in a man of such predominant and lively feelings—did not always express himself after the same manner; yet when he had become acquainted. from his own experience, with the corruption of the church, he often declared himself with great energy against the want of Christian love among the better disposed, who in solitude lived only for their own improvement, instead of employing the gifts bestowed on them for the good of others. "Behold what perverseness now reigns," says he in one passage. "They who possess some of the joy of a good conscience dwell on the tops of mountains, and have torn themselves from the body of

* Hom. VII. Hebr. s. 4.
† Homilia in Seraphim, s. 1. Montfaucon, VI. f. 138.

the church, as if it were inimical and alien to them; something not their own."* Thus, too, he complains in his *sixth*
homily on the first epistle to the Corinthians,†‡ that they in
whom there were still some remains of the old Christian wisdom, had forsaken the cities, the market, and the intercourse
of life, and, instead of forming others, took possession of the
mountains. " How shall we conquer the enemy," he exclaims,
" when some have no care for virtue, and those who are interested for it, retreat to a distance from the order of battle?"
And in another discourse he very justly refers to the parable
of the talents, as a proof that there can be nothing truly good,
the advantage of which does not extend also to others; and he
goes on to say: "Though you fast, though you sleep on the
ground, though you eat ashes and mourn perpetually, but
without benefiting any other individual, you will not bring
much to pass. Though you exercise the highest perfection of
the monk, but give yourself no concern that others are going
to ruin, you cannot maintain a good conscience in the sight of
God.‡ Neither voluntary poverty, nor martyrdom, nor anything else we may do, can testify in our favour, if we have not
attained to the crowning virtue of love."§

As we here perceive, Chrysostom attacked the exaggerated
opinion of Monachism, by assuming for his position the consciousness of the universal Christian calling, the sense of the
principle of holy living, which he recognized as belonging in
common to all true believers; but he was still too much influenced by the prevailing views of his time to be able always to
carry out and apply that position with logical consistency. It
is apparent here, as it often is in his case, that on one side he
was confined by the prevailing spirit of his age; while, on the
other, by his profound insight into the essence of the gospel,
he rose above it and was thus betrayed into self-contradiction.
On the other hand, there arose in the Western church, at Rome,
another man, who had the courage and freedom of spirit to
express and apply that fundamental principle, in direct opposition to the prevailing views of the time, and, from this main
position, to attack the whole ascetic way of estimating moral

* Hom. VII. Ephes. s. 4.   † Hom. VI. ep. i. ad Corinth. s. 4.
‡ Κᾂν τὴν ἄκραν φιλοσοφίαν ἀσκῇς, τῶν δὲ λοιπῶν ἀπολλυμένων ἀμελῆς,
οὐδεμίαν κτήσῃ ταρὰ θιῷ παῤῥησίαν.
§ Epist. i. ad Corinth. h. 25.

worth. This was the monk Jovinian, who flourished near the
end of the fourth century. It may appear singular, that this
reaction against Monachism should proceed from Monachism
itself; but this was a natural reaction springing from the inner
Christian life, which in many was roused into action by Monachism—a phenomenon which often occurred. Thus we saw
already the indications of such a reaction in the case of a Nilus
and of a Marcus.

Jovinian, the protestant of his time, went on the principle,
" that there is but one divine element of life, which all believers share in common; but one fellowship with Christ, which
proceeds from faith in him; but one new birth. All who possess this in common with each other—all, therefore, who are
Christians in the true sense, not barely in outward profession—
have the same calling, the same dignity, the same heavenly
blessings; the diversity of outward circumstances creating no
difference in this respect." Accordingly, he supposes an opposition altogether universal, admitting of no intermediate link,
no grade of difference, between those who find themselves in
this state of grace and those who are shut out from it. Hence
he derives the conclusion, that the life of celibacy, or that of
marriage, eating, or fasting, the using or forbearing to use
earthly goods, all this can make no difference between Christians, where the same one ground of the Christian life is present. Everything depends on the inward Christian life, on the
temper of the heart, not on the outward forms of life and on
outward works by themselves considered, in which forms and
works the temper which makes the Christian only reveals itself.
Of course, the whole theory respecting a loftier, ascetic stage
of Christian perfection, respecting the difference between the
counsels which Christ gave to those only who strove after that
stage of perfection, and the ordinary duties incumbent on all
Christians respecting the merit of certain outward works, fell
to the ground. " Virgins, widows, and married women," said
he, " who have been *once* baptized into Christ, have the same
merit, if, in respect to works, there is otherwise no difference
between them.* The apostle Paul says, 'Know ye not, that
your body is a temple of the Holy Ghost?' He speaks of one
temple, not in the plural number, to denote that God dwells

* Virgines, viduas, et maritatas, quæ semel in Christo lotæ sunt, si non
discrepant cæteris operibus, ejusdem esse meriti.

after the same manner in all.   And as the Father, Son, and
Holy Ghost are one God, so should there be also but one
people in them, John xvii. 21, that is, his dear children, who
are partakers of the divine nature.*   The apostle John makes
no other distinction than one, between those who are born of
God and sin not, and those who are not born of God.   Christ
makes no other separation than that between those who stand
on the right and those who stand on the left hand, the sheep
and the goats."

Jovinian did not allow himself to be hurried on by an inconsiderate zeal unconditionally to condemn fasting, the life of
celibacy, Monachism, considered purely by themselves, though,
in other respects, he seems to have been inclined to extremes
in polemical matters.   Estimating the power and worth of
Christianity only by its influence on the temper, it was therefore the temper only which he attacked in the present case ;
the presumption and arrogance which attributed to the unmarried and ascetic life, a peculiar merit beyond the other tendencies of the Christian life generally.   Hence he continued
to live as a monk himself, and so refuted the charge that he
had devised such doctrines merely for the sake of liberating
himself from a yoke which was irksome to him.   " It amounts
to the same thing," said he, " whether a person abstain from
this or that food, or partake of it with thanksgiving.   I do
thee no injustice," he remarked, addressing those who lived
in celibacy ; " if thou hast chosen the unmarried life on the
ground of a present necessity, be careful only not to exalt
thyself.   Thou art a member of the same church to which the
married also belong."   He merely sought to show, that men
were wrong in recommending so highly and indiscriminately
the life of celibacy and fasting, though he was ready to admit,
that both, under certain circumstances, might be good and
beneficial.

In respect to marriage, he appealed in its defence to the
fact, that so great worth was ascribed to it immediately at the
creation ; and that it might not be said that this had reference
to the Old Testament alone, the same testimony had been confirmed by Christ, Gen. ii. 24, Matth. xix. 5.   He adduced the

* Et quomodo Pater et Filius et Spiritus Sanctus unus Deus ; sic et
unus populus in ipsis sit, hoc est quasi filii carissimi, divinæ consortes
naturæ.

example of the married saints, from the Old Testament, to defend himself against the common objection, that this applied only to the early infancy of mankind, when the multiplication of the race was particularly necessary; and added such proof passages from the New Testament as 1 Tim. v. 14; Heb. xiii. 4.; 1 Cor. vii. 39; 1 Tim. ii. 14.* He pointed to the fact, that Paul required of the bishop and deacon only that each should be the husband of one wife, that he accordingly sanctioned the marriage of the clergy. In respect of fasts, he cited Rom. xiv. 20; 1 Tim. iv. 3; that, according to the declaration of Paul, to the pure all things are pure; that Christ was pronounced by the Pharisees a man gluttonous and a wine-bibber, a friend of publicans and sinners; that he did not disdain the banquet of Zaccheus, and that he attended the marriage-feast at Cana.† Christ chose the wine for the sacrament of the supper, the wine as a holy symbol.‡ He says, justly, that those mortifications could not be possessed of any peculiar Christian character, since they were practised also among the Pagans in the worship of Cybele and of Isis.§ But it must have been an extremely contracted notion of final ends,

---

* It is worthy of notice, that Jerome (I. I. s. 30. contra Jovinian.) cited the whole book of Solomon's Song as an evidence in favour of marriage. From this we might infer, that he rejected the mystical interpretation of that book, which was then common; and in this case we should have here another proof of the more liberal inquiring spirit of the man. But the language which he employs respecting the church (Jerome, l. II. s. 19), sola novit canticum Christi, seems, notwithstanding, to point to a mystical interpretation of Solomon's Song. In the present case we can understand the argumentation of Jovinian only as follows: The holiest of things, the union of Christ with his church, would not have been represented here under such images, so carried out, if the union betwixt the two sexes were not a sacred thing.

† Jovinian's manner is characteristically presented in the words: Porro aliud est, si stulta contentione dicitis, eum isse ad prandium jejunaturum, et impostorum more dixisse: hoc comedo, illud non comedo, nolo vinum bibere, quod ex aquis creavi.

‡ In typo sanguinis sui non obtulit aquam, sed vinum. From the fact that the word "typus" is here employed, it cannot be directly inferred, that he ascribed to the sacrament of the supper only a symbolical significancy; for this name is given to the external symbols, as such, even by those who attached other notions to them; for example by Cyril of Jerusalem.

§ Quasi non et superstitio gentilium castum matris Deum observet et Isidis.

which led him to understand the proposition, that all other creatures are made for the use of man, in the sense that they were intended only *to subserve man's sensual wants.* Accordingly he reckoned up a number of animals, which, if they were not to serve as food for man, were created by God to no purpose, and he inferred that therefore it must have been the Creator's design that man should eat flesh ;* a conclusion which Jerome found it quite easy to refute.

Not merely in reference to the outward works of *asceticism,* but also in other respects, Jovinian took a decided stand against that false direction of the moral spirit of his age, which looked to external works alone, instead of looking only at the temper of the heart; as was seen, for example, in the exaggerated opinion entertained of martyrdom, solely on the ground of the outward suffering. He expressed himself as follows —" A person may be burnt, strangled, beheaded, in a time of persecution, or he may flee or die in the prison. These are, indeed, different kinds of conflict; but there is only one crown of victory."

The false direction of morals against which Jovinian took his stand, having its ground in the fact that men did not apprehend the Christian life on the side of its inward connection with faith, it came about for this very reason, that to outward works was ascribed a meritoriousness of various degrees; and the fear of future punishment, the aspiration after the higher stages of blessedness, were employed as incentives to moral and ascetic exertions. Jovinian, on the other hand, went on the principle that the true Christian, who by faith has become partaker of a divine life, is already certain of his salvation. He has nothing higher to aspire after than that which is already secured to him by faith : he needs only to preserve what he has received, to seek to persevere in the state of grace in which he has once been placed ; and this can be done only in the progressive life of holiness. "If you ask me," said he, " wherefore the just man should be actively exerting himself, whether in times of peace or of persecution, when there is no progress, when there are no greater rewards, I answer, he

---

* Quis usus porcorum absque esu carnium ? Quid capreæ, cervuli, etc. Cur in domibus gallina discurrit ? Si non comeduntur, hæc omnia frustra a Deo creata sunt.

does this, not that he may deserve something more, but that he may not lose what he has already received."*

Wherever there is a living faith, there, according to Jovinian, is fellowship with the Redeemer; there is divine life; and wherever this is, there it comes off victorious, by its own intrinsic power over all evil; there sin can find no entrance. The good tree can bring forth only good fruit; the evil tree must bring forth evil fruit. He who is born of God doth not commit sin. Hence it also followed that whoever had, by regeneration, received the divine life, could not any longer live in that slavish fear of sin to which the monastic asceticism had linked itself, together with its preventive remedies and cunningly devised tricks for foiling Satan. See above. In opposing this painful asceticism, Jovinian remarked, " He who is baptized, cannot be tempted of the devil." As he proceeded on the principle of referring the *inward life* to Christ as its source, he must have understood here by baptism, not so much an outward baptism, operating with the power of a charm, as the inward baptism, growing out of faith, the baptism of the Spirit. " In those who are tempted," says he, " it is seen that, like Simon Magus, they have received only the water, not the spiritual baptism. The spiritual baptism they only have received who have been baptized with the genuine faith by which regeneration is obtained."† The first of the above-cited passages might be so understood as if Jovinian considered the state of the regenerate to be one beyond the reach of all temptations; in which view he might justly be charged with teaching a practically mischievous error. But this assuredly could *not* be his meaning; for otherwise he could not have spoken of the moral efforts of the just man.

---

* As we have remarked already, that the views of Jovinian are not to be considered as wholly insulated from all other phenomena of the age, but as connected with a more general reaction of the Christian spirit excited by Monachism itself; so we may observe, in the present case, a remarkable analogy between Jovinian's expressions and those of the monk Marcus; for also Marcus says: " We who have been deemed worthy of the laver of regeneration, offer good works, not for the sake of a reward, but to preserve the purity which has been imparted to us." Ὅσοι τοῦ λούτρου τῆς παλιγγενεσίας ἠξιώθημεν, τὰ ἀγαθα ἔργα οὐ δι' ἀνταπόδοσιν προσφέρομεν, ἀλλὰ διὰ φυλακὴν τῆς δοθείσης ἡμῖν καθαρότητος. Bibl. patr. Galland. T. VIII. f. 14, s. 22.

† Plena fide in baptismate renati.

See above. And, moreover, he himself clearly explains how he understands the phrase "to be tempted" in that proposition, when he says that such a person cannot be overcome by Satan in temptations, cannot be plunged into guilt.*

Without doubt, however, Jovinian must have supposed, according to this assertion, that he who had been once really regenerated could not again fall from the state of grace;—that whenever one who appeared to have been baptized, to believe, was surprised into sin, this was evidence that he did not as yet possess living faith, had not as yet been really renewed.

As it is extremely easy for a man in combating one error, to fall into another of an opposite kind, so it seems to have happened with Jovinian. We noticed how, in opposition to the over-valuation of a certain species of outward works, and to the theory of a certain loftier ascetic Christian perfection, he gave prominence to the unity of the divine life in all believers. Again, Jovinian attacked the arbitrary theory, grounded on a misconception of the passage in 1 John v. 17, according to which sins were classified by reference solely to the outward act, into mortal (peccata mortalia), and venial sins (peccata venialia), a division by which the number of sins excluding from eternal life was often extremely limited. In opposition to such a theory, he maintained that the gospel required and brought along with it a new holy disposition, with which every sin, of whatever kind it might be, stood directly opposed; that the new man, the new life from God, excluded everything sinful; that as all goodness springs out of the same disposition of love to God, so, too, all sin, however different it might be in outward appearance, proceeded from the same fountain, manifested the same ungodly life. Christ says,—"Whoso eateth my flesh and drinketh my blood, dwelleth in me, and I in him." As Christ then dwells in us without any grade of distinction whatever, so we also dwell in Christ without any degree of difference. "If a man love me," saith the Lord, "he will keep my words; and my Father will love him, and we will come unto him and make our abode with him." Whoever is righteous loves, and whoever loves, to him come the Father and Son, and they dwell in his tabernacle. But where such an inhabitant is, there, I

* Eum a diabolo non posse subverti. According to Jerome, in the beginning of his first book against Jovinian.

think, nothing can be wanting to the owner of the dwelling. The gospel presents five virgins that were foolish, and five that were wise: the five who had no oil remained without; the other five, who had prepared themselves with the light of good works, entered with the bridegroom into the bride chamber. The righteous were saved with Noah, the sinners were destroyed together. In Sodom and Gomorrah, no other distinction was made account of than that between the righteous and the wicked. The just were delivered, all the sinners were consumed by the same fire. One salvation for those that were saved, one destruction for those that remained behind. Lot's wife is a witness how no allowance can be made for swerving from righteousness, even in the least respect. Whoever says to his brother, "Thou fool, and Raca," is in danger of hell-fire. And whoever is a murderer, or an adulterer, is in like manner cast into hell-fire. So, too, he maintained that it was the same thing whether a man became converted early or late. The moment men entered through faith into fellowship with the Redeemer, there was no longer any difference between them; they all possessed the same. " Between the brother who was always with the father, and him who was received afterwards because he had repented, there was no difference. The labourers of the first, the third, the sixth, the ninth, and the eleventh hour, received each alike one penny; and that you may wonder the more, the payment begins with those who had laboured the shortest time in the vineyard." But Jovinian did not here consider that, although the divine life, as a common property of all who believe, is one and the same, yet different stages are to be found in its development, and in the degree in which man's nature is assimilated and pervaded by it: that, along with the divine life, the principle of sin still continues to linger in believers, which may more or less prevail, or be overcome and suppressed by the divine principle of life; and that in this respect it is assuredly right to speak of a *more or less*, of a distinction of degrees, as well with regard to goodness as to sin.* This error lies at the root also of Jovinian's mode of

* Excellent are the remarks which Lücke takes occasion to introduce respecting Jovinian, in his beautiful commentary on the epistles of John, for which, certainly, many will join me in thanking him. P. 166. " Jovinian stood at the same ideal position with John; and his ethico-critical

expression, whereby he represents sanctification as a mere preserving of that which had been once received,* but not as a progressive development of it.†

If, then, in connection with this doctrine, he maintained that a person once regenerated could not be drawn into sin, and if he allowed of no distinction between the outward manifestations of sin, the consequence necessarily follows that the regenerate individual might indeed be tempted to sin, but could never be so overcome by temptation as to be led into actual sin.   Thus his theory would unquestionably conduct to a result contradictory to the universal experience of Christians,

efforts, in the spirit of a reformer, were aimed especially in opposition to the mock holiness, the externality and half-way character of the Christian life of his time, to re-assert, in its full clearness, precision, and truth, the fundamental moral conception and ideal of the gospel." I could only wish to say, in addition, that Jovinian, in opposing the ideal standard of Christianity to that which, having regard barely to the manifestation, and hence overlooking its connection with the idea, respected the mere appearance, failed to distinguish sufficiently between the ideal position, and that of the manifestation—a distinction which John was careful to observe. Thus he was led in a certain sense to confound the two positions with each other.

* Undoubtedly this expression, in itself considered, may admit also of being understood in an altogether faultless sense, so far as all pure development may be regarded as a preserving, securing, and maintaining in its purity of the original principle ; and so, too, all progressive sanctification may be considered as the preserving of the divine life imparted by regeneration ; as the preserving of the state of innocence into which man has entered through justification.   Yet, at the same time, it seems to me to follow necessarily from the whole connection of ideas to be found in the rest of Jovinian's writings, that he gave such undue prominence to the notion of constancy, as was inconsistent with the notion of progressive development in the Christian life.

† In the case above cited, where Jovinian remarks that there is no difference between virgins, widows, and married women, provided only they do not differ in respect to their other works, the passage might, to be sure, be so understood as if he meant to assert a possible difference in respect to good works, and accordingly would admit the existence of distinctions in the estimation of moral character.   But according to the connection of his ideas, as elsewhere exhibited, with which this assertion would otherwise clash, we must conceive, unless we are willing to suppose him inconsistent with himself, that he understood his own position in the following sense: provided only they did not so differ in respect to their other works, as that some of them manifested by their conduct the true baptism of the Spirit, while the others showed by their conduct that they had not received any such baptism, but only the outward baptism of appearance.

which could only be adhered to by a system of self-deception. How far he was really involved in this his one-sided theory, plainly appears from the extremely tortuous methods of explanation by which he seeks to bring the passages of scripture, adduced against him by the other party, into harmony with that theory.*

We must notice, too, by the way, a point which belongs strictly to the evolution of the idea of the church, but which we bring in here on account of the connection in which this point stands also with Jovinian's whole mode of thinking. As he begins and proceeds in his entire theory, by immediately referring the inner life of each individual, through faith, to Christ, without presupposing any external medium of communication; as, in his way of thinking, the notion of fellowship with Christ had precedence of the notion of the church, so this latter notion, too, must, in his system, take an altogether different position. The notion of the invisible church, as a community of believers and redeemed sinners, spiritually united, was by him made far more prominent than the notion of the visible church, derived from outward tradition. "The church, founded on hope, faith, and charity, is exalted above every attack. No unripe member is within it—all its members are taught of God. No person can break within its enclosure

---

* Thus when, in objection to his views, the parable was cited of a different measure of increase from the scattered seed, according to the different quality of the soil on which it fell, Matth. xiii., Luke viii., Mark iv., he maintained that the only point to be held fast here was, the difference between the good and the bad ground. All the rest belonged not to the matter of comparison, but to the decoration of the figure ; and in favour of this explanation he urged the absurd argument, that the difference of numbers could be of no importance here, because Mark pursued the reverse order in his enumeration. Numerum non facere præjudicium, præsertim quum et evangelista Marcus retrorsum numeret. To defend himself against the application of the words in John xiv. 2, "In my Father's house are many mansions," which in fact could be employed by his adversaries in favour of their own side only in a way running directly counter to the connection in which they are found, he opposed it by another interpretation no less contradictory to the connection of the passage, maintaining that by the different mansions were to be understood simply the *different* church communities on earth, which still constituted, however, but one church of God. Non in regno cœlorum diversas significat mansiones; sed ecclesiarum in toto orbe numerum, quæ constat una per septem (h. e. in septem ecclesiis apocalypseôs nonnisi una ecclesia).

by violence, nor creep in by fraud."* It is plainly evident
that Jovinian could only have understood by the church here,
the *invisible* church. So, too, in the following predicates
which he applies to the church—"The titles bride, sister,
mother—and whatever other names you may think of—refer
to the community of the one church, which is never without
her bridegroom, without her brother, without her son. She
has one faith, and within her there arise no schisms by means
of erroneous doctrines. She ever remains a virgin to whom
the Lamb goes; him she follows, and she alone knows the
song of Christ." Of course he can understand by the church
here only the community of true believers.

Jovinian's reasons against the worth of the unmarried life
found admittance among the laity, monks, and nuns in Rome.†
But it was natural that the Roman bishop Siricius, with whom
we have already become acquainted as a zealous opponent of
married priests, should declare strongly against the doctrines
of Jovinian. At a Roman synod, held in 390, he pronounced
in the harshest and most unjustifiable language ‡ sentence of condemnation on Jovinian and eight of his adherents.§ Jovinian
betook himself to Milan, and there perhaps sought to shelter
himself under the protection of the emperor, then residing in
that place. But here he was opposed by the mighty influence
of the bishop Ambrose, who had already been made acquainted with the affair by the synodial letter of Siricius, and
who, as a zealous promoter of the ascetic tendency and of
Monachism, could be no otherwise than a zealous opponent of
Jovinian. In his reply to Siricius, written in the name of a
synod held at Milan, he declared his agreement with the
judgment pronounced by the latter. Jovinian and his friends
were banished from Milan. But perhaps the silent working

---

* Scimus ecclesiam spe, fide, caritate, inaccessibilem, inexpugnabilem;
non est in ea immaturus, omnis docibilis, (scil. a Deo, as the Vulgate
translates the term θεοδιδάκτος,) impetu irrumpere vel arte eludere, (it
should read perhaps, *illudere*, enter in by trick, by deception,) potest
nullus.

† Augustin. Hæres. 82, Retract. ii. 22.

‡ He calls Jovinian luxuriæ magister.

§ Incentores novæ hæresis et blasphemiæ divina sententia et nostro
judicio in perpetuum damnati. For the rest, even Siricius witnesses of
the spread of these doctrines, when he says: Sermo hæreticorum intra
ecclesia cancri more serpebat.

of his influence continued to be felt there, if it were not the case that, independent of him, a similar reaction proceeding out of Monachism itself, called forth there an opposition to the spirit of monkish morality.

Ambrose must also witness the influence of these principles among his own monks at Milan. Two persons of this order, Sarmatio and Barbatianus, attracted notice, who, like Jovinian, disputed the peculiar merit of the unmarried life.*. Not being allowed freely to express their principles in the cloister, they released themselves from that yoke.† Next, they repaired to the church at Vercelli, where, perhaps, as the church happened at that time to be without a bishop, they hoped to find a better reception, and to be able to propagate their principles with less danger of disturbance. But the bishop Ambrose immediately sent warning of them in a letter which he addressed to the church.‡ He accused them of spreading such doctrines as that the baptized needed not concern themselves about striving after virtue; that excess in eating and drinking could do them no harm; that it was foolish in them to abstain from the enjoyments of life; that virgins and widows ought to marry. But, in a statement of this sort, it is easy to see the distorting influence of passion. Taking these charges in connection with the doctrine of Jovinian and the other positions held by these men, it becomes probable, that with Jovinian they intended merely to affirm : " Whoever received the baptism of the Spirit possessed means enough for overcoming sin, and needed not to have recourse to a painful asceticism."

As to the rest, Jerome, the warm opponent of Jovinian, by the exaggerated statements into which he continually fell in conducting his attacks, served rather to place the cause which

* When Ambrose accuses them besides of asserting: Delirare eos, qui jejuniis castigent carnem suam, ut menti subditam faciant,—this may perhaps be a consequence of his own drawing.

† Ambrose intimates himself, that nothing could be objected to them as long as they were at Milan. He points to the reason which chiefly induced them to leave the cloister, when he says . interdicta ludibriosæ disputationi licentia. But it was an ungrounded inference of his own making, when he accuses them of having left the cloister because they could not indulge, as they wished, in riotous living, nullus erat luxuriæ locus.

‡ Lib. X. ep. 52, ed. Basil.

he defended in an unfavourable light, and to further that of
his opponent ; for it seemed, according to the statements of
the former, that his opponent was right in asserting that men
could not extol the life of celibacy without depreciating the
state of marriage, which Christ has sanctioned, and thereby
outraging the common sense and feeling of Christian men.
Augustin, perceiving this, was led to write his book *de bono
conjugali*, in which he sought to do away with the above-
mentioned objection by acknowledging the worth of marriage,
and yet ascribing a still higher state of Christian life to the
state of celibacy when chosen out of a right temper of heart.
In this tract he distinguishes himself, not only for his greater
moderation, but also for a more correct judgment of the
ascetic life in its connection with the whole Christian temper ;
as it is in fact the great merit generally of his mode of apprehending the Christian system of morals, that, like Jovinian, he
opposed the tendency to set a value upon the outward conduct,
outward works, as an opus operatum, without regard to their
relation to the disposition of the heart. By giving prominence
to the latter, Augustin approached Jovinian, and he would
have come still nearer to him, had he not been on so many
sides fettered to the church spirit of his times.*

Among the opponents of the ascetic spirit and of Monachism should be noticed also a person respecting whom we shall
have occasion to speak again, as an antagonist of the prevailing tendencies of the church spirit,—the presbyter *Vigilantius*.
He probably believed that the words of our Lord to the rich
young man were misapprehended (see above), when taken, as
they were by many, in the sense of an invitation to give all
they possessed at once to the poor, and to retire among the
monks. *They*, he maintained, who managed their own property and distributed its income gradually among the poor,

---

* Thus Augustin, as well as Jovinian, says, that true martyrdom consists in the disposition of the mind ; and that a man who had no outward
call to become a martyr, yet, in the temper on which all moral worth
depends, might be quite equal to the martyrs. Thus it was also with regard to abstinence. So Abraham, although he lived in marriage, because
this was agreeable to the then stage of the development of God's kingdom, might, in the Christian virtue of abstinence and self-denial, be fully
equal to the Christians who led a life of celibacy in a holy temper.
Continentiæ virtutem in habitu animi semper esse debere, in opere autem pro rerum et temporum opportunitate manifestari.

did better than those who gave away the whole at once. It behoved each individual to provide rather for the wants of the poor of his own neighbourhood instead of sending his money to Jerusalem for the support of the poor who were there (the monks). "Should all retire from the world and live in deserts," said he, " who would remain to support the public worship of God? Who would exhort sinners to virtue? This would be not to fight but to fly."

But such individual voices could effect nothing of importance against a tendency of the church which was so decided, nor could they counteract a form of church life which had already become so prevalent. Monachism, in fact, was to be preserved, furnishing, as it did, so important a means for the diffusion of Christianity and of Christian culture in the succeeding centuries.

II.—Christian Worship.

1. *Relation of Christian Worship to the whole sphere of the Christian Life.*

As the consciousness of the universal Christian priesthood was gradually supplanted by the idea of a class of men particularly consecrated to God, whose peculiar business it was to devote their time and thoughts to divine things; so, too, the original relation, grounded in the essence of Christianity, of the common worship of Christians to the whole circle of Christian life, respecting which we spoke in the preceding period, was continually becoming obliterated. Men forgot that Christian worship is not confined to any particular place, times, or actions, but was meant to embrace the entire life, consecrated to God. Yet the more distinguished church teachers, such as Chrysostom and Augustin, well understood that living Christianity could proceed only out of that original Christian consciousness to which the whole Christian life presented itself as a worship of God in spirit and in truth, and they laboured to revive this consciousness,—to counteract in every way that delusive notion which placed the essence of Christianity in the opus operatum of joining in outward acts of worship, and to introduce the point of view into practical life, that instruction in divine truth, reading of the holy scriptures, and prayer, were not to be confined solely to the church assemblies, but

should be diffused through the whole of the Christian life.
Accordingly Chrysostom, in his sixth discourse against the
confounding of Christianity and Judaism,* observes that
" God permitted the single temple at Jerusalem to be destroyed, and erected in its stead a thousand others of far
higher dignity than that : for the apostle declares, 'Ye are
the temple of the living God.' Adorn *this* house of God,
drive from it all wicked thoughts, so that you may be a
temple of the spirit, and make others do so too." " Christians," he remarks in another discourse, "should not merely
celebrate one single day as a feast, for the apostle says,
1 Corinth. v. 8 : 'Let us keep the feast, not with old leaven,'
&c. We are not to stand by the ark of the covenant and by
the golden altar,—we, whom the Lord of all existence himself
has made his own dwelling; and who continually hold con-
verse with him by prayer, by the celebration of the holy
supper, by the sacred scriptures, by alms, and by the fact that
we bear him in our hearts. What need therefore of the Sabbath to him who celebrates a continual feast, who has his conversation in heaven? Let us then celebrate a continual feast,
and let us do no sin, for *this* is the keeping of the feast."† In
opposition to those who thought themselves righteous because
they regularly attended church, he says : " If a child daily goes
to school and yet learns nothing, would that be any excuse for
him ?—would it not rather serve to aggravate his fault? Just
so it is with us ; for we go to the church, not merely for the
sake of spending a few moments there, but that we may go
away with some great gain in spiritual things. If we depart
empty, our very zeal in attending the sanctuary will redound
to our condemnation. But that this may not be the result, let
us, on leaving this place, friends with friends, fathers with
their children, masters with their servants, exercise ourselves
in reducing to practice the lessons we have here learned. This
momentary exhortation cannot extirpate every evil ; the husband should hear it again at home from his wife, the wife
from her husband."‡ And in another discourse :§ " When
you have sung together two or three psalms, and superficially

* Adv. Judæos, VI. s. 7, T. I. 661.
† H. 39, in Matth. s. 3, ed. Montf. T. VII. f. 435.
‡ H. 5, de statuis, s. 7, T. II. f. 71.
§ Hom. 11, in Matth. s. 7.

gone through the ordinary prayers, and then return home, you suppose this suffices for your salvation. Have you not heard what the prophet, or rather what God, through the mouth of the prophet, says: 'This people honour me with their lips, but their heart is far from me?'" He was ever pressing this point, that every house should be a church; every father of a family a shepherd for his household; that he was equally responsible for the welfare of all its members, even for that of the domestics, whom the gospel placed on a level with all other men in their relation to God.* He complains that, whilst in the early Christian times the house was by the love of heavenly things converted into a church, the church itself was now, through the earthly direction of thought in those that visited it, converted into an ordinary house.† Augustin likewise says to the members of his community: "It is your business to make the most of your talent: each man should be a bishop in his own house; he must see to it that his wife, his son, his daughter, his servant (since he is bought with so great a price), persevere in the true faith. The apostolical teaching placed the master above the servant, and bound the servant to obedience towards his master; *but Christ has paid one ransom for both.*"‡

In respect particularly to prayer, Chrysostom often took ground against the delusive notion which grew out of that Jewish tendency, that unevangelical distinction of secular and spiritual things which we must so often allude to, as though this duty might not and ought not to be performed in every place, and during the ordinary business of life, which indeed should be sanctified thereby, as well as in the church. "When Christ came," says he, "he purified the whole world; every place became a house of prayer. For this reason, Paul exhorts us to pray everywhere with boldness, and, moreover, without doubting, 1 Tim. ii. 8. Mark you, how the world has been purified? As it regards the place, we may *everywhere* lift up holy hands; for the whole earth has become consecrated, more consecrated than the holy of holies.§ After

---

* Hom. 6 in Genesin, s. 2. Ἐκκλησίαν ποίησόν σου τὴν οἰκίαν, καὶ γὰρ καὶ ὑπεύθυνός εἶ καὶ τῆς τῶν παιδίων καὶ τῆς τῶν οἰκετῶν σωτηρίας.

† In Matth. H. 32, s. 7. Τότε αἱ οἰκίαι ἐκκλησίαι ἦσαν, νῦν δὲ ἡ ἐκκλησία οἰκία γέγονεν.

‡ S. 94. § Homil. 1, de cruce et latrone, s. 1, T. II. f. 404.

having remarked that all the works of the frail earthly life should flow from prayer, and find support in the same, he supposes it objected by a worldly man of those times: "How can a man of business, a man tied to the courts of justice, pray and resort to the church thrice in a day?" And he replies: "It is possible and very easy; for if you cannot easily repair to the church, you may at least pray before the door; and that even though you may be tied to the courts of justice, for it needs not so much the voice as the disposition of the heart; not so much the outstretched hands as the devotional soul; not so much this or the other posture as the mind." He then goes on to say: " It is not here as in the Old Testament. Where-ever you may be, you still have the altar, the sacrificial knife, and the offering by you; for you yourself are priest, altar, and sacrifice. Wherever you are, you may raise an altar by sim-ply cherishing a devout and serious temper. Place and time are no hindrance. Though you bow not the knee, though you beat not the breast, though you stretch not your hands to heaven, but only manifest a warm heart, you have all that belongs to prayer. The wife, while she holds in her lap the spindle and spins, can with her soul look up to heaven, and call with fervency on the name of the Lord. It is possible for this man to offer a fervent prayer while he is on his way alone to the market; for that other to lift up his soul to God, who sits in his shop and sews leather; and the servant who makes purchases, goes errands, or sits in the kitchen, has nothing to hinder him from doing the same thing."*

To this period also was transmitted from the primitive Christian times the right, closely connected with the consci-ousness of the universal Christian priesthood, and belonging to all Christians, of instructing and edifying themselves by going directly to the fountain of the divine word. Hence manu-scripts of the Bible were multiplied and exposed for sale.†
It was regarded as the chief part of a pious Christian educa-tion, both in men and women, to become early familiar with the holy scriptures. Thus Jerome notices it of Læta, a noble Roman lady, that she taught her daughter, from early child-hood, to cultivate a love for the sacred scriptures instead of

---

* De Anna S. IV. s. 6, T. IV. f. 738.

† Scriptura venalis fertur per publicam. Augustin. in Ps.' xxxvi. S. I. s. 2.

jewelry and silks ;* that she learned patience from the example of Job; that she never suffered the gospel to be out of her reach.† Among both women and men, of whatever rank in society, it was regarded as the characteristic mark of those with whom Christianity was a serious concern of the heart, that they were much occupied with the study of the Bible :— as the examples of Monica and Nonna show. The rhetorical preacher who pronounced the funeral discourse on the younger Constantine, mentions it to his praise that he constantly nourished his soul out of the sacred writings, and formed his life by their precepts.‡ This, perhaps, may be regarded as nothing more than empty eulogy ; but it enables us, nevertheless, to see what was reckoned in this age as belonging to the qualities of a pious prince. When Pagans who were inquiring after the truth, found difficulties in the Christian doctrines, they did not repair at once, as a matter of course, to the clergy, but oftentimes to their friends among the Christian laity. These sought for a solution of the questions proposed to them in the holy scriptures; and when they met with difficulties there too hard for them to solve, Augustin invites them not so much to seek instruction from their spiritual guides, as to pray for light from above.§ For those who were awakened by the public worship of God to more serious reflection on divine truth, or who were desirous of studying the scriptures in a more quiet way, rooms were provided and furnished with Bibles in the galleries of the church (φροντιστήρια), to which they could retire for the purpose of reading and meditation.‖ Jerome complains of it as an evil that men and women all thought themselves competent to discourse, however deficient their knowledge, on the right interpretation of the sacred volume.¶

* Ep. 107, s. 12. Pro gemmis et serico, divinos codices amet.

† In Job virtutis et patientiæ exempla sectetur, ad evangelia transeat, nunquam ea positura de manibus. Compare above, the examples from the rule of Basil, and what Gregory of Nyssa says respecting the education of Macrina.

‡ Anonymi monod. in Constantin. jun. p. 7, ed. Morell. Ἐντεῦθεν καὶ βίον ἐκόσμει καὶ ἤθας ἐρρύθμιζε.

§ Ad ipsum Dominum pulsa orando, pete, insta. Sermo 105, s. 3.

‖ Paulinus of Nola, ep. 321. T. I. p. 209.
   Si quem sancta tenet meditanda in lege voluntas,
   Hic poterit residens sacris intendere libris.

¶ Sola scriptura ars est, quam sibi omnes passim vindicant, hanc

The clergy were not the first to derive from the unevangelical theory respecting a distinct priestly caste, the inference,
which lay not very remote, that the fountain of the divine
word was to be approached only by themselves; that the laity
must depend for all their instruction in divine things simply on
the clergy, without being entitled to go to the original source
itself; but it was the altogether worldly-minded laity, who, as
they had taken advantage of the distinction between a spiritual
and a secular class, to set up for themselves a convenient
Christianity, subservient to their pleasures, so made use of the
same pretext as a reason for avoiding all intercourse with the
divine word, and an excuse for their indifference to higher interests, alleging that the study of the Bible was a business properly belonging to ecclesiastics and monks. But distinguished
church-teachers, such as Chrysostom and Augustin, contended
strenuously against this way of thinking.   The former denominates the excuses: "I am a man of business; I am no monk;
I have a wife and children to provide for,"* cold and exceedingly censurable words; and maintained, on the contrary, that
just those persons who were in the midst of the storms of the
world and exposed to its many temptations, stood most of all
in need of those means of preservation and safety which the
holy scriptures furnish—more even than those who led a life
of silent retirement, far from all strife with the outward
world.† Frequently, both in private conversation and in his
public discourses, he exhorted his hearers not to rest satisfied
with that which they heard read from the scriptures in the
church, but to read them also with their families at home;‡
for what food was for the body, such the holy scriptures were
for the soul,—the source whence it derived substantial
strength.§ To induce his hearers to study the scriptures,

garrula anus, hanc delirus senex, hanc sophista verbosus, hanc universi
præsumunt, lacerant, docent, antequam discant. Alii adducto supercilio
grandia verba trutinantes, inter mulierculas de sacris literis philoso-
phantur, alii discunt a feminis quod viros doceant. Ep. 53 ad Paulinum,
s. 5.

* ᾿Ανηρ εἰμι βιωτικός· οὐκ ἔστιν ἐμον, γράφας ἀναγινώσκειν, ἀλλ᾿ ἐκείνων
τῶν ἀποταξαμένων.   † H. 3 de Lazaro, T. I.

‡ Καὶ ἐπὶ οἰκίας σπουδαζώμεν τῇ ἀναγνώσει τῶν θείων προσέχειν γραφῶν.
Hom. 29, in Genes. s. 2.

§ ῞Οπερ ἡ σωματικὴ τροφὴ πρὸς τὴν σύστασιν τῆς ἡμετέρας ἰσχύος, τοῦτο
ἡ ἀνάγνωσις τῇ ψυχῇ γίνεται. L. c. T. IV. f. 281.

he was often accustomed—when there was as yet no set lesson of the sacred word prescribed for every Sunday—to give out for some time beforehand the text which he designed to make a subject of discourse on some particular occasion, and to exhort them in order that they might be better prepared for his remarks, in the meantime to reflect upon it themselves.[*] In like manner, Augustin says: "Do not allow yourselves to be so immersed in present earthly things, as to be obliged to say, I have no time to read or to hear God's word."[†] Among the characters of the zealous Christian, whom he describes under the figure of the ant, as one that treasures up from the divine word that which he may have occasion to use in the time of need, he places the following: "He goes to church and listens to God's word; he returns home, finds a Bible there, and opens and reads it."[‡] Often does Chrysostom trace the corruptions of the church, as well in doctrine as in life,—the spread of error and of vice,—to the prevailing ignorance of the scriptures.[§]

Two hindrances to the general reading of the Bible might then, for the first time, unquestionably have been removed, had Christianity been directed also to multiply and diffuse the means of general mental cultivation, and by associations formed in the spirit of love, to supply what individuals could not obtain for themselves. These two hindrances were, first, the fact that but few knew how to read, and second, the high price of manuscripts.[||]

In respect to this second hindrance, of poverty, which for-

* This he describes as his method in the discourse on Lazarus, referred to in the preceding note. T. I. f. 737.

† Non mihi vacat legere. In Psalm lxvi. s. 10.

‡ Audire sermonem, audire lectionem, invenire librum, aperire et legere. In Psalm lxvi. s. 3.

§ E. g. Prooem. in epist. ad Rom. T. IX. f. 426.

|| Cyrill of Jerusalem adduces as a reason why all could not read the Bible, "ignorance and the pressure of business," οὐ πάντες δύνανται τὰς γράφας ἀναγινώσκειν, ἀλλὰ τοὺς μὲν ἰδιωτεία, τοὺς δὲ ἀσχολία τις ἐμποδίζει. Cateches. V. s. 7. Augustin makes a distinction between the book of creation and the book of the sacred writings: In istis codicibus non ea legunt, nisi qui litteras noverunt, in toto mundo legat et idiota. In Psalm xlv. s. 7. Augustin was in want of a Bible, when the desire first arose in his mind at Milan to become more accurately acquainted with the divine doctrines: Ubi ipsos codices quærimus? Unde aut quando comparamus? Confess. l. VI. s. 18. A difficulty which, to be sure, he could easily surmount, when he was in right earnest about the matter.

bade the purchase of a Bible, Chrysostom reckoned it among those pretexts which would certainly give way to real earnestness and zeal about Christianity. "As many of the poorer class," said he, "are constantly making this excuse, that they have no Bibles, I would like to ask them can poverty, however great it may be, hinder a man when he does not possess, complete, all the tools of his trade? What, then! is it not singular that in this case he never thinks of laying the blame to his poverty, but does his best that it may not hinder him; while, on the other hand, in a case where he is to be so great a gainer, he complains of his poverty?"*

As to those who were prevented from studying the scriptures themselves, the reading of the scriptures in the church, as Chrysostom explains in the passage last referred to, and in other places, was to serve as a remedy for this want; for on these occasions not single passages merely, but entire sections and whole books of the Bible were read in connection. Hence many who could not read had still been able, by a constant attendance at church, and by carefully listening to the portions read in each year, to treasure up in their memories a familiar knowledge of the sacred scriptures.†

2. *Relation of Public Worship to Art. Church Buildings; their Embellishments, Images.*

We remarked in the preceding period, that the primitive Christian way of thinking was averse to the employment of art, as being a heathen practice. This stern opposition to art would naturally cease as the opposition to the now constantly declining Paganism relaxed. Christianity might, and indeed by its very nature should, appropriate to its own use, purify, ennoble, and sanctify even art; but the danger now threatened, that the artistic element would become too predominant for the healthful development of religious morals; that external splendour and ornament would supplant the simple devotion of the heart; that sense and the imagination would be called into

---

* Hom. 11, in Johan. s. 1.

† As was done by Parthenius, afterwards bishop in Lampsacus, in whose youth it is related, literarum imperitus, sanctarum autem scriptu rarum vel maxime valens memoria. See his life, which seems to be at least not without a genuine foundation. Acta Sanctorum mens. Febr. T. II. f. 38.

exercise more than the mind and the affections.   Yet it is evident, nevertheless, that the primitive evangelical temper, directed to the worship of God in spirit and in truth, maintained the struggle with this new tendency which threatened to turn devotion away from the inner essence of religion.

As, in the preceding period, the whole outward form of the church and of church life betokened a community propagating itself in opposition to the dominant power, a community persecuted and oppressed ; so, in the present, the altered situation of this community manifested itself in its whole external appearance.   The churches destroyed under the Dioclesian persecution were again rebuilt in greater magnificence ; the Christian emperors emulated each other in erecting splendid structures, and in embellishing and enriching them in every way.   Wealthy and noble laymen followed their example ; and the delusive notion insinuated itself, that in so doing men performed a work of peculiar merit and of the highest service to religion.   Many believed that by thus contributing to adorn the churches, by presenting them with costly vessels, mounted with gold, silver, and precious stones, they could atone for their sins.   Hence Chrysostom felt himself constrained to say : " God forbid that we should believe it is enough for our salvation, if *we* rob widows and orphans, and present to the altar a golden chalice, set with precious stones ! Wouldst thou honour the offering of Christ?   Then present him thy own soul as an offering, for which he himself has offered up his life.   Let this become a golden one ; for the church is not a storehouse of gold and silver manufactures, but it is the community of angels ; hence we ask for souls ; for even this (donation made to the church) God accepts only for the sake of souls." *   The pious and enlightened abbot, Isidorus of Pelusium, in a beautifully written letter, complains of his bishop, that he superfluously decorated, with costly marbles, the outward structure of the church ; whilst

* Chrysost. in Matth. h. 50, s. 3.   So also he says in his 80th homily on Matthew, s. 2 : " Instead of presenting to the church splendid vessels, and expending large sums in ornamenting the walls and the grounds of the church, it would be better to provide first for the support of the poor."   There were, on the other hand, to be sure, bishops like Theophilus of Alexandria (who hence bore the surname of λιθομάνης), that were very willing to deprive the poor of what was their due, and expend it on the erection of splendid buildings.

402

he persecuted the pious, and thus destroyed the true church,
consisting of the community of believers. He admonishes
him to be careful, and distinguish between the church building and the church itself; the latter being composed of pure
souls, the former of wood and stone.* In the time of the
apostles, said he, church buildings did not as yet exist; but
the church consisting of the communities was rich in the gifts
of the Spirit. Now, the church structures were resplendent
with marbles, but the church itself was barren of those gifts
of the Spirit.†

Magnificent public buildings, already erected, and pagan
temples, were also occasionally presented as gifts to the
churches, and were consecrated and altered for the purposes
of Christian worship. Yet it might well be that, in the provincial towns, the more simple places of assembly, which bore
the impress of Christian antiquity, continued for a long time
to form a striking contrast with the splendid church edifices
in the large cities. Zeno, bishop of Verona (who lived after
the middle of the fourth century), labours to show, in one of
his discourses, that the distinguishing mark of Christianity, as
compared with Judaism and Paganism, could not consist in
the beauty of its outward buildings, in which it was excelled
by both those religions; but what constituted the peculiarity
of Christianity, what it had in preference to both these religions, was, the spiritual being of the church, the community
of believers, God's true temple. The living God would have
living temples. In this discourse he remarks, that no Christian churches were to be found, or at least but very few,
which could be compared with the ruins of the neglected
heathen temples.‡ Doubtless this language is not to be taken
as literally true. We must make allowance for what should
be attributed to rhetorical exaggeration, or explained as too
general a conclusion from individual examples.

The Christian churches were planned after the pattern of
the temple at Jerusalem; and this threefold division was

* Ὅτι ἄλλό ἐστιν ἐκκλησία καὶ ἄλλό ἐκκλησιαστήριον, ἡ μὲν γὰρ ἐξ
ἀμώμων ψυχῶν, τὸ δ᾽ ἀπὸ λίθων καὶ ξύλων οἰκοδομεῖται.
† See lib. II. ep. 246.
‡ Lib. I. Tract. 14. Quod aut nullum aut perrarum est per omnem
ecclesiam Dei orationis loci membrum, quod possit quavis ruina in se
mergentibus idololatriæ ædibus nunc usque aliquatenus comparari.

closely connected with the whole peculiar form of worship, as it had sprung out of the idea of a Christian priesthood, corresponding to the Jewish, and of a New Testament sacrificial service corresponding to that of the Old Testament.   The three parts were, *first*, the front court,* where all the unbaptized, Pagans, Jews, and Catechumens, could stand and hear the sermon and the reading of the scriptures: the place assigned to all the uninitiated; *next*, the proper temple, the place assigned to the community of laymen, believers and baptized persons;† *finally*, the sanctuary,‡ the place appro-·priated to the offering of the New Testament sacrifices, and to the priests who presented them, and therefore separated by a veil § and railing ‖ from the other parts of the church. Here . stood the altar; here stood the θρόνος, the chair (cathedra) of the bishop; and in a semicircle around it were seats for the clergy.   The clergy alone had the privilege of receiving the holy supper within the limits which separated the altar from the other parts of the church.¶

The consecration of new churches was celebrated with great solemnity.   It was a popular festival, which such bishops as Theodoret courteously invited even pagans to attend; and the day of the year in which this consecration had been made was likewise solemnized.   The unevangelical notion which, like so many other errors of church life, grew out of the confusion of outward things with spiritual, was already becoming fixed,

* Πρόναος, νάρθηξ, ferula, so called from its oblong form.

† The νάος, the ἱερον in the more restricted sense of the term; called from its shape ἡ ναῦς or navis ecclesiæ (the nave), where also was the chancel, from which the holy scriptures were read, and occasionally the sermon was delivered (ἀμβων, pulpitum, suggestus). Usage was not always alike in this respect. Sometimes the sermon was preached from the steps of the altar, sometimes from the tribune, βῆμα, or exedra of the bishop.

‡ Τὰ ἄγια τῶν ἁγίων, τὰ ἄδυτα, sanctuarium, βῆμα metonymice.

§ Ἀμφιθύρα.   ‖ Κίγκλιδες, cancelli.

¶ As in this distinction of the clergy is exhibited the false notion of the priesthood, so the Byzantine spirit, which tended to drag into the church even the distinctions of worldly rank, is betrayed in the circumstance that an exception was made in this case with regard to the emperors, who were also permitted to take their place within the limits of the sanctuary. Ambrose is reported to have been the first to make a change in this respect in favour of the emperor Theodosius; he assigned the latter a place at the head of the church, immediately in front of the limits (πρὸ τῶν δρυφάκτων). Sozom. hist. eccles. VII. 25.

that by this consecration the churches acquired a peculiar
sanctity of their own ; although, as may be gathered from what
has already been said, an evangelical tendency of spirit, which
placed the essence of the church rather in the communion
of hearts, and derived all true consecration and holiness solely
from the direction of the spirit, opposed itself to this error.*
Chrysostom represents the benefit of prayer in the church to
consist, not in *the holiness of the place*, but in the *elevation
of the feelings by Christian communion*, by *the bond of love;* †
although the very men who, *on the one hand*, under the impulse of their purely Christian consciousness, uttered so many
noble thoughts in opposition to the sensuous and Judaizing
tendency of the spirit of those times, were nevertheless urged
on by that spirit, unconsciously, to warrant and confirm many
a practice which was at war with that purely Christian consciousness. Thus Chrysostom, for example, who, as is evident
from the proofs already given, understood so well how to distinguish and hold apart the New Testament point of view
from that of the Old, yet, for the purpose of showing the
superiority of the church to the temple of the Old Testament,
mentioned, among other things, the higher virtue of the sacred
lamp in the church, compared to that in the temple ; since, by
the oil of the former, miraculous cures had been wrought by
those who used it in the exercise of true faith.‡   It was charged
as a high misdemeanour on Athanasius, that on the Easter festival he had assembled the community, whom the other churches
had not room enough to accommodate, in a large edifice recently founded by the emperor Constantine, before it had been
consecrated according to the usual form.   Prayer and worship,
it was alleged, ought never to be offered on any unconsecrated
spot.   Athanasius met his accusers with the words of our Lord,
that he who would pray should shut himself in his chamber : no

* The term "church," says Chrysostom, is a designation of fellowship
—ἐκκλησία συστήματος καὶ συνόδου ἐστιν ὄνομα.   In Psalm cxlix. T. V. f.
498.   The church is not wall and roof, but faith and life—ἡ ἐκκλησία οὐ
τοίχος καὶ ὄροφος, ἀλλὰ πίστις καὶ βίος.   Sermo in Eutrop. T. III. f. 386.

† 'Ἐνταῦθα ἐστι τὶ πλίον, οἷον ἡ ὁμονοία, καὶ ἡ συμφωνία, καὶ τῆς ἀγάπης
ὁ σύνδεσμος.   It is true, he adds, of the false principle of the priesthood,
by which he too was fettered : καὶ αἱ τῶν ἱερίων εὐχαί.   De incomprehen-
sibili, T. I. f. 469, s. 6.

‡ Hom. 32, Matth. s. 6.   'Ἰάσιν ὅσοι μιτὰ πιστίω; κzι εὐκαιρῶς ἰλαίω
χριάμινοι νοσήματα ἔλυσαν.

place therefore was, in itself considered, too profane for prayer.*

As it regards the decoration of churches with representations of religious objects, it is necessary first to distinguish here, from other images, the symbol of the cross, the sign of the victory of Christ over the kingdom of evil, the token of redemption. From the actions of daily life, in which this sign was everywhere customarily employed, and which were thus to be consecrated and sanctified, the sign probably passed over, at an early period, to the places where the Christian communities assembled for worship,† although other symbols were still kept away from them as savouring of Paganism. A true and genuine Christian feeling lay at the basis of the practice, when this symbol was employed not only in the consecration of all ecclesiastical transactions, as in baptism, clerical ordination, the ordinance of the supper, the religious celebration of marriage, but also in other transactions of life, whether of a more sorrowful or joyful kind ; the feeling, that the Christian's whole life, in sorrow and in joy, should be passed with one constant reference to the redemption, and sanctified thereby. But with most, this resort to the sign of the cross had become a mere mechanical act, in performing which they either were not conscious themselves of the ideas thus symbolized, or else transferred to the outward sign what should have been ascribed to

---

* Athanas. apologia ad Constantium, s. 17. To what profanation of holy things that superstitious reverence for the external signs of the holy was capable of leading, this example may show. Two bishops in Libya, about the year 420, were engaged in a quarrel about the possession of a place which may have been of some importance as a fortified place of refuge from the incursions of the barbarians. To secure this spot for his church, one of them resorted to the following stratagem. He pressed his way in by force, caused an altar to be brought, and consecrated upon it the sacrament of the supper. Now in the opinion of the superstitious multitude the whole place was consecrated, and could no longer be used for any ordinary purpose of social life. Very justly was it remarked by the bishop Synesius, complaining of this transaction to Theophilus, patriarch of Constantinople, that in this way the holiest ordinances could be abused for the accomplishment of the vilest purposes. He said it was not the manner of Christianity, to exhibit the divine as a thing which could be charmed with magical necessity by certain formulas of consecration ; but as something that had its dwelling in the pure and godlike temper of mind : "Ὥστε παρεῖναι ταῖς ἀπαθέσι καὶ ταῖς οἰκείαις τῷ θεῷ διαθέσισιν. Synes. ep. 67, ad Theophilum.

† See vol. I. p. 406.

faith and to the temper of the heart alone, and thus fell into a superstitious veneration of the symbol itself. The cross, hitherto simple and destitute of all ornaments, was now gorgeously decorated, as the altered condition of the church was thought to require, with gold, pearls, and precious stones. The universal use of this symbol is thus described by Chrysostom: "The sign of universal execration, the sign of extremest punishment, has now become the object of universal longing and love. We see it everywhere triumphant: we find it in houses, on the roofs and the walls; in cities and villages; on the market place, the great roads, and in deserts; on mountains and in valleys;* on the sea, on ships; on books and on weapons; on wearing apparel, in the marriage chamber, at banquets, on vessels of gold and of silver, in pearls, in pictures on the walls, on beds; on the bodies of brute animals that are diseased;† on the bodies of those possessed by evil spirits;‡ in the dances of those going to pleasure, and in the associations of those that mortify their bodies."§ Men like Augustin denounced the mere mechanical practice of making the sign of the cross, and, on the other hand, gave prominence to that which it was designed to indicate, the inward bent of the affections, to that which should have a living existence in the temper of the heart. The sign of the cross was to remind believers of the nature of the Christian calling, of their destination to suffer for the cause

* Also on windows,—54 in Matth. s. 4. 'Επὶ τῶν θυρίδων; pavements, too, were laid with signs of the cross; a practice forbidden by the second council of Trulla, 691, c. 73.

† See above, the account of the rhetorician Severus.

‡ It being the intention to expel evil spirits by the power of the cross.

§ See the homily on Christ's divinity, s. 9. T. I. f. 571. We frequently find it mentioned, also, that Christians wore *the sign of the cross on their foreheads*, effingere crucem in fronte, ἐκτυποῦν ἐν τῷ μετώπῳ, portare crucem in fronte;—and in several places, we are to understand by it, or at least may without hazard understand by it, that they frequently made the sign of the cross with the finger on their foreheads. But there are also several places where this explanation does not suffice, and which, perhaps, can be understood in no other sense than that Christians actually imprinted in some way or other, or hung the sign of the cross on their foreheads. Augustin, in Psalm lxxiii. s. 6. Jam in frontibus regum pretiosius est signum crucis, quam gemma diadematis. In Ps. xxxii. Enarrat. III. s. 13, compared with what Chrysostom says, Exposit in Ps. cix. p. 6, T. V. f. 250. Πάντες ἐπὶ τοῦ μετώπου τὸν σταυρὸν περιφέρομεν, οὐ μὴν ἰδιῶται μόνον, ἀλλὰ καὶ αὐτοὶ οἱ τὰ διαδήματα περικείμενοι ὑπὲρ τὰ διαδήματα αὐτὸν βαστάζουσι.

of God, and through sufferings to follow Christ to glory. God wanted not such as described this sign on their foreheads, but such as practised what this sign denoted in their daily lives, such as bore the imitation of Christ's humility in their hearts.*

It was a somewhat different case, where *representations of the human form were employed with religious allusions.* That tendency of the Christian spirit, of which we spoke in the preceding period, still expressed, at the beginning, its opposition to such representations. But as Christianity gradually pressed its way into popular and domestic life, the cases must continually become more frequent, where, in place of the objects of pagan worship, those would be substituted which were dear to the faith and feelings of Christians. Besides this, a change had now taken place in the views and in the taste of the Christians. Those who, at an earlier period, had shrunk from the outward splendour of religion as savouring of Paganism, as opposed to the idea so often mentioned of Christ's appearance in the form of a servant, were, by the altered condition of the church, led rather to wish to see Christianity emblazoned by external pomp; and the conversion of many was of such a kind, that in truth their tendency to materialism in religion merely took another shape and turn. They would fain have, in Christianity too, a religion presented under images of sense. This tendency, the imperial family of the Constantines certainly had to a remarkable degree, and in many things they gave the tone to others. As a substitute for the remains of old pagan art, Constantine lavished on the public monuments with which he embellished the new imperial city, the representations of religious objects taken from the circle of the Old and New Testaments; as, for example, Daniel in the lion's den, Christ under the image of the Good Shepherd.† The sister of this emperor, Constantia, the widow of Licinius, petitioned the bishop Eusebius of Cæsarea for a figure of Christ.

It was not the church-teachers, then, nor the leaders and heads of the communities, but the great mass of the Christians, with whom we reckon also the lofty ones of the earth, that introduced the use of religious images. At Rome, the names of the apostles Peter and Paul being often coupled together as martyrs, and the memory of both celebrated on the same day, it came about, that the figure of Christ, attended by these

* Augustin. p. 302, s. 3. p. 32, s. 13. † Euseb. de v. c. iii. 49.

two apostles, was painted on the walls; a fact by which many of the heathen were misled to suppose that Paul had been chosen among the apostles by Christ during his earthly lifetime.* Images of martyrs, venerated monks, and bishops, were dispersed far and wide.† The Antiochians had the likeness of their deceased bishop Meletius engraven on their signets, and painted on cups, goblets, and on the walls of their chambers.‡ The figure of Abraham offering up Isaac was a favourite subject of Christian art.§ Among the rich and noble men and women in the large cities of the Byzantine empire, Christianity was affected even in the mode of dress; and, as often happens, it was supposed the corrupt inclinations which remained essentially the same, were sanctified by the seemly show of a Christian outside. When it was the fashion for men and women of rank to wear garments on which the whole representation of a chase was embroidered in gold and silver threads, they who made pretensions to piety, on the other hand, chose the representation of the marriage feast at Cana; of the man sick of the palsy, who took up his bed and walked; of the blind man restored to sight; of the woman with the issue of blood; of the Magdalene who embraced the feet of Jesus; of the resurrection of Lazarus. Bedizened with such figures, they supposed—as Austerius, bishop of Amasia, in Pontus, in the last half of the fourth century, asserts—that their dress must be well approved in the sight of God.‖ This excellent church-teacher advises them rather to dispose of such garments for as much as they would bring, and use the avails to honour the *living* images of God; instead of carrying about the sick of the palsy on their garments, rather to look up the actually sick and relieve them; instead of wearing on their bodies a kneeling penitent in embroidery, rather to mourn over their own sins with a penitent spirit.¶

At the same time, we should take pains to distinguish the

* Christus simul cum Petro et Paulo in pictis parietibus. Augustin. de consensu Evangelistarum, l. I. s. 16.

† As, for example, Simeon the Stylite. See above.

‡ Chrysostom. Homil. in Meletium, T. II. f. 519.

§ See Gregor. Nyss. orat. in Abrah. T. III. opp. Paris. 1638, f. 476. Comp. Augustin. c. Faustum, l. XXII. c. 73, tot locis pictum.

‖ Asterius de divite et Lazaro: Ταῦτα ποιοῦντις εὐσέβειν νομίζουσιν, καὶ ἱμάτια κεχαρισμίνα τῷ θιῷ ἀμφιννύσθαι.

¶ See above.

different points of view in which images were regarded by individual church-teachers. If they opposed the use of images in the church, because they feared it would degenerate into an idolatrous veneration ; if they strove to elevate the religion of the senses to that of the spirit ; if they especially rejected the images of Christ on the score of some particular principle of doctrine, yet we are not warranted for these reasons to conclude that they condemned, in general, all representations of religious objects.

Against images of Christ in particular, there might be the more decided opposition, inasmuch as the whole tradition of the church witnessed that no genuine likeness of Christ existed : in fact, the very reason why men resorted so much to symbolical and parabolical representations, in reference to the Saviour and his work, was, that they were conscious of possessing no genuine image of his person.

The strongest to declare himself against images, was Eusebius of Cæsarea, in his letter in reply to Constantia's request for an image of Christ. On the one hand, we observe, still manifesting itself in Eusebius, that aversion to images which was closely connected with the more ancient Christian view of Christ's appearance, and with that sterner opposition to every thing bordering on Paganism ; not less, too, the by no means ungrounded anxiety, lest the devotion of the princess, taking too sensuous a direction, might be turned wholly aside from the essence of Christianity : on the other hand, along with these common traits of Christianity, we see a great deal besides, derived from the peculiar notions in Origen's system of faith, which Eusebius was inclined to favour "What do you understand, may I ask, by an image of Christ?"—says Eusebius. "You can surely mean nothing else but a representation of the earthly form of a servant, which, for man's sake, he for a short time assumed. Even when, *in this*, his divine majesty beamed forth at the transfiguration, his disciples were unable to bear the sight of such glory ; but now the figure of Christ is become wholly deified and spiritualized,— transfigured into a form analogous to his divine nature.[*]

* Πῶς δὲ τῆς οὕτω θαυμαστῆς καὶ ἀλήπτου μόρφης, εἴγε χρὴ μόρφην ἔτι καλεῖν τὴν ἔνθεον καὶ νοεράν οὐσίαν, εἰκόνα τίς ζωγραφήσειεν; We recognize the Origenist. Comp. vol. I. s. 3. Τῆς τοῦ δούλου μόρφης τὸ εἶδος εἰς τὴν δεσπότου καὶ Θεοῦ δόξαν μετεσκευάσθη.

Who, then, has power to draw the image of such a glory, exalted above every earthly form? Who, to represent in lifeless colours the splendour which radiates from such transcendent majesty?* Or could you be satisfied with such an image as the pagans made of their gods and heroes, which bore no resemblance to the thing represented? But if you are not seeking for an image of the transfigured godlike form, but for one of the earthly, mortal body, so as it was constituted before this change, you must have forgotten those passages in the Old Testament, which forbid us to make any image of that which is in heaven above or on the earth beneath. Where have you ever seen any such in the church, or heard of their being there from others? Have not such things (images, therefore, of religious objects) been banished far from the churches over the world?"† He said he once saw in a woman's possession, two figures of men in the garb of philosophers, which she pretended were Christ and Paul. But he made her give them up, lest some scandal might result from them either to herself or to others; lest it might seem that the Christians, like idolaters, carried about their God in an image.‡ Paul, he observed, exhorts all Christians to cleave no longer to the things of sense,§ saying: "Though we have known Christ after the flesh, yet now henceforth know we him thus no longer." The godless sect of the Simonians had an image of Simon Magus; and he himself had seen among the Manicheans a figure of Mani. "But we," he concludes, "who confess that our Lord is God, we must let the whole longing of our hearts be directed to the intuition of him in his divine character; we must therefore cleanse our hearts with all earnestness, since none but the pure in heart can see God. Still, should any one be anxious to see an image of the Saviour, instead of beholding him face to face, what better could we have, than that which he himself has drawn in the sacred writings?"‖ Thus, a truer image of Christ could be

* Τίς δ' οὖν τῆς τοσαυτῆς ἀξίας τε καὶ δόξης τὰς ἀποστιλβούσας καὶ ἀπαστραπτούσας μαρμαρυγὰς οἷος τε ἂν εἴη καταχαράξαι νεκροῖς καὶ ἀψύχοις χρώμασι καὶ σκιογραφίαις.

† Οὐχὶ δὲ καθ' ὅλης τῆς οἰκουμένης ἐξώρισται καὶ πόρρω τῶν ἐκκλησιῶν πεφυγάδευται τοιαῦτα;

‡ Ἵνα μὴ δοκῶμεν δίκην εἰδωλολατρούντων τὸν θεὸν ἡμῶν ἐν εἴκονι περιφέρειν.

§ Παύλου τε ἀκούω ἡμᾶς παιδεύοντος, μήκετι τοῖς σαρκίκοις προσανέχειν.

‖ A fragment of this letter is preserved among the transactions of the

found in the exhibition of his life, as recorded in the gospel history, than in the representation of his bodily form. The manner in which Eusebius speaks, in his church history, concerning the busts of Christ, which it was said the woman cured of the issue of blood at Cæsarea Philippi had made, as a memorial of her gratitude to Christ; and the manner in which he there speaks of other ancient images of Christ and of Paul, perfectly accord with the views expressed by him in the present letter: for in this latter passage also, he considers it as a pagan way of expressing reverence to the benefactors of mankind.*

In respect to Asterius, his polemical attacks were directed, as may be gathered from the passages already cited, not so much against the use of religious images generally, as against that pomp and display, which, to the injury of active Christian charity, followed in its train. Yet even he expressed his disapprobation on the same grounds with Eusebius, particularly of images to represent Christ; and maintained that men ought not to renew and multiply the servant-form which Christ once, during the days of his flesh, voluntarily assumed for the salvation of mankind. "Bear," said he, "the Logos, who is a spirit, in a spiritual manner, within your souls."† In these views of Eusebius and Asterius there was manifestly, however, something of a one-sided character. They betray, in part, the restricted notions peculiar to the earlier Christian period, of Christ's servant-form; and in part they show a certain Neo-Platonic contempt of the body. The earthly human nature of Christ was not recognized here in the profound meaning which it must and should have for the Christian feelings: for to these, every thing that pertains to the purely human nature, even now,

---

council of Iconoclasts at Constantinople, A.D. 754; and from these it has been adopted into the sixth action of the seventh œcumenical council, or of the second council of Nice, A.D. 787. More of it has been published by Boivin, in the remarks on the second volume of Nicephorus Gregoras, f. 795.

* "Ὡς εἰκὸς τῶν παλαίων ἀπαραφυλάκτως οἷα σωτῆρας ἐθνικῇ συνηθείᾳ παρ' ἑαυτοῖς τούτον τιμᾶν εἰωθότων τὸν τρόπον. Euseb. VII. c. 18.

† "Ἀρκεῖ γὰρ αὐτῷ ἡ μία τῆς ἐνσωματώσεως ταπεινοφροσύνη, ἣν αὐθαιρετῶς δι' ἡμᾶς κατεδέξατο. Ἐπὶ δὲ τῆς ψυχῆς σου βαστάζων νοητῶς τὸν ἀσώματον λόγον περίφερε. Respecting the connection of these views with the peculiar form of his system of faith, see below, in the fourth section.

in its present earthly form, has been sanctified and ennobled by Christ; and on this side, the universal Christian feeling would naturally plead in favour of the images of Christ against their opponents; although, on the other side, the truly evangelical direction of these latter, which points away from the sensible to the spiritual Christ, communicating himself in spiritual fellowship, is not to be mistaken. With this tendency, Asterius could nevertheless approve of the pictures of suffering martyrs, and speak with lively interest of the impression which a picture of this sort had made on himself.*

In the same sense in which Asterius spoke against those who were in the habit of displaying on their dress the representation of sacred stories as a mark of piety, in this same sense another church-teacher, near the close of the fourth century, Amphilochius, bishop of Iconium in Phrygia, rebuked those whose piety consisted in multiplying dead images of the saints, instead of copying their example in the practice of Christian virtues.† Thus, too, Chrysostom agrees with Eusebius in disclaiming all knowledge of a sensuous image of Christ, but ever speaking of Christ's moral image alone in the copying of his holy walk, or pointing away to the intuition of Christ glorified in the eternal life. In respect to the former, he remarks: "Teach the soul to form a mouth which is like the mouth of Christ; for she can form such a one if she will. And how is this to be done? By what colours? By what materials? By no colours, no materials; but only by virtue, by meekness, and humility. How many are there amongst us who wish to see his form? Behold we can not only see him, but also be like him, if we are really in earnest."‡ And with regard to the latter he says, after having spoken of the majesty of Christ's appearance: "Perhaps you are now seized with the desire of beholding that image. But if we *will*, we may see a far better one."§ The same spirit is manifest also in Augustin, as when he says: "Let us hear the gospel with such a mind, as if we saw the Lord present before us; and

---

* See his discourse on the martyrdom of Euphemia.

† Οὐ γὰρ τοῖς πίναξι τὰ σάρκικα προσώπα τῶν ἀγίων διὰ χρωμάτων ἐπιμελὲς ἡμῖν ἐντυποῦν, ὅτι οὐ χρῆζομεν τουτῶν, ἀλλὰ τὴν πολιτείαν, αὐτῶν δι' ἀρετῆς ἐκμιμεῖσθαι. See this fragment in the VI. act. of the second Nicene council.

‡ In Matth. H. 78, vel 79, s. 4.   § In Matth. H. 27, vel 28, s. 2.

let us not say to ourselves, ' Blessed are they who could see him ;' since many among those who saw him have perished ; but many among us who have not seen him, believe on him. The Lord is above ; but here, too, in the very midst of us, is the Lord of truth."*

In the course of the fourth century, men began, by degrees, to decorate the churches also with images—a practice, however, which did not become general until near the close of this century.† Men of wealth and rank who founded churches, wished them to be set out with all the embellishments of art, and so, too, with the rich ornament of pictures ; and, in particular, the churches dedicated to the memory of martyrs were adorned with the representations of their sufferings, and with pictures from the historical parts of the Old and New Testaments. When, on the festivals of the martyrs, great multitudes of the people flocked to these churches, these paintings were to serve the purpose of entertaining, touching, edifying, and instructing the rude and ignorant, who could not be instructed and edified by means of books.‡ Still, many influential voices were heard objecting to the superfluity of picture ornaments ; and others, against the use of them at all in the churches. A respectable man at Constantinople, who wished to erect a church in memory of the martyrs, conceived the plan of ornamenting it with various pictures from nature, which perhaps were to have some symbolical meaning, and also with many signs of the cross. But the pious Monk Nilus, a worthy disciple of Chrysostom, to whom he communicated his design, advised him to be sparing of picture ornaments : it was a childish thing, said he, to dissipate the eyes and atten-

---

* In Evang. Joh. Tract. 30, s. 4.

† In the sermons delivered by Chrysostom at Constantinople, as well as at Antioch, there is not to be found—though he frequently alludes in his figures, metaphors, and comparisons, to the manners and customs of his time—any reference to images in the churches. Montfaucon, indeed, supposed that he found such an allusion in the H. 10, Ephes. s. 2, but wrongly ; for, in this place, Chrysostom is speaking, not of the visible but of the invisible church,—of the pillars in this according to a spiritual sense ; and in truth he there compares the invisible church, not with a splendid *church edifice*, in which case unquestionably we should find an allusion here to images in the churches, but with the palace of a lord, which is ornamented with columns and statues.

‡ See Paulinus of Nola, carmen IX. et X. de S. Felicis natali.

tion of the faithful by such objects.* Instead of this, he
should erect in the sanctuary, and in each compartment of the
nave of the church, a single cross, and decorate the church
with paintings of stories from the Old and New Testaments;
so that those who could not read the sacred scriptures themselves might be reminded, by looking at the paintings, of
those examples of piety, and thus excited to imitate them.
He ought to abstain from all superfluities, and seek rather,
by fervent prayer, by steadfast faith, by invincible hope in
God, by alms, humility, *study of the* holy scriptures, compassion towards his fellow-men, kindness to *servants*, and observance of all the commands of the Lord, to adorn and to preserve himself and all his family.† When the aged bishop,
Epiphanius of Salamis, or Constantia, in the isle of Cyprus,
in making a visit to Jerusalem, came to a church in one of
the neighbouring villages, and there found on a curtain a
human image, whether it was of some representation of Christ
or of a saint, he immediately rent the cloth, expressing great
indignation. It was contrary, said he, to the authority of
holy scripture, that the image of a man should be hung up in
a Christian church.‡ The cloth would be in better use to
shroud the body of some poor man. This arbitrary proceeding having excited dissatisfaction, after his return he sent to
the parish priest of the church another curtain, to replace the
one he had torn down, and called upon the bishop John of
Jerusalem to see to it that for the future no such church-
hangings, so contradictory to the Christian religion, should
be used.§ We see in this the pious, indeed, but impatient
and narrow zeal which characterized this man generally.
Had he better understood the spirit of the Old Testament
command, and been capable of duly distinguishing from each
other the Old and the New Testament economies, he would
not have been so greatly excited by what he saw. Still, however, it was the way of thinking of the ancient church, which

---

* Νηπιῶδες καὶ βρεφοπρέπες, τὸ τοῖς προλεχθεῖσιν περιπλανῆσαι τὸν
ὀφθαλμὸν τῶν πίστων.

† Nil. l. IV. ep. 61.

‡ Detestatus in ecclesia Christi, contra auctoritatem scripturarum, hominis pendere imaginem.

§ Quæ contra religionem nostram veniunt. See ep. 51, Hieronym.
ejusd. opera ed. Vallarsi, t. I. f. 252.

he followed out in this case; and at all events it is to be remarked that it was not the *principle,* as it seems, on which he proceeded here, but simply his arbitrary *mode* of proceeding, which excited opposition.* But, without much question, this zeal of pious men is justified, when we reflect how easily the prevailing spirit of piety, which was directed on sensible and outward things, might betray the rude multitude, who were to be gradually weaned from Paganism to the superstitious veneration of images; especially, as the excessive reverence paid to saints would soon be transferred also to their pictures, and as reports of the marvellous effects produced by the images which men were accustomed to regard with peculiar veneration, as also by the reliques of the saints, soon became widely spread.

Augustin, as early as the last times of the fourth century, was forced to complain of the fact that many worshippers of images were to be found among the rude Christian multitude†

* The council of the Iconoclasts at Constantinople cited several writings of Epiphanius against images, in which he maintained that they ought to be used neither in the church, nor at the cemeteries of the martyrs, nor in private dwellings; but the genuineness of these pieces is extremely liable to suspicion. As well the enemies as the friends of images indulged themselves in fabricating writings under ancient venerated names, in favour of their respective principles. The friends of Images appealed to the fact that these writings, ascribed to Epiphanius, had remained hitherto unknown to everybody. And though this cannot be considered a decisive proof against their genuineness, yet these fragments bear on their face many marks of having been fabricated. The first cited words of Epiphanius (Concil. Nic. ii. actio vi. Concil. ed. Harduin. T. IV. f. 390) correspond, in fact, too nearly with the ordinary modes of expression among the enemies of images in the period. Next occurs a letter of Epiphanius to the emperor Theodosius, f. 391, in which he writes to him, that he had often called on his colleagues to abolish the images, but they would not listen a moment to his representations. It is hardly probable, however, that at this early period Epiphanius would have found any occasion for resorting to the authority of an emperor against the images; and this very incident with John, bishop of Jerusalem, renders it improbable that Epiphanius, in his declarations against the images, could have found at that time so violent a resistance. It should rather seem that the enemies of images in the eighth century fabricated, in this case also, occurrences of an earlier period, corresponding to what was done in their own time. Probably that single incident in the life of Epiphanius which has been related, was the occasion of such writings being forged in his name.

† Novi multos esse picturarum adoratores. De moribus ecclesiæ catholicæ, l. 1. s. 75.

—which worship of images the Manicheans laid as a reproach against the whole church; .but he reckoned those image-wor-shippers as belonging to the great mass of nominal Christians to whom the essence of Christianity was unknown.[*]

In the Western church this modern tendency, between unconditional opposition to images and image-worship, main-tained itself till late into the following period ; as we see, for example, in the case of the Roman bishop, Gregory the Great, with whom we shall begin the next following period.

But this moderate tendency did not so maintain itself in the Eastern church. Here the progress was rapid from one step to another. The spirit of the East, prone to excess in the expression of feelings; its more lively, warm imagination; its confounding of the sign with the thing represented; its predominant artistic sense; all this brought it about at an early period in the Oriental church, that not only *the multi-tude* passed from the use of images to the worship of them, but even the church-teachers suffered themselves to be carried along by the prevailing spirit, and sought to defend their course on scientific grounds. In the course of the sixth cen-tury, it was already a ruling custom in the Greek church for persons to prostrate themselves before images as a token of reverence to those represented by them (the προσκύνησις). Already did the Jews lay hold of this prevailing worship of images to accuse the Christians of apostacy from the divine law, which forbade the use of images in religion, and of idola-try. Leontius, bishop of Neapolis, in the isle of Cyprus, who, near the end of the sixth century, wrote an apology for Christianity and for the Christian church, against the accusa-tions of the Jews, was forced already to pay particular atten-tion to these charges. What remains to us of this writing [†] is of importance, as giving us information respecting the character of the veneration paid to images in this period, and respecting the light in which this practice was regarded by those who expressed with consciousness the prevailing spirit of the times.

He maintains, against the Jews, that the Mosaic law was

---

[*] Professores nominis Christiani nec professionis suæ vim aut scientes aut exhibentes.

[†] The fragments in the fourth action of the second Nicene council. Harduin. Concil. IV. f. 194.

not directed unconditionally against all devotional use of images, but only against the idolatrous use of them; since, in fact, the tabernacle and the temple both had their images. But from the idolatrous adoration of images, the Christians were assuredly far removed. They showed, in the sign of the cross, their love and reverence towards Christ, who was represented by it, in accordance with a principle grounded in human nature. As affectionate children, whose father is on a journey, if they do but see his coat, his hair, or his mantle in the house, embrace every such article and kiss it with tears, so, too, we believers, out of transcendent love to Christ, reverence everything which he did but touch; and for this reason we represent the symbol of his passion in churches, in houses and shops, in the market place, on the articles of clothing; so that we may have it constantly before our eyes, and may be reminded of it, and not forget it, as the Jews have forgotten their God. He argues that in the Old Testament the ceremony of prostration sometimes occurs as a mark of respect even to men, and therefore could not by any means imply the notion of idolatry. He refers to the cures said to have been wrought on energumens by means of images;— and indeed it may easily be conceived that the impression made on the imagination and feelings by the sight of such objects might, in the case of diseases of this sort, arising from the peculiar nervous system and disposition of the individual, produce extraordinary effects. In the same manner may be explained also what he says about the sudden conversions wrought by the sight of images, as evidence of the virtue residing in them;—that, in almost every part of the world, abandoned men, murderers, robbers, profligates, idolaters, were every day, by the sight of the cross, awakened to conviction, and not only so, but led to renounce the world and practise every virtue. All which, though rhetorically overwrought, yet cannot be pure fabrication, but was probably drawn from some few individual examples in which rude minds, by the sight of the cross or of other images, were suddenly overpowered, and quit a life wholly abandoned to sin for penitence in Monachism. But it may indeed be a question whether the crisis to which men were brought by sudden impressions of this sort had not been prepared long beforehand, and whether the effect produced was of a permanent cha-

racter. To that which really occurred, the ready imagination
of the East now added a great deal that never happened.
Thus arose the stories about miraculous images, from which
blood had been seen to trickle. Such facts, also, Leontius
adduces in defending the worship of images.* Summing all
together, he says : " The images are not our gods ; but they
are the images of Christ and his saints, which exist and are
venerated in remembrance and in honour of these, and as
ornaments of the churches." † We see here how closely the
veneration paid to images was connected with the whole Oriental mode of intuition ; how this expression of reverence by
no means amounted to so much, at the beginning, among the
Orientals, as the same ceremony would have done among the
people of the West, whose colder temperament was less inclined to any violent expression of the feelings. So much the
more dangerous, however, would this tendency of the Oriental
spirit to sensualize everything threaten to become to Christianity, if the prevailing spirit of Christianity had not opposed
to it, as it did at the beginning, a sufficient counterpoise.
Yet even in this century there are still to be found the ves-
tiges of an opposition, growing out of the purely Christian
spirit, against the spreading superstition. The respectable
Monophysite church-teacher, Xenayas, or Philoxenos, bishop
of Hierapolis, in Syria, in the early times of the sixth century,
decidedly opposed the representations of angels in the human
form, and the representation of the Holy Ghost in the shape
of a dove ; doubtless led to it by the rude sensuous notions
which were attached to these symbols. He said men should
not think they honoured Christ through the images of Christ ;
no worship was pleasing to him but the worship in spirit and
in truth. Such images, with which a superstitious reverence
had probably become connected, he removed from the churches.‡

We now proceed to consider the seasons for divine worship
and the festivals.

---

* Πολλάκις αἱμάτων ῥύσεις ἐξ εἰκόνων γεγόνασι.

† Πρὸς ἀνάμνησιν καὶ τιμὴν καὶ εὐπρεπείαν ἐκκλησίων προκείμενα καὶ προσ-
κυνούμενα.

‡ So relates the monophysite historian, John the Schismatic, 'Ιωάννης
ὁ διακοινόμενος, in his church history, from which a fragment has been
preserved in the fifth action of the second Nicene council. Harduin.
Concil. IV. f. 306.

3. *Seasons for holding Divine Worship and Festivals.*

Although the habit of confounding the Old and New Testament points of view had already in various ways, as we have seen in the earlier sections, struck deeply into the church life, yet the most distinguished church-teachers of this period continued still to express the purely Christian idea of the relation of the festivals to the whole Christian life, which, as we remarked in the preceding period, had first grown out of Christianity in its opposition to Judaism. Thus Jerome asserts,[*] that, considered from the purely Christian point of view, all days are alike, every day is for the Christian a Friday, to be consecrated by the remembrance of Christ crucified; every day a Sunday, since on every day he could solemnize in the communion the fellowship with Christ though risen. But festivals and meetings for divine worship at stated seasons were instituted for the good of those who were not yet capable of rising to this position, who were not yet so minded or so disciplined as every day of their life, before engaging in the business of the world, to offer God the sacrifice of prayer. Chrysostom delivered a discourse at Antioch, in which he showed that those who never attended church, except on the principal festivals, adopted the Jewish point of view; that on the other hand, the Christian celebration of festivals was not necessarily restricted to certain times, but embraced the whole life grounded in faith, and that this was so, he endeavoured to demonstrate from the nature and design of the principal Christian festivals. " Our first feast," said he, " is the feast of Christ's appearance (the Epiphany, τὰ ἐπιφάνια). What then is the object of this feast? To show that God appeared on earth and dwelt with men; that the only-begotten Son of God was with us. *But he is ever with us.* We may then every day celebrate the feast of Christ's appearance. What is the meaning of the feast of the passover? We then announce the Lord's death. But this too we do not signify merely at one stated season, for when Paul would free us from being confined to stated times, he showed that it was possible continually to celebrate the passover, and said, ' As often as ye eat

---

[*] L. II. ep. ad Galat. c. iv. ed. Martianay, T. IV. f. 272.

this bread and drink this cup, ye do show forth the Lord's death.' And what is the import of the feast of Pentecost? That the Spirit has visited us. Now as *Christ* is ever with us, so the Holy Spirit too is ever with us ; we may then continually celebrate also the feast of Pentecost."* In like manner, the church historian Socrates remarks, that Christ and the apostles, conformably to Christian freedom, gave no law respecting feasts, but left everything open here to the free expression of the feelings. The diversity that existed in the celebration of festivals among the Christian churches of different countries he traces to this very fact, that everything here had from the beginning, with perfect freedom and by slow degrees, spontaneously shaped itself after different ways.† In the principle lying at the basis of the state laws on this point, and from which many of the arrangements of the Roman church proceeded, we do, indeed, perceive already the predominance of Jewish notions, which had repressed the original Christian consciousness.

The reference to Christ crucified, arisen, and glorified, continued to be, as in the preceding period, the central point of the weekly and of the yearly festivals and fast-days. The celebration of the *dies stationum*, of Wednesday and of Friday, respecting the origin of which we have spoken in the preceding period, passed over into this, but was observed only iu several of the churches, and in these not after the same manner. Socrates mentions it as a peculiarity of the Alexandrian church, that on Wednesday and on Friday,‡ the holy scriptures were there read in the church and expounded by homilies, and in general the whole service conducted as on Sunday, the celebration of the communion excepted. This custom probably vanished by degrees in most of the churches,§

---

* In Pentecost. h. 1. s. 1, T. f. 458.   † Socrat. V. 22.

‡ On the τίτρας and on the παρασκιύη. Respecting the service which was held at Alexandria on Friday morning, see Athanas. hist. Arianor. ad monachos, s. 81. Συνάξις τῇ παρασκιύῃ.

§ Yet Epiphanius, in his exposit. fid. cathol. c. 22, still mentions fasting on the τίτρας and on the προτάββατον as a universal custom of the church. Also in the churches of Milan, it seems to have been the custom to assemble on these days about noon, sing together, and partake of the communion, and with this terminated the fast. Ambros. expositio in Psalm 118, s. 48, in case we are to understand the plerique dies in this passage, as we probably should, to refer to the dies stationum. Accord-

only Friday continued to be consecrated to the memory of Christ's passion. The emperor Constantine, as Sozomen relates,[*] enacted a law that on Friday, as on Sunday, there should be a suspension of business at the courts and in other civil offices, so that the day might be devoted with less interruption to the purposes of devotion.[†] At Antioch the communion was celebrated on Friday as well as on Sunday.[‡] Also at Constantinople Friday was observed by the more serious Christians as a day of penitence and fasting, consecrated to the memory of Christ's passion,[§] and the sacrament of the supper was distributed. It is true the great mass of the citizens took no concern in it, as we learn from a discourse of Chrysostom's,[||] complaining of the people because while he, with a few who had met with him, were rendering thanks to God on a Friday, for deliverance from threatening famine; most of them had flocked to the public games of the circus.

We noticed in the preceding period the origin of the difference which prevailed as to the celebration of the Sabbath. The custom, derived from the Jews, of paying a certain respect to the Sabbath still continued to be handed down in the *Oriental* communities.[¶] In several of the Eastern churches the Sabbath was celebrated nearly after the same manner as Sunday. Church assemblies were held, sermons delivered, and the communion celebrated on this day.[**] The

ing to Epiphanius, these assemblies convened about three o'clock in the afternoon. [*] L. 8.

[†] This may have stood in the law, which has not been preserved to our times, by which Constantine ordered this in respect to Sunday already before the year 321. See cod. Theodos. l. II. Tit. VIII., l. I.

[‡] See Chrysostom, hom. 5, in epist. i. ad Timoth. s. 3.

[§] Chrysostom. h. in the sermon first published by Montfaucon, T. VI. f. 272, s. 1. Ἡμέρα, ἐν ᾗ νηστεύειν καὶ ὁμολόγειν ἔδει.

[||] The one just referred to.

[¶] In the apostolic constitutions, II. 59, the Sabbath is particularly mentioned along with Sunday as a day for the assembling together of the church; VIII. c. 33, that on the Sabbath and on Sunday the slaves should rest from their labours, and attend church with the rest to hear the sermon. L. V. 15, that the Easter Sabbath excepted, there should be no fasting on the Sabbath, when God rested from the work of creation. The 66, among the apostolic canons, excludes from the fellowship of the church those who fasted on the Sabbath and on Sunday.

[**] As it concerns the last at Antioch, see the passage referred to above respecting Friday.

direction given by the council of Laodicea deserves to be
noticed,* viz. : that on the Sabbath, the gospels should be read
along with the other parts of the holy scriptures.   It may be
that the new arrangement which this council designed to introduce by the above-cited canon was simply that the scriptures
generally should be read in church on the Sabbath in the same
manner as on Sunday ; and in this case we must suppose the
council wished to restore the custom, formerly observed, of
assembling for worship on the Sabbath as well as on Sunday,
which had now become obsolete in many of the Eastern
churches.   Or this ordinance may be understood as simply
indicating the design of the council, that in the meetings for
divine worship on the Sabbath the gospels should be read,
together with other parts of the holy scriptures ; whence we
might infer that, as the celebration of the Sabbath had been
taken from the Jews, it had been the custom also to make use
of the *Old Testament only* on this day in the church lessons.†
In many districts a punctual Jewish observance of the Sabbath
must doubtless have become common, hence the council of
Laodicea considered it necessary to ordain that Christians should
not celebrate this day after the Jewish manner, nor consider
themselves bound to abstain from labour.‡   It was a general
rule in the Eastern church that there should be no fasting on
the Sabbath, hence the Sabbath also, as well as Sunday, was
excepted from the period of fasting before Easter.§   But in
many of the Western churches, particularly in the Roman and
the Spanish, opposition to the Jews and Judaists‖ had led to the

* C. 16. Περὶ τοῦ ἐν σαββάτῳ εὐαγγέλια μετὰ ἑτέρων γραφῶν ἀναγινωσκίσθαι.

† It is an objection to the last interpretation, that both εὐαγγέλια and
ἑτέρων γραφῶν stand without the article ; accordingly do not express here
any antithesis ; but the whole of the sacred writings, according to their
different parts, seems to be indicated here generally.   Moreover, if such
an antithesis had been intended, instead of ἑτέρων γραφῶν, the phrase
παλαίας διαθήκης would doubtless have been used.   But the difficulty
with the first interpretation is, that the customary celebration of the
Sabbath is everywhere presupposed by this council, and they considered
themselves bound rather to moderate the Judaizing tendency to carry
this celebration to an extreme.

‡ C. 29. Ὅτι οὐ δεῖ χριστιανοὺς ἰουδαΐζειν καὶ ἐν τῷ σαββάτῳ σχολάζειν.

§ Hence, by the decrees of the council of Laodicea, c. 49 and 51, the
communion and the commemoration of the martyrs might be celebrated,
during the period of fasting, on the Sabbath as well as on Sunday.

‖ See vol. I. p. 408.

custom of observing the Sabbath rather as a day of fasting.* They who were truly enlightened by the gospel spirit, and knew how to distinguish essentials from non-essentials in religion, such men as Ambrose of Milan, Jerome, and Augustin, sought to avoid all controversy on matters of this sort which had not been decided by divine authority, and which had no particular connection with the essence of faith and of sanctification. They held it as a principle, that, in such matters, each individual should follow the custom of his own church, or of the country in which he resided, and strive that the bond of charity might not be broken by differences in such unimportant matters, and that occasion of offence might not be given to any man. Ambrose, when questioned on this point, replied that at Rome he was accustomed to fast on the Sabbath, but in Milan he did not. Augustin rightly applies the rules given by Paul, in the fourteenth chapter of the epistle to the Romans, to this diversity of practice. He complains that weak minds were disturbed by the controversial obstinacy or the superstitious scruples of many who would insist on that practice as being the only right one, for which they supposed they had found certain reasons, no matter how weak, or which they had brought with them as the ecclesiastical usage of *their own* country, or which they had seen in foreign lands, although neither the holy scriptures nor the universal tradition of the church decided any thing as to the point, and although it was a matter of perfect indifference as to any practical advantage.† But that rigid hierarchical spirit of the Roman church, which from a very early period required uniformity in things unessential, would in this case also put a

* See Cassian. institut. cœnobial. l. III. c. 9 et 10. Hieronym. ep. 71 ad Lucinium, s. 6.

† Ep. 54 ad Januarium, s. 3. Sensi sæpe dolens et gemens multas infirmorum perturbationes fieri per quorundam fratrum contentiosam obstinationem vel superstitiosam timiditatem, qui in rebus hujusmodi, quæ neque scripturæ sanctæ auctoritate, neque universalis ecclesiæ traditione, neque vitæ corrigendæ utilitate, ad certum possunt terminum pervenire (tantum quia subest qualiscunque ratiocinatio cogitantis, aut quia in sua patria sic ipse consuevit, aut quia ibi vidit, ubi peregrinationem suam, quo remotiorem a suis, eo doctiorem factam putat), tam litigiosas excitant quæstiones, ut, nisi quod ipsi faciunt, nihil rectum existiment. To this point of dispute, the two beautiful letters of Augustin relate, the one just cited, and ep. 36 ad Casulanum.

restraint on religious freedom. In the Roman church it was affirmed that this custom came down from Peter, the first of the apostles, and hence ought to be universally observed. The idle tale was there set afloat, when the origin of that custom from the old opposition between the originally pagan and the originally Jewish communities was no longer known, that the apostle Peter instituted a fast on the Sabbath, in preparing for the dispute with Simon Magus.* The Roman bishop Innocent decided, in his decretals addressed to the Spanish bishop Decentius (at the very time that men like Augustin expressed themselves with so much liberality on this difference), that the Sabbath, like Friday, must be observed as a fast day.† In defence of this rule he offered a better reason at least than those monks, viz.: that, in its historical import, the Sabbath necessarily belonged to the period of sorrow which preceded Sunday, the joyful day of the feast of the resurrection, since on both the former days the apostles were plunged in grief, and on the Sabbath had hid themselves for fear.

As to the celebration of Sunday, the custom, which had long prevailed in the church, of consecrating this day in a special manner to religious employments, and of abstaining from all worldly business, was established by a synodal law, the twenty-ninth canon of the council of Laodicea, yet with this restriction, that all Christians should abstain from their worldly business if they were able.‡ A collision betwixt this ecclesiastical ordinance and the relations to the state, which must have arisen in the earlier situation of the church, could now be easily removed, when the state itself recognized the church as such, and endeavoured to uphold her in the prose-

---

* That Roman spirit expresses itself after a characteristic manner in the following language of a treatise which was probably composed by some member of the Roman clergy, and was intended to procure the general recognition of the Roman custom: Petrus, apostolorum caput, cœli janitor et ecclesiæ fundamentum, extincto Simone, qui diaboli fuerat, nonnisi jejunis vincendi figura (that Simon Magus could be vanquished by Peter only through fasting, was represented as a typical allusion to the fact, that Satan also, whom Simon Magus represented, could be conquered only by fasting), id ipsum Romanos edocuit, quorum fides annuntiatur universo orbi terrarum.

† S. 7. Sabbato jejunandum esse ratio evidentissima demonstrat.

‡ Εἴγε δυναίντο σχολάζειν.

cution of her principles and the attainment of her ends. We
have already said, that the emperor Constantine, in a law
enacted previous to the year 321, commanded the suspension
of all suits and courts of justice on Sunday. It was a beautiful exception, wholly in accordance with the spirit of Christianity, by which he provided that the emancipation of slaves,
after the usual forms, should be permitted to take place on
Sunday.* As Eusebius, in his life of Constantine, relates, he
also forbad all military exercises on this day.† By a law of
the year 386, those older changes effected by the emperor
Constantine were more rigorously enforced, and, in general,
civil transactions of every kind on Sunday were strictly forbidden. Whoever transgressed was to be considered, in fact,
as guilty of sacrilege (as a sacrilegus). ‡

Owing to the prevailing passion at that time, especially in
the large cities, to run after the various public shows, it so
happened, that when these spectacles fell on the same days
which had been consecrated by the church to some religious
festival, they proved a great hindrance to the devotion of
Christians, though chiefly, it must be allowed, to those whose
Christianity was the least an affair of the life and of the heart.
Church teachers, such as Chrysostom (see above) were, in
truth, often forced to complain, that in such competitions the
theatre was vastly more frequented than the church. And
among those who gave up the church for the theatre, many
might be found not wholly unsusceptible of right feelings,
who, if they had not been hurried along by the prevailing
corruption, would have employed Sunday in a way more
serious and more healthful for their inner life. Moreover, by
the civil relations of those times, many were obliged, on
account of their particular place among the citizens, to take
part in the arrangements necessary for the support of the
public shows, and so to be interrupted in their devotions even
against their will. Hence, the North-African church resolved,
at an ecclesiastical convention held at Carthage in 401, to
petition the emperor, that the public shows might be transferred from the Christian Sunday and from feast days to some
other days of the week.§ Owing to the prevailing passion for

* L. II. Tit. VIII. l. I.: † Euseb. vit. Constantin. IV. 18, 19, 20.
‡ Cod. Theodos. lib. VIII. Tit. VIII. l. 3.
§ It is adduced as a reason: Populi ad circum magis quam ad

the shows, this petition could not be granted, perhaps, without considerable difficulty. First, in the year 425, the exhibition of spectacles on Sunday, and on the principal feast days of the Christians, was forbidden, in order that the devotion of the faithful might be free from all disturbance.* In this way the church received help from the state for the furtherance of her ends, which could not be obtained in the preceding period. But had it not been for that confusion of spiritual and secular interests; had it not been for the vast number of mere *outward conversions* thus brought about, she would have needed no such help. The spirit of church fellowship could effect more in those ancient times than all which the outward force of political law and a stricter church discipline could now do, towards restraining or expelling such as had never been brought to feel the inward power of that spirit; and the church of those times could well dispense, therefore, with the outward support.

In respect to the yearly festivals, those still continued, at first, to be universally observed, which answered to the weekly feast-days; for, as we observed in the preceding period, the circle of yearly feasts had sprung out of that of the weekly feasts, and both had arisen from the same fundamental idea, around which the whole Christian life revolved.† Hence, Augustin, about the year 400, still mentions, as the celebrations recognized in the whole church, only those of Christ's passion and resurrection, of his ascension, and of the outpouring of the Holy Ghost.‡

ecclesiam conveniunt,—and on the score of those obligations devolving on many classes of citizens: Nec oportere quemquam Christianorum cogi ad hæc spectacula, maxime, quia in his exercendis, quæ contra præcepta Dei sunt, nulla persecutionis necessitas a quopiam adhibenda est; sed, uti oportet, homo in libera voluntate subsistat sibi divinitus concessa. Cod. can. eccles. Afr. c. 61.

* Totæ Christianorum ac fidelium mentes Dei cultibus occupentur. Cod. Theodos. l. XV. Tit. VII. l. 5.

† This was acknowledged even by the Roman bishop Innocentius, and from this very fact he inferred, that as fasting was practised not merely on Good Friday, but on the Friday of each week, the same practice should be observed also in respect to the Sabbath. (L. c. s. 7. Quod si putant semel atque uno sabbato jejunandum; ergo et Dominica et sexta feria semel in Pascho erit utique celebranda.)

‡ Quæ toto terrarum orbe servantur,—quod Domini passio et resurrectio et adscensio in cœlum et adventus de cœlo Spiritus Sancti anni-

The difference of views with regard to the feast of the passover, which we had occasion to notice in the preceding period, continued to exist also in this; but men were wise enough not to allow the bond of Christian fellowship to be ruptured by this difference.* Yet the spirit of church uniformity which sprung up in the West, sought to insinuate itself also here. The council of Arles, in 314, already decreed that the paschal feast should be celebrated on the same day throughout the world ;† but this ecclesiastical assembly, to which the people of the East paid little attention, had no such great and general influence as to be able to triumph over the old Asiatic custom. Now, to the emperor Constantine it seemed scandalous, that the commemoration of the fact which laid the foundation for the recovery of mankind should not be celebrated by all Christians on the same day ; and that, while some were fasting, others should be feasting. To him, such a difference would perhaps appear more grave, and less compatible with the unity of the Catholic church, than an important dogmatical difference, known by him to exist about this time, in respect to the doctrine of Christ's divinity. He attempted, first through the negotiations of Hosius, bishop of Cordova, to bring the churches together in one usage. In this, however, he did not succeed ; he therefore convoked, partly for this object, the general council of Nice, in 325. As the reason which, in earlier times, had led to the Oriental custom, and which especially contributed to preserve it, viz., the adherence to Judaism, no longer existed,—but, on the contrary, a polemical tendency, in opposition to the Jewish spirit, rather predominated,—this change in the way of thinking would naturally lead to the laying aside of the ancient custom. ‡ Accordingly, an agreement was entered into, at this council, to abandon the old Jewish custom, and to celebrate the remembrance of Christ's passion always on Friday ; the

---

versaria solennitate celebrantur, ep. 54 ad Januar., and the passage above referred to from Hieronym. comment. ep. ad Galat. l. II. c. 4.

* Sozom. I. 16.   † C. 1.

‡ This reason, that it was so disgraceful a thing for the Christian church to govern itself by the pattern of the unbelieving Jews, who had crucified the Lord, is made particularly prominent therefore by the emperor, μηδὲν ἔστω ἡμῖν κοινὸν μετὰ τοῦ ἐχθίστου τῶν Ἰουδαίων ὄχλου. See Euseb. de vita Constantini, l. III. c. 18.

remembrance of Christ's resurrection on Sunday. It was acknowledged that, by the sacrifice of Christ for mankind, the feast of the passover had lost its significance; that the thanksgiving for the sacrifice of Christ in the sacrament of the supper had taken the place of the passover, and that the former was restricted to no particular time.* But, as it usually happens, there were still many communities and individuals in the East who refused to depart from the old traditional custom, on account of its very antiquity, without assigning any further reason for their refusal. Instead of winning them over by love, the church excluded them from her communion.† Persecution made the old custom still dearer to them; they accused the Nicene council of having altered it out of flattery to Constantine.

The council of Nice, it is true, had decreed ‡ that the feast of the passover should, for the future, be celebrated on one and the same day; but they had suggested no means for securing uniformity in the reckoning of the time; and the purpose of the council, therefore, was still far from being attained. In the Alexandrian churches, where astronomical and mathematical knowledge was very generally diffused, the most accurate calculations were instituted, which the whole Eastern church followed. The bishop of Alexandria made known every year, at the feast of Epiphany, by a circular letter § to his whole diocese, the day on which the next Easter festival would fall. But, as the Roman church was not so exact, differences arose as to the time of Easter, between the Eastern churches and those of the West, which amounted sometimes to a week, occasionally even to a month; until at length, particularly by means of the Roman abbot, Dionysius Exi-

---

* This is now τὸ πάσχα ἐπιτίλιιν, says Chrysostom against the advocates of the Jewish custom. Orat. c. Judæos. III. s. 4, T. I. f. 611.

† They were denominated as a separate sect (after that fourteenth day of the month Nisan), Quartodecimani, τισσαρισκαιδικατίται, τιτραδίται (probably by an abbreviation), πρωτοπασχίται.

‡ It is remarkable that this decree occurs only in the letter in which the emperor Constantine (see above) made known and recommended the decisions of this council, and that among its own canons no one is to be found which has any reference to it. Perhaps it was omitted out of indulgence to the adherents of the ancient custom, who, it was hoped, would be induced to yield by degrees.

§ Libellus paschalis, γράμματα πασχαλία.

guus, in the sixth century, the Alexandrian mode of reckoning was introduced also into the Roman church.*

It became, by degrees, as we have observed already in the preceding period, a more universally prevailing custom to prepare for the jubilee of the feast of the resurrection by a season of penitence and fasting. This fast was compared with the forty days' fast of Christ (see vol. i. p. 408); hence it received the name of τεσσαρακοστή, quadrigesima; although the whole time of forty days was by no means observed so generally as the name was applied.† It was sought by degrees, however, to make the period of fasting, in its whole extent, actually correspond to the ancient name (quadrigesima). In determining, then, the number of weeks before Easter, that difference ·of usage between the Eastern and the Western church by which the Sabbath was excepted from the fast-days in the former and not in the latter church, must have had its influence.

This period of fasting was designed to furnish the Christians an opportunity of preparing themselves, by a more moderate indulgence of the sensual appetites, by abstinence from the pleasures of the world, and by the diligent reading of God's word, to enter more worthily upon the celebration of the days consecrated to higher spiritual enjoyments,—to commemorate the new creation in humanity which came from the resurrection and glorification of Christ,—to engage, by means of self-examination and repentance, in a worthy celebration of

* The more accurate and detailed development of this point is to be found in a dissertation of F. Walch, in the novis commentariis Soc. Reg. Gottingensis, T. I. Ideler's Chronology, T. II. p. 202, etc.

† About this difference Socrates treats, V. 22. At Antioch the number of forty days was accurately observed as early as the fourth century ; for Chrysostom says, orat. 3, c. Judæos, s. 4, T. I. f. 611, in a discourse delivered during the fast : Νηστεύομεν τὰς τεσσαρακόντα ταύτας ἡμέρας, where the only question that arises is, whether the Sundays and Sabbaths, in which no fasts were observed, were also reckoned among these forty days. The difference related not alone to the number of days, but also to the extending of the fast to each day, and to the kind of abstinence which was practised at meals during this period. Not only among the communities of different countries, but also among individuals, a different custom existed in this respect. Some, who would be eminently pious, passed two entire days without food. Others not only refrained, like the rest, from wine, flesh, and oil at their meals, but supported themselves wholly on bread and water. H. IV. de statius, s. 6.

the holy supper, in which so many participated at the time of the Easter festival.*

A portion of the year so consecrated might also send a healthful influence through the rest of it. An occasion was offered to those who divided their whole time between worldly business and sensual pleasures, for collecting their thoughts from this dissipation and for self examination. The holy scriptures, which at least they heard read in the church, and sermons pointedly exhorting to repentance, would lead them to this. Their minds, less absorbed in the things of sense, would be more open to spiritual impressions. The solemn, earnest stillness following at once upon tumult and dissipation in the large cities, the sudden change in the aspect of public life, was calculated to arouse the trifling mind out of its sleep of security, and render it susceptible of higher influences. In truth, the commencement of the fasts must have produced a striking change in the large towns. "Quiet, to-day, is nowhere disturbed," says Chrysostom in a fast sermon preached at Antioch,† "nowhere do we hear cries ; nowhere the noise of the shambles, the bustle of cooks. All this is past ; and our city presents to-day the appearance of a sedate and modest matron. To-day there is no difference between the table of the emperor and that of the poor man." And in another sermon : ‡ "Then, no songs are heard in the evening, no revels of the drunkard in the day ; the voice of clamour and contention is hushed, and profound quiet everywhere reigns." Still, as it usually happens with such sudden revolutions of life, this change was more often transient than enduring, more apparent than real. If there was a horse-race at the circus during the fast, all was over ; the city rapidly assumed another look. The same persons who had been momentarily aroused by the earnest, impressive words of a Chrysostom, who had beaten their breasts and sighed over their sins, now filled the circus, and took a passionate interest in

* This aim is assigned to the institution by Chroysostom, orat. adv. Judæos, III. s. 4, T. I. f. 611. Οἱ πατέρες ἐτύπωσαν ἡμέρας τεσσαράκοντα νηστείας, εὐχῶν, ἀκροάσεως, συνόδων, ἵν᾽ ἐν ταῖς ἡμέραις ταύταις καθαρθέντες μετ᾽ ἀκριβείας ἅπαντες καὶ δι᾽ εὐχῶν καὶ δι᾽ ἐλεημοσύνης καὶ διὰ νηστείας καὶ διὰ παννυχίδων καὶ διὰ δακρύων καὶ δι᾽ ἐξομολογήσεως καὶ διὰ τῶν ἄλλων ἁπάντων, οὕτω κατὰ δύναμιν τὴν ἡμετέραν μετὰ καθαροῦ συνειδότος προσίωμεν.

† H. 2 in Genesin, s. 1, T. IV. f. 8.
‡ In Annam. II. 1, s. 1, T. IV. f. 700.

the contending sides.* True, men soon returned back again to their previous quiet and repose of the fast; but, if this could be so easily disturbed by other impressions from abroad, it is plain how superficial must have been the change produced on these occasions. As is usually the case with such changes, prescribed by law and enforced by constraint, the end often failed of being attained, because confounded with the means. Men looked for justification and increase in holiness in outward fasting, and entirely forgot in this the essential things, true repentance and sanctification, which the period of fasting was only designed to remind them of. Or the end was missed because men submitted to the laws of the church from constraint and in opposition to their inward feelings, partly influenced by the sense of shame, and partly by the dread of the divine punishment. Hence many sought to indemnify themselves beforehand for the forced abstinence imposed on them by the fasts, by indulging in the more riotous excess on the days immediately preceding them.† Many only complied with the laws of fasting in their literal sense; refraining from meat, but taking care to provide themselves with the daintier fare out of what was permitted by the fast laws literally interpreted.‡

The more eminent church-teachers of this period, Chrysostom, Augustin, Maximus of Turin, Cæsarius of Arles, Leo the Great, often warned against this hypocritical tendency of the fasts. They showed that fasting was without force or meaning, except as accompanied with the hearty forsaking of sin and sincere penitence. They exhorted Christians to use fasting as a means of learning how to subdue sinful passions and desires, propensities and habits. They gave examples, especially Chrysostom, to show how this must be done. They took this occasion to rebuke the corrupt tendencies particularly prevailing in their own times and under their own eyes, and warned men against them. They called upon Christians to unite charity

---

* See the admonitory discourse of Chrysostom, preached after an incident of this sort at Antioch. H. 6 in Genesin, T. IV. opp.

† Chrysost. de Pœnitentia, H. 5, s. 5, T. II. f. 315. Παραίνω ὥστε μὴ τὴν ἐκ τῆς νηστείας ἐσομένην ὠφελίαν προανέλειν λαιμαργίᾳ καὶ μέθῃ.

‡ Augustin. p. 209, s. 3, et 108, s. 1. Pretiosiores sine carnibus animalium escas. On the other hand, Restringendæ sunt deliciæ, non mutandæ.

and benevolence with fasting; to appropriate to these purposes what they saved by abstinence; to forgive each other's
offences; to lay aside contentions; as, in fact, the bishops
made it a point, at this particular season of fasting, to close
all disputes in the communities, and bring about a reconciliation between the contending parties; using as a means for
this end, the conviction of universal sinfulness and need of
redemption awakened by the season, and the approaching
celebration of the remembrance of Christ's sufferings for the
sins of mankind; they moreover called on masters in particular to treat their servants with kindness.

The season of fasting ended with the week which, on account of the great events connected with the salvation of
mankind, and commemorated in it, was called the *great* week
($\dot{\epsilon}\beta\dot{\delta}o\mu\dot{\alpha}\varsigma$ $\dot{\eta}$ $\mu\epsilon\gamma\dot{\alpha}\lambda\eta$).* It began with Palm Sunday ($\dot{\eta}\mu\dot{\epsilon}\rho\alpha$
$\tau\tilde{\omega}\nu$ $\beta\alpha\dot{\iota}\omega\nu$), and closed with the great Sabbath, as it was called.
The approach of the Easter festival reminded all, high and
low, of their individual sins, and of the grace to which they
owed their forgiveness. Hence the emperors made laws † to
release those who had been arrested for minor offences; and
on Palm Sunday special decrees of mercy were frequently
issued by them. " As on this day," says Chrysostom in one
of his discourses, " our Lord delivered men from the chains of
sin, so his servants will do all in their power to imitate his
love to mankind, and as they cannot deliver men from spiritual
fetters, will release those who are bodily bound."

In this week of solemnities, some days were particularly
distinguished, Thursday, for example, in which was commemorated the last supper of Christ with his disciples, and the
institution of the Eucharist.‡ On this occasion great numbers
were accustomed to participate in the sacrament of the supper.§
While, on other occasions, the holy supper was only to be received with fasting, it was dispensed on this day in memory of
the original institution, in the afternoon, and could be received
after a meal.‖ Next, came the day commemorative of Christ's

---

* See the Homily of Chrysostom respecting the meaning of this name.
† See in the Codex Theodos. the titulus de indulgentiis.
‡ 'Η ἁγία πέντας, quinta feria Paschæ, dies anniversarius, quo cœna
Dominica celebratur.
§ See Chrysostom's discourse delivered on this day. T. II. f. 386.
‖ Thus it was at least in the North-African church, by the decree of

passion.* At Antioch, perhaps also in other churches of the East, it was customary for the church on this day to hold its assemblies in the grave-yard, to commemorate the crucifixion of Christ without the gates of Jerusalem.† The week was closed by the great *Sabbath* (τὸ μέγα σάββατον), on which many were baptized, and put on their white robes ; and in the evening the cities were illuminated, and appeared like streams of fire. The whole population poured along with torches to church, and vigils were kept till the dawn of the morning of universal jubilee, the feast of the resurrection. The small number of pagans who still dwelt amongst the Christians must also, in one way or another, have been affected, in spite of themselves by what so moved the whole multitude on this occasion of general Easter vigils.‡

The custom having been borrowed from the Jews of holding a last festival on the eighth day after the commencement of the series, the celebration of the passover was concluded with the following Sunday as the eighth day of the feast. Throughout the whole of this week, from the Easter Sabbath and onward, the persons then baptized had worn their white garments, and, as new Christians, the new-born,§ had formed a separate division of the community, easily distinguished by their dress. This sacred time of the celebration of their new birth being now over, they laid aside their white robes ; the bishop exhorted them to a faithful observance of their baptismal vow, and they joined the rest of the community. This important transaction gave its name to this Sunday. So it was at least in the Western church.‖ Thus, then, the whole

---

the council of Hippo, A.D. 393, in the cod. canon. eccles. Afr. c. 41. Augustin. ep. 54 ad Januar. s. 9.

* The ἡμέρα τοῦ σταυροῦ, also called in a more restricted sense, Pascha.
† See the discourse of Chrysostom on this day, V. 2.
‡ Respecting this Sabbath : Λαμπροφορία καὶ φωταγωγία, ἣν ἰδίᾳ τὶ καὶ δημοσίᾳ συνεστησάμεθα· πᾶν γένος ἀνθρώπων μίκρου καὶ ἀξία πάσα δαψίλει τῷ πύρι τὴν νύκτα καταφωτίζοντες. Gregor. Nazianz. orat. 2 in Pascha V. orat. 42, at the beginning. Augustin : Clara vigiliæ hujus celebritas toto orbe terrarum. Respecting the Pagans : Ista nocte multi dolore, multi pudore, *nonnulli etiam, qui fidei propinquant*, Dei jam timore non dormiunt, p. 219. § Novi, infantes.
‖ Octava infantium, dies novorum, dominica in albis, κυριάκη ἐν λευκοῖς. Augustin. p. 376. Hodie octavæ dicuntur infantium ; miscentur hodie fidelibus infantes nostri. P. 260. Hodie completis sacramentum octa-

period of fourteen days, reckoning from Palm Sunday, was a festival. As such it was recognized also by the civil authority, and in it no court of justice could be held.* Moreover, the fifty days after Easter were specially distinguished, although the feast of Ascension, and the feast of Pentecost in the more restricted sense—the feast of the outpouring of the Holy Ghost, were selected from the rest for particular celebration. In the Eastern church, the Acts of the Apostles were read during this time, in the public worship, as recording what the risen and glorified Christ had wrought through the apostles ; and in the year 425, it was decreed, that during this whole period the devotion of Christians should not be disturbed by any public sports.†

To these were added two principal festivals, which, as we observed in the preceding period, most probably existed in their germ in very early times, but which first began to be more generally observed during the course of the fourth century, and that in an opposite order,—the one coming from the East to the West, and the other from the West to the East ; the *festival of Christ's baptism*, and the festival of his nativity.

As to the first, we find it mentioned by Chrysostom, as an ancient principal feast of the church in Eastern Asia, under the name of the feast of the appearance or manifestation of Christ, who had till then been hidden from the world ; ἡ ἐπιφάνεια or τὰ ἐπιφάνεια according to Tit. II. 11.‡ But if, in the region where this feast originated, another festival having

---

varum vestrarum. Comp. ep. 55, s. 35. Respecting the newly baptized, Veste dealbatus intra octavas suas. Ep. 34, s. 3. It may perhaps have been otherwise in the Eastern church, where, as it seems, the newly baptized wore their white garments until the end of the feast of Pentecost. See the passage presently to be referred to from the Cod. Theodos.

* Dies feriarum, sancti quoque Paschæ dies, qui septeno vel præcedunt numero vel sequuntur. Cod. Theodos. l. II. T. VIII. l. 2.

† Cod. Theodos. l. XV. T. VII. l. 5. Quamdiu cœlestis lumen lavacri imitantia novam sancti baptismatis lucem vestimenta testantur (which is probably said only in conformity with the use of the Eastern church) quo tempore et commemoratio apostolicæ passionis, totius Christianitatis magistræ, a cunctis jure celebratur. Which refers to the reading of the Acts.

‡ Chrysostom in his Homily on this feast, s. 2, T. II. f. 369. Ἐπειδὴ οὐχ' ὅτι ἐτέχθη, τότε πᾶσιν ἐγίνετο κατάδηλος, ἀλλ' ὅτι ἐβαπτίσατο.

reference to the first appearance of the Logos in human nature, a feast of Christ's nativity, was already existing, the latter would hardly have become so entirely lost sight of, and a name which belonged to it transferred to the feast of Christ's baptism. More probably this was the only festival which in that district had reference to the first appearance of Christ. Accordingly, Chrysostom actually denominates it in the discourse already cited, which he pronounced at the feast of Pentecost in Antioch, the festival of Epiphany, the first among the principal feasts, and the only one which had reference to the appearance of Christ among men.* He speaks here according to the views of Christian antiquity which prevailed in those countries where a Christmas festival was as yet wholly unknown. In a certain sense, men doubtless had some reason for placing this festival in special connection with the baptism of Christians,—inasmuch as the divine life, which was to proceed forth from Christ to all the faithful, here first began to reveal itself in a visible way to the greater portion of men. But as the age, confounding the outward sign with the inward grace, ascribed to the water in baptism a supernatural power to sanctify, so it supposed that Christ first imparted to the water its power to sanctify by his own baptism.† The first indication of the celebration of this feast having spread to the Western church we find about the year 360; for the historian Ammianus Marcellinus relates ‡ that the emperor Julian, then residing at Vienna in the month of January, celebrated the feast of Epiphany in the Christian church. By means of the union of the Greek colonial and mercantile towns in the south of France with the East, this feast may have been adopted, perhaps, in these districts at an earlier period than in the other countries of the West. It was

---

* H. 1, in Pentecost. s. 1, T. II. f. 458. Παρ' ἡμῖν ἑορτὴ πρώτη τὰ ἐπιφάνια· τίς ἡ ὑπόθεσις τῆς ἑορτῆς; ἐπειδὴ θεὸς ἐπὶ τῆς γῆς ὤφθη καὶ τοῖς ἀνθρώποις συνανεστράφη.

† Τὴν τῶν ὑδάτων ἡγίασε φύσιν. Chrysostomus. Out of this false notion also sprung the custom at Antioch, of very zealously drawing water about midnight of this feast, to which water was attributed the wonderful property of remaining fresh several years. Even Chrysostom partook of this superstition, h. de baptismo Christi, s. 2. Being the feast of Christ's baptism, and of baptism generally, it was also called in the Eastern church, ἑορτὴ τῶν φώτων, or τὰ φῶτα. So in Gregory of Nazianzen.

‡ L. XXI. c. 2.

because this festival was originally unknown to the Western church that the Donatists, who had separated themselves from the dominant church at a time when as yet no knowledge of any such feast existed among the people of the West, rejected it as an innovation; as they did other regulations that arose after their secession.* And as this festival was originally unknown to the Western church, so it happened that its meaning also was changed, though in such a way as to be easily connected with the fundamental idea of the festival. The general conception of a manifestation of Christ in his divine dignity, or in his divine calling as a Redeemer, was applied in a way which must have been more agreeable to the point of view taken by the communities of the West, which were formed of pagan Christians, than the view of it which had first sprung out of the peculiar conceptions of Jewish Christians (see vol. i. sect. 3, p. 408): and, at the same time, this festival was brought into closer connection with Christmas, which had been established here for a long time already. While, in the countries where the feast of Christ's baptism had its distinct traditional meaning as the feast of Epiphany, and where it was adhered to, therefore, without any change, everything which had reference to Christ's infancy was connected with the festival of Christmas; in the Eastern church, on the other hand, the idea of the manifestation of Christ was applied in a pre-eminent sense to his manifestation to the heathen world as the Redeemer of all mankind. The festival was referred to the coming of the three wise men from the East, who were supposed to be heathens; and so this feast became the feast of the first announcement of salvation to the heathen world, of the first conversion of some heathens, as the precursors of the approaching general conversion of the pagan nations.† When these two points of view became united in one, the general conception of the Epiphany was referred to the first manifestation of the miraculous power of Jesus after

* Augustin. p. 202, s. 2. Merito istum diem nunquam nobiscum Donatistæ celebrare voluerunt, quia nec unitatem amant, nec Orientali ecclesiæ communicant.

† Augustin. p. 203. Hodierno die manifestatus redemptor omnium gentium, fecit sollennitatem omnibus gentibus. The mystic interpretation of Psalm lxxii. 10, led to the converting of the three Magi into three kings. See Tertullian. adv. Judæos, c. 9.

his baptism, in the first miracle at Cana, the dies natalis virtutum Domini.*

The case was directly the reverse with the festival of Christ's nativity, which in its origin belonged to the Western church. As it was particularly from the church of the West the dogmatic tendency proceeded, by which the doctrine of original sin cleaving to all men from their birth, and of the necessity of their being renewed and sanctified in order to deliverance from this corrupt nature, was clearly unfolded— as it was in the church of the West that the practice of infant baptism first became generally spread, so too in the Western church originated the festival which refers to the sanctification of man's nature from its first germ by participation in a divine life. This feast first makes its appearance as one generally celebrated in the Roman church, under the Roman bishop Liberius, after the middle of the fourth century.† The general participation in the celebration of this feast leads to the inference that it was not at that time a festival wholly new. It was not till later, however, that it spread from the Roman church to Eastern Asia. From what we have previously observed respecting the celebration of the feast of Epiphany in this part of the church, it would already seem clear that the Christmas feast could not be one which originated there; but Chrysostom says expressly, in a discourse pronounced at Antioch in celebration of this festival, on the 25th of December of the year 386, that it *had first become known there less than ten years before.*‡ In a sermon which Chrysostom

---

* Maximus of Turin, in the beginning of the fifth century, says, after having cited all the three modes of explaining the feast: Sed quid potissimum hoc factum die, novit ipse, qui fecit. H. 6. He calls it a certain tradition, that the three facts collectively occurred on the same day, the sixth of January; but in H. 7 he says, that although the tradition respecting what occurred on that day, and respecting that to which the feast alluded, was different, yet there was but one faith and one devotion.

† Ambrose relates, that when his sister Marcella was consecrated as a nun on the dies natalis Salvatoris, in St. Peter's church, by the bishop Liberius, the latter said to her, Vides quantus ad natalem sponsi tui populus convenerit. Ambros. de virginib. l. III. c. 1.

‡ Hom. in diem natal. Christi, s. 1, T. II. f. 355. Οὔπω δέκατόν ἐστιν ἔτος, ἐξ οὗ δῆλη καὶ γνώριμος ἡμῖν αὕτη ἡ ἡμέρα γεγένηται. True, he is speaking in that place particularly of *the celebration of this feast on the twenty-fifth of December;* yet the course and mode of his argument

pronounced on the 20th of December in the same year, on the feast of a martyr,* he digresses from the proper subject of his discourse for the purpose of inviting his hearers to participate in the approaching festival of Christmas.† The way in which he speaks of it shows how desirous he was of making the interest more general, which he himself felt in a festival still new to this portion of the church.‡ In the next following discourse, on the 25th of December, he says, indeed, that this feast, although still new in that part of the world, yet soon acquired equal authority with the more ancient high festivals: of this the crowded assemblies, which the churches could scarcely contain, bore witness. But still, it is evident from his own remarks that, as usually happens with new

shows that it was only on the assumption of the twenty-fifth of December as the birth-day of Christ, a distinct feast for the celebration of this birth-day had there been founded. If it had already been the custom there at an earlier period to celebrate some festival of this sort, but on a different day, he would without doubt have separated the celebration of such a feast generally from the assumption of the twenty-fifth of December for its celebration. He would have endeavoured to show the want of foundation for reckoning of the time previously fixed upon, before he adduced the reasons for the new calculation. Moreover, it would assuredly have been yet more difficult to introduce the determinate time adopted at Rome into the Antiochian church, if another time had there already been fixed upon. The authority of the Roman church would hardly have been such as to induce the whole community to transfer a feast already existing, to another day. It may be conjectured, that, previous to this time, people were as far from thinking to consecrate a feast to the birth-day of Christ, as they were from the thought of chronologically determining when this birth-day occurred: for we find the bishop of Edessa still declaring in the seventh century, that nobody knew on what day Christ was born. See Assemani bibl. oriental. T. II. f. 1636. It was not until men believed that there was some account which could be relied on respecting this last-mentioned fact, that they were led to connect with it the celebration of a particular feast. At the same time it may be said, perhaps with truth, that the interest in behalf of a festival which must have commended itself to the feelings of Christians, contributed to create the belief and admission that the time had been truly determined.

* Philogonius. T. I. f. 492.   † L. c. s. 3.

‡ Which he here styles "the mother of all other feasts, μητρόπολις πασῶν τῶν ἑορτῶν," as indeed all the others presuppose the birth of Christ; and he names on this occasion the principal feasts, ἀπὸ γὰρ ταύτης τὰ θεοφανία καὶ τὰ πάσχα καὶ ἡ ἀνάληψις καὶ ἡ πεντηκοστὴ τὴν ἀρχὴν καὶ τὴν ὑπόθεσιν ἔλαβον.

church regulations, all were not satisfied with the celebration of this new festival. A controversy arose about it. While some denounced the festival as an innovation, others affirmed in its defence that it had been known of old from Thrace to Cadiz.* This difference of opinion led him into a detailed argument in support of the festival. Its object would of course be acknowledged by every Christian of the orthodox church at that time as worthy of commemoration. The grounds of opposition, therefore, could relate only to the arbitrary determination of the time: hence Chrysostom laboured only to show that the true time was determined.

He appeals, in the first place, to the rapid and general reception of the festival, to its authority increasing every year, as evidence that the time had been rightly assumed; applying here the well-known remark of Gamaliel. But it is plain that in the settling of a date this argument can decide nothing; although there is certainly good reason for supposing that the natural propriety of such a festival, its entire accordance with the feelings which glowed in every Christian breast, promoted its reception on its own account, and created a general belief that the true time for it had been rightly determined. Next he appeals to the precise time, preserved in the Roman archives, of the census of the Procurator Quirinus. On this point it is possible he may have been deceived by false reports; or perhaps, at Rome itself, certain apocryphal records had been allowed to pass as genuine. In other homilies, also, written towards the close of the fourth century, by Greek fathers, who notice this festival as one which Christians very generally observed, there are nevertheless marks of its comparatively recent introduction.†

* Ἄνωθεν πᾶσι τοῖς ἀπὸ Θρᾴκης μέχρι Γαδείρων οἰκοῦσι καταδῆλος καὶ ἐπίσημος γέγον. Though this assertion cannot pass for a credible historical testimony, yet it is something in favour of the supposition, that the festival existed from early times in many countries of the West.

† It seems to be the wish of Gregory of Nyssa to defend the authority of this festival against those who were not disposed to place it on the same level with the ancient principal feasts, which commemorated the passion, the resurrection, and the ascension of Christ, when he says (Hom. in natalem Christi, T. II. ed. Paris, 1638, f. 352): Μηδεὶς τῷ κατὰ τὸ πάσχα μυστηρίῳ μόνην τὴν τοιαύτην εὐχαριστίαν πρέπειν ὑπονοείτω, and therefore endeavours to show, like Chrysostom, that that which constituted the object of this festival was presupposed by everything else

On account of this more recent introduction of the Christmas festival from the West into the East, the Christians in many countries of the East preferred, instead of adopting a festival altogether new, to unite the commemoration of Christ's nativity with the ancient feast of the Epiphany. Thus it was at Jerusalem, and in the Alexandrian church. And it was attempted to justify this simultaneous celebration on the authority of Luke iii. 23, from which passage it was inferred that the baptism of Christ took place on the very day of his nativity.[*] Hence again it was, that, in many of the Greek churches where from the earliest times neither of the two feasts had been observed, and where the feast of Christ's nativity was now introduced because it appeared the more important of the two, the name *Epiphany* or *Theophany* was transferred to the latter.[†]

But to explain how the Christmas festival came to be ob-

Christ had wrought for the salvation of mankind. So, in a homily, ascribed incorrectly to Basil of Cæsarea (T. II. opp. ed. Garnier, f. 602, s. 6), it is said: Οὐδεὶς ἀσυντέλης (let there be no one but what contributes something to the general joy), οὐδεὶς ἀχρίστος, φθεγξώμεθα τίνα καὶ ἡμεῖς φωνὴν ἀγαλλιάσεως, ὄνομα θώμεθα τῇ ἑορτῇ ἡμῶν θεοφανία,—from which passage we may infer, perhaps, that in the country where this was said, not even the old Epiphany festival of the Syrian church was as yet introduced; since, were it otherwise, its name would hardly have been transferred to the new feast of Christ's nativity.

[*] See Cosmas Indicopleust. topographia Christiana in Montfaucon, collectio nova patrum, T. II. 1, V. f. 194: Cassian. Collat. X. c. ii, respecting the simultaneous celebration of these festivals by the Egyptians. This custom of the Alexandrian church must have been altered, it is true, at a later period; for in a homily delivered at Alexandria, in the year 432, by Paulus, bishop of Emisa in Phœnicia, we find the feast of Christ's nativity described as an independent feast by itself. According to the title, this festival was held on the twenty-ninth of the Egyptian month Choyac, which answers to the twenty-fifth of December. See acta concilii Ephesini pars iv. Harduini Concil. T. I. f. 1694. It might be, that the intimate connection of the Alexandrian church with the Roman in the time of Cyril, the posture of opposition in which the former stood at that time to the churches of Eastern Asia; the dogmatical interest in the polemics waged against the Antiochian type of doctrine—all this contributed to bring about the change.

[†] So in the passage above cited from the sermon extant under the name of Basil, and in the expositio fidei of Epiphanius: Ἡμέρα τῶν ἐπιφανίων, ὅτι ἐγεννήθη ἐν σάρκι ὁ κύριος. Jerome disputed the propriety of this use of the term *Epiphania*, in his Commentary on Ezekiel, c. 1: Epiphaniorum dies non, ut quidam putant, natalis in carne, tum enim absconditus est et non apparuit.

served first in the Roman church, and to pass from this to the other churches; and how the time for its observance came to be transferred to this particular date of the 25th December; certain antagonistic tendencies were referred to, growing out of the peculiar circumstances of the Roman church, of which mention is already made in older writings.*

Precisely in this season of the year, a series of heathen festivals occurred, the celebration of which among the Romans was, in many ways, closely interwoven with the whole civil and social life. The Christians, on this very account, were often exposed to be led astray into many of the customs and solemnities peculiar to these festivals. Besides, these festivals had an import which easily admitted of being spiritualized, and with some slight change transformed into a Christian sense. First came the *saturnalia*, which represented the peaceful times of the golden age, and abolished for a while the distinction of ranks, the distance between servants and free men. This admitted of being easily transferred to Christianity, which, through the reconciliation of man with God, through the restoration of the fellowship between God and man, had introduced the true golden age, representing the equality of all men in the sight of God, and brought the like true liberty as well to the freeman as to the slave. Then came the custom, peculiar to this season, of making presents (the strenæ),† which afterwards passed over to the Christmas festival; next, *the festival of infants*, with which the saturnalia concluded, —the sigillaria, where the children were presented with images;‡ just as Christmas was the true festival of the children. Next came a festival still more analogous to the Christmas, that of the shortest day, the winter solstice; the birth-day of the new sun about to return once more towards

* The account of Johannes, bishop of Nice, in Combefis. auctarium bibliothecæ patrum novissimum, Paris, 1648, T. IL, and with supplementary additions in the edition of the patres apostolici, by Coteler. T. I. 313, is from too late a period, and too fabulous, to possess any historical importance whatever.

† The participation in the customs of this pagan festival, as well as the mutual sending of presents, were practices for which the Christians were already reprimanded by Tertullian.

‡ Macrob. Saturnal. l. I. c. XI. quæ lusum reptanti adhuc infantiæ oscillis fictilibus præbent.

the earth (dies natalis invicti solis).* In the case of this last named feast, a transition to the Christian point of view naturally presented itself, when Christ, the sun of the spiritual world, was compared with that of the material. But the comparison was carried still further; for, as in the material world, it is after the darkness has reached its highest point that the end of its dominion is already near, and the light begins to acquire fresh power; so, too, in the spiritual world, after the darkness had reached its utmost height, Christ, the spiritual sun, must appear. to make an end of the kingdom of darkness. In fact, many allusions of this kind are to be found in the discourses of the church fathers on the festival of Christmas.†

That Christian festival which could be so easily connected with the feelings and presentiments lying at the ground of the whole series of pagan festivals belonging to this season, was now, therefore, to be opposed to these latter; and hence the celebration of Christmas was transferred to the 25th of December, for the purpose of drawing away the Christian people from all participation in the heathen festivals, and of gradually

* The Manichæan Faustus actually brings it as a charge against the Christians of the Catholic church, that they celebrated the solstitia with the Pagans : Solennes gentium dies cum ipsis celebratis, ut kalendas et solstitia. See Augustin. l. XX. c. Faustum. The Roman bishop, Leo the Great, complains that many Christians had retained the pagan custom of paying obeisance from some lofty eminence to the rising sun; so too, when in the morning they were ascending the steps of St. Peter's church. Leo, p. 26, c. 4. The second Council of Trulla, or quinisextum, 691. were still under the necessity of forbidding the Christians to take any part in the celebration of the Brumalia. Now, if it was the case that the remains of heathen customs still existed among the Greeks at a time when Paganism had already almost wholly vanished, much more must this have been the case among the Roman Christians in the earlier centuries.

† Thus says Gregory of Nyssa, in his sermon on this festival, T. III. f. 340.—It was not a matter of chance that Christ's nativity took place at this season, ἐν ᾗ μειοῦσθαι τὸ σκότος ἄρχεται καὶ τὰ τῆς νυκτὸς μέτρα τῷ πλεοναζόντι τῆς ἀκτῖνος συνωθεῖται πρὸς ἐκλείψιν· μυστήριον τι διὰ τῶν φαινομένων τοῖς διορατικωτέροις διηγεῖται ἡ κτίσις. Augustin. p. 190, s. 1. " Since the infidelity which covered the whole world like a night, was to diminish, while faith increased; for this reason, on the nativity of the Lord Jesus Christ, the night begins to grow less. and the day to increase. Let us, then, celebrate this festival, not like the unbelievers, on account of this sun. but on account of the Creator of this sun." So, too, Leo the Great (p. 25, s. 1) says, that this day, more than any other, presents, by the new light beaming forth even in the elements, an image of this wonderful birth

drawing over the pagans themselves from their heathen customs to the Christian celebration. This view of the matter seems to be particularly favoured in a New Year's discourse by Maximius, bishop of Turin, near the close of the fourth century, where he recognizes a special divine providence in appointing the *birth of Christ to take place in the midst of the pagan festivals*; so that men might be led to feel ashamed of pagan superstition and pagan excesses.*

But these allusions to the series of heathen festivals happening in this season of the year, furnish, however, no decisive evidence that the Christian festival was instituted on this account generally, or that it was transferred to this particular time for the purpose of being opposed to the pagan celebrations. In fact, the resorting to this means for drawing away men from the pagan superstitions was a very hazardous experiment, which might easily lead men to confound Christianity with Heathenism, and to lose out of sight the true import of the Christian festival. Of this, indeed, Leo the Great found it necessary to give warning.† Yet we must allow that, from the unsuitableness of the means, it in nowise follows that such a means was not then resorted to. Easily might it happen that, with their eyes intently fixed on the single object proposed, men might overlook the evil naturally connected with it. In a later period such a mode of proceeding would be no matter of surprise. But it may be questioned whether we could rightly presume it of the period to which, according to what has been said, the origin of the Christmas festival must be referred. We can hardly separate the origin of this festival, considered by itself, from the particular designation of its time; for it can hardly be conceived that, after a tradition had once obtained credit respecting the day of Christ's nativity, and after the festival of Christmas had been fixed on this day, the

---

* Maximus Taurinens. H. 5, in Kal. Jan. bibl. patr. Galland. T. IX. f. 353. Bene quodammodo Deo providente dispositum, ut inter medias gentilium festivitates Christus Dominus oriretur et inter ipsas tenebrosas superstitiones errorum veri luminis splendor effulgeret, ut perspicientes homines in vanis superstitionibus suis puræ divinitatis emicuisse justitiam, præterita obliviscerentur sacrilegia, futura non colerent.

† P. 21. c. 6. Diabolus illudens simplicioribus animis de quorundam persuasione pestifera, quibus hæc dies sollennitatis nostræ non tam de nativitate Christi, quam de novi, ut dicunt, solis ortu honorabilis videatur.

specific time would be altered out of regard to the festivals of the pagans. Yet it should be remarked, in general, that the accommodation of Christian to pagan institutions proceeded, in most cases, from the side of the people; the church-teachers resisted, at first, the intermingling of pagan customs with Christian; afterwards they gave way, or were themselves carried along by the spirit of the times. Individual exceptions, it is true, are to be met with; yet in no point which could be compared with the institution of such a principal festival, and which reached back to so early a period as the origin of Christmas. Originally the prevailing mode of procedure in the Western church was by no means to connect the celebration of Christian festivals with pagan; but rather to set over against the pagan festivals days of fasting and penitence.* The passage of Faustus, in which Christians of the Catholic church are accused of taking part in the festivities of Paganism (see above), seems, it is true, at first glance, to confirm the conjecture above mentioned; but on closer examination it will be found rather opposed to it. Faustus accuses the Christians, first, of merely changing the heathen into a Christian superstition; for example, substituting the worship of the martyrs in place of the worship of idols;† and secondly, of imitating, without any change, heathen festivities as heathen; and here he names the *kalendæ* and the *solstitia*. Now, with regard to the first of these charges, we know certainly—a fact presently to be mentioned—that the church never had anything to do with those pagan festivities, but constantly expressed the warmest opposition to all participation in them. The same would be true therefore of the celebration of the solstitia, since this belonged in the same category with the rest. But if Faustus had had any ground whatever for accusing the Christians of altering the pagan celebration of the solstitia into a seeming Christian celebration of the nativity, it is the less to be supposed that he would have omitted to bring such an

---

* Leo the Great cites it, in his vii. Sermo, as an old tradition, ut quoties cœcitas paganorum in superstitionibus esset intentior, tunc præcipue populus Dei orationibus et operibus pietatis (under which he comprised alms and fasts, which were not allowable on the principal festivals) instaret.

† Idola eorum vertistis in Martyres, to which passage we shall again revert on a future occasion.

accusation against them, as the feast of Christ's nativity must have been particularly disagreeable to him as a Manichæan, who looked upon the birth of Christ in the flesh as a sorry superstition.

And what necessity is there, in truth, of searching for outward causes to account for a fact which, as we have already remarked, explains itself as growing out of the inner development of the Christian life? As it respects, however, the specific time of the 25th of December, designated for the festival of Christmas, it should not be forgotten that, in the earlier ages, there were several different determinations of the day of Christ's nativity; and we might, with the same good reason, repeat the question with regard to each one of these, How was this ascertained? It is very probable that, in the Roman church, this point was settled by the authority of some historical tradition, founded on apocryphal records. Now it is very possible, we may admit, that, allowing the existence of such an apocryphal tradition, it might have been helped along —not indeed by any design of imitating or rivalling the pagan ceremonies, but quite independently of these—by the mystical interpretation given to that season of the year.*

We find that it was originally a principle with teachers and governors of the church to resist the tendency, among the multitude, to confound pagan rites with Christian. We see this particularly illustrated in the case of the New Year's festival, the Kalendæ Januariæ. The celebration of this grandest of the Roman festivals, which began with the end of December and lasted several days, was, more than that of any other, interwoven with the whole public and private life of the Romans; with all civil, social, and domestic arrangements, manners, and customs. It was, in fact, the commencement of the civil year, according to which all sorts of business had to be adjusted and arranged. It was the time when the magistrates entered upon their several offices. 'It was therefore the ordi-

---

* How easily the determination of chronological questions of this sort might proceed from mystical interpretations of scripture texts, may be seen, e. g., by consulting Hieronym. in Ezechiel. c. i. v. 1, where, on the principle that the first month of the civil year of the Jews must nearly correspond to the month of October, the fourth month therefore to January, the author concludes that the baptism of Jesus, on the fifth of January, is here typified.

nary season of congratulations, when presents were mutually given and received. Tertullian already found reason to complain that Christians participated in all these customs. In defence of this participation it could ever be alleged, as it was still alleged by many in the beginning of the fifth century, that this whole festival was in truth of a purely civil nature, having no necessary connection with religion, and that it might be joined in, therefore, without the least danger to the faith.[*] But *with* this celebration were united customs standing directly at variance with the principles of the Christian faith and the rules of Christian conduct—riotous excesses, abandoned revelry, and various kinds of heathen superstition, which sought, by means of omens and the arts of divination, to unveil the destinies of the whole year. The first day was spent by many of the pagans in an unrestrained indulgence of sensual enjoyments, under the persuasion that such a beginning would be followed by a corresponding year of pleasure.[†] It is manifest what a corrupting influence this contagious example of pagan immorality and superstition would exert on the Christian life: indeed, the Christian teachers were often forced to complain of it in their homilies.[‡] Yet even in this case, the pagan festival could have been converted into a Christian one, having no connection with the pagan in religion, by simply giving to the commencement of the *civil* year a Christian import, on the principle that every change and new beginning in earthly things should be sanctified by religion. Thus the commencement of the year, as it was to be regarded from the Christian point of view, would be most appropriately opposed to the pagan celebration of the day. Such considerations are to be met with; for instance, in Chrysostom's discourse on the commencement of the new year. But to no one does the obvious thought seem to have occurred, of converting the civil observance wholly into an ecclesiastical one; for this thought lay too remote from the original Christian point of view, conformably to which all festivals were referred exclusively to the momentous facts connected with man's salvation,

---

[*] Petrus Chrysologus, p. 155. Esse novitatis lætitiam, non vetustatis errorem, anni principium, non gentilitatis offensam.

[†] See Liban. ἐκφρασις Καλενδων. Chrysost. Homil. Kalend.

[‡] See the homilies of Asterius of Amasea, of Maximus of Turin, of Chrysostom, Augustin, Leo the Great.

and had their origin in a purely religious interest ; while, at the same time, there was a strong reluctance to fall in with the pagan custom of celebrating the commencement of the year with religious observances. It would have been nearer the Christian point of view, to separate the ecclesiastical year from the civil, and to make the year begin either with Easter or the Christmas festival.* It was only *to oppose a counter influence to* the pagan celebration, that Christian assemblies were finally held on the first day of January ; and they were designed to protect Christians against the contagious influence of pagan debauchery and superstition. Thus, when Augustin had assembled his church, on one of these occasions, he first caused to be sung the words, " Save us, O Lord our God! and gather us from among the heathen," Psalm cvi. 47 ; and hence he took occasion to remind his flock of their duty, especially on this day, to show, that as they had, in truth, been gathered from among the heathen, to exhibit in their life the contrast between the Christian and the heathen temper ; to substitute alms for New-Year's gifts (the strenæ), edification from scripture for merry songs, and fasts for riotous feasting. This principle was gradually adopted in the practice of the Western church, and three days of penitence and fasting opposed to the pagan celebration of January,† until, the time being designated, the festival of Christ's circumcision was transferred to this season ; when a Jewish rite was opposed to the pagan observances, and its reference to the circumcision of the heart by repentance, to heathen revelry.

Besides these festivals, should be mentioned also the days consecrated to the memory of holy men, who had endeared

.* With the Easter festival, since the resurrection of Christ was the beginning of a new creation, and the spiritual spring might be associated with the spring of nature. With the Christmas festival, since the nativity of Christ was the beginning of his life, which laid the foundation for man's salvation, and the festival was the one from which all the others proceeded.

† See Isidor. l. I. c. 40, de officiis and Concil. Turonense II. A.D. 567, c. 17. Triduum illud, quo, ad calcandum gentilium consuetudinem, patres nostri statuerunt privatas in Kalendis Januariis fieri litanias, ut in ecclesiis psallatur, et hora octava in ipsis Kalendis circumcisionis missa Deo propitio celebretur. It may be a question, whether the latter refers to the circumcisio cordis, or already to the memoria circumcisionis Christi.

themselves to the church as teachers, or as martyrs to the faith. Of these we shall speak more particularly hereafter. We now pass to consider the particular acts of Christian worship.

4. Particular Acts of Christian Worship.

The principal acts of Christian worship, respecting the origin of which we spoke in the preceding period, continued to be observed also in the present. To this class belongs first the *reading of the holy scriptures.* We have already spoken of the important influence which the reading of large portions of the sacred scriptures had on the church life of this period. At the beginning, it was left for each bishop to appoint such portions of the Bible as he chose, to be read at each meeting of the church. The historical and practical allusions to the above-mentioned parts in the cycle of Christian festivals, first led to the practice of selecting certain portions of scripture with reference to the principal feasts; and this practice was gradually converted, by tradition, into a standing rule.*

As to the relation of the sermon to the whole office of worship, this is a point on which we meet with the most opposite errors of judgment. Some, who looked upon the clergy as only offering priests, and who considered the main part of Christian worship to consist in the magical effects of the priestly

---

* What Augustin says, in the prologue to his homilies on the first epistle of John, may serve as a proof: Solennitas sanctorum dierum, quibus certas ex evangelio lectiones oportet recitari, quæ ita sunt annuæ, ut aliæ esse non possint. Thus, in Easter week, the history of Christ's resurrection was read in turn from all the gospels. See Augustin. p. 231 and 39. Chrysostom. in Hom. 4, in principio actorum, T. III. f. 85, says, the fathers had introduced such apportionments of scripture to particular times, not for the sake of abridging Christian liberty (οὐχ ἵνα ὑπὸ ἀνάγκης καίρων τὴν ἐλευθερίαν ἡμῖν ὑποβάλωσιν), but out of condescension to the necessities of the weak. But the natural propensity of men to bind themselves to forms once sanctioned by use, was shown also in the present case. In the African church it was customary to read on Good Friday the history of the passion from Matthew. When Augustin, to give his church a more varied and full knowledge of the history of the passion, proposed to read the different gospels yearly, in turn, and on a certain Good Friday caused the portion to be read from another gospel, disturbances arose, for many were disappointed not to hear what they had been accustomed to: Volueram aliquando, ut per singulos annos secundum omnes evangelistas *etiam passio* legeretur. Factum est, non audierunt homines quod consueverant, et perturbati sunt. P. 232, s. 1.

services, were hence inclined greatly to overvalue the liturgical, and wholly to overlook the necessity of the didactic · element of worship. The gift of teaching they regarded as something foreign from the spiritual office, as they supposed the Holy Ghost, imparted to the priest by ordination, could be transmitted to others only by his *sensible mediation*. Others, however,—and on account of the rhetorical style of culture which prevailed among the higher classes in the large cities of the East, this was especially the case in the Greek church— gave undue importance to the didactic and rhetorical part of worship ; and did not attach importance enough to the essentials of Christian fellowship, and of common edification and devotion. Hence the church would be thronged when some famous speaker was to be heard ; but only a few remained behind when the sermon was ended and the church prayers followed. " The sermons," said they, " we can hear nowhere but at church ; but we can pray just as well at home."* Against this abuse Chrysostom had frequent occasion to speak, in his discourses preached at Antioch and Constantinople. Hence, too, without regard to the essential character of the church, a style borrowed from the theatre or the lecture rooms of declaimers was introduced into the church assemblies; as these were frequented for the purpose of hearing some orator, celebrated for his elegant language, or his power of producing a momentary effect on the imagination or the feelings. Hence the custom of interrupting such speakers, at their more striking or impressive passages, with noisy testimonials of approbation (κρότος). Vain ecclesiastics, men whose hearts were not full of the holy cause they professed, made it the chief or only aim of their discourses to secure the applause of such hearers, and hence laboured solely to display their brilliant eloquence or wit, to say something with point and effect. But many of the better class, too, such men as Gregory of Nazianzen, could not wholly overcome the vanity which this custom tended to foster, and thus fell into the mistake of being too rhetorical in their sermons.† Men of holy seriousness, like Chrysostom, strongly rebuked this declamatory and theatrical style,‡ and said that,

---

* See Chrysostom. H. 3, de Incomprehensib. s. 6, T. I. 469.

† Gregory of Nazianzen says himself, in his farewell discourse at Constantinople : Κροτήσατε χεῖρας, ὀξὺ βοήσατε, ἀράτε εἰς ὕψος τὸν ῥήτορα ὑμῶν.

‡ Thus on one occasion he says : " This is no theatre ; you are not

through such vanity the whole Christian cause would come to be suspected by the heathens.

Many short-hand writers eagerly employed themselves in taking down on the spot the discourses of famous speakers, in order to give them a wider circulation.* The sermons were sometimes—though rarely—read off entirely from notes, or committed to memory; sometimes they were freely delivered, after a plan prepared beforehand; and sometimes they were altogether extemporary. The last we learn incidentally, from being informed that Augustin was occasionally directed to the choice of a subject by the passage which the " prælector " had selected for reading; when, he tells us, he was sometimes urged by some impression of the moment, to give his sermon a different turn from what he had originally proposed.† We are also informed by Chrysostom, that his subject was frequently suggested to him by something he met with on his way to church, or which suddenly occurred during divine service.‡

Church music was cultivated, in this period, more according to rule. In connection with the " prælectors,"§ were appointed church-choristers, who sung sometimes alone, sometimes interchangeably with the choirs of the congregation. It was considered very important that the whole church should take part in the psalmody.‖

sitting here as spectators of comedians." Οὐδὲ γὰρ θεάτρον ἔστι τὰ παρόντα, οὐ τραγῳδοὺς καθῆσθε θεώμενοι νῦν. In Matth. H. 17, s. 7.

* Hence Gregory of Nazianzen, in his farewell discourse, preached at Constantinople, says: Χαίρετε γράφιδες φανέραι καὶ λανθανοῦσαι. Hence the complaint of Gaudentius of Brescia, that his sermons had been inaccurately transcribed by note-takers, who sat out of sight. See the Præfat. to his Sermones. Hence the different recensions we have of so many of the ancient homilies.

† Augustin. in Psalm cxxxviii. s. 1. Maluimus nos in errore lectoris sequi voluntatem Dei, quam nostram in nostro proposito.

‡ See the sermon of Chrysostom, of which the theme was chosen on his way to church, when he saw, in the winter time, lying in the vicinity of the church, many sick persons and beggars, and touched with pity, felt constrained to exhort his hearers to works of brotherly kindness and charity. T. III. opp. ed. Montf. f. 248. Compare also the turn which he gave to his discourse in a certain sermon, when the lighting of the lamps drew away the attention of his hearers. See T. IV. f. 662.

§ Ψάλται, cantores, who, like the lectores, were taken from the younger clergy.

‖ In the fifteenth canon of the council of Laodicea, it was ordered, that no others besides the regularly appointed church cantores should

Besides the Psalms, which had been used from the earliest times, and the short doxologies and hymns, consisting of verses from the holy scriptures, spiritual songs composed by distinguished church-teachers, such as Ambrose of Milan and Hilary of Poictiers, were also introduced among the pieces used for public worship in the Western church. To the last-named practice, much opposition, it is true, was expressed. It was demanded that, in conformity with the ancient usage, nothing should be used in the music of public worship but what was taken from the sacred scriptures. And as sectaries and heretical parties often had recourse to church psalmody, as a means for giving spread to their own peculiar religious opinions, all those songs which had not been for a long time in use in the church, were particularly liable to suspicion.*

It must already have become a matter of complaint, however, as well in the Western as in the Greek church, that the ecclesiastical music had taken too artificial and theatrical a direction, and departed from its ancient simplicity ; for we find the Egyptian abbot Pambo, in the fourth century, inveighing against the introduction of heathen melodies into church psalmody,† and the abbot Isidore of Pelusium complaining of the

sing in divine service (περὶ τοῦ μὴ δεῖν πλίον τῶν κανονίκων ψάλτων τῶν ἐπὶ τὸν ἀμβώνα ἀναβαινόντων καὶ ἀπὸ διφθέρας (the church song-books), ψαλλόντων ἑτέρους τίνας ψάλλειν ἐν ἐκκλησία). But this is hardly to be understood as meaning that the participation of the congregation in the church music was to be wholly excluded. At least, if this were the case, it must be regarded as a temporary and provincial regulation ; and it would be in direct contradiction to the usage of the Eastern church, in which the distinguished church teachers, such as Basil of Cæsarea and Chrysostom, expended much labour in improving the style of church music. Most probably this canon is to be understood in the sense that none but persons of the clerical order should hold the post of professed church-singers, so that the singing of the congregation was to be regarded as a wholly independent thing.

* See Concil. Laodicen. c. 59. Ὅτι οὐ δεῖ ἰδιωτίκους ψάλμους λέγεσθαι ἐν τῇ ἐκκλησίᾳ. The first council of Braga, in the year 561, c. 12, against the Priscillianists, directed, ut extra psalmos vel scripturas canonicas nihil poetice compositum in ecclesia psallatur. On the other hand, the fourth council of Toledo, A.D. 633, c. 13, defended the use of such sacred hymns as were composed by Hilary and Ambrose. Even the ancient hymns and doxologies taken from scripture were not, they said, wholly free from human additions. As prayers and liturgical forms of human composition were used in divine service, the same use might be made also of sacred hymns indited by men.

† See the conference of the abbot Pambo with his disciples, on the too

2 G 2

theatrical style of singing, particularly among the women, which, instead of exciting emotions of penitence, served rather to awaken sinful passions;* and Jerome, in remarking on the words of the Apostle Paul, in Ephes. v. 19,† says, " Let our youth hear this; let those hear it whose office it is to sing in the church.   Not with the voice, but with the heart must we make melody to the Lord.   We are not like comedians, to smooth the throat with sweet drinks, in order that we may hear theatrical songs and melodies in the church : but the fear of God, piety, and the knowledge of the scriptures, should inspire our songs; so that not the voice of the singer, but the divine matter expressed, may be the point of attraction ; so that the evil spirit, which entered into the heart of a Saul, may be expelled from those who are in like manner possessed by him, rather than invited by those who would turn the house of God into a heathen theatre."

We now proceed to consider the administration of the sacraments.

And, first, as it respects baptism : it may be remarked that infant baptism—as we have observed that the fact was already towards the close of the preceding period—was now generally recognized as an apostolical institution ; but from the theory on this point we can draw no inference with regard to the practice.   It was still very far from being the case, especially in the Greek church, that infant baptism, although acknowledged to be necessary, was generally introduced into practice. Partly, the same mistaken notions which arose from confounding the thing represented by baptism with the outward rite, and which afterwards led to the over-valuation of infant baptism, and partly, the frivolous tone of thinking, the indifference to all higher concerns, which characterized so many who had only exchanged the pagan for a Christian outside,—all this toge-

---

artificial church music of Alexandria, in imitation of the heathen melodies (κανόνις καὶ τροπάρια).   " The monks," says he, " have not retired into the desert, to sing beautiful melodies, and move hands and feet :" Μιλῶ- δοῦσιν ᾄσματα καὶ ῥυθμίζουσιν (βάλλουσι?) πόδας.   See the Scriptores ecclesiastici de Musica, published by the abbot Gerbert, T. I. 1784, p. 3.

* Isidor. Pelus. I. I. ep. 90. Κατάνυζιν μὶν ἐκ τῶν θσίων ὕμνων οὐχ' ὑπομίνουσι, τῇ δὲ τοῦ μιλοῦς ἡδυτῆτι εἰς ἰριθίσμον παθημάτων χρώμινοι, οὐδὲν αὐτην ἔχιιν πλίον τῶν ἐπὶ σκηνῆς ἀσμάτων λογίζονται.

† See his Commentar. in ep. Ephes. l. III. c. 5, T. IV. f. 387, ed. Martianay.

ther contributed to bring it about that among the Christians of
the East, infant baptism, though in theory acknowledged to
be necessary, yet entered so rarely and with so much difficulty,
into the church life during the first half of this period.

Accustomed to confound regeneration and baptism, believing that they were bound to connect the grace of baptism with
the outward ordinance, with the performance of the external
act; failing to perceive that it should be something going
along with, and operating through, the entire life; many
pious but mistaken parents dreaded entrusting the baptismal
grace to the weak, unstable age of their children, which grace,
once lost by sin, could never be regained. They wished rather
to reserve it against the more decided and mature age of man-
hood, as a refuge from the temptations and storms of an uncertain life.

To a mother who acted on this principle, says Gregory of
Nazianzen: " Let sin gain no advantage in thy child; let it
be sanctified from the swaddling clothes, consecrated to the
Holy Ghost. You fear for the divine seal, because of the
weakness of nature. What a feeble and faint-hearted mother
must you be! Anna consecrated her Samuel to God, even
before he was born; immediately after his birth she made him
a priest, and she trained him up in the priestly vesture. Instead of fearing the frailty of the man, she trusted in God! "*
Others, unlike this mother, were induced, not by an error of the
understanding, but by a delusion springing from an altogether
ungodlike temper, to defer their baptism to a future time.
They had formed their conception of God, of whom they would
gladly have been relieved from the necessity of thinking, only
as an almighty judge, whose avenging arm appeared to their
unappeased conscience ready to strike them; and they sought
in baptism a means of evading the stroke, without being willing, however, to renounce their sinful pleasures. They were
disposed to enter into a sort of compact or bargain with God
and Christ,† to be permitted to enjoy, as long as possible,
their sinful pleasures, and yet in the end, by the ordinance of
baptism, which like a charm was to wipe away their sins, to
be purified from all their stains, and attain to blessedness in a

---

* Orat. 40, f. 648.
† They are very justly styled by Gregory of Nazianzen, l. c. f. 643:
Χριστοκαπήλους καὶ χριστέμπορους.

moment.* Hence many put off baptism until they were reminded by mortal sickness, or some other sudden danger of
approaching death. † Hence it was, that in times of public
calamity, in earthquakes, in the dangers of war, multitudes
hurried to baptism, and the number of the existing clergy
scarcely sufficed for the wants of all. ‡

In the case of many who first received baptism in the later
period of life, this proceeding was no doubt attended with one
advantage,—that the true import of the baptismal rite might
then be more truly expressed. It was not until after they
had been led, by some dispensation affecting the outward or
the inner life, to resolve on becoming Christians with the
whole soul, that they applied for baptism, and the ordinance,
in this case, was not a mere opus operatum; but really constituted to them the commencement of a new era of life, truly
consecrated, in the temper of the heart, to God. Thus it was,
that many made it a point, from the time of their baptism, to
enter upon the literal observance of Christ's precepts; they
would no longer take an oath; and not a few outwardly renounced the world and became monks, which, at all events,
shows what importance they attached to this ordinance. But,
on the other hand, the cause of delaying baptism, with numbers, was their want of any true interest in religion, their
being bred and living along in a medley of pagan and Christian
superstitions; nor can it be denied, that the neglect of infant
baptism contributed to prolong this sad state of things. By
means of baptism, children would have been immediately introduced into a certain connection with the church, and at
least brought more directly under its influence; instead of

---

* Gregory of Nyssa, de baptismo, T. II. f. 221, aptly calls it: Καίνη
καὶ παράδοξος ἐμπόρια, οὐ χρύσου καὶ ἐσθῆτος, ἄλλα πληθοὺς ἀνομίων, καπηλεία
περίεργος τῆς κατὰ ψύχην καθάρσεως.

† Πρὸς τὰς ἐσχάτας ἀναπνοὰς τὴν οἰκείαν ἀναβαλλόμενοι σωτηρίαν. Chrysostom. b. 18, in Joh. s. 1.

‡ Gregory of Nyssa, in the sermon above cited, mentions a case which
is said to have proved to many a warning example. A young man of a
respectable family in the town of Comana in Pontus, was fatally wounded
by the Goths—who had already taken the suburb—as he was going out
to reconnoitre. As he fell dying, he begged with a cry of despair for
baptism, which at the moment no one was at hand to bestow on him. To
be sure, if he had been more correctly taught respecting the nature of
baptism, and of the forgiveness of sin, he would not have been reduced
to such a strait.

being exposed as they now were, from their birth, to pagan superstition, and often kept at a distance, in their first training, from all contact with Christianity. To commend their children to God and to the Saviour in prayer, was not the custom of parents; but rather to call in old women, who were supposed to possess the power of protecting the life of infants by amulets and other devices of heathen superstition.*

We observed, in the preceding period, that the catechumens were distributed into two classes. To these, at the beginning of the fourth century, was added a third. At first a distinction was made, generally, between those who professed Christianity, though, they had not as yet attained to a complete knowledge of the Christian doctrines, nor received baptism—the catechumens, who were, in the common meaning of the word, called also Christians,† though in a vaguer sense,—and the fully instructed baptized Christians. ‡ The lowest class among these constituted the ἀκροώμενοι, ἀκροαταί, or auditores, audientes, who took his name from the circumstance that they were admitted to hear only the reading of the scriptures and the sermon, and then were immediately dismissed. §

* Chrysostom contrasts the Christian consecration which the child ought to receive from the first, with the pagan superstition to which it was immediately exposed : Τὰ περίαπτα καὶ τοὺς κωδώνας τοὺς τῆς χειρὸς ἐξηρτημένους καὶ τὸν κόκκινον στήμονα καὶ τὰ ἄλλα τὰ πολλῆς ἀνοίας γέμοντα, δέον μηδὲν ἕτερον τῷ παιδὶ περιτιθέναι ἀλλ᾽ ἢ τὴν ἀπὸ τοῦ σταυροῦ φυλακήν. Hom. 12, in ep. 1 ad Corinth. s. 7.

† Hence the act of the bishop or presbyter, who received those who were not Christians, as candidates for the Christian church, into the first class of catechumens, by making over them the sign of the cross : Ποιεῖν χριστιανούς. Concil. œcum. Constantinop. I. c. 7. Ποιεῖν χριστιανόν.

‡ The distinction Christiani ac fideles and Christiani et catechumeni. Cod. Theodos. de apostat. l. II.

§ Some have supposed that there was a still lower class, those who were not as yet permitted to attend the meetings of the church, the ἐξωθούμενοι. But as this attendance was allowed even to Pagans and Jews, it is scarcely possible to suppose that a class of catechumens were particularly designated by a name which signified their present exclusion. Neither would the term ἐξωθούμενοι, denoting, as it does, not the fact that persons have not yet been received, but that those once received have been excluded, be suited to the case in question. The fifth canon of the council of Neo-cæsarea (in which it was simply ordered that those ἀκροαταί who had fallen into any sin rendering them unworthy of the Christian ¦name, inasmuch as they could not be transferred to a lower class of catechumens, should be wholly excluded from the list) furnishes no warrant for the hypothesis of a particular class of excluded persons

The second class consisted of those who had already received more full and accurate instruction in Christianity. In behalf of these a special prayer of the church was offered, and they received, kneeling, the blessing of the bishop: whence their name ὑποπίπτοντες, γονυκλινόντες, Genuflectentes, Prostrati; also Catechumens in the stricter sense of the term. This prayer of the church was so composed and arranged, as to bring directly before the consciousness of these individuals their need of being enlightened by the Holy Spirit, without which the divine doctrines could not be vitally apprehended, and the necessary connection between faith and practice; as well as to assure them of the sympathy of the whole community in all their concerns.*

On leaving *this class*, they next took their place among those who proposed themselves for baptism, the baptismal can-

---

among the catechumens: on the contrary, the canon here speaks of such as were no longer to be considered as belonging to the catechumens in any sense. |

* As an example of the manner in which the Christian feeling expressed itself in these prayers, we will insert here the form of this prayer according to the liturgy of the ancient church of Antioch: "That the all-merciful God would hear their prayer, that he would open the ears of their heart, so that they might perceive what eye hath not seen nor ear heard; that he would instruct them in the word of truth; that he would plant the fear of the Lord in their hearts, and confirm the faith in his truth in their souls; that he would reveal to them the gospel of righteousness; that he would bestow on them a godly temper of mind, a prudent understanding, and an upright and virtuous walk, so that they might at all times meditate and practise what is of God, might dwell in the law of the Lord day and night; that he would deliver them from all evil, from all devilish sins, and from all temptations of the evil one; that he would vouchsafe to them, in his own time, the new birth, the forgiveness of sins, the investiture of the new, imperishable, divine life (ἔνδυμα τῆς ἀφθαρσίας. See sect. 3, and below, the doctrine concerning baptism); that he would bless their coming in and their going out, their families, their domestics; that he would multiply their children, bless them, preserve them to the ripeness of age, and make them wise; that he would cause all things that awaited them to work together for their good." The deacon then bade the catechumens, who had remained kneeling during this prayer, to arise, and invited them to pray themselves, " for the angel of peace, for peace upon all that awaited them, peace on the present days, and on all the days of their life, and for a Christian end." He concluded by saying, " Commend yourselves to the living God and to his Christ." They then received the blessing from the bishop, in which the whole community joined by saying, Amen. See Chrysostom. in epist. 2, ad Corinth. Hom. 2, s. 5.

didates,* the Competentes,† φωτιζόμενοι. They learned by
heart the confession of faith, since this was to be orally transmitted, as written on the living tablets of the heart, and not
in a dead, outward letter (see vol. i. sect. 3, p. 422); and this
confession, as containing the sum and essence of Christian doctrine, was explained to them by the lectures of the bishop or
the presbyter. To the symbolical usages connected with the
preparation for baptism, of which we have spoken in the preceding period, new ones were added, yet not the same in all
the churches. It seems to have been a custom which very
generally prevailed, for the candidates until the time they
were incorporated, on the octave of the festival of Easter, by
the complete rite of baptism (in the Western church, see
above), with the rest of the church, to wear a veil on the
head and over the face, which perhaps was meant in the first
place as it is explained by Cyrill of Jerusalem, to serve as a
symbol, expressing that the attention should not be diverted
by foreign objects; afterwards, on the ground of St. Paul's
declaration in the First Epistle to the Corinthians, the additional meaning was given to it, that, as the act of veiling was
a sign of dependence and of tutelage, so the removing of the
veil was a sign of freedom and of maturity conceded to them
as regenerated persons.‡ To exorcism was now added in-
sufflation, or breathing on the candidate (ἐμφυσᾷν, insufflare),
to denote the communication of the Holy Ghost, as the former
had denoted deliverance from unclean spirits. The bishop
next touched the ear of the candidate, saying, in the words of
Mark vii. 34, " Ephphatha, Be opened, and may God send
thee an open understanding, that thou mayest be apt to learn

* Their names were inscribed for this purpose in the church books,
the *diptycha*, the matricula ecclesiæ; which was nomen dare baptismo.
The ὀνοματογραφία is mentioned in Cyrill's prologue to his Catecheses, s.
1, and to this the mystical exposition of Gregory of Nyssa alludes, de
baptismo, T. II. f. 216, where he says, " that, as he inscribed the names
with ink in the earthly roll, so might the finger of God write them down
in his imperishable book:" Δοτέ μοι τὰ ὀνόματα, ἱνὰ ἔγω μὶν αὖτα ταῖς
αἰσθήταις ἐγχαράξω βίβλοις. In the fifth act of the council under Mennas,
A.D. 536, a deacon occurs, Ὁ τὰς προσηγορίας τῶν εἰς τὸ βαπτίσμα προ-
σιόντων ἐγγράφειν τεταγμένος.

† Simul petentes regnum cœlorum. Augustin. p. 216.

‡ Cyrill. Prolog. c. 5. Ἐσκεπάσται σοῦ τὸ προσώπον, ἱνα σχολάσῃ
λοίπον ἡ διανοία. Augustin. p. 376, s. 2. Hodie octavæ dicuntur infantium, revelanda sunt capita eorum, quod est indicium libertatis.

and to answer." * In the North-African church, the bishop
gave to those whom he received as competentes, while signing
the cross over them as a symbol of consecration, a portion of
salt, over which a blessing had been pronounced. This was
to signify the divine word imparted to the candidates as the
true salt for human nature.† When the baptism was to be performed, the candidate was led to the entrance of the bap-
tistry, where he first stood with his face towards the West as a
symbol of the darkness which he was now to renounce, and
pronounced, addressing Satan as present, the formula of renunciation, the origin and meaning of which were explained
under the preceding period : " I renounce thee, Satan ; all thy
works, all thy pomp, and all thy service." ‡ Next he turned
to the East, as a symbol of the light into which he would now
enter from the darkness, and said : " To thee, O Christ !
I devote myself." §

We noticed as existing already in the preceding period the
custom of anointing at baptism.‖ In this period, when there
was an inclination to multiply symbols, the custom arose of a
double unction ; one as a preliminary rite, denoting the consecration to be imparted to the believer by his fellowship with
Christ, whereby he was to be delivered from the sins of the
old man, the putting away of whom had just been symbolized
by the laying aside of the garments.¶ The second unction,
with the consecrated oil (the χρίσμα), the same symbolical
act which we found existing already in the preceding period,
denoted the completion of baptism by a perfect communion
of divine life with the Redeemer,—the communication of
the Holy Spirit consecrating the individual to the spiritual
Christian priesthood.** At the first anointing, the head only
was marked ; at the second, the forehead, ears, nose, and

* The sacramentum apertionis. Ambros. de iis qui mysteriis initian-
tur, c. 1. See the work ascribed to him, de sacramentis, l. I. c. 1.
† Augustin. de catechizandis rudib. c. 26. Confession. l. I. c. 11.
‡ Ἀποτάσσομαί σοι, σατανα, καὶ πάσῃ τῇ πόμπῃ σου, καὶ πάσῃ τη λατρείᾳ
σου.
§ Συντάσσομαί σοι, Χρίστε.   ‖ See vol. I. sect. 3, p. 436.
¶ Cyrill. Mystagog. II. c. 3. Κοινῶναι ἐγίνεσθε τῆς καλλιελαίου Ἰησου
Χρίστου. Constitut. apostol. VII. 22.
** Τούτου τοῦ ἁγίου χρίσματος καταξιωθέντις, καλεῖσθε χριστιανοί, says
Cyrill of Jerusalem, Cateches. Mystagog. III. c. 4, conf. Concil.
Laodic. c. 48.

breast,—to show how this consecration by the divine life should pervade and ennoble the entire human nature.

We noticed in the preceding period how, in the western church, a distinct sacrament had arisen out of *confirmation*, or the laying on the hands of the bishop as a symbol of the communication of the Holy Spirit (see above), which originally made a part of the rite of baptism. The ideas which men associated with the administration of that chrism, and with the imposition of hands by the bishop, were originally so kindred that they might easily be led to comprehend them both under one and the same conception, and to unite them in one transaction. Yet on this point the usage was still unsettled.*

The baptized now arrayed themselves in white robes, as a sign of regeneration to a new divine life of infantile purity, as in fact the laying aside of the old garments had been a symbol of the putting away of the old man. Next followed a custom in the western churches, also handed down from the foregoing period, of giving them a mixture of milk and honey as a symbol of childlike innocence (a foretype of the communion which was to be received by them).†

---

* Jerome reckons among the things reserved to the bishop the manus impositio and invocatio Spiritus Sancti, as constituting together only one act. *Adversus Luciferianos*, s. 8. Moreover, Augustin, in his work de baptismo contra Donatistas, l. V. s. 33, considers the manus impositio to be the only thing necessary in the case of those who had already received baptism in a heretical church (and so, too, Siricius, ep. ad Himerium, s. 2); so that, according to this, confirmation would consist simply in the laying on of the hands of the bishop. But the seventh canon of the council of Laodicea ordains, that the Fideles from several sects whose baptism was recognized as valid, should not be admitted to the communion till they had received the chrism. The Roman bishop, Innocent, finally decided, in his Decretals to the bishop Decentius, A.D. 416, s. 6, that the anointing of the forehead belonged to the act of consignation (in the middle age called confirmation), which was especially appropriated to the bishop. Hoc autem pontificium solis deberi episcopis, ut vel consignent vel paracletum Spiritum tradant. Presbyteris chrismate baptizatos unguere licet, sed quod ab episcopo fuerit consecratum, non tamen frontem ex eodem oleo signare, quod solis debetur episcopis, cum tradunt Spiritum paracletum.

† Hieronym. adv. Lucif. s. 8, Cod. canon. eccles. Afr. canon. 37. Mel et lac et quod uno die solennissimo,—probably Easter Sabbath or Easter Sunday—(more probably the former, because on Easter Sunday they already united together in the communion)—in infantum mysterio solet offerri.

To the times of administering this rite, more particularly observed in the preceding period, among which, however, the Easter Sabbath ever continued to be the principal one, was now added, in the Greek church, the *feast of Epiphany*,—a favourite season for the administration of this ordinance, on account of its reference to the baptism of Christ; while, by the same church, the feast of Pentecost was not reckoned among the other customary seasons for administering baptism.* The free evangelical spirit of Chrysostom declared strongly against those who would confine baptism to particular seasons, and who imagined that a genuine baptism could not be administered at any other; he brings against this opinion the examples in the Acts of the Apostles.† The narrow spirit of the Roman church, on the other hand, was here again the first to lay a restraint on Christian liberty. The Roman bishop Siricius, in his decretal addressed to Himerius, bishop of Tarraco in Spain, A.D. 385, styled it arrogant presumption in the Spanish priests that they should baptize multitudes of people at Christmas, at the feast of Epiphany, and at the festivals of the apostles and martyrs, as well as at the other regular times ; and decreed, on the other hand, that, except in the case of new-born infants, and other cases of necessity, baptisms should only be administered at the festivals of Easter and Pentecost.‡

With reference to these two constituent portions of the church assemblies, the *catechumens* § and baptized believers, the whole

* Chrysost. H. 1, in act. ap. s. 6. He here intimates as the reason, that fasts belonged, with other things, to the preparation for baptism, and that no fasts were held during the season of Pentecost.

† H. 1, in act. ap. s. 8.   ‡ See the Decretals, s. 3.

§ In respect to what took place between the two portions of time, the arrangements seem not to have been everywhere alike; and this is true especially so far as it concerns the number of the single prayers of the church appointed for the different classes of Christians. In the nineteenth canon of the council of Laodicea, the prayer for the catechumens is mentioned first after the sermon; then after their dismission, the prayer for the penitents (Pœnitentes). In the Apostolic Constitutions, there occurs also a special prayer for the baptismal candidates (Competentes); but the author of these Constitutions seeks in every way to multiply the liturgical services, and it may be questioned whether such a church-prayer was ever in actual use. We find no indication of it in Chrysostom. There certainly occurs, however, in the latter writer (H. 3, de incomprehensib. s. 6. T. I. f. 469), the notice of a special church-prayer for the Energumens, while the same is not mentioned in the above-cited canon of the Laodicean council. But it may be well sup-

service was divided into two portions: one in which the catechumens were allowed to join, embracing the reading of the scriptures and the sermon, the prevailing *didactic* portion; and the other, in which the baptized alone could take part, embracing whatever was designed to represent the fellowship of believers, —the communion and all the prayers of the church which preceded it. These were called the missa catechumenorum and the missa fidelium ($\lambda\epsilon\iota\tau o\upsilon\rho\gamma\iota a$ $\tau\tilde{\omega}\nu$ $\kappa\alpha\tau\eta\chi o\upsilon\mu\epsilon\nu\omega\nu$ and $\tau\tilde{\omega}\nu$ $\pi\iota\sigma\tau\omega\nu$);* which division must of course have fallen into disuse after the general introduction of infant baptism.

We now leave the Missa Catechumenorum to speak of the Missa Fidelium; and first of the preparations for the celebration of the communion.

The separation of the sacrament of the supper from the agapæ had, as we have observed (see vol. i. sect. 3, p. 450), been made long before in the preceding period. The original celebration of the latter was a thing so remote from the views and feelings of this present period, that the homeletic writers find it difficult even to form a just conception of it.† The agapæ had lost their original meaning. They were at pre-

posed that persons of this description would be found only in the larger towns, and under particular circumstances of climate, in sufficient numbers to constitute a class by themselves in the public worship, for whom a particular prayer would be offered. All these church-prayers, however, are known to us only from Eastern sources. The question comes up, whether these special church-prayers were in use also in the Western church, in addition to the universal prayer of the church for the different classes of Christians. Augustin, Sermo XLIX, s. 8, represents the dismission of the catechumens, and next the Paternoster, which was designed only for baptized believers, the $\epsilon\check{\upsilon}\chi\eta$ $\tau\tilde{\omega}\nu$ $\pi\iota\sigma\tau\omega\nu$, as following immediately after the sermon.

* The term *missa*, in the Latinity of this period, is a substantive, and synonymous with *missio*. The dismission of any assembly was called missa. Avitus of Vienna, ep. 1. In ecclesia palatioque missa fieri pronuntiatur, cum populus ab observantia dimittitur. In this sense Augustin used the word, p. 49, s. 8. Post sermonem fit missa catechumenorum. As the term then properly denoted the dismission of the catechumens, so it was next applied metonymically to the different portions of divine service which preceded or followed this dismission; and finally, in an altogether peculiar sense, to the communion which came afterwards, and by synecdoche to the whole of a complete service. Thus the word missa, *mass*, in its ordinary acceptation, came gradually into use.

† As, for example, Chrysostom in the twenty-seventh homily on the first epistle to the Corinthians.

sent banquets with which the wealthier members of the community sometimes entertained the poorer Christians, and at which the latter enjoyed a somewhat better fare than ordinarily fell to their lot.* The more gloomy and morose spirit, whose opposition to the agapæ we have already noticed in the preceding period, continued to show the same dislike to them in this. The above-mentioned council of Gangra, which manifested some resistance to this one-sided ascetic tendency, took the agapæ under its protection, pronouncing sentence of condemnation in its eleventh canon on those who treated these festivals with contempt when they were made from Christian motives, and discourteously refused to attend them when the brethren were invited in honour of the Lord. Other councils did not object to the agapæ, *in themselves considered*, but only forbad them to be held *in the churches*.†

In respect to the liturgical service connected with the sacrament of the supper in this period,‡ it is to be observed that it was based on the genuinely Christian view of the holy supper as representing the fellowship of divine life subsisting between believers, their Redeemer, and one another. The whole design, therefore, was to bring up to lively exercise in the minds of Christians the thought that they were now entering into communion with the ascended Christ, and should, in spirit, ascend up to where he is in heaven : that though the whole was a free gift of divine grace, yet they should be prepared to receive it by the direction of their affections to the Redeemer and by faith in him ; that without mutual love towards each other, they could not enter into communion with the Saviour. The deacon invited all present to bestow the mutual kiss of charity, as a sign of the fraternal communion of hearts, without which no true celebration of the sacred supper could be observed.§ Next the deacon called upon the assembled church

* Augustin. c. Faustum I. XX., c. 20. Agapes nostræ pauperes pascunt, sive frugibus sive carnibus. Plerumque in agapibus etiam carnes pauperibus erogantur.

† Concil. Laodicen. c. 28. Concil. Hippou. 393, or Cod. canon. eccles. Afr. 42. Later Concil. Trullan. II. c. 74.

‡ As we learn from the apostolic Constitutions, from the V. among the λόγοις μυσταγωγίκοις of Cyrill, and from the scattered fragments in the homilies of Chrysostom; also from single hints in the sermons of Augustin and of others.

§ Ἀσπάσισθε ἀλλήλους ἐν φιλήματι ἁγίῳ, or in Cyrill, ἀλλήλους ἀπολά-

to examine themselves and one another to see that no unworthy person was among them;[*] meaning by this that they should see, not merely that no catechumens, unbelievers, or heretics were present, but also that there was no one who harboured wrong feelings against his brother, no one playing the part of a hypocrite.[†] "Let us all stand up ; our eyes directed to the Lord, with fear and trembling (in the sense of our own unworthiness and weakness, and the exalted character of him who is willing to commune with us").[‡] Then, for the purpose of making it still more distinctly felt, that none but the heart whose affections were bent on heavenly things could take any part in communion with the Saviour, the deacon once more said—" Lift up your hearts :"[§] to which the church responded, " Yes, to the Lord we have lifted them up."[||] Next, in conformity with the original meaning and celebration of the ordinance, followed the invitation of the bishop, calling on the church to unite in giving thanks for all the blessings of creation and redemption ;[¶] and the church replied to the bishop's invitation in the words—" Yes, it is meet and right to give thanks unto the Lord."[**] Before the elements were distributed, the bishop, to signify that only a holy temper was prepared to participate in a holy ordinance, exclaimed, " The holy, to the holy."[††] But the church expressed the consciousness that no man is holy out of his own nature ; that only one is holy, and the sinful could be made holy only through faith in him, by exclaiming, " One is holy, one Lord, Jesus Christ,

βιτι και αλλήλους ασπαζώμεθα: which last formula doubtless was to show, that the clergy should consider this as addressed not only to the flock, but also to themselves.

[*] 'Επιγινώσκετε αλλήλους, according to Chrysostom.

[†] Μη τις κατα τινος, μη τις εν υποκρίσει.

[‡] Ορθοι προς κύριον μετα φόβου και τρόμου εστώτες ωμεν προσφέρειν. In the word προσφέρειν lies, it is true, the notion of sacrifice ; yet in this connection the term may still have reference to the notion of sacrifice, taken in the spiritual, symbolical sense. See vol. I. s. 3, p. 458; and it is singular to observe, that here the sacrificial act is set forth *according to the original view*, which held the clergy to be only the representatives of the church in the exercise of the universal Christian priesthood, as a common transaction of the priest and the flock, not as a special act of the priest alone.

[§] "Ανω τας καρδίας, or ανω τον νουν, or both together, ανω τας καρδίας και τον νουν, sursum corda.

[||] "Εχομεν προς τον κύριον.

[¶] See vol. I. s. 3. p. 456.

[**] "Αξιον και δίκαιον.

[††] Τα αγία τοις αγίοις.

blessed for ever to the glory of God the Father."* During
the celebration of the supper the 34th Psalm, particularly the
9th verse, was sung, as an invitation to the communicants.

In the consecration of the elements, it was considered to be
essentially important that the words of the institution, according to the gospel, and according to the apostle Paul,
should be pronounced without alteration; for it was the
general persuasion that when the priest uttered the words of
Christ, "This is my body, my blood," by virtue of the magical power of these words, the bread and wine were, in some
miraculous way, united with the body and blood of Christ.†
Concerning the particular notions on this point, see section iv.
These words of institution were, however, introduced into a
prayer,‡ in which God was invoked graciously to accept this
offering.§ When the bishop or presbyter was about to finish
the consecration, the curtain which hung before the altar was
drawn up,‖ and the consecrating minister now showed to the
church the outward elements of the supper, which till now
had been concealed from their eyes, lifting them up, as the
body and blood of Christ.¶ That the church then fell on
their knees, or that they prostrated themselves on the ground,

---

* Εἷς ἅγιος, εἷς κύριος, εἷς Ἰησοῦς Χριστός, εἷς δόξαν Θεοῦ πάτρος εὐλογητὸς
εἷς τοὺς αἰῶνας, ἀμήν.

† See Chrysostom. hom. 1, de proditione Judæ, s. 6, T. II. f. 384.
Τοῦτο τὸ ῥῆμα μεταρρύθμιζει τὰ προκείμενα· ἡ φωνὴ αὕτη ἅπαξ λιχθεῖσα καθ'
ἑκαστην τράπεζαν ἐν ταῖς ἐκκλησίαις ἐξ ἐκείνου μέχρι σήμερον καὶ μέχρι τῆς αὐτοῦ
παρουσίας τὴν θυσίαν ἀπερτισμένην ἐργάζεται. De sacramentis, lib. IV. c.
4. Ubi venitur, ut conficiatur sacramentum, jam non suis sermonibus
sacerdos, sed utitur sermonibus Christi; ergo sermo Christi hoc confecit
sacramentum.

‡ Basilius, de Sp. S. c. 27, says, that besides the words taken from the
gospels and from Paul, many others were here used from tradition.
Προλέγομεν καὶ ἐπιλέγομεν ἕτερα.

§ Such a form of prayer has been preserved to us in the work de
sacramentis, l. c.; and it is remarkable, that here, too, the primitive
way of thinking and feeling still manifests its presence, since it was
not Christ, but the bread and wine, the symbols of his body, which
were represented as the object of the sacrificial act. Hanc oblationem—it
runs—quod est figura corporis et sanguinis domini nostri, offerimus tibi
hunc panem sanctum.

‖ Chrysostom. hom. 3, in epist. ad Ephes. s. 5. Ἀνελκόμενα τὰ
ἀμφίθυρα.

¶ Basil. de Sp. S. c. 27: Ἀναδείξις τοῦ ἄρτου καὶ τοῦ ποτηρίου. Dionys.
Areopagit. hierarch. 3. Of the consecrating officer it is said: Τ͞τ' ὄψιν
ἄγει ἀνακαλύψας.

cannot indeed be proved by the authority of any ecclesiastical writer of this period. We know it was not until a much later period that this usage was introduced into the Western church; but the custom, to say the least, fell in with the prevailing views and language of the Greek church;* and this outward sign of reverence was, in fact, more frequently used by the latter, and in a less rigid sense, than among the people of the West.

The confounding of the inward thing with the outward sign in the sacrament of the supper, gave rise to many expressions of a superstitious reverence for the external symbols of the ordinance;† while this superstitious reverence had no tendency whatever to promote the worthy use of it as a means of grace. On the contrary, the more men were accustomed to look upon the holy supper as possessing a power to sanctify by some magical operation from without, the less they thought of what was requisite on the part of the inner man, in order to a right use of this means of grace in its religious and moral purport; a fact made sufficiently evident by the censures and admonitions which the Greek fathers found it necessary so frequently to introduce in their homilies.

We already noticed, in the preceding period, the origin of the diversity of custom which prevailed in respect to the less frequent or the daily participation in the communion. This difference of practice continued to prevail also in the present period. In the *Roman*, the *Spanish*, and the *Alexandrian* churches,‡ daily communion was still practised, at least in the fourth century. In other churches the custom was to observe the communion less frequently; each individual, in fact, joining in it according as his own inward necessities required. This diversity of practice also grew out of the different views which prevailed respecting the use of this means of grace. Some, who were in favour of the less frequent participation of

---

* See Theodoret. Dial. II. in confus. respecting the outward elements in the supper: Προσκυνεῖται ὡς ἐκείνα ὄντα ἅπερ πιστεύεται.

† Thus Cyrill of Jerusalem, Mystagog. v. 17, recommends that, as long as any moisture remained in the mouth, Christians should apply it to the hand, and with the hand so moistened touch the forehead, the eyes, and the other organs of sense, and thus sanctify them.

‡ Respecting the two first, see Hieronymus, ep. 71, ad Lucinium, s. 6; —respecting the latter, Basilius of Cæsarea, ep. 93.

the sacrament, said, certain seasons ought to be chosen in which Christians might prepare themselves, by a life of severity and abstinence, by collecting the thoughts, and by self-examination, for a worthy participation, so as not to join in the holy ordinance to their own condemnation. Others maintained that Christians ought never to keep away from the ordinance, except when, on account of some great transgression, they were by the sentence of the bishop suspended from the communion and condemned to church penance; on all other occasions they ought to look upon the Lord's body as a daily means of salvation.* Augustin and Jerome reckoned these differences also among the ones where each individual, without prejudice to Christian fellowship, was bound to proceed according to the usage of his own church, and according to his own subjective point of view. " Each of them," says Augustin, " honours the Lord's body in *his own way;* just as there was no difference between Zaccheus and that centurion, when one of them received the Lord joyfully into his house, Luke xix. 6, and the other said, ' Lord, I am not worthy that thou shouldst come under my roof,' (Matt. viii. 8,)—both honouring the Saviour in different, and, so to speak, opposite ways, both felt themselves wretched in their sins, both obtained grace." Chrysostom inclines to the opinion that, as the celebration of the communion of believers with the Lord and with one another, in the sacred supper, belonged to the essential being of every church assembly, therefore, whenever the communion was celebrated in the church, all should participate in it: but here assuredly everything depends on its being done in the right temper of heart, else it must only redound to the condemnation of him who unworthily participates in the ordinance. " Many," says he, in a discourse preached at Antioch,† " partake of the sacrament *once* in the year, others *twice.* The anachorets in the deserts oftentimes can partake of it only once in two years. Neither of these cases can be approved, in itself considered. We can give our unqualified approbation only to those who come to the communion with a pure heart, a conscience void of offence, and a blameless life. Such may continually repair to the sacrament of the supper; but those who are not so disposed eat and drink condemnation to them-

---

* See Augustin. ep. 54, ad Januar. s. 4.
† H. 17, in ep. ad Hebr. s. 4.

selves, even though they partake of it but once." He was obliged to complain that many who, on ordinary occasions, felt themselves unworthy to participate in the communion, still had no scruples to communicate once a year, after the fasts, at the festival of Easter, or of the Epiphany; just as if they did not incur the same condemnation, whether they received the holy supper at these or at any other times in an unholy temper of mind.* He complains† that of those who, on other days when the church assembled, attended the entire missa fidelium, very few participated in the communion, to which the whole liturgy had reference; so that the whole act in this case was a mere formality. "They either belong to the class of the unworthy, who are notified (see above) to depart from the assembly, or they remain behind as belonging with the worthy, in which case they ought to partake of the communion. What a contradiction, that, while they join in all those confessions and songs, they yet cannot participate of the Lord's body!"

In those cases, however, where the custom of daily communion still prevailed, but divine service was held and the sacramental supper consecrated only once or twice on Sunday and Friday, or at most but four times a week, on Sunday, Saturday, Wednesday, and Friday, no other course remained for those who were desirous of having the body of the Lord for their daily nourishment, except to take home with them a portion of the consecrated bread—for a superstitious dread prevented them from taking with them the wine, which might be so easily spilled—and to reserve it for future use, so that now they might every day, before engaging in any worldly employment, participate of the sacrament, and consecrate and strengthen themselves by communion with the Lord.‡ In voyages by sea, also, Christians were in the habit of taking with them a

---

* H. 5, in ep. 1, ad Timoth. s. 3. In ep. ad Ephes. homil. 3, s. 4.

† The last-cited place, s. 5.

‡ This is said by Jerome, in ep. 48, ad Pammachium, s. 16, concerning Rome: Romæ hanc esse consuetudinem ut fideles semper Christi corpus accipiant; and subsequently in reference to those who, although they were afraid to come to church, yet had no fear of participating in the Lord's body at home, he says: An alius in publico, alius in domo, Christus est? In like manner, Basil of Cæsarea says of Alexandria ep. 93, that in that place each one communicated, whenever he pleased, at home.

portion of the consecrated bread, so as to have it in their power to partake of the sacrament by the way.*

This abuse, so contradictory to the original design of the holy supper, whereby it was converted into a sort of amulet,† was the occasion, too, of bringing about the first deviation from the original form of institution ; for Christians were now satisfied when they partook of the consecrated bread without the cup.   In other respects, the full participation of the sacrament in both kinds was uniformly held to be necessary.   The contrary practice was condemned as savouring of Manichæism; since the Manichæans, conformably to their ascetic principles, avoid a partaking of the wine in the sacrament of the supper.‡

The preceding period shows us how, by a change of the idea of the Christian priesthood, another shape and direction was given also to the original idea of a sacrificial act in the sacrament of the supper.   In the present period we may still trace, by various marks, the separate existence of these very different elements, out of which the notion of a sacrifice in the Lord's Supper gradually arose.   On the one hand, was the *older form of intuition* and the *older phraseology*, according to which the name sacrifice was referred to the *outward elements*, so far as these represented the gifts of nature, all to be consecrated to God in the temper of grateful, child-like love : on the other, was the later form of intuition, which referred the sacrifice to the body of Christ himself.   Again, considerable prominence was given, it is true, on one side, to the assertion that, if the

---

* See Ambros. oratio funebris de obitu fratris Satyri. This notion of a magical virtue residing in the bread, is illustrated by an example which Ambrose here relates in the case of his own brother. The latter, at some period before he had received baptism, being on board a ship which ran ashore and was wrecked, obtained from some of his fellow voyagers who had been baptized, a portion of the consecrated bread, which they carried with them. This he bound round his neck, and then confidently threw himself into the sea. He was the first to get to the land, and of course ascribed his deliverance to the power of this charm.

† Meanwhile we find, in the third canon of the council of Cæsaraugusta, (Saragossa,) A.D. 380, and in the fourteenth canon of the first council of Toledo, A.D. 400, a stringent decree against those who did not partake of the sacrament of the supper at church ; but this decree may perhaps have been directed, not so much against the abuse of treasuring up the consecrated element, by itself considered, as against the hypocritical catholicism of the Priscillians.

‡ See Leo the Great, Sermo 41.

sacrament of the supper must, in the last reference, be called a sacrifice, yet by this was to be understood simply the celebration of the memory of Christ's sacrifice once for all; but still the notion here crept in, of effects and influences similar to those of a priestly sacrifice.

At this point came in many traditional usages from the preceding period, which, though they sprung originally out of a purely Christian feeling, yet, on account of their connection with the false notion of a sacrifice, received an unevangelical meaning. With the prayer of thanks at the celebration of the Lord's Supper, were united intercessions for all the different classes of Christendom, and also intercessions for the repose of the souls of the dead. · In the uniting together of these objects, the idea lying at bottom was, that all the prayers of Christians, both thanksgivings and intercessions, derived their Christian significancy from their reference to the Redeemer and to the redemption; that the spirit of love which actuated the community of believers longed to have the blessed effects of the redemption experienced by all the individual members of Christ's body, and also by those who did not as yet belong to it, who must first be incorporated into it by divine grace; that nothing could be alien from this love, which concerned the individual members of the body of Christ; that the fellowship between those who had died in the faith of the Lord, and the living members of the same community of the Lord, still endured, and could not be interrupted by death; that the celebration of the remembrance of Christ's sufferings for the redemption of mankind was especially suited to call forth all these feelings. It is this combination of ideas, too, though not so distinctly apprehended, which lies at the basis of those rhetorico-poetical representations in the Greek homilists, concerning the connection of these church-prayers for the celebration of the Lord's supper.[*] Petitions were offered for those who had fallen asleep in Christ, and for those who celebrated their memory.[†] On this occasion, too, the individuals were particularly mentioned by name, who had made donations to

---

[*] E. g. Chrysostom. h. 21, in act. apostol. s. 4. Καταγγέλλεται τότε τὸ μυστήριον τὸ φρίκτον, ὅτι ὑπὲρ τῆς οἰκουμένης ἰδώκεν ἑαυτόν ὁ Θεός, μετὰ τοῦ θαύματος ἐκείνου εὐκαιρῶς ὑπομιμνήσκει αὐτὸν τῶν ἡμαρτηκότων.

[†] Ὁ διάκονος βοᾷ: ὑπὲρ τῶν ἐν Χριστῷ κεκοιμημένων καὶ τῶν τὰς μνείας ὑπὲρ αὐτῶν ἐπιτελουμένων.

the church; a practice certainly calculated to inspire the more wealthy with a false confidence, by leading them to imagine that by such gifts they could purchase the remission of their sins, or to flatter their vanity, since they considered it a special honour to have their names thus publicly proclaimed.* Parents, children, husbands, and wives, celebrated the memory of their departed friends by laying a gift on the altar at their death and on each returning anniversary of it, thus causing them to be particularly remembered in the prayers of the church.†

But now, when the idea of a commemorative celebration of the sacrifice of Christ for mankind passed insensibly into the idea of an efficacious sacrificial act of the priest standing as a mediator between God and men, it was just from the connection of these intercessions and offerings with this sacrificial act that a special efficacy was attributed to them.‡ The expressions, more rhetorical than dogmatically precise, which were employed by the Greek homilists, for the purpose of representing to the imagination the efficacy of these intercessions,§ like-

---

* See Hieronymus, lib. II. in Jeremiam opp. ed. Martianay, T. III. f. 584. Nunc publice recitantur offerentium nomina, et redemptio peccatorum mutatur in laudem,—also the 29th canon of the council of Elvira, nomen alicujus ab altare cum oblatione recitare. The Roman bishop Innocent directed that all the gifts presented should first be commended to God, as consecrated to his service by the love of the Christians; and that then all the individuals should be mentioned by name in the prayers of the church at the celebration of the communion. Prius oblationes sunt commendandæ. ac tunc eorum nomina, quorum sunt, edicenda, ut *inter sacra mysteria* nominentur, ep. 25, ad Decentium, s. 5. The patrons of the church were also specially mentioned on this occasion: for Chrysostom represents it as a special privilege of the proprietor who allows a church to be built on his land, τὸ ἐν ταῖς ἁγίαις ἀναφόραις ἀεὶ τὸ ὄνομα σοῦ ἐγκεῖσθαι. H. 28, in act. ap. s. 5.

† Chrysost. h. 29, in act. ap. s. 3. Ἔθος ὁ δεῖνα ἔχει ποιεῖν τὴν ἀνάμνησιν τῆς μήτρος ἢ τῆς γυναικὸς ἢ τοῦ παιδίου. Epiphanius cites among other ancient usages of the church, expos. fid. cathol. Ἐπὶ τῶν τελευτησάντων ἐξ ὀνόματος τὰς μνήμας ποιοῦνται, προσευχὰς τελοῦντες. καὶ λατρείας καὶ οἰκονομίας. Chrysostom distinguishes expressly the presentation of the Lord's Supper, in reference to the departed, from the prayer and the alms connected therewith. Οὐκ εἰκῆ προσφοραὶ ὑπὲρ τῶν ἀπελθόντων γίνονται, οὐκ εἰκῆ ἱκετηρίαι, οὐκ εἰκῆ ἐλεημόσυναι. In act. ap. H. 21, s. 4.

‡ Thus the words of Innocent, in the above-cited passage from his Decretals, refer to this connection: Ut ipsis mysteriis viam futuris precibus aperiamus.

§ See Chrysostom. H. 21, in act. ap. s. 4. "As, on the celebration

wise contributed to promote the tendency, already existing in the popular belief, to regard this ordinance in the light of a charm, just as in other cases we may often observe a similar action and reaction between the dogmatical and the liturgical departments.

Still, however, the opposite purely evangelical way of regarding the relation of the sacramental supper to Christ's sacrifice is expressly adopted by Chrysostom, when he says: "Do we not offer every day? We do offer, it is true; but only in this sense, that we celebrate *the memory of Christ's death.*[*] We ever present the same offering; or rather we *celebrate the remembrance of that one offering.*"[†] This purely Christian way of regarding the ordinance is presented also by Augustin, when he says that Christians, by the presentation and participation of the body and blood of Christ, celebrate the memory of the offering made once for all;[‡] when he styles the Lord's Supper an offering in *this* sense, that it is the sacrament which celebrates the remembrance of the sacrifice of Christ.[§] His mode of apprehending the idea of sacrifice seems to proceed from a genuinely Christian spirit. The true sacrifice consists, according to him, in this: that the soul, consumed by the fire of divine love, consecrates itself wholly to God. All actions which flow from such a temper are, in this sense, sacrifices. The whole redeemed city of God, the community of saints, is the universal offering presented to God by the High Priest, who has offered himself for us, that we, following his example, might become the body of so great a head. This, the celebration of Christ's sacrifice in the sacrament of the holy supper represents; in the sacrifice of Christ, the church at the

of an imperial victory, the imprisoned obtain their liberty, but he who lets this opportunity slip obtains no further grace, so it is here." And Cyrill of Jerusalem, Cateches. Mystagog. v. s. 7. "Just as when the emperor condemns one to banishment, but if his kinsmen present a chaplet in his behalf, the emperor is induced to show him some favour; so we present to God, in behalf of those who are asleep, though they were sinners, the Christ who was offered for our sins."

* H. 17, in ep. ad Hebr. s. 3. 'Αλλ' ἀναμνήσιν ποιούμινοι τοῦ θανάτου αὐτοῦ.

† Μᾶλλον δὲ ἀναμνήσιν ἐργαζόμιθα θυσίας.

‡ Peracti ejusdem sacrificii memoriam celebrant. c. Faust. l. XX., c. 18.

§ L. c. c. 21. Sacrificium Christi per sacramentum memoriæ celebratur.

same time presents itself as a sacrifice to God. That is, the living celebration of the memory of Christ's sacrifice in Christian communion necessarily includes in it, that they who are united together, by faith in the Redeemer, in one community of God, should in spirit follow the Saviour, and, as they have been redeemed, in order wholly to belong to him and to serve him, give themselves unreservedly to God.* But had Augustin conceived and expressed this in a way so entirely clear, and introduced into the sacramentum memoriæ nothing besides, no room would have been left for the notion of a sacrificial act working on for the salvation of others. He did connect with it, however, the idea already implied in the practice of the church, of an offering for the repose of departed souls.† It was thus, then, that the germ of the false idea of sacrifice still continued to be propagated; and so it passed over, by means of Gregory the Great (with whom we shall commence the next period), in its fully developed form, to the succeeding centuries.

To that which, in itself considered, had sprung out of a purely Christian root, but had received a different turn by becoming diverted and estranged from the original Christian spirit, belonged also the *celebration of the memory of the great teachers of the universal church, divinely enlightened by the Holy Spirit*, or of distinguished individual confessors of the faith. By itself considered, a purely Christian feeling and interest manifested themselves in this fact, that men not only looked for and acknowledged the working of the Holy Spirit in the great whole of the church, but had their attention particularly directed also to the special forms of this activity in the sanctified and enlightened human minds which had specially served as the organs of that Spirit; that in these, and the labours of these, men specially honoured the power and grace of God, the Redeemer and Sanctifier, and gave this particular direction to the views of their contemporaries and of the following generations, which should go on to develop themselves under the influence of Christian remembrances. The

---

* De civitate Dei, l. X. c. 6. Quod etiam sacramento altaris fidelibus non frequentat ecclesia, ubi ei demonstratur, quod in ea re, quam offert, ipsa offeratur.

† Ep. 32, ad Aurelium, s. 6. Oblationes pro spiritibus dormientium, quas vere aliquid adjuvare credendum est.

commemorative days of holy men passed over from the preceding period into this; many such days were celebrated in those particular portions of the church where these men were born, or where they had laboured; and some of them throughout the whole church, with more than usual pomp and circumstance. The latter was the case with festivals in commemoration of the martyrdom of Peter and Paul, which were among the principal festivals at Rome, and with the feast in honour of St. Stephen.*

The Christian mode of judgment was shown also in this, that men no longer shrunk from the contact of a dead body as if it were unclean and defiling, but looked upon the body as the organ of a purified soul, destined to be transfigured to a higher form of existence. Hence it was, that the repose of such bodies was watched with the faithful memory of reverence and love; that they were gladly received and deposited in newly erected churches, so as to connect these places, as it were, by an outward historical bond with the Christian deeds of the church achieved in more ancient times. But we observed already, in the preceding period, how the multitude began to incline towards a deification of human instruments. The church-teachers, who in one respect resisted this popular bent,† yet in another were hurried along themselves by the same spirit; and they certainly fostered in the germ that ten-

---

* The fact that this last-mentioned festival was transferred by the Western church to the day after Christmas is not to be ascribed to any exaggerated reverence for Stephen, that ventured to compare him in some sense with Christ; but the reason of it is to be found rather in the right apprehension of Stephen's relation to his Saviour and Master, to whom he bore witness by his confession and death. In this way it was intended to represent Stephen as the first witness of Christ, who was born on the day before; it was intended by this to make it manifest, that without the Saviour's birth, Stephen could not have suffered this martyrdom; that his martyrdom was a standing memorial of what human nature had attained by Christ's nativity. The Western homilists, especially Augustin, understood very well how to unfold and turn to good account this connection of ideas.

† At the death of a venerated monk, contentions might arise between the people of the city and the country about the possession of his body. See Theodoret, hist. religios. c. 21, T. III. p. 1239. But pious monks, as has been already seen in the case of Anthony, took care beforehand to have the place of their burial concealed, and to prevent their bodies becoming objects of worship. See hist. religios. p. 1148 and 1221, in the vol. just cited.

dency, the extravagances and manifestly pagan-like offshoots of which they were contending against. The churches now erected over the tombs of the martyrs tended to promote the veneration for them. The feelings and remembrances here awakened by the place itself, might in many cases lead to extraordinary effects on the mind. Thus it may be explained how the conscience of many a guilty individual might here be aroused, and impel him to the confession of his crime; * how many kinds of diseases, where a particular bent of the imagination or state of the nervous system had special sway, might here be relieved,—especially mental diseases, as indeed many of the churches of the martyrs were celebrated for the cure of demoniacs. The same effects were attributed to the reliques of saints and martyrs, the sight and touch of which often produced great effects, by virtue of what they were for the mind of the beholder. The fact was triumphantly appealed to, that the divine grace, revealed itself in so manifold ways through these consecrated organs, that the body of each martyr was not preserved in a single burial place, but cities and villages shared it between them; and that although the martyr's body was thus distributed in fragments, yet the gracious virtue of the remains continued to be undivided. † But in this way it came about, that the people, on whom what was immediately present, and made a direct impression on their own senses, exerted the greatest influence, instead of adhering steadfastly to the one Saviour and Mediator for sinful humanity, forgot him in their admiration of men standing in equal need of redemption with themselves, and made the latter their mediators; and that much which was essentially heathen became incorporated, under a Christian form, with Christian modes of feeling and thinking. There were to be found in the churches of the martyrs, as formerly in the temples of pagan gods, representa-

---

* Augustin tells the story of a thief, who was about to perjure himself in the church of a martyr, but was so wrought upon as to confess his theft, and restore the stolen property. Novimus Mediolani apud memoriam sanctorum, ubi mirabiliter et terribiliter dæmones confitentur, furem quendam, qui ad eum locum venerat, ut falsum jurando deciperet, compulsum fuisse confiteri furtum et quod abstulerat reddere. Augustin. ep. 78, s. 3.

† Theodoret. Ἑλληνικ. Θεραπευτικη παθήματ. Disputat. 8. p. 902. Πόλυς καὶ κῶμαι ταῦτα διανειμάμιναι· μεριϲθέντος τοῦ ϲώματος ἀμερίϲτος ἡ χάρις μεμίνηκε.

tions in gold or silver, of limbs supposed to have been healed by help of the martyrs, and which were suspended there as consecrated gifts.* Transferring to these churches the old practice of incubation in the temples of Æsculapius, sick persons laid themselves down in them, and sought for the cure of their complaints by such remedies as it was supposed the martyrs would reveal in dreams, during the night; and many were the legends told of their appearances on these occasions. If a man was about to start on a journey, he besought some martyr to accompany and protect him; and on his safe return, he repaired again to the church to return thanks. As, under paganism, every province and city had its tutelary deity, so now the martyrs were converted into these tutelary beings.† Sometimes pagan myths were mixed up with Christian legends, martyrs converted into mythical personages, and others invented who never lived. Thus the fable of Castor and Pollux was transferred to Phocas, a martyr, said to have been a gardener at Sinope, in Pontus,—whether any such person ever lived, or the whole was but a mythical invention,—and he was converted into a patron saint of sailors, whose opportune appearance and friendly interposition formed the subject of many a legend.‡ The pagan celebrations in memory of the dead (the parentalia), offerings and sacrificial banquets in honour of the manes, were transferred to martyrs and other deceased persons, at whose graves the people prepared feasts, which they were invited to attend as guests. Well-meaning bishops had over-

* Theodoret. l. c. T. IV. f. 922.

† As Theodoretus says himself, l. c. 902: Σωτῆρας καὶ ψύχων καὶ σωμάτων καὶ ἰατροὺς ὀνομαζοῦσι καὶ ὡς πολιούχους τιμῶσι καὶ φύλακας· and Synesius says of the Thracian martyrs :—

> Θέους
> Δρησστῆρας ὅσοι
> Γόνιμον Θράκης
> "Εχουσι πέδον.

' Hymn III. v. 458.

‡ Connected with this was the following beautiful, though not purely Christian custom. During a voyage at sea, in preparing the common table for the whole crew, a dish was set for Phocas, who was supposed to be an invisible guest. The different individuals of the crew purchased this dish in turn. The amount of all the days of the voyage was reckoned up, and, the vessel having prosperously terminated her voyage, the crew distributed all the money thus collected among the poor, as a testimony of gratitude for the successful journey. Asterius in Phocam.

looked these things in the untutored multitude, hoping that by
the triumph of Christianity over sensual rudeness, these abuses
would disappear of themselves.* But it was by means of this
unwise connivance, springing from an anxiety to promote conversion by masses, that encouragement was given to the habit of
confounding pagan and Christian customs, and the pervading
influence of the Christian spirit greatly retarded. The abuse,
which might have been more easily suppressed at the beginning, was now upheld by the authority of the older bishops,
and by length of time became so inveterate, that a North-
African council could only decree that these banquets should
be discontinued as far as possible,† and that it required all the
firmness and pastoral prudence of an Augustin, which few
possessed in the same eminent degree, to get the better here
over the rudeness and superstition of the multitude.‡

Pagans and Manichæans already frequently reproached the
catholic church with deifying the saints. As it regards the
pagans, it was indeed oftentimes the very circumstance which
most completely accorded with the *Christian feelings*, that
was most repugnant to their own. The church fathers defended themselves against this reproach, by affirming that it
was far from being the design of the church to deify the martyrs; that they were only honoured and loved as instruments
of the divine working. Thus, Augustin says: §—" The
Christian people celebrate the memory of the martyrs, as well
that we may be excited to emulate their virtues as that we
may share in their merits and be supported by their prayers.
Yet it is not to the martyrs, but only to the God of the
martyrs, even in churches consecrated to their memory, that

* See vol. I. sect. 3.
† Concil. Hippou. A.D. 393, quantum fieri potest.
‡ See the report on this matter in Augustin, ep. 29, ad Alypium. This
pagan celebration was transferred particularly to the festival which was
held originally in remembrance of the power to bind and to loose, conferred on Peter, the natalitia ecclesiæ et episcopatus. As this festival
fell on the 22nd of February, the usages connected with various kinds
of sin-offerings, the *parentalia februationes*, which happened in the
month of February, came to be mixed in with it. Perhaps, too, the idea
of the keys to the kingdom of heaven being given to Peter gave occasion
for the introduction of various pagan ideas and customs of this sort. See
concil. Turon. II. A.D. 567, c. 22, against those qui in festivitate cathe-
dræ Petri cibos mortuis offerunt.
§ C. Faust. l. 21. c. 21.

we erect altars.   What bishop has ever stood at the altar near the grave of a martyr, and said, ' We offer to thee Peter, Paul, or Cyprian!'   Whatever is offered, we offer to the God who crowned the martyrs, and we present it on the holy spots consecrated to the memory of those whom he has crowned; so that, by the very recollections of the place, our feelings may rise upward, and our love be enkindled as well towards those whose example we would imitate, as towards Him by whose help we may be enabled to do so.   We honour the martyrs, then, with that reverence of love and communion which even in this life we pay to the holy men of God, who, in the temper of their hearts, appear to us to be prepared to suffer such things for the gospel truth.   But the former we reverence with the greater devotion, as the confidence is greater with which it can be done, after the conflict is over,—as the assurance with which we praise the conquerors is more complete than we can have with regard to those who are still engaged in the conflict."   So Theodoret: " We honour them as witnesses and well-disposed servants of the most High."[*]   The church-teachers, as well as the rest, shared in that wide-spread faith in the operations of divine grace through the remains which had once served as the sanctified bodily organs of these men.   They looked upon these as an evidence of the importance which a *sanctified* man, in whatever state or condition, had in the sight of God; they spoke on this subject with enthusiasm: but at the same time they constantly referred back from these sanctified men to God the author of all, and represented them as only living monuments of the Redeemer's grace.   Teachers like Chrysostom and Augustin exhorted their hearers not to place their dependence on the intercession of the martyrs without any holiness of their own; not to use them as a crutch for their own inactivity; representing the martyrs and saints as being, after all, but *men*, in their *sinful nature* the same with all others; and calling upon their hearers to reverence them truly by imitating their virtues.   In a word, we find here various conflicting elements of a Christian estimation of true worth, and an unevangelical overvaluation of human instruments.

So also the liturgy of the Eastern church, where it makes

---

[*] L. c. 903.   'Ως Θεοῦ γε μάρτυρας καὶ εὐνοῦς θεραπόντας.

mention of the martyrs, contains something at variance with the exaggerated reverence bestowed on them. For as the original custom of *oblationes pro martyribus* arose from the fact that they were placed on the same level with other redeemed sinful men, so this view of the case passed over into the liturgical forms, and the martyrs were mentioned in like manner with others, in the intercessions.* We must endeavour to reconcile this element, originating in the primitive Christian way of thinking, with the prevailing notions concerning the martyrs, by some such explanation as the following: that although the martyrs were mentioned in the same rank and series, yet this was done with a different reference and in another sense; the martyrs being considered as a standing witness of the redeeming power of Christ's sufferings, the remembrance of which was celebrated in the sacrament of the supper, and also of his victory over death; † just as in the celebration of a triumph of the emperor, all those partook of the honour who had borne any share in obtaining the victory.

Much, however, as the more distinguished teachers of the church laboured to reconcile with the essence of the pure Christian worship of God, and so to spiritualize, the worship of the saints, still the extravagant encomiums which they bestowed on them, in their rhetorico-poetical style of writing and speaking, could not fail to result in promoting the popular superstition. And by the same principle on which they here proceeded to spiritualize the worship of the saints, the New-Platonic philosophers could sublimate and spiritualize polytheism itself.

But here, too, as in the case of the overstrained ascetic tendency, respecting which we have already spoken, an opposition manifested itself, which grew out of the original Christian spirit still remaining in the church. The extravagant veneration paid to the martyrs, which, among the people bordering on idolatry, moved the presbyter Vigilantius of Barcelona, a native of Gaul—whom we have mentioned in another connection as an opponent of the one-sided ascetic tendency and of Monachism—to call the whole thing in ques-

---

* In the general προσφορα for the community of believers, it was said also: Κᾄν μάρτυρις ὦσι κᾄν ὑπὲρ μαρτύρων. Chrysostom. h. 21, in act. ap. s. 4.

† Chrysostom.: Καὶ τοῦτο τοῦ τι θανατῶσθαι τὸν θάνατον σημεῖον.

tion. He seems to have been a man possessed, indeed, of
too headstrong a temper, yet actuated by an honest and pious
zeal for preserving the purity of the Christian faith.* Had
he used greater moderation in attacking aberrations of the
religious spirit which still had some foundation in the feelings, although misinterpreted, of the Christian heart, he might
have accomplished more. In a tract written against the
abuses of the church in his time, he calls the venerators of
martyrs and reliques "ashes-worshippers and idolaters."† He
represents it as supremely ridiculous to manifest such veneration, nay, adoration, of a miserable heap of ashes and
wretched bones; to cover them under costly drapery, and
kiss them.‡

In answer to this reproach of worshipping the martyrs,
Jerome replies, that Christians were far from intending to pay
creatures the honour which is due to the Creator alone; they
so honoured the reliques of the martyrs as to worship Him only
of whom the martyrs had borne testimony. The honour they
showed to the servants had reference to the Master himself,
who says, Matt. x. 40, " He that receiveth you, receiveth me."
*But was the thought which Jerome here makes so prominent
actually present to the consciousness of the people in their
veneration of reliques and martyrs?*

When Vigilantius spoke of *wretched bones*, Jerome could
very justly reply, that the devotion of believers saw and felt
somewhat more than this in them; that to the eye of faith,
there was nothing here which was dead; but that, through
these, believers looked up to the saints living with God:
that God is, in truth, not the God of the dead, but of the
living.

Vigilantius complained that the heathen practice of placing
lighted lamps before the images of their gods had been transferred to the martyrs; that wax tapers were burned during

* Hence may have proceeded the somewhat ignorant zeal which he
manifested in the Origenistic controversies. See below.

† Cinerarios et idololatras. Hieronym. ep. 109, ad Riparium.

‡ Quid necesse est, te tanto honore non solum honorare, sed etiam
adorare illud nescio quid, quod in modico vasculo transferendo colis?
ubicunque pulvisculum nescio quod in modico vasculo pretioso lintea-
mine circumdatum osculantes adorant. Hieronym. c. Vigilant. s. 4.
The nescio quod intimates, perhaps, that the bones of some unknown
person were often given out for reliques.

the day-light in the churches of the martyrs;*—how could they think of honouring those martyrs by the light of miserable wax candles, on whom the Lamb in the midst of God's throne reflected all the brightness of his majesty? To this Jerome replies:—"Even though some of the laity or pious women might, in their simplicity, suppose the martyrs were so honoured, yet we are bound to recognise and to respect the pious feelings evinced, though they may err in the mode of their expression. Thus Christ approved the pious feelings of the woman who anointed him, and reproved the disciples who found fault with her." Such considerations ought, indeed, to teach indulgence towards errors of religious feeling ; yet not the less on this account ought those errors to be censured which might prove so dangerous to pure Christianity. True, the charity which seeks out and indulgently embraces what-ever of truth may be lying at the ground of the error, ought not to fail ; and it is only in connection with this charity that zeal for truth can work rightly ; but neither should the cor-rective zeal for truth be wanting, if the error must not be suffered at length wholly to supplant the fundamental truth, and Christianity to be completely subverted by the unchristian element. Zeal for truth, actuated by the spirit of love, must operate constantly as a corrective and refining energy in the life of the church, if its divine foundation is to be preserved pure and entire.

Vigilantius inveighed also against the nocturnal assemblies (the vigils) held in the churches of the martyrs; asserting, what his antagonist Jerome could not deny, that these assem-blies, in which both the sexes participated, frequently served as a pretext and as an occasion for gross immoralities. He seems also to have thought it unbefitting that the vigils— which, according to ancient usage, were a distinctive feature of the Easter festival—should be transferred to the festival of the martyrs. He inveighed next against the *reliance placed on the intercessions of the martyrs.* "According to the holy scriptures," says he, "the living only should mutually pray for each other." To this Jerome replies, that, if the apostles and martyrs in this earthly life, before they had yet come

---

* Prope vitium gentilium videmus sub prætextu religionis introduc-tum in ecclesiis, sole adhuc fulgente moles cereorum accendi.

safely out of the conflict, were able to pray for others, how much more could they do so after they had obtained the victory. But what word of scripture bids the faithful call upon such departed saints to be their intercessors, as it invites the living to mutual intercession for each other, in the fellowship of love?

As an argument against such innovations, Vigilantius affirms that the martyrs could not be present wherever they were invoked to hear men's petitions, and to be ready to succour them. Here he may have conceived of the habitation of the blessed spirits after a manner somewhat confined and local, and possibly may have taken various figurative expressions of the New Testament in too material and literal a sense.* On the other hand, Jerome asserts of the glorified saints, that they follow the Lamb whithersoever he goes, Rev. xiv. 4. If, then, the Lamb is everywhere present, so must we believe that they also who are with the Lamb are everywhere present; thus the faithful are, in spirit, everywhere present with Christ. Both Vigilantius and Jerome, although in opposite ways, were for knowing too much respecting those things of a higher world which are hidden from the eye of man, and of which he cannot judge by the forms of his earthly perception.

When the miracles said to have been wrought at the graves of martyrs, and by their reliques, were alleged in defence of the propriety and great importance of honouring them, we do not find that Vigilantius took much pains to examine into the credibility of these reports, but he simply opposed to this prevailing passion for the miraculous, the Christian principle of judgment respecting miracles. "The Christian who is certain of his faith," says he, "neither seeks nor asks for miracles; nor does he need them. Miracles were wrought not for the believing, but for the unbelieving." Perhaps Vigilantius intended by so saying to have it understood, on the one hand, that those who were seeking miracles from the martyrs showed, by this very circumstance, how far removed they were from the genuine Christian spirit, and on the other, that, in the main, these pretended miracles were nothing but a delusion;

---

* We perceive here the advocate of the grossly literal interpretation of the Bible, the opponent of Origen, when he says: Vel in sinu Abrahæ vel in loco refrigerii vel subter aram Dei animas apostolorum et martyrum consedisse.

for, as the end for which all miracles were performed no longer
existed in the minds of believers, miracles ought, among
Christians, no longer to be admitted.

This extravagant, superstitious tendency manifested itself
also particularly in the *worship of the Virgin Mary.* The
ascetic spirit venerated in Mary the ideal of the unmarried
life; the name "mother of God" (Θεοτόκος), which it had
become the custom to apply to her ever since the last times of
the fourth century, and which afterwards became the occasion
of so many controversies,—this name itself might, by a natural
misconstruction of the people, contribute some share towards
the deification of Mary.   Among a small sect of women, who
came from Thrace and settled down in Arabia, the superstition had already advanced to an idolatrous worship of the
virgin Mary; a practice universally condemned, it is true, by
the church.   They looked upon themselves as the priestesses
of Mary.   On a set day, consecrated to her as a festival, they
conveyed about in chariots (δίφροι), similar to those used by
the pagans in religious processions, cakes or wafers consecrated to Mary (κολλύριδες, κολλύρια, hence their name
κολλυριδιάνιδες, Collyridians), which they presented as offerings to her, and then ate themselves.   It would seem that
this was a transfer of the oblations at the Lord's Supper to the
worship of Mary, the whole taking the shape of a pagan ceremony.   The truth perhaps was,* that a corruption was here
introduced from the pagan worship of Ceres, that the customary bread-offerings at the heathen feast of the harvest
(Thesmophoria), in honour of Ceres, had been changed for
such offerings in honour of Mary.   The excessive veneration
of Mary had, as a further consequence, however, to call forth
still more violent opponents; and these seem to have been
antagonists at the same time of the one-sided ascetic tendency
which chose Mary as its ideal.   This controversy grew more
particularly out of a disputed question of history and exegesis.
Many teachers of the church had in the preceding period
maintained that by the brethren of Jesus, mentioned in the
New Testament, were to be understood the later born sons of
Mary.   But the ascetic spirit, and the excessive veneration of
Mary, were now shocked at the renewal of this opinion.   Thus
it came about that, at the close of the fourth century, a layman

* A conjecture of bishop Münter of Seeland.

of Rome, by the name of *Helvidius*, destitute as it would seem of a regular theological education, supposed that in the New Testament he found reasons for this opinion, while at the same time he appealed to the authority of Tertullian and Victorinus of Petavio. He affirmed, also, that by this opinion he nowise infringed on the honour of Mary; and he was thus led to attack also the exaggerated opinion of the unmarried life. He quoted the examples of the patriarchs, who had maintained a pious life in wedlock; while, on the other hand, he referred to the examples of such virgins as had by no means lived up to their calling. These opinions of Helvidius might lead us to conclude, that the combating of a one-sided ascetic spirit was a matter of still more weight with him than the defence of his views with regard to Mary. Perhaps, also, he may have been led into these views simply by exegetical inquiries and observations, and so had been drawn into this opposition to the *over-valuation* of celibacy, merely for the purpose of defending his opinion against an objection on the score of propriety.

But when we consider, that at the very time when Helvidius appeared at Rome, the presbyter Jerome, by his extravagant encomiums on the unmarried and his depreciation of the married life was creating there a great sensation, and by his extreme statements, giving every provocation which, according to the common course of things, would be likely to call forth opposition from the other side; it seems more probable that both Helvidius and Jovinian were excited by this very counter-action of their own polemical efforts, although, in the case of the latter, the opposition doubtless was based on a deeper inward ground in the whole connected system of his Christian faith. Jerome wrote against Helvidius, to whom, in scientific culture and erudition, he was confessedly superior, with all the violence and heat which characterized him.

Among these opponents of the reigning opinion belongs also another contemporary, Bonosus, a bishop, probably of Sardica, in Illyria, against whose views several synods, as well as the bishops Ambrose of Milan, and Siricius of Rome, protested.*

* See the letter to Anysius, bishop of Thessalonica, probably written by the Roman bishop Siricius. Both Siricius and Ambrose held this opinion to be an essentially false doctrine. The latter says: Hoc tantum

The idolatrous veneration of the virgin Mary, in Arabia, of which we have just spoken, was probably the occasion also of the same views being advanced by many, whom the blind zealot Epiphanius denominates enemies of Mary (ἀντιδικομαρια-νίται).

In the preceding period, we already noticed the devotion with which places in Palestine consecrated by religious remembrances were regarded and sought out by the Christians. The tendency towards the outward, in the religious spirit of these times, must have contributed to increase the veneration for these monuments of sacred history. Especially since the empress Helena and other members of the Constantine family had been so eager to visit these spots, and had decorated them with magnificent churches, the number of pilgrims began greatly to multiply. Chrysostom says, that from all quarters of the earth men flock to see the places where Christ was born, where he suffered and was buried.* Emperors made pilgrimages to the tomb of the apostle Peter in Rome, and before they visited it laid aside all their imperial insignia, in memory of this hero of the faith. Even the memory of Job drew many pilgrims to Arabia, to see the dung-heap and to kiss the earth on which the man of God had suffered with such resignation.† Very justly did it appear a great thing to Chrysostom, that, while the monuments of earthly glory were overlooked, the places, in themselves inconsiderable, consecrated by nothing but the remembrances of religion, should be searched out, after hundreds and thousands of years, by the common devotion; and very properly might he say, that great profit could be derived from visiting those spots, from the recollections and thoughts which they suggested, while the sight of imperial magnificence left but a transient impression. It was in consonance with a

---

sacrilegium—and we see it was nothing but the ascetic spirit which attributed so much importance to this dispute—cum omnes ad cultum virginitatis s. Mariæ advocentur exemplo. De institutione virginis, c. V. s. 35.

* Exposit. in Psalm cix., s. 6, T. V. 259, 'Η οἰκουμένη συντρέχει. In Matth. h. 7, s. 2. 'Απὸ τῶν περάτων τῆς γῆς ἔρχονται, ὀψόμενοι τὴν φάτνην καὶ τῆς καλύβης τὸν τόπον.

† Chrysostom. Homil. 5, de statuis, s. 1, T. II. p. 59. Πολλοὶ νῦν μακράν τινα καὶ διακόντιον ἀποδημίαν στίλλονται ἀπὸ τῶν περάτων τῆς γῆς εἰς τὴν 'Αραβίαν τρέχοντες, ἵνα τὴν κόπριαν ἐκείνην ἰδῶσι καὶ θεασάμενοι καταφιλήσωσι τὴν γῆν.

deep-seated feeling of human nature, that these places should possess a peculiar worth for the Christian heart. The only mischief was when too great stress was laid on these sensible and outward means of exciting devotion, since they usually made a momentarily, all-absorbing, and transitory, rather than a deep and lasting impression; although certainly some allowance should be made here for the different temperaments of southern and northern races of men. The effect was especially disastrous, when men began to attribute to these visits to holy places, in themselves considered, a sanctifying and justifying power. And it must be allowed that this would very soon happen, since men so easily inclined to overlook the inward grace in the outward form, the end in the means. Yet even here, a remarkable opposition of the pure evangelical spirit manifested itself against the sensual tendency. Thus Jerome declared* that " the places of the crucifixion and of the resurrection of Christ profited those only who bore their own cross, and rose each day with Christ; but those who said, 'The temple of the Lord, the temple of the Lord,' should hearken to the apostle, ' Ye are the temple of the Lord, the Holy Spirit dwells within you.' Heaven stands open to us in Britain, as well as in Jerusalem; the kingdom of God should be within ourselves." He relates, that the venerable monk Hilarion, in Palestine, had visited the holy places but once in his life, although he lived in their vicinity, so that he might not give countenance to the exaggerated veneration of them. And Gregory of Nyssa said (ep. ad Ambrosium et Basilissam) : " Change of place brings God no nearer. Wherever thou art, God will visit thee, if the mansion of thy soul is found to be such that he can dwell and rule in thee. But if thou hast thy inner man full of wicked thoughts, then, whether thou art on Golgotha, on the Mount of Olives, or at the monument of the crucifixion, thou art still as far from having received Christ into thy heart, as if thou hadst never confessed him." The moral corruption which prevailed in these very regions, beyond what was the case in any other country, he very justly cites as a proof of the little influence which those impressions on the senses could of themselves have on the sanctification of the heart.

Thus, throughout this entire section, we perceive still going

* Ep. 49, ad Paulin.

on, the conflict between the original, free, and purely Christian spirit directed to the worship of God in spirit and in truth,
and the encroaching, sensuous, half-Jewish and half-pagan
spirit, which would rob the inner man of the liberty achieved
for him by Christ, and make him a slave to outward, earthly
things, and to the maxims of this world.

In concluding this section, we may bring forward another
witness of this struggle, who appeared as an opponent of various novel tendencies of the church life, even of such as had
their origin in the preceding period. This was Aërius, a youthful friend of that Eustathius, bishop of Sebaste, in Armenia,
whom we have already mentioned. When Eustathius was
made bishop, he placed his friend, as presbyter, over a house
of paupers. But subsequently to this, Aërius fell into a quarrel with the bishop. He accused him of not remaining true to
the ascetic life, which had originally brought them together,
and of being too much interested in the acquisition of earthly
property:—Whether the fact was that Eustathius deserved
this reproach, or that Aërius, owing to the strength of his prejudices, did him injustice, and would make no allowance for
the change of conduct to which he was impelled by his office
and the wants of the church placed under his care.   Probably
also he had been drawn into disputes with his bishop respecting the proper administration of ecclesiastical affairs; against
whom he advocated the equality of bishops and presbyters,
according to the original system of church polity.   As evidence
of this he brought the fact, that presbyters as well as bishops
baptized and consecrated the elements of the holy supper.
Finally, he became the author of a schism, and attacked various usages of the dominant church.   He inveighed against
the practice of attaching value to intercessions and to the celebration of the eucharist as an offering for the dead.   If such
an ordinance could help the departed to bliss, there would be
no need of moral efforts in the present life; it would only be
necessary for each to make or purchase for himself friends,
who could be induced to pray and offer the oblation of the
supper in his behalf.   (See above.)   It is worthy of notice,
that, although an ascetic, he was opposed to the laws regulat-
ing fasts, and to the confining of fasts to set times, as Wednesday, Friday, the Quadrigesima and Good-Friday.   All this,
he maintained, ought to be done according to the spirit of the

gospel, with freedom, according to the inclinations and necessities of each individual. He found fault with the ordinances of the church on this point, because they had substituted the yoke of a Jewish bondage to the law, in place of the gospel liberty. He disputed, moreover, the custom of celebrating the passover, which, handed down from more ancient times, was still observed in these parts of Asia. By the sufferings of Christ, that which this type foreshadowed was fulfilled once for all. Such a celebration was, in his opinion, a confounding of Jewish rites with Christian. It is easy to see, that the spiritual bent of Aërius required a total separation of Christian ordinances and doctrines from Jewish.

The hierarchical sentiment occasioned violent persecutions against Aërius and his party. Driven from all quarters, they were often obliged to hold their assemblies in the open fields, in groves and on the mountains.*

---

* The principal authority, hæres. 75.

SECTION FOURTH.

HISTORY OF CHRISTIANITY APPREHENDED AND DEVE-LOPED AS A SYSTEM OF DOCTRINES.

I. GENERAL INTRODUCTORY REMARKS.

THIS period introduced important changes as well in the evolution of the conceptions of Christian doctrine as in other branches of Christian development. The change proceeding from outward relations, which formed the groundwork of this new period, was not, it is true, so *immediately* connected with that which, by its very nature, must take its outward shape from a power residing within. But, in tracing the course of development of human nature, no single branch can be contemplated without some reference to the others; much rather do all stand in a relation of mutual action and counteraction. Changes having their beginning from without extend their influence also to the inner world; and seldom does an important revolution take place in outward relations, until the way for its transforming influence has been prepared in the more inward development. This was particularly true with reference to the influence on the inward development of doctrines, produced by the great change which had taken place in the outward relations of the church since the time of Constantine. For the effects which actually resulted from this influence, the way had long since been prepared by the course of development within the church itself. It was not all at once, and through the influence of an external force, that the Christian doctrine was first delivered from the struggle with Judaism and Paganism; but the development of the Christian doctrine in intelligent consciousness had of itself so far pushed on its way triumphantly, through the oppositions of Judaism and Paganism, that these were forced to retire, when now the peculiar essence of Christianity, as a whole, and as it appeared in its several great doctrines, had come to be more clearly and distinctly apprehended by means of the conflict with these antagonists.

The agreement in the essentials of Christianity, expressed in the struggle against those heresies which sprung up out of impure commixtures of Judaism or Gentilism, continued from the preceding period into the present. In the mean time, however, notwithstanding the agreement in essentials, various germs of opposition in respect to the mode of apprehending particular Christian doctrines had sprung up; as indeed we observed to be the case in the preceding period. These might, at first, subsist peacefully side by side, while fellowship as to the essentials of Christianity still overbalanced the individual peculiarities arising out of different modes of apprehension, and the common opposition to those tendencies of spirit which appeared in the struggle against the peculiar doctrines of Christianity, diverted men's attention from these subordinate differences. But it lay in the very essence of human nature, that the germs of these oppositions should ever proceed to unfold and shape themselves into a more distinct form of subsistence. But the common opposition to the Jewish and Judaizing, to the pagan and paganizing spirit, having begun to relax; the church, delivered from the hostile tendencies which assailed her from without, being left more entirely to herself; it now happened that those differences in the mode of conceiving individual doctrines, unfolded to downright opposition, came into conflict with each other. According to the regular course of the development of human nature, it could not well happen otherwise. The process of development once begun could not stand still; as human nature is constituted, the harmonious apprehension of Christianity in all its parts could only proceed out of these opposite views of doctrine. If the entire substance of humanity, in thought as well as in life, was to be thoroughly pervaded by Christianity, it must necessarily enter also into these oppositions. But the melancholy fact was, indeed, the same here as often recurs in the history of the church; that, amid these oppositions, the unity of Christian consciousness which embraced and included them all, could be wholly forgotten; that each party apprehended and judged the opposite views of the other, only from its own particular position; and, contemplating them from without, instead of entering into their principles, and examining them according to their internal coherence and connection, charged them with consequences which lay utterly remote from them. Thus to each of the contending doctrinal parties, the struggle for their *own peculiar* modes of apprehension seemed identical with the struggle for Christianity itself. Had men but clearly seized and fixed in their own consciousness the exact relation of the *speculative* system of faith to the *life of faith*, and the relation of the single Christian doctrines to that which constitutes the peculiar and *essential foundation* of the gospel, to the doctrine concerning Christ as the Redeemer of mankind, the whole would have turned out otherwise. The oppositions, which often existed only in the speculative mode of apprehending doctrines, would not have been able to disturb and break up the fellowship and unity of the Christian consciousness; and a peaceful mutual understanding would have soon taken the place of oppositions rigidly set over against, and mutually excluding each other.

But, as men were not prepared to acknowledge that different speculative modes of apprehending doctrines might subsist side by side, provided only that the unity in the fundamental essence of Christianity was also held fast in the speculative conception, it was attempted to bind the unity of Christian consciousness to a unity of speculative apprehension, excluding all differences; and hence the effort after a narrow and narrowing uniformity, which would force all the different bents and tendencies of mind under one yoke, and which must necessarily check the free and natural evolution of the Christian system of faith, and thereby in the end of the Christian life of faith itself.

Still more hurtful was the course taken by these doctrinal controversies when disturbed by the interference, especially in the East Roman empire, of a foreign power, namely, that of the state, which hindered the free development and the free expression of the different opposite opinions. Owing to this, the purely dogmatic interest of the controversies was oftentimes extremely vitiated by the intermixture of a foreign secular interest and foreign secular passions. Not unfrequently did it happen that the opposite views of doctrine, which, after being developed outwardly from within, had already proceeded to such extent, indeed, as to be prepared for collision with each other, were first called forth into actual collision by outward foreign occasions, arising out of the confusion of ecclesiastical with political matters. And the consequence of this was, that, from the very first, a foreign interest was superinduced, which increased the difficulty of arriving at a mutual understanding, and disturbed the pure course of development. In remarking this, however, many too superficial observers have been led falsely to suppose that these disputes were due *solely* to their outward occasions, and to the conflict of passions; when the truth is, that the outward occasions could only call forth what had long since been prepared in the course of development within the church itself; as in fact we saw, when we traced the incipient germs of these oppositions in the preceding period, and, as will be still more clearly shown in detail, when we come to consider their progressive movement in the period before us. The interference of that foreign power might, moreover, for certain transient periods of time, bring about some other result of the controversies than that which corresponded to the natural relation of the conflicting elements to each other; but such results, forced on from without, could not, as the history of their doctrinal controversies shows, be anything permanent. The theological spirit of that portion of the church on which such results were forced was moved to resist them, and the foreign element was spurned away again, though not without a violent struggle.

The different dogmatic tendencies of spirit, which in the preceding period could unfold and express themselves with some degree of universality and completeness, now presented themselves for the most part in a more precise and definite shape, in controversies about single doctrines,—and, as a general thing, did not proceed to unfold themselves in wider compass and with more logical consistency. For this reason the controversies about single doctrines also furnish us with the most important help towards understanding the different general tendencies of the dogmatic spirit. While, in the preceding period, the conflict of universal spiritual tendencies fully carrried out, in the oppositions of Judaism, of Gnosticism, of the Roman church tendency, of Montanism, and of the Alexandrian tendency, predominated; in the present period, on the other hand, the oppositions manifested themselves rather in the history of single doctrines, than in the tendencies of the dogmatic spirit generally. Had the universal ground-tendencies which lay at the foundation of the controversies respecting single doctrines been allowed to express themselves in their entire compass, this circumstance would have been attended with very important consequences, affecting the entire development of Christianity.

Amidst the doctrinal controversies of this period, the characteristic difference between the tendency of the dogmatic spirit in the eastern and in the western church became apparent, while, at the same time, it went on to shape itself into a more precise and determinate form. In the eastern church, the Greek mobility of intellect and speculative direction of thought predominated. In the western church the more rigid and calm, the less mobile but more practical tendency of the Roman spirit prevailed.* Hence it happened that while, in the eastern church, the development of doctrines had to pass through the most various forms of opposition before they could come to any quiet adjustment, the result to which the eastern church first arrived, after manifold storms and conflicts, was, in a certain sense, anticipated by the church of the west; and she subsequently appropriated to herself the accurate definitions of doctrine which had been devised in the eastern church from the conflict of opposite parties.

In the next place, the doctrinal controversies of the eastern

* This difference between the two churches was rightly perceived by Greek theologians, as early as the twelfth century, and made use of as an argument in defending the Greek church against the reproach, that all the heresies had sprung out of her bosom. See the remarks of Nicetas, archbishop of Nicomedia, in Anselm. Havelbergem. Dialogg. l. III. c. xi. D'Achery spicileg. T. I. f. 197. Quoniam nova et pluribus inaudita fides subito publicæ prædicabatur, et in hac civitate studia liberalium artium vigebant, et multi sapientes in logica et in arte dialectica subtiles in ratione disserendi prævalebant, cœperunt fidem Christianam disserendo examinare et examinando et ratiocinando deficere. Next, to the vana sapientia, by which the Greek false teachers had suffered themselves to be misled, is opposed the simplicitas minus docta of the Romans, which is derived vel ex nimia negligentia investigandæ fidei, vel ex grassa tarditate hebetis ingenii, vel ex occupatione ac mole secularis impedimenti. So far as the intellectual phenomena of different times admit of being compared, we might find some analogy in the relation existing between the *theological development among the Germans and the English*; but with this difference, so important in its bearing on the result, that in Germany the more active intellectual life has not been checked and hampered in the development of its opposition by anything which resembles Byzantine despotism.

church sprung out of the speculative theology, although at the same time there was also an interest for practical Christianity at bottom. But the only doctrinal controversy belonging properly to the *western* church took its beginning from that which constitutes the central point of all practical Christianity, anthropology in its connection with the doctrine of redemption.

All the doctrinal controversies of the eastern church stand closely connected, as the following exhibition of them will show, with the controversy about the speculative mode of apprehending and defining the doctrine of the Trinity. This was fraught with very important consequences on the peculiar direction of the system of faith in both churches. As it had already happened, in the preceding period, that, in the doctrine of the Trinity, the form of speculative apprehension and the essential, practically Christian, object-matter had been too much confounded; as the custom had been to apprehend this doctrine in too isolated a way,—not enough in its vital connection with the doctrine of redemption, in the right connection with which it can alone have its true significancy; so the course taken by the doctrinal controversies in the Greek church contributed still more to establish and confirm this method of treating the doctrine of the Trinity. And hence it came about that, in the Greek church, the whole system of faith was built on a foundation too entirely speculative; that matters of philosophy and matters pertaining to the system of faith were too frequently jumbled together; that speculative definitions with regard to the divine essence were held to be just the most important; and that so much the less interest was taken, therefore, in that which is the most important thing for practical Christianity in the true sense, namely, with Christian anthropology, in its connection with the doctrine of redemption; and the doctrines bearing on this subject were held to be of inferior importance.*

* Thus Gregory of Nazianzen names, among the subjects discussed in the public teaching of those times, the question whether there was but one world, or whether there were many worlds; the questions, what is matter, what is soul and spirit; questions about the different kinds of higher spirits (ὅσα περὶ κόσμων ἢ κόσμου πεφιλοσόφηται, περὶ ὕλης, περὶ ψύχης, περὶ νοῦ καὶ νοέρων φύσεων), and having spoken next of the appearance and sufferings of Christ, he names as the principal thing (τὸ κεφαλαίον), the doctrine of the Trinity (see his orat. I. f. 16), although this doctrine surely derives its *Christian* importance only from its con-

Since, then, the systematic theology of the Greeks placed at the centre of its system a certain speculative form of apprehending Christian truth, a certain speculative definition of the Christian idea of God, rather than that which constitutes the natural centre of the whole Christian life : the consequence was, that doctrines of faith and doctrines of practice could not be evolved from a common centre, and hence the vital organic connection between the two could not be fairly presented to the conscious apprehension, and so a system of legal morality grew up by the side of an excessively metaphysical, cold, and lifeless system of faith.   Thus the adoption of a wrong method in treating the doctrines of faith must exert an influential reaction also on Christian life itself.

It was otherwise in the church of the west.   The only doctrinal controversy which properly had its origin in this church, related to Christian anthropology in its connection with the doctrine of redemption.   Owing to this circumstance, systematic theology here received at once its peculiar practical direction, and the inner connection between doctrines of faith and of practice was clearly presented to consciousness ;—and the honour of bringing about this result belongs preëminently to Augustin, the man who bore the most distinguished part in the controversy above mentioned.

The most significant phenomenon in the general history of the system of faith, and one whose influence reached from the

nection with that doctrine which Gregory represents as a subordinate one ; although entire Christianity starts not from a speculative doctrine concerning the Divine Being, but from the actual revelation of God, as a fact in history.   In another place, he speaks, it is true, as he frequently does elsewhere, against those who made the investigation of Christian truth to consist merely in speculating on the doctrine of the Trinity, and warns against the tendency which seeks to determine too much concerning the essence of the Godhead—a subject, the full knowledge of which is reserved for the future life ; but then he names in connection, as subjects on which men might employ their thoughts more profitably, and in which also there was no danger of going astray (τὸ διαμαρτάνειν ἀκίνδυνον), the φιλοσοφεῖν περὶ κόσμου ἢ κόσμων, περὶ ὕλης, περὶ ψυχῆς, περὶ λογικῶν φυσίων βελτιόνων τε καὶ χειρόνων, περὶ ἀναστάσεως, κρίσεως, ἀνταποδόσεως, χριστοῦ παθημάτων.   Orat. xxxiii, f. 536.   An error in respect to the relation of Christ's sufferings to the work of redemption, seemed to him, then, less dangerous than an error in respect to the relation to one another of the hypostases in the Trinity.   It is worthy of notice, also, that nothing occurs here which has any bearing whatever on the distinguishing character of Christian anthropology.

preceding period over into the present, was the struggle betwixt the speculative spirit of Origen's school, and the opposite tendency of practical realism. True, at Alexandria itself the spirit of this school did not maintain itself as one vigorously working onward in its wide embracing compass, and with its whole vital energy. The catechetical school at Alexandria was no longer such as it had been under Clement and Origen. Didymus, the last and the only distinguished teacher of this period, wanted the *original* and profound intellect of Origen, wonderful as was the erudition which this person, blind from his early youth, had found means to store up in his mind. Only one thing peculiar to the spiritual tendency of Origen passed over to the *Alexandrian church* as a whole. The contemplative, mystical, and, in part, speculative element continued to be cherised there; and out of this the peculiar dogmatic character of that church gradually formed itself; but Origen's free and enlarged spirit of inquiry vanished away from it. Origen's greatest influence, on the other hand, proceeded from his writings, which had no small share in forming the minds of some of the most eminent church teachers of the East, who were distinguished in the doctrinal controversies for their free spirit and their theological moderation. Such were Eusebius of Cæsarea and the great church-teachers of Cappadocia, Gregory of Nazianzen, Basil of Cæsarea, and his brother Gregory of Nyssa, on whose strong mind the speculative spirit of Origen had a very great influence.

In general, though the *realism* of the church spirit offered a counterpoise to the speculative spirit of Origen's school, and though many of Origen's peculiar ideas were universally rejected ; partly such as the development of the theological spirit in these times was not ripe enough to receive, and partly such as had grown out of a combination of Platonism with Christianity, and which were really foreign from the essence of the gospel; yet the school of Origen had served, in this struggle, to introduce, throughout the entire church, a more spiritual mode of apprehending the system of faith, and to purge it everywhere of a crude anthropomorphism and anthropopathism, and of the sensuous notions of Chiliasm. And in the treatment of the most weighty single doctrines we may discern the after-working of the influence of that great church-teacher on the development of antagonisms which made their appearance in the fourth century, as will be more particularly shown in the history of those controversies.

As Platonism had been chiefly employed by the Alexandrian school in giving shape to Christian theology, and as the *philosophical character* of this school had been formed under the influence of Platonism, so this peculiar form of the scientific spirit continued to be the prevailing one with all those in the Greek church who made it their special object to obtain a scientific understanding of the system of faith. It was only the narrow dogmatism of the understanding which sprung from Eunomius, that sought wholly to suppress the element of Platonism. Had this latter succeeded in its struggle, a complete revolution would have been brought about in the system of faith. But the three great church-teachers of Cappadocia, who had been formed in the school of Origen, took strong and decided ground against this whole new tendency. We shall treat more particularly of this struggle hereafter, in relating the history of doctrinal controversies.

A new mixture of Platonism with Christianity, independent of Origen, in which, moreover, the Platonic predominated in a far greater measure over the Christian element, is seen in the case of Synesius of Cyrene, afterwards bishop of Ptolemais, the metropolitan town of Pentapolis, in the early times of the fifth century. We have here a remarkable exemplification of the manner in which a transition might be gradually made from fundamental ideas of the religious consciousness, conceived under the form of Platonism, to Christianity. But we see, also, how a transformation of Christian doctrines into mere symbols of Platonic ideas might be brought about in the same way. Precisely as, in earlier time (see vol. I. sec. 1, p. 47), this Platonism had attached itself to the pagan cultus, and to the hierarchical system of paganism, out of which combination arose a mystico-theurgical system of religion; so a similar phenomenon, under the Christian form, might arise out of a combination of Platonism with the dominant religion of the church. The false notion of the priesthood, by which it was represented as a mediatory organ between heaven and earth, between God and man, as a vehicle for the conveyance of heavenly powers to the earth, as man's representative before God; the false notion connected with this other of the sacraments, as the bearers of those heavenly powers—all this might easily be laid hold of as a basis for theurgical mysteries. A theurgical system, or mystical symbolism of this sort, formed out of a mixture of Christianity and Platonism, we find completely elaborated in the writings forged under the name of Dionysius the Areopagite, which might have been composed some time in the course of the fifth century.

The influence of Origen had been very great, also, in giving form and direction to a thorough exegetical study of the scriptures with all the helps of learning. This method, in truth, was first called into existence by him, in opposition to a crass, literal interpretation of the Bible. The exegetical bent of a Eusebius of Cæsarea and of a Jerome, the latter of whom was the first to create an interest in the more thorough method of studying the scriptures in the western church, had been first awakened by Origen. But by the introduction of his speculative principles, and by his allegorizing tendency, which was in part owing to this fondness for speculation, the free development of that exegetical method, and the unbiassed application of it to the exposition of the system of faith, had, in Origen's own case, been greatly hindered. Up to this time there had existed only the opposite extremes of that crass literal method of biblical interpretation, and this arbitrary allegorizing tendency. But already, at the close of the preceding period, we observed how a grammatical and logical method of interpreting the Bible, holding the medium between these two extremes, had begun to be formed under the direction of the Antiochian church teachers. The beginnings of this tendency were still further developed by distinguished men in the fourth century and in the commencement of the fifth;— by Eustathius, bishop of Antioch; Eusebius, bishop of Emisa, in Phœnicia; Diodorus, bishop of Tarsus, in Cilicia; and, above all, by the sagacious and original Theodore, bishop of Mopsuestia, in the same country. Now, as the Alexandrian church had continued to preserve the allegorizing tendency, it could scarcely fail to happen, as a matter of course, owing to the great influence which different hermeneutical and exegetical tendencies naturally have on the treatment of the system of faith, that opposite tendencies of doctrine would also spring up between the theological schools of the two churches. The allegorizing tendency could, without much difficulty, accommodate itself wholly to the form of the tradition in the

dominant church, and explain the Bible in conformity therewith. The more unprejudiced, grammatical, and logical interpretation of the Bible would tend, on the other hand, to
purge the existing system of church doctrine of the various
foreign elements which had found entrance through the church
tradition, guided as that tradition had been by no clear consciousness of the truth. The allegorizing interpretation of
the Bible was closely connected with that extreme theory of
inspiration which made no distinction whatever between
essence and form in the communication of divine things, but
regarded everything alike as having come from divine suggestion. The followers of this mode of interpretation looked
upon every word as equally divine; they sought mysteries on
all sides; they would not admit that there was any human
element to be taken account of; they would not construe this
element according to its human individuality of character
and human origin—would explain nothing by reference to
human modes of apprehension and development. Under the
idea of showing particular respect to the Bible, they undesignedly detracted from its authority; because, instead of
understanding its human form from the history of its human-
becoming, and of perceiving the divine Spirit revealing itself
therein, they explained the whole as a single production after
a system, foreign indeed from the sacred word, but pre-con-
ceived and pre-established as a divine one by themselves, thus
foisting or implying in the Bible what really was not there.
Moreover, according to the above mode of interpretation, no
insurmountable difficulties, forcing men to perceive that such
notions of inspiration were untenable, could occur; for by
resort to the mystical sense (the ἀναγωγὴ εἰς τὸ νοητόν), all
difficulties could be easily set aside, all striking discrepancies
in the representation of scriptural facts explained away. On
the other hand, the grammatico-logical interpretation of the
Bible must take notice of the human as well as of the divine
element in the sacred scriptures; in this case difficulties
would necessarily present themselves, not to be reconciled
with the adoption of those extreme notions of inspiration;
men must be led to perceive the diversity of human individualities of character in the style of the inspired writers,—
the discrepancies between historical accounts in particular
matters; and the clear perception of these facts must lead to

a different way of apprehending the idea of inspiration. True, men generally proceeded in this period, as in the preceding, upon the idea of a divine inspiration of the holy scriptures, without accurately investigating or defining the idea itself; but still these differences would of themselves, ever and anon, distinctly come up to view, although few or none proceeded at once to unfold them in their whole extent; and although sometimes, even unconsciously, conflicting elements of different modes of apprehending the idea of inspiration might practically be united by the same person. The fact is, accordingly, that we meet with no instances of the more free mode of apprehending the idea of inspiration in this period, except in those persons who had been led to it by an unprejudiced, grammatico-logical interpretation of the Bible, as was the case, for instance, with Jerome, Theodore of Mopsuestia, and Chrysostom.* The applying of such a different notion of inspiration to the investigation of the scriptures, with a view to educe from them the system of faith, would also of itself lead to many differences in matters of doctrine. In connection with this different mode of conceiving the idea of inspiration, there would come to be fixed also a different point of view, from which to consider the divine and the human elements in the life of the apostles, and in the life of Christ himself; since the Antiochian school was led, by the exegetical tendency above described, to take up the human along with the divine, while the Alexandrian school, taking a more partial view of the matter, gave prominence to the divine element alone. To this we must add the general difference of intellectual bent in the two schools; which difference, again, lay at the root of the other difference between their respective

* As, for example, when Chrysostom says, Hom. 1, in Matt. that differences in the gospels on matters not essential constituted no objection to their credibility, but rather served to place their argrement in essentials in the light of a stronger evidence for their truth; since thus it would not be alleged that their agreement and harmony was the effect of design. So when Jerome, commenting on the passage in Gal. v. 12, finds no difficulty in supposing that St. Paul, in the choice of an expression, is governed by the vehemence of an emotion, arising, however, out of a pure temper of heart. Nec mirum esse, si apostolus, ut homo, et adhuc vasculo clausus infirmo, vidensque aliam legem in corpore suo captivantem se et ducentem in lege peccati, semel fuerit hoc loquutus, in quod frequenter sanctos viros cadere perspicimus.

tendencies in exegesis and interpretation. In the Alexandrian
school, an intuitive mode of apprehension, inclining to the
mystical; in the Antiochian, a logical reflective bent of the
understanding predominated; although that hearty and sincere
Christianity which may consist with every variety of intellectual bent, was not wanting to either. The first of these
tendencies inclined to give prominence to the transcendent,
the ineffable, the incomprehensible side of the divine matter
revealed in Christianity;* to place by itself the incomprehensible as not to be comprehended, as an object of faith and
of religious intuition: to oppose all attempts at explanation;
and, in order to express this in the strongest possible manner,
it sought after expressions whereby to push the matter to the
utmost extreme, and which were certainly liable to misconstruction. On the other hand, the Antiochian intelligential
bent, while it was for allowing faith its just due, and would
not attempt to explain the incomprehensible, strove to unfold
the matter of revelation by the understanding, to present it in
the clearest form in which it could be apprehended, and to
provide against all possible misapprehensions (particularly
such as might arise from confounding together and inter-
changing the divine and the human elements) by means of
precise conceptions. Thus arose out of the relation of these
two schools to each other the most important theological antagonism in the eastern church, the effects of which were most
decidedly manifested in the doctrinal controversies. This antagonism would have been attended with still more important
consequences on the theological development, had it been permitted to go on and express itself in its fullest extent. The
tendency of the Antiochian school is seen in its more moderate
form, and deeply pervaded by the Christianity of the heart, in
the case of two individuals, both of whom present models of
biblical interpretation for the period in which they lived, while
one of them furnishes the best pattern of a fruitful homiletic
application of the sacred scriptures: these were Theodoret
and Chrysostom. The example of the latter shows particularly
the great advantage of this exegetical tendency, when accompanied by a deep and hearty Christian feeling, and a life
enriched by inward Christian experience, to any one who

* Τὸ ἄῤῥητον, τὸ ἄῤῥαστον, τὸ ἀπεριόνκητον τοῦ μυστηρίου.

would cultivate a talent for homiletic exposition, and indeed for the whole office of the preacher.

The same important part which Origen had borne in directing the theological development of the eastern church, was sustained by Augustin with reference to that of the western church. His influence was, in many respects, still more general and long-continued than the influence of that great father of the church. To remarkable acuteness and depth of intellect he united a heart filled and thoroughly penetrated ᚼ with Christianity, and a life of the most manifold Christian experience. In system and method, he was doubtless superior ᚼ to Origen; but he wanted the erudite historical culture, for ᚼ which the latter was distinguished. If to his great qualities of mind and heart he had united this advantage, he would thereby have been preserved from many a partially conceived dogma, from many a stiff abstraction pushed to the utmost extreme, into which he was hurried by his speculative turn of mind, his rigid systematic consistency, combined with the peculiar direction of his religious feelings.

We noticed, in the case of the Alexandrian Gnosis, a twofold element; the Platonic view of the reciprocal relation between esoteric, philosophic knowledge of religion and of the symbolical faith of the people (of ἐπιστήμη and of δόξα), and on the other side, the view derived from the Christian consciousness of the relation of doctrinal knowledge to faith. Augustin was the first who clearly separated, in his own consciousness, these two forms of knowing, and placed the latter above the former. Augustin's scientific discipline, as well as Origen's, came from Platonism; but with this difference, however, that in the case of Origen, the Platonic element was sometimes confounded with the Christian, and Christianity subordinated to Platonism. In the case of Augustin, on the other hand, his theology disentangled itself from Platonism, and the forms of Christian intuition and thought were expressed in an independent manner, and even in opposition to the Platonism from which the scientific discipline of Augustin's mind had taken its first direction. And in connection with this, while in Origen's case the philosophical and the dogmatic interest were often confounded, in that of Augustin, on the other hand, with whom the central point of his inner Christian life constituted also the central point of his system of faith,

the dogmatic element unfolded itself in the main with more
purity and independence. But even in his case, the philosophical interest and element of his speculative intellect unconsciously mixed in with the Christian and theological : and
it was from him that this mixture of elements was transmitted
to the scholastic theology of the middle age, which stood in
immediate connection with his own. We see in Augustin the
faith for which the anti-gnostic party had contended, reconciled with the Gnosis which came from the Alexandrian
school. The peculiar training of his life enables us to understand how he came to occupy this important place in the
development of the system of faith. The transition, in Augustin's case, from the Platonic philosophy of religion to the
peculiar gnosis of Christianity, was not a mere speculative
change, but a process in his own life. The development of
doctrinal ideas proceeded, in his case, conformably to the
natural order of things out of his own internal experience.

Let us recur here, in the first place, to a fact stated in an
earlier part of this history, that a truly pious mother had
seasonably scattered the seeds of Christianity in Augustin's
heart while yet a child. The incipient germs of his spiritual
life were unfolded in the unconscious piety of childhood.
Whatever treasures of virtue and worth, the life of faith, even
of a soul not trained by scientific culture, can bestow, was set
before him in the example of his pious mother. The period
of childlike, unconscious piety was followed, in his case, by
the period of self-disunion, inward strife and conflict. For at
the age of nineteen, while living at Carthage, he was turned
from the course which a pious education had given him, by
the dissipations and corruptions of that great city. The fire
of his impetuous nature needed to be purified and ennobled by
the power of religion : his great but wild and ungoverned
energies, after having involved him in many a stormy conflict,
must first be tamed and regulated by a higher, heavenly
might ; must be sanctified by a higher spirit, before he could
find peace. As it often happens that a human word, of the
present or the past, becomes invested with important meaning
for the life of an individual, by its coincidence with slumber-
ing feelings or ideas, which are thus called forth at once into
clear consciousness, so it was with Augustin. A passage
which he suddenly came across in the Hortensius of Cicero,

treating of the worth and dignity of philosophy, made a strong impression on his mind. The higher wants of his spiritual and moral nature were in this way at once brought clearly before him. The true and the good at once filled his heart with an indescribable longing ; he had presented to the inmost centre of his soul a supreme good, which appeared to him the only worthy object of human pursuit; while, on the other hand, whatever had, until now, occupied and pleased him, appeared but as vanity. But the ungodly impulses were still too strong in his fiery nature, to allow him to surrender himself wholly to the longing which from this moment took possession of his heart, and to withstand the charm of the vain objects which he would fain despise and shun. The conflict now began in his soul, which lasted through eleven years of his life.

As the simplicity of the sacred scriptures possessed no attractions for his taste—a taste formed by rhetorical studies and the artificial discipline of the declamatory schools ;—especially since his mind was now in the same tone and direction with that of the emperor Julian, when the latter was conducted to the Platonic theosophy ; as, moreover, he found so many things in the doctrines of the church which, from want of inward experience, could not be otherwise than unintelligible to him, while he attempted to grasp by the understanding from without, what can be understood only from the inner life, from the feeling of inward wants, and one's own inward experiences ;—so, under these circumstances, the delusive pretensions of the Manichean sect, which, instead of a blind belief on authority, held out the promise of clear knowledge and a satisfactory solution of all questions relating to things human and divine, presented the stronger attractions to his inexperienced youth. He became a member of that sect, and entered first into the class of *auditors*. It was the sum of his wishes to be received into the class of the *elect,* so as to become acquainted with the mysteries of the sect,— which were the more alluring to his eager thirst for knowledge, by reason of their enigmatical character,—and thus finally attain to the clear light he was so earnestly in pursuit of. But his interviews with Faustus, one of the most eminent teachers of this sect, so entirely baulked his expectations, that, after having spent ten years as a member of the sect, he was thrown into complete bewilderment. At length he was fully

convinced that Manicheism was a delusion ; but from this he
was in danger.of falling into absolute scepticism, from which
nothing saved him but that faith in God and truth which remained planted in the deepest recesses of his soul.   During
this inward struggle, the acquaintance which he had gained,
by means of Latin translations, with works relating to the
Platonic and New-Platonic philosophy, proved of great service to him.   He says himself, that they enkindled in his
mind an incredible ardour.*   They addressed themselves to
his religious consciousness.   Nothing but a philosophy which
addressed the heart,—a philosophy which coincided with the
inward witness of a nature in man akin to the divine,—a philosophy which, at the same time, in its later form, contained
so much that really or seemingly harmonized with the Christian truths implanted in his soul at an early age ;—nothing
but such a philosophy could have possessed such attractions
for him in the then tone of his mind.   Of great importance
to him did the study of this philosophy prove, as a transition-
point from scepticism to the clearly developed consciousness
of an undeniable objective truth ;—as a transition point to the
spiritualization of his thoughts, which had by means of Manicheism become habituated to sensible images ;—as a transition-
point from an *imaginative* to an intellectual direction ;—as a
transition-point from *Dualism* to a consistent *Monarchism.* He
arrived, in this way, first to a religious idealism, that seized and
appropriated to itself Christian elements ; and was thus prepared
to be led over to the simple faith of the gospel.   At first, this
Platonic philosophy was his all ; and he sought nothing further.   It was nothing but the power of that religion implanted
during the season of childhood in the deepest recesses of his
soul, which, as he himself avowed, drew him to the study of
those writings which witnessed of it.   He argued that, as
truth is but one, this religion could·not be at variance with
that highest wisdom ; that a Paul could not have led such a
glorious life as he was said to have led, had he been wholly
wanting in that highest wisdom.   Accordingly, in the outset,
he sought in Christianity only for those truths which he had
already made himself acquainted with from the Platonic philosophy, but presented in a different form.   He conceived of

* L. II. c. academicos, s. 5.   Etiam mihi ipsi de me ipso incredibile
incendium in me concitarunt.

Christ as a prophet, in illumination of mind and holiness of character exalted, beyond all comparison, above all others; one who had been sent by God into the world for the purpose of transplanting what, by philosophical investigation, could be known only to a few, into the general consciousness of mankind, by means of an authoritative faith. From this point of view, he contrived to explain all the Christian doctrines on the principles of his Platonic idealism. He imagined that he understood them, and spoke of them as a master who was certain of his matter. As he afterwards said himself, he wanted that which can alone give the right understanding of Christianity; and without which, any man will have only the shell of Christianity without its kernel—the *love which is rooted in humility.**

But this theory, as it frequently happens with theories, and especially theories on religious matters erected on some other basis than living experience, was demolished, in his case, by the energy of life; for the Platonic philosophy presented before him, it is true, ideals which ravished the intellectual vision, but could give him no power of obtaining victory over the flesh. The ideals retreated from him whenever he attempted to grasp them: he was continually borne down again by the ungodly impulses which he thought he had already subdued. As he was conducted, therefore, by his living experience to an acquaintance with the want which Christianity alone can satisfy, and without the feeling of which it cannot be vitally understood, to a knowledge of the want of redemption from the sense of inward schism; so he found in Christianity more than he was seeking for in it, having in fact been led to it chiefly in the way of speculation. The study of St. Paul's epistles in particular, which he began in this epoch of his life, made the more powerful impression on his soul, because so much in the fundamental idea of these epistles respecting that which is law, spirit, and that which is flesh, and respecting the conflict between both, connected itself with his own inner experiences and conflicts, and became clearly evident to him from them. Much that had been un-

---

* As he says himself, in his confessions, speaking of this period of his life: Garriebam plane quasi peritus, jam enim cœperam velle videri sapieus; ubi erat illa caritas, ædificans a fundamento humilitatis, quod est Christus Jesus.

intelligible to him before he had made these experiences, he could now understand ; and, in general, he became better acquainted with Christianity, the more he found himself at home in it by means of his own inner life, and the more he experienced the sanctifying power of the divine doctrines on his own soul. Thus, then, by degrees, the relation was completely reversed: it was no longer the Platonic philosophy which was most certain to him ; and it was no longer barely the prejudice in favour of the religion of his childhood, which made what had been imparted to him by that philosophy appear to him under a more familiar and popular form ; but as he had found in Christ his Saviour, so all that Christ taught him was infallible truth, which required no other confirmation. It was the highest criterion of all truth. He himself had experienced the power of this doctrine in his inmost soul ; and this was to him a subjective testimony of its divinity and truth. His religious and moral consciousness was now satisfied ; his desire of knowledge alone still sought satisfaction. He longed to see that what was certain to him by faith in divine authority and by inward experience, was also true and necessary on internal grounds ; and the means to this were to be furnished him by the Platonic philosophy.*

Now the fact was, that, at this stage of his development, the same thing happened to him which is so liable to occur in similar cases. He deprived biblical ideas of their *full, peculiar* significance, by translating them into the language of the Platonic philosophy. Thus, for example, he called the wisdom of this world simply a wisdom which is still entangled in the forms of sense, which does not elevate itself to *ideas ;* and the kingdom of Christ, as not being a kingdom of this world, he styled one which has its foundation in the world of ideas.†

* Thus he said, on entering upon his thirty-third year, in this very epoch of his life: Mihi autem certum est, nusquam prorsus a Christi auctoritate discedere, non enim reperio valentiorem. Quod autem subtilissima ratione persequendum est—ita enim jam sum affectus, ut quid sit verum, non credendo solum, sed etiam intelligendo apprehendere, impatienter desiderem,—apud Platonicos me interim, quod sacris nostris non repugnet—reperturum esse confido. C. Academicos, l. III. s. 43.

† In his critical examination of his own writings, his retractationes, l. I. c. iii. Augustin himself passes censure on this translation of the notions of faith, into the philosophical language of the Platonic school, in which he had indulged himself in those writings which belonged to the epoch

Nor was this merely a change of expression, in which nothing was lost to the matter; but the form of expression was intimately connected with the ethical point of view peculiar to this school. Augustin was, at this time, particularly inclined to dwell in his thoughts exclusively upon the opposition between the spiritual world and the world of sense;—to contemplate the divine rather as simply opposed to the things of sense and to sensuous appearance, than as opposed to the self-seeking tendency of the spirit;—to derive moral evil expressly from man's propensity to the things of sense and sensual appearances. Yet by degrees, in proportion as Christianity penetrated from the inner life through his whole mode of thinking, he came to perceive the difference between Platonic and Christian ideas, and unshackled his system of faith from the fetters of Platonism.

Augustin had learned from his own experience, that, in reference to the knowledge of divine things, the *life* must precede the *conception;* that the latter could only come out of the former; for, in truth, the reason why the simple doctrines of the gospel had, at the beginning, appeared so foolish to him, and the delusive pretensions of that boastful mock-wisdom of the Manicheans had so easily drawn him into its current, was, that those truths had as yet found no point of union whatever in his inner life. It was from the life within that he had learned to believe in these truths, and to understand them. By love for the god-like, by the power of the religious, moral temper of heart, he had conquered the scepticism with which he had for a while been threatened. Thus—as his system of faith was throughout the copy and expression of the development of his eternal life, and hence possessed so much

of his life just mentioned, as also in his work de ordine, l. I. c. xi. When Christ says, " My kingdom is not of this world," he does not mean by this the ideal world (the κόσμος νοητός), as opposed to the world of sense (the κόσμος αἰσθητός); but rather the world in which there should be a new heaven and a new earth, when that came to pass which we pray for in the words, " Thy kingdom come." At the same time we may notice the freedom from prejudice with which he acknowledges that the idea of a *mundus intelligibilis*, in the Platonic sense, by no means contained in it, absolutely considered, any unchristian view, but, rightly understood, was a truth altogether undeniable; the mundus intelligibilis being nothing other than the eternal, invariable order of the world as it lies grounded in the divine reason.

vitality—it became with him a fundamental idea, that *divine things must be incorporated with the life and the affections, before we can be capable of an intellectual knowledge of them.* While a Manichean, he had entertained the opinion, that perfection was to be attained by speculative illumination, by the wisdom of the perfect man. At present, this way to the knowledge of divine things appeared to him as one which, since it reversed the natural order of things, must necessarily fail of its end ;* for it was clear to him, that the perfect knowledge of divine things presupposed the perfection of the inner man. At present he was convinced, that man must first humbly receive, from a divine authority, the truth which is to sanctify him, ere he could be sanctified, and so fitted with an enlightened reason for the knowledge of divine things. Although *that* could only be revealed to men by divine authority which in its intrinsic nature was truth, hence also cognizable as true on grounds of reason,—yet, in the order of time, implicit faith, the faith of authority, must have the precedence,† as a means of preparation and culture, in order to a capacity for this knowledge, the process of which is outward from within. Yet he was still, in some sense, bound up in that view of Platonism respecting the relation of δόξα to ἐπιστήμη in religion ; and as he perceived, that, without the scientific culture to which but comparatively few Christians could attain, that rational knowledge was not possible, but as without it there seemed to him to be something still wanting to Christianity ; so he was of the opinion, therefore, that those few only attained to the real blessedness of this life by Christianity, who combined with its scientific culture. But in proportion as his views became more clearly unfolded with the progress of his Christian *life ;* as the life of faith appeared to him possessed of a loftier nature, from the experience of his own heart ;‡ and as he became acquainted with this life among

---

* So he says in the work de moribus ecclesiæ Catholicæ, 1. I. s. 47, in opposition to the Manicheans : Quamobrem videte, quam sint perversi atque præposteri, qui sese arbitrantur Dei cognitionem tradere, ut perfecti simus, cum perfectorum ipsa sit præmium. Quid ergo agendum est, quid quæso, nisi ut eum ipsum, quem cognoscere volumus, prius plena caritate diligamus?

† Augustin. de ordine, l. II. c. 9. Tempore auctoritas, re autem ratio prior est.

‡ This is an important point, also, in its bearing on the development

all conditions and forms of culture, in the same proportion he became convinced, that reason (ratio) did but unfold the essential contents of what was given by faith, into' the form of rational knowledge, but could impart to it no higher character. He distinctly set forth this relation of reason proceeding out of faith, and the life of faith, to faith itself; especially in his disputes with the Manicheans, who reversed this relation.[*]

. Thus it was first by him that the great principle out of which the subsequent doctrinal system developed itself in its independent self-subsistence—" fides præcedit intellectum "— was established in a logically consistent manner. We find, therefore, in Augustin, two tendencies, by which he exerted a special influence on the development of· Christian knowledge in this century, and in the following ones; a tendency to assert the dignity and independence of faith, as opposed to a proud, speculative spirit, which rent itself from all connection with the Christian life; and to point out in opposition to the advocates of a blind faith, the agreement of faith with reason, the development of faith from within itself by means of reason.[†]

of Augustin's views respecting grace and predestination which we shall hereafter examine more closely when we approach the history of these doctrines. In the outset, when his faith was still more purely the faith of authority, the latter appeared to him as the human element, to which alone the divine could attach itself. When he had penetrated more deeply into the essence of that which is the life of faith, faith itself seemed to him already to presuppose the communication of the divine element to the man: it seemed to him, that in faith the divine and human elements were already conjoined.

[*] As in the tract de utilitate credendi.

[†] On this point, the letter of Augustin to Consentius, ep. 120, is particularly worthy of notice. He here proposes the problem, ut ea, quæ fidei firmitate jam tenes, etiam rationis luce conspicias. " Even faith," says he, " has its eyes, with which, in a certain sense, it sees that to be true which still it does not see, and with which it sees with the utmost confidence that it does not yet see what it believes." In faith lies also the yearning after more perfect knowledge, for faith cannot exist without the longing after, and without the hope of, that which one believes. Against an absolute antagonism of fides and ratio he says: " Far be it from us to suppose, that God should hate in us that by means of which he has made us superior to all other creatures. Far be it from us to suppose, that we are to believe in order that we may be under no necessity of receiving or of seeking rational knowledge, since we could not even believe, unless we were possessed of rational souls. Even this, too, is beyond all question in conformity with reason, that in some things pertaining to the doctrines of salvation, which we are as yet not able to pene-

But it is necessary to add here, what we have before remarked, that Augustin assumed as that on which faith must fix, and from which it must take its departure, *every thing given in the tradition of the church;* hence he was led to admit into his *ratio* many foreign elements, as though they were given by *fides;* and his well-exercised speculative and dialectic intellect made it easy for him to find reasons for everything,—to construe, as necessary, everything which had once become fused, although originally composed of heterogeneous elements, with his life of faith. His system of faith wanted that historical and critical direction whereby alone, returning back, at all periods of time, to the pure and original fountain of Christianity, it could *make* and *preserve* itself free from the foreign elements which continually threaten to mix in with the current of impure temporal tradition.

We now pass to consider the history of the principal doctrines of Christianity singly considered, and of the prominent antagonism in the modes of apprehending and treating these doctrines; and, in so doing, we shall see still more clearly presented, in their peculiar features, the different and opposite main tendencies of the theological spirit.

trate by our reason, faith precedes rational knowledge, that so the disposition may be purified by faith, in order to be in a condition, at some future period, to receive the light of so great truth."

END OF VOL. III.

LONDON: PRINTED BY W. CLOWES AND SONS, STAMFORD STREET.

BOHN'S CLASSICAL LIBRARY.

A Series of Literal Prose Translations of the Greek and Latin-Classics,
with Notes and Indexes.

Uniform with the Standard Library, *5s. each (except Thucydides, Æschylus, Virgil,
Horace, Cicero's Offices, Demosthenes, Appendix to Æschylus, Aristotle's Organon,
all of which are 3s. 6d. each volume).*

1. HERODOTUS. By the Rev. Henry Cary, M.A. *Frontispiece.*

2 & 3. THUCYDIDES. By the Rev. H. Dale. In 2 Vols. (3s. 6d. each). *Frontispiece.*

4. PLATO. Vol. I. By Cary. [The Apology of Socrates, Crito, Phædo, Gorgias, Protagoras, Phædrus, Theætetus, Euthyphron, Lysis.] *Frontispiece.*

5. LIVY'S HISTORY OF ROME, literally translated. Vol. I., Books 1 to 8.

6. PLATO. Vol. II. By Davis. [The Republic, Timæus, and Critias.]

7. LIVY'S HISTORY OF ROME. Vol. II., Books 9 to 26.

8. SOPHOCLES. The Oxford Translation, revised.

9. ÆSCHYLUS, literally translated. By an Oxonian. (Price 3s. 6d.)

9* ———— Appendix to, containing the new readings given in Hermann's posthumous edition of Æschylus, translated and edited by G. Burges, M.A. (3s. 6d.)

10. ARISTOTLE'S RHETORIC AND POETIC. With Examination Questions.

11. LIVY'S HISTORY OF ROME. Vol. III., Books 27 to 36.

12 & 14. EURIPIDES, literally translated. From the Text of Dindorf. In 2 Vols.

13. VIRGIL. By Davidson. New Edition, Revised. (Price 3s. 6d.) *Frontispiece.*

15. HORACE. By Smart. New Edition, Revised. (Price 3s. 6d.) *Frontispiece.*

16. ARISTOTLE'S ETHICS. By Prof. R. W. Browne, of King's College.

17. CICERO'S OFFICES. [Old Age, Friendship, Scipio's Dream, Paradoxes, &c.]

18. PLATO. Vol. III. By G. Burges, M.A. [Euthydemus, Symposium, Sophistes, Politicus, Laches, Parmenides, Cratylus, and Meno.]

19. LIVY'S HISTORY OF ROME. Vol. IV. (which completes the work).

20. CÆSAR AND HIRTIUS. With Index.

21. HOMER'S ILIAD, in prose, literally translated. *Frontispiece.*

22. HOMER'S ODYSSEY, Hymns, Epigrams, and Battle of the Frogs and Mice.

23. PLATO. Vol. IV. By G. Burges, M.A. [Philebus, Charmides, Laches, The Two Alcibiades, and Ten other Dialogues.]

24, 25, & 32. OVID. By H. T. Riley, B.A. Complete in 3 Vols. *Frontispieces.*

26. LUCRETIUS. By the Rev. J. S. Watson. With the Metrical Version of J. M. Good.

27, 30, 31, & 34. CICERO'S ORATIONS. By C. D. Yonge. Complete in 4 Vols. (Vol. 4 contains also the Rhetorical Pieces.)

28. PINDAR. By Dawson W. Turner. With the Metrical Version of Moore. *Front.*

29. PLATO. Vol. V. By G. Burges, M.A. [The Laws.]

33 & 36. THE COMEDIES OF PLAUTUS, By H. T. Riley, B.A. In 2 Vols.

35. JUVENAL, PERSIUS, &c. By the Rev. L. Evans, M.A. With the Metrical Version of Gifford. *Frontispiece.*

37. THE GREEK ANTHOLOGY, translated chiefly by G. Burges, A.M., with Metrical Versions by various Authors.

38. DEMOSTHENES. The Olynthiac, Philippic, and other Public Orations, with Notes, Appendices, &c., by C. Rann Kennedy. (3s. 6d.)

1 c

64. **PLINY'S NATURAL HISTORY,** translated, with copious Notes, by the late J BOSTOCK, M.D., F.R.S., and H. T. RILEY ESQ. B.A. Vol. 1.

65. **SUETONIUS.** Lives of the Cæsars, and other Works. THOMSON's transla revised by T. FORESTER.

BOHN'S ANTIQUARIAN LIBRARY.

Uniform with the STANDARD LIBRARY, *price 5s.,*

1. BEDE'S ECCLESIASTICAL HISTORY, & THE ANGLO-SAXON CHRONI

2. MALLET'S NORTHERN ANTIQUITIES. By BISHOP PERCY. With Abs of the Erbyggia Saga, by SIR WALTER SCOTT. Edited by J. A. BLACKWELL.

3. WILLIAM OF MALMESBURY'S CHRONICLE OF THE KINGS OF ENGLA

4. SIX OLD ENGLISH CHRONICLES: viz., Asser's Life of Alfred; the Chron of Ethelwerd, Gildas, Nennius, Geoffry of Monmouth, and Richard of Cirences

5. ELLIS'S EARLY ENGLISH METRICAL ROMANCES. Revised by J. ORCH HALLIWELL. Complete in one vol., *Illuminated Frontispiece.*

6. CHRONICLES OF THE CRUSADERS: Richard of Devizes. Geoffrey de Vin Lord de Joinville. Complete in 1 volume. *Frontispiece.*

7. EARLY TRAVELS IN PALESTINE. Willibald, Sæwulf, Benjamin of Tu Mandeville, La Brocquiere, and Maundrell. In one volume. *With Map.*

8, 10, & 12. BRAND'S POPULAR ANTIQUITIES OF GREAT BRITAIN. SIR HENRY ELLIS. In 3 Vols.

9 & 11. ROGER OF WENDOVER'S FLOWERS OF HISTORY (formerly asc to Matthew Paris.) In 2 Vols.

13. KEIGHTLEY'S FAIRY MYTHOLOGY. Enlarged. *Frontispiece* by CRUIKSH

14, 15, & 16. SIR THOMAS BROWNE'S WORKS. Edited by SIMON WIL *Portrait.* In 3 Vols. With Index.

17, 19, & 31. MATTHEW PARIS'S CHRONICLE, containing the Histo England from 1235, translated by DR. GILES, with Index to the whole, inclu the portion published under the name of ROGER OF WENDOVER, in 3 Vols. 9 & 11). *Portrait.*

18. YULE-TIDE STORIES. A collection of Scandinavian Tales and Traditions, e by B. THORPE, Esq.

20 & 23. ROGER DE HOVEDEN'S ANNALS OF ENGLISH HISTORY, A.D. 732 to A.D. 1201. Translated and edited by H. T. RILEY, Esq., B.A. 2 Vols.

21. HENRY OF HUNTINGDON'S HISTORY OF THE ENGLISH, from the R Invasion to Henry II.; with The Acts of King Stephen, &c. Translated edited by T. FORESTER, Esq., M.A.

3 e

22. **PAULI'S LIFE OF ALFRED THE. GREAT.** To which is appended **ALFRED'S ANGLO-SAXON VERSION OF OROSIUS**, with a literal translation. Notes, and an Anglo-Saxon Grammar and Glossary, by B. THORPE, Esq.

24 & 25. **MATTHEW OF WESTMINSTER'S FLOWERS OF HISTORY,** especially such as relate to the affairs of Britain, from the beginning of the world to A.D. 1307. Translated by C. D. YONGE, B.A. In 2 Vols.

26. **LEPSIUS'S LETTERS FROM EGYPT, ETHIOPIA,** and the **PENINSULA OF SINAI.** Revised by the Author. Translated by LEONORA and JOANNA B. HORNER. With Maps and Coloured View of Mount Barkal.

27, 28, & 30. **ORDERICUS VITALIS.** His Ecclesiastical History of England and Normandy, translated, with Notes and the Introduction of Guizot, by T. FORESTER, M.A. In 3 Vols.

29. **INGULPH'S CHRONICLE OF THE ABBEY OF CROYLAND,** with the Continuations by Peter of Blois and other Writers. Translated, with Notes and an Index, by H. T. RILEY, B.A.

32. **LAMB'S SPECIMENS OF ENGLISH DRAMATIC POETS** of the time of Elizabeth; including his Selections from the Garrick Plays.

33. **MARCO POLO'S TRAVELS,** the translation of Marsden, edited, with Notes and Introduction, by T. WRIGHT, M.A., F.S.A., &c.

34. **FLORENCE OF WORCESTER'S CHRONICLE,** with the Two Continuations; comprising Annals of English History, from the Departure of the Romans to the Reign of Edward I. Translated, with Notes, by T. FORESTER, Esq.

35. **HAND-BOOK OF PROVERBS,** comprising the whole of Ray's Collection, and a complete Alphabetical Index, in which are introduced large Additions collected by HENRY G. BOHN.

BOHN'S PHILOLOGICAL LIBRARY.

Uniform with the STANDARD LIBRARY, *price* 5s. *per Volume.*

1. **TENNEMANN'S MANUAL** of the HISTORY of PHILOSOPHY, revised and continued by J. R. MORELL.

2. **ANALYSIS** and SUMMARY of HERODOTUS, with synchronistical Table of Events, Tables of Weights, Money, &c.

3. **TURNER'S (DAWSON W.) NOTES TO HERODOTUS,** for the use of Students. With Map, Appendices, and Index.

4. **LOGIC,** or the SCIENCE OF INFERENCE, a popular Manual, by J. DEVEY.

5. **ANALYSIS** and SUMMARY of THUCYDIDES, by T. WHEELER. New Edition, with the addition of a complete Index.

BOHN'S BRITISH CLASSICS.

Uniform with the STANDARD LIBRARY, *price 3s. 6d. per Volume.*

1, 3, 5, 8, 11 & 14. **GIBBON'S ROMAN EMPIRE**; Complete and Unabridged, with variorum Notes, including, in addition to all the Author's own, those of Guizot, Wenck, Niebuhr, Hugo, Neander, and other foreign scholars. Edited by an ENGLISH CHURCHMAN, *with Portrait and Maps.*

2, 4, & 6. **ADDISON'S WORKS**, with the Notes of BISHOP HURD. *With Portrait and Engravings on Steel.*

7. **DEFOE'S WORKS**, Edited by SIR WALTER SCOTT. Vol I. Containing the Life, Adventure, and Piracies of Captain Singleton, and the Life of Colonel Jack. *Portrait of Defoe.*

9. **DEFOE'S WORKS**, Vol. 2. Containing Memoirs of a Cavalier, Adventures of Captain Carleto n, Dickory Cronke, &c.

10. **PRIOR'S LIFE OF BURKE.** (forming the 1st Volume of BURKE'S WORKS), new Edition, revised by the Author. *Portrait.*

12. **BURKE'S WORKS**, Vol 1, containing his Vindication of Natural Society, Essay on the Sublime and Beautiful, and various Political Miscellanies.

13. **DEFOE'S WORKS**, Edited by SIR WALTER SCOTT. Vol. 3. Containing the Life of Moll Flanders, and the History of the Devil.

15. **BURKE'S WORKS.** Vol. 2, containing Essay on the French Revolution, Political Letters and Speeches.

BOHN'S ECCLESIASTICAL LIBRARY.

Uniform with the STANDARD LIBRARY, *price 5s. per Volume.*

ı **EUSEBIUS' ECCLESIASTICAL HISTORY**, Translated from the Greek, with

BOHN'S SHILLING SERIES.

*Those marked *, being Double Volumes, are 1s. 6d.*

3. GERVINUS' INTRODUCTION TO THE HISTORY OF THE NINETEENTH
CENTURY, translated from the German (*with a Memoir of the Author*).
4. CARPENTER'S (DR. W. B.) PHYSIOLOGY OF TEMPERANCE AND TOTAL
ABSTINENCE, being an Examination of the Effects of the excessive, moderate,
and occasional use of Alcoholic Liquors on the Human System (or *on fine paper,
bound in cloth, 2s. 6d.*)

BOHN'S MINIATURE LIBRARY.

Foolscap 12mo. elegantly bound in morocco cloth.

ARBAULD AND AIKIN'S EVENINGS AT HOME. *Frontispieces.* 3s.

OURRIENNE'S MEMOIRS OF NAPOLEON. *Portrait and Frontisp.* 3s. 6d.

UNYAN'S PILGRIM'S PROGRESS. With a Life and Notes by Scott, containing
all in Southey's Edition. *25 Woodcuts, by* HARVEY, *Frontisp.* &c. 3s. 6d.

———— CHEEVER'S LECTURES ON, *Frontisp.* 2s. 6d.

YRON'S POETICAL WORKS, in 1 thick Volume, including several suppressed Poems
not included in other editions. *Beautiful Frontispiece.* 3s. 6d.

DON JUAN, complete. *Frontispieces.* 2s. 6d.

OLERIDGE'S SELECT POETICAL WORKS. 2s.

OWPER'S POETICAL WORKS, with Life by SOUTHEY, including all the copyright
Poems (700 pages). *Beautiful Frontispieces after* HARVEY, *by* GOODALL. 3s. 6d.

RYDEN'S POETICAL WORKS, complete in 1 Vol., with *a Portrait, Frontispiece, and
Vignette Title.* 3s. 6d.

NCYCLOPÆDIA OF MANNERS AND ETIQUETTE, comprising an improved
edition of Chesterfield's Advice to his Son on Men and Manners. 2s.

EBER'S (BP.) & MRS. HEMANS' POETICAL WORKS. 3 Vols. in 1. *Fronts.* 2s. 6d.

ERRICK'S POETICAL WORKS, complete. *Frontispiece.* 3s.

OE MILLER'S JEST BOOK. *Frontispiece.* 3s.

ONGFELLOW'S POETICAL WORKS, viz.—Voices of the Night—Evangeline—Sea-
side and Fireside—Spanish Students—Translations. *Portrait and Frontisp.* 2s. 6d.

PROSE WORKS, viz.—Outre-Mer—Hyperion—Kavanagh. 2s. 6d.

ILTON'S POETICAL WORKS, with Life and Notes by DR. STEBBING; and Dr.
Channing's Essay on Milton. *Frontispiece.* 3s. 6d.

EW JOE MILLER, a Selection of Modern Jests, Witticisms, Droll Tales, &c. 2s. 6d.

SSIAN'S POEMS, with Dissertations by MACPHERSON and Dr. Blair. *Frontisp.* 3s.

OPE'S HOMER'S ILIAD. Essay on Homer. Notes and Essays. *Frontispiece.* 3s.

———— ODYSSEY, (uniform). *Frontispiece.* 3s.

COTT'S POETICAL WORKS, and Life, in one volume. *Port. and Frontisp.* 3s. 6d.

TURM'S REFLECTIONS ON THE WORKS OF GOD. *Frontisp.* 3s.

HOMPSON'S SEASONS. With his Castle of Indolence, 4 *beautiful Woodcuts.* 2s.

ATHEK, AND THE AMBER WITCH. 2 vols. in 1. 2s. 6d.